Second Edition, Fully Revised and Updated

Latin American Politics and Development

EDITED BY HOWARD J. WIARDA AND HARVEY F. KLINE

Westview Press / Boulder and London

First edition published in 1979 by Houghton Mifflin Company

Published in 1985 in the United States of America by Westview Press, Inc., 5500 Central Avenue, Boulder, Colorado 80301; Frederick A. Praeger, Publisher

Library of Congress Cataloging in Publication Data
Main entry under title:
Latin American politics and development.
   Includes bibliographies and index.
   1. Latin America—Politics and government.
I. Wiarda, Howard J., 1939– . II. Kline, Harvey F.
F1410.L39   1985   320.98   84-21937
ISBN 0-8133-0097-5
ISBN 0-8133-0098-3 (pbk.)

Printed and bound in the United States of America

10   9   8   7   6   5   4

Contents

PART 4   Conclusion: Latin America and Its Alternative
          Futures, *Howard J. Wiarda and Harvey F. Kline*

Illustrations

Preface
to the Second Edition

Six years have passed since publication of the first edition of this book. A lot has happened in Latin America since that time—and in our interpretations of the area. The highlights include the Nicaraguan Revolution and the coming to power of the Sandinista government; a guerrilla challenge in El Salvador and upheaval elsewhere in Central America; a greatly increased U.S. presence throughout Central America and the Caribbean; the restoration of democracy in Argentina, Ecuador, Peru, Honduras, and Bolivia and the transition toward democracy in Brazil and Uruguay and maybe Chile; and financial and economic instability throughout the hemisphere.

These changes have forced us to update, reorient, and in some cases entirely rewrite our country chapters. But they have also forced us as editors and authors to rethink some of our general ideas and intellectual concepts about Latin America, as found in Part 1. The second edition thus puts more emphasis on political economy, public policy, and the relations of dependency in which the Latin American nations find themselves. We feel these changes reflect both changing realities through-out the hemisphere and our sense of the newer directions in political science and Latin American studies.

The first edition of this book largely captured the field of Latin American politics courses organized on a country-by-country basis. The book begins with an extensive introduction, almost a separate book in itself, and then proceeds to a country-by-country treatment of all the Latin American nations. For reasons of space we have not included chapters on the former British, French, and Dutch colonies in the area.

A word about our principle of organizing the country chapters, which in the first edition was a source of some puzzlement to readers. The editors organized the book in terms of how they teach their courses, proceeding from a "sleepier" nineteenth-century society (Paraguay in South America, Nicaragua in Central America) as examples of what Latin American politics *used* to be like, to the dynamics of alternative models of modernization throughout the region—military and democratic systems, one-party regimes, multiparty systems, revolutionary regimes, and so on. It is clear Nicaragua is no longer a sleepy, backward-looking dictatorship. We have also reorganized the other country chapters so that (1) the bigger and more important countries come first in each section; (2) the sequence of countries flows generally from south to north; and (3) some of the "crisis countries" (Nicaragua, El Salvador) receive expanded coverage. But the book is sufficiently flexible and the treatment of individual countries sufficiently independent from one another that a teacher or reader may employ any one of the several ordering principles noted in the preface to the first edition.

H.J.W.   H.F.K.

Preface
to the First Edition

It has been nearly a decade since the last comprehensive, country-by-country textbook on Latin American politics was written. So much has transpired since that time that only a few of the most significant events can be highlighted: the Peruvian revolution; the Chilean experience with socialism; the Brazilian economic "miracle"; the return of the Peróns to Argentina and the subsequent end of Peronist rule; the institution-alization of the Cuban revolution; the rise of new Caribbean independence and black power movements; the collapse of Uruguayan democracy; the new issues in Mexico and in Mexican-U.S. relations; the great debate over the Panama Canal; the resurgence of many authoritarian regimes throughout the area, and the resulting concern for human rights; the debate over the status and future of Puerto Rico; the nationalization of the oil industry in Venezuela; the swing to the left of an entire generation of young Latin Americans; and the search throughout the hemisphere for new development models. All these major events and others cry out for analysis and assessment.

This book not only chronicles the foregoing events; it presents new scholarly interpretations of Latin American politics. Recent writing and thought represented here include the literature on Latin American dependency; the innovative focus on corporatism and authoritarianism in Latin America; the new interpretations of what makes Latin America culturally distinctive; the emphasis on class and structural forces; the new stress on the state and on public policy; and the effort to examine Latin American politics and development on their own terms, rather than through the culture-bound perceptions of North America.

The book takes a country-by-country approach. The Introduction and Conclusion by the editors set the tone of the book, present the major themes, and pull the entire work together. The seven chapters of the Introduction describe the overall context of Latin American politics; the pattern of historical development; the acceleration of the modernization process; the major interest groups and parties; the structure of the state; public policy issues and practices; and the overall political process. The chapters on individual countries that follow explore the themes of the Introduction in greater detail, analyzing both the comparative patterns that exist in Latin America and specific national variations. The parallel structure of these chapters facilitates comparative analysis and makes this an integrated book about Latin American politics and development.

The authors of the various chapters are among the leading scholars in the field. All are experts on the countries about which they have written. It is hoped that some of the dynamism and enthusiasm that they and the editors feel for their subject, some of the excitement and challenge that mark Latin American politics and development today, will be conveyed to the readers of this book.

As editors, we have not sought to impose any single conceptual framework or set of rigid orthodoxies on the contributors. We have cast the book in comparative terms and within a broad framework of general developmental themes, economic, social, and political. Inevitably, our own and the contributors' individual biases will manifest themselves. But our primary aim has been to provide a comprehensive treatment of Latin America by its foremost scholars, regardless of their ideological or methodological views.

This book is designed to be used in several ways. In a one-semester course, the chapters in Part 1 can serve as a convenient introduction to Latin American politics, which may then be followed by a treatment of the more important countries (here, Argentina, Brazil, Cuba, and Mexico receive especially detailed treatment) or of other countries the instructor knows especially well or is particularly interested in. In a two-semester sequence, the introductory materials and chapters on selected South American countries might serve for the first semester; and then in the second semester (after a brief repetition of the Introduction for the benefit of new students) the chapters on Central America and the Caribbean might be taken up. Or a course might begin with the introductory chapters and then turn to a comparative analysis of Latin American social revolutions (Bolivia, Costa Rica, Cuba, Mexico, Peru). Still other methods of organization might be devised. We have tried to make the book's coverage sufficiently comprehensive to accommodate a wide range of approaches.

The author of the chapter on Brazil would like to thank the following persons for their helpful criticisms and suggestions: Warren Dean, Daniel Gross, Michael M. Hall, Robert Laurenty, Robert M. Levine, Ronald M. Schneider, and Amory de Souza. The authors of the chapter on Chile likewise wish to thank Edmundo Fuenzalida. The author of the chapter on Peru thanks Cynthia McClintock, Frederick Pike, and Steve Stein.

Finally, the editors are grateful to the following persons for reading all or part of the manuscript and extending valuable suggestions: G. Pope Atkins, U.S. Naval Academy; Enrique A. Baloyra, University of North Carolina at Chapel Hill; Douglas A. Chalmers, Columbia University; and Edward Gonzalez, University of California at Los Angeles.

H.J.W.   *H.F.K.*

Part 1

The Latin American tradition and process of development

HOWARD J. WIARDA
HARVEY F. KLINE

1
The Context of
Latin American Politics

Latin America is one of the most interesting and exciting research areas in the world. In Cuba, Mexico, Peru, Venezuela, Argentina, Nicaragua, Colombia, Brazil, and elsewhere throughout the continent, some of the globe's most innovative social and political experiments are being carried out. Latin America is undergoing profound revolutionary change— socially, economically, politically, psychologically—and it is seeking to devise new institutional arrangements to manage the complex transformations currently under way. Industrialization, urbanization, accelerated social change, and the "revolution of rising expectations" are having momentous effects, altering old political relationships and forging new ones. Latin America is vibrant, dynamic, and changing. At the same time, the area has achieved a new status in terms of its rising strategic importance and wealth of natural resources in an age when we have become acutely aware of our dependence on such resources. Because of our common New World heritage and because we have always considered this area as lying within our sphere of influence— a situation that is now changing—we have thought of Latin America as having a special relationship with the United States.

The nature of the transformations going on in Latin America is different than is commonly imagined. Most North Americans have a picture, based on news headlines and *New Yorker* cartoons, of a Latin America governed by comical, mustachioed men on horseback who gallop in and out of the presidential palace with monotonous regularity. Our other image is of poor but happy peasants with big sombreros either taking siestas under the palm trees or dancing gaily in the streets. Neither of these images conforms to the realities of the area. The revolutionary transformations now taking place are not just palace revolts that substitute one man on horseback for another but profound social revolutions that affect all areas of national life. Latin America is no longer comic opera or the stuff of cartoons. Instead, politics and the clash of social forces have become deadly serious, with the stakes high and the outcome still uncertain.

We speak of Latin America in our writings and policy pronouncements as if it were a single entity. It is and it isn't. In fact, the area is

characterized by immense diversity. Argentina is as different from
Paraguay as France from Portugal. There is a world of difference between
the cosmopolitan societies of Rio de Janeiro, São Paulo, Buenos Aires,
and Mexico City and the provincialism of Asunción or Santo Domingo.
Yet within this context of diversity, which makes it imperative that we
know each country of the area individually, there are also important
common characteristics of language, culture, institutions, and social and
historical background. This factor of unity amid diversity makes Latin
America an exciting living laboratory for the study of comparative social
and political change.

Latin America is not only diverse but it faces—and has always faced—
a profound identity crisis. We must therefore ask not only whether Latin
America exists as a unit, but what it is, what is its essence. Is it Western,
non-Western, developing, Third World, or what? The answer is complex.
With its strong roots in Roman law, Catholicism, and the Iberian
sociopolitical tradition, Latin America is Western; yet it represents a
particular Luso-Hispanic variant of the Western tradition and is obviously
quite different in its social and cultural underpinnings from the variant
established by the British in North America. Moreover, because of its
strong Indian and—in the circum-Caribbean and Brazil—African sub-
cultures, Latin America is sometimes classified as a non-Western area.
Although integrated into an emerging Western, capitalist world economy
as colonies and exporters of precious metals (it is seldom mentioned
that the gold and silver from Latin America helped initiate the Industrial
Revolution), Latin America as a whole received few of the benefits, long
remained at the margins of the world economic system, and was
considered as a supplier of raw materials, destined to lag behind in
terms of economic growth.

Nor, with some 160 years of independent life behind them, can the
Latin American countries be included in the category of "new nations."
And, though Latin America is seldom considered a part of the First
World of developed capitalist countries (the United States, West Europe,
Japan) or the Second World of developed socialist countries (Soviet
Union, China, East Europe; Cuba and Nicaragua are the only socialist
states in the Western Hemisphere), it does not comfortably fit into the
Third World category either. By virtually any criterion, almost all the
Latin American nations are more developed than the Third World nations
of Africa or Asia; they tend to be *transitional* countries, neither fully
developed nor wholly underdeveloped. Moreover, when the Latin American countries follow a Third World foreign policy, they usually see
themselves as leaders of the Third World, not merely members of it.
Many scholars, emphasizing the ill fit of any of the existing categories
and pointing to the distinctive features of its tradition, have begun
referring to Latin America as a Fourth World of development. By this
they mean not just what economists sometimes have in mind when
they talk of the more advanced developing nations, but an entire political-

cultural tradition and a developmental model that are fundamentally different from the rest of the world.

But if Latin America has evolved as a unique fragment of the Western tradition, albeit with strong indigenous features and with its own social institutions and political dynamics, then we must try to comprehend what that tradition is and how its institutions function. We must deal with the issue of how and why Latin American development has taken the paths it has, as well as how the Latin American tradition reflects and interacts with broader patterns of change and modernization. Moreover, in coming to grips with the main themes of Latin American development, we must seek to understand that tradition on its own terms, shedding commonly held prejudices about the area and our frequently ethnocentric biases. We must put away our stereotypes and come to know Latin America through an understanding of its institutions and processes rather than an idealized conception of our own. A greater modesty regarding the supposed superiority of North American civilization and an appreciation of another culture area with which we are less familiar are indispensable if we are to comprehend Latin America.

Latin America today is an area of immense vibrancy and sometimes dizzying change, of clash and conflict, of complex efforts to deal with developmental issues of great importance, of attempts to reconcile what is valuable in its own traditions and past (personalism, a strong sense of community, intense individualism, an ethical view of people and society) while also accommodating itself to the modern world. Though the traditional institutions and holders of power remain strong, the winds of revolution are sweeping through the area. The conflicts between these forces are fierce and deep-rooted and lie at the heart of Latin American politics and the process of change.

James Reston of the *New York Times* once remarked that people in the United States seemed willing to do anything for Latin America except read about and seek to comprehend it. It is our hope that in this book you will not only read about Latin America but also try to understand it. Given the United States' strategic interests in the area and also our vulnerability to commodity and raw materials shortages, Latin America now has added reasons for being important to this country. And given also the crisis of our own social and political institutions, it may be that we can learn something from the way Latin Americans have dealt with contemporary change—instead of their always "learning" from us.

LATIN AMERICA

Latin America—broadly defined as Middle, Central, and South America and the Caribbean—is a vast area. It encompasses 8 million square miles (21 million square kilometers) of land (19 percent of the world's total) with roughly 350 million people. It comprises eighteen Spanish

American countries, Brazil, Haiti, seven new states (six former British colonies and one Dutch one), and a number of dependencies of France, Britain, the Netherlands, and the United States. For the purposes of this book and to facilitate comparison among countries, we shall be concentrating on the Luso-Hispanic countries of Latin America—the vast area colonized by Spain and Portugal, which includes Puerto Rico. References to Latin America thus can be understood to exclude the present or former British, Dutch, and French colonies or territories: Guyana, Suriname, Belize, Jamaica, Haiti, Trinidad and Tobago, and the other smaller islands.

The countries of Latin America are diverse. Some are, or think of themselves as, predominantly white and European (Argentina, Chile, Costa Rica, Uruguay); some are heavily Indian and mestizo, or mixtures of Indian and European (the Andean countries of Ecuador, Peru, and Bolivia and Mexico and Central America). In some the racial mix is black and mulatto or black, mulatto, and white (Northeast Brazil, the Caribbean islands, and the circum-Caribbean countries); in others the social and racial configurations involve the complex interrelations of Indian, European, and black. Some are based largely on subsistence agriculture, some have heavy industry, but the majority are mixes of the most backward areas and the most modern urban centers. Per capita income, literacy rates, and other social indicators show remarkable variation.

Though the diversity of the area and the special features of each country must be recognized, the common features are equally significant. And though we may lament the simplistic notions of journalists and government officials when they talk of a single "Latin America policy" for all twenty-odd nations of the area, we must acknowledge the cogent reasons for treating the countries comparatively and as part of a single culture area. For in their common Iberian colonial past, their institutional foundations, their struggles for independence, their cultural commonalities and continuities, and their often parallel development processes, the nations of Latin America have had some remarkably analogous experiences. This book seeks to understand both the distinctiveness of the Latin American nations and, especially in its introductory and concluding sections, their common patterns and experiences.

Latin America is diverse not only in terms of its peoples and societies but also in terms of its geography and resources. It contains one of the world's highest and most majestic mountain ranges, the Andes, whose peaks serve as the backdrop for the Pacific countries of South America (Colombia, Ecuador, Peru, Chile) and continue northward, leveling out in lower ranges and plateaus, through Central America and Mexico. Its vast fertile plains in Argentina, Uruguay, Brazil, and Venezuela support large-scale agri-industry, whereas the meager soil in the highland areas makes it impossible to eke out even subsistence. Natural resources are abundant in some areas (Venezuela, Brazil, Mexico, Chile, Peru) and almost nonexistent in others. For the resource-poor nations, the absence of natural resources implies that no national development plan or formula can effect more than modest changes in the basic pattern of poverty. Even Fidel Castro has cautioned that revolution in countries of slim resources would sometimes cause more harm than good.

The tropical coastal regions of Brazil and the circum-Caribbean are suitable for sugarcane production (and also in earlier times for slave-plantation agriculture—hence the large importation of Africans to these regions), and the highlands of Central America, Brazil, and Colombia are suitable for coffee. There are also vast areas (the Llanos of Colombia, much of the Amazon Basin, the denuded mountainsides) that may not be able to support any form of profitable agriculture. And even though Latin America has some of the world's great river systems (the Orinoco, Amazon, and Río de la Plata), they are often unsuitable for internal transportation.

Geography has not always been kind to Latin America and has retarded efforts toward development and national integration. In the early years, the Andes on the Pacific and the coastal escarpments on the Atlantic slowed internal colonization and helped account for the fact that almost all the major cities lie on or close to the coast. The steep mountains and the secluded valleys partly explain the historical lack of contact among the towns of the area and the localism of the small community or the patria chica ("little country"). The "whole world" could be encompassed by an isolated valley, and the patria chica or the local hacienda, often self-sufficient and virtually self-governing, was the setting for all of one's life experiences. Before the onset of modern communications and transportation, geographic provincialism impeded development and growth of a sense of national loyalty. It also did—and still does—help prevent the development of an integrated national economy, political community, and nation-state.

Latin America's main population centers lie on the coast, while the interior of the continent remains largely empty. With such vast empty spaces and with a population density about one-sixth that of the United States or West Europe and one-ninth that of Asia, Latin America would appear not to have a severe population problem. But many of the interior areas are not particularly hospitable from a health and climate point of view, and much of the land is infertile and unsuitable for agriculture. To date, the Latin American interior has represented a static frontier, not a dynamic one.

Latin America has an abundance of natural resources, but they are often not juxtaposed in a way conducive to the development of modern industry, or they are the wrong kind of resources. The abundant gold and silver found during the colonial era were used largely to benefit the colonizing countries rather than for internal development. Gold and silver also contributed to a get-rich-quick mentality, repeated cycles of boom and bust, and a system of exploitation that still marks the area.

There is some coal and iron ore in Latin America, but they are generally of inferior quality, and because the two are seldom in proximity, the coal cannot readily be used in iron smelting. If steel is the key to the development of a modern industrial base, few of the Latin American nations possess the resources to produce it in sufficient quantity. Venezuela and perhaps Brazil are the major exceptions.

Oil is another story. Venezuela, much of which literally floats on oil, was for a long time the richest Latin American nation in known reserves; today Mexico claims to have the largest reserves. It is no accident that Venezuela has the highest per capita income in the area, and the wealth generated by oil helps explain why Venezuela is one of the few Latin American nations that still enjoys democratic government. Ecuador, Colombia, Argentina, Brazil, and Peru are also oil producers, and new finds in the Caribbean may transform that area. Latin America holds other mineral resources: copper and nitrate in Chile; tin in Bolivia; bauxite in Jamaica; emeralds and coal in Colombia; and small deposits of nickel, gold, manganese, and bauxite in several other countries. Brazil's Amazon Basin contains huge and largely untapped quantities of numerous precious and industrial metals, and this in part explains why Brazilians think of Brazil as the future of Latin America.

Nature, however, has been relatively stingy with Latin America, and there is nowhere near the amount of resources possessed by the United States during its historical development period. In Latin America the obstacles to development have been all but insuperable: steep mountains coming right to the water's edge, dense tropical jungles, an incredibly chopped-up geography, rivers and farmland whose location hindered development, scarce and inaccessible minerals. Geography and nature have often played critical and not necessarily friendly roles in Latin American history.

THE ECONOMIES

Latin America was settled as a colonial area and exploited chiefly for the benefit of the colonizing countries. Under the economic conceptions then prevalent (mercantilism), the colonies existed to enrich Spain and Portugal. Much of Latin America's wealth was drained away to Europe, through Spain and Portugal and on to the Netherlands and Britain, where it helped stimulate the rise of capitalism. From the beginning Latin America has been at the margins of the emerging world system of capitalist economies, an area to be milked dry by the exploiting powers but with little of its wealth used for internal improvements.

One need not be an economist to recognize poverty, and the impoverished state of this area is what will first strike most visitors. The poverty, based on a rigid socioeconomic structure that benefits chiefly the wealthy and on centuries of exploitation and deprivation, is most visibly present in the bloated bellies of the children, the widespread malnutrition-related diseases, the shacks that pass for houses, and the malformed bodies of both old and young. It is toward relieving this poverty that the contemporary revolution in Latin America is aimed. Poverty is the way of life of perhaps 70 percent of the Latin American population, and it ranges from a depressingly severe level in most countries to the relative prosperity of Argentina or Venezuela.

Historical economic patterns throughout Latin America have varied considerably, and these different patterns still help account for the differing socioeconomic configurations of the area. In Brazil and the Caribbean islands, and on the low-lying mainland rim of the Caribbean, slave-plantation systems were established, necessitating the large-scale importation of Africans as laborers. In Mexico, Peru, and Bolivia in the early days, mining was critically important; and since those areas were also the centers of some of Latin America's largest indigenous civilizations, the Indians became forced laborers. In other areas, large cattle ranches sprang up and were gradually concentrated; many of today's immense estates have their origins in the vast tracts the Spanish Crown granted to the conquistadores. Some areas that had neither precious metals nor vast numbers of Indians to enslave remained largely empty during the colonial era and thus escaped the full weight of the Spanish colonial heritage. When these areas, such as Costa Rica, were finally settled, less of the get-rich-quick attitude prevailed, and a society of mostly self-sufficient medium-sized family farms emerged instead of the usual pattern of large estates dominated by a European elite with a large servile class, either black or Indian.

The hacienda was probably *the* classic institution of the nineteenth century. During this period the system of great estates begun in the colonial period was expanded and consolidated: The Argentine pampa was enclosed and divided into private estates, communal Indian lands were brought under private ownership, areas of cultivation and grazing were expanded. The hacienda was a self-contained unit socially, economically, politically, religiously. The *hacendado* had absolute sway, his tenants and peasants largely cast in a system of peonage that differed little from earlier slavery. The hacienda not only generated wealth for its owner, but the number of acres, cattle, and peasants were also symbols of social status or prestige. The large estate was thus both a capitalist enterprise and a feudal one. It helped perpetuate the two-class, exploitative, authoritarian structure first established during the colonial period.

The hacienda economy was agriculturally centered. The peasants continued to eke out a subsistence existence on their small plots, and the hacienda produced not food but commodities (tobacco, coffee, sugar) largely for the world market. Even today, although many of the Latin American economies remain predominantly agricultural ones, they are oriented toward producing for the world market and hence must import basic foodstuffs to feed their own populations.

Toward the end of the nineteenth century, commerce was increasingly stimulated and the process of industrialization began. Industry remained incipient and small-scale until after World War I and the market crash of 1929, however, when the markets for Latin America's exports dried up and it was impossible to import manufactured goods. Industrialization thus took the form of "import substitution"—that is, the production locally of goods that had previously been imported. Although industrialization proceeded rapidly, with the pace obviously varying from country to country, agriculture remained predominant and subsistence the way of life of most Latin Americans. Today in the majority of countries, the amount of gross national product (GNP) generated through agriculture and the amount generated through industry are approximately the same.

Industrialization quickened the pace of life and led to accelerated social change. It served to break down the traditional isolation of the *patria chica* and to integrate further the Latin American economies into the world marketplace. It also stimulated foreign investment in the area and paved the way for growth of the modern multinational corporation. These changes brought some economic betterment, but they also cast Latin America into a position of subservience and dependency with regard to the advanced industrial nations, principally the United States.

Although some of the bigger and richer countries like Mexico, Argentina, Brazil, and Venezuela have at times made progress in becoming more self-sufficient in terms of both food production and industrial output, the majority of the Latin American countries remain locked in the historical pattern of exporting raw materials for the world market and importing manufactured goods. That pattern was beneficial to Latin America up to the 1920s, so long as the price Latin America received for its exports remained roughly equivalent to what it had to pay to import manufactured goods. But since that time the costs of the imported manufactured goods have risen far faster than has the price Latin America receives for its exports. The result has been that while the countries of the northern tier (North America, West Europe, Japan) forged ahead, Latin America lagged increasingly behind, with mounting trade deficits, balance-of-payments problems, woefully low wages, and underdeveloped economies. The gap between the industrialized nations of the North and the raw-materials-producing ones of the South widened instead of narrowed.

The situation was made worse by the fact that the essentially one-crop or one-resource economies of Latin America (tin for Bolivia, nitrate and then copper for Chile, sugar for Cuba and the Dominican Republic, coffee for Brazil, Colombia, and Central America, bananas for Ecuador) were subject to fluctuating world market prices, changing demands and consumption habits, and the import quotas set by the major powers, chiefly the United States. If, as occurred during World War I, nitrate could be produced chemically instead of being mined, the bottom would drop out of the Chilean economy. If the price of sugar were to fluctuate downward by a few cents per pound, the Cuban and Dominican economies could be ruined and their political systems toppled. If we were to decide to drink beer instead of coffee, Colombia and Brazil could similarly slide into chaos. Or, if the United States were to decide to punish Cuba or the Dominican Republic, all it would have to do is reduce the quota of sugar imported from them. The Latin American economies are vulnerable to impersonal, outside forces over which they have no control.

The vagueness of both world market prices and consumption habits subjects the Latin American countries to political pressures and to boom-and-bust cycles whose effects are devastating and, to those countries, intolerable. They are now bargaining for stable markets and prices, and the rising demand for commodities and raw materials has given them a stronger negotiating position. Many are banding together to form blocs of commodity and raw-materials producers similar to the Organization of Petroleum Exporting Countries (OPEC) oil cartel (of which Venezuela is a leading member). There are now cartels of bauxite-producing countries, copper-producing countries, coffee-producing countries, and banana-producing countries. Other countries are making renewed efforts to diversify their economies and to industrialize. But the very effort to industrialize is producing new social forces (the rise of sizable middle-class and trade-union organizations) that are challenging the internal structure of social and political power. The dynamics of these changes, the processes of social, economic, and political modernization lie at the heart of the analysis of this book.

The Latin American economies are no longer ranked as "underdeveloped" or "Low Income," but they have not reached the stage of being "Industrial Market Economies" either. Rather they are classified by the World Bank as "Middle Income Countries," with Bolivia, Honduras, El Salvador, and Nicaragua at the lower end of that scale; Brazil, Mexico, Argentina, Chile, Uruguay, and Venezuela at the upper level; and the other countries occupying intermediary positions. In various measures of social and political modernization, as we shall see, the Latin American countries are also intermediary, neither so backward and uninstitutionalized as other Third World areas nor so developed as the industrial nations (Table 1.1).

Though the Latin American economies have modernized rapidly during the past four decades, there remain important continuities with the past. Increasingly drawn into a world capitalist system, the Latin American systems have nonetheless retained a number of distinct historical features. We are apt to go astray if we think of the Latin American economies in terms of the U.S. capitalist model. Yes, Latin America is a part of the capitalist world, but it often practices its own special form of

Table 1.1 Indices of Modernization in Latin America

	GDP[a] per capita (US$) (1981)	Manufacturing as % of GDP (1981)	% of Urbanization (1981-preliminary est.)	Life Expectancy (years) (1981)	Literacy Rate (%) (1980)
Argentina	1,795.9	25	86.3	71	93
Bolivia	549.9	14	33.0	51	63
Brazil	1,554.9	27	69.0	64	76
Chile	1,674.6	22	80.6	68	90
Colombia	924.9	21	78.1	63	81
Costa Rica	1,446.1	20	47.0	73	90
Cuba	840.0[b]	—	66.0	73	96
Dominican Republic	1,043.9	15	55.4	62	68
Ecuador	1,053.2	11	44.0	62	81
El Salvador	604.7	15	40.5	63	63
Guatemala	1,182.8	—	32.2	59	47
Honduras	616.3	17	36.8	59	60
Mexico	1,953.7	22	65.9	66	83
Nicaragua	888.8	26	59.2	57	90
Panama	1,982.7	10	54.7	71	85
Paraguay	1,205.0	17	36.5	65	84
Peru	1,294.0	25	72.6	58	80
Puerto Rico	3,502.0[c]	—	61.8[d]	72	90
Uruguay	2,155.9	26	81.6	71	94
Venezuela	2,615.2	15	79.0	68	85

[a]Gross domestic product
[b]Per capita income (1977)
[c]Per capita income (1981)
[d]1975

Sources: Inter-American Development Bank, *Economic and Social Progress in Latin America: 1982* (Inter-American Development Bank, Washington, D.C., 1982); World Bank, *World Development Report 1983* (Oxford University Press, New York, 1983).

capitalism. In keeping with Latin America's historical traditions of central control, the capitalism of Latin America is not generally one of laissez-faire and individual initiative but often a system of *state capitalism*, with a comparatively large public sector and much central direction over the whole system. Let us keep in mind this concept of state capitalism and its implications, and the hypothesis that the modern Latin American economies represent an updated, modernized extension of the semifeudal, exploitative "milk-cow," mercantilist system of the colonial period.

CLASSES AND SOCIAL FORCES

Latin America has always been essentially a two-class society of lords and peasants, elites and masses. There has been at all times a small middle sector composed of artisans, craftsmen, soldiers, and petty bureaucrats, even during the colonial era. But the system remained basically two-class with a small group of Spanish (or Portuguese) elites at the top and a large mass of peasants, workers, Indians, and slaves at the bottom. Within these major sectors, additionally, there was ample room for rivalries and further gradations.

The pattern was that of a small European elite never numbering more than a few percent of the population and of a huge Indian, African, or racially mixed mass. The system was sharply pyramidal and rigidly hierarchical; there was almost no possibility of social mobility or movement from one class to another. Implied here is the fact that the society had caste overtones as well as class criteria: The elite was not only wealthy but white; the lower classes were not only poor but Indian, African, or of mixed racial background.

It should not be surprising that this two-class pattern was established in the sixteenth century. What is remarkable is that it lasted so long; once established, it persisted through the seventeenth and eighteenth centuries. The institution of the hacienda perpetuated the same two-class system throughout the nineteenth century, despite the achievement of independence and the writing of a host of democratic constitutions. Social anthropologists tell us that the same two-class pattern, albeit modified in various particulars, exists today.

The onset of modernization and industrialization in the nineteenth century, however, gave rise to some new social forces that made the historical system more complex. The growth of commerce helped stimulate the emergence of a new class of business people that in some instances challenged the power of the traditional *hacendados*. In most cases, however, this newer wealth was gradually joined with the older wealth, through marriage and other means, so that the historical oligarchic pattern was strengthened.

The new immigrant communities—Italians, Germans, Syrians, Jews, Japanese, English, North Americans—that began coming to Latin America in the late nineteenth century were often co-opted and assimilated in much the same fashion. Though in some ways maintaining a sense of separate identity, many of the new immigrants prospered, married into the elite Latin American community, and became leading members of society.

The growing middle class or middle sectors in Latin America represent a distinctive but parallel phenomenon. As economic growth accelerated, a sizable (20–40 percent of the population, depending on the country) middle sector began to emerge, consisting of small-business people, merchants, clerks, government workers, and the like. But the middle sectors were deeply divided on political issues and showed little consciousness as a class. They aped aristocratic ways, despised the lower classes (from which they had recently risen), and frequently were more politically conservative than the real aristocrats. Hence although in terms of income there appears to be a growing "middle class" in Latin America, in terms of social and political attitudes the old two-class system has been perpetuated. The basic dividing line lies between those who work with their hands and those who do not. Neither the upper nor the middle classes work with their hands; manual labor is done only by peasants and workers. The continuing two-part division of society seems to mean that no middle-class society, with all its presumed middle-class virtues—moderation, pragmatism in politics, democratic social and political ideas—has as yet emerged in Latin America.

But within this basically two-class system, the lower classes have become further differentiated. There are varying forms of tenancy and of wage labor in the countryside. Other peasants have migrated en masse to the cities, where they have formed a large but unorganized subproletariat. Trade unions, consisting of skilled workers, the "elite" of the lower classes, have secured a place as major power contenders in many of the countries.

Thus while Latin America remains an essentially two-class society, within that structure there are various gradations. And though Latin American society remains rigidly hierarchical and pyramidal, and though social mobility is limited, new avenues for advancement have opened up. Business, the army, government service, and university or technical training all provide ways for the upwardly mobile to rise in the social scale. Nevertheless, many of the old class barriers persist, and the basic two-part division of society implies a situation of on-again, off-again class warfare. No apathetic, "safe," middle-of-the-road bourgeois society appears to have emerged anywhere in Latin America. All this most likely signals the continuation of what Kalman Silvert called a conflict society.

THE POLITICAL CULTURE

Political culture is a term used to describe the basic values, ideas, and behavioral patterns that govern a society. It covers a large terrain and is fraught with dangers of misuse. We must avoid stereotyping cultures as the old "national character" studies did in the past. We must also recognize that any society may have several cultural currents existing simultaneously; additionally, we must realize that political culture presents a general and composite picture and that individual persons and behavior within the society may sometimes fit the ideal type at best imperfectly and sometimes not at all. Nevertheless, when employed carefully, the concept of political culture is a useful one and helps us get at the differing assumptions on which distinct political societies are based.

It is probably safe to say that although North American political culture is strongly Lockean and liberal, that of Latin America, historically at least, is strongly elitist, hierarchical, authoritarian, corporatist, and patrimonialist. The elitism of Latin American society stems from the Iberian tradition of nobility and grandees, a medieval tradition that had reached its fruition in Spain and Portugal precisely at the time the discovery of the Americas provided new lands and slaves that allowed any aspiring Spanish conquistador to live like an aristocrat. Elitism stemmed also from the long history of Spanish political theory, which argued that society should be governed by its "natural elites" and which was skeptical of the capacity of the masses to govern wisely and well.

Elitism, hierarchy, and authoritarianism all had a powerful basis in traditional Spanish Catholicism, particularly as articulated in the writings of Saint Thomas Aquinas and his disciples. This was not the only tradition in Spanish thought, but for a long time it remained the dominant one. Political authority emanated directly from God or from the "natural order" of the universe. Both power and society were organized hierarchically and from the top down: God, archangels, angels, cherubim, seraphim, and so on down to humans. But only certain types of humans. First came kings, who received their power directly from God, and then nobles, whose authority over land and men was similarly assumed to be God-given. Occupying positions progressively further down the hierarchy were the lesser nobility; then soldiers, artisans, craftsmen; then workers, day laborers, peasants. And in the New World, there were Indians and African slaves still lower in the hierarchy.

Although Latin society was thus structured hierarchically by rank, it was also structured vertically in terms of society's major corporate groups: army, Church, bureaucracy, university, and so on. In the twentieth century, corporatism as a manifest ideology received a deservedly bad reputation because of its association with fascism; but in Latin America, corporatism was not necessarily fascistic but had to do with the historical Latin tendency to divide society vertically and functionally. Latin American society is hence a society of place, of position. External appearance and manners are essential in signaling to others what rank or status one holds and therefore how one should be treated. It is a system organized along both class and corporate lines.

All these features, grounded in Catholic political philosophy and natural law, served to reinforce each other. Corporatism, elitism, hierarchy, and authoritarianism helped foster a rigidly stratified system in which mobility was difficult at best. If one was born into a certain position in society, one generally stayed in that position. At each level in the hierarchy one was expected to accept one's station in life as God-given and conforming to the natural ordering of the universe. There could be no questioning of the system. Society was thought of as fixed and immutable; for over three hundred years it remained locked in this pattern.

But even though Latin American society was authoritarian and hierarchical, it was also patrimonialist and paternal. Thus, although elitism and authoritarianism were viewed as natural and God-given, the elites had a Christian obligation to take care of those less fortunate than themselves. Those who owned land and labor might run their estates in absolute fashion but, in theory, they had also to be just and fair. Although the peasant or worker owed an obligation of labor to the *patrón*, he in turn was obligated to look after the welfare of his workers. And even though those in political authority could rule autocratically and expect loyalty from their subjects, they had an obligation not to overstep the bounds of "right" behavior. Patron-client relations were thus a two-way process, whether at the level of the local hacienda or in the national political system. Patrimonialism as it applied to the state system emphasized the features of centralization, authoritarianism, and modernization under elite hegemony, but within some quite carefully defined bounds. In many ways these traditions of hierarchy, authoritarianism, elitism, corporatism, and patrimonialism are still strongly present in Latin American political society.

In the nineteenth century, however, a new framework of ideas and values—liberal, republican, and egalitarian, sometimes secular and rationalist—was superimposed upon the earlier tradition. Scholars continue to argue about the degree to which these values took hold and the variations among countries. Liberal ideas were often incorporated in laws and constitutions, but the underlying structures of landownership and authority often remained elitist. By now, however, in most Latin American societies there exist two basic conceptions, two political cultures, side by side: the one elitist, hierarchical, authoritarian; the other liberal and democratic. Although frequently these two traditions are so far apart that they do not touch and provide little basis for social and political compromise, most Latin American nations now represent complex fusions of both (as in the growth of Christian democracy or authoritarian socialism). These two fundamentally opposed conceptions of society and the role and functions of people in it lie at the heart of much nineteenth- and twentieth-century political conflict. They help account for the concepts of "the two Brazils," "the two Venezuelas," for instance, frequently found in the literature. They also help explain the deep divisions found in Latin American political society.

While from the nineteenth century a second tradition has been superimposed on the first, in the twentieth century a third and socialist tradition was in turn superimposed on the first two. In most of Latin America, socialism is still a minority strain. But socialism has come to power in Cuba and Nicaragua; in Chile political opinion is about equally divided electorally among conservative, liberal, and socialist conceptions; social democratic governments have come to power in several countries;

and clearly, among young people generally, socialist sentiment is growing. Hence the real question may be not whether socialism is coming to Latin America, for it is; but rather whether it will be fused into the older traditions, or whether, as in Cuba, it will seize power by itself and proceed to discard or eliminate the other, older traditions.

In this way, what was once a fairly unified, stable, monolithic Latin American political culture has now become a deeply divided and unstable one. The old values are no longer universally held, yet the newer ones are sometimes only incompletely established. Moreover, the distances between such wholly different societal conceptions—feudalism, liberalism, socialism—are so vast as to be virtually uncompromisable. The overlaps and fusions between quite distinct and often wholly opposed ideas and world views of society tend to make Latin America even more a conflict society than was the case before.

Of course, not all of the Latin American countries exhibit all of these traits and patterns, nor to the same degree. The pattern of elitism, authoritarianism, hierarchy, corporatism, and patrimonialism here ascribed to traditional Latin American culture provides an "ideal type" that does not always mirror existing reality. It fits only some countries, or if all, then to varying degrees. In some countries traditional Spanish institutions were strong; in others, weak. Some countries that lacked strong Hispanic institutions endeavored later to create them; in others (such as Chile) the liberal and republican tradition was strong right from the beginning; and in still others both the traditional Hispanic and the liberal institutions were historically so weak that chaos, clan politics, and caudilloism remained endemic. These variations stand out clearly in the country chapters.

CONCLUSIONS AND IMPLICATIONS

Latin American society has long been riven by geographic, economic, social, and political-cultural divisions that retarded both national integration and development. But the great motor force of twentieth-century change is now overcoming those barriers and altering the foundations on which Latin American society has rested. These are no longer the sleepy "banana republics" they once were; rather, Latin American society has become vibrantly alive, with far-reaching social changes sweeping the area.

Although the changes have been immense, the problems remain at least equally large. Poverty, malnutrition, and malnutrition-related diseases are endemic. Illiteracy remains high; the majority of the population is ill housed, ill clothed, ill fed. Health care is poor, wages are low, inflation is rampant, and the standards of living of peasants and slum dwellers are woefully inadequate. In addition, the existing social and political institutions are unable to cope with the immense changes in process. The fabric of Latin American society is being torn apart, whereas the institutional structure to manage these changes has not developed at the same pace.

And yet Latin America is not failing altogether in dealing with its developmental dilemmas. New formulas are being tried and new institutions experimented with. A single-party system in the context of an institutionalized—now somewhat tired—revolution has proved more or less functional in Mexico. Colombia, Costa Rica, and Venezuela have developed into more or less democratic systems. Peru, Panama, Bolivia, Ecuador, and Honduras have had military regimes come to power that, with varying degrees of enthusiasm and success, have stressed nationalist and developmentalist themes; more recently in all these countries democracy has again been tried. In Paraguay an old-time caudillo regime remains in control, but it too has brought change. Conservative, authoritarian, state-capitalist military regimes had established themselves in Brazil, Chile, and Uruguay, but they are also in transition. And in Cuba, a socialist regime remains in power that has not been as successful in encouraging economic growth as other Latin American countries but that has carried out some of the most successful social programs—in housing, health care, education, and social services—in all of Latin America. Nicaragua has also embarked on a socialist course. The variety of alternatives being weighed and experimented with to handle the new pressures and social forces of modernization makes Latin America exciting to study. An exploration and assessment of these varied alternatives and their degrees of success or failure form the basis of the analyses presented in this book.

2
The Pattern of
Historical Development

Latin America is a product of its past in ways that North America is not. Latin America remains dominated in large measure by institutions and practices first established during the colonial era; in many aspects it is still a semifeudal area. Because the weight of history is so strong, we must come to grips with Latin America's past in order to understand its present.

THE CONQUEST

The conquest of the Americas by Spain and Portugal fully a century before the English colonies were established was one of the most incredible epic adventures of all time. Its significance reached beyond the Americas. Columbus's first steps in the New World and the subsequent conquest in the next several decades of almost all of Latin America were the initial phase of a European expansionism and colonialism that would eventually encompass the entire world. Latin America was the first non-European continental area to be Westernized.

The contact of Europeans with the native Indian population gave rise to a clash of cultures that persists today. It gave rise also to some of the earliest comparative anthropological and sociological studies of non-European cultures and societies. It resulted in the Christianization, to a greater or lesser degree, of Latin America. We have already remarked how the gold and silver brought back by the Spanish in part made possible the Industrial Revolution. The conquest immensely expanded human knowledge and frontiers. It stimulated worldwide exploration and trade and helped turn the focus of commerce and power from the Mediterranean to the Atlantic. The conquest led to new patterns of social, political, and race relations and to innovative experiments in seeking to colonize and govern distant lands. In a very short period of time the known world had doubled in size; so had human vistas.

Although it is conventional to begin a history of Latin America in 1492, this is yet another reflection of our Western biases. Latin America was already settled by large-scale Indian civilizations long before the

Europeans arrived. It has been estimated that, whereas the Indian population of North America numbered only 3 million at the time of European colonization and was organized generally in dispersed and small-sized tribes, the number of Indians in Latin America was about 30 million, many grouped into settled large-scale civilizations. These differences in size and numbers shaped the subsequent histories of the two areas to a major extent and help explain the differences in society and race relations that persist in the two parts of the Americas.

North America largely solved its Indian problem by either killing the Indians or, later, confining them to reservations. In Latin America there were, in many areas, too many Indians to be killed; although the Spanish conquest involved barbarism toward the Indians at least equal to that of the English colonists, the sheer number of Indians in Latin America spoke for a policy of assimilation rather than of annihilation. The Indians were generally subdued rather than slaughtered; Indian leaders were often co-opted into working with or for the Spaniards; and the Spanish usually replaced the Indian aristocracy at the top of the social pyramid without destroying the pyramid per se.

North America was *settled* by families, whereas Latin America was *conquered* by conquistadores who did not bring their families along because they viewed the conquest as a military campaign. The immense differences in the number of Indians and the level of their civilizations between the two parts of the Americas implied also greater racial intermingling and less manifest racial prejudice in Latin America than in North America. This applied to blacks as well as Indians. Miscegenation and more relaxed racial attitudes led to predominantly mestizo or mulatto societies in many countries of Latin America, and this situation helps explain the sense of national inferiority (on racial and cultural grounds) that many Latin Americans still feel and the sense of superiority—bolstered by old-time racial prejudices—that North Americans still harbor.

Indian culture was so strong and well established that it pervaded the Spanish and Portuguese colonies to a degree as yet perhaps unrecognized. The larger-scale Indian civilizations practiced a form of elitism and theocracy on which the Spaniards simply imposed a new layer. The tradition of political absolutism and arbitrary rule by local caciques has its roots as much in Indian traditions as in the Spanish. Moreover, the Aztec, Inca, and Mayan civilizations of Latin America were proud cultures of major accomplishments; they affected the Spaniards almost as much as the Spaniards did the native Indians. Hence the clash of cultures in Latin America was far more a two-way process of interaction between Indian and European than in North America. In many realms of life Indian ways prevailed; in other realms such as religion there are complex mixtures of Catholicism and native Indian beliefs. Some nations like Mexico and Peru are immensely proud of and preoccupied with their Indian pasts and have sought to elevate the mestizo to a new racial and national type.

Although assimilation and the fusion of Indian and European cultures were the rule in some areas, separation remained the rule in others. In the highlands of Latin America the Indians remained all but untouched by the conquest. The conquest was such a shock to the Indians in some regions that they withdrew into a shell of isolation. In Guatemala, Peru, Bolivia, and elsewhere, the distance between the Indian and European cultures is still almost unbridgeable; in these countries there exist two nations within the same borders. In Guatemala, for example, where some 50 percent of the population does not speak the national language, lives completely outside the money economy, is wholly uninvolved in national social and political life, and may not even be cognizant of being part of an entity called Guatemala, the problem of integration makes that in the United States seem far less severe by comparison.

The conquest proceeded in stages and took different forms in different areas. It is useful to review this process and the distinct patterns of colonization, race relations, landholding systems, and colonial structures to which it gave rise, since these early patterns strongly shaped the internal structures of the independent nations that eventually came into being.

The first area to feel the impact of Spanish conquest and colonization was the island of Hispaniola, which flourished for some thirty years until the supplies of gold and Indian labor began to decline. Hispaniola also served as the launching pad for the conquests of Cuba and Puerto Rico. But these islands, like Hispaniola, had little gold or silver and as the Indian population was decimated, African slaves were brought in. The islands were eventually dominated by grazing, agriculture, and, later, large plantations (not by mining); and their socioracial patterns were henceforth shaped by the relations between Africans and Europeans rather than Indians and Europeans.

Hernando Cortés undertook the conquest of Mexico from Cuba. In Mexico, Yucatan, and present-day Guatemala the Spanish found not small tribes as on the islands but large-scale civilizations with populations numbering in the millions. The incredible impact the discovery and presence of these civilizations had on the Spanish and how Cortés captured the Aztec chief Montezuma and conquered his empire are now the stuff of legend. The Spanish were awed and impressed but hardly immobilized by the riches and cities of the Indians. The conquest of such an extensive civilization was aided by several factors: the use of the horse, which the Indians had never seen before and which was probably more effective than firearms; the resentment of the Aztecs by other tribes whom Cortés cleverly employed as allies; the fortuitous circumstance that Cortés arrived the same year Indian prophesies foretold of a "great god" who would sail across the waters from the east; and the disintegration of Indian resistance once Montezuma himself was captured.

But in Mexico, unlike the islands, Indian civilization was stronger and so never entirely subdued or eliminated; there were simply too many Indians. The result was a sometimes thin Spanish veneer of "civilization" with a huge Indian subculture, incompletely Hispanicized and Westernized, underneath. The Spanish became the overlords and absolute rulers and the Indians the laborers and peasants. The Spanish Crown granted the conquistadores the right to Indian labor (*encomienda*), a right that carried the obligation to Christianize the Indians and treat them justly. But Spain was far away and unable to enforce its edicts completely and regularly; there were many abuses of the system and grants of labor soon de facto became grants of land also, with the Christianizing duties often forgotten. The later hacienda system, so important in shaping Latin American history and society, was formed on this same two-class lord and peasant relationship, a relationship that was based as much on race and caste as it was on class. Few African slaves were brought to the mainland (except along the coasts of the Caribbean) since the supply of Indian labor seemed inexhaustible; hence, race, class, and social relations in Mexico and most of the mainland would be written in terms of the interactions between Europeans and Indians, not Europeans and blacks.

From Mexico the conquest proceeded south to Guatemala and down the isthmus through Central America. In the meantime, Brazil was being settled by the Portuguese, and other Spanish galleons had explored the Venezuelan coast and sailed up the Río de la Plata to claim Argentina, Paraguay, and Uruguay. Balboa had crossed Central America at Darien (present-day Panama) to gaze out upon the Pacific. And in an epochal feat, the Pizarro brothers and a handful of men conquered the Inca empire stretching across Ecuador, Peru, and Bolivia. In the process the area of what is now Colombia came under the hegemony of the Spanish Crown, and Chile followed shortly thereafter. From Bolivia the conquest spilled across the Andes into Argentina, which, despite its fronting on the Atlantic, was initially settled more from the western than the eastern side. The conquest of the entire continent was completed within the first eighty years, as compared with the three centuries that it took for North America to be settled.

Where the Spaniards found large numbers of Indians to enslave or to force to work in the mines or on the land, as in Peru, Ecuador, and Bolivia, the same kind of rigid two-class landholding and hacienda system emerged as in Mexico and Guatemala. What is now Paraguay with its Guaraní Indians was a fascinating special case, since their overlord through a grant from the Spanish Crown was the Jesuit order. In Central America, Venezuela, and Chile precious metals were less readily available and there were smaller numbers of Indians to enslave; hence, the Spanish presence was generally weaker, the Church less important as an institution, and the system of the hacienda less pervasive. In Uruguay and Argentina, there were neither precious metals nor more than a few Indians. These areas were only lightly and generally later colonized and never felt the full weight of the authoritarian Spanish colonial system that fell upon Mexico and Peru.

There were thus degrees by which the Spanish presence and institutions were experienced; not all areas were equally affected. Characterized by colonial neglect, these less-affected areas often developed a stronger sense of self-reliance. With fewer Indians to enslave, the Spanish who settled there often had less aversion to manual labor; nor were class and caste lines so rigidly drawn. Finally, because the yoke of the past was often lighter, these areas frequently had fewer obstacles to overcome in their later drive to develop and modernize. The possibilities for national development and democratization in Latin America were generally inversely proportional to the degree these areas experienced the Spanish colonial heritage. Where Indians and gold and hence Spanish institutions were strong, as in Mexico, Guatemala, Peru, Ecuador, and Bolivia, the difficulties of development and democratization have (except perhaps in Mexico—and then only by violent revolution) proved almost insuperable. Where Indians and precious metals were scarce and hence Spanish institutions weak, as in Venezuela, Chile, Costa Rica, Argentina, and Uruguay, the possibilities for development and democratization have been better.

The conquest of Brazil by the Portuguese represents a parallel but distinctive case. Brazil was established on an authoritarian, elitist, hierarchical, corporatist, patrimonialist, and semifeudal basis just as the Spanish colonies were. But Portugal had neither the will nor the power to colonize effectively such an immense area, and Portugal's colonization efforts were always more relaxed and easygoing than those of the Spanish. Further, the Portuguese enclaves were largely limited to the coast and only later spilled over the mountainous escarpment into the interior. Additionally, since there were few Indians to enslave, the Portuguese imported African slaves. But here again the plantation system and race relations in Brazil were never so rigid and unyielding as in the Spanish colonies. Brazil represents a variant on the main themes here presented of conquest and colonization, although in the Portuguese colony too, elitist, oligarchic, and two-class patterns prevailed.

By 1570, several decades before the first British colonies were established in North America, the Spanish and Portuguese conquest had been all but completed. It was a remarkable feat in a short span of time, and Spain became, briefly, the major power in Europe.

COLONIAL SOCIETY:
PRINCIPLES AND INSTITUTIONS

The institutions colonial Spain and Portugal carried with them to the New World were a direct reflection of the Spanish and Portuguese themselves in 1492. An understanding of these institutions serves as the beginning point for comprehending modern-day Latin America and also for contrasting the foundations of Latin American society with those of North America.

Spain in 1492 had just completed the reconquest of its own peninsula from the Moors, North Africans of the Muslim faith who had dominated Iberia since the eighth century. The effort to drive out the Moors was both the culmination of a long effort at national unification and a religious crusade. No mercy was asked for—or given to—the infidels. The conquest of the Americas was similar in this sense, for the Indians were also heathens, who had to be Christianized and Hispanicized— or else! The conquest of the Americas was an extension of Spain's reconquest and "purification" of its own peninsula.

Because of Spain's and Portugal's long struggles against the Moors, the development of feudalism and a stable lord-vassal system was slower and distinctly different from that in the rest of Europe. Feudalism in Iberia was tied to conquest: As the fighting knights and nobles drove the Moors farther south, they received the right to the lands they had conquered and the labor of those who lived on the lands. Spain had just begun to develop a pattern of feudal landownership when the conquest of the Americas occurred.

Feudalism was then brought to the New World, where it received a new lease on life—at a time when it had already begun to fade away elsewhere in Europe. The Spanish Crown used the New World lands and grants of Indian labor to reward middle-class elements and the lower nobility—who would not have been able to gain such extensive wealth and the titles that went with it in the peninsula itself—and thus to buy their loyalty and keep them from rebelling against royal authority. The Crown employed the time-honored practice of doling out lands, labor, and titles in return for loyalty and the further centralization of authority in the Crown itself. When they arrived in the New World, the Spaniards found the conditions particularly propitious for a new form of feudalism: abundant lands, a ready-made peasantry, and a virgin society ripe for conquest in which they would constitute the new elite. Whereas in the peninsula the available land and labor had already been partitioned, in the New World every would-be Spanish grandee could become the overlord of vast estates.

The late fifteenth century was also important because it was during that period that the principal Spanish kingdoms of Aragon and Castile were unified through the marriage of Ferdinand and Isabella. Further, Spain had been unified under authoritarian, absolutist, centralized, and patrimonialist auspices, and these features too were carried over to the New World through the Spanish colonial system. The early-sixteenth-century model of a pyramidal, centralized, authoritarian, corporate-contractual state system, the ideal of Spain's golden century of national accomplishment, would continue to serve as an ideal for many years. In several countries of Latin America, this sixteenth-century model is still regarded as the ideal toward which a nation should strive (see Figure 2.1).

The institutions that Spain brought to the New World beginning in 1492 were reflections of Spain itself and of its historical developmental

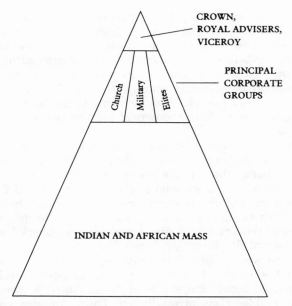

Figure 2.1 The Corporate-Authoritarian Structure of Latin American Political Society, Sixteenth Century

drives. The political tradition that Spain enshrined was one of authoritarian and patrimonialist rule. Power emanated from the top down, from king to viceroy (literally *vice king*) to local cacique, *hacendado*, or landowner. It was absolutist and centralized to the core.

Beneath the king came the major corporate and vested interests: Church, army, nobility. Each of these interests had its own powerful traditions and prerogatives, its own courts and codes of conduct, its own jurisdictions and responsibilities. Each owed loyalty to the king and constituted his strong right arm in religious, military, and economic affairs, respectively. The king could not always enforce his decrees in colonies several thousand miles away, but centralized absolutism nonetheless remained the ideal. So did the idea of a harmonious, vertically organized structure of corporate orders, all similarly authoritarian and hierarchical in their respective spheres but ultimately revolving around and subservient to the Crown or the central state.

The religious institutions of Catholicism and the Church bolstered and reinforced the state concepts. The Church was an instrument of the state and of the conquest. Because of the long crusade against the Moorish infidels and the preoccupation with maintaining the purity of the Catholic faith, the Spanish Church was more intolerant and absolutist than its European counterparts. Catholic beliefs at the time, inspired by Saint Thomas and a remarkable group of sixteenth-century political theorists, emphasized authority, absolutism, and the natural inequalities and hence hierarchy of humankind. These concepts not only helped undergird and bolster the idea of a strong central state and monarchy, but they provided convenient rationalization for subjugating the Indians. In Spain, the Church was more than just another interest group and Catholicism more than merely another religion: They were the backbone of the regime, a part of the state system, at the base of the political culture and the moral and theoretical foundations of society and the political order.

The economic system was organized on an exploitative basis. The colonies were considered to exist solely for the benefit of the colonizing country, and hence their ample resources were drained away. To fight their European wars and to provide glitter to Crown and Church, Spain and Portugal milked the colonies dry. This marked the beginning of Latin America's being cast in a dependency position in relation to the major colonial powers. The Latin American "periphery" was exploited for the benefit of the European "core."

Society was set up along similarly hierarchical and two-class lines. Except in a few localized cases, Latin America never developed a class of medium-sized family farmers as in North America, nor did a sizable commercial middle class arise. Rather, Latin America consisted of a small elite with a huge mass of Indian or African slaves, serfs, tenant farmers, peasants, and day laborers at the bottom. These social classes had been rigidly stratified in the Old World; in the New World class considerations were further reinforced by racial ones. Each class and caste in the hierarchy enjoyed its own special rights and obligations. This was the "feudal ideal," although it was seldom mentioned that the upper classes monopolized most of the rights and the lower classes most of the obligations. Since this structure was thought to be natural and in conformity with God's just ordering of the universe, little change was possible. The structure of an essentially two-class, patron-client system persists today, almost as rigid and unyielding as in colonial times.

Intellectual life and the educational system were grounded upon many of the same principles. Education was private and reserved only for the elites; it followed from the hierarchical and nonegalitarian premises that there was no need of mass public education. Education and intellectual life were infused with Catholic, Thomistic premises. The method of learning was scholastic and deductive, based upon the rote memorization of absolute truths from which principles of correct conduct could be deduced. There was no sense of science, empiricism, or observation to arrive inductively at agreed-upon knowledge. Learning, education, and intellectual life were closed and absolutist.

It should not be surprising that the Spanish and Portuguese colonies were established on the basis of semifeudal institutions. True, Spanish Catholicism was probably more intolerant than that of other areas of

Table 2.1 Contrasting Foundations of Latin and North American Society

	Latin America, 1492–1570	North America Seventeenth Century
Political	Authoritarian, absolutist, centralized, corporatist	More liberal, early steps toward representative and democratic rule
Religious	Catholic orthodoxy and absolutism	Protestantism and religious pluralism
Economic	Feudal, mercantilist, patrimonialist	Emerging capitalist, entrepreneurial
Social	Hierarchical, two-class, rigid	More mobile, multiclass
Educational and Intellectual	Scholastic, rote memorization, deductive	Empirical, scientific, inductive

Europe, and the special nature of Iberian feudalism, the way the Spanish kingdom had been unified, and a distinct political tradition helped make Spain and Portugal different. But of at least equal importance was the time period in which the colonies were settled, a factor that makes the colonies the product more of historical accident than of some supposed evils residual in the Hispanic tradition.

The Spanish and Portuguese colonies were founded on a set of institutions that were absolutist, authoritarian, hierarchical, Catholic, feudal or semifeudal, two-class, corporatist, patrimonialist, orthodox, and scholastic to their core. By contrast, the British colonies to the north, founded fully a century and more later, derived from a set of institutions and practices that were fundamentally different from those prevailing when the Iberians came to America. By the seventeenth century, when colonial North America was effectively settled, the first steps toward limited, representative government were already under way, and the Protestant Reformation had broken the monopoly of Catholic absolutism and led to greater religious (and political) pluralism. Economically, capitalism had begun to supersede the feudal and patrimonialist conceptions. Socially, a more pluralistic and predominantly middle-class society had come into existence. And intellectually, the revolution ushered in with Galileo and Newton had taken place, with its emphasis on science and experimentation. The differences between the sixteenth century, when the Latin American colonies received their indelible imprint, and the seventeenth, when North American society took firm shape, and the the major distinguishing characteristics of the two cultures that developed in the Americas are summarized in Table 2.1.

The differences are stark. They imply entirely different life-styles and world views, wholly distinctive social, economic, and political institutions and behavior. They provide clues to explain why one part of the Americas was condemned to lag behind while the other forged ahead. For if there is validity to our dividing a course on the basic history of Western civilization into pre–A.D. 1500 and post–A.D. 1500 components, then it is important to see that Latin American institutions were grounded on essentially feudal conceptions dating from the period before that historical breaking point, while those of the United States were based upon the more modern world emerging from the seventeenth century on. This has nothing to do with any alleged inherent superiority of liberal, Protestant, northern, Anglo-Saxon civilization. Rather it has to do with the contrasting time periods in which the societies in Latin and North America took definitive shape, and the distinct, alternative sets of institutions that these earlier and later colonizers, respectively, transplanted to the New World.

Given the times and circumstances, therefore, it should not be surprising that the Latin American colonies were founded on a semifeudal basis. What is remarkable is the perseverance of these institutions. The absolutist, authoritarian, two-class, patrimonialist, Catholic, scholastic, mercantilist, and corporatist institutions of Latin America lasted through the period of conquest and settlement in the sixteenth century, the era of institutionalization in the seventeenth century, and the reforms of the eighteenth century. Indeed, efforts to reform colonial institutions in the Americas to bring them abreast of the rest of Europe generated so much antipathy that they helped precipitate the separation of the colonies from Spain. Moreover, many of these same institutions, although necessarily remodeled, were carried over after independence into the nineteenth century and continued to survive on into the twentieth.

THE WARS OF INDEPENDENCE—AND AFTER

The wars of independence in Latin America did not bring about such a sharp break with the past as is often imagined. They meant more a separation from Spain and Portugal than a profound transformation in the social structure. Although the apex of the pyramid, the Crown, had been removed, the basic hierarchical and elitist order of society remained intact. Where social revolt did accompany the independence struggle (as in Mexico, where a major Indian uprising occurred), it was quickly snuffed out and conservative rule reestablished.

The causes of the independence struggles in Latin America were complex. The example of the United States, as well as the ideals of liberty, equality, and fraternity stemming from the French Revolution of 1789, had an effect, particularly on Latin American intellectuals, who used these concepts to frame a rationalization for independence. The liberal, Enlightenment reforms of the Spanish Bourbons (such as the expulsion of the Jesuits in 1767) had also stimulated resentment in the colonies, and the ineptness of the Spanish and Portuguese kings in the late eighteenth and early nineteenth centuries led to a belief on the part of the colonists that they could manage their own affairs better than the colonizing countries could. A rising merchant class in the colonies had grown impatient with the monopoly systems of Spain and Portugal and wished to be free to trade with whomever it wished.

A critical factor was the growing impatience of the Spanish *criollos* (those of Spanish descent born in the New World) with the monopoly on colonial positions held by the *peninsulares* (colonial officials sent from the Iberian peninsula). The *criollos* wished to have political power, and doubtless the salaries and perquisites, commensurate with their growing economic wealth, yet they were blocked in this desire by the Crown's policy of appointing peninsula-born officials to the major posts. Frustrated, the *criollos* became increasingly impatient, and independence sentiment grew. When Napoleon Bonaparte captured Spain in 1808 and placed his brother on the throne, the Latin American *criollos* refused to accept his authority and moved to take power until the legitimate king could be restored. Later, when the legitimate king did return to the throne but refused to accept the liberalizing reforms proposed by the colonies, the final break came.

The wars of independence lasted some fifteen years, involving epic struggle. But since the Spanish garrisons stationed in the Americas were small (it is a measure of the success of the Spanish colonial enterprise that such modest armed force was used to maintain it for three hundred years) and located only in the major centers, the actual fighting was limited. The first revolts, in Argentina and Mexico, were quashed. Simón Bolívar carried out a long struggle against the Spanish in Venezuela, then helped to liberate the present countries of Colombia and Ecuador. José de San Martín finally defeated the Spanish forces in Buenos Aires and then marched his army over the Andes to drive the Spanish from Chile.

But the key to the liberation of South America was the large Spanish force centered in the viceroyalty at Lima. San Martín proceeded north by ship while Bolívar went south over land. In the decisive battle of Ayacucho in 1824, the royalists were routed. Ayacucho marked the virtual end of the wars for independence in South America. Meanwhile, the revolt in the other main center, Mexico, had foundered for several years until in 1821 the victory over the loyal Spanish forces was also won. Once Mexico had been freed, Central America followed halfheartedly, although there had been little fighting. Because the Spanish colonial system was so highly centralized, once the main centers at Caracas, Buenos Aires, Santiago, Bogotá, Quito, Lima, and Mexico were liberated, the rest of the colonies followed suit, chiefly by administrative fiat.

In Brazil the situation was different. When Napoleon's forces occupied Portugal, the royal family set sail for Rio de Janeiro—the first time European royalty had ever set foot in the New World. Later, when the French were driven out of Portugal and the king called back, he left his son Pedro in Brazil. Although summoned subsequently to succeed his father in Lisbon, Pedro determined to stay in Brazil. Hence, when

Brazil became independent, it did so as an independent monarchy, not as an independent republic. The republic would come later. The transition to independence in Brazil was thus peaceful, and the continuity provided by the monarchy enabled Brazil to escape the chaos characteristic of the Spanish colonies during their early years of independence.

The disintegrative tendencies set loose during the wars of separation continued for a time after independence. The confederation of Gran Colombia split up in 1830 into the separate nations of Venezuela, Colombia, and Ecuador. The United Provinces of Central America fragmented in 1838 into five small separate city-states. Bolivia's independence also came late and was, in the words of historian Hubert Herring, a "vague afterthought of the wars of independence," while Paraguay gained independence more as a result of its struggles with the Argentines than of those with the Spanish. The Dominican Republic was forcibly united with Haiti from 1822–1844 before the island of Hispaniola was permanently divided into these two nations, and Uruguay was established with British assistance as a buffer state between the two giants of South America, Argentina and Brazil. Panama was a distant province of Colombia until the United States helped guarantee its independence in 1903 as a means of securing the rights to build the canal. Cuba and Puerto Rico remained Spanish colonies until the war of 1898, a fact that shaped both islands' history of frustrated nationalism.

Within each of the new republics the situation was similarly chaotic, disorderly, and fragmented. The removal of the Spanish Crown had eliminated the one unifying element in the colonies, setting loose a variety of centrifugal forces and creating a legitimacy vacuum. The *criollo* conservatives attempted to fill the vacuum along with the caudillos and the armies left over from the independence struggles. But neither could effectively stem the disintegrative forces at work, and power continued to drain away from the center. In the absence of an effective central authority, power came to be lodged in local or regionally based caudillos, rival elite factions, and the self-contained haciendas. Power was diffuse, decentralized; little real authority was exercised by those occupying the presidential palace. The semifeudal system was perpetuated.

Almost universally the new nations of Latin America adopted constitutions providing for democratic, representative rule. At the time this seemed the only acceptable alternative to colonialism and monarchy. But often enshrined in these constitutions were numerous articles that helped preserve corporate privilege and autocratic rule. The constitutions were thus more a reflection of the area's historical forms and traditions than a sharp break with the past, including as they did extensive powers for the executive, various measures to limit the suffrage and preserve oligarchic rule, and a special place and privileges for such groups as the Church or the army. Much of subsequent Latin American history would be written in terms of the conflict between these divergent republican and autocratic tendencies.

The political instability of the time was often accompanied by economic disorder and, in some countries, reversion to a more primitive form of existence. With the disruption of old trade patterns, commerce came virtually to a standstill and many mines and plantations ceased to function. The comings and goings of various caudillos led to such disruption that markets and prices were unstable, crops and cattle were destroyed, fields were abandoned, and agriculture and production declined. In many areas, peasants and Indians went back to a pre-Columbian type of subsistence agriculture.

The politics of the first decades after independence, roughly 1820–1850, are more easily understood if we remember that the wars of independence had been conservative movements, not liberal ones. They were aimed at preserving oligarchic privilege and the status quo, not sweeping them away. Many royalist commercial and landed elites had only reluctantly come around to the independence cause when they grew convinced it could result in an increase in their wealth and trade. The wars of separation from Spain were aimed at reasserting the power and institutions of traditional society, not at destroying them. The wealth and power of the Church remained largely intact after independence. The importance of the hacienda and of the semifeudal two-class system was similarly enhanced after independence. It was not flaming radicals or liberals who inherited power after Spain was driven out but generally conservative oligarchs and their agents. The independence armies frequently stepped in to fill the vacuum left by the withdrawal of the Crown.

But the *criollo* oligarchy was often a bedraggled element unable to rule effectively or maintain order. In some countries rival regionally based oligarchic families competed for the national palace and all the spoils and opportunities for land and social advancement that holding presidential power implied. Juan Manuel de Rosas in Argentina and Antonio López de Santa Anna in Mexico were caudillos in this early classic mold, dominating their countries by force and bravura during the first thirty years of independence. The prevailing pattern, however, was the frequent coming and going of rival caudillos and elite or would-be elite families, whose constant alternation in power helped retard the development of most of the nations of the area. Only Brazil under its emperor and Chile, whose conservative elite quickly reasserted itself after independence, escaped this era of chaotic, disruptive, caudillo politics.

Hence the first thirty years after independence were marked by a general lack of progress throughout Latin America and by efforts to devise new institutional formulas necessitated by the withdrawal of royal authority. Precisely because it was so chaotic, so prone to breakdown, this era also gave rise to a number of what would become the historic drives of Latin American development policy. These may be identified as the quest, given the prevailing chaos, to secure and maintain order at all costs; to populate and thus to fill the area's vast empty spaces; to control and civilize the Indian and African elements so as to prevent future social upheavals; to strengthen the oligarchy through immigration and a general Hispanicizing of the population; to maintain and strengthen existing structures such as the army and, in many areas, the Church; to fill the organizational void and correct the historic *falta de organización;* and to resurrect a political model that reflected the area's earlier glory and its hopes for the future. That model was frequently the authoritarian-autocratic model of sixteenth-century Spain and Latin America.

THE EARLY STAGES OF MODERNIZATION

By the 1850s in most countries, some order had been brought out of the earlier chaos. The first generation of postindependence caudillos and *criollos* had died or faded from the scene. Newer Liberal parties had emerged to vie with the traditional Conservatives. The Liberals were not often very liberal, however, and usually consisted of one group of rival first families organized to contest the power and privileges held by another elite group. The Liberals stood for some of the classic nineteenth-century freedoms, including separation of Church and state and free trade. By stimulating a greater competition for power, the rise of the Liberals resulted in an expansion of the suffrage and an increase in the voting population to perhaps 3–5 percent.

The 1850s was a period of gradual, incipient socioeconomic changes as well. Cattle ranches and plantations began to recover from the earlier devastations, and new lands were opened for cultivation. In the Argentine pampa and elsewhere, common land gave way to private ownership, and the system of large estates started to expand. There was a commercial quickening, new banks opened, and in the cities a merchant and artisan class, often stimulated by European immigrants, emerged. Foreign capital, chiefly British, provided a catalyst for investment and production. New national industries began to grow: guano in Peru, sugar in Cuba, mining in Chile, agriculture (meat, hides, wool) in Argentina and Uruguay, rubber and coffee in Brazil. The first railroads and highways were laid; docks and port facilities were constructed; a national economic infra-structure began to develop. In economic terms, the 1850s and 1860s represented the first stages of modernization; the "preconditions for takeoff" were established.

Yet these preconditions were different in Latin America than in the United States or Europe, simply because the northern countries had gone through the process first. In many Latin American countries there were debates between policymakers who favored high tariff barriers, in order to encourage nascent industry, and those who favored low tariffs, in order to base economic growth on foreign trade. The key economic fact was that, at least in the short run, British (and later U.S.) manufactured goods were less expensive than those produced locally, because of economies of scale and higher levels of technological development.

Increasingly the policymakers favoring low tariffs, often but not always calling themselves Liberals, won the debate. The most beneficial policy seemed clear, as indicated in this statement by Colombian treasury minister Florentino González in 1847:

> In a country rich in mines and agricultural products, which can sustain a considerable and beneficial export trade, the law should not attempt to encourage industries that distract the inhabitants from the agricultural and mining occupations. . . . Europe with an intelligent population, and with the possession of steam power and its applications, educated in the art of manufacturing, fulfills its mission in the industrial world by giving various forms to raw materials. We too should fulfill our mission, and there is no doubt as to what it is, if we consider the profusion of natural resources with which Providence has endowed this land. We should offer Europe raw materials and open our doors to her manufactures, to facilitate trade and the profit it brings, and to provide the consumer, at a reasonable price, with the products of the manufacturing industry.[1]

Following hence what later was to be called "comparative advantage," the decisions made reinforced the dependency position of Latin America that had begun during colonial times. Latin America was cast as an exporter of primary products and its industry lagged. The ramifications of these decisions were evident from then on in Latin America, even in the energy crisis of the 1970s and the debt crisis of the 1980s, as discussed later.

Although there was considerable economic resurgence during the 1850s and 1860s, the political situation had not stabilized. Rival caudillos, frequently at the head of competing Liberal and Conservative factions, continued to vie for control of the national palace. Instability remained the rule. In some countries the Conservatives and Liberals alternated in the presidency; in others a Conservative or a Liberal caudillo might manage to hold on to power indefinitely. Despite the frequent instability, however, the economic structure continued inexorably to change, giving rise to new social forces as yet only dimly foreseen.

In the 1870s and 1880s the political situation began to stabilize. There were two basic patterns, with a third one to emerge somewhat later. The first, exemplified in Argentina, Brazil, and Chile, involved the gradual consolidation and joining of older (landed) and newer (commercial) wealth into a system of strong oligarchic rule. With few interruptions, oligarchic rule continued until 1930; it was a period of unprecedented stability *and* economic growth. Indeed, the entire span from the 1880s to 1930 may be considered the heyday of oligarchic power throughout Latin America.

The second pattern, similarly stabilizing and consolidating, involved the coming to power of a new type of order-and-progress caudillo.

Porfirio Díaz in Mexico is the prime example, although in Guatemala, Venezuela, and the Dominican Republic the situation was parallel. No longer so unrefined as their caudillo predecessors and no longer interested solely in power for its own sake, the new order-and-progress caudillos sought to promote national economic growth and bring Latin America abreast of the rest of the world. They surrounded themselves with advisers who brought a positivistic, scientific, and progressive approach to national development. Under both the consolidating oligarchies and the order-and-progress caudillos (frequently intertwined, since the new breed of caudillos often ruled at the behest of powerful national oligarchies), the Latin American nations began their "takeoff."

Law and order were now established, often brutally. New national armies and police forces were set up, replacing the unprofessional and caudillo-led armed bands of the past. The police and army enforced order in the countryside and served as agencies for increased national and central direction. As oligarchic power was consolidated, furthermore, peasants and Indians were impressed into the labor force and obliged to sacrifice their communal lands and small holdings as the great estates expanded.

Along with political consolidation came greater economic growth. New roads and railroads were built. The first telegraph and telephones were introduced. Import and export facilities—docks, storage, ships— were constructed and improved. Large amounts of capital began to flow in, initially chiefly from Europe; however, by the 1890s in at least some of the countries, the United States had replaced Britain as the major source of foreign investment and trade. Manufacturing and industry were burgeoning. Immigration from Europe was encouraged. Previously empty areas began to be filled, and new lands were opened for rubber, coffee, sugarcane, cacao, and tobacco production. The number of commercial establishments multiplied; previously sleepy towns and port cities began to grow and come alive with activity. There was a general economic quickening as more money became available and business and trade picked up. New governmental agencies were established to administer these new activities. The national infrastructure—bureaucracies, communications structures, armies, and so on—started to take definitive shape. The drive to modernity had commenced. Some of the historical goals and aspirations of Latin American development policy began to be fulfilled.

It must be remembered, however, that in the majority of countries development and modernization came under elite, authoritarian, and oligarchic auspices, not democratic ones. Still, the general economic stimulus gave rise to new sociopolitical forces whose growth helped undermine the oligarchic order. A new middle class appeared in the urban areas and began pushing for political influence commensurate with its increased economic wealth. By the first decades of the twentieth century some strong trade unions, often rural as well as urban—cane cutters and tobacco workers, for example—had emerged, similarly demanding a bigger piece of the omelet and threatening to scramble it if their demands were not met. These pressures mounted. In 1910 dissatisfaction with the Díaz regime and impatience on the part of the nascent Mexican middle class with the barriers to advancement and spoils, coupled with deep-seated and long-smoldering resentment by peasants and Indians over encroachments of the big estates onto lands they had previously held, led to a revolt against the old dictator that triggered the twentieth century's first great social revolution. In 1916, Argentina's newly enfranchised middle-sector voters wrested control from the oligarchy for the first time, and in 1920 Chile's middle sectors made common cause with the workers to unseat the oligarchy. This pattern would be repeated in numerous countries of the area when the big upheaval of 1930 came.

In addition to the consolidating-oligarchy and order-and-progress caudillo patterns in evidence during this period, a third pattern involved direct U.S. intervention in the smaller countries of Latin America and the Caribbean, both to ensure political stability and to secure and expand U.S. economic and strategic interests. In the aftermath of the Spanish American War of 1898 the United States had emerged as a major industrial and economic center and an aspiring world power. In that war, the United States acquired Puerto Rico (and other areas) as territories and established a protectorate over Cuba. Panama also took on independence as a protectorate of the United States, with its national territory divided by the U.S.-controlled Canal Zone. Under the now-infamous Roosevelt Corollary to the Monroe Doctrine, the United States intervened in the Dominican Republic in 1905 to prevent European creditors from using force to collect unpaid debts and to take over the administration of all customs receipts. During the first two decades of the twentieth century the U.S. Marines intermittently occupied and intervened in the Dominican Republic, Haiti, Nicaragua, Panama, and Cuba.

The role of the United States in these countries was in many ways like that of the order-and-progress caudillos and produced many of the same results. The marines pacified the countryside. They built roads and port facilities. Through the establishment of marine-created national guards, power and administration were centralized just as in the caudillo regimes. Moreover, by bringing order to the national finances, conducting land surveys, and reorganizing the national systems of land titles, the United States helped facilitate further U.S. investment and production. Naturally those who were in a position most to benefit from these changes (again similar to the order-and-progress caudillos) were the large foreign investors and those Latin Americans who already possessed land, capital, and good connections. The third major developmental pattern of the period thus involved the wedding of foreign and domestic capital and the use of North American military power to join the emerging Latin American bourgeoisie with U.S. strategic and private economic interests. This pattern too served generally in Latin America to reinforce conservative, oligarchic rule.

But by the 1920s a change in the situation was due. The pressures were beginning to mount on the United States to withdraw its military forces from the Caribbean. The Latin American middle sectors and trade unions were insisting on the need for a national restructuring—or else! The military officer corps, no longer from aristocratic ranks, was becoming restless. The final triggering cause was the world market crash of 1929, which forced the bottom to fall out of the market for Latin America's exports, undermined oligarchic rule, and made the need for basic change obvious to all. In 1930 a rash of revolutions swept Latin America and signaled not just another dreary round of military coups but a profound reordering of the sociopolitical structure. The heyday of the oligarchy was over, and a new era of middle-sector-dominated politics had begun.

CONCLUSIONS AND IMPLICATIONS

The weight of the feudal and semifeudal past, of the colonial era and its institutions, hung heavier over Latin America than over North America. Indeed, in many ways the heavy hand of the past continues to weigh upon and shape the present-day Latin American countries in a fashion not true of the United States. In many countries, authoritarianism, elitism, a two-class system, hierarchy, patrimonialism, and corporatism have proved to be remarkably persistent, durable features.

But we have already seen that within this context considerable change is nevertheless possible. Latin American history is hardly the total failure that some detractors of the area would have us believe it to be. Indeed, given Latin America's background and the geographic, social, and economic barriers to development present historically, the accomplishments have been notable. It must be remembered, however, that the changes ushered in to this point have most often come under oligarchic auspices, not democratic ones. However, these changes gave rise to new social forces, principally labor and the new middle sectors, that challenged and helped undermine oligarchic rule.

NOTES

1. Quoted in Miguel Urrutia, *The Development of the Colombian Labor Movement* (Yale University Press, New Haven, Conn., 1969), pp. 6–7.

3
The Acceleration of Modernization, 1930 to the Present

The year 1930 was a turning point in Latin American history. Not only did the older oligarchic order break down—at least temporarily—but the modernization process greatly accelerated. The middle sectors became a dominant force in politics but were deeply divided. The trade unions were now a power group to be reckoned with. The new rulers of Latin America, cognizant of the weaknesses of economies based solely on raw materials and commodities exports, turned increasingly to industrialization as a means of stimulating growth and lessening reliance on expensive imports. But accelerated industrialization led to even more accelerated social transformations. A new set of pressures began to be felt that, cumulatively, added up to profound social revolution. Let us trace the chronology of these changes and analyze the major areas of Latin American society presently undergoing restructuring.

THE POST-1930 PERIOD
OF LATIN AMERICAN DEVELOPMENT

The political response to the wave of revolts that swept Latin America in 1930 was far from uniform. A variety of alternative development strategies were tried. The host of new parties and movements that emerged, ranging from moderate to social democratic to Communist, challenged and sometimes defeated the older elitist Conservative and Liberal factions. Socialist, anarchist, Communist, and anarcho-syndicalist influences were strong within the trade unions. A number of Christian-Democratic parties and Catholic trade unions, business groups, and student associations were formed. Fascist and manifestly corporatist movements and regimes also attracted support.

Despite the wide variety of new movements and ideologies that sprang up in the 1920s and 1930s, there were common political responses as well. In general, the Latin American systems in the 1930s and on into the 1940s sought to adapt to change, but that did not imply the destruction of the system per se. They attempted to accommodate themselves to the newer currents and forces that recent modernization had spawned without sacrificing entirely the institutions of the past. Their formula was not to destroy the older established order but to mold and reorder it to fit the new realities.

The general Latin American way of responding to the social pressures of the times was to add on and assimilate the new corporate groups and power contenders that had recently risen up to challenge the system (the middle sectors and the trade unions) without necessarily repudiating or destroying the older centers of influence. (See especially Anderson, *Politics and Economic Change in Latin America.**) Latin America sought to expand and remodel the prevailing hierarchical and elitist order, but it did not necessarily shake off its traditions of elite-dominated rule. The new groups were to be accommodated and brought into the system, but they would have to play by the rules of the game and not seek to topple the prevailing structure. They had to go along with and accept the benefits that accrued, or they would be suppressed.

The management of this change process involved some clever politics on the part of those elite groups that had historically governed Latin America and those newer middle-sector elements that now were moving into positions of power. They saw that for things to remain the same, they would have to change, and this implied a granting of recognition and certain benefits to the middle and labor sectors, but at a price. In return for legal standing and certain social programs, for example, the labor movement was often organized under strict government control and regulation. The status quo was hence changed, but it was also preserved. The nature of this evolution, as well as the continuity with the older tradition, is presented in Figure 3.1.

Three major arenas of change are apparent between these two images and time frames of the Latin American sociopolitical structure. First, in the post-1930s period the number of vertical corporate groups or power contenders has been expanded to include both the older (army, Church, oligarchy) and the newer (business, middle-sector, labor) elements. Second, the size of the middle sectors has been expanded horizontally. Third, skilled and organized workers have been differentiated from the peasants and/or Indian masses and have been given a special place in the hierarchy. In these ways, the Latin American systems have sought to respond to change and modernization and have proved adaptable in the process.

But of at least equal importance are four points: (1) the hierarchical, pyramidal societal structure has been retained; (2) the top-down system of rule by elites remains intact (although the relative power of the several elites may have shifted); (3) the line separating the "effective nation" (elites and middle class, a few from the organized working class) from

---

*All references are to the suggested readings found at the end of Chapter 7.

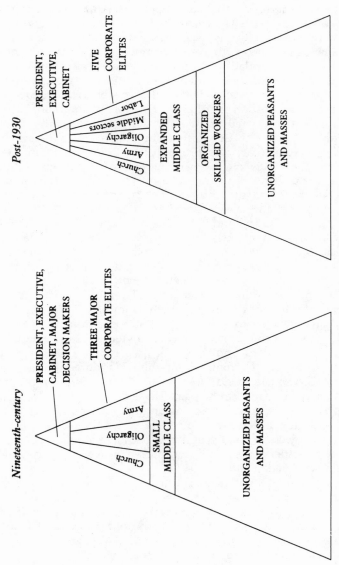

Figure 3.1 Continuity and Change in the Latin American Sociopolitical Structure

the rest is still sharply drawn; and (4) the essentially two-class nature of Latin American society, in which the middle sectors come frequently to share the values of the historical elites (such as disdain for the common people and for manual labor), persists. Note also the remarkable continuity of the post-1930s structure with the sixteenth-century model pictured in Figure 2.1. Thus, although much had changed in Latin America since the nineteenth century, much also remained the same. Whether such an essentially elitist, hierarchical, and pyramidal system as outlined here can continue to cope with and manage the forces that modernization sets loose, or whether that system will be overthrown in revolution, is a question that lies at the heart of the political struggle in virtually all the national political systems treated in this book.

Although the effort to adapt to change while also preserving the traditional structure intact was probably the dominant Latin American pattern from the 1930s on, a great number of variations within that basic pattern could and did occur, and in some nations the basic model itself was attacked and overthrown. The middle sectors emerged predominant in some countries; instead of oligarchic rule, the prevailing pattern in Chile, Uruguay, and Venezuela was one of general dominance by the new (albeit frequently internally divided) middle-class groups and parties. Mexico developed a single-party system, although power within the official party came to be lodged not so much with the labor and peasant sectors as with an emergent bourgeoisie.

In Brazil and Argentina, a new kind of populist leader rose up in the persons of Getúlio Vargas and Juan Domingo Perón, respectively, who both gave benefits to and expected support from the new middle and labor sectors. Social democratic parties vied for and sometimes won power in Costa Rica, Peru, and Venezuela. In contrast, strongarm dictators emerged in Cuba, the Dominican Republic, Honduras, Nicaragua, Paraguay, and Guatemala, who despite all their authoritarian practices signaled a partial break with the past. These dictators were from middle-class and often racially mixed social origins, rather than from the old oligarchy, and they undertook a considerable number of nation-building development projects. In many countries, democratic rule was established for a time; in others, the elites recaptured power after having been temporarily deprived of it.

But the prevailing situation in all the countries was a new legitimacy crisis, deepening fragmentation, and hence a pattern often of oscillation between any or all of these phenomena. Latin America had become increasingly a conflict society in which the old norms and institutions were being questioned while the various newer groups were badly divided as to what future directions their country should take. A democratic government might come to power briefly, only to be followed by a new military regime, or else populist politicians would instigate a needed reform program only to be replaced by a conservative-oligarchic government. There were strong challenges from the left in Brazil, El

Salvador, and other nations, defensive actions from the right, increased fragmentation in the center—and repeated clashes among all these groups.

A few of the countries of the area—Mexico, Chile, and Uruguay for a time, Costa Rica, Venezuela, perhaps Colombia—seemed able to deal fairly well with these competing, divisive crosscurrents. But in the rest (and eventually even in some of the countries mentioned), the divisions helped produce a worsening situation of fragmentation. The conflicts were often so deep, the gaps among the contending groups and classes so vast, the bitterness so intense that no government—left, right, or center—could come to power, govern effectively, and hope to survive for long. As the divisions became more intense, government and the political system were increasingly rendered unable to function effectively. Breakdown and national disintegration seemed imminent in such leading countries as Argentina, Brazil, Chile, and Uruguay. Again, as in the nineteenth century, it was the army that stepped into the vacuum.

The collapse of the older oligarchic order in 1930 had left a political lacuna that neither the old elites nor the new ones seemed capable of filling more than temporarily or with anything resembling majority support. Meanwhile, social and economic change continued to transform underlying realities. The 1930s were a decade throughout all of Latin America of rapid, albeit uneven, industrialization; the pace of change quickened.

Heavy industry—steel, manufacturing, petrochemicals—was built up during this period. Prosperity accelerated further during World War II, both because of the difficulty of receiving goods from abroad and because of the demand for Latin American products occasioned by the war itself. Although in the postwar period the political instability seemed generally unrelieved, economic growth continued, pushing ahead at unspectacular but often steady rates. The share of gross domestic product (GDP) generated by industry and manufacturing gradually rose. Other social transformations, often undramatic but nonetheless cumulative, occurred: Literacy rates rose, as did life expectancy; new communications and transportation grids penetrated deeply into the interior; the middle sectors continued to grow; organized labor increased in strength; the population grew and empty areas were filled; production expanded; peasants migrated in droves to the cities; rural elements were organized for the first time; social problems multiplied; and workers and the middle class became impatient for larger numbers of goods and services.

As social and political pressures continued to mount in the 1950s, 1960s, 1970s, and on into the 1980s, the possibilities for a genuinely revolutionary transformation increased. Conflicts and divisions within the middle sectors and among the various groups (army, parties, business, students) deepened; at the same time the struggle between these groups and the emerging labor movements took on aspects of class warfare. Peasant elements were by now sufficiently mobilized in some countries that they also constituted a force to be reckoned with, particularly in situations where peasant violence was accompanied by workers' strikes, student unrest, and middle-class discontent.

Seeking to break out of the immobility and conflict of the traditional system, the revolutionary alternative began to appear more attractive. In 1952 in Bolivia, a revolution destroyed the power of the traditional landed elites and mining interests and brought to prominence a movement dedicated to transforming the prevailing social and economic patterns. In Argentina Perón in 1946 had also come to power as a populist and on the basis of working-class support. On January 1, 1959, Fidel Castro ushered in his revolution in Cuba, transforming that society into the first socialist nation in the Western Hemisphere.

In Guatemala in 1944 and in the Dominican Republic in 1965, social revolutions took place as well, but these were frustrated by U.S. military intervention. In Chile, the Socialist-Communist Popular Unity government of Salvador Allende was overthrown in 1973 with the aid of the United States. But in Peru a revolutionary military regime successfully destroyed the power of the traditional landed oligarchy, and nationalist military regimes took power for a time in Ecuador, Bolivia, Honduras, and Panama. Nicaragua had a revolution, and revolutionary upheaval threatened to spread throughout Central America. Meanwhile, in some of the most important nations of the area—Argentina, Brazil, Chile, and Uruguay—authoritarian military regimes took over, determined to eliminate by brutal means if necessary the challenge from the left and from below. Some of these regimes later began going back toward democracy.

THE CONTEMPORARY REVOLUTION
IN LATIN AMERICA

Although the preceding discussion has of necessity focused on the political elites of Latin America, on the efforts of various regimes to control and manage the development process, and on what is (with perhaps three or four major revolutionary exceptions) still a predominantly conservative political order, attention must now be turned to the newer revolutionary currents sweeping over the area. These often operate below the surface and do not get the headlines that major events occurring at the top do, but their importance is real and is certain to increase. The changes under way are so immense and far-reaching that they add up to a situation of genuine social revolution.

When we talk of the contemporary revolution in Latin America, we are not speaking of the usual palace revolts and *pronunciamientos* (pronouncements against the government) but of deep-rooted social change whose cumulative effects add up to full-scale, long-term social transformation. We propose to discuss these basic changes under six broad headings: changes in values and political culture, the economic transformation of the area, changes in social structure, the emergence of new political forces and movements, the new policies fashioned by governments in response to the new demands, and changes in the international context. These measures not only give us a working definition of *development* in Latin America, but they provide a list of key indicators to watch for as we measure the relative strength of the change forces in the country chapters that follow.

Values and Political Culture

Latin America was founded upon a value system that stressed authority, hierarchy, and elitism. Although these values are still often strongly present throughout the area, in many countries the traditional beliefs that long undergirded the social and political system are undergoing transformation or are being fused with new values: social justice, democracy, participation, development, socialism, and the like.

It is no longer so easy as in the past to convince a peasant that one must be poor because poverty is good for the soul, or that one must accept a low station in life as part of the natural order. The old myths simply do not wash anymore. Instead of the fatalistic rural worker who is resigned to his or her lot because Saint Thomas or the Church said this is the way things must be, the countryside is now full of increasingly restless people who question traditional values for the first time and who are impatient for change. Challenging new ideas are filtering in.

The agents of these changes are modern transportation and communications, particularly the cheap transistor radio. Whereas before the rural peasant lived with almost no contact with the outside world, today it is practically impossible to go anywhere in Latin America where the transistor radio is not heard broadcasting news, sports, and a wider conception of the outside world. New roads have also brought the rural elements in contact with urban markets. Party organizers, U.S. officials, government agencies, and young revolutionaries have fanned out into the countryside, carrying with them new concepts of how to order one's life. The historic isolation of the *patria chica* is breaking down.

But while the old values are being undermined and new ideas introduced, we cannot be sure of what the long-term meaning of these changes will be. For the new values—democracy, socialism, communism, capitalism—are also frequently in competition with each other. Not only do Radio Havana and the Voice of America come in loud and clear, but also competing for the listener's ear are the government station, the Church station, the voice of the armed forces, and various political parties. Hence, while the old assumptions are challenged, the newer values are still inchoate and at best incompletely digested. There are too many ideas to be absorbed all at once. The value and belief systems of most transitional persons represent a mixture of old and new. There is no clear-cut or unilinear progression from traditional beliefs to modern ones.

A good number of efforts are also under way on the part of conservative interests and governments to control these changes or to manipulate the educational system so as to preserve intact historical institutions. Education and social mobilization can be manipulated to produce conservative results as well as revolutionary ones. At this point we do not know definitely whether we should expect increasingly sharp breaks with the past, whether the traditional elites will succeed in their quest to control this change process, or whether, as seems most likely, Latin America will continue to represent a mixture of old and new—although always in a dynamic, changing relationship.

Economic Transformations

Latin America is also being transformed economically, but here, too, the outcome of the process remains in doubt. Along with the acceleration of the industrialization process, beginning in the 1930s and continuing to the present, has come a steady rise in per capita income and standards of living. Two-thirds of the Latin American countries have now passed the threshold, arbitrarily put at US$1,000 income per person per year, that separates the underdeveloped nations from the developed. Although the standard of living is still not comparable to that of the United States, West Europe, or Japan, neither are the Latin American nations basket cases. By most indices, the Latin American nations are transitional systems, neither fully developed nor wholly underdeveloped.

A comparison of present-day per capita income in Latin America (see Table 1.1) with the situation in 1960 or 1950 shows significant change. In most cases, per capita income has doubled and in some it has trebled in the preceding thirty years. These figures are impressive, but they do not tell the whole story since they fail to indicate how income is distributed. Most of the income is still concentrated in upper- and middle-class pockets, while the standard of living of the urban and rural poor remains abysmally low. In many areas, the standard of living of the poor, especially rural peasants and subsistence farmers, has actually *declined*. But the general picture, obviously varying from country to country, is one of gradual improvement, although as shown in Figure 3.2, which uses data from Brazil, the rate of improvement of the distinct social strata is highly uneven.

The Brazilian case, which was fairly typical for the countries of Latin America through the 1970s, shows some interesting patterns. Most obvious is the steep rise in income for the upper classes. The middle sectors also profited significantly from the recent economic growth. Skilled workers (the working class) similarly improved their lot. The so-called marginals managed to achieve some improvement, though in many Latin American countries that has not been the case. But for many lower-class Brazilians living standards went down even under conditions of "miracle growth" on a national level.

Three points bear emphasizing in Figure 3.2. First, the income levels of the major organized groups have shown improvement over the years.

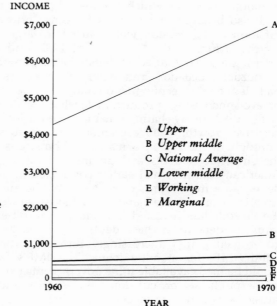

INCOME

A Upper
B Upper middle
C National Average
D Lower middle
E Working
F Marginal

Figure 3.2 Average Income in Brazil by Social Strata, 1960 and 1970 (constant dollars)

YEAR

Source: Based on Albert Fishlow, "Brazilian Size Distribution of Income," in Alejandro Foxley, ed., *Income Distribution in Latin America,* Cambridge University Press, Cambridge, 1976, pp. 61, 72.

Second, it is clear that middle- and upper-class income and living standards have improved far faster and more disproportionately than those of the working class (and, hence, the gaps between the classes have widened, not narrowed). Third, marginal elements, rural and urban, have been left behind. At issue in Latin America, therefore, except for the poorest, unorganized, and marginal elements, is not so much the sheer deprivation as the relative deprivation of some classes vis-à-vis others. Most Latin American governments have sought to channel sufficient benefits to their lower classes, at least to those organized elements constituting a potential threat, to head off revolution. In this, so far, most have succeeded. Thus while organized working-class elements have often gained salary increases, the very poor, who are not seen as a threat, continue to live a hand-to-mouth existence.

This system of growth and some political stability has been severely threatened by the economic crisis that began in Latin America in 1979 and deepened thereafter. The crisis was first caused for the oil-importing countries of Latin America by the two shocking oil-price increases of the 1970s. Next, the changed nature of the post-OPEC world negatively affected the Latin American countries through effects on the importing capacity of the industrial countries of the world (including inflation on imports needed by Latin American countries) and through the world economic recession, which diminished demand in the industrial countries and also brought lower prices for other primary-goods products. Both inflation and recession were caused in large part by the OPEC price increases. Finally, the "oil glut" of 1982, and the decline of petroleum prices, negatively affected those Latin American members of OPEC (Venezuela, Ecuador) and other oil exporters (especially Mexico) that had planned their economies on both rising petroleum prices and constant, or even increasing, production levels.

By 1982 many Latin American countries were recording zero or negative growth. Their economic pies turned stagnant or even shrank. Throughout the region a major economic crisis set in, made worse by the stupendous debts at high interest rates that almost all the Latin American countries had earlier contracted. In large part these increased debts came from loans, to both the public and private sectors in Latin America, from private banks of the industrial world, which were recycling the petrodollars invested in them by the oil-exporting nations. As the threat of default on these debts was faced by various Latin American governments, they increasingly turned to the International Monetary Fund (IMF) for standby loans. The IMF's formula was clear: Loans would be made available if the governments froze wages; cut employment in the public sector; cut down on deficit spending and inflation; ended subsidies, which were especially for the lower- and middle-income sectors; devaluated the national currencies; and cut down on foreign imports, while encouraging additional exports.

The economic crisis not only left many Latin American lower- and middle-class elements worse off but also threatened political stability. At a time of rising expectations, there were fewer pieces of the pie to hand out, and discontent spread. Not only were many governments throughout the area faced with threats of destabilization but the whole Latin American *system* of gradualist, accommodative, evolutionary politics (described in Chapter 7) was undermined as well.

There are other changes in the economic structure of which you must be aware when reading the country chapters that follow. One involves the growth of increasingly state-directed economies throughout Latin America, whether socialist economies or capitalist ones. A second concerns the spread of the big multinational corporations throughout Latin America and their capacity to shape internal markets and governments. A third relates to the growing interrelationships between the Latin American economies and outside market prices (such as for oil) and forces.

Changes in Social Structure

With economic development have come changes in the social structure. The Latin American societies are no longer the simple lord and peasant societies of the past. Rather, they are now much more complex systems with a far greater differentiation among social groups. Many aspects of the two-class system have been retained, but that should not blind us to the changes.

Industrialization helped give rise to new social forces. A new larger middle class has emerged, but it is further split into upper, middle, and lower substrata and is additionally divided along vertical lines: clerics, army officers, university students, government workers, shop owners, small farmers, small-business people. The middle sector is also divided politically, so that if we say the army officer corps or the political party executive committees are dominated by middle-sector representatives, that may be insufficient to tell us their political ideologies. Indeed, it could be said that since 1930 virtually all institutions in Latin America— armed forces, Church, parties, universities, bureaucracy—have come to be dominated by the middle sectors and that, hence, politics in much of Latin America is essentially middle-class politics. But given the divisions within the middle sectors, a great variety of developmental solutions—ranging from far left to far right and all positions in between— are possible.

The trade unions have also shown themselves to be a significant new social force that must now be discussed in any consideration of Latin American politics. Peasants too have been mobilized and partially organized, however unevenly, in most countries of the area. Urban marginals, the recent peasant arrivals in the major cities, who are generally underemployed and as yet not organized, have also emerged as a new social force.

It is not just within the newer social groups that change has occurred but within the more traditional sectors as well. The military and the Church hierarchies are not recruited from upper-class ranks but from the middle sectors, and this has had some important implications in terms of their political behavior. Neither the Church nor the army can any longer be depended on as automatic defenders of the status quo. Rather, both these institutions are severely divided internally, and particularly within the army, nationalist and developmentalist ideologies are strong, cutting across the traditional ideological divisions. Within the Church, the large number of foreign-born clergy (French, Spanish, North American) has also acted as a stimulus to new ways of thinking about society and participation. The oligarchy similarly consists no longer just of an aristocratic class tracing its origins to colonial times but of a business-commercial elite, of old-rich and new-rich elements, and frequently now of powerful foreign communities. To understand the dynamics of contemporary Latin American politics, we must come to grips with these new complexities.

New Political Groups

Along with accelerated social change has come a host of new political associations and movements. The old Liberal and Conservative elite factions have lost their monopoly on power. Beginning in the 1920s and 1930s and continuing into the post–World War II period, a variety of new middle-class and worker movements emerged to challenge the historical dominance of the old elites. Led often by charismatic, populist political leaders, these movements showed themselves able to break the monopoly of power that the upper class had long maintained. They helped make the political situation much more fluid—and unstable—than it had been before.

The first Communist and socialist parties were organized during this period, led usually by middle-class intellectuals and with a strong base in the emerging trade unions. Parties that called themselves Radical, patterned after the French Radicals but ultimately not very radical, had grown up earlier in Argentina and Chile, based on middle-class support. A variety of social-democratic or Aprista-like parties (named after the APRA—American Popular Revolutionary Alliance—in Peru) challenged the established order starting in the 1930s and in some cases came to power. New Christian-Democratic movements were organized. A variety of agrarian, worker, peasant, anarchist, and other organizations added to the party potpourri.

But it was not just parties that were organized but an entire associational vacuum that began to be filled. Many of the new associations called themselves nonpartisan, but they frequently acted like partisan groups. The new trade-union movements, split into Communist, socialist, Christian-Democratic, and anarcho-syndicalist groups, were as much parties as the groups that used that label. There were new associations of students, business people, peasants, and women. Military lodges, sometimes secret, were formed; landowners began to band together to protect their interests. The organizational void that had always plagued Latin America began to be filled—either through free association or by government fiat. The state frequently created its own official associations, trade unions, and the like, as a way of heading off possible revolutionary change that a genuinely independent and pluralist associational life posed.

New Policies and Institutional Arrangements

A fifth area of major change involves the greater complexity of governmental institutions and the policies flowing from them. With the "revolution of rising expectations," government was called upon to perform a host of services and carry out a variety of programs it never had to before. Government was expected to deliver social-security programs, health care, housing, rural electrification, roads, dams, water supplies, and a great number of other services. Moreover, with the Great Depression, World War II, and growth of the economy, the government's regulatory role was vastly expanded.

The result was the creation in all the countries of the area of many new ministries, agencies, and institutes to carry out the new programs. New ministries of labor, commerce, industry, planning, and social security were set up; hundreds of other agencies to administer agrarian reform, community development, water resources, and the like came into existence. Moreover, to administer the new programs, bureaucratic behavior had to change. No longer could the line between the public and the private domains be so easily blurred. New norms of honesty, rationality, and effectiveness in public administration were called for. The patrimonialist conception remained strong, but the point is that it was no longer the only one. Graft, family favoritism, political payoffs, and special privileges still provided the grease that helped turn the wheels of government, but now real programs and not just paper ones had to be carried out—or else! For although traditional bureaucratic behavior remained strongly in evidence and was widely tolerated up to a point, the success of any government came to be judged on its capacity effectively to implement programs of social and economic development.

One result of this new thrust was the enormous growth of the public sector. The Latin American state assumed the role of national patron, industrialist, and chief capitalist. The government became the largest employer in the country. Even greater power was concentrated at the central state level. Local and regional authority and that of the local caudillos were undermined. The historical tendency to look to the central government to solve all of society's ills was greatly strengthened. These changes in the structure and central role of the state implied some major transformation, probably equal in importance to the other social and political changes discussed earlier. Such enormous power and funds concentrated at the central state level made the competition to capture these higher stakes that much more intense.

Changes at the International Level

Latin America's traditional isolation, not only internally in terms of the separate existence of its *patrias chicas*, but also externally in terms of its relations with the outside world, is breaking down. Latin America is no longer an isolated backwater of the West but has been increasingly integrated into world trade patterns, communications networks, alliances, and the like. This too adds up to a major change in the way Latin America sees itself and relates to the rest of the world.

Modern communications and transportation networks are making all nations interdependent in ways they never were before. Markets and trade patterns have also become increasingly international. Latin America must sell its coffee, sugar, tobacco, and bananas abroad at favorable prices, or its entire economic (and political) structure will be threatened with collapse. At the same time, most of Latin America is absolutely dependent on the importation of oil at reasonable prices.

The web of dependent and interdependent relations is complex and difficult to sort out. The Latin American economies are heavily dependent on international markets, and they are particularly dependent on their exports to and imports from the United States. Economic dependence has often been translated into political dependence—the capacity of the United States through its control over markets and international lending agencies to manipulate the internal politics of the Latin American nations. Many nations are now trying to break out of this historical dependence by diversifying their economies and increasing their trade and contacts with West Europe, East Europe, Japan, the Soviet Union, and other areas; but these strategies have not been altogether successful, and dependency upon the United States is still the situation for many countries.

Latin America is also tied into a web of international political and defense arrangements similarly dominated by the United States. The cold war altered the face of Latin America's internal politics and, as in Cuba, Chile, Guatemala, and the Dominican Republic, made several countries pawns in the worldwide rivalry between the superpowers. Latin America's communications media are also tied in closely with U.S. news agencies. The big multinationals have gained immense power throughout the area, often with the ability to manipulate Latin American governments and their policies. Some would argue that even Latin American culture is becoming heavily Americanized, as the "Coca-Cola-ization" of the continent goes forward. But in more recent years, many of these big companies, fearing instability and tired of extensive regulation by the governments of the area, have begun pulling out of the area and investing elsewhere.

Latin America is thus breaking out of its historical isolation, but in some areas that has brought decidedly mixed results. Latin America has become more a part of a modern and interdependent world, but that has frequently also meant accepting increased dependence with independence.

CONCLUSIONS AND IMPLICATIONS

The pace of change has accelerated throughout Latin America. In the past four decades, new and revolutionary transformations have begun to sweep across the continent. These changes, taken together and cumulatively, add up to a profound social transformation in Latin American society and polity. The changes have generally been gradual, but are no less profound for having taken this slower route. Since the 1930s the newer social and political forces have fundamentally altered all areas of Latin American life.

Still the power of traditional forces has also remained strong, and the question must be raised as to whether the changes have been thorough enough. Has Latin America experienced fundamental change, or is it still engaged in a holding action? Have the changes noted affected basic power relationships, or is the essentially elitist, hierarchical, and authoritarian structure still in place? To what extent have the newer groups gained genuinely independent bargaining power? Conversely, have the benefits channeled to them served to co-opt them into the older pattern of elitist rule and to prevent more fundamental changes? These are critical issues; they lie at the heart of the Latin American political process—and of the analyses presented in this book.

4
Interest Groups and Political Parties

The Latin American political tradition differs in many ways from that of the United States and West Europe. The distinct political tradition of Latin America is reflected in the composition and interrelationships of political groups in the area.

There is considerable disagreement whether Latin America has a politics of interest-group struggle comparable to that of the United States. Of course there is competition among various groups and factions throughout Latin America. But whereas in the United States group politics is looked upon as a natural, generally wholesome aspect of the political system, in Latin America the emphasis is often on creating an administrative state above party and interest-group politics. Another difference has to do with the fact that although in the United States the major groups, religious agencies, and the like are assumed to be independent from the government, in Latin America such agencies as the Church, the army, the university, and perhaps even the trade unions are often more than mere interest groups: They are a part of the state system and inseparable from it. Of course there are degrees of government control over these groups, ranging from almost complete control to almost complete freedom as under liberalism. But the usual pattern involves considerably more state control over interest groups than in the United States, and this helps put interest- (or what some have preferred to call corporate-) group behavior in Latin America in a different framework than is the case in the United States.

Latin America, as Charles Anderson has suggested, never experienced a definitive democratic revolution—that is, a struggle resulting in agreement that mobilization of votes would be the only legitimate way to obtain public power. In the absence of such a consensus, political groups do not necessarily work for political power by seeking votes, support of political parties, or contacts with elected representatives. The groups might seek power through any number of other strategies. Other resources used include coercion (the military), economic might (upper-class groups and foreign enterprises), technical expertise (bureaucrats), and controlled violence (labor unions, peasants, and students). Any group that can mobilize votes is likely to do so for an election. Since that is not the only legitimated route to power, the result of any election is tentative. The duration of any government is uncertain, given the varying power of the competing groups and the incomplete legitimacy of the government itself.

Further, group behavior in Latin America is conditioned by a set of unwritten rules, leading to what Anderson has called the "living museum" effect. Before a new group can participate in the political system, it must tacitly demonstrate both that it has a power resource and that it will respect the rights of already existent groups. Until a new group has demonstrated that it has some capacity to challenge or even overthrow a government, there is little reason for the established groups to take it seriously. Equally important, this potential participant in the political process must give assurances that it will not use its power to harm or eliminate those groups that already exist. The result is the gradual addition of new groups under the two conditions but seldom the elimination of the old ones. The newest, most modern groups coexist with the oldest, most traditionalist ones.

A related factor is the tradition of *co-optation or repression.* As new groups emerge as potential politically relevant actors, already established actors (particularly political parties or strong national leaders) sometimes offer to assist them in their new political activities. The deal struck is one mutually beneficial to both: The new group gains acceptance, prestige, and some of its original goals, and the established group or leader gains new support and increased political resources. The co-opted group drops some of its original goals, leading many observers to be critical of the system. But those leaders and observers who prefer stability to change see the co-optation system as beneficial to the political system.

In some circumstances, new groups refuse to be co-opted and fail to accept the rules of the game. Instead, they take steps indicating to established groups and leaders that they might act against the interests of the established elites. In the case of a group that violates the ground rules by employing mass violence, for example, an effort is made by the established interests to repress the new group, either legally by refusing it legal standing or in some cases through the use of violence. The army or hired thugs are employed to suppress the group that ventures outside the system. Most commonly, such repression has proved successful, and the new group, at least for the time being, disappears or atrophies, accomplishing none of its goals. The general success of repression makes co-optation seem more desirable to new groups, since obtaining some of their goals through co-optation is preferable to being repressed.

In a few cases, the result is quite different. The established political groups fail to repress the emergent groups, and the latter come to power through revolutionary means, proceeding to eliminate the traditional power contenders. These are known as the "true," genuine, or social revolutions in Latin America and include only the Mexican Revolution of 1910–1920, the Bolivian Revolution of 1952, the Cuban Revolution of 1959, and the Nicaraguan Revolution of 1979. Examples of the reverse process—utilization of violence and repression to eliminate the newer challenging groups and to secure in power the more traditional system— are Brazil in 1964 and Chile in 1973. Both led to the elimination of independent political parties, student associations, and labor and peasant unions as power groups.

It is in this context of often patrimonial, corporative tradition, now overlain with the trappings of liberalism (and in some countries more than mere trappings), and of a set of elaborate though unwritten rules of the game that we should view the politically relevant groups of Latin America. After independence three groups, often referred to as the "nineteenth-century oligarchy," were predominant: the military, the Roman Catholic Church, and the large landholders. These groups were once staunch defenders of the status quo; now they are more hetero- geneous. Through the process of economic growth and change new groups emerged: first commercial elites; later industrial elites, students, and middle-income sectors; most recently industrial labor unions and peasants. Throughout the process, political parties have existed. Par- ticularly since the end of the nineteenth century, the United States has been a politically relevant force in the domestic politics of the Latin American countries, in both its governmental and its private business incarnations. The U.S. Embassy is a leading actor, not only in terms of Latin America's trade and diplomatic relations but in internal affairs, comparable in importance to such major forces as the Church, the oligarchy, and the army.

THE ARMED FORCES

During the wars for independence, the Spanish American countries developed armies led by a great variety of individuals, including well- born *criollos*, priests, and people of more humble background. The officers did not come from military academies but were self-selected or chosen by other leaders. Few of the officers had previous military training, and the armies were much less professional than the armies we know today.

Following independence, the military element continued as one of the first important power groups. The national army was supposed to be preeminent, and in some countries national military academies were founded in the first quarter century of independence. Yet the national military was challenged by other armies. The early nineteenth century was a period of limited national integration, with the *patrias chicas* or regional subdivisions of the countries often dominated by local land- owners or caudillos—men on horseback who had their own private armies. One aspect of the development of Latin America was the struggle

between the central government and its army on the one hand and the
patrias chicas and local caudillos on the other, with the eventual success
of the former.

The development of Brazil varied somewhat from the norm because
of the different colonizing power and because of the lack of a struggle
for independence. The military first gained preeminence in the Paraguayan
War (1864–1870). Until 1930, the Brazilian states had powerful militias,
in some cases of comparable strength to the national army.

Although Latin American militaries varied in the nineteenth century,
a study of them reveals two general themes. First, various militaries,
including the national one, became active in politics. At given times
they were regional or personal organizations; at others, they were parts
of political parties that were the participants in the civil wars frequently
waged between rival factions. But, second, the national military often
played the role of a moderating power—staying above factional struggles,
preferring that civilians govern, but taking over power temporarily when
the civilians could not effectively rule. Although this moderating power
did not emerge in all countries, it is seen in most, especially in Brazil,
where, with the abdication of the emperor in 1889, the military became
the chief moderator in the system.

As early as the 1830s and 1840s in Argentina and Mexico, and later
in the other Latin American countries, national military academies were
established. Their goal was to introduce professionalism into the military,
requiring graduation for officer status. Aided in the first decades of the
twentieth century by military missions from Germany and France, and
later by Chilean missions, these academies were for the most part
successful in making entry and promotion in the officer corps proceed
in a routinized manner. No longer did individuals become generals
overnight; rather, they were trained in military tactics and procedure.
By the 1950s a Latin American officer was named a general, with
potential political power, only after a career of some twenty years.

Through professionalization, the military career was designed to be
a highly specialized one that taught the skills for warfare but eschewed
interest in political matters. Officership would absorb all the energy of
its members, and this functional expertise would be distinct from that
of politicians. Civilians were theoretically to have complete control of
the military, which would stay out of politics. Yet this model of professionalism, imported from West Europe and the United States, never
took complete root in the Latin American political culture. The military
continued to play politics and to exercise its moderating power, and
coups d'état continued.

By the late 1950s and early 1960s, a change occurred in the nature
of the role of the military in Latin America and in the developed countries
of the West. The success of guerrilla revolutions in China, Indochina,
Algeria, and Cuba led to a new emphasis on the military's role in
counterinsurgency and internal defense functions. In addition, Latin

American militaries—encouraged by U.S. military aid—began to assume responsibility for civic-action programs, which assisted civilians in the construction of roads, schools, and other public projects. This led to a broader responsibility for the military in nation building.

The new professionalism of the past two decades is more in keeping with the Latin American political culture than the old professionalism was. Military skills are no longer viewed as separate or different from civilian skills—management, administration, nation building. The military was to acquire the ability to help solve those national problems that might lead to insurgency—which is, in its very essence, a political rather than apolitical task. The implication of the new professionalism is that, besides combating active guerrilla factions, the military will take care that social and economic reforms necessary to prevent insurgency are adopted if the civilians prove incapable of doing so. Although the new professionalism has also been seen in the developed Western world and in other parts of the Third World, it has been particularly prevalent in Latin America, where it coincided with the moderating power tradition. Professionalism in Latin America therefore has led to more military intervention in politics, not less.

It is difficult to compare the Latin American militaries cross-nationally. Trying to distinguish "civilian" from "military" regimes is also a meaningless task sometimes or at best a difficult one. Often military personnel temporarily resign their commissions to take leadership positions in civilian bureaucracies. Frequently they hold military and civilian positions at the same time. In some cases, an officer might resign his commission, be elected president, and then govern with strong military backing. In almost all instances, coups d'état are not just simple military affairs but are supported by civilians as well. It is not unheard of for civilians to take a significant part in the ensuing governments. In short, Latin American governments are usually coalitions made between certain factions of the militaries with certain factions of civilians in an attempt to control the pinnacles of power of the system.

Few would argue that all Latin American governments are exactly alike in the degree of military influence. Various attempts have been made to categorize military intervention in politics. Although this is not the place to present a definitive classification, we suggest that several dimensions be considered in the country chapters that follow.

1. How often does the military forcefully remove chief executives, either elected ones or the victors in previous military coups? Colombia, for example, has had only two successful coups in this century. Ecuador has had many more. Bolivia has had more than two hundred in 160 years of independent life.

2. How often are military men elected to the presidency? And if they are elected, to what extent are they "Dwight D. Eisenhower civilians" and to what extent is this a way to bring the military to power and yet remain "democratic"?

3. To what degree do military officers occupy key positions in the civilian bureaucracy, having resigned their commisssions but fully expecting to be recommissioned at the same level without losing seniority when their civilian days are over?

4. To what extent do the leaders of the military have a say in nonmilitary matters, issues other than the size of the military budget and the nature of defense?

5. In what way does the moderating power of the military obligate it to step in and unseat an incompetent president or one who has violated the rules of the game?

Besides the degree of military influence in the political system, several other interrelated questions should be kept in mind during the reading of the country chapters.

1. Why is the military active in politics? Is this normal behavior in the country, or does it occur only in times of severe crisis?

2. Whom does the military respresent? Is it acting in its own corporate interests, for the perceived good of the entire nation, or in the interests of the middle class, from whose ranks most members of the officer corps come?

3. Is the result of military rule conservative, maintaining or returning to the status quo, or is the military the handmaiden of social change?

4. How is the military divided? In no country does it seem to be a monolithic entity. Splits have occurred between branches of service (the more upper-class navy against the middle-class army), between age groups of officers (the young colonels against the old generals), between factions with different perceptions of the military's role in society (officers preferring civilian rule versus those who like military governments), and between groups with various ideologies (the traditionalists versus the radicals).

The military is one of the traditional pillars of Latin American society, with rights (*fueros*), responsibilities, and legal standing that can be traced back to colonial times. This means the military will and must play a different role than it does in the United States. Hence, it is advisable to look at the military's role in any country in the context of the interaction of these traditions with the problems that the individual countries face. Little is gained from blanket condemnation or blanket approval of military intervention.

THE ROMAN CATHOLIC CHURCH

All Latin American countries are nominally Catholic, although the form of that religion varies from country to country. The Spanish and Portuguese came to "Christianize the heathens" as well as to seek precious metals. In areas of large Amerindian concentrations, religion became a mixture of pre-Columbian and Roman Catholic beliefs. To a lesser degree, Catholicism later blended with African religions, which also exist on their own in certain areas, especially in Brazil and Cuba. In contrast, religion in the large cities of Latin America is similar to that in the urban centers of the United States and West Europe. But in the more isolated small towns, Roman Catholicism is still of fifteenth-century vintage.

The power of the Church hierarchy in politics also varies. Traditionally the Church was one of the main sectors of Spanish and Portuguese corporate society, with rights and responsibilities in such areas as care for orphans, education, and public morals. During the nineteenth century, the Church was one of the three major groups in politics, along with the military and the landed interests. Yet during the same century, some lay people wanted to strip the Church of all its temporal power, including its lands. Generally speaking, the conflict over the role of the Church had ended by the first part of the present century, with some exceptions.

Today the Church is changing—expecially if by *Church* we mean the top levels of the hierarchy that control the religious and political fortunes of the institution. These transformations were occasioned by the new theologies of the past hundred years, as expressed through various papal encyclicals, Vatican II, and the conferences of the Latin American bishops at Medellín, Colombia, in 1968 and Puebla, Mexico, in 1979. There are significant numbers of bishops (and many more parish priests and members of the various orders) who subscribe to what is commonly called liberation theology. This new theology stresses that the Church is of and for this world and should take stands against repression and violence, including the "institutionalized violence"—the life-demeaning and -threatening violence—experienced by the poor of the area. Liberation theology also stresses the equality of all believers—lay people as well as clerics and bishops—as opposed to the former stress on hierarchy. The end result has been, in some parts of the area, new People's Churches, with lay leadership and only minimal involvement of priests.

It would be a mistake, however, to assume that all, or even most, members of the Latin American clergy subscribe to liberation theology. Many believe that the new social doctrine has taken the Church more into politics than it should be. Some are concerned with the loss of traditional authority that the erosion of hierarchy has brought. As the various countries of Latin America differ substantially in Church authority and adherence of the bishops to liberation theology, we raise this issue now; additional information is given in the country chapters in Parts 2 and 3 of this book.

The result of the changes is a clergy that is no longer uniformly conservative, but rather one whose members differ on the role that the Church should play in socioeconomic reform and on the nature of hierarchical relations within the Church. At one extreme of this conflict is the traditional Church elite, usually with social origins in the upper class or aspirations to be accepted by it, still very conservative, and with close connections to other supporters of the status quo. At the other end of this intraclergy conflict are those priests, of various social backgrounds, who see the major objective of the Church as assisting the masses to obtain social justice. In some cases (the most notable of which was Camilo Torres in Colombia, who left the clergy to fight in the guerrilla wars), these priests are openly revolutionary. Other priests fall between these two extremes of political ideology, and still others favor a relaxing of the rigid hierarchy, giving more discretion to local parish priests.

The Church still participates in politics to defend its material interests, although in most cases its wealth is no longer in land. Certain Church interests are still the traditional ones: giving religious instruction in schools and running parochial high schools and universities, the cost of which has traditionally made higher education possible only for people of middle income or higher; and occasional attempts to prevent divorce legislation and to make purely civil marriage difficult. At times, the Church has been a major proponent of human rights, especially when military governments deny them. A touchier issue is that of birth control, and in most cases the Latin American hierarchies have fought artificial methods. However, in the face of the population explosion, many Church officials have assisted in family-planning clinics, turned their heads when governments have promoted artificial methods of birth control, and occasionally even assisted in those governmental efforts.

Nominally Latin America is the most Catholic area of the world, although many individuals are not active communicants. The general religious ethos that permeates some of the Latin American countries gives the Church an indirect power, making it unnecessary for the archbishop or the clergy actively to lobby for or against legislation or to state the formal position of the Church on a traditional issue. Decision makers usually have been exposed to religious education at some point and know perfectly well the Church's position.

Some analysts feel the Church is no longer a major power contender. They argue that on certain issues its sway is still considerable, but that the Church is no longer as influential politically as the army, the wealthy elites, or the U.S. Embassy. Other analysts, pointing to the liberation theology People's Churches, argue, on the contrary, that the Church or individual clerics connected to it are powerful as never before. Later we will examine these contradictory hypotheses in our studies of the various countries.

LARGE LANDOWNERS

In all the countries of Latin America, save Costa Rica and Paraguay, the colonial period led to the establishment of a group of large landowners who had received their lands as royal grants. With the coming of independence, these *latifundistas* (owners of large land tracts called *latifundios*) were more powerful than before and developed into one of the three major groups of nineteenth-century politics. This is not to say that they operated monolithically; in some cases they were divided against each other.

In recent times, these rifts have remained among the large landowners, usually along the lines of crop production. They might disagree on a governmental policy favoring livestock raising to the detriment of crop planting. However, the major conflict has been between those who have large tracts of land and the many landless peasants. In those circumstances the various groups of large landowners tend to coalesce, burying their differences. In some cases, there is an umbrella organization to bring all of the various producer organizations together formally; in other cases, the coalition is much more informal.

In the 1960s, the pressures for land reform were considerable, both from landless peasants and from foreign and domestic groups who saw this reform as a way to avoid Castro-like revolutions. In some countries, such as Mexico, land reform had previously come by revolution; in others, such as Venezuela, a good bit of land had been distributed to the landless; in still others, the power of the landed, in coalition with other status quo groups, led to the appearance of land reform rather than the reality. More and more of the landless moved to the cities. In many of the Latin American countries, especially those in which the amount of arable land is limited and where the population explosion has led to higher person-land ratios, the issue of breaking up large estates will continue for the foreseeable future. Given the power of the landed, such change is likely to be slow in the absence of something approaching a social revolution.

One failure of the land reforms of the 1960s was not achieving the vision, about which U.S. Agency for International Development (AID) officials and sociologists waxed poetic, of countries of middle-class farmers reflecting all of the Jeffersonian virtues of tilling the land and encouraging liberal democracy. Only three countries in Latin America have significant numbers of these family farms—Costa Rica, Colombia, and Mexico—and these predated the 1960s. In the absence of wholesale land reform (and even with it, if the policymakers decide that the economies of scale call for collective or state ownership of land), a middle-class farmer group seems very unlikely for the future.

COMMERCIAL AND INDUSTRIAL ELITES

Commercial elites have existed in Latin America since independence; one of the early political conflicts was between those who wanted free trade (the commercial elites and allied landed interests producing crops for export) and those who wanted protection of nascent industry (industrial elites with allied landed groups not producing for export).

Although the early industrial elites were important in this conflict, the real push for industrialization in Latin America did not come until the Great Depression and World War II, when Latin America was cut off from trade with the industrialized world. Before those crises, industrial goods from England and the United States were cheaper, even with transportation costs and import duties, than locally produced goods. The one exception to this generalization was the textile industry.

Over the past forty years, the Latin American countries have experienced industrialization of the import-substitution type—that is, producing goods that formerly were imported from the industrialized countries. This has been the case in light consumer goods—in some consumer durables—including assembly plants for North American and European automobiles, and in some other heavy industries such as cement and steel. Because import substitution necessitates increased foreign trade in order to import capital goods, there no longer is much conflict between commercial and industrial elites: Expanded trade and industrialization go together.

Much of the industry that exists in Latin America today is of a subsidiary nature—parts of large multinational corporations based in the United States, West Europe, and Japan. This detracts from the industrial elite's status as an independent power contender in the political process, although the multinationals have their own power. Likewise, private industry is not as strong a group as it might be, since Latin American governments themselves have developed or nationalized many of the industries that traditionally are private in the United States: steel, railroads, and petroleum, among others.

Another complicating factor in the consideration of the industrial elite is its relationship with the landed elite. In some countries, such as Argentina, the early industrialists were linked to the landed groups; later, individuals who began as industrialists invested in land. The result was two intertwined groups, a marriage of older landed and newer moneyed wealth, with only vague boundaries separating them and some families and individuals straddling the line. Although this might not be true of all Latin American countries, the interrelationship between the two has been offered as a reason for industrialist opposition to land reform. The land to be received by the *campesinos* (those living on the land) was that of the industrialist, his family, or his friends!

Industrialists and commercial elites are highly organized in various chambers of commerce, industrial associations, and the like; they are strategically located in major cities of Latin America; and generally they favor a status quo that profits themselves. They are seen as the driving forces in Latin American economic development and for these reasons and because they are frequently represented in high official circles no matter what government is in control, they are very powerful.

STUDENTS

Student activism in politics is a long-standing tradition in Latin America, not only at the university level, but at high-school levels too. University students are an elite group in Latin America in that they have the leisure to study rather than work. Although the figure varies from country to country, it is estimated that only about 3 percent of the university-aged population at any time has the opportunity to pursue post-secondary education.

University students tend to have power beyond their numbers. They are a highly prestigious group, traditionally held in high regard in Spanish and Portuguese culture and seen as the leaders of the coming generation. They are often looked to by workers and peasants as their natural leaders. Major universities are located in the capital and other large cities. Since much of Latin American politics is urban politics, students are in the right place to have maximum input with street demonstrations and, sometimes, urban guerrilla activities. The traditional autonomy of university campuses means the military and police cannot enter to make an arrest, even in hot pursuit of urban guerrillas.

Although most students are of various leftist persuasions, political parties of all ideologies have attempted to include the students in their ranks. Each party tends to have its own student branch. The parties also sponsor "professional students," who dedicate more of their time to organizing than to studying. This attempt to organize students is based on their proven ability in politics, although students tend to be more successful opposing than supporting groups in the government.

Yet students are not so strong a group as those discussed in the preceding sections. Deep political divisions among the students militate against their exercising greater power, as does the fact that students are a transitory group, with nearly 100 percent turnover every five or six years. This is a disadvantage for a group, as recruitment to political activity and training must be constant. Finally, students have less influence than they might since some are much more concerned with education as a method of social mobility or of preserving their social status than they are with politics.

Students can be expected to remain a politically relevant group, especially if economic growth is slow or nonexistent. In alliance with workers or a faction of the military, they can play an important role in making or breaking a government. Latin American universities, although they train a relatively small percentage of the population, are producing more potential white-collar workers than there are places for in government bureaucracy and private enterprise. Students who see slight possibilities of a professional career after college are likely to be drawn into politics because of frustration and insecurity.

THE MIDDLE SECTORS

Although the Latin American countries began independence with a basically two-class system that still exists today, there have always been individuals who fell statistically into the middle ranges, neither very rich nor abjectly poor. These few individuals during the nineteenth century were primarily artisans and shopkeepers and, later, doctors and lawyers. More recently, the number of these middle elements has significantly grown.

The emergence of a larger middle sector was a twentieth-century phenomenon, associated with urbanization, technological advances, industrialization, and the expansion of public education and the role of the government. All of these changes necessitated a large number of white-collar, managerial workers. New teachers and government bureaucrats constituted part of this sector, as did office workers in private businesses. In addition, small businesses grew, particularly in the service sector of the economy. Many of these new nonmanual professions have been organized—teachers' associations, small-business associations, lawyers' associations, organizations of governmental bureaucrats, and so forth. Frequently these and such other new groups as organized labor and the students have taken up liberal and socialist values at odds with the older hierarchical, Thomistic notions.

The people who filled the new middle-sector jobs were the product of social mobility. Some came from the lower class; others were "fallen aristocrats" from the upper classes. They lacked a prolonged, common historical experience. This, together with their numerous and heterogeneous occupations, temporarily impeded the formation of a sense of common identity as members of a middle class. Indeed, in some of the countries of Latin America this identification has yet to emerge—and may not emerge. In the United States, there has always been an idealization of the middle class; in Latin America, in contrast, the ideal is to be a part of "society," preferably high society.

In those countries of Latin America in which a large middle-sector group has emerged, certain generalizations about its political behavior can be made. In the early stages of political activities, coalitions tended to be formed with groups from the lower classes against the more traditional and oligarchic groups in power. Major goals included expanded suffrage, the promotion of urban growth and economic development, a greater role for public education, increased industrialization, and social-welfare programs. The principal means of accomplishing these goals was through state intervention.

In the later political evolution of the middle sectors, the tendency has been to side with the established order. In some cases the middle-class movements allied with landowners, industrialists, and the Church against their working-class partners of earlier years; in other cases, when the more numerous lower class seemed ready to take power on its own, the middle sectors were instrumental in fomenting a middle-class military coup, to prevent "premature democratization." Over the years, then, middle-class movements changed dramatically.

Yet this transformation was sometimes more apparent than real. All the original goals of the middle-sector movements had as their effect, if not their intention, the creation of new white-collar, nonmanual jobs for teachers, government bureaucrats, and private bureaucrats in industry. Further, when the middle-sector movements took political control, they did not completely replace the traditional elite; they came to terms with that elite, entered into compromises with the members of it, and, in the process, came to be identified with the very elite institutions that they had planned to take over.

This general introduction, based largely on the more industrially advanced countries of the southern cone of South America should raise a number of questions that students should consider in reading the country chapters that follow.

1. How large are the middle-income sectors of the country?
2. To what extent do the middle sectors tend to act together politically? Do they tend to work in one or several political parties, or are they split between parties on loyalties predating the emergence of the middle class?
3. To what degree do the members of the middle sectors identify themselves as such? Is there a perceived commonality of interests? Or alternatively, although objectively they have the same class interests, do they fail to see them?

Many publications dealing with Latin America used to assume that there was a kind of progressive spirit inherent in the individual members of the middle class and that this spirit would be defined in terms of a desire for economic development and political democracy. This assumption was based on an idealized vision of what the middle classes had done in the United States and West Europe. The evidence now suggests that in some, but surely not all cases, the growth of middle-class movements in Latin America might retard economic development and impede liberal democracy, encouraging instead military rule.

LABOR UNIONS

From its inception, organized labor in Latin America has been highly political. Virtually all important trade-union groups of the area have been closely associated with a political party, strong leader, or government. On some occasions, labor unions have grown independently until they were co-opted or repressed. In other cases, labor unions have owed their origins directly to the efforts of a party, leader, or government.

Two characteristics of the Latin American economies have favored partisan unionism. First, Latin American unions came relatively early in the economic development of the countries, in most cases earlier than in the United States and West Europe. In Latin America the labor pool of employables has been much larger than the number who can get the relatively well-paid jobs in industry. An employer in that situation can almost always find people to replace striking workers unless they are protected by a party or by the government. Further, inflation has been a problem in Latin America in recent decades, making it important for unions to win the support of political groups in the continual renegotiation of contracts to obtain higher salaries, which often need governmental approval.

The Latin American legal tradition requires that unions be officially recognized by the government before they can collectively bargain. If a group cannot obtain or retain this legal standing, it has little power. Further, close attention must be paid to labor legislation. In some countries, labor codes have made it mandatory that labor organizers be employed full time by the industry that they are organizing, limiting the power of unions lacking leaders who are paid full salary to spend part of the working day in union activities. This is only one of the many governmental restrictions placed on labor unions.

Labor groups of some kind have long existed in Latin American industry. Before the early years of this century, they tended to be mutual benefit societies, a collective insurance and Catholic charity agency formed in the absence of governmental social-security programs. Labor movements moved to the next stage with the arrival of large numbers of Europeans in the early years of this century, especially in Argentina, Uruguay, Brazil, and Cuba. Anarcho-syndicalism was the dominant philosophy of the period, with Marxism as its main competition. From these original countries the labor movement and its competing ideologies spead to other countries of Latin America.

The influence of anarcho-syndicalism waned after World War I, when factory industry grew and with it the need for collective bargaining, which the anarcho-syndicalists did not accept as a tactic. Various national parties entered into the labor field, as well as the socialists and Communists with their international connections. Since World War II, the older, international-type organizations have lost influence, and in most countries of Latin America the major labor federations have had few international ties, although some have belonged to Catholic associations and others have received support from the American Federation of Labor–Congress of Industrial Organizations (AFL-CIO). Attempts to convert Latin American labor unions into something more like unionism in the United States have failed.

Yet the co-optation–and–repression system has by no means taken over the labor unions of Latin America. Some union organizations have been co-opted; others remain outside the system. For the country chapters to follow, certain questions are relevant.

1. To what extent are industrial (and middle-class) workers organized?
2. How is the labor code used to prevent or facilitate labor organization?
3. What is the nature of the relationships between labor and political parties, or between labor and government? Who has gained what from these associations?
4. To what extent are there labor unions that have not been co-opted or repressed? Is there a potential for new labor federations with new leaders outside of the unions themselves?
5. When labor allied with political parties, did it do so with one single party or are there various co-optive relationships with several parties?

PEASANTS

The term *peasants* refers to many different kinds of people in Latin America. Some prefer the Spanish term *campesinos* rather than the English term with its European-based connotations. The major groups of *campesinos,* who vary in importance from country to country, include the following:

1. Amerindian groups, who speak only their native language or who are bilingual in that language and Spanish
2. workers on the traditional hacienda, tilling the fields in return for wages or part of the crops, with the owner as a *patrón* to care for the family or, more frequently, a manager-patron who represents the absentee owner
3. workers on modern plantations, receiving wages but remaining outside of the older patron-client relationship
4. persons with a small landholding (*minifundio*), legally held, of such a size that a bare existence is possible
5. persons who cultivate small plots, with no legal claim, perhaps moving every few years after the slash-and-burn method and the lack of crop rotation deplete the soil
6. persons who are given a small plot of land to work by a landowner in exchange for work on the large estate

What all of these *campesinos* have in common, in the context of the extremely inequitable distribution of arable lands in Latin America, is a marginal existence due to their small amount of land or income and a high degree of insecurity due to their uncertain claims to the lands they cultivate. It was estimated in 1961 that over 5 million very small farms (below 30 acres—74 hectares) occupied only 3.7 percent of the land, while, at the other extreme, 100,000 holdings of more than 1,500 acres (3,706 hectares) took up some 65 percent of the land. Two decades later, the situation had changed little. At least 80 million people still live on small landholdings with insufficient land to earn a minimum subsistence, or they work as agricultural laborers with no land at all. For many of these rural masses, their only real chance of breaking out of this circle of poverty is by moving to an urban area, where they face another—in some ways even worse—culture of poverty. For those who remain on the land, unless there is a dramatic restructuring of ownership, the present subhuman existence is likely to continue.

Rural peasant elements have long been active in politics. The traditional political structure of the countryside was one in which participation in national politics meant taking part in the patronage system. The local *patrones,* besides expecting work on the estate from the *campesino,* expected certain political behavior. In some countries, this meant that the *campesino* belonged to the same political party as the *patrón,* voted for that party on election day, and, if necessary, served as cannon fodder in its civil wars. In other countries, the national party organizations never reached the local levels, and restrictive suffrage laws prevented the peasants from participation in elections. In both patterns, there was no such thing as national politics, only local politics, which might or might not have national party labels attached to the local person or groups in power.

This traditional system still exists in many areas of Latin America. But since the 1950s, signs of agrarian unrest and political mobilization have been more and more evident. In many cases, major agrarian movements have been organized by urban interests—political parties, especially those of the Marxist left. Some of these peasant movements have been openly revolutionary, seeking to reform and improve the land tenure system and to reform significantly the entire power structure of the nation. They have employed strategies that include the illegal seizure of land, the elimination of landowners, and armed defense of the gains thus achieved. We could call these movements ones of revolutionary agrarianism. Less radical are the movements that seek to reform the social order partially, through the elimination of a few of the most oppressive effects of the existing power structure that weighs on the peasant subculture, but without threatening the power structure as such.

The peasants, numerically the largest group in Latin America, remain politically weak. That is so chiefly because the peasant sector is largely unorganized—a situation that those of wealth and power have a vested interest in maintaining. Because of the diversity of land and labor patterns, the dispersed nature of the countryside, and high illiteracy, it is difficult to mobilize a strong peasant movement. Their distance from the urban centers of power also makes it hard for peasants to effect change. Hence, they remain subjects of the political system rather than participants in it, despite the activities of revolutionary agrarianism.

The country chapters will demonstrate a wide spectrum of peasant organizations and a wide variation of peasant success in Latin America. In some countries, one or two political parties have been instrumental in the organization of peasants, who have received a fair degree of land as a result. In other cases, governments have facilitated the organization of peasants, who for reasons of economy of scale do not receive private land titles. In still other instances, the landed elites have been successful in preventing significant agrarian reform. The variation is so great (and the issue so constant) that the reader is referred to the country chapters for individual cases.

THE UNITED STATES

Another important power element in Latin American politics is the United States. This influence has been seen in at least three interrelated ways: U.S. governmental representatives, U.S.-based private business, and U.S.-dominated international agencies. Some people would deny the validity of this separation. The United States, they would argue, presents a common front either by design or by effect. Their position is party substantiated by the following quote from Maj. Gen. Smedley D. Butler, U.S. Marine Corps:

> I helped make Mexico and especially Tampico safe for American oil interests in 1914. I helped make Haiti and Cuba a decent place for the National City Bank boys to collect revenue in. . . . I helped purify Nicaragua for the international banking house of Brown Brothers in 1909–1912. I brought light to the Dominican Republic for American sugar interests in 1916. I helped make Honduras "right" for American fruit companies in 1903.[1]

The general concern of this section is the activities of various U.S. groups in the Latin American political process. At times these groups work in harmony, and at times they operate at cross-purposes.

The U.S. government has been interested in the area since Latin America's independence. Its first concern, that the new nations not fall under the control of European powers, led to the Monroe Doctrine in 1823. Originally a defensive statement, the doctrine was later changed through various corollaries to a more aggressive one, telling the Latin Americans that they could not sell lands to nonhemispheric governments or businesses (if the locations were strategic) and that the United States would intervene in Latin America to collect debts owed to nonhemispheric powers (the Roosevelt Corollary). At various times, the U.S. government has set standards that must be met before full diplomatic recognition is accorded to a Latin American nation. This de jure recognition policy, most memorable in the Wilson, early Kennedy, and Carter administrations, favors elected democratic governments, exclusion of the military from government, and a vision of human rights that should be applied in Latin America. At other times the United States has pursued a de facto recognition policy, according full diplomatic standing to any government with effective control of its nation's territory.

Whatever recognition policy is followed, the U.S. ambassador to a Latin American country has impressive powers. One ambassador to pre-Castro Cuba testified that he was the most influential individual in the country, second only to the president. This ambassadorial power has typically been used to support or defeat governments, to focus governmental policy of the Latin American countries in certain directions, and often to assist U.S.-based corporations in the countries. In Central America recently a number of U.S. ambassadors have played this strong proconsular role.

From their early beginnings, particularly in agribusiness (especially sugar and bananas), U.S.-based corporations in Latin America have grown dramatically. In addition to agribusiness, corporations have now entered the extractive field (petroleum, copper, iron ore), retailing (Sears, Roebuck, among others), the services industry (accounting firms, computer outfits), and communications (telephones, telegraphs). The most recent kind of U.S. corporation introduced to Latin America is the export-platform variety—that is, a company that takes advantage of the low wages in Latin America to produce pocket calculators in Mexico or baseballs in Haiti, mainly for export to the industrialized world.

U.S. corporations in Latin America often enter into the politics of their host countries. Some of the instances are flagrant: bribing public officials to keep taxes low or threatening to cut off a country's products if certain policies are approved by its government. But most political activities of the gringo corporations are probably much less dramatic. Almost always Latin Americans in the host countries buy stock in the U.S. corporations and hold high managerial positions in them. In many cases, U.S. corporations purchase Latin corporations, the leaders of which then work for the new owners. The result is that the U.S. corporation develops contacts and obligations like those powers possessed by Latin American industrialists and commercial interests. But there are now indications that the era of large U.S. corporate holdings and hence influence in Latin America may be in decline. Many U.S. corporations are pulling up stakes in Latin America, withdrawing their capital, and moving on to more profitable and stable areas.

Most foreign-aid and international lending organizations are dominated by the United States. These agencies, especially active since the early 1960s, when aid to Latin America began in large quantities, include the U.S. Agency for International Development, which administers most of our foreign aid, the World Bank, the International Monetary Fund (IMF), and a variety of others. The World Bank and the IMF are international agencies, results of post–World War II agreements between the countries of the West. However, the representation of the United States on the governing boards of both is so large (based on the amount of money donated to the agencies) and the convergence of interests of the two with those of the U.S. government is so great that they can be considered U.S.-oriented groups. Since economic development has been a central goal of the Latin American states for the past twenty years, since loans for that development have come predominantly from AID and the World Bank, and since those loans are contingent many times on a monetary policy judged as healthy by the IMF, the officials of these three groups have much influence in the day-to-day policies of the governments of the area.

This power of the lending agencies was probably greatest during the 1960s. AID had most leverage or "conditionality" during the Alliance for Progress. This foreign-aid program, initiated by the Kennedy administration, attempted to change Latin America dramatically in a decade. Even though it failed, it did lead to large loans from the U.S. government, substantial progress in some fields, and along with it much influence for the local AID head in the domestic politics of some Latin American countries. Some AID representatives sat in on cabinet meetings and wrote speeches for and gave advice to the local officials with whom they worked, and others largely ran the agencies or even ministries of the host government to which they were assigned.

The Alliance for Progress was terminated by the Nixon administration. Further, the power of the World Bank has waned in the wake of the crisis of the industrialized economies of the West following the Arab oil embargo of 1973–1974 and with the growing power of OPEC. Many leaders of the industrialized nations are searching for a new international system of monetary and trade stabilization. In the meantime, the economies of Latin America are undergoing crisis while in the importing nations protectionist measures have risen. The Latin American nations are clamoring for access to U.S. markets, and they are likely to be partially successful in that quest. The U.S. government has also proposed a new massive assistance program for Central America and the Caribbean designed to restore solvency and preserve stability.

The influence of U.S-directed and -oriented groups—diplomatic, business, foreign-assistance—in Latin America is considerable. This does not mean that the power is equal in all the Latin American countries. One might venture the hypothesis that U.S. influence is greater for security reasons in those countries nearer the continental United States and/or where U.S. private investments are larger. When a Latin American country is important strategically to the United States and when U.S. private investors have established a large investment in the economy (Cuba before Castro), U.S. elements are extremely powerful in domestic Latin politics. This does not mean that the United States cannot have considerable influence in domestic politics in distant countries with relatively little private investment by U.S. corporations, as the example of Allende's Chile has shown.

POLITICAL PARTIES

In Latin America, political parties are oftentimes only one set of groups among several, probably no more (and perhaps less) important than the army or the economic oligarchy. Elections are not the only legitimated route to power, nor are the parties themselves particularly strong or well organized. We do not want to denigrate the place of parties in Latin America, for they are important actors in the political process and in some of the more democratic countries they represent the chief means to gain high office. But neither do we want to give parties a significance they do not have, since frequently the parties are peripheral to the main focal points of power and the electoral arena is considered only one arena among several.

General elements of the groups just discussed have combined in political parties in their pursuit of governmental power. One must be careful with the term *political party*, as the term *partido* has a much more general application than the English equivalent. For example, *el partido militar* is used in the press of the Dominican Republic and other countries to refer to the military, although clearly the officers do not use electoral tactics such as those normally associated with a U.S. political party. Further, some civilians belonging to political parties have been known to plot with factions of the military to take power in a coup d'état.

There have been a myriad of political parties in the history of Latin America; indeed, someone once quipped that to form a political party, all you needed was a president, vice president, secretary-treasurer, and rubber stamp. (If times were bad, you could do without the vice president and the secretary-treasurer!) Nevertheless, there have been certain characteristics common to parties, although the country chapters that follow show great national variation.

Groups calling themselves political parties have existed from the early years of independence. The first parties were usually founded by elite groups in competition with other factions of the elite. Mass demands played only a small role, although *campesinos* were mobilized by the party leaders, often to serve as cannon fodder. In many cases, the first cleavage was between individuals in favor of free trade, federalism, and anticlericalism (the Liberals) and those for protectionism for nascent industry, centralism, and clericalism (the Conservatives). In some countries these original party divisions have long since disappeared, replaced by other cleavages; in other countries they are still very much alive.

With social and economic change in some countries of Latin America, the emergence of new social strata led to the founding of new political parties. A portion of these attracted those in the growing middle sectors who were quite reformist in the early years but later changed as they became part of the system. In other cases, new parties were more radical, calling for a basic restructuring of society and including elements from the working classes. Some of these originally radical parties were of international inspiration; most of the countries have had Communist and socialist parties of differing effectiveness and legality. Other, more radical parties were primarily national ones, albeit with ideological inspiration traceable to Marxism.

One such party, founded in 1923 by the Peruvian Víctor Raúl Haya de la Torre while in exile in Mexico, was the American Popular Revolutionary Alliance (APRA). Although APRA purported to be the beginning of a new international of like-minded democratic-left individuals in Latin America, this goal was never fully reached. An inter-American organization was established, but it never had great importance. At the same time, inspired by Haya and APRA, a number of national parties were founded by young Latin Americans. The most successful Aprista-like party has been Democratic Action (AD) in Venezuela, but the same programs have been advocated by numerous other parties of this group, including the Party of National Liberation in Costa Rica and the National Revolutionary Movement in Bolivia, as well as parties in Puerto Rico, Paraguay, the Dominican Republic, Guatemala, Honduras, and Argentina. Only in Venezuela and Costa Rica did the APRA-like parties come to power more than temporarily, and by that time, twenty years after the founding of APRA, they were no longer extremely radical. They favored liberal democracy, rapid reform, and economic growth. In most cases, the APRA-like parties were led by members of the middle sectors, and they received much of their electoral support from middle- and lower-class ranks.

A newer group of political parties are the Christian-Democratic ones, particularly successful in Chile and Venezuela. These parties call for fundamental reforms but are guided by Church teachings and papal encyclicals rather than Marx or Engels, even though they are nondenominational and open to all. The nature of the ideology of these parties varies from country to country.

Other parties in Latin America have been based on the leadership of one or few persons, and hence do not fit into the neat party spectrum just described. Quite often the "man on horseback" is more important than the program of a party. This tradition of the caudillo is seen in the case of Brazil, where Getúlio Vargas founded not one but two official political parties; in Ecuador, where personalistic parties have been strong contenders for the presidency; and in Communist Cuba, where in the 1960s the party was more Castroist than Communist.

The system of co-optation further complicates the attempt at classification. How is one to classify a political party traditional in origin that includes at the same time large landowners and the peasants tied to them, as well as trade-union members organized by the party with the assistance of parts of the clergy? How does one classify a party such as the Mexican Institutional Revolutionary party (PRI), which has made a conscious effort ot co-opt and include all politically relevant sectors of the society?

Even further complicating the picture is the question of party systems— that is, how many parties are there in a country and how often does power pass from party to party (or for that matter, from party to military)? All parties are coalitions; but is a party still only a single party if it offers more than one candidate for president or more than one list of candidates for congressional seats? Both have occurred in recent years in the only two-party systems of Latin America—Colombia's and (formerly) Uruguay's. These kinds of things do not happen by accident; they are the results of electoral laws drawn up by political elites with various goals in mind.

As in the case of the military, the literature on parties in Latin America is replete with contradictions, misleading classifications, and misunderstandings. We suggest for the country chapers keeping in mind these questions:

1. How many major parties are there? What are their historical origins, their formal programs as enunciated by candidates and platforms, and their policies when in power?

2. How is the electoral law written, favoring or impeding parties? Since proportional representation, with countless variations, is most common, is this a reflection of societal circumstances when electoral laws are written, or rather does unwitting legislation change party systems?

3. What is the electoral behavior in the countries? Do voting patterns show regionalism, urban-rural dichotomies, class voting, or some combination of the three?

4. What kinds of contacts are there between the political parties and the military? Are they friendly and cooperative or hostile? The military is still the ultimate arbiter of the nation's politics, and mere political parties must take care not to go beyond the "dikes of military opinion," to paraphrase Harvard professor V. O. Key's statement about U.S. politics.

5. How often in national history have civilian political parties been in power? If they are weak, is it because the military institution so quickly monopolized power after independence, or did the military do so because the parties were weak? No matter which is the chicken and which the egg, is this a situation that can be changed by Latin America or is the area to follow the historical patterns in the near future?

6. What roles do parties play and how do they vary from country to country? Is their function to devise platforms and run candidates in elections? Or are they really just another giant patronage agency? Are they independent of government or simply mechanisms of the state? Do they serve a public interest or are they merely a means by which the ambitious may gain status and a following?

On two notable occasions in the past three decades, students of Latin America have been told to study political parties. Perhaps the time has now come to change this advice, to urge not just a study of parties per se but, more importantly, of the relations of parties to the military, to the state, and to the system as a whole.

CONCLUSIONS AND IMPLICATIONS

The preceding discussion has indicated that there are many politically relevant groups in Latin America and that they use various means to secure and retain political power. Yet at least two other themes should be introduced that tend to complicate the picture.

First, it should be noted that the urban and rural poor—outside the labor unions—have not been included in the discussion. This shows one of the biases of the system. Preceding the first step in attaining political relevance is another—being organized. This means that potential groups, especially poorly educated and geographically dispersed ones like the peasants and the urban poor, face difficulties in becoming politically relevant since they have difficulties in organizing themselves or being organized from the outside. Peasants have become increasingly organized. The same is not the case of the urban poor, working in cottage industries, as street vendors, or not at all. Their numbers are swelling rapidly, with the growing exodus from the countryside to the cities. Although to this point the urban poor have not been organized, political party leaders are increasingly aware of their large numbers and are beginning organizational attempts that employ, not surprisingly, co-optation or repression tactics common to the Latin American practice. As *campesinos* were increasingly organized in the 1960s, perhaps the urban poor will be the next addition to the "living museum" in the 1980s.

Second, not all politically relevant groups fall into the neat categories of this chapter (which, of course, are familiar to both liberals and Marxists of the European and North American traditions). Anthony Leed's research in Brazil has shown (at least in small towns, probably larger cities, and even perhaps the whole nation) a politically more relevant series of groups to be the *panelinhas* ("little saucepans").[2] These are composed of individuals of common interest but different occupations—say, a doctor, a large landowner, surely a lawyer, and a governmental official. The *panelinha* at the local level controls and endeavors to establish contacts with the *panelinha* at the state level, which might have contacts with a national *panelinha*. Of course, at the local level there are rival *panelinhas*, which contacts with rival ones at the state level, with contacts. . . . As is generally the case with such patrimonial-type relations, all interactions (except those within the *panelinhas* themselves) are vertical, and one level of *panelinha* must take care to ally with the winning one at the next higher level if it wants to have political power.

Similar research in other countries has revealed a parallel pattern of informal, elitist, patronage politics. Whether called the *panelinha* system in Brazil or the *camarilla* system in Mexico, the process and dynamics are the same. The aspiring politician (almost always a man) connects himself with an aspiring politician at a higher level, who is connected with an aspiring . . . and so forth on up to an aspiring candidate for the presidency. If the person in question becomes president, the various levels of *camarillas* prosper; if he remains powerful without becoming president, the *camarillas* continue functioning in expectation of what will take place in six years (in Mexico, the next presidential election); but if the aspiring candidate is disgraced, dismissed from the official party, or dies, the whole system of various levels of *camarillas* connected with him disintegrates. Although this *camarilla* phenomenon is also known in the United States and the Soviet Union, it is more common in the personalistic politics of Latin America. The *camarilla* system operates outside, while overlapping with the formal structure of groups and parties decribed here.

This discussion of *panelinhas* and *camarillas* raises the question again of whether U.S.-style interest groups and political parties are operating and are important in Latin America. The answer is: They are and they aren't. In the larger and better-institutionalized systems, the parties and interest groups are often important and function not unlike their North American or European counterparts. But in the less-institutionalized, personalistic countries of Central America (and even behind the scenes in the larger ones), it is frequently family groups, cliques, clan alliances, and patronage networks that are more important—often disguised behind the appearance of partisan or ideological dispute. One must be careful therefore in some countries not to minimize the importance of a functional, operational party and interest-group system, while recognizing that in others it is the less formal network through which politics is carried out.

NOTES

1. Quoted in John Gerassi, *The Great Fear in Latin America* (Collier Books, New York, 1965) p. 231.

2. Anthony Leeds, "Brazilian Careers and Social Structure: A Case History and Model," *American Anthropologist* 66 (1964):1321–1347.

5
Government Machinery and the Role of the State

Neither the classic Marxian categories nor the theory of liberalism gives more than secondary importance to the role of the state. In the Marxian paradigm the state or governmental system is viewed as part of the superstructure shaped, if not determined, by the underlying structure of class relations. In the liberal model the state is generally conceived as a referee, umpiring the competition among the interest groups but not itself participating in the game, a kind of "black-box" intermediary into which the "inputs" of the system go in the form of competing interests and pressures and from which come "outputs" or public policies. Neither of these two classic models adequately explains the Latin American systems.

In Latin America the state has historically held an importance that it lacks in the classic models. The state is viewed as a powerful and independent agency in its own right, above and frequently autonomous from the class and interest-group struggle. Whether in socialist regimes such as Cuba's or rightist ones like Brazil's, it is the state and its central leadership that largely determine the shape of the system and its developmental directions.

The state does not merely reflect the class structure but, through its control of economic and political resources, itself shapes the class system. The state is viewed as the prime regulator, coordinator, and pacesetter of the entire national system, the apex of the Latin American pyramid from which patronage, wealth, power, and programs flow. The critical importance of the state in the Latin American nations helps explain why the competition for control of it is so intense and sometimes violent. Determining who controls the pinnacles of the system is a fundamental, all-important, and virtually everyday preoccupation.

Related to this is the contrasting way citizens of North America and Latin America tend to view government. In North America government has usually been considered a necessary evil requiring elaborate checks and balances. Political theory in Iberia and Latin America views government as good, natural, and necessary for the welfare of society. If government is good, there is little reason to limit or put checks and balances on it. Hence, before we fall into the trap of condemning Latin America for its powerful autocratic executives, subservient parliaments, and weak local government, we must remember the different assumptions on which the Latin American systems are based.

It is around these issues concerning the role of the state that much of Latin American politics revolves. The following list provides some keys as to what to look for in the discussions that will come later: (1) the fundamental issue of who controls the state apparatus and the immense power and funds at its disposal; (2) the constant efforts historically of the state or strong presidents to expand their power, versus the efforts of others (university students, peasant or Indian communities, municipalities) to resist; (3) the requirement that governments have to somehow reconcile theory and constitutionalism, which are often liberal and democratic, with the realities, which are frequently authoritarian and elitist; (4) the issue of whether and when a strong government oversteps the bounds of permissible authoritarianism and becomes an outright tyranny, thus justifying the "right of rebellion." After a successful coup the cycle may begin all over again.

THE THEORY OF THE STATE: CONSTITUTIONS AND LEGAL SYSTEMS

After achieving independence early in the nineteenth century, the Latin American nations faced a severe legitimacy crisis. Socialism had not yet produced its major prophets and therefore was not an alternative. Monarchy was a possibility (and some nations did consider or experiment briefly with monarchical rule), but Latin America had just struggled through years of independence wars to rid itself of the Spanish imperial yoke, and monarchy had been discredited. Liberalism and republicanism were attractive and seemed the wave of the future, but Latin America had had no prior experience with liberal or republican rule.

The solution was ingenious, though often woefully misunderstood. The new nations of Latin America moved to adopt liberal and democratic forms, while at the same time preserving many of the organicist, elitist, and authoritarian principles of their own tradition. The liberal and democratic forms provided goals and aspirations toward which society could strive; they also helped present a progressive picture to the outside world. But the liberal and republican principles were circumscribed by a series of measures authoritarian in content that were truer to the realities and history of the area and to its existing oligarchic power relationships. It has been the ongoing genius and challenge of Latin American politics to seek to blend and reconcile these conflicting currents.

Virtually all the Latin American constitutions have provided for the historical, three-part division of powers among executive, legislature, and judiciary. But in fact the three powers are not coequal and were not intended to be; the executive is constitutionally given extensive powers to bypass the legislature, and judicial review is largely outside the Latin American legal tradition. Knee-jerk condemnations of a Latin American government that rules without giving equal status to the legislature or courts often reveals more about our own biases, ethno-centrism, and lack of understanding than it does about the realities of Latin America.

The same kinds of apparent contradictions exist in other areas. Although one part of the constitution may be devoted to civilian institutions and the traditional three branches of government, another may give the armed forces a higher-order role to protect the nation, preserve internal order, and prevent internal disruption. In this sense, the military may be considered a fourth branch of the state. Military intervention, therefore, should not necessarily be condemned as an extraconstitutional and illegitimate act since it is often an implied prerogative of the armed forces. The military thus generally sees itself as the defender of the constitution, not as its usurper—although it is the armed forces who decide when the constitution needs defending.

The same is true of human rights. Even though all the Latin American constitutions contain long lists of human and political rights, these same constitutions also give the executive power to declare a state of siege or emergency, suspend human rights, and rule by decree. The same applies to privilege. While one section of the constitution may proclaim democratic and egalitarian principles, other parts may give special privileges to the Church, the army, or the landed elites. While repre-sentative and republican precepts are enshrined in one quarter, au-thoritarian and elitist ones are legitimated in another.

Of course this is not meant to imply approval of human-rights violations or of overthrows of democratic governments but only to point out how these are often perceived differently in Latin America. Hence, the real questions may concern not the right of the armed forces to intervene in politics or the executive to prorogue the legislature (since those are often givens of the system), but the degrees of military intervention or limits on legislative authority and how and why these actions are taken. It is not simply a matter of the military usurping the constitution, since it is often the constitution itself that gives the military the right, even obligation, to intervene in the political process under certain circumstances. Similarly, when human-rights violations are re-ported, we must understand this within the Latin American constitutional and legal tradition rather than within our own. Human rights are not conceived as constitutional absolutes, and frequently there is a consti-tutional provision for their suspension. When, however, torture is practiced or, as in Paraguay, a state of siege has been in effect and human rights suspended almost continuously since 1947, we may have legitimate suspicions that basic rights are being violated not just on our terms but theirs as well.

The most important issues of Latin American politics, therefore, revolve not around haughty condemnations from the point of view of some "superior" political system, but around the dynamics of change and process from the Latin American perspective. We cannot understand the area if we look only at the liberal and republican side of the Latin American tradition while ignoring the rest; nor should we simply condemn some action from the point of view of the North American constitutional tradition without seeing it in the Latin American context. If the civil and military spheres are not strictly segregated as in the U.S. tradition, then what are their dynamic relations in Latin America and what are the causes of military intervention? If strict separation of powers is not seen in the same light in Latin America and if the branches are not equal, what *are* their respective powers and interrelations? If hierarchy, authority, and special privilege are legitimated principles along with democratic and egalitarian ones, then how are these reconciled, glossed over, or challenged, and why?

The Latin American constitutions are misunderstood in another way that has to do with their sheer number. We frequently smile condescendingly on Latin America for its many constitutions (thirty-odd in Venezuela, Ecuador, and the Dominican Republic) as compared with our one. But these figures ignore the fact that in Latin America a new constitution is generally promulgated whenever a new amendment is added or when a major new interpretation requires official legitimation. The situation would be comparable to the United States' proclaiming a new constitution every time an amendment was passed or a major judicial reinterpretation decided upon. The facts are: First, the Latin American constitutional tradition has been far more stable than the number of constitutions implies, and second, in most countries of the area there are only two main constitutional traditions, the one authoritarian and the other liberal and democratic, reflecting the main currents of Latin American politics. The many constitutions, then, signify the repeated alternations between these two basic traditions, with variations.

These perspectives on the constitutional tradition also provide hints as to the distinct legal tradition of Latin America, as compared with that of the United States. Whereas the U.S. laws and constitution are based upon a history and practice derived from British common law, those of Latin America derive from a code-law tradition. This difference has several implications. Whereas the U.S. legal system is founded on precedent and reinterpretation, the Latin American codes are complete bodies of law allowing little room for precedent or judicial reinterpretation. The codes, like the Latin American constitutions, are fixed and absolute; they embody a comprehensive framework of operating principles; and unlike the common-law tradition with its inductive reasoning based upon cases, enforcement of the codes implies deductive reasoning. One begins not with facts or cases but with general truth (the codes or constitution) and deduces rules or applications for specific circumstances from this.

Although one should not overstress the point and although mixed forms exist throughout Latin America, an understanding of the code-law system and its philosophical underpinnings carries us a considerable distance toward understanding Latin American behavior. The truths embodied in the codes and constitutions and the deductive method have their origins and reflection in the Roman and Catholic-scholastic tradition. The authoritarian, absolutist nature of the codes also finds reflection in (and helps reinforce) an absolutist, frequently authoritarian political culture. The effort to cover all contingencies with one code or to engage in almost constant constitutional engineering to obtain a "perfect" document tends to rule out the logrolling, compromise, informal understandings, and unwritten rules that lie at the heart of U.S. or British political culture. And because courts and judges, in their role as applicators and enforcers of the law rather than creative interpreters of it, are bureaucrats and bureaucratic agencies, they do not enjoy the respect their counterparts do in the United States, thus making judicial review and even an independent judiciary difficult at best.

EXECUTIVE-LEGISLATIVE-JUDICIAL RELATIONS

The tradition of executive dominance in Latin America is part of the folklore. Power in the Latin American systems has historically been concentrated in the executive branch, specifically the presidency. Terms like *continuismo* (prolonging one's term of office beyond its constitutional limits), *personalismo* (emphasis on the person of the presidency rather than on the office), to say nothing of *machismo* (strong, manly authority) are all now so familiar that they form part of our political lexicon. The noted Latin America scholar Frank Tannenbaum has argued that the power of the Mexican presidency is comparable to that of the Aztec emperors; we can also say that the present-day Latin American executive is heir to an imperial and autocratic tradition stemming from the absolute, virtually unlimited authority of the Spanish and Portuguese crowns. Of course, modern authoritarianism has multiple explanations for its origin (a reaction against earlier mass mobilization by populist and leftist leaders, the result of stresses generated by modernization, and the strategies of civilian and military elites for accelerating development) as well as various forms (caudillistic and more institutionalized arrangements). In any case, the Latin American presidency is an imperial presidency in ways that not even Richard Nixon conceived.

The formal authority of Latin American executives is extensive. It derives from a president's powers as chief executive, commander in chief, and so on and from the broad emergency powers to declare a state of siege or emergency, suspend constitutional guarantees, and rule by decree. The presidency in Latin America is such a powerful position that the occupant of the office can rule almost as a constitutional dictator.

The powers of the Latin American president are far wider than is implied in the provisions of the constitutions. The presidency has been a chief beneficiary of many twentieth-century changes: among them, radio and television, concentrated war-making powers, broad responsiblity for the economy. In addition, many Latin American chief executives serve simultaneously as heads of state and presidents of their party machines. If the potential leader's route to power was the army, the president also has the enormous weight of armed might for use against foreign enemies and domestic foes. Considerable wealth, often generated because the lines between the private and the public weals are not so sharply drawn as in North American political society, may also become an effective instrument of rule.

Perhaps the main difference lies in the fact that the Latin American systems, by tradition and history, are more centralized and executive oriented than in the United States. The president is *the* focal point of the system. It is around the person occupying the presidency that national life swirls. The president is responsible not only for governance but also for the well-being of society as a whole. The Latin American president is the symbol of the national society in ways that a U.S. president is not. Not only is politics concentrated in the office and person of the president, but it is by presidential favors and patronage that contracts are determined, different clientele are served, and wealth, privilege, and social position parceled out. The president is *the* national *patrón*, replacing the local landowners and men on horseback of the past. With both broad appointive powers and wide latitude in favoring friends and those who show loyalty, the Latin American president is truly the hub of the national system. Hence, when a good, able executive is in power, the system works exceedingly well; when this is not the case, the whole system breaks down.

Various gimmicks have been used to try to limit executive authority. None has worked well. These range from the disastrous results of the experiment with a plural (nine-person government-by-committee) executive in Uruguay to the varied unsuccessful efforts at parliamentary or semiparliamentary rule in Chile, Brazil, Cuba, and Costa Rica. Constitutional gimmickry does not work in limiting executive rule because it is an area-wide tradition and cultural pattern that is in effect, not just some legal article.

The role of the congress in such a system is not generally to initiate or veto laws, much less to veto or to serve as a separate and coequal branch of government. Congress's functions can be understood if we begin not with the assumption of an independent branch but with one of an agency that is subservient to the president and, along with the executive, a part of the same organic, integrated state system. The congress's role is thus to give advice and consent to presidential acts (but not much dissent), to serve as a sounding board for new programs, to represent the varied interests of the nation, and to modify laws in some particulars (but not usually to nullify them). The legislature is also a place to bring some new faces into government as well as to pension off old ones, to reward political friends and cronies, and to ensure the opposition a voice while guaranteeing that it remains a minority.

Except in a handful of countries, only a very brave or foolhardy legislature would go much beyond these limited functions. Legislatures that do are often closed and their members sent home. In any case, most legislative sessions in Latin America are of relatively short duration, since to fulfill the limited functions listed above requires little time. These legislative restrictions and short sessions explain why few legislators see their jobs as full time. Nor do their limited functions and part-time roles demand elaborate staffs and offices.

If the president in Latin America is the heir of royal absolutism, then the congress is in a sense a descendent of the old royal curia or *cortes*. The curia, generally representative of the major estates or elites, was a body of royal advisers to the Spanish and Portuguese crowns that evolved into the *cortes*. But the *cortes* never developed the independent budgetary and law-making capacities of the British Parliament, nor did the supremacist doctrines put forth by the British Parliament ever become a part of Spanish or Portuguese public law. The king remained the focus, not the *cortes*. In all these ways the modern-day Latin American congress is a direct descendant of the *cortes*. Moreover, in some countries it was determined early on not only that the congress would be an advisory body but that those chiefly represented there would be society's major corporate groups—army, Church, *hacendados*, industrialists, and perhaps some middle sectors and labor groups (though generally only those recognized and legitimated by the state). Popular representation, the idea of one person, one vote, has only recently been institutionalized in Latin America, and only partially and not altogether enthusiastically. Many countries have combined systems of geographic, political, and functional representation.

This is not to say that the legislatures of Latin America are worthless. The functions in the preceding discussion are important ones. Moreover, in some countries (Chile in the past, Colombia, Costa Rica) the congress has come to enjoy considerable independence and strength. A few congresses have gone so far as to defy the executive—and gotten away with it. In some there are strong staffs and important committee work. The congress may serve additionally as a forum that allows the opposition to embarrass or undermine the government, as a means of gauging who is rising and who is falling in official favor, or as a way of weighing the relative strength of the various factions within the regime.

Many of the same comments apply to the courts and court system. First, the court system is not a separate and coequal branch—nor is it intended or generally expected to be. A Latin American supreme court would declare a law unconstitutional or defy a determined executive only at the risk of embarrassment and danger to itself, something the courts have assiduously avoided. Second, within these limits, the Latin

American court systems function not altogether intolerably; particularly in the everyday administration of justice, they are probably no worse than the U.S. system. Third, the courts, through such devices as the writ of *amparo* (Mexico and Argentina), popular action (Colombia), and *segurança* (Brazil), have played an increasingly important role in controlling and overseeing governmental action, protecting civil liberties, and restricting executive authority even under dictatorial regimes.

The court system has its origins in the Iberian tradition, upon which French and Anglo-American practices have been superimposed and which has been shaped by indigenous influences and national variations. The chief influences historically were Roman law, Christianity and the Thomistic hierarchy of laws, and the traditional legal concepts of Iberia, most notably the Siete Partidas of Alfonso the Wise. In Latin America's codes, lists of human rights, and hierarchy of courts, the French influence has been pronounced. And in the situation of a supreme court passing (in theory at least) upon the constitutionality of executive or legislative acts, the U.S. inspiration is clear.

It should be remembered, however, that what makes the system work is not the legislature or judiciary but the executive. The former two still meet or sit largely at executive discretion, and they have no delusions that they are independent and coequal branches. The modern Latin American president is thus still a man on horseback, although the means of transportation is now likely to be a helicopter. The formally institutionalized limits on executive power in terms of the usual checks and balances are not extensive and frequently can be bypassed. More significant is the informal balance of power within the system and the set of generally agreed upon understandings and rules of the game beyond which even the strongest of Latin American presidents (like a Trujillo, Somoza, Stroessner, or Pinochet) goes only at severe risk to his regime's survival.

LOCAL GOVERNMENT AND FEDERALISM

There have been four full-fledged federal systems in Latin America: in Argentina, Brazil, Mexico, and Venezuela. Federalism in Latin America emerged from exactly the reverse of the situation true in the United States. In the United States in 1789, a national government was reluctantly accepted by thirteen self-governing colonies that had never had a central administration. In Latin America, by contrast, a federal structure was adopted in some countries that had always been centrally administered.

It is difficult to judge where federalism was the greatest failure. In the United States, the federal principle survived, however inefficiently and precariously at times, in the face of gradual centralization of power in the national government. In Latin America, the principle of unitary government has survived, also precariously at times, despite such weak central power historically that regionalism and an almost de facto form of federalism existed whether specified in the constitution or not.

The independent power of the states in those few Latin American countries organized on a federal basis was greatest in the nineteenth century when the central government was weak. For a long time Mexico, Argentina, and Venezuela were dominated by caudillos operating from a regional base that often corresponded to federal boundaries. In Argentina, the disparity of wealth and power between Buenos Aires and the interior was so great that adoption of federalism seemed eminently sound. Brazil was so large that the federal principle also made sense there.

But although these nations were federal in principle, the central government reserved the right to "intervene" in the states. As the authority of the central government grew during the 1920s and 1930s, its inclination to intervene also increased, thereby often negating the federal principle. These major countries have since been progressively centralized with virtually all power concentrated in the national capital. Nevertheless, the dynamics of relations and tensions between the central government and its component states make for one of the most interesting political arenas.

Local governments in Latin America may be described by employing many of the same caveats. The Latin American countries are structured after the French system of local government. Virtually all power is concentrated in the central government. Authority flows from the top down, not from the grass roots up. Local government is ordinarily administered through the ministry of interior, which is also responsible for administering the national police. Almost all local officials are appointed by the central government and serve as its agents at the local level.

Local governments have almost no power to tax or to run local social programs. These activities are administered by the central government according to a national plan. Centralized rule is of course a part of the entire Iberian and Latin American tradition. Only persons entirely unfamiliar with the area, such as those who often inhabit U.S. AID missions, would try to impose a decentralized New England town-meeting style of local government on a system that has always been highly centralized. The results in this, as in other reform areas myopically and ethnocentrically perceived by AID, were predictable.

And yet, even though the theory has been that of a centralized state, the reality in Latin America has always been somewhat different. Spanish and Portuguese colonial power was concentrated mostly in coastal enclaves, while the vast hinterland was subdued but only thinly settled. The Spanish and Portuguese crowns had difficulty enforcing their authority in the interior, which was far away and virtually autonomous.

With the withdrawal of the Crown early in the nineteenth century, centrifugal tendencies were accelerated. Formerly large viceroyalties and captaincies general fragmented into smaller nation-states. Within these new nations, decentralization proceeded even further until the local region, parish, municipality, or hacienda became the focal point of the system. Power drained off into the hands of local landowners or regional men on horseback, who competed for control of the national palace. With a weak central state and powerful centrifugal tendencies, a strong de facto system of local rule did emerge in Latin America, contrary to what the laws or constitutions proclaimed.

Thereafter, nation building in Latin America consisted of two major tendencies: populating and thus "civilizing" the vast empty interior, and extending the central government's authority over the national territory. Toward the end of the nineteenth century, national armies and bureaucracies were created to replace the unprofessional armed bands under the local caudillos; national police agencies enforced the central government's authority at the local level; and the collection of customs duties was centralized, thereby depriving the strong men of the funds for their *pronunciamientos*. Authority became concentrated in the central state, the regional isolation of the *patria chica* broke down as roads and communications grids were developed, and the economy was similarly centralized under the direction of the state.

In most of Latin America the process of centralization, begun in the 1870s and 1880s, is still going forward. Indeed, that is how *development* is often defined throughout the area. A developed political system is one in which the central agencies of the state exercise control over the disparate and centrifugal forces that make up the system. In many countries this process is still incomplete, so that in the vast interior, in the highlands, in diverse Indian communities, and among some groups (such as landowners, large industrialists, and big multinationals), the authority of the central state is still tenuous. Indeed, this also constitutes one of the main arenas of Latin American politics: the efforts of the central government—any government—to extend its sway over the entire nation, and the efforts of the local and component units (be they regions, towns, parishes, or Indian communities) to maintain some degree of autonomy.

A FOURTH BRANCH OF GOVERNMENT: THE AUTONOMOUS STATE AGENCIES

One of the primary tools in the struggle to centralize power has been the government corporation or the autonomous agency. The growth of these agencies, in many ways parallel to that of the "alphabet agencies" in the United States, has given the central government a means to extend its control into new areas. These agencies have become so large and so pervasive that they could be termed a separate branch of government. Some Latin American constitutions recognize them as such.

The proliferation of these agencies has been such that in some countries they number in the hundreds. Many are regulatory agencies, often with far broader powers than their North American counterparts, with the authority to set or regulate prices, wages, and production quotas. Others administer vast government corporations: among them, steel, mining, electricity, sugar, coffee, tobacco, railroads, utilities, and petrochemicals. Still others are involved in social programs: education, social security, housing relief activities, and the like. Many more participate in the administration of new services that the state has been called upon to perform: for example, national planning, agrarian reform, water supplies, family planning.

The purposes for which these agencies have been set up are diverse. Some, such as the agrarian-reform or family-planning agencies, were established as much to please the Americans and to qualify a country for U.S. and World Bank loans as to carry out agrarian reform or family planning. Others have been created to bring a recalcitrant or rebellious economic sector (such as labor or the business community) under government control and direction. Some have been used to stimulate economic growth and development, to increase government efficiency and hence its legitimacy, or to create a capitalist structure and officially sanctioned entrepreneurial class where none had existed before. They also enable more job seekers to be put on the public payroll.

But the common feature of all these myriad agencies is that they tend to serve as agents of centralization in that historic quest to "civilize" and bring order to what was, in the past even more than now, a vast, often unruly, near-empty territory with strong centrifugal propensities. The host of official agencies, bureaus, boards, commissions, corporations, offices, directorships, institutes, and juntas that are now part of the state structure have all been instruments in this process.

The growth of these agencies, specifically the government corporations, has meant that the degree of central state control and even ownership of the means of production has increased significantly as well. We make a fundamental mistake if we think of the Latin American economies as private enterprise–dominated systems. It is not just Cuba that has a large public sector; in fact, all the Latin American economies are heavily influenced by the state.

If one asks who owns Brazil, for example, the answer will not be Coca-Cola, General Motors, or International Telephone and Telegraph (ITT). The answer is the Brazilian government. The Brazilian national government, either by itself through the ownership of major public corporations or through joint ventures with private entrepreneurs, generates 35–40 percent of the total gross national product (GNP). The second largest generator of GNP in Brazil is not Ford or Volkswagen but the Brazilian state governments, and the third largest is municipal government. Between these three levels of government, roughly 55–60 percent of the GNP is generated by the public sector. It is only after these three levels of public ownership that one can begin talking about General Motors, Chrysler, and other multinationals. And the situation is similar, although the percentage of public ownership varies somewhat, throughout Latin America. Contrary to popular notion, these are not free enterprise, capitalist economies. Rather they tend increasingly to be state-capitalist (state-socialist in Cuba) economies with a very high percentage of the GNP generated by the public sector.

This phenomenon has important implications. It means the stakes involved in the issue of who controls the central government, with the vast resources involved, are very high. It belies economist Milton Friedman's advice to the governments of Latin America, posited as it is on the assumptions of a free market system, which the Latin American economies are not. It also implies that very rapid structural change is readily possible. In countries where between 40 and 60 percent of the GNP (far higher than in the United States) is generated by the public sector and where so much power is concentrated in the central state, the transformation from a state-capitalist to a state-socialist system is relatively easy and can happen almost overnight (as in Cuba or Peru). All that is required is for a left or socialist (instead of the usual rightist or middle-of-the-road) element to capture the pinnacles of these highly centralized systems.

The growth of all these centralized state agencies has another implication deserving mention. Though established as autonomous and self-governing bodies, the state corporations have in fact become heavily political agencies. They provide a wealth of sinecures, a means to put nearly everyone on the public payroll. They are giant patronage agencies by which one rewards friends and cronies and finds places for (and hence secures the loyalty or at least neutrality of) the opposition. Depending on the country, 30–50 percent of the gainfully employed labor force now works for the government. Many of the agencies are woefully inefficient, and the immense funds involved provide nearly endless opportunities for private enrichment from the great public trough. In performing these patronage and spoils functions, the state agencies have preserved the status quo, since large numbers of people, indeed virtually the entire middle class, are dependent upon them for their livelihood and opportunities for advancement.

ARMY, CHURCH, BUREAUCRACY: FIFTH, SIXTH, AND SEVENTH BRANCHES OF GOVERNMENT?

In the previous chapter we saw that the army, the Church, and the vast bureaucracy are sometimes more than mere pressure groups in the North American sense. Historically they constituted the backbone of nearly every Latin American regime, inseparable from it. Many scholars argue that these agencies should not be considered as pressure groups distinguishable from the institutions of government but more accurately as part of the central state apparatus. They deserve brief mention here as perhaps the fifth, sixth, and seventh branches of government.

The army is the most clear-cut case. Although most Latin American constitutions proclaim that government should be civil and republican and that the armed forces are to play an apolitical role, they also give certain special functions to the army that make it constitutionally the ultimate arbiter of national affairs. The army not only plays a moderating role but it is frequently given the power to defend national integrity and preserve order. If these functions are not mentioned in the constitution, they are often given full expression in the organic law of the armed forces, literally a separate constitution that both establishes the internal structure of the military and defines its relations with the state.

All this is foreign to the U.S. experience. The usual distinction implied by the term *civil-military relations* is inapplicable in Latin America. There the distinction between the military and the civilian spheres is blurred, and in fact most regimes are coalitions, albeit in varying degrees, of civil and military elements. Not only do the armed forces have the right and obligation to intervene in politics under certain circumstances, but they are urged and expected to do so by the rest of the population. In this sense, the army is an integral part of the central state apparatus. It functions almost literally as a separate, perhaps even coequal, branch of government. Though often internally divided, when its own interests are threatened the army may still operate as a monolith to protect itself.

Some of the same comments apply to the Church, although in most Latin American constitutions Church and state are now officially separated. Still the Church, like the military, has its organic law, usually in the form of a concordat, signed by the government and the Vatican, that defines the rights and obligations of both. The concordat may give the Church certain privileges in the areas of education, social services, charity, health care, and the like; it may obligate the state to aid the Church with public funds and may grant it autonomy in the appointment of ecclesiastic authorities.

In addition, the Church may participate in a variety of quasi-official ceremonies (openings, blessings, and dedications of bridges, highways, and public buildings) and take quasi-official stands on a variety of matters that are undefined in any official document: stands on abortion, divorce, or family planning; unofficial advice proffered the president or the voting population. The Church is not as strong and influential as it once was, and certainly not as powerful as the army or the business elites. But its position remains more than that of a mere pressure group. In this way the Church could also be said to function as a distinct branch of government, no longer of first-rank importance but probably at least as influential as the legislature or the judiciary.

The third major corporate pillar deserving mention in this context is the bureaucracy. It too has its organic law, with certain carefully defined powers and responsibilities and the relations of its members to the state carefully spelled out. Whereas the Church may be a declining power, the bureaucracy, thanks to the growth of the autonomous agencies and government corporations, is a rising one. Because of the strategic position of its members within the state system, its role like the army's is particularly critical in the making or breaking of existing governments.

There are other quasi-branches, discussed in the previous chapter as "interest groups," that merit brief mention in this context. The tendency in many Latin American countries to create and structure *official* trade-union organizations and *official* peasant associations—to say nothing of the university community governed by its separate charter or organic law—adds still other branches to the state system. Such a categorization is not merely fanciful but may reflect more accurately the structure of power in Latin America than the Montesquieuian three-part division into which many of our analyses of Latin America are locked. One important study found there were no fewer than sixteen "powers" or "branches," each with its own carefully defined functions and responsibilities. That may be a more realistic and fruitful line of approach than our usual efforts, which involve gauging the success of Latin American government using criteria that stem largely from the North American constitutional tradition.

CONCLUSIONS AND IMPLICATIONS

There are numerous instances in this chapter where it is suggested that in the organization of power the Latin American systems differ fundamentally from that of the United States. These are not so much underdeveloped political systems as ones with philosophical underpinnings and cultural traditions distinctive from our own. What emerges from this study is a sense of the considerable variation that exists among the Latin American nations themselves. Throughout the country chapters ahead, the reader should be thinking both of these variations within Latin America and of the even more fundamental differences between these systems and that of the United States.

Certain hints also surface as to what we should look for in the upcoming country chapters. Five critical arenas may be identified:

1. the relations between the various branches of government within the system, including not only executive-legislative relations in the U.S. mold but also, in the Latin American mold, executive-military and other relations
2. the competition among the rival elites, interest groups, factions, and mass organizations to capture the pinnacles of political power as represented by the state system
3. the relations between the central state apparatus and the various components of the system, particularly the constant struggle of

the state seeking to expand its power and the efforts of such
agencies as universities, trade unions, and the like to maintain
their autonomy

4. the relations of the central state with federal, regional, or local
   units and the effort of the state to extend its suzerainty over these
   distant areas

5. the historical process of the expansion of state power, including
   the growth of new national agencies such as armies and bureaucracies, the emergence of a plethora of regulatory agencies and
   public corporations, the growth of public ownership in all levels
   of the economy, the issue of toward whose benefit the emerging
   systems of state capitalism are directed, and the growth of public
   bureaucracy and its political implications

These are some major domestic political arenas. To them must now
be added the issue discussed in previous chapters of how the Latin
American nations cope with the international forces affecting them—
the pressures from the United States, the conditions of loan arrangements,
the influence of the big multinational corporations and of such major
international agencies as the World Bank and the IMF, world market
forces—as well as how these international issues and pressures interrelate
with domestic policymaking.

6
Public Policy and the Policy Process

Before focusing on the major issues and problems of public policy in Latin America, several analytical distinctions should be made. By *public policy* we mean the actions of groups in authority to implement their decisions. These policies are attempts by the relevant actors in a political system to cope with and to transform their environment by deliberate measures. These measures may involve the commitment of physical or symbolic resources. Alternatively, these measures include non-acts, decisions against responding or even taking up an issue. These non-decisions are extremely difficult to study because often they are not even detected.[1]

No political system is completely successful in accomplishing what it wishes. This is certainly the case in those societies that are under-developed politically and economically and hence it applies to the Latin American countries in varying degrees. Further, there are certain uniquely Latin American traits, over and above the area's underdeveloped character, that militate against effective public policies. For this reason, it is analytically useful to distinguish between a *policy output*, which is a deliberate act or non-act of the ruling coalition to allocate resources for a determined purpose, and a *policy outcome*, which reflects the impact of a policy.[2] Although the output and the outcome are related, they are not the same. Output is much easier to study than outcome and is the subject of most studies of Latin American public policy.

Any government has a large number of policy outputs. Philippe Schmitter, in his ground-breaking study of public policy in Latin America, measured in quantified form eighteen policy outputs, as well as nine outcomes. All of these are *allocative policies*, decisions that confer direct material benefit upon individuals and groups. Left out of his analysis (as well as most other studies) are those allocations of symbolic benefit and *structural and regulatory policies*, which establish structures or rules to guide future allocations.[3] These symbolic, structural, and regulatory policies, though important, are as yet little examined in Latin America because they are difficult to study with the same rigor as one would the allocative policies.

MAJOR ISSUES OF PUBLIC POLICY

Most of the historic issues of the nineteenth century—the role of the Church, centralism or federalism, free trade or protectionism—have been resolved or at least placed on the back burner in post–World War II Latin America. Although from time to time these old issues reemerge in some countries, the newer issues of economic development, agrarian reform, urban reform, and population growth have largely replaced them in the past two decades.

Economic Development

One goal of almost all sectors in the Latin American political process is economic development, although they disagree on its nature and the way to obtain it. For some, economic development means no more than a growth in the national economy, with a resulting larger gross domestic product. In this conception, the nature and structure of the economy would not change at all, only the size. The kinds of products would remain the same, and the nature of trade relations with the outside world would vary only slightly, albeit expanded in amount.

Other Latin Americans, probably the majority of the political leaders, define economic development as the industrialization and diversification of their economies. Traditionally, Latin American countries have produced agricultural or other primary goods that are traded with the more developed countries of the North for industrial goods. Many Latin American countries have concentrated on only one such primary good. Although they might have comparative advantage in those primary products, the national economies suffer when there is a world oversupply of them and are also vulnerable to quotas fixed by the industrial nations. By the early 1960s, it became evident that there was a general decline in the terms of trade for all such primary goods. The long-term trend was for industrial articles to go up in price more rapidly than primary goods. Although a frost in Brazil might mean a short-term increase in the price of Colombian coffee, by the 1960s a tractor imported to Colombia from the United States cost more bags of coffee beans than it had twenty years before. Although this example did not pertain to Venezuelan oil before 1982, almost all other Latin American countries have lost income from the declining terms of trade.

The middle position on economic policy, then, would call for two major policies of an economic nature: industrialization and diversification. The former would be for the purpose of import substitution. Rather than importing industrial goods, the Latin American country imports capital goods and technology, which it then uses to produce the goods that formerly were imported. Further, in order to lessen the dependence on one crop, a government makes tax and credit decisions that will encourage production of goods other than the traditional one for export. The vision of the new, economically developed society is one in which more goods of greater variety are produced for export, while fewer manufactured goods are imported. Increased trade is an important facet of this policy, since hard currency is needed for the purchase of these capital goods.

A more radical position, held by most socialists and Marxists and by some who fit into neither of those categories, also posits industrialization and diversification as goals. But this position further calls for a wholesale restructuring of society, with redistribution of income from the rich to the poor and from the cities to the countryside. At the same time, proponents of the position call for all kinds of social reforms: ending stratification on the basis of the manual, nonmanual distinction; terminating the subservient position of women; and building a whole series of governmental programs in health, housing, and other fields. The reformist, slower, and parliamentary-democratic version of this position is exemplified by the Democratic Action party in Venezuela and the National Liberation party in Costa Rica. The more radical, rapid, and total transformation of this type has taken place in Castro's Cuba, Allende's Chile, and Sandinista Nicaragua.

An even more radical economic policy espoused by some intellectuals, as yet untried in Latin America, is to cut the nation off completely from trade with the industrialized world. This policy option is based on the observation that most industrial development by Latin Americans themselves occurred during those three periods of recent history—the first and second world wars and the Great Depression—when industrial goods were not available from the developed countries of the North. The argument is that autonomous Latin American development will happen only when most trade ties are severed with the industrial world and Latin Americans are forced to generate their own capital and develop their own technologies. These radicals argue that the technology now imported is too *capital intensive*, calling for much machinery and little labor, and that industrialization in Latin America should be *labor intensive*, employing more people.

The more radical proponents of autonomous economic development are likely to continue to voice these opinions, and in some cases their ideas might be partially adopted. However, two key assumptions of the radicals, which cannot be verified or disproved a priori, make the complete acceptance of this route to economic development unlikely, even in revolutionary situations. First, the autonomous development model assumes that the political leaders can convince or coerce the inhabitants of a Latin American country to forgo consumption of industrial goods until national industry emerges. Second, this policy assumes that the individual Latin American countries can generate capital and develop technologies on their own. Both assumptions are tenuous, the first in all countries of Latin America, and the second in all but those large countries most endowed with national resources.

These four positions are ideal types, and governmental economic policy in all the countries of Latin America tends to be a combination of elements of the four. But economic policy is much more complex than the preceding discussion indicates. What to do about inflation? Latin American countries have experienced "stagflation" (the combination of a stagnant economy and high inflation) for at least two decades. Is this to be solved by monetary measures (printing less money, balancing budgets, maintaining a balance of trade between imports and exports), or is the real cause for the inflation a structural one, based on the declining terms of trade and the concentration of economic power in the small group at the top in most of the Latin American countries? If the reason is structural, more dramatic public policies are needed. Who is to develop industry? Will national enterprise do it (and if so, will it be the government or private investors)? Or alternatively will laws be written to encourage foreign multinational corporations? How will the generally negative balances of payment be redressed? What kinds of laws are needed to encourage the importation of capital goods and infrastructure materials while discouraging the purchase of consumer goods from foreign countries? If national industry is to be developed, how is capital to be generated? Is this to be done by stopping capital flight, by reducing consumption by the lower and middle classes through forced savings, or by some combination of techniques?

After October 1973 a new economic issue arose—that dealing with the value of petroleum. For the oil-exporting countries, the question became how best to use the new wealth while keeping inflationary pressures at a minimum and protecting national industry. For the petroleum importers, the questions revolved around how to keep economic growth going while using more of the scarce hard-currency export earnings and reserves to purchase needed oil. By the early 1980s, whether these policy issues were successfully resolved or not, the question changed to how the debt crisis could or would be resolved.

Almost all Latin American groups agree that economic development and growth are desirable. It is only in that way that incomes can be raised, social services increased, and the revolution of rising expectations dealt with or managed satisfactorily. There is much disagreement on the policy to obtain these goals and on who should be the beneficiaries.

Agrarian Reform

A second major issue is that of the ownership of land. Land is very inequitably distributed, with a small number of very large landholders and a great number of landless, illegal squatters and owners of very small holdings. Only in a few countries are there substantial numbers of middle-class farmers. During the 1960s, in large part because of the influence of the United States and fear of an agrarian revolution (such as the Cuban one was perceived to have been), many countries of Latin America set up agencies to deal with the problems of land. Yet in only Venezuela and Mexico were there significant land reforms. Even though land reform was not the issue in the 1970s that it had been in the

1960s, the problem still exists: Land ownership is very unevenly distributed, and at least 80 million Latin Americans live in the countryside under subhuman conditions.

One very important reason that more dramatic land reforms have not occurred is the power of the large landowners, who have attempted to prevent this attack on their property. In some countries, the landowners have given up a little to avoid giving up a lot. Another reason for the failure of land reform is the lack of good technical information about who owns what land and what it is being used for. If the land were divided among peasants, what would be the best crops? Which kinds of seeds and fertilizers would be best? What does the peasant need in addition to land?

Further, there were economic reasons for not breaking up the large tracts of land. The *latifundios* or estates vary greatly in their use and economic output. If a sizable estate is not used or is used very inefficiently, any granting of the land to *campesinos* would lead to increased agricultural production for either national consumption or export. If, however, the estate is effectively utilized by the large landowner, the goals of land reform and increased agricultural production are, at least for the short run, in conflict. Evidence from many countries shows that agricultural production in this second situation will decrease for at least the better part of a decade. Moreover, there are certain agricultural products that have economies of scale—that is, they cannot be successfully grown on a family-sized farm. In this case, agrarian reform means long-term lower production unless the land holdings are held collectively. There are both Spanish (the *ejido*) and Amerindian traditions of collective ownership of lands, and the Peruvian case shows such traditions being used through communal ownership. The Cuban case shows that state farms—those owned by the government with *campesinos* receiving wages for work—can be another alternative.

Urban Reform

One reason that agrarian reform is not the issue that it was twenty years ago is that many people have left the countryside to seek a better life in the cities. There are both push and pull factors for this internal migration. Some *campesinos* are pushed off the land, either because there are more children than the land can support or because the large landowners have mechanized production. Others are pulled to the cities by the better life that they believe will be found there. The movement has been dramatic: It is estimated that every year from 1970 to 1985 a population of some 8.75 million persons has been incorporated into the cities of Latin America, and in the 1985–2000 period this will increase to between 11 and 12 million a year. Caused by both internal migration and the high birthrate, this urban growth affects the major cities, many of which have doubled or tripled in size over the past decade.

Cities in Latin America were not prepared for such rapid growth; this was true of U.S. cities during similar growth periods at the end of the last century and beginning of this one. But there are important differences. Unlike that of the United States and West Europe, Latin American urbanization has not been accompanied by a surge of industrial growth. Not many of these new urbanites receive jobs in industry. Only the lucky ones do, with others settling for hand-labor construction work and many more underemployed or unemployed. The political dimension is also different in Latin America, given the greater centralization of the state. Policies to meet the new problems of the cities are more likely to come from national than city governmetns.

The problems that these national governments face are numerous and difficult. One is housing. Although some of the urban migrants rent rooms in large old houses where certain public utilities already exist, even more build makeshift homes in the open areas around the cities. Called different names in different countries (*callampas* or mushroom towns in Chile, *favelas* in Brazil, *barrios* in Peru, *tugurios* in Colombia), most of these new slums are built illegally on private or state-owned land. They are completely devoid of such urban services as water, sewerage facilities, electricity, roads, effective police and fire protection. Some studies have shown that the life expectancy is lower for the dwellers of these shantytowns than for the *campesinos*.

One author at the beginning of the 1970s suggested that decade would be one of urban reform as the 1960s had been one of agrarian reform. Perhaps he was correct, since urban reform has been no more a success than agrarian reform was a decade back. One key reason for the lack of urban reform so far, although there has been progress in some of the countries, is that the urban dwellers have yet to organize into effective political movements. There are no doubt many explanations for this. The following have been mentioned in the literature:

1. The new urban poor are too busy in the day-to-day attempt to make enough money to feed themselves and their children. They work fourteen to sixteen hours a day and have little time for political activities.

2. In the shantytowns, people often develop a sense of community that seems to provide considerable security and often engenders resentment against government interference in their internal affairs.

3. Additional security is received from the extended family (one survey indicated that a typical resident of a São Paulo *favela* can identify by name anywhere from thirty to five hundred relatives, many of whom live in the city or even in the same *favela!*) and from the ceremonial kinship relationship in which friends or people slightly higher in the social structure are godparents of a person's children.

4. Close contact is maintained between the urban poor and the rural areas from which they came. If things get extremely bad economically, they can return.

5. A high percentage of the urban poor are engaged in service work and petty commercial activities such as street vending. Such people tend to form an atomized labor force, and their lack of association with others like themselves makes organization difficult.

6. Many who do obtain factory jobs work in very small factories, often of the cottage variety. The owner fills the traditional *patrón* function, dispensing all the benefits and liabilities, and this prevents other forms of organization.

7. Business people, industrialists, and governments participate in strategic activities designed to give the urban poor a bit of what they want, but of course not all that they really need.

8. The same elite groups participate in sanctions against the urban poor, who often have jobs in which they can be easily replaced by the unemployed if they engage in political activities. Many urban poor have illegally built houses from which they could be removed if the government saw fit.

9. Whether they will live longer or not, the new urban poor perceive themselves to be better off—or at least their children to be better off—than they have been in the countryside.

One does not have to accept all of these arguments. The causes vary from country to country and among individuals. Yet the conclusion seems clear that the urban poor do not have the power yet that their numbers would indicate. They do have the advantage of being in the center of Latin American politics, which has always been essentially urban. Some governments and political parties have begun their co-optation-or-repression techniques (see the introduction to Chapter 4), and it seems likely that the urban poor will become organized. With that organization will come increased power for the urban poor and, as a result, some policy outputs favoring a better life for them.

Population Policy

Another issue of Latin Americans politics, at least for some groups, is population growth. Latin America has the highest growth rate in the world. Although the birthrate is higher in certain parts of Asia and Africa, death rates are lower in Latin America, and the result is a population growth rate for the area of roughly 3 percent per year. This of course varies from country to country: Argentina and Uruguay both increase in population at about 1.0 percent a year, roughly comparable to the United States. But other countries, such as Brazil and Mexico, are between 3 and 4 percent a year, which means that the population doubles every twenty-five to thirty years.

Population growth is related to another issue area previously discussed. Economic growth must be at least equal to population growth for a country just to stand still in per capita income terms. If an increase in per capita income is a target, then it must be greater than the population growth rate. The Alliance for Progress of the 1960s led to impressive growth in the GDPs of many Latin American nations, but the GDP per capita gained only slightly in the face of population growth. Likewise, agrarian reform was an issue, in part because of the increasing numbers of rural inhabitants. And of course the population growth rate, as well as internal migration, is what led to the relatively recent issue of urban reform.

One of the key reasons for population growth is the increasing life expectancy and the lower infant mortality rates, which have changed dramatically since World War II. These improved rates are the result of better health care, more doctors, better sanitary conditions, and the eradication of some diseases, such as smallpox and malaria, through public-health programs. Meanwhile, the birthrate, with the exception of the countries of the southern cone of South America, has not decreased dramatically. Few would suggest that the solution to the growth problem lies in lowering life expectancy. The way to slow this growth, therefore, has to be through some control of the high birthrate.

Some people believe that if the population problem can be resolved, so can other public policy issues. In many cases, the groups taking this position are not Latin Americans but officials of international population agencies. Whereas in the 1960s a precondition for foreign assistance was having in place an agrarian-reform program, today the precondition is having a program of family planning. Part of the motivation for this is humane: If Latin America cannot adequately feed its current population, how can it expect to feed a doubled population in thirty years? But there are other motivations, relating to U.S. strategic and economic needs. A growing population in Latin America will lead to nations in which there is so much human misery that there will be radical revolutions, whose protagonists are likely to ally themselves with the international enemies of the United States and take over the U.S.-based multinationals in the area.

Some groups in Latin America agree with this reasoning, particularly those upper-class groups who would lose in a radical revolution. But the traditional ally of the secular status quo groups—the Church—sees the matter differently. As the papal directives are against all artificial forms of birth control, in those places where it is strongest the Church hierarchy has tended to oppose anything more than family-planning clinics and natural birth-control methods. Yet even Church officials are split on the issue. Some, for either the humane reasons of caring for the flock or in fear of what a radical revolution would do to them, have quietly supported artificial birth control.

In this particular policy area, the Church has found itself in the unusual position of taking the same stand as radical, nationalistic, and even Marxist groups. These argue that population growth is desirable, either because (1) the nations can absorb more population and in the process will become more powerful in relation to the United States, or

(2) with increased population, things will get so bad as to ensure revolution, which the radical groups see as desirable.

It is not clear where the majority of the poor Latin Americans—those who are having the large families—stand on this matter. If they are practicing Catholics, they have been taught that artificial methods of birth control are wrong. But if they are finding it increasingly difficult to feed, clothe, educate, and house their growing families, their perceptions might be different.

Although it is among the poor that the population growth rates are highest (the middle and upper classes have no difficulty obtaining contraceptives), this is precisely the group least organized to lobby for an effective program of family planning. And with the ruling elites divided on the issue, population policy has largely been ineffectual, piecemeal, and often shifting because of changing government coalitions. The only constant proponents of birth control have been those international agencies that use their power and the leverage of foreign assistance to push toward their goal.

Meanwhile, it has become evident that even in those countries that have no effective family-planning programs, the birthrate has begun to fall. This decline seems related to increased urbanization, education, and knowledge concerning ways to limit family size. After all, it may make some sense for a rural peasant to have lots of children, both to put to work in the fields and to take care of the parents (in nations that have few effective social-security programs) in their old age. But for the urban poor the argument for more rather than fewer children makes less sense, and it is precisely in the urban areas that the population growth rate has begun to fall.

CONSTRAINTS IN LATIN AMERICAN POLICYMAKING

In the previous section some of the major issues of Latin American public policy were considered. The aim of this section is to outline some of the constraints—conditions that affect political decisions as well as those that impede effective transition from policy outputs to policy outcomes. These constraints are divided into three areas: (1) those that come from economic underdevelopment, (2) those that stem from the nature of the Latin American political systems, and (3) those that are due to the position of these countries in a hemisphere dominated by the United States and to their position in the international political economy. Although these three are clearly related, for the purpose of analysis they have been separated.

Underdevelopment

The key feature of economic underdevelopment is that even a government wishing to change many things does not have the revenue to do so. All allocative policies have money costs. If the governing coalition of a Latin American country decides that economic development (through governmental ownership of industry), agrarian reform, urban reform, and birth control are desirable, there might not be enough money adequately to fund all four policies. Similar restraints might plague the more specific levels of policies. For example, Castro's policies have included governmental construction of schools, hospitals, rural housing, and urban housing. Yet the reality of underdevelopment in the Cuban case is that there are not enough construction materials for all four kinds of projects. In some instances in Latin America, policymakers honestly cannot do all that they would like; in other cases legislation creates programs that are never funded. Governmental policy in Latin America, therefore, should be analyzed not only by studying established law but by looking at the actual expenditures of governmental revenues.

Yet another feature of underdevelopment, more political than economic, is the lack of bureaucratic expertise. Bureaucracies in Latin America have one very important purpose: to provide white-collar, nonmanual employment for the members of the middle sectors, especially "the best and the brightest," who in the absence of such employment would be likely to join the political opposition. Because of this co-optive function, the bureaucracies of the area are not generally efficient in the day-to-day running of governmental programs. They contain people who have jobs only because of personal connections, people who do not have the necessary educational background, and people who hold multiple bureaucratic jobs, working only briefly or not at all in any one.

For this reason, some governments of Latin America have gone the route of decentralized agencies set up for specific policies in an attempt to insulate them from the more corrupt regular bureaucracy. But in many countries even this has failed to produce an effective bureaucracy. Therefore, even in the case of a policy that is accepted by the ruling coalition and adequately funded, the policy consequence might not be what was intended.

The Political System

The rules of the Latin American political game were described in Chapter 4. Here it is sufficient to repeat that a new group entering into the accepted circle of power groups must tacitly demonstrate that it will not do anything to harm already existent groups. This means that many alternatives are closed for public policy by the rules of the game. How is there to be an agrarian reform if, although supported by international groups, the *campesinos*, and perhaps by organized labor, the governing coalition includes the large landowners and their industrialist friends? How is there to be an urban reform when governing coalitions generally include those real-estate interests that would be adversely affected?

In most countries of Latin America, there are two possible ways to solve this dilemma. First, governmental policy will work in such a political system if the economy is expanding and increasing governmental income. In such a case, new revenues can be allocated to public policies in a *distributive* fashion—that is, by dividing up the bigger pie. Governments still have difficulties with such distributive policies, since industrialists, for example, would prefer that the new revenue used for urban reform, which benefits them little, be employed for infrastructure improvements (roads, railroads) that would help them economically. However, the controversy over distributive policies is much less than that over *redistributive* ones—that is, policies that would take something away from one group and give it to another. For this reason, land reform encountered many difficulties. It is not surprising that Venezuela has had one of the most successful reformist governments in Latin America, made possible by governmental taxes on foreign oil producers, and one of the most successful agrarian reforms, using lands that the government already owned.

Yet not all the governments of Latin America have the luxury of participating in only distributive policies. If the economy is stagnant, and even worse if it is shrinking, there may be no governmental policy. So a second possibility is a case-by-case, eclectic policy situation in which one group wins on one policy issue, another group on another issue, and so forth. Although politically this is good short-run strategy, the long-term result might have contradictory effects, with detrimental ramifications for the economy, the people, and even the political system.

This dilemma of policymaking in the Latin American context is most evident in those countries where almost all individuals have organized into groups that have accepted the rules of the game. This case (well documented in Mexico by Raymond Vernon,[4] with Argentina the only other example to date) is at worst one of almost complete governmental stalemate or at best one of very eclectic and contradictory policies. Since all groups are politically relevant and involved, and since all groups have agreed not to harm the interests of others, practically no agreed-upon policy is possible.

Still another feature of the Latin American political tradition, affecting public policy implementation, is the tentative nature of the political system. One question just beginning to be researched is whether public policies change when military governments replace civilian ones or vice versa. Early evidence suggests that policies do change with regime shifts, at least in most cases.[5] Furthermore, one might speculate that during the crisis periods of very tentative regimes, ones likely to fall at any time, policy implementation suffers. Why should a bureaucrat (who might be jockeying for a more powerful position in a new government) spend time trying to carry out a policy that might be reversed by the new regime? This aspect of public policy applies only in those most "tentative" systems and not so much in stable ones, be they military or civilian.

The United States and the International Political Economy

A third set of constraints on Latin American public policymaking relates to the position of these countries in a hemisphere dominated politically and economically by the United States and to their position in the international political economy. Some of the constraints on policymaking are dramatic, appearing on the front pages of newspapers. Guatemala in 1954 demonstrated that a Central American government could not enact a dramatic land reform adversely affecting U.S. business interests or launch a general social revolution backed and participated in by the Communist party. Eleven years later, the case of the Dominican Republic showed that the U.S. government might intervene militarily even if a coalition about to come to power only appeared dangerous to certain U.S. economic and security interests. Chile in the 1970s illustrated that no matter how geographically remote and economically unimportant a country might be to the United States, the "giant of the north" can intervene through both governmental and private business agencies. The lesson of Chile for public policymaking in the rest of Latin America seems to be "Thou shalt not institute a socialist economy, call it that, nationalize U.S. businesses, and follow a foreign policy independent of U.S. government interests." There are certain things that Latin American governments cannot consider. The obvious exception to these generalizations is Cuba, where certain issues were raised and the U.S. opposition was foreseen, but by planning and a lot of luck the revolution survived. In Peru and Venezuela, major U.S. properties were nationalized without provoking a marine intervention. So far, however, these cases are the exceptions and not the rule. Nicaragua remains an uncertain case.

There are other more subtle ways in which the United States manipulates Latin America. The Agency for International Development (AID) of the U.S. government uses its leverage to push certain programs: land reform in the 1960s, birth control in the 1970s, private-sector initiatives in the 1980s. Within these areas and elsewhere, AID officials assist the Latin American governments in operational plans. Likewise, international agencies dominated by the United States, such as the World Bank and the International Monetary Fund, traditionally encourage the Latin American governments to make certain economic and fiscal policy decisions. For example, the IMF might push a Latin government to devalue its currency. If the country refuses, World Bank loans become unlikely, AID will be hesitant to offer credit to the country, and even the private banks of New York will be reluctant to extend credit.

Other issues never arise and remain nondecisions because of the position of Latin America in the world political economy. Increasing national wealth means, in large part, obtaining higher prices for goods exported to the industrial world. This, in turn, leads to higher costs and less wealth for those industrial countries, something that they resist. Industrialization in Latin America often leads to products that are *more* expensive in the short run than those that can be imported from the industrial world. The examples are many. The major point is that as a group of small, poor, and weak countries, the Latin American nations are severely constrained in their public policy options by the international political economy.

This position has led to a school of thought—the dependency approach—whose basic premise is that Latin American underdevelopment is due not to the attitudes and institutions inherited from the Spanish and Portuguese but rather to the dependent position of Latin America in the world economy. Although there are many kinds of dependency theorists, two basic strains of thought are predominant.

One group of dependency theorists sees the separation of an industrialized North from a primary-product-oriented South as the result of a conspiracy in which international capitalism works in trusts whose various holdings are intentionally meant to complement, not compete with, each other. If one subscribes to this conspiracy theory of capitalism, then the devils can be identified, perhaps eliminated, and presumably the plight of the poor ameliorated.

Other theorists of dependency see it more as a natural and inevitable happening, rather than as a conspiracy. They argue that the development of the North and the underdevelopment of Latin America and the rest of the Third World go hand in hand. Latin America has been and is financing the development of the United States and Europe, since those countries take more out of the region than they put in. Further, these theorists argue that all this began when the European nations started their capitalist and mercantilist development in the sixteenth and seventeenth centuries.

Viewing the economic development of the world in this way, the dependency theorists reject certain theses often advanced by North American and Latin proponents of U.S. investment. The underdevelopment of Latin America was not caused by general backwardness or by the traditionalism of the area. Underdevelopment in Latin America results from development in other parts of the world. By way of corollary, this means that Latin America is *not* in one of the various aeronautical stages postulated by W. W. Rostow.[6] Latin America has at no time paralleled the United States and West Europe in its development, and this lack of similarity is due to the northern countries having developed in the absence of more advanced countries. Further, the dependency theorists add that real economic development of Latin America will not come from import substitution. Although this might help the balance of payments in the short run, in the long run dependency on the industrialized North is even greater because of the need for continuing importation of technology, replacement parts, new machinery, and foreigners to run the industries.

Real economic development in Latin America will come, the dependency theorists argue, only when the diffusion of foreign capital and culture is ended. The empirical evidence demonstrates that during the two world wars and the Great Depression was the only time that Latin Americans developed their own technologies and industries on a large scale. The prescription for the future, if development is wanted, is to divorce themselves from the industrialized countries once again.

For Latin American public policymaking, it is irrelevant whether there is a conspiracy or an inevitable dependency. The fact remains that industrial goods can frequently be imported more cheaply from the developed world than they can be produced in the nascent industries of Latin America. The dilemma thus posed is how to convince the present generation to abstain from buying these goods so that the future generation will have a better life. Further, in the smaller countries of Latin America, relatively autonomous development might be impossible, even if a generation or two of potential consumers make sacrifices. Some countries simply do not have the natural resources or the market size to make this goal possible. For this reason, a common policy of the past thirty years, so far with mixed results, is for the smaller countries of the area to join in common markets, such as the Central American Common Market and the Andean Pact. In such cases, public policy has decided against purely national development and opted instead for economic development through cooperation and division of labor.

In addition, and regardless of the arguments of the dependency theorists, most Latin American governments recognize they must deal realistically with the United States. For better or worse, the United States is the major political and economic power in the hemisphere. Latin American is stuck in a dependency position. Hence, the real question is not whether Latin America can dispense with the United States but whether the Latin American countries can reap some advantages from this relationship. Clever Latin American presidents as adeptly manipulate the U.S. Embassy as the Embassy does the politics of the Latin American countries—particularly if they have commodities that the United States must have.

CONCLUSIONS AND IMPLICATIONS

In the previous pages, we have generalized about the issues and constraints of public policy in Latin America. Although there are great commonalities among the Latin American countries on these matters, there are also notable differences. We suggest that the following questions be considered as the country chapters are read:

1. What are the major issues of public policy in the individual Latin American countries? Are they the same as those analyzed here or are there others of equal or greater importance?
2. Which of these issues lead to governmental policies and which do not, and why?

3. What kinds of policies are designed? Are they distributive or redistributive?
4. What does the nature of the governing coalition suggest about which issues become policies? What variations exist among the several countries?
5. How effective is the bureaucracy in translating official policy outputs into policy outcomes? What are the ramifications, from a policy standpoint, of having or not having an effective bureaucracy?
6. In the case of each country, what are the major constraints on policymaking?
7. Who benefits from public policy: elites? the public?

We should warn that definitive answers to these questions should not always be expected. The study of public policy in Latin America is primarily one of the last dozen years. The authors of the individual chapters have been hindered by lack of empirical studies on which to base their conclusions, a condition that, it is hoped, will soon be rectified.

NOTES

1. Philippe C. Schmitter, "Military Intervention, Political Competitiveness, and Public Policy in Latin America: 1950–1967," in *Armies and Politics in Latin America*, ed. Abraham Lowenthal (Holmes & Meier, New York, 1976), p. 120.
2. Ibid., pp. 121–122.
3. Ibid., pp. 113–161.
4. Raymond Vernon, *The Dilemma of Mexico's Development* (Harvard University Press, Cambridge, 1963).
5. Schmitter, "Military Intervention."
6. W. W. Rostow, *The Stages of Economic Growth* (Cambridge University Press, Cambridge, 1960).

7
The Latin American Political Process and Its Present Crisis

North Americans often have difficulty conceiving of a Latin American political process or system. With their frequent coups and repeated violations of constitutional precepts, the Latin American nations are instead thought of as having no system and only chaotic political processes. Such a view is myopic and mistaken. It is based on a North American conception of what constitutes a system and the proper political processes. Politics in Latin America is every bit as systematic as in North America and Latin American political processes no more irregular.

It is not that Latin America has failed to develop a political system of its own but that residents of the United States have seldom attempted to understand it or how it functions. A close examination reveals that the Latin American political systems are as rational (given the distinctiveness of Latin American political society), as complex, and as interesting as the North American. In this chapter we shall be pulling together the various ideas and threads developed in earlier chapters to show the nature of the Latin American political system, broadly conceived, its various component parts and their interrelationships, and the system's present crisis.[1]

THE LATIN AMERICAN POLITICAL PROCESS

As a product of the Spanish and Portuguese political traditions, the Latin American political process is distinct from that of the Anglo-American nations. It rests often on different assumptions regarding the nature of humankind and how best to order its social and political institutions. These differing traditions make Latin American politics distinct from North American and not necessarily less developed.

The Latin American political process is grounded historically on a set of assumptions and characteristic features that emphasize hierarchy, authority, personalism, family and kinship ties, centralization, the need for organic national unity, elaborate networks of patron-client relations, patrimonialism, and a pervasive pattern of vertical-corporate organization. Many of these assumptions and concepts derived originally from Catholic precepts, particularly the Thomistic notions of hierarchy and authority, and to a large extent the givens of Catholic political culture still undergird the workings of the Latin American systems. But since the nineteenth century, many of these same assumptions have been given republican and/or secular bases, although the form in which they appear often may have been only slightly altered.

Centralized, almost imperial rule is one of the chief characteristics of the Latin American political process. Much of Latin American history can be studied in terms of the effort to develop a centralized state capable of asserting its authority over distant territories and the diverse groups that make up national society.

The president is the center of national political life. In theory and constitution, the president is the focus of decision making. The legislature, courts, and local government are subordinated to the principle of strong, personalistic, executive-centered rule. It makes little difference whether one speaks of authoritarian right-wing regimes like Brazil's or revolutionary regimes like Cuba's; what is important is the system of executive-centered rule. The president is the focus of the system to an extent unknown in the United States. Presidential charisma, strength, and personality (or the lack thereof) are what make the system work or fail.

In nineteenth-century Latin American society the three main societal actors were the Church, the army, and the large landowners. These three constituted an impregnable system of power and were closely joined. It used to be said that the ambition of a Latin American oligarch was to have his first son inherit the land, his second become a general, and his third become an archbishop. In the absence of other organized centers of power, these three groups were the main corporate pillars of a traditional, agrarian, elite-dominated, and status quo–oriented society.

But toward the end of the nineteenth century and in the first decades of the twentieth century, new groups began to demand admission to the system. These included the business-industrial bourgeoisie, the new middle class, and eventually trade unions and peasants. In other societies, such as Britain or the United States, the emergence of these new groups tended to give rise to a more liberal, pluralist, and democratic polity. But in Latin America the process was frequently different.

Although one should not understate the degrees of liberalism and republicanism present in Latin America, and though some countries evolved in a pluralistic fashion, the more common pattern involved an effort to structure the admission of new groups to the system. Voting and the franchise were often carefully restricted. Political party activity was similarly controlled. Rather than allowing the free-wheeling, tumultuous pluralism of North American interest-group competition, the Latin American nations tried to regulate the process. They either policed closely the already existing groups or created official, government-run trade-union federations and peasant associations. In this way, they sought to co-opt the emerging middle sectors through the provision of government jobs and other benefits and characteristically fashioned some strongly corporate (as distinct from pluralist) structures so as to keep the group struggle—particularly labor relations—under control. They sought to maintain the unity of state and society, to forge links between workers and employers, and thus to avoid class struggle and the potential for revolutionary upheaval.

New groups could be admitted to "the system" and some change could go forward, but only under government and elite auspices and regulation. The hierarchical, structured, and elite-dominated system of the past was thus generally retained. Two conditions were necessary for the admission of a new power contender into the system. The first was that the group had to demonstrate a power capability: that it was strong enough to challenge the system and therefore deserved to have its voice heard. This helps explain why organized labor was admitted to the system in the 1930s and 1940s and the peasants only in the 1960s and 1970s—if at all. The second condition was that the group had to agree to abide by certain rules of the game. It was not permitted to destroy other groups in the system by revolutionary means. Those that tried were often suppressed. And each group had to agree to accept its place in the system, which meant that it was not allowed to put forward what were considered exorbitant demands.

This system, implying the gradual absorption of new groups into the political process without the old ones being destroyed or the basic hierarchical structure of society being upset, had several important implications. It tended to concentrate power in the hands of the state and its growing administrative apparatus. It was the state that regulated the entire process by which new groups were admitted, licensed them, and gave them *juridical personality*—that is, recognition and the right to bargain in the political process. In the chapters that follow it will be interesting to see the different patterns by which these new groups in Latin America were admitted to the system (for example, through the populist corporatism of Cárdenas in Mexico, the rigid controls of Trujillo in the Dominican Republic, the liberalism of Chile, the authoritarian systems of Vargas in Brazil or Perón in Argentina), as well as to contrast these with some parallel phenomena in the United States.

The state now has become the great national *patrón*, replacing the local landowners and oligarchs of the past. It is from the state and its head that jobs, patronage, money, favors flow. Political disputes tend to be handled administratively and bureaucratically, rather than through the open competition of party politics. The oft-stated goal of both leftist and rightist regimes is a technocratic administration devoid of divisive party squabbling and conflict-prone interest groups. That helps explain why political parties in Latin America have seldom enjoyed the importance they do in U.S. politics, since it is the state system and administration—and who controls them—that are critical and not so much the political parties. It also explains the effort oftentimes to incorporate the interest groups directly into the state apparatus as direct creations of the state or appendages of it.

Politics in Latin America revolves not just around ideological and class issues but around patronage, kinship, and friendship—except that now the patronage networks are larger and more elaborate than ever before. Who controls the presidential palace and its patronage opportunities is a matter of critical importance. A group of officials, and sometimes entire trade unions or peasant leagues, may tie themselves to one person to whom they are often related by blood or marriage and ride with this individual to the pinnacles of power—or crash down in the event of failure. In return for loyalty and support, the group or individual expects jobs and favors. It is a classic patronage pattern now greatly elaborated in a complex network of national, often highly institutionalized patron-client relations.

Elections in such a system are important but they do not always carry the definite legitimacy that elections have in the Anglo-American democracies. Elections serve chiefly to ratify the authority of a *patrón* (president, labor leader, or the like) who is already in power, rather than to give the voters a clear choice. Where elections are competitive, they are often manipulated to ensure that the government candidate wins. And even where the ballots are honestly counted, elections are viewed as providing only a tentative mandate. There are other routes to power that also enjoy legitimacy: the general strike, the coup d'état, the heroic guerrilla struggle. This makes the entire Latin American political system more tentative, more unstable, more open to rapid changeovers than is true in the United States. It also makes the job of the Latin American president, who must juggle all these contending forces without losing control of any of them, difficult and complex. In the shifting quicksands of Latin American politics, the president's power base may be eroded; the president's *clientela* will go elsewhere if they feel they have not received certain goods and favors; and there is always the potential for the president to be ousted from power at almost any time.

The accommodative, co-optive nature of the Latin American systems has also tended to rule out revolutionary transformations. That may sound strange, for we know there have been many revolutions in Latin America. But these have generally been revolutions in the palace guard, implying the substitution of one elite for another. Full-scale social revolutions have been rare. Only in Mexico, Cuba, and to a more limited extent Bolivia, Nicaragua, and Peru have genuinely social revolutionary transformations occurred; and even in some of these (Cuba constituting the major exception) the restructuring that resulted showed considerable continuity with the past. Co-optation, the gradual absorption of new groups, the creation of official agencies of the state to meet the challenge of rising new groups, and the elaboration of larger patronage networks have helped militate against the possibility of violent revolution from below.

The role of the United States in this regard is interesting. The United States is not only the most important external actor with which the Latin American nations must deal, but the U.S. Embassy is one of the most influential internal forces as well. Most of the considerable U.S. assistance over the last few years has been oriented toward support of the existing order in Latin America and the defense of the status quo. Although many U.S. officials are liberals and interested in change, the changes they have proposed have been gradual, piecemeal, evolutionary, and in support of the accommodative, nonrevolutionary politics described earlier. U.S. aid has also been based on the assumption of a fundamental commonality of interests between the United States and Latin America. These assumptions and policies have served to support the system in Latin America; by the same token, U.S. aid and influence have been employed to frustrate revolutionary challenges to it.

These brief comments cannot do full justice to the richness and complexity of the Latin American political system and processes, or to the variations within the several countries. But they do serve to indicate some of the main features of the system and how it operates.

THE BIASES OF THE SYSTEM

All political systems have biases of one sort of another, favoring certain class, regional, or political intersts at the expense of others. Let us look at the biases built into the Latin American system.

It should be said first that, contrary to numerous popular prejudices, many of the Latin American systems, with their distinct institutions, have proved to be quite effective in managing the twentieth-century change process. Economic growth and industrialization have been greatly stimulated, sometimes (as in the cases of Brazil or Mexico) at almost miraculous rates; per capita income and living standards have risen; social services and programs have been vastly expanded; rising social forces have been progressively admitted as new participants in the system. Under the right circumstances, the centralized, technocratic, executive-centered, elite-directed, corporatist-controlled, frequently au- thoritarian and hierarchical, national patronage-dominated systems of Latin America can be quite efficient and responsive, providing for a great deal of growth and modernization.

But there are also biases within these systems that command attention. This section will comment on the value, class, political, and economic assumptions that undergird the system, showing both how it has worked historically and why it is now being so strongly challenged.

First, the system is based on the assumption of a wide community of interest within the nation and shared popular values and outlooks. Such a community of interest was probably stronger in the sleepier, more Catholic nineteeneth century than it is now. Where those values still hold or have been successfully secularized and popularized, the Latin American systems will likely continue to function as before. But where newer values and concepts have been strongly felt, where Marxist and other revolutionary ideologies have gained mass appeal, and where groups have organized on bases other than those previously considered the only legitimate ones, the challenges are no longer simply a way of demonstrating power capability (and hence the desire to be admitted to the system) but may be aimed at toppling it altogether and replacing it with an alternative form. In addition, the assumed community of interest between the United States and Latin America is being increasingly questioned.

Second, within the Latin American systems is a strong bias in favor of the political status quo. This is not to say that change never occurs but that the changes tend to be within carefully defined boundaries and according to the rules of the game. The accommodative nature of the politics outlined earlier means that while new groups are assimilated into the system, old ones cannot be disposed of. Hence the army, the Church, and the landed elites in Latin America continue to enjoy power and a privileged place all out of proportion to their numbers. The persistence of many anachronistic groups and practices has given rise to a certain "mausoleum effect," whereby Latin America retains features from its semifeudal past that have been confined to the ash cans of history in other nations but serve in Latin America to perpetuate the status quo.

Third, there is a class bias built into the Latin American systems. New groups are admitted but only on the condition that they accept the rules of the game established by the older wielders of power, the elite and the rising middle sectors. A patron-client system similarly involves two-way give-and-take, but it is the patrons who receive most of the benefits while their clients are obligated to accept their station in life and the usually meager rewards that come their way. The trade unions may gain certain benefits, but these are generally doled out paternalistically. The government, dominated by the elites and bourgeoisie, controls the process by which labor participates, and the unions themselves tend to be headed not by rank-and-file members but by officials acceptable to the elites and often appointed by them. Peasants, Indians, and marginal laborers may be wholly excluded from participation. Similarly the economic growth that has occurred has benefited the lowest classes very little, raised living standards somewhat for organized workers, profited the middle sectors to a greater extent, and enriched the elites most of all. Although much development has occurred throughout Latin America, it is the elites and upper bourgeoisie that have continued to control the entire process and who have been its prime beneficiaries.

Finally, there is the necessity and assumption of sustained economic growth built into this accommodative, co-optive political process. In order to provide more pieces of pie to the newer groups, without depriving any of the older groups of their share, the pie must be steadily enlarged. During the 1930s, 1940s, 1950s, and early 1960s, precisely the heyday of the system here described, economic growth occurred at steady, if seldom spectacular, rates. With their economies expanding, the Latin American systems could afford to give more benefits to labor, to peasants—to all groups in the system. The model of the political process described here, implying the gradual assimilation of new groups, greater benefits, and rising living standards, was predicated on continued steady growth rates and hence more and more funds to buy off revolutionary challengers. But what if, as at present, the Latin American nations should face a situation where the pie would no longer be an expanding one but a stagnant or, in the case of some nations, a contracting one? Then how long could the political model outlined here—a relatively peaceful, stable, consensual, and accommodative one—be expected to last? These are the questions the Latin American nations must now face up to.

THE PRESENT CRISIS

The Latin American political systems are not the entirely rigid, static, unchanging systems of popular stereotype. Up to a point, in fact, they have proved to be quite flexible, adaptive, and accommodative. They have accepted and assimilated a great deal of modernization, but without undergoing much change in their basic order or power relationships. The question now is whether they have reached the point where the old assumptions no longer hold, where the older model is no longer effective, where it is being increasingly challenged and in some cases superseded by alternative conceptions.

Sustained economic growth is an absolute requirement for the maintenance of the system, but that can no longer be taken for granted. Brazil's economic "miracle" is over, as is Mexico's; both countries are now being riven by severe economic and political tensions and conflicts. Sugar and coffee prices were up for a time, but now they are down again, and, in any case, such boom-and-bust cycles cannot be the basis for steady, sustained growth. U.S. economic assistance is way down since the high point of the 1960s, and the long terms-of-trade imbalance between the commodity-producing nations of Latin America and the industrial countries of the North is still tipped disastrously in favor of the latter. Many Latin Americans are therefore questioning their situation of dependence vis-à-vis the United States: whether Latin American economic interests instead of being compatible with those of the United States are not at loggerheads with them; whether U.S. prosperity is in part based on keeping Latin America underdeveloped.

Most of the Latin American nations, additionally, are experiencing a stagflation far worse than our own. The GDP has leveled off and in some countries is actually decreasing. Inflation runs from 30 percent to over 200 percent per year. Unemployment and underemployment affect between 20 percent and 40 percent of the work force. The price most Latin American nations must pay for oil has almost ruined them, leading to huge balance-of-payments deficits and immense foreign debts. Argentina, Brazil, and other countries may have to default on their outstanding debts, and several other nations of the area are on the brink of financial disaster. It is clear that a political order based on the absolute necessity of an expanding pie cannot last long when the pie stops expanding or shrinks.

Coupled with the economic crisis is a rising popular challenge. This challenge has by now taken on strong class overtones and is increasingly evidenced by mass discontent, violence, and sporadic upheaval. The students are often in revolt; workers are taking direct action; peasants are seizing private lands. In the past, such protest movements could be contained through either mild authoritarianism or else partial acquiescence to their demands. But now the protests have multiplied into genuine class disputes and in some areas are getting out of hand; the response to them has hence grown fiercer and more brutal. These protests have sometimes been exacerbated by the Soviet Union and the Cubans seeking to advance their own interests in the region.

Finally, the historical model is being questioned by a variety of political actors who were once its staunchest supporters. As Juan Velasco Alvarado, former president and general of Peru, has stated:

> Our revolution is not interested in the false participation demanded by traditional politicians of the old system.
> The legitimacy of this Revolutionary Government cannot rest on the respect for the rules of a politically decadent game which only benefits the privileged groups of the country. Our objectives have nothing to do with the traditional form of politics, of a political system which is rotten to the core because it has never served to defend the authentic interests of the Peruvian people.[2]

In short, even the armed forces of Latin America, or some factions thereof, have come to consider the traditional co-optive model as inadequate for today's needs. As Fidel Castro has neatly put it, "The fire has spread to the firehouse." Similar splits have occurred within the once monolithic Church, and the divisions within the middle class over the continued relevance and appropriateness of the older pattern have also widened. The present student generation is strongly oriented toward nationalism and socialism. There is among all groups a general sense of malaise and discontent, of uncertainty and impending change, a feeling that one epoch and pattern of rule may have ended and that another, although ill defined, may be about to begin. These comments also imply that our interpretations of Latin America must be based not just on the traditional patterns of politics but on other interpretations as well: class analysis, dependency analysis, and the political economy of the international system.

REVOLUTION AND REACTION: THE NEW ALTERNATIVES

In a period of economic stagnation and downturn, the competition for the few available pieces of pie has accelerated, and throughout Latin America violence has increased. At the same time, the conflict among the various participating groups in the Latin American political process has in some countries produced a situation of paralysis and immobility, of spiraling discord and conflict. With no one group able to command a majority or rule by itself; with power often more or less evenly shared among eight or nine leading power contenders (army, Church, oligarchy, business elites, middle sectors, bureaucracy, professionals, labor, universities); and with deep internal division and fragmentation present within each of these groups, decision making and policy implementation have been stymied. Not only have the problems multiplied of late, but Latin America's historic way of resolving them seems no longer to work.

These challenges and crises have increasingly brought into question the capacity of the traditional Latin American system to respond as in the past. One should not sell short the ability of the traditional elites to survive the present crisis as they have others previously, to fashion new formulas designed to co-opt the newest challengers to their rule while retaining the historic structure intact. But there is no doubt that this traditional system is being challenged, questioned, and undermined to a degree never before experienced.

At least nine major alternatives seem possible at present, with the likelihood high of continued experimentation with new formulas or the borrowing from several to form new permutations. These models, the reasons for them, and the distinct national variations should be kept in mind as one reads the country analyses in Parts 2 and 3. The nine alternatives are these:

1. the maintenance of traditional, authoritarian, almost nineteenth-century politics and society in a country largely unaffected by the revolutionary currents here described (Paraguay)
2. a situation in the more advanced nations of recurrent crisis, breakdown, and fragmentation with seemingly no formulas available for successfully resolving the national malaise (leading case: Argentina since the 1930s)
3. a full-scale socialist revolution (Cuba under Castro, perhaps Nicaragua)
4. a situation of revolution or social transformation frustrated through U.S. intervention (leading cases: Guatemala, the Dominican Republic, Chile; El Salvador may be a special case)

5. a pattern of societal mobilization, conflict, paralysis, and endemic civil war, to the point where the military is compelled to step in, restore order with a vengeance, and suppress groups such as workers and peasants who had previously been mobilized (leading cases: present-day Brazil, Chile, Uruguay; formerly Argentina)
6. a democratic breakthrough, as in Costa Rica, Venezuela, and perhaps Argentina in 1983 (encouraging democratic developments have also occurred in Peru, Ecuador, Bolivia, Panama, Honduras, and Brazil)
7. a single-party regime combining elements of both mass mobilization and control (Bolivia for a time, Mexico)
8. a military regime that takes a leftist rather than rightist approach, that stakes out a nationalist position and ushers in revolution from above before it occurs from below (leading case: Peru, with some aspects of this pattern also present for a time in Bolivia, Ecuador, El Salvador, Honduras, Panama)
9. a hodge podge regime combining elitist features with democratic ones and continuing to muddle along largely in the historical pattern (best examples: Colombia, Dominican Republic, perhaps El Salvador, Honduras, Panama)

Puerto Rico, tied to the United States in a commonwealth arrangement, constitutes a special case.

NOTES

1. The discussion here and in the followng section derives from Charles W. Anderson, "The Latin American Political System," chap. 4 of his *Politics and Economic Change in Latin America* (Van Nostrand, Princeton, N.J., 1967); reprinted in *Politics and Social Change in Latin America: The Distinct Tradition*, rev. 2d ed., ed. Howard J. Wiarda (University of Massachusetts Press, Amherst, 1982).

2. Quoted in David Scott Palmer, *"Revolution from Above": Military Government and Popular Participation in Peru, 1968–1972*, Cornell University Dissertation Series, Latin American Studies Program, Ithaca, N.Y., 1973.

SUGGESTIONS FOR FURTHER READING

Adams, Richard N., et al. *Social Change in Latin America Today.* Vintage, New York, 1961.

Adie, Robert F., and Guy E. Poitras. *Latin America: The Politics of Immobility.* Prentice-Hall, Englewood Cliffs, N.J., 1974.

Alba, Victor. *Politics and the Labor Movement in Latin America.* Stanford University Press, Stanford, Calif., 1968.

———. *The Latin Americans.* Praeger, New York, 1969.

Alexander, Robert J. *Organized Labor in Latin America.* Harper & Row, New York, 1965.

———. *Agrarian Reform in Latin America.* Macmillan, New York, 1974.

Anderson, Charles W. *Politics and Economic Change in Latin America*. Van Nostrand, Princeton, N.J., 1967.

Blackman, Morris J., and Ronald G. Hellman. *Terms of Conflict: Ideology in Latin American Politics*. Institute for the Study of Human Issues, Philadelphia, 1977.

Blasier, Cole, ed. *Constructive Change in Latin America*. University of Pittsburgh Press, Pittsburgh, 1968.

Boxer, C. R. *Four Centuries of Portuguese Expansion*. University of California Press, Berkeley, 1969.

Burnett, Ben G., and Kenneth F. Johnson, eds. *Political Forces in Latin America*. Wadsworth, Belmont, Calif. 1970.

Burns, E. Bradford. *Latin America: A Concise Interpretative History*. Prentice-Hall, Englewood Cliffs, N.J., 1977.

Cardoso, F. H., and E. Faletto. *Dependency and Development in Latin America*. University of California Press, Berkeley, 1978.

Cespedes, Guillermo. *Latin America: The Early Years*. Knopf, New York, 1974.

Chalmers, Douglas. "The Politicized State in Latin America." In *Authoritarianism and Corporatism in Latin America*, edited by James Malloy. University of Pittsburgh Press, Pittsburgh, 1977, pp. 23–46.

Chalmers, Douglas A., ed. *Changing Latin America*. Academy of Political Science, Columbia University, New York, 1972.

Chaplin, David, ed. *Population Policies and Growth in Latin America*. Lexington, Lexington, Mass., 1971.

Chevalier, François. *Land and Society in Colonial Mexico*. University of California Press, Berkeley, 1970.

Chilcote, Ronald H., and Joel C. Edelstein. *Latin America: The Struggle with Dependency and Beyond*. Schenkman, Cambridge, Mass., 1974.

Cockcroft, James D., et al. *Dependence and Underdevelopment: Latin America's Political Economy*. Doubleday, Garden City, N.Y., 1972.

Collier, David. *The New Authoritarianism in Latin America*. Princeton University Press, Princeton, N.J., 1979.

Cortes Conde, Roberto, *The First Stages of Modernization in Spanish America*. Harper & Row, New York, 1974.

Cotler, Julio, and Richard Fagen, eds. *Latin America and the United States: The Changing Political Realities*. Stanford University Press, Stanford, Calif., 1975.

Davis, Stanley M., and Louis Wolf Goodman. *Workers and Managers in Latin America*. Heath, Lexington, Mass., 1972.

Dealy, Glen. *The Public Man: An Interpretation of Latin American and Other Catholic Countries*. University of Massachusetts Press, Amherst, 1977.

Duncan, W. Raymond. *Latin American Politics: A Developmental Approach*. Praeger, New York, 1976.

Duncan, W. Raymond, and James N. Goodsell. *The Quest for Change in Latin America*. Oxford, New York, 1970.

Einaudi, Luigi R., ed. *Beyond Cuba: Latin America Takes Charge of Its Future*. Crane, Russak, New York, 1974.

Elliot, J. H. *The Old World and the New, 1492–1650*. Cambridge University Press, Cambridge, 1960.

Erickson, Kenneth Paul. *The Brazilian Corporative State and Working-Class Politics*. University of California Press, Berkeley, 1977.

Feder, Ernest. *The Rape of the Peasantry*. Doubleday, Garden City, N.Y., 1971.

Fitch, John Samuel. *The Military Coup d'Etat as a Political Process: Ecuador, 1948–1966*. Johns Hopkins University Press, Baltimore, 1977.

Freyre, Gilberto. *The Masters and the Slaves.* Knopf, New York, 1964.

Gibson, Charles. *Spain in America.* Harper & Row, New York, 1966.

Glade, William P. *The Latin American Economies: A Study of Their Institutional Evolution.* Van Nostrand, New York, 1969.

Gott, Richard. *Guerrilla Movements in Latin America.* Nelson, London, 1970.

Graham, Lawrence, and Clarence E. Thurber, eds. *Development Administration in Latin America.* Duke University Press, Durham, N.C., 1973.

Greenfield, Sidney M. "The Patrimonial State and Patron-Client Relations in Iberia and Latin America." Occasional Paper no. 1, University of Massachusetts, Program in Latin American Studies, 1976.

Halperin Donghi, Tulio. *The Aftermath of Revolution in Latin America.* Harper & Row, New York, 1973.

Haring, Clarence. *The Spanish Empire in America.* Harcourt Brace, New York, 1963.

Harris, Louis K., and Victor Alba. *The Political Culture and Behavior of Latin America.* Kent State University Press, Kent, Ohio, 1974.

Heath, Dwight, and Richard Adams, eds. *Contemporary Cultures and Societies of Latin America.* Random, New York, 1965.

Herring, Hubert. *A History of Latin America.* Knopf, New York, 1968.

Hirschman, Albert O. *Journeys Toward Progress: Studies of Economic Policy-Making in Latin America.* Doubleday, Garden City, N.Y., 1965.

Horowitz, Irving L. *Masses in Latin America.* Oxford University Press, New York, 1970.

James, Preston. *Latin America.* Odyssey, New York, 1969.

Johnson, John J. *Political Change in Latin America: The Emergence of the Middle Sectors.* Stanford University Press, Stanford, Calif., 1958.

_____. *The Military and Society in Latin America.* Stanford University Press, Stanford, Calif., 1964.

Kantor, Harry. *Patterns of Politics and Political Systems of Latin America.* Rand McNally, Chicago, 1969.

Karst, Kenneth, and Keith Rosen. *Law and Development in Latin America.* University of California Press, Berkeley, 1975.

Kirkpatrick, F. A. *The Spanish Conquistadores.* World, New York, 1962.

Landsberger, Henry A. *Latin American Peasant Movements.* Cornell University Press, Ithaca, N.Y., 1969.

Landsberger, Henry A., ed. *The Church and Social Change in Latin America.* Notre Dame University Press, Notre Dame, Ind., 1970.

Lewis, Oscar. *The Children of Sanchez.* Random, New York, 1961.

Lieuwen, Edwin. *Arms and Politics in Latin America.* Praeger, New York, 1961.

Lipset, Seymour, and Aldo Solari, eds. *Elites in Latin America.* Oxford University Press, New York, 1967.

Lowenthal, Abraham F., ed. *Armies and Politics in Latin America.* Holmes & Meier, New York, 1976.

Lynch, John. *The Spanish-American Revolutions, 1808–1826.* Norton, New York, 1973.

McCoy, Terry, ed. *The Dynamics of Population Policy in Latin America,* Ballinger, Cambridge, Mass., 1974.

McDonald, Ronald H. *Party Systems and Elections in Latin America.* Markham, Chicago, 1971.

_____. "Nación y Estado en America Latina." *Estudios Andinos* 10 (1974–1975).

Malloy, James, ed. *Authoritarianism and Corporatism in Latin America*. University of Pittsburgh Press, Pittsburgh, 1977.

Mander, John. *The Unrevolutionary Society: The Power of Latin American Conservatism in a Changing World*. Knopf, New York, 1969.

Martz, John, ed. *The Dynamics of Change in Latin American Politics*. Prentice-Hall, Englewood Cliffs, N.J., 1971.

Mecham, J. Lloyd. *Church and State in Latin America*. University of North Carolina Press, Chapel Hill, 1966.

Mercier Vega, Luis. *Roads to Power in Latin America*. Praeger, New York, 1969.

Moreno, Francisco J., and Barbara Mitrani, eds. *Conflict and Violence in Latin American Politics*. Crowell, New York, 1971.

Morison, Samuel Eliot. *The European Discovery of America*. Oxford University Press, New York, 1971.

Mutchler, David E. *The Church as a Political Force in Latin America*. Praeger, New York, 1971.

Needler, Martin. *Political Development in Latin America*. Random, New York, 1968.

Needler, Martin, ed. *Political Systems of Latin America*. Van Nostrand, New York, 1970.

O'Donnell, Guillermo A. *Modernization and Bureaucratic Authoritarianism*. Institute of International Studies, University of California, Berkeley, 1973.

Paz, Octavio. *The Labyrinth of Solitude*. Grove, New York, 1961.

Petras, James. *Politics and Social Structure in Latin America*. Monthly Review, New York, 1970.

Petras, James, and Maurice Zeitlin, eds. *Latin America: Reform or Revolution?* Fawcett, New York, 1968.

Pike, Frederick B. *Spanish America, 1900–1970*. Norton, New York, 1973.

Pike, Frederick B., and Thomas Stritch, eds. *The New Corporatism*. University of Notre Dame Press, Notre Dame, Ind., 1974.

Powelson, John P. *Latin America: Today's Economic and Social Revolution*. McGraw-Hill, New York, 1964.

Sarfatti, Magali. *Spanish Bureaucratic Patrimonialism in America*. Institute of International Studies, University of California, Berkeley, 1966.

Sigmund, Paul. *Multinationals in Latin America*. University of Wisconsin Press, Madison, 1980.

Sigmund, Paul, ed. *Models of Change in Latin America*. Praeger, New York, 1970.

Silvert, Kalman H. *The Conflict Society: Reaction and Revolution in Latin America*. American Universities Field Staff, New York, 1966.

Smith, T. Lynn, ed. *Agrarian Reform in Latin America*. Knopf, New York, 1965.

Stavenhagen, Rodolfo, ed. *Agrarian Problems and Peasant Movements in Latin America*. Doubleday, Garden City, N.Y., 1970.

Stein, Stanley J., and Barbara H. Stein. *The Colonial Heritage of Latin America*. Oxford University Press, New York, 1970.

Stepan, Alfred. *The State and Society: Peru in Comparative Perspective*. Princeton University Press, Princeton, N.J., 1978.

Stycos, J. Mayone. *Human Fertility in Latin America*. Cornell University Press, Ithaca, N.Y., 1968.

──────. *Ideology, Faith, and Family Planning in Latin America*. McGraw-Hill, New York, 1971.

Tannenbaum, Frank. *Ten Keys to Latin America*. Vintage, New York, 1962.

Vallier, Ivan. *Catholicism, Social Control, and Modernization in Latin America.* Prentice-Hall, Englewood Cliffs, N.J., 1970.

Van Niekirk, A. E. *Populism and Political Development in Latin America.* University Press, Rotterdam, 1974.

Veliz, Claudio. *The Politics of Conformity in Latin America.* Oxford University Press, New York, 1967.

————. *The Centralist Tradition in Latin America.* Princeton University Press, Princeton, N.J., 1980.

Veliz, Claudio, ed. *Obstacles to Change in Latin America.* Oxford, New York, 1965.

Wagley, Charles. *The Latin American Tradition.* Columbia University Press, New York, 1968.

Wauchope, Robert, ed., *The Indian Background of Latin American History.* Knopf, New York, 1970.

Whither Latin America? Monthly Review, New York, 1963.

Wiarda, Howard J. *Corporatism and Development in Latin America.* Westview Press, Boulder, Colo., 1981.

————. *In Search of Policy: The United States and Latin America.* American Enterprise Institute, Washington, D.C., 1984.

Wiarda, Howard J., ed. *Politics and Social Change in Latin America.* Rev. ed. University of Massachusetts Press, Amherst, 1982.

————. *Rift and Revolution: The Central American Imbroglio.* American Enterprise Institute, Washington, D.C., 1984.

Willems, Emilio. *Latin American Culture.* Harper & Row, New York, 1975.

Williams, Edward J. *Latin American Christian Democratic Parties.* University of Tennessee Press, Knoxville, 1967.

————. *The Political Themes of Inter-American Relations.* Duxbury, N. Scituate, Mass., 1971.

Williams, Edward J., and Freeman Wright. *Latin American Politics: A Developmental Approach.* Mayfield, Palo Alto, Calif., 1975.

Worcester, Donald E., and Wendell G. Schaeffer. *The Growth and Culture of Latin America.* Oxford University Press, New York, 1970.

Zea, Leopoldo. *The Latin American Mind.* University of Oklahoma Press, Norman, 1963.

Part 2

The political systems of South America

8
Argentina: Politics in a Conflict Society

PETER G. SNOW

Argentina is one of the most highly developed nations in the world— if development is thought of in exclusively social and economic terms. The people of Argentina are literate, urban, and relatively prosperous. And, in spite of the nation's image as a beef and wheat producer, three times as much of the gross domestic product comes from manufacturing as from agriculture. There is a large middle class, and a huge part of the urban working class belongs to powerful trade unions.

The political side of the picture, however, is quite different. During the last half century, there has been very little political stability. (Thirteen presidents have been removed from office by force; not a single civilian president has served a full term.) And, during the last quarter century, the level of political violence and repression has been higher than in any other Latin American nation (and, during the 1970s, perhaps as high as anywhere in the world).

Since economic, social, and political development are often thought of as going hand in hand, the vast disparity in Argentina between political development and social and economic development seems paradoxical. A great deal of time and effort has been expended in an attempt to find an intrinsically Argentine explanation for this apparent paradox. Only recently have scholars begun to question the very existence of the paradox and to examine the possibility that the high levels of social and economic development are the cause of political instability.

Samuel Huntington has written that violence and instability are "in large part the product of rapid social change and the rapid mobilization of new groups into politics coupled with the slow development of political institutions."[1] It is not at all difficult to make the case that this is exactly what has occurred in Argentina. New social groups were politicized earlier, more thoroughly, and more rapidly than in any other Latin American nation. The dramatic increases in political participation in 1912 and again in 1945 were not fully accepted by the older elites; the political system that allowed first the middle class and then the

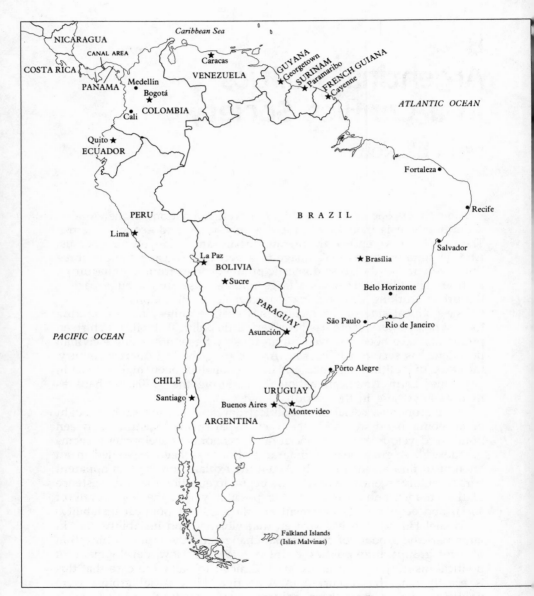

South America

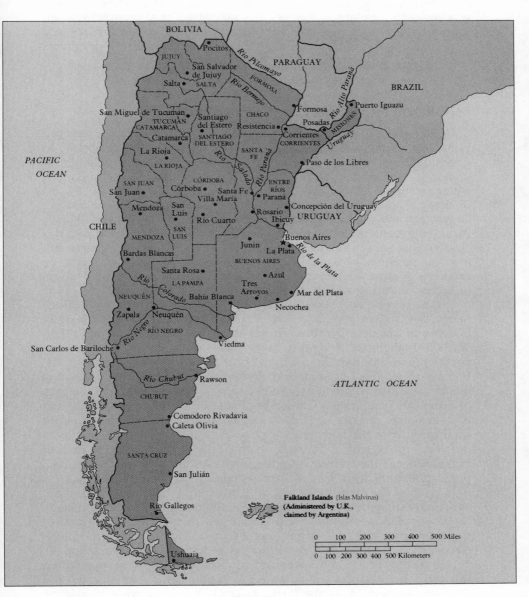

Argentina

working class to gain an important voice in the government lost much of its legitimacy in the eyes of the upper class, and yet no new system was created to replace it. The result was that political groups began to confront each other nakedly, for there were neither institutions nor leaders that were recognized as legitimate intermediaries.[2] This, unfortunately, is a problem for which there are no simple solutions.

THE SOCIOECONOMIC BACKGROUND

Of all nations of Latin America, Argentina is the one farthest removed from the stereotypical impressions held by many North Americans. In Argentina, one finds 28 million highly literate, well-fed people almost uniformly of European ancestry, who inhabit the world's eighth largest nation, virtually all of which lies in the Temperate Zone. Almost a third of these people live in metropolitan Buenos Aires, one of the world's largest and most cosmopolitan cities. Even those living outside Buenos Aires fail to conform to the stereotypical image that sees them as poverty-stricken peasants working someone else's land. Certainly there are landless peasants in Argentina, but not nearly as many as might be expected. Almost three-fourths of the non-Buenos Aires population lives in urban centers, a fourth in cities of over 100,000 people.

For many years now, Argentina has been an almost completely "white" nation. The Indian population has steadily decreased, not just relatively but also in absolute numbers. Today there are probably no more than 100,000 Indians in Argentina, and these are concentrated near the northwestern frontier. In the nineteenth century, when most of the Indians were killed in order to push the frontier to the south, the mestizos (a mixture of Indian and European) were absorbed by waves of European immigration. Presently about 10 percent of the population is classified as mestizo, and these people appear to be concentrated in rural areas near the northern and western borders. There are virtually no blacks in Argentina. Although numerically significant at the time of independence, they have been rapidly assimilated into the general population until their number has dropped to about five thousand.

In spite of the swift move toward urbanization and industrialization, agriculture still provides the livelihood for about a fifth of the economically active population. Another third is engaged in the industrial sector of the economy, with the largest number working in food processing, construction, textiles, and metallurgical industries. The remaining 45 percent is engaged in commerce and services. The largest groups within this sector are business people and their employees, public officials, and domestic servants. It is the tertiary sector that is growing in relative size, while the percentage of the population engaged in agriculture is declining and the industrial sector remains relatively constant. A major part of the growth of the tertiary sector is a result of the ever increasing size of the bureaucracy, which now employs almost one out of every ten economically active citizens.

The often-repeated bromide about the lack of a middle class in Latin America simply is not true of Argentina, where about half of the population can be so classified (at least in terms of being neither upper class nor working class). However, this middle class—or, more appropriately, middle sector—is in almost no way a cohesive group. Wealthy business people, members of the liberal professions, and clerks in government offices have little in common and certainly lack a single coherent world view that could be translated into political action.

PRE-1930 POLITICAL HISTORY:
THE PERIOD OF DEVELOPMENT

The area that is now Argentina was originally settled by two separate streams of colonization. The first, coming from Peru, entered from the northwest and founded the towns of Mendoza, San Luis, Tucumán, San Juan, and Córdoba during the last half of the sixteenth century; the second, coming directly from Spain, settled along the Río de la Plata estuary. Throughout most of the colonial period the people of Buenos Aires and those of the interior lived quite separate existences. The interior was developed primarily to provide food, livestock, and textiles for the mining areas of Peru, while Buenos Aires remained oriented toward Europe.

Prior to 1776, Argentina was part of the viceroyalty of Peru. The area was of little importance to Spain, largely because of its lack of precious metals. However, as the population increased and as the Portuguese in Brazil came to be seen as a threat, a new viceroyalty was created with its seat in Buenos Aires. Nevertheless, peninsula-born Spaniards continued to monopolize all high political offices, while those born in the colony were denied any appreciable influence in political affairs. Of greater significance, perhaps, is the fact that effective political control of the region was exceptionally difficult if not impossible. Although the lines of authority (running from the king of Spain, through the viceroy, to the local intendants) were clear, a number of factors militated against the uniform implementation of policy. Among these factors were (1) the great distance between population centers; (2) the overall scarcity of population (at the end of the colonial period there were fewer than 500,000 inhabitants in an area half the size of the United States); and (3) a largely rural, almost nomadic population. These factors led to deep-seated feelings of regional loyalty that later increased greatly the difficulty of creating a nation.

In 1808, Spanish authority in the New World was weakened immeasurably by the French invasion of Spain and the overthrow of King Ferdinand VII. Two years later, when the last vestiges of Spanish authority on the Iberian peninsula were gone, the lines of legitimacy were blurred, at best, and the viceroys found themselves in virtually untenable positions. On May 25, 1810, the Buenos Aires city council deposed the viceroy and assumed control of the city. This was the beginning of the independence movement, although independence was not formally declared for another six years.

Between 1810 and 1819 the Argentines fought not only the Spaniards, but also the Paraguayans, Uruguayans, Brazilians, and, most frequently, each other. Although the southern part of the continent was free from Spanish control by 1819, a series of juntas, triumvirates, and supreme directors came and went without any success in the quest for national unification. Although the level of violence declined after 1819, until 1862 very little progress was made toward the creation of a single nation. During this period there existed only an amalgamation of autonomous provinces. Seldom was there even a semblance of a national government, and even in the provinces, if political order existed it was usually forcibly imposed by a local caudillo.

In 1852, most of the provincial governors agreed to attempt to form a national union, and the following year a constitution was written that, except for the interval between 1949 and 1955, has been Argentina's fundamental law ever since. Buenos Aires, however, boycotted the constitutional convention and maintained a separate existence. A single nation could not be created until the bitter struggle between the interior provinces and Buenos Aires was resolved.

Politically, this conflict was over the kind of national government to be established. The political leaders of the interior, referring to themselves as Federalists, tended to equate federalism with democracy and liberty. They remembered the intense centralization of the colonial period and wanted no part of a continuance of the unitary system. They recognized the economic and social differences between some of the provinces, especially between those of the interior and Buenos Aires, and felt that federalism was the best way to reconcile these differences. On the other hand, the Unitarians of Buenos Aires were convinced that only a unitary system could weld the warring provinces into a single nation; they were afraid that if federalism were adopted, there would be no nation.

In the realm of economics, the conflict revolved around the fact that the dominant source of income for the new nation was the import duties collected in Buenos Aires, which had the nation's only developed port. During and immediately after the war for independence, most of the interior provinces were in extremely bad shape financially. They were cut off from their traditional markets in Peru, and all their goods entering or leaving the country through the Río de la Plata estuary were taxed in Buenos Aires, with the revenue going into the treasury of that province.

In very general terms, the Buenos Aires Unitarians wanted to form a strong national government run by and for the people of Buenos Aires. To many of the political leaders of the interior, federalism meant only provincial autonomy and the right of the local caudillo to exploit his province as he saw fit.

This conflict increased in intensity until it came to civil war in 1858 and again in 1861. In 1861, the forces of Buenos Aires, under the leadership of Bartolomé Mitre, defeated the provincial army at Pavón. After the adoption of relatively minor constitutional amendments, Buenos Aires agreed to join the union, and the next year Mitre became Argentina's first truly national president.

The inauguration of Mitre in 1862 marked the beginning of a new era in Argentina. For half a century the country had endured chaos and anarchy, interrupted only by the dictatorship of Juan Manuel de Rosas (1835–1852); the next seven decades were characterized by peace and stability and by rapid economic and political development.

Mitre and the two presidents who succeeded him concentrated most of their efforts on pacification and the creation of the institutions of government. The Congress was moved from Paraná to Buenos Aires and began meeting regularly. A national judiciary was created and staffed with extremely competent people. The city of Buenos Aires was removed from the province of that name and converted into a federal district, much like Washington, D.C. And, most importantly, general acceptance was gained for the existence of a single national government.

Beginning in 1880, emphasis was shifted from politics to economics. The next group of presidents set out to increase production by importing Europeans and European capital. At the time, there were barely 1.5 million Argentines occupying 1 million square miles (2.6 million square kilometers). The majority of those people were rural, and most were engaged in subsistence agriculture. Infrastructural development was accomplished primarily through British financing; the rail system, for instance, was British owned until World War II. When Mitre took office, there were perhaps 2,000 miles (3,200 kilometers) of track: fifty years later, there were 20,000 (32,000 kilometers). During the same period, the amount of cultivated land was upped from less than 1.5 million acres (.6 million hectares), to more than 60 million (24.3 million hectares), and the amount of land devoted to grazing was increased almost as dramatically. These and similar factors changed Argentina from a subsistence agricultural system to a major exporter of primary products, and the transformation took place with amazing rapidity. By the time of World War I, Argentina was exporting 350,000 tons (317,450 tonnes) of beef and 5 million tons (4.5 million tonnes) of cereals annually.

During this same period, there were important changes in the nature of Argentine society, largely as a result of massive immigration. The author of the 1853 constitution said, "To govern is to populate," and the dictum was taken to heart by the country's nineteenth-century rulers. A concerted effort was made to attract Europeans to Argentina, an effort that was incredibly successful. Immigration began in the 1850s as little more than a trickle but increased at an astronomical rate during the next forty years. In 1870, 40,000 immigrants arrived; in 1885, 110,000; and in 1890, 200,000. Between 1869 and 1929, 60 percent of the nation's population growth came from immigration.[3]

Although a great many Argentines attained some degree of economic well-being between 1862 and 1916, the average person remained almost completely removed from the political process. Government machinery revolved around the person of the president. In the provinces the legislatures were subservient to the governors, to whom most members owed their election. The governor was also quite influential in the selection of congressional representatives from the province. The provincial legislature chose the members of the upper house, and the governor and the Conservative party had control over the electoral machinery so that "safe" representatives were returned to the lower house. The governors, in turn, were virtually the personal agents of the president, who could keep the governors in line with the use or just the threat of his presidential power to remove them from office. The system was self-perpetuating, as the president and the governors kept each other in office through the use of fraud and, when necessary, force. A number of political parties were active in this period, but until the turn of the century all were essentially conservative organizations representing different sectors of the aristocracy—primarily the large landowners of the interior and the commercial and livestock interests of the city and province of Buenos Aires.

This political system was perhaps appropriate for Argentina as long as its society was composed almost exclusively of a small landowning elite and a large politically inarticulate mass; however, such ceased to be the case when the nation's social structure underwent fundamental alteration. The most important of the societal changes was the rapid formation of a middle class composed largely of immigrants and their offspring.

It was this newly emerging middle class that formed the base for the Radical Civic Union (UCR), founded in 1890. During the first forty years of its existence, this party was dominated by a single enigmatic politician named Hipólito Yrigoyen. Convinced that UCR participation in elections supervised by the Conservatives would only serve to place the party's stamp of approval on inevitable electoral fraud, Yrigoyen saw to it that the Radicals boycotted all elections prior to 1912. Instead, they attempted to come to power by force, instigating rebellions in 1890, 1893, and 1905. When these revolts proved unsuccessful, the Radicals still did not nominate candidates for office or write specific programs; rather, they contented themselves with denunciations of the oligarchic nature of the government and insisted that it be replaced by a "national renovation" led by the UCR.

In an effort to bring more people to the polls and thus increase the legitimacy of the regime, the conservatives wrote a new election law in 1911. The law provided for universal and compulsory male suffrage, a secret ballot, permanent voter registration, and minority representation in the Congress. Within five years, the honest administration of this law cost the Conservatives their monopoly on public office.

In 1916, in what may have been the country's first truly honest presidential election, Hipólito Yrigoyen became Argentina's first non-Conservative president. Unfortunately, the Radicals, still lacking a definite program, had no clear idea how to put into effect the national renovation they had so long promised. The UCR held power for fourteen years; but even though relatively minor reforms were enacted, no fundamental changes were even attempted and the economic power of the Conservatives remained intact. It may be that by that time the Radicals had lost their revolutionary zeal and their goal had become simply recognition of the right of the middle class to participate fully in the economic, social, and political life of the country—or at least recognition of its right to a share of the spoils of office.

In 1912 the Conservatives had been willing to share power with the Radicals, although certainly not on the basis of equality. They apparently saw the provision in the new election law guaranteeing minority representation in the Congress as a means of co-opting their middle-class opponents. (The congressional debate on the law made it clear that the Conservatives did not envision the possibility of their becoming the minority party.) What the Conservatives were unwilling to do was to relinquish power to the Radicals, yet that is exactly what happened. Voter participation increased dramatically (from 190,000 in 1910 to 640,000 in 1912 and 1,460,000 in 1928), and as it grew so did the percentage of the vote obtained by the Radicals. By 1930, it was clear that the Conservatives were quite unlikely to win any national elections in the foreseeable future. Although the policies adopted by the Radicals had not been particularly disadvantageous to the nation's elite, the large and growing Radical electorate meant that this was a definite possibility at any time in the future. The institutions of liberal democracy that had served the elite in the past were called into question.

In September 1930 an economic crisis, ever increasing corruption in the government, President Yrigoyen's senility (at the age of seventy-two he was serving a second term), recognition by the Conservatives that the rules of the game had to be changed if they were to return to power, and widespread popular disillusionment with the Radicals led to their overthrow and the establishment of Argentina's first military government.

POST-1930 POLITICAL HISTORY: THE PERIOD OF STAGNATION AND FRAGMENTATION

The 1930 military coup marked the beginning of a new era in Argentina. The preceding seventy years had been characterized by a degree of political stability almost unknown in Latin America and by a level of economic development that led to the attainment of a standard of living comparable to that of southern Europe. The years since 1930, on the other hand, have been characterized by exactly the opposite: economic stagnation and an incredible degree of political instability.

Following the overthrow of Yrigoyen, the armed forces retained power for less than two years before returning control of the government to the Conservatives by means of elections as fraudulent as those conducted prior to 1912. In fact, the period between 1932 and 1943 is frequently referred to as the Era of Patriotic Fraud. According to the Conservatives, it was their patriotic duty to engage in electoral fraud, for otherwise the Radicals would hoodwink the immature voters, return to power, and once again lead the country down the road to ruin.

The social, economic, and political elite that governed Argentina between 1862 and 1916 was dedicated to national development. Such was decidedly not true of the elite in power following the 1930 coup. The government did lead the country out of the depression and restore a degree of prosperity; however, it also saw to it that this prosperity was distributed even more inequitably than before. Argentina was run almost exclusively for the benefit of the landed aristocracy.

At about the same time, there occurred a profound change in the character of the urban working class. During World War I, the majority of the urban workers were recent immigrants, almost none of whom became naturalized citizens; but by World War II, they were primarily recent migrants from the countryside and, to a lesser extent, the children of immigrants. During the 1930s and early 1940s, the wave of migration to the cities was of truly incredible proportions. For example, it has been estimated that in one four-year period alone one out of every five rural dwellers moved into an urban center, most into greater Buenos Aires.[4] Politically, this new urban working class differed from its earlier counterpart in at least one important way: Its members were citizens and hence potential voters.

Unfortunately, the nation's political institutions were not equipped to handle large new groups of political participants. Neither the structures, nor the programs, nor the leaders of the existing political parties were able (or willing, perhaps) to offer anything of value to this working class. Until 1940, the Congress was dominated by the Conservatives, who seemed totally uninterested in the plight of the workers; for the next three years, the Radicals used their congressional majority to harass the president and to prevent the enactment of any sort of program.

Such was the scene in 1943 when the leaders of the armed forces again assumed the role of keeper of the national conscience and deposed the Conservative government. In the military administration that followed the coup, power gradually came to be concentrated in the hands of a colonel who was to dominate the course of Argentine politics for the next thirty years: Juan Domingo Perón.

Perón was the one army officer who appears to have seen the political potential of the labor movement. Content with a quite secondary position in the revolutionary government, that of secretary of labor, he almost immediately began an active campaign for working-class support. He saw to it that wages were raised substantially and that existing ameliorative labor legislation was enforced for the first time. He presided over the formation of new trade unions and the enormous expansion of existing unions that were friendly to him. For example, under his influence, membership in the Textile Workers Union grew from 2,000 in 1943 to over 84,000 in 1946; the Metallurgical Workers Union grew from 2,000 to 100,000 in the same period.[5] By 1945, his labor secretariat was the nation's sole collective-bargaining agency, and unions utilizing its auspices were virtually certain to obtain whatever they sought.

In the presidential election of February 1946, Perón was the candidate of the hastily formed Argentine Labor party. Although opposed by a single candidate representing all the nation's traditional political parties, Perón won. In 1916, it had been the newly emerging middle class that was largely responsible for the election of Yrigoyen; thirty years later it was the new urban working class that could claim most of the credit for the election of Juan Perón.

As president, Perón continued to do a great deal for the working class, both materially and psychologically. The process of unionization was continued, wages and fringe benefits were dramatically increased, and a modern social-security system was created. To an appreciable extent, there was a redistribution of income that favored the wage earners. At least as important in the long run was the thorough politicization of the working class, which came to realize its potential political strength. Nevertheless, the material benefits obtained by the workers during the Perón administration were essentially gifts from above rather than the result of working-class demands. The Peronist party (the name given the former Labor party) functioned primarily as a vehicle for mobilizing working-class support for the regime; it did not, in fact, participate in the governing of Argentina.

Although honestly elected in 1946 and reelected in 1951, Perón moved steadily in the direction of authoritarian rule. Freedom of the press was virtually destroyed, the judiciary was purged as were the universities, and opposition leaders were harassed, exiled, or imprisoned. Perón originally came to power with the support of the Church, the armed forces, and organized labor. By 1955, his labor support had declined somewhat, and the Church had moved completely into the opposition. Most important, an appreciable sector of the armed forces had decided that he must go.

In September 1955, Perón was deposed; he went into exile, from which he did not return for eighteen years. It was relatively simple to get rid of Perón, but it was much more difficult to rid the country of Peronism. For two and a half years, Gen. Pedro Aramburu presided over a provisional regime dedicated to destroying Peronism and returning the country to civilian constitutional rule. With regard to the first goal, there was almost a total lack of success; in fact, the extreme anti-Peronism of the military government seems to have served only to convince Perón's followers that they must remain united in support of their exiled leader or see the political clock turned back to pre-1946. The second goal met with only limited success, for although elections were held, as far as the military was concerned the wrong man won.

The 1958 elections were swept by the faction of the old UCR calling itself the Intransigent Radical Civic Union (UCRI). Its leader, Arturo Frondizi, attained the presidency due largely to a deal with Perón, who traded the votes of his followers for a promise of legality for the Peronist party. This bargain gave Frondizi the presidency, but it cost him the ability to govern effectively. The anti-Peronist sector of the population and especially the leaders of the armed forces considered his election tainted and his administration illegitimate.

For four years, Frondizi made a concerted effort to accelerate the nation's rate of economic development and to integrate the Peronists back into political life. By 1962, his economic policies appeared to be on the verge of success, but his political maneuvers by then had cost him his job. Restored to legality, the Peronist party emerged victorious in the congressional and gubernatorial elections held in March 1962. This was the last straw as far as the anti-Peronist military leaders were concerned, and Frondizi was deposed.

After a year of near total chaos and virtual civil war within the military, elections were held once again. This time they were won by the People's Radical Civic Union (UCRP), the faction of the old UCR that had lost the 1958 elections to Frondizi's Intransigent Radicals. Elected to the presidency was Arturo Illia, a mild-mannered country doctor who received only a fourth of the popular vote. (Peronists were denied the right to nominate candidates for executive office.) The three years of the Illia administration were characterized by lack of action. In 1962, Frondizi had been overthrown because the leaders of the armed forces disapproved of his actions; in 1966, Illia was deposed because he refused to act.

By 1966, the military had witnessed the failure of two civilian administrations to resolve the Peronist problem and to bring about an acceptable rate of economic growth—and these were the administrations of the only two political parties with popular support approaching that of the Peronists. The military this time closed the Congress, dissolved all the nation's political parties, and granted almost complete authority to a retired general, Juan Carlos Onganía.

General Onganía was put in power to bring about a fundamental restructuring of the nation's political system. The leaders of the armed forces seemed to realize that the existing system was incapable of adapting to the myriad of demands placed on it. However, there was little in the way of consensus as to the form a new political system should take, and thus very little was accomplished during the seven years of military rule. An attempt was made to exclude the working class from the political process and to depoliticize groups such as the unions and the student organizations. However, unlike their Brazilian counterparts, whom they emulated to some degree, the Argentine military was unwilling to resort to extreme levels of repression, and thus these attempts were doomed to failure. Student organizations were banned by law, yet students engaged in violence to a greater degree than ever before. The labor movement was not depoliticized, and the working class refused to accept passively a reduction in its standard of living.

By 1970, it was clear that Onganía was accomplishing very little, that the public acquiescence he originally had enjoyed had almost vanished, and that the nation was experiencing a completely intolerable level of political violence. The leaders of the armed forces appear to have decided that they had no choice but to hold elections and return to constitutional government. (There was evidently some hope that the return to constitutionalism would relieve the frustrations contributing to the violence and that even if constitutionalism failed the armed forces would not be to blame.) When Onganía refused to go along with this, he was deposed, as was his successor a few months later when he too showed no signs of moving toward elections. Finally, the army commander in chief, Gen. Alejandro Lanusse, assumed the presidency and announced that he would hold office only long enough to stop the violence and hold elections.

It was obvious to all that if a newly elected government was to have any claim to legitimacy the Peronist movement would have to be given complete electoral equality. Yet, since many military leaders opposed the prospect of a Peronist government, changes were made in the election law to require a runoff election if no presidential candidate received an absolute majority of the popular vote. (There was general agreement that the Peronist candidate, whoever that might be, would win a plurality of the vote but would be defeated in a runoff by a coalition of non-Peronist parties.) Moreover, a number of complicated maneuvers effectively prevented Perón himself from being a candidate.

When the elections were held in March 1973, the Peronist candidate, Héctor Cámpora (whose slogan was Cámpora to the Presidency; Perón to Power), received 49.6 percent of the vote, more than double that of his nearest competitor. In violation of his own regulations, Lanusse decided that the results were close enough to the required absolute majority to cancel the runoff. Upon Cámpora's inauguration, all political prisoners received amnesty, the universities were turned over to the far left, and in general the government took on a vaguely leftist tint. However, after only fifty days in office Cámpora and his vice president resigned, necessitating new elections—this time with Juan Perón himself a candidate.

Eighteen years and eighteen days after he was forced into exile, Perón once again became the president of Argentina. Now the government moved decidedly to the right. In the universities, the Marxist admin-istrators were replaced with neofascists; several leftist governors were removed from office; and, most important, Perón openly sided with the relatively conservative labor sector of the Peronist movement against the leftist youth sector. On July 1, 1974, Perón died, leaving his widow, María Estela Martínez de Perón (Isabel) as the nation's chief executive.

The political violence, which had abated while Perón was president, reached an incredible level shortly after his death. Inflation, which was already high, increased until it approached 1 percent per day. Corruption became rampant. And, quite predictably, the armed forces once again assumed power. Isabel was arrested, and the army commander in chief, Gen. Jorge Videla, was inaugurated as president.

The major goals of the new military government were the elimination of antiregime terrorism and the achievement of economic recovery. With regard to the former, appreciable success was attained within three years, but at a very high price, as the government itself resorted to terrorist tactics. Thousands of people were subjected to arbitrary arrest, impris-onment, and torture, and many more just disappeared. The nation's economic problems, on the other hand, proved far more difficult to resolve. In spite of some short-term successes, such as the rapid ac-cumulation of foreign currency, seven years of military rule left the country in even worse shape than it had been in in 1976. During this period the exchange rate for the peso went from 80 to 260,000 to the dollar, and the foreign debt increased equally astronomically to $43 billion.

By 1982 the military government was very much in disrepute. This situation changed quite rapidly, but equally briefly, on April 2 with the invasion of the Malvinas (Falkland) Islands. Although virtually all Argentines were delighted at the "recuperation" of the islands, they were also totally disillusioned with the loss of the war with Great Britain that followed. This rather ignominious defeat led almost immediately to the creation of a provisional government whose only purpose was the holding of elections and the return to constitutional government.

On October 30, 1983, Argentines went to the polls for the first time in more than a decade, and to the amazement of most observers, they chose as their new president a Radical, Raúl Alfonsín. For the first time since the party's formation in 1946, the Peronists lost a presidential election—and lost decisively, as their presidential candidate, Italo Luder, received only 40 percent of the popular vote, while Alfonsín obtained 52 percent.

The Alfonsín administration has inherited a multitude of problems, including an inflation rate in excess of 400 percent, a level of unem-ployment approaching 25 percent, and a foreign debt perhaps the largest in the world in per capita terms. Nevertheless, the return to constitutional government in December 10, 1983, seemed to be greeted with a degree of optimism that Argentines have not exhibited in a very long time.

POLITICAL GROUPS

As in most nations, in Argentina a large number of groups, institutions, and associations have played prominent political roles. In terms of relative importance, three stand out above all others: the political parties, the armed forces, and the trade unions.

Political Parties

During the last quarter century, a great many political parties have attained legal recognition, but only the Radicals and the Peronists have gained sufficient popular support to hope to win an honest national election.

The Radicals

Formed in 1890, the UCR was Argentina's first nonaristocratic party and the first with grass-roots organization. Unlike the Radical party in Chile, however, it has seldom formulated a coherent program. Instead, it has demanded adherence to constitutional norms and promised change of an unspecified nature. Allegedly a middle-class organization, it has never effectively challenged the prerogatives of the nation's economic elite, nor has it appreciably alleviated the plight of the poor. For example, Peter Smith has shown that between 1916 and 1930, the period during which the Radicals first controlled the national government, ninety bills beneficial to the nation's livestock producers were introduced in the Congress; 60 percent of these bills were introduced by Radicals, 29 percent by Conservatives.[6] Even the rather bland reformism of the Radicals seems to have died in 1933 with Yrigoyen. Shortly thereafter, the party's right wing gained control and retained it until 1957.

Throughout much of its history, the catchwords of the UCR have been *nationalism* and *intransigence*. Radical nationalism has been, to a large degree, rhetorical. When out of power, the party has often espoused greater control of multinational corporations, a more independent foreign policy, and freedom from the strings frequently attached to loans by the International Monetary Fund or World Bank. With one major exception, however, the Radicals have failed to do very much that could be labeled nationalistic. That exception lies in the area of petroleum policy. In 1919, President Yrigoyen declared that petroleum was the property of the nation and thus no longer open to private exploitation. Three years later, a government corporation was given a monopoly on the production of all petroleum products. Since then, petroleum policy and especially foreign oil concessions have been major issues in Argentine politics—and the number one symbols of economic nationalism.

Intransigence, a word used constantly by Yrigoyen and repeated by most Radical politicians ever since, in practice means opposition to electoral alliances, to coalition governments, to any relationship with other political groups that might endanger "the purity of Radical ideals."

(This messianism is itself characteristic of the Radicals, who deny that the UCR is a political party, instead insisting that it is a movement of national regeneration.) Although intransigence may have been a successful tactic for the UCR at times, it has rarely been beneficial to the political system. It was most detrimental in 1973 when in all probability the leader of the Radicals, Ricardo Balbín, could have been Juan Perón's running mate in the September presidential election. The party evidently refused to permit this, and the vice presidential slot was filled by Perón's third wife, who was unable to govern effectively when her husband died less than a year after his election. Although one cannot be sure that things would have been different with Balbín as president, the possibility exists that Radical intransigence contributed to the 1976 military coup.

In 1957, the followers of Arthur Frondizi left the main body of radicalism to form the UCRI. These Radicals departed from both the tactics and the program of the traditional UCR. The direction of this change may be described in terms of two words constantly repeated by this group: *integration* and *development*.

Integration was an attempt to reincorporate Peronism into national political life, preferably by attracting individual Peronists to the banner of the UCRI. While most Radicals maintained their opposition to electoral alliances and Peronism, Frondizi's supporters made a deal with Perón. Perón told his followers to vote for Frondizi in the 1958 presidential election (thus ensuring his election) in return for a promise of legality for the Peronist party. With the legality granted by President Frondizi, the Peronists won the gubernatorial and congressional elections of 1962; Frondizi was deposed by the armed forces eleven days later.

The economic counterpart of integration was the attempt at total industrialization based on the creation of heavy industry. Directly contrary to the economic nationalism of the UCR, Frondizi's economic policies included free convertibility of the peso, loans from the International Monetary Fund, and the granting of petroleum concessions to foreign oil companies. In addition to being a political liability, *desarrollismo* (developmentalism) was less than successful from an economic point of view. Some progress was made toward the goal of total industrialization— steel production was increased dramatically, and the nation became virtually self-sufficient in petroleum—but during the period of *desarrollismo* the cost-of-living index went up more than 300 percent and the value of the peso declined from 28 to 140 to the U.S. dollar.

After Frondizi was overthrown in 1962, the electoral success of his party declined steadily. Frondizi received 42 percent of the vote in the 1958 presidential election; his UCRI could manage only 25 percent in 1962, 16 percent a year later, and 10 percent in 1965. The Frondicistas were little more than a junior partner in the Peronist coalition that swept the 1973 elections, and ten years later their presidential candidate received less than 2 percent of the vote.

Peronism

The Peronists, like the Radicals, have failed to develop a clear ideological position. This might be attributed to the party's originally heterogeneous social composition and to the fact that until 1974 it was dominated almost totally by Juan Perón. Between 1946 and 1955, while Perón was president, the party was essentially an alliance of three socioeconomic sectors: the urban working class, especially in and around the federal capital; the dependent middle class of the poorer interior provinces; and the newer industrialists, who prospered during World War II but needed government protection soon thereafter. After 1955, although much of the party's middle-class and industrialist following was won over to the Intransigent Radicals, leaving Peronism a more clearly working-class movement, it still failed to develop a coherent program. In the industrial areas of the country, Peronism resembled a European labor party, but elsewhere it was closer to being a Social Christian party, a Catholic nationalist organization, or, in many rural areas, simply a personal vehicle for the local caudillo.

For several years followng the overthrow of Perón, his movement was divided into two main sectors: a hard-line syndicalist group centered in Buenos Aires and its industrial suburbs and a soft-line or neo-Peronist group, whose strength was concentrated in several of the interior provinces. The former was by far the more important in terms of the number of votes it could deliver. Its leaders dominated the General Confederation of Labor (CGT) and its vast financial resources. Calling for nothing more than a return to the "good old days" of 1946–1955, the hard-line group played an essentially negative political role. It was vehemently opposed to both the Frondizi and Illia administrations and was overjoyed by the fall of each (even though neither the 1962 nor the 1966 coup worked to its immediate advantage).

The neo-Peronists formed an appreciably more moderate group. Without strong ties to the CGT, this sector of the Peronist movement was essentially a loose alliance of virtually autonomous provincial parties, most of which were more willing than their syndicalist counterparts to work within the system. The neo-Peronists showed a degree of independence from Perón, even to the extent that some of their leaders spoke of "Peronism without Perón." They lacked the class consciousness of the hard liners, and in many provinces the party was more personalist than ideological, with the personality involved often a local political leader, not Juan Perón. It should not be surprising that neo-Peronism tended to be strongest in the least-developed provinces, where caudilloism plays an important role in the political process.

Many neo-Peronist leaders accepted positions in the military government of 1966–1973, thus abdicating to the syndicalists the role of the Peronist opposition. However, at this time a far more significant cleavage within the Peronist movement became apparent; it pitted the working-class sector of the party (whether urban or rural) against the increasingly radical youth sector. One of the country's leading urban guerrilla groups, the Montoneros, was in effect the Peronist youth movement. Given a good deal of moral support by Perón (then in exile in Madrid), the Montoneros were quite useful to Peronism *as long as they were an opposition party*. Their bombings, kidnappings, and assassinations were instrumental in persuading the leaders of the armed forces to hold elections and return to civilian rule. That same Montonero movement was very much a thorn in the side of Peronism when it came to power. To most of the nation's union leaders, a Peronist election victory was first a means of attaining greater political power and second a means of raising the standard of living of their rank-and-file union members. To the Peronist youth, on the other hand, Perón's election was to be the beginning of a socialist revolution.

The bitterness of the labor-youth cleavage became apparent to all the day Perón returned from exile. Hundreds of thousands—perhaps a million—Argentines made their way to Ezeiza International Airport to cheer his return. However, shortly before his plane was scheduled to land a gun battle broke out between the labor and youth sectors. Twenty people were killed and hundreds wounded. There is still controversy over which side began the shooting, but the episode left no doubt as to how far each side would go to impose its brand of Peronism.

With the election of a Peronist president in March 1973, the Montoneros ceased, or at least drastically reduced, their terrorist activities. However, soon after Perón's inauguration in October, he openly sided with the trade-union sector of the movement. In 1975–1976 the Peronist youth movement was openly at war with the Peronist government—a war replete with atrocities by both sides.

With the death of Perón in 1974 and the overthrow and arrest of Isabel two years later, Peronism was left virtually leaderless. After Isabel was allowed to go into exile in Spain she remained completely aloof from the party's internal struggles; she even refused to take part in the process of nominating candidates for the 1983 elections. The selection of candidates for most major offices seems to have been dictated by a few Peronist labor leaders who must now assume responsibility for their defeat.

The Minor Parties

Completely dominant on the political scene prior to 1916 and again between 1932 and 1943, the Conservative party disintegrated rapidly during the first Peronist period. Although still an important force in two or three provinces, at the national level the Conservatives pose no electoral threat to the Radicals and Peronists. In 1983 there were two conservative presidential candidates, neither of whom received as much as 2 percent of the popular vote.

The Socialist party, which received a great deal of electoral support during the 1930s, when the Radicals were boycotting all elections, also lost most of its importance soon after Perón came to power. The Communist party has never been an important force at the polls; it made an enormous tactical error in the 1940s when it vehemently opposed Perón, who was considered simply another Fascist dictator. In the 1983 presidential election there were four Marxist candidates, none of whom received as much as 1 percent of the vote.

The Lack of a Loyal Opposition

Although political parties in Argentina are susceptible to indictment on a number of counts, the one that has proved especially detrimental to the political system is the failure to form a loyal opposition. Given the nature of the Argentine political system, which concentrates power in the hands of the president, the losing parties seldom have accepted electoral defeat as definitive. To accept defeat at the polls and agree to act as a loyal opposition would have meant almost complete impotence for at least six years. Thus opposition parties traditionally have turned to other means of attaining power, most often a military coup. If the leaders of the armed forces could be convinced of the necessity to overthrow the government, the opposition parties might be able to gain power in the revolutionary government, or failing in this, they might fare better in new elections—especially if the party overthrown was denied participation at the polls.

All of Argentina's military governments have been supported, at least initially, by most of the major parties in opposition to the deposed government. In many instances, opposition parties were also active in revolutionary conspiracies. Generally speaking, only the party removed from power has condemned the armed forces for breaking the constitutional order; the other parties have praised the removal of an "illegitimate" regime. In 1930 the Conservatives, unable to win honest elections, supported the coup that deposed Yrigoyen and soon inherited the government. The Radicals applauded the 1943 coup and moved into the opposition only when they realized that the military was not going to install them in power. Both Conservatives and Radicals were deeply involved in plots against the Peronist government, and each supported the revolutionary government. After the Peronist electoral victories in 1962, the Radicals might have been able to save the Frondizi administration by agreeing to serve in a coalition government; instead, they joined the chorus of those demanding that Frondizi resign. Frondicistas reciprocated four years later when they were influential in persuading the military to depose the Radical government. The single important exception to this rule came in 1974 and 1975 when the Radicals, and especially their leader, Ricardo Balbín, played a very responsible opposition role, thus helping to forestall, temporarily, the overthrow of Isabel Perón.

The Armed Forces

With regard to the armed forces, the major questions to be answered are, What sorts of political roles do they play? Why have they become so deeply involved in politics? and Why have they been so unsuccessful in governing the country?

Types of Political Activity

The political activity of the Argentine armed forces has not been limited to deposing civilian presidents. One can discern four distinct political roles played by the military during this century: (1) a simple pressure group with limited objectives (1922–1930, 1932–1943, 1963–1966, and 1973–1976); (2) a governmental partner or, as many put it, "a cogovernment" (1946–1955 and 1966–1970); (3) a wielder of veto power (1958–1962); and (4) a national ruler (1930–1932, 1943–1946, 1955–1958, 1962–1963, 1970–1973, and 1976–1983).

When the military establishment has acted as a simple pressure group, its behavior has not placed great strain on the stability of the political system; its goals have been limited in scope, and its demands have dealt almost exclusively with military affairs. The armed forces played a more forceful role during the Perón and Onganía administrations, when they served as a partner of the government. In each government, the president was a retired army officer dependent to a great extent, but not exclusively, on the support of the military. During the Frondizi administration, the armed forces seem not to have actually formulated policy but rather to have insisted that major presidential policy decisions be submitted to the leaders of the armed forces for their approval. The last role is that of actually running the country. What factors lead the military leaders to take this most drastic final step?

Major Causes of Military Coups

The Argentine armed forces are frequently accused of assuming control of the government to maintain the status quo and to prevent any meaningful change, yet the reasons given by military leaders for their revolutionary actions rarely include complaints about the major policy decisions of the deposed governments. Instead of being criticized for their actions, these governments are more frequently criticized for their lack of action. It is impossible to find a single factor to explain any of Argentina's coups, much less all of them. Nevertheless, there are three or four factors that collectively help explain most of the coups.

Contributing to the first three military coups was the manner in which the government dealt with the armed forces. Particularly unacceptable was political interference in what the military considered its internal affairs. For example, both Yrigoyen and Perón promoted officers with little regard for military regulations such as time in grade; they also rewarded military personnel for past services and promised further benefits for future services. Frondizi was accused of playing off one faction or branch of the armed services against another and of capitulating to officers who were in rebellion against civilian and military authorities while disciplining those who were attempting to maintain legality. It is more than slightly ironic that this sort of action angered precisely the segment of the military that ordinarily would be most inclined to support constitutional government.

In the case of each military coup, the leaders of the armed forces claimed that they simply acceded to popular demands. It is true that all deposed presidents have faced widespread civilian opposition, and at the time of the coups, only one, Perón, had any appreciable popular support (and his support was very definitely on the decline). An important feature of this opposition is that its leaders have not been willing to await its manifestation at the polls but instead have gone to the military in an effort to convince it of the necessity of revolution. As one Argentine sociologist put it, "Although they must all deny it publicly, Argentine politicians cannot ignore the fact that at one time or another during the past quarter century they have gone to knock at the doors of the barracks."[7]

Within all but possibly the last of the revolutionary governments, there has been a group of military leaders intent on changing the very nature of the political system. Many of those responsible for the 1930 coup were interested in replacing liberal democracy with some form of corporatism; in 1943, several army colonels wanted to establish a neofascist state; in 1966, there was near unanimity among military leaders that the political system had to be modified substantially; and in 1955 and 1962, several military leaders were intent on not only eliminating Peronism as a political force but changing the system that had allowed the rise of Peronism.

The last four coups have, to varying degrees, been a result of anti-Peronism. When first inaugurated in 1946, Perón certainly had the support of most of the leaders of the armed forces; however, by 1951 this support had begun to wane, and in 1955 it was the military that forced his removal from office. The first source of friction between the two seems to have been Perón's wife Evita. As the illegitimate child of a poor provincial family and later a radio and movie actress, she was not considered fit to be the wife of a high-ranking army officer, much less a president; her openly antimilitary attitude did not improve the situation. Another source of friction was the extreme anticlerical stance taken by Perón in 1954 and 1955. Legalization of divorce, abrogation of religious instruction in the public schools, and the jailing and deportation of clergymen caused divided loyalties in the Catholic officer group. After 1952, when economic problems forced Perón to abandon his nationalistic posture, he lost the support of those military men who had been attracted by his economic nationalism. Also, government corruption during the Perón administration became so rampant that it began to cast suspicion on the honesty of the armed forces, which have always been eager to protect their reputation.

Above all, the major source of friction almost certainly was Perón's relationship with the organized labor movement. Many upper-middle-class military personnel were never prolabor (although certainly they were not opposed to using the labor movement for their ends). The conflict intensified in the early 1950s when the CGT adopted an increasingly arrogant attitude toward the armed forces. Particularly galling was the fact that the CGT managed to have the death penalty reinserted into the Code of Military Justice. The last straw came in 1955 when Perón appeared to be considering the establishment of armed workers' militias.

Military opposition to Peronism during the last quarter century has been based partly on the fear that a return of the Peronists to power would mean a resurrection of the issues mentioned earlier. Military anti-Peronism became self-perpetuating. The bitterly anti-Peronist generals of 1955 were responsible for promoting the next generation of generals, and so on; many officers must have feared that a relaxation of their anti-Peronism would leave them open to widespread purges by their fellow officers or by the Peronists, should they return to power. Still, the most important reason for the anti-Peronism of the leaders of the armed forces between 1950 and 1970 was an unwillingness to accept any regime with power to deprive the military of its role as an arbiter or to eliminate it as *the* decisive power factor. Only Peronism, with its mass following centered around organized labor, was a potential threat to the continued hegemony of the armed forces.

There is one additional factor to be mentioned as a rationale for military intervention. This is the new national-security doctrine. National security is thought of as not only connected to but also *dependent on* economic development. Although there is some disagreement on what form economic development should take, there is a broad consensus that it must involve total industrialization. Since the maintenance of national security is clearly the responsibility of the armed forces and since national security is conceived of as an unobtainable objective without economic development, it is a short step to the conclusion that if civilian governments are not doing an adequate job in this realm it is the duty of the armed forces to assume responsibility for economic development. Many military leaders are willing to go a step further and claim that the military is uniquely qualified to direct the development process. According to this perspective, not only does the military have the necessary hierarchical organization and discipline, it is, unlike most civilian groups, not tied to any specific economic interest and thus is able to represent the interests of the nation as a whole. (In this connection, it is frequently pointed out that the armed forces have done a better job of developing the steel industry than the state corporation has done developing the petroleum industry.)

Factionalism and the Failure of Military Regimes

Ever since 1930, when the armed forces became deeply involved in the nation's political life, the military has been plagued by the existence of antagonistic ideological factions. The problem seems most serious (and certainly most obvious) following military coups. Lack of agreement within the armed forces as to goals and the means of achieving them severely limits the ability of a military regime to carry out a coherent program.

In 1930, one group of officers thought of the military coup simply as a means of removing an inefficient, corrupt administration and of returning the government to more responsible elements—meaning the Conservatives; another group looked on the coup as the beginning of a revolution that would replace liberal democracy with a neofascist corporate state. Following the 1943 coup, a group of young ultranationalistic officers looked at the urban working class as a group capable of legitimating a revolutionary regime; a far more conservative faction was as opposed to such a military-labor alliance as to the civilian administration just deposed. After the overthrow of Perón in 1955, military leaders were separated only by the degree of their anti-Peronism. In 1962 and 1963, the extreme anti-Peronists and their somewhat more moderate opponents within the armed forces quite literally went to war. The first battle, involving only army units, was won by the moderates, who immediately imprisoned or forcibly retired their opponents; the next year they put down an attempted putsch by the navy, whose leaders were almost uniformly extremists. As a result of the second battle all the nation's admirals were forced into retirement, and the Naval Marine Corps was reduced to nearly insignificant size. The military regime of 1976–1983 appears to have been less subject to factionalism than its predecessors; nevertheless, the palace coups of 1981 and 1982 show that something less than complete consensus reigned within the armed forces.

The Labor Movement

Throughout much of Latin America, organized labor has recently attained a position of some political importance; this is especially true in Argentina, where the labor movement is very large, relatively wealthy, quite well organized, and thoroughly politicized. The leader of a large union in Argentina is almost automatically considered a prominent national politician; the secretary-general of the CGT holds potential political power equal to that of a major political party leader. This political prominence of the labor movement is a relatively recent phenomenon, and thus before examining the current political role of labor it is necessary to review the development of the movement.

Tomás R. Fillol has written that "the history of Argentine trade unions is largely an account of internal strife, of disunity, struggle and rancor."[8] Prior to the mid-1940s, this internal struggle was among the anarchists, syndicalists, socialists, and Communists, who all had radically different ideas about the ultimate goals of the labor movement and the proper means of attaining those goals. In the decade 1945–1955, organized labor was relatively well united under Peronist control, but with the fall of Perón the movement split once again.

Before 1910, the dominant ideological faction within the union movement was that of the anarchists, who looked upon political authority as unnecessary and undesirable. Preferring solidarity strikes, general walkouts, and sabotage to negotiation, the anarchists resorted frequently to violence and assassination. Largely because of government repression, the anarchists lost control of the labor movement in 1910, and for the next quarter century dominance passed into the hands of the syndicalists. Theoretically apolitical, Argentine syndicalists accepted the Marxist analysis of class struggle but denounced political action on the part of the proletariat. About 1935, control of the labor movement passed into the hands of the socialists, who differed from the anarchists and syndicalists in that they were willing to work within the existing political system; they insisted that improvement of the conditions of the working class could be attained by legislative action.

The development of an effective union movement was opposed not only by employers but by the government. Prior to 1916, both looked on unions as inherently subversive. This attitude changed somewhat after the Radicals came to power. Yrigoyen protected both the right to organize and the right to strike, but the UCR had no specific labor program and very little labor legislation was enacted. The administrations of the second Conservative era (1930–1943) were somewhat less hostile toward labor than their predecessors of 1862–1916, probably because by this time the labor movement was under the control of socialists willing to abide by the rules of the game. During this period some labor legislation was enacted, largely through the initiative of Socialist deputies, but the Conservative governments were quite willing to look the other way when employers ignored it.

A great deal changed during the 1943–1955 period. For the first time the labor movement had an ardent supporter in the government. Perón began his appeal to the workers as secretary of labor in the 1943–1946 government and continued it throughout his term as president. Wages, fringe benefits, and working conditions all improved appreciably; however, none of this was the result of pressure from below but instead was essentially a gift from Perón. The price paid by the labor movement was near total subservience to Perón. The Labor party was dissolved; non-Peronist unions were subjected to government intervention; and personal friends of the president were appointed to the top positions in the CGT. The constitution of the CGT was amended to declare that the fundamental purpose of the organization was to support Perón and to carry out his policies.[9] The labor movement benefited considerably during the Peronist administration, but given the means by which these benefits were obtained, they were certain to cease when Perón was overthrown.

Shortly after that happened, the military government intervened in all the nation's unions, replacing Peronist leaders with military men. However, when union elections finally were allowed, a majority of the unions reverted to Peronist leadership; a few were captured by the Communists, while others elected radical, socialist, or anarchist leaders as they had in the pre-Perón period. These political sectors soon came to be called by the number of union elections won at this time: The 62 organizations referred to the Peronist-dominated group; the 19 was the Communist group; and the 32 was the non-Communist, anti-Peronist sector. Most of the unions of white-collar workers (*empleados*), such as the commercial employees and government workers, belonged to the 32, while those of blue-collar workers (*obreros*)—the metallurgical and textile workers, for example—most often affiliated with the 62.

In 1963, the General Confederation of Labor held its first national convention since the fall of Perón. At this time, the Peronists regained effective control of the national apparatus of the trade-union movement; however, this was also when the 62 began to experience internal dissension. A so-called orthodox faction, unconditionally loyal to Perón, was in violent opposition to the administrations of Presidents Frondizi and Illia. A more moderate group, while claiming loyalty to Perón, preferred negotiation over open confrontation with the government. Also at about this time, the conflict between the Peronist and non-Peronist unions intensified, further diluting the political strength of the union movement.

The methods employed by the Argentine labor movement have varied a great deal, depending largely on two things: the ideological faction in control of the labor movement and the type of government in power. During the period of anarcho-syndicalist domination, when the national government considered the very idea of labor organization as subversive, there was an attempt by labor to destroy the state completely with general strikes, widespread violence, and assassination. During the period of socialist control, when the national administrations were less hostile to labor, emphasis was placed on legislative enactment, which failed almost as completely as had the violence of the earlier period. Between 1943 and 1955, when the government was openly sympathetic to the aspirations of labor, there was almost exclusive reliance on the good will of the president. Since that period, labor has been badly split ideologically, giving rise to a number of different political methods.

Following the 1943 revolution, labor began to flex its muscles at the polls. In the presidential elections of 1946, 1951, and 1973, the bulk of the Peronist votes came from the urban working class. Labor provided much of the margin of victory in 1958 and 1963. In 1958, the workers voted en masse for Frondizi—in accordance with the orders of Perón, and in 1963 a large number of workers voted for Illia in an attempt to defeat General Aramburu. After the overthrow of Perón in 1955, the electoral strength of labor lost much of its significance as the armed forces refused to permit Peronism any opportunity to regain executive power. Thus while the votes of labor certainly were influential in 1958 and 1963, the workers were forced to choose between lesser evils, as Peronist candidates were prohibited. In 1962, when the Peronists were given full electoral freedom, their victories were ephemeral, since they led to a military coup and an annulment of the election results. With its electoral strength thus virtually nullified, the labor movement was forced to turn to other means of political expression.

Labor attempted to intimidate President Frondizi by means of a number of politically motivated strikes and sporadic violence; however, the 1964 Plan de Lucha is the best example of post-1955 political bargaining. Shortly after his inauguration, Illia was faced with labor demonstrations, inflammatory public speeches, and a general strike. Then in May 1964, the executive committee of the CGT decided to adopt a plan of systematic seizure of industrial plants. The country was divided into eight zones, each of which was subjected to a twenty-four-hour demonstration of labor's ability to seize control of the sources of industrial production. Within a month, eleven thousand plants were occupied by over 3 million workers.

The ostensible purpose of the Plan de Lucha was to show labor's disapproval of the economic policies of the Illia administration. In actuality, its basic goal was to demonstrate the government's intrinsic weakness and to invite a military coup. The nation's labor leaders hoped the government would react either by applying massive repression, thus making martyrs of the workers, or by doing nothing. President Illia chose the latter course, refusing to call out the army to dislodge workers from the factories. Under different conditions, this might have been the proper response; however, in the Argentina of 1964 it satisfied no one. It failed to placate labor, it angered the business and industrial community, and it infuriated the leaders of the armed forces.

The military governments of 1966–1973 were harassed by the labor movement in much the same manner, although less successfully. When Perón returned to power in 1973, organized labor was once again rewarded for its support, but certainly not to the extent it had been between 1943 and 1955. Following the 1976 military coup the government intervened in all the nation's larger unions, not only removing the elected leaders but also barring them from future election. And, once again, the unions split on the question of how best to deal with a military government.

Other Groups

The Church and Catholic Lay Groups

Throughout most of Latin America, nineteenth-century politics was dominated by a bitter conflict over the proper relationship between

Church and state, as the original cleavage between Conservative and Liberal political parties was in large part a conflict between Catholic and anticlerical forces. Such was not the case in Argentina, where relations between Church and state were relatively serene until the 1880s when religious instruction in the public schools was abolished and civil wedding ceremonies required. These laws were bitterly resented by the Church and by many of the country's more devout Catholics, who formed a very short-lived confessional party. This party was completely unsuccessful at the polls, and religious issues soon disappeared from the political agenda.

It was not until 1943 that religious issues again attained a degree of political importance. In December, the military government reestablished religious instruction in the public schools. This and other similar measures led the Church to support not only the revolutionary government but its candidate—Juan Perón—in the presidential election of 1946. Shortly before the election, a pastoral letter forbade Catholics to vote for candidates who supported separation of Church and state, secular education, or legalization of divorce. Since Perón's single opponent was in favor of all these items, the nation's Catholics were told, in effect, to vote for Perón or to stay home on election day. In what turned out to be a relatively close election, it is quite possible that the Church swung enough votes to put Perón in office.

Although Perón had the near total support of the Church in 1946, by 1951 its position had changed to neutrality and by 1955 to complete opposition. By 1955, the Perón administration had legalized divorce and prostitution and discontinued religious instruction in the schools. Also, a number of churches were sacked and several clergymen imprisoned. In June 1955, Perón was excommunicated by Pope Pius XII. Since that time the Argentine Church as an institution has remained relatively aloof from partisan politics. However, this behavior does not carry over to all Catholic groups.

One organization of Argentine clergymen that has attracted a great deal of attention is the Movement of Third World Priests. In mid-1967, eighteen bishops from several nations issued a statement entitled "A Message from Bishops of the Third World." Stating that the primary duty of the Church is to aid the poor and the oppressed, this document called for the immediate implementation of the encyclical *Populorum Progressio*. This statement was immediately countersigned by 270 Argentine priests, who soon thereafter formed the Movement of Third World Priests. This group called for a Latin American brand of socialism (without explaining exactly what it meant). The Third World Priests supported peasant organizations, union demonstrations, and strikes and were accused of aiding, if not taking part in, terrorist organizations.

During the last half century, a number of extreme nationalist organizations have been founded by militant Catholics who tend to equate liberalism with anticlericalism. The Argentine Catholic nationalists are especially opposed to formal structures of liberal democracy such as political parties and legislative bodies. The alternative they propose is most frequently referred to as communitarianism, which is essentially Catholic corporatism similar to that described in the encyclicals *Rerum Novarum* and *Divini Redemptorus.* Communitarianism is based on the assumption that society is not a cluster of individuals or social classes but instead an organic body composed of natural parts that must cooperate for the good of the whole. Thus politics should not be organized on the basis of participation by individuals, political parties, or social classes—for this will lead to conflict, anarchy, and class warfare—but on the basis of confederations of workers and employers in each branch of economic activity. Catholic nationalist organizations have been most prominent and influential during the military governments of 1930, 1943, 1955, and 1966. They have not been able to attain any appreciable popular support however, and have been of negligible importance during periods of civilian rule.

The only Catholic political party to attain any real significance was the Christian Democratic party, founded in 1956. Although it elected a few congressional representatives in 1963 and 1965, the party was never able to obtain as much as 5 percent of the national vote. Roughly two-thirds of its votes came from women, most of whom appear to have been members of the upper and upper-middle classes. In 1973, the Christian Democrats split into separate parties: One supported Perón; the other joined the Communists and some Intransigent Radicals in a coalition of the moderate left. In 1983 a reunited party elected only one congressman.

Economic Groups

It is much easier to identify those economic groups that possess considerable political authority than it is to explain exactly how much authority is exercised and by what means. Most students of Argentine politics would agree that there are three associational groups of landowners, business people, and industrialists that traditionally have influenced the course of Argentine politics: the Rural Society, the Argentine Industrial Union (UIA), and the General Economic Confederation (CGE).

Since its fonding in 1866, the Rural Society has spoken for the nation's largest and wealthiest agricultural interests. Although no longer quite as elite an organization as formerly, it still has only about ten thousand members, including almost all the rural elite of the pampas. The potential influence of the Rural Society may be seen in the fact that during the course of the last century, most ministers of agriculture have come from its ranks. The minister of economics between 1976 and 1981, previously minister of agriculture, was a former president of the Rural Society, as were his father and great-uncle; his great-grandfather was one of the founders and the first president of the organization.

There are two important associations of industrialists and business people. The older and more powerful of the two is the UIA, founded in 1887. It tends to represent the nation's largest industries, especially those centered in and around Buenos Aires. The CGE, founded in 1951, represents the smaller businesses and industries of the capital and interior provinces. Very much committed to free trade policies, the UIA was bitterly opposed to the first Perón administration, which allowed it very little political influence. The CGE enjoyed a good deal of political say from the time of its formation until Perón was overthrown; it then suffered a dramatic decline in power until 1973 when the Peronists returned to power and it became the official spokesman for the business community.

Guerrilla Movements

Argentina's first guerrilla movements began operations in isolated rural areas of the northwest in the early 1960s; however, the rural guerrillas were never much of a menace and were rather quickly wiped out by the nation's security forces. A much more serious threat was the urban guerrilla movements that came to prominence about 1970. There were a large number of such groups, but by far the most important were the Montoneros and the People's Revolutionary Army (ERP).

The Montonero group was organized in 1968 by a number of young Peronists who saw in Peronism a means of national liberation within a neo-Marxist framework. The Montoneros first gained widespread attention in June 1970 when they kidnaped Pedro Aramburu, president from 1955 to 1958. In a series of well-publicized communiqués, it was announced that Aramburu had been tried, convicted, and executed for crimes against the Argentine people; his crimes were evidently the anti-Peronist measures taken while he was provisional president.

The ERP was the armed wing of the Trotskyite Revolutionary Workers party (PRT). Formed in 1970, the ERP was active in kidnappings and assassinations. Among its more prominent assassination victims were an army general, two navy admirals, the president of Fiat, and a secretary-general of the General Confederation of Labor. An enormous sum of money has been paid to ransom several ERP kidnapping victims; Esso allegedly paid more than US$14 million for the return of one of its executives, and a large landowner may have paid much more than that for the return of his sons.

The ideologies of these two groups were extremely eclectic. That of the Montoneros was a curious blend of Marxism, Catholicism, and Peronism. The ERP claimed to have taken from Lenin its ideas on the vanguard party, from Trotsky the concept of permanent revolution, from Mao the idea of a party army, and from Che Guevara the belief that the objective conditions for revolution can be created. Despite their common desire to overthrow the government, to destroy the liberal, capitalist system, and to create some form of national socialism, the Montoneros and the ERP were unable completely to coordinate their actions because of strategic differences and differing attitudes toward

Juan Perón and Peronism. The Montoneros were ardent supporters of Perón until 1973 when he openly sided with their opponents in the labor movement; even then, they found it very difficult to attack the government as long as Perón was president. The ERP, on the other hand, never identified with Peronism and thus was not as confused by Perón's adoption of an essentially rightist stance upon his return to power.

During the administrations of Juan and Isabel Perón, right-wing terrorist groups entered the fray. The best known of them was the Argentine Anticommunist Alliance (AAA), which assassinated a number of leftists, including politicians, intellectuals, and union leaders.

Following the 1976 coup the role of the AAA was assumed by groups organized by, or actually part of, the government. In the so-called dirty war the armed forces themselves adopted terrorist tactics, and by 1979 antiregime terrorism was virtually at an end.

The Role of the United States

Many people are convinced that the United States plays an important role in Argentine politics. This may be true, but it is extremely difficult to demonstrate. Private investments from the United States amount to about US$1 billion (roughly two-thirds of it in manufacturing), and this is almost half the total foreign investment in Argentina.[10] Still, it is virtually impossible to determine the degree of political influence exercised by the U.S. business community. Most U.S. business enterprises in Argentina are affiliated with the Argentine Industrial Union, and it is probably through the UIA that their interests are articulated, although from time to time they may use diplomatic channels.

The amount of political influence exerted by the U.S. government is likewise difficult to measure. In those few cases where it is known that the U.S. government attempted to influence the course of events in Argentina, the results were quite unsuccessful. The most blatant intervention (and also the best known) occurred during the 1946 election campaign. Spruille Braden, the U.S. ambassador to Argentina, made a series of speeches denouncing the military government and most of its officials. Later, when Braden became assistant secretary of state, he continued his scathing denunciations of Perón; and then just two weeks before the election, he issued a Blue Book calling Perón a "Nazi-fascist." This attempt to destroy Perón's bid for the presidency was a marked failure. Equally unsuccessful was the effort of the U.S. Embassy to prevent the military coup of 1966.

The preceding paragraphs should not be taken to mean that the United States plays no role in Argentine politics, but rather that the role played is largely covert and thus difficult to assess. It may well be that the more U.S. influence is hidden from public view the more successful it is, for no Argentine government, whether civilian or military, Radical or Peronist, can afford to be thought of as subservient to foreign interests.

GOVERNMENT MACHINERY
AND THE ROLE OF THE STATE

The organizational structure and formal powers of most governmental institutions in Argentina closely resemble their counterparts in the United States. Political authority is divided between a national government and twenty-two semiautonomous provinces, each of which has a constitution that allocates power among the various branches of the provincial government. At the national level, there is a president chosen for a fixed term of office by an electoral college, a bicameral congress composed of a senate and a chamber of deputies, and a judiciary headed by a supreme court. Nevertheless, in practice there is a great deal of difference between the two countries.

To begin with, Argentina has long been a highly centralized state. Ever since the federal district was created in 1880, there has been near total hegemony on the part of the national government, which now dominates the allegedly autonomous provinces both politically and financially.

All the constitutional provisions to ensure provincial autonomy are easily negated by the power of the national government to intervene in any province to guarantee a republican form of government. Since it is the national government itself that is empowered to define republicanism, this means that the national government may assume total control of a province at any time; however, more often than not, the mere threat of intervention is sufficient to obtain provincial compliance.

As was mentioned earlier, the only major source of government income during most of the nineteenth century was the import and export duties collected at the Buenos Aires port. With the nationalization of Buenos Aires, that revenue was monopolized by the national government. Then, with the passage of time, Buenos Aires became the commercial and industrial center of the nation, further increasing the disparity of wealth between that city and the remainder of the nation. For at least half a century, the provincial governments have been dependent upon financial assistance from the national government. Because the provinces have lacked political and fiscal autonomy, decision making has come to be concentrated almost exclusively in the federal capital.

The centralization of authority does not stop there, for within the national government the president holds most power. Except for a brief period between 1912 and 1930, the Congress has not played a major political role. Before 1912, the Congress was a preserve of the conservatives, who appear to have seen their function as that of rubber-stamping the proposals of the chief executive. Decisions tended to be made by the president and a small group of friends and advisers; some of the members of this group may have been congressional representatives, but it was their socioeconomic status that made them members of the political elite, not the offices they held. Between 1912 and 1930, the

Congress did gain a degree of political influence. After the election of Radical and Socialist representatives to the Congress, it became an open arena for conflict and, to a lesser extent, for conflict resolution. This short-lived situation ended with the 1930 revolution. By the late 1930s, "representative institutions like the Congress were discredited and useless."[11] Once again it was the president who was almost completely dominant.

The Argentine judiciary has never played a prominent political role. Although possessing the power of judicial review, the Supreme Court has used considerable restraint in its exercise. Like its U.S. counterpart, it has always refused to hear political questions, and it has defined as *political* any issue that might lead to a major conflict with the executive branch—a conflict that all justices realize they would certainly lose. Damaging to both the power and the prestige of the court is the fact that in spite of constitutional guarantees of life tenure for its members there were major purges in 1946, 1955, 1966, and 1976. Also detrimental to its public image is its tradition of formally recognizing the de facto status of revolutionary governments. (In fact, during periods of military rule, the court seems to limit itself to an attempt to protect individual liberties.) Although it would be an overstatement to claim that the Argentine judiciary has no political power, it is certainly true that the courts are exceptionally weak in comparison to the president and even in comparison to their counterparts in the United States.

Political power, then, is concentrated to an enormous degree in the hands of a single individual, the president of the Argentine Republic. This is a situation well understood not just by politically active groups and individuals but also by the average citizen (who quite frequently refers to the president as the government). In a presidentialist system such as this, where the president is considered both omnipotent and all responsible, there is a tendency for all political demands to be brought to him (or, between 1974 and 1976, to her). Those speaking for most groups are well aware that the president can meet their demands by issuing an executive decree, by bringing pressure to bear on the bureaucracy, or, if necessary, by obtaining the enactment of legislation by the Congress.

The president is constantly faced with a range of demands that far exceed the resources at his disposal and by sets of demands that are mutually incompatible. It is the president who must decide which to grant and which to deny. Most politically active groups, unwilling to leave this decision entirely to presidential discretion, back up their demands with threats. Wheat farmers may threaten to cut down on the number of acres planted, or cattle raisers to slaughter their breeding stock, thus reducing the exportable surplus and aggravating the balance-of-payments problem; students may threaten violent antigovernment demonstrations, or the General Confederation of Labor a general strike. And, since the military is best equipped to threaten the president, many groups try to find a sector of the armed forces willing to articulate their demands. Since the participants in this game assume, probably correctly, that the president will accede only to those demands accompanied by the most dire threats, the level of the threats is ever increasing.

In such a situation, the president becomes powerful only in comparison to other individuals and institutions within the government. The government itself, buffeted by a myriad of unsatisfied (and in large part unsatisfiable) demands, is relegated to a position of weakness.

This position of relative governmental weakness is somewhat paradoxical considering that the state traditionally has played a very active role in Argentina. In the realm of economics, for example, the state performs a multitude of functions. It is actively involved in the collective-bargaining process, even to the point that in recent years the General Confederation of Labor bargained first with the labor ministry, with the barganing between individual unions and industries proceeding only after general guidelines had been established. Foreign trade is controlled to a great extent through the use of a complicated multiple exchange rate; and for a while during the first Peronist administration, foreign trade was monopolized by a government agency. The state is responsible for the licensing of all professions, for the legal recognition of political parties and trade unions, and so forth. It was actively engaged in the political mobilization of the working class during the late 1940s and in an attempted demobilization during the late 1960s and 1970s. The concept of limited government, so dear to the hearts of the framers of the U.S. constitution, is virtually unknown in Argentina, where the state is considered virtually all responsible.

PUBLIC POLICY

Given the preceding discussion of Argentine politics, it should not be surprising that there has been relatively little continuity of public policy in Argentina, especially during the last sixty years or so. This is largely because major political issues have usually been defined by the administration in power. Prior to 1916, the Conservatives were intent upon creating a modern nation, and most public policies were a means of attaining that aim. On the other hand, between 1916 and 1930 the Radicals appear to have had no clearly defined goals and thus no consistent policies. Policies seem to have been ad hoc reactions to events rather than part of an overall framework. Although the Yrigoyen administration was often prolabor, in 1919 the army was used to put down a strike of the metal workers; the 1918 university reform was not a part of a larger educational policy, but was simply a reaction to a student strike. Such examples could go on indefinitely. Everything changed back when the Conservatives regained power in 1932. Once more, public policies appear to have been aimed at a single goal, but this time that goal was the protection of the economic interests of the landowning elite.

During the first Peronist period (1946–1955), public policy was designed primarily to maintain working-class support. There was a dramatic redistribution of income, with the percentage of gross national product going for wages and salaries increasing from 45 percent to almost 60 percent.[12] However, except in relative terms this shift was quite painless for the nation's economic elite, for the bulk of the increase in wages was a result of the government's spending most of the credits built up during World War II, when Argentina had a favorable balance of trade. Rather than investing this money in an industrialization process, the government used it to raise the standard of living of the working class without appreciably reducing the standard of living of the middle and upper classes.

A concerted policy of industrialization, especially the creation of heavy industry, did not come until the administration of Arturo Frondizi. Lacking domestic capital sufficient for the massive scope of industrialization envisioned, Frondizi was forced to seek foreign investment (even in the previously sacrosanct realm of petroleum) and to borrow large sums of money from international lending agencies. Some of the strings attached to loans by the International Monetary Fund reversed the income redistribution that had taken place during the Perón administration, although this was not intended by the government. Despite extensive planning and four years of concerted effort, not a great deal of progress was made; in 1962, total industrial production was not appreciably greater than in 1958. The economic policy priorities of Frondizi were turned upside down during the Illia administration (1963–1966), which seemed unconcerned with industrialization and instead tried to stimulate agricultural production (an area virtually ignored by Frondizi).

When Perón returned to power in 1973, the Social Pact became the keystone of economic policy. The Social Pact was an attempt to obtain both labor (CGT) and management (CGE) approval for a very general policy to increase production, reduce unemployment, and raise wages and profits—while maintaining social harmony. There was an initial wage increase and a freeze on many prices, with the understanding that future wages and prices would be determined by a commission representing the General Confederation of Labor, the General Economic Confederation, and the government. The social harmony did not last long, as an ever increasing inflation rate soon destroyed any possibility of labor-management cooperation.

The military administrations of 1976–1983 returned to a liberal, free market economy, with emphasis upon increased foreign investment. Such a policy was clearly something less than a panacea and the return to civilian government almost certainly will mean a more statist economic policy.

More interesting perhaps than the policies adopted by recent administrations are those that appear to have never seriously been discussed. For example, in spite of the nation's dependence on agricultural exports and the concentration of landownership in relatively few hands, agrarian reform has never been a major political issue. Also, although there has long been a quite visible foreign sector in banking and manufacturing, nationalization seems never to have been seriously considered. In fact, between 1966 and 1973, and again between 1976 and 1983, the trend was toward denationalization—that is, the sale of domestic firms to foreigners. This denationalization almost certainly will be stopped, and perhaps reversed by the Alfonsín administration.

FUTURE PROSPECTS

During the last few months of 1983 and the first few months of 1984 the general mood in Argentina was one of optimism. On the evening of October 30, long before the final results of the election were known, the streets of Buenos Aires were full of celebrating crowds. Many of those celebrating were Radicals who were reasonably sure that Alfonsín had won, but many more were simply celebrating the end of military rule and the return to constitutional government. One wondered if these celebrators believed that the elections in and of themselves had, or would, solve all the nation's problems.

During his first two months in office Alfonsín appears to have lost very little of the support he enjoyed at the time of his inauguration. In a poll taken in February 1984 Argentines were asked to evaluate the government's performance during its first sixty days. "Good" or "very good" was the response of 58 percent of those polled, while only 8 percent responded "poor" or "very poor." In what must have been a pleasant surprise for Alfonsín, the response of unskilled workers, most of whom one would have thought to be Peronists, was 50 percent "good" or "very good" versus 6 percent "poor" or "very poor."[13]

Potential future problems with the Congress came to light in March 1984, when the government's first major legislative proposal failed to gain passage. The Union Democratization bill, which called for government supervision of almost immediate elections in all the nation's unions, passed the Chamber of Deputies, but failed by a very narrow margin in the Senate. Unfortunately, this could well become the norm for major legislation proposed by Alfonsín. Although the Radicals have only a bare majority in the lower house (129 of the 254 seats), there are another 6 to 8 minor party members who can be expected to side with the president far more often than not. The composition of the upper house is far less favorable; in it there are 18 Radicals, 21 Peronists, and 7 members of minor parties, only 2 of whom can be counted on to support the administration. Assuming that the Peronists vote as a bloc, as they almost certainly will on many issues, they need the support of only 3 of the minor party senators to block legislation.

Even if Alfonsín can manage to put together a relatively stable majority coalition in the Senate, he must then weather important elections in 1985 and 1987. In 1985 half of the membership of the lower house of congress will be renewed, and without executive elections to polarize the voters, the nation's minor parties are almost certain to increase their representation in the Chamber of Deputies. Unless Alfonsín has by that time made enormous progress on the economic front, he is likely to lose his majority in that body. In 1987 the other half of the deputies will be chosen, as will most provincial governors. Major losses in either of these elections would be hailed by Alfonsín's opponents as a public repudiation of his administration; it could also set the stage for still another military coup.

* * *

In the first edition, this chapter closed on a quite pessimistic note:

It is, of course, exceptionally difficult to forecast with any degree of accuracy the political future of any nation; however, it may not be as difficult in the case of Argentina as with most nations. In fact, it seems relatively simple to predict that during the next several years (or decades) Argentine politics will resemble that of the past few decades. At least since 1955, and some would say since 1930, instability has been the dominant feature of the political system, and there is no reason to believe that such will not continue to be the case.

Six years later, it is still difficult for a foreign observer to be optimistic; however, it may be that a lesser degree of pessimism is now appropriate.

NOTES

1. Samuel P. Huntington, *Political Order in Changing Societies* (Yale University Press, New Haven, Conn., 1968), p. 4.

2. This is almost exactly the situation Huntington describes in *Political Order*, p. 196.

3. David Rock, *Politics in Argentina, 1890–1930: The Rise and Fall of Radicalism* (Cambridge University Press, London, 1975), p. 11.

4. Carlos F. Díaz Alejandro, *Essays on the Economic History of the Argentine Republic* (Yale University Press, New Haven, Conn., 1970), p. 95.

5. Roberto Carri, *Sindicatos y poder en la Argentina* (Editorial Sudestada, Buenos Aires, 1967), p. 27.

6. Peter Smith, "Los radicales argentinos y la defensa de los intereses ganaderos, 1916–1930," *Desarrollo Económico* 7 (April-June 1967):826.

7. José Luis de Imaz, "Los que mandan: Las fuerzas armadas en la Argentina," *América Latina* 7 (October-December 1964):68.

8. Tomás Roberto Fillol, *Social Factors in Economic Development: The Argentine Case* (MIT Press, Cambridge, Mass., 1961), p. 76.

9. Robert J. Alexander, *Organized Labor in Latin America* (Free Press, New York, 1965), p. 36.

10. Juan Eugenio Corradi, "Argentina," in *Latin America: The Struggle with Dependency and Beyond*, ed. Ronald H. Chilcote and Joel Edelstein (Schenkman, Cambridge, Mass., 1974), p. 406.

11. Peter H. Smith, *Politics and Beef in Argentina: Patterns of Conflict and Change* (Colombia University Press, New York, 1969), p. 246.

12. Peter H. Smith, *Argentina and the Failure of Democracy: Conflict Among Political Elites* (University of Wisconsin Press, Madison, 1974), p. 104.

13. *Somos* 8 (February 17, 1984):12–16.

SUGGESTIONS FOR FURTHER READING

Baily, Samuel L. *Labor, Nationalism and Politics in Argentina.* Rutgers University Press, New Brunswick, N.J., 1967.

DiTella, Guido. *Argentina Under Peron, 1973–76.* St. Martin's Press, New York, 1983.

Fraser, Nicholas, and Marysa Navarro. *Eva Peron.* W. W. Norton, New York, 1980.

Gillespie, Richard. *Soldiers of Peron: Argentina's Montoneros.* Oxford University Press, London, 1982.

Goldwert, Marvin. *Democracy, Militarism and Nationalism in Argentina.* University of Texas Press, Austin, 1972.

Imaz, José Luis de. *Los que mandan.* State University of New York Press, Albany, 1964.

Kennedy, John J. *Catholicism, Nationalism and Democracy in Argentina.* University of Notre Dame Press, Notre Dame, Ind., 1958.

Kirkpatrick, Jeane. *Leader and Vanguard in Mass Society: A Study of Peronist Argentina.* MIT Press, Cambridge, Mass., 1971.

O'Donnell, Guillermo A. *Modernization and Bureaucratic Authoritarianism.* University of California, Berkeley, 1973.

Page, Joseph. *Perón: A Biography.* Random House, New York, 1983.

Potash, Robert A. *The Army and Politics in Argentina, 1928–1945.* Stanford University Press, Stanford, Calif., 1969.

———. *The Army and Politics in Argentina, 1945–1962.* Stanford University Press, Stanford, Calif., 1980.

Rock, David. *Politics in Argentina, 1890–1930: The Rise and Fall of Radicalism.* Cambridge University Press, London, 1975.

Smith, Peter H. *Argentina and the Failure of Democracy: Conflict Among Political Elites.* University of Wisconsin Press, Madison, 1974.

Snow, Peter G. *Political Forces in Argentina.* Praeger Special Studies, New York, 1979.

Timerman, Jacobo. *Prisoner Without a Name, Cell Without a Number.* Alfred A. Knopf, New York, 1981.

Walter, Richard. *Student Politics in Argentina.* Basic Books, New York, 1968.

Wynia, Gary. *Argentina in the Postwar Era: Politics and Economic Policy Making in a Divided Society.* University of New Mexico Press, Albuquerque, 1978.

9
Brazil: Corporative Authoritarianism, Democratization, and Dependency

KENNETH PAUL ERICKSON

Brazil is by almost any standard an impressive country. In 1980, it was the world's fifth largest nation in terms of land surface, the sixth largest in terms of population (121 million), and the ninth largest in terms of economic output. Viewed by social scientists, Brazil is a fascinating living laboratory, offering a range of cultures from Stone Age tribal groups to modern metropolises. The casual visitor cannot but be struck by the beauty of the beaches, the rhythm of the music, the audacity of the architecture, the sophistication of the literature, and the splendor of the wealthy.

Brazil impresses in other ways, too. The acrid urban smog of Rio de Janeiro and São Paulo, the unpotable water, the obvious signs of unemployment and underemployment, and the poverty, begging, malnutrition, and disease leave lasting memories on those visitors who take the initiative to venture beyond the luxury-hotel zone along Rio's beachfront.

Brazil, because of its size, population, natural resources, and dramatic and sustained economic development, also holds substantial potential in international politics. This importance is not lost on foreigners or on the Brazilians themselves. Indeed, during the height of Brazil's industrial expansion in the 1970s, Brazil's ruling military officers asserted that their country would be a world power by the year 2000. In 1977, a former high-ranking U.S. intelligence official placed Brazil sixth in the world in terms of perceived power, ahead of the United Kingdom, Canada, and Japan![1]

The Brazilian bid for great-power status, if successful, will necessarily destabilize the international political scene, just as the emergence of

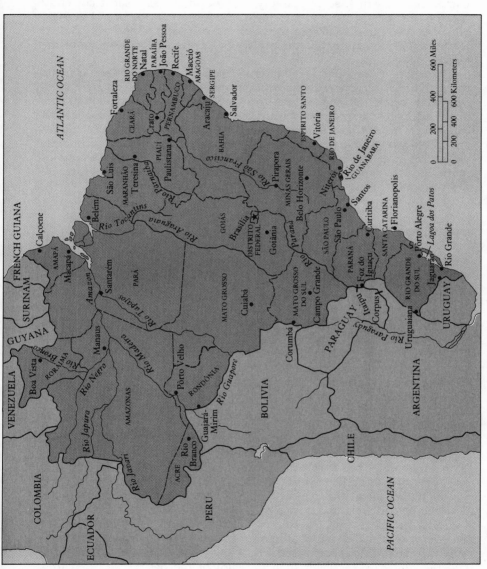

Brazil

other great powers upset it in earlier eras. This inevitably will cause friction—friction that has already begun to manifest itself—between Brazil, which seeks to shake off the shackles of dependency, and the United States, which seeks stability in a world system that it currently controls. Brazil's present foreign debt, the largest in the world at $100 billion in 1984, and its severe recession have at least temporarily halted its drive for international autonomy while increasing the leverage of the United States.

This chapter describes and analyzes Brazil's political system. It treats the authoritarian corporative tradition on which military rule from 1964 has been based, as well as the growing civilian movement that has extracted major concessions toward a return to democratic practices. It highlights institutions and processes that have enabled this South American giant to marshal its resources for almost unparalleled economic expansion and for anticipated great-power status. It also discusses domestic and foreign institutions and processes that not only perpetuate the poverty of many Brazilians but even aggravate it.

THE APPROACH: TWO THEMES

Corporatism

Brazil is an elitist country. One sees elitism in the structure of its political institutions and in the dominant values of its political culture, both of which reflect the ideology of corporatism. National political and economic institutions were styled along explicitly corporative lines during the fifteen years that Getúlio Vargas and his modernizing nation builders controlled Brazil after seizing power in the Revolution of 1930. A later section of this chapter treats that period in greater detail.

What is corporatism? Although ignored by most of today's political theory textbooks, it is a third major contemporary Western ideology, along with liberalism and Marxism. It owes its origins to such philosophers as Aristotle and Saint Thomas Aquinas.

The principal philosophical component of corporatism, for the purposes of this discussion, is the organic view of the state. Corporative theorists draw an analogy between society and the human body. They note that the parts of the body perform specific functions and that these parts are organized in a hierarchical fashion, with the brain deciding what is in the best interest of the person as a whole. In organic-state thought, the ruler or rulers take the role of the brain and are supposed to see that the *general will* or national interest prevails over the specific interests of which the society is composed. This view, then, holds that a discernible general will exists—greater than the sum of the desires and demands of the individuals who make up the society—and that a nation's rulers are capable of identifying it. The prevalence of this view reinforces the dominant position of the state elites, because they can discredit specific interest groups or opposition forces for trying to deform the national interest in order to achieve their own private gain.

In corporative theory, people are ordered and ranked according to their function in society and, in the modern era, according to their economic function. They are to participate politically through state-approved and -regulated (and often, as in the case of Brazil, state-created) interest associations.

Corporatism contrasts sharply with liberalism, the philosophy of most North Americans. Liberalism is individualistic and seeks to promote individual freedom, which, it is believed, will lead to the greatest good for the greatest number. Liberalism differs significantly from corporatism in that it does not accept the notion that an empirically discernible general will exists, apart from the sum of individual wills in society. The national interest can therefore be determined by majority vote, and the political activity of private groups cannot be branded illegitimate. Corporatism is thus the direct opposite of participatory democracy, for it assumes that elites acting in the name of the nation will possess the ability and integrity necessary to choose the best policies. And because these will be the "best" policies, the masses should, in their own interest, acquiesce rather than interfere.

Corporatism also contrasts with Marxism. Because of contemporary Marxism-Leninism's short- and medium-run prescription for the dictatorship of the proletariat, it, like corporatism, is elitist, and the elites who exercise this dictatorship presume to know and act in the national interest. Marxism and corporatism differ, however, in their visions of social class and the future of society. For Marxists, the social class that should shape a future democratic, classless society is the working class. For Latin American corporatists, on the other hand, a classless society would be disastrous. Their vision ultimately goes back to medieval natural-law theories that hold that class distinctions are *natural*—that is, divinely ordained and socially necessary. The upper class occupies a superior social, economic, and political rank because it *is*, in this view, superior. The duty of the upper class, in the tradition of noblesse oblige, is to maintain social harmony and to look after the interests of its inferiors. The corporatist vision of the future social order, then, is a vision of the past, albeit adapted in detail to the modern industrial age.

One can trace corporatism's origins in Brazil back to Portuguese colonial officials, for colonization coincided with a revival and adaptation of Saint Thomas's thought in Iberia. The elitist, paternalistic, corporative principles emphasized by the neo-Thomistic thinkers of the time shaped colonial institutions and practices.

Two major enduring institutions served to perpetuate corporative principles in Brazil, thus keeping them available for the modernizing elites who restructured the political system in the 1930s. First, the Brazilian legal system, with its roots in the Roman law tradition, has protected the supremacy of government elites by actively subordinating interest groups to the state. In this tradition, the state therefore regulates minutely the activity of such groups as trade unions and employers' organizations. For example, workers may form an association at a factory, but they have no right to make demands of their employers or to attempt to bargain with them unless their association has first obtained official recognition by the ministry of labor and has agreed to follow the principles of organization and behavior laid down by the state.

Second, the Roman Catholic Church provided a key vehicle for another major revival of the corporative elements of Thomistic thought in the late nineteenth and early twentieth centuries. Pope Leo XIII (1878–1903), the first pontiff to encourage a social conscience for the Church, was a Thomistic scholar. His work modernized Church thought and brought it into the industrial age, but his vision of the good society was neither liberal or democratic. Rather, it was organic, paternalistic, authoritarian, and corporative. The poor were to accept unquestioningly their inferior station in life, while the wealthy were to endeavor to improve life for all classes.[2]

In 1931, on the fortieth anniversary of *Rerum Novarum*, Leo's famous encyclical calling for the wealthy to act with social responsibility, Pope Pius XI issued a new encyclical, *Quadragesimo Anno*. In it he advocated explicitly corporative social and political institutions in order to eliminate class conflict. From the time of Leo XIII right through Brazil's Revolution of 1930, Catholic social organizations, intellectuals' associations, and workers' circles propagated corporative ideas in Brazil. Corporatism was, by the 1930s, a concept for which Brazil was well prepared.

Dependency

The second major theme is that of dependency. Brazil is a dependent capitalist country whose economy, society, polity, and policies have reflected its dependence. To understand the dynamics of dependency and its impact upon poorer countries, one must view the world capitalist system *as a system* that conditions the behavior of individual nations within it. Nations, like individuals, seek to enrich themselves—that is, to accumulate capital—and the dominant nations usually possess the political and economic power to do so at the expense of the poorer ones. The prizes that the dominant nations have sought in poorer countries are raw materials, markets, and investment opportunities. Brazilian history illustrates this process well and shows how wealth flows upward from the very poor to the very rich nations, sometimes through intermediaries.

To begin, who received the gold and riches of the New World? Contrary to common belief, this wealth did not come to rest in Spain and Portugal. They soon became dependencies of the dominant and increasingly powerful capitalist countries, notably England, the Netherlands, and France. "By the end of the sixteenth century, the Dutch controlled about 66 percent of the shipping between Brazil and Portugal, the Dutch owned a large share of the sugar exported from the colony, and Amsterdam not Lisbon had about 25 sugar refineries using semi-processed Brazilian sugar." General economic ascendancy passed to the English once they had defeated the Dutch fleet in combat. The English then successfully pursued the raw materials and markets of Spain's and Portugal's American colonies, so that "in a variety of ways the English, Iberian, and Ibero-American economies were interlocked by 1700."[3] The fabled gold of the Americas wound up in the vaults of England, the Netherlands, and France, for in the final reckoning the Spanish and Portuguese merely served as intermediaries between the growing industrial capitalist economies of northern Europe and the purchasers of textiles, hardware, and mining and milling equipment in the Iberian colonies.

The British based their economic primacy upon their military (particularly naval) supremacy. Indeed, control of the seas facilitated a British strategem that ultimately shaped the Brazilian road to independence. When Napoleon invaded Portugal in 1807, British diplomatic agents convinced Prince Regent Dom João VI, then ruling on behalf of his demented mother, to pack up the royal treasury, library, and documents of state and move the government of the Portuguese empire to Rio de Janeiro. Convoyed by British warships, the Portuguese royal family, court, and some ten thousand followers reached the colony in January 1808. Safely behind the British naval umbrella, João set out to bring this rustic, backward, and insalubrious colony up to a level befitting a European royal family and its court. He quickly created institutions that carried out great advances in education, commerce, agriculture, defense, culture, and the fine arts. So dramatically did the government's arrival change the life of Brazil over the next fifteen years that when Portugal sought, in 1821 and 1822, to turn back the clock by uprooting these institutions and returning them to Europe, Brazil's local notables reacted bitterly. Prince Regent Pedro, João's son, declared Brazil's independence in 1822.

Britain, of course, was richly rewarded for its role in the escape of the Portuguese rulers. With Portugal itself occupied first by the French and then by the British between 1807 and 1814, the government in Rio necessarily had to open its ports to foreign vessels. The British were in the strongest position to profit from the opening of Brazil, because although Napoleon controlled the continent, the British controlled the seas and hence, the access to Brazil. Moreover, the Portuguese badly needed the British at this time, for only the British could provide them with indispensable manufactured goods. The British consolidated their strong position in the Treaty of 1810, in which they obtained a tariff rate even lower than that for the Portuguese, whereas Brazil's tropical agricultural products, which competed with similar ones from British colonies, entered Britain only after paying a high tariff. Thus, the British assured that even after the Napoleonic wars, they would remain supreme in trade with Brazil.

HISTORY TO 1930

The Empire of Brazil, 1822–1889

Brazil, unlike any other country in Latin America, was a colony of Portugal, giving it a distinctive language, culture, and national identity. And while Hispanic republics won their independence through long violent wars that shook their social structures, laid waste their economies, and destroyed the authoritarian political institutions established by the colonial powers, Brazil shook off Portuguese control comparatively quickly and easily. Brazil's independence was declared by none other than the Portuguese crown prince, who announced in 1822 that he would remain in Brazil as monarch instead of returning to Portugal as the Portuguese constituent assembly had ordered him to do. The Empire of Brazil, the only hereditary constitutional monarchy in Latin America, endured from 1822 until 1889.

And although the Spanish empire ultimately disintegrated into eighteen nations, Portuguese America remained intact. That the empire protected Brazil's territorial integrity in the face of great centrifugal pressures is surely its outstanding achievement. Independent Brazil's continuity with the past helped hold the nation together.[4] Monarchy, the only form of government with which Brazilians were familiar, was the one with the greatest legitimacy—that is, general public acceptance—at the time of independence, a legitimacy strengthened by the presence of the same royal family on the throne.

Pedro I, emperor from 1822 to 1831, gave his political system an aura of nationalism and responsiveness from the beginning by consulting closely with important political figures, some of whom were openly anti-Portuguese. In 1824, the emperor promulgated a constitution, satisfying those intellectuals whose reading of liberal European Enlightenment literature led them to desire constitutional limitations upon the monarch. Yet the constitution also satisfied the partisans of strong personal rule, for it not only specified that the emperor's person was "inviolable and sacred," but it conferred on him the "moderating power" (*poder moderador*), the power to stand above and harmonize the legislative, executive, and judicial branches of government. Reflecting an organic, corporative concept of society, the moderating power charged him to be the conscience of the nation and to act to defend the national interest when he believed private or partisan interests threatened it.

By exercising the moderating power, the emperor assured that the political system would not be liberal; rather, it would remain autocratic and consonant with the colonial past. The emperor's will, not popular sovereignty, explains the alternation in power of the Liberal and Conservative parties. When the emperor decided it was time for a change, he exercised his right to dismiss the cabinet and appoint a new prime minister who would put his own party's officials in charge of government agencies and purse strings (and, hence, in a position to indulge or deprive voters) at national, state, and local levels. This done, he called elections. Public opinion followed rather than caused the change in government. And, of course, the new government held the trump cards, for it controlled the electoral machinery, thus eliminating any chance that it would lose.

Had the Brazilian political system been built upon liberal, instead of conservative, principles, Brazil might well have fragmented in the early decades after independence. Liberalism would have weakened the central government and devolved its power on the regional landed oligarchies. In that period, the oligarchies in the distant reaches of the empire backed dozens of unsuccessful rebellions, many of which sought greater local autonomy or even secession. Only after the coffee boom of the 1840s provided the revenues to strengthen the imperial navy, leading to the imposition of central authority throughout the land, did the waves of rebellion cease.

The empire endured to 1889, when the military overthrew Pedro II, emperor from 1840. A popular monarch for the first decades of his reign, Pedro saw support for his political system dissipate under a variety of pressures. A costly, debilitating war with Paraguay from 1865 to 1870 not only put the nation in debt and diverted its energies from more productive pursuits, but it built up a military institution that later resented its postwar reduction in personnel, money, and prestige. The Church, in the wake of a Church-state conflict during which Pedro imprisoned two bishops, ceased to back the monarchy. The government generally left the planters of the principal crops to shift for themselves on the world market, and so the producers of the two declining crops—sugarcane and cotton—felt they owed little to the empire. In the mid-1880s, the snowballing abolition movement encouraged slaves to flee the coffee plantations in great numbers and to take refuge in the cities. In 1888, therefore, the most progressive coffee planters had the Conservative government pass an abolition bill in order to stem the intensifying socioeconomic disintegration in the countryside and to regularize the supply of field hands on the basis of wage labor. The less-enlightened and economically declining majority of landowners, disoriented or despondent as their way of life crumbled about them, lost their principal reason to support the empire or the party to which most of them had belonged.

Urban interests also ceased to support the monarchy. Among the expanding bureaucratic, commercial, and professional middle classes, republican and positivist ideas circulated widely in the last two decades of the empire, creating a growing receptivity for alternative forms of government. Industrial entrepreneurs did not get the protective tariffs or credit policies they wanted, which slowed Brazil's first steps toward industrialization and frustrated the incipient bourgeoisie. Finally, the emperor himself, aging, in ill health, and with no male heirs, saw his earlier prestige diminish. Furthermore, Crown Princess Isabel's French husband was a very unpopular figure in Brazilian society, and the nation viewed the succession with grave misgivings. Military officers, sensitive to this widespread discontent, took on themselves the moderating power, seized the government, exiled the emperor, and—after a brief military dictatorship—ultimately allowed a constituent assembly to draft a republican constitution.

Throughout the nineteenth century, Brazil remained dependent upon the world's central capitalist country, Great Britain. The Treaty of 1810, renewed in 1827, gave Britain great advantages in tariffs and trade and required Brazil to take steps to curb the slave trade and end the institution of slavery. The Brazilians protested that this would badly damage their economy and make them more dependent upon the British. Nonetheless, the British navy sought to force Brazilian compliance by regularly seizing Brazilian ships suspected of carrying slaves, until a Brazilian law put an end to the slave traffic in the early 1850s. Although British anti-slavery policies reflected the Victorian moralism of the rising English middle classes, it must be recognized that economic considerations also motivated their implementation. These British measures were intended to hold down Brazil's labor force and, hence, to put a lid on Brazilian production of sugar. In this way, the British protected their sugarcane growers in Jamaica and other tropical colonies.[5]

A typically colonial umbilical cord linked Brazil to Britain. Brazil sent raw cotton, coffee, sugar, hides, and other primary products to England, buying in return finished textiles and leather goods, iron, hardware, and other manufactures. British capital built the railroads to link field and mine to the ports, where it deepened the harbors and built warehouse facilities. Surely British Foreign Secretary George Canning's hope of the 1820s that "England will be the world's workshop, and Latin America its farm" became a reality in nineteenth-century Brazil.[6]

The Old Republic, 1889–1930

The republic differed from the empire in several important respects. First, the two principal parties of the empire collapsed with it, and in nearly every state there arose a single party controlled by the landed oligarchy. Although each of these state parties took the label "Republican party," no permanent national Republican party existed to coordinate or control them. Second, the liberal constitution of 1891 eliminated the moderating power, so no official stood above political parties to force their alternation in office. Third, in the absence of a central moderating power to speak in the name of the national interest, the reality of political power gravitated to the oligarchies of the two most powerful states, São Paulo and Minas Gerais, which treated their own interests as the "national" interest. Their dominance of the political system brought an alternation of national governments, this time between the top political figures of these two states.

Thus, in what came to be known as the "politics of the governors," the president spoke for his own state and, in consultation with the governor of the other major one, negotiated with the heads of the Republican parties of the lesser states. The federal government, in return for electoral support, funded public works such as railroads, highways, harbor facilities, and drought-control projects. These patronage projects usually enabled the landed elites in the recipient states to increase their income by producing or marketing a larger crop, and they in turn used the additional receipts to build and maintain their political clienteles. Elections generally ratified the slates composed by the outgoing executive at each level, and the electorate averaged less than 3 percent of the population. Machine control explains why the winning candidates received more than 90 percent of the vote in six of eleven presidential races and pulled more than 70 percent in two others. For most Brazilians, therefore, the democracy of the Old Republic was only a sham.

The planter oligarchies espoused liberalism because its decentralizing principles enabled them to take possession of many government agencies and functions denied them under the empire. The new Brazilian federal system left most initiative to the states and, thus, to their ruling oligarchies. It was the São Paulo government, not the federal one, that first addressed Brazil's chronic labor shortage by recruiting European immigrants. And the São Paulo government devised the coffee-valorization scheme to warehouse the product and thus protect planters from devastating cyclical price fluctuations. The states could contract foreign loans. State banks fostered industrial development, and state governments built railroads and expanded transport facilities. The states even had the authority to levy export taxes on products destined for other states, although industrializing states like São Paulo eliminated them in order to boost the sales of their manufactures. Finally, the states maintained militias stronger than the local contingents of the weak federal army.

Brazil's achievements under the Old Republic were mainly economic and diplomatic. Along with the previously mentioned programs and policies, ever growing world demand for coffee increased the capital available for industrial expansion. World War I, which cut off supplies of European manufactured goods, forced the Brazilians themselves to produce such goods and thus lent impetus to domestic industry.

During the first decades of the Old Republic, the Brazilian foreign ministry settled outstanding border disputes with neighboring countries and gave the Brazilian map the contours it has today. Baron Rio Branco, first as diplomat and then as foreign minister, negotiated so skillfully that Brazil took definitive possession of 342,000 square miles (886,000 square kilometers—an area greater than France) also claimed by its neighbors.[7]

In politics, the Old Republic proved unable to adapt to changing conditions. First, the system depended on the alternation of presidents between São Paulo and Minas Gerais. In 1930, the outgoing Paulista president violated the agreement by selecting another Paulista to succeed him, provoking the opposition of the Minas political machine. Second, the system managed tensions successfully when only two states had the power to claim the presidency. The rise in power and importance of Rio Grande do Sul had already added a measure of instability to the system when, in 1930, that state's governor, Getúlio Vargas, linked his state's political machine to that of Minas and opposed the Paulista candidate for the presidency. He lost, but his supporters claimed the election was tainted with fraud.

Third, the system was based on and responsive to landed interests. It could not cope with the expansion of the urban working class and middle sectors generated by recent industrialization and rising foreign trade. The landed oligarchy vigorously suppressed labor unions and maneuvered to exclude all urban interests from meaningful political participation. This provoked a series of army revolts by urban-oriented junior officers. In 1930, the urban groups supported Vargas, who actively courted their favor. Finally, the liberal laissez-faire economic theory of the oligarchy left Brazil's rulers, like those of most other countries, unequipped to deal with the blow of the Great Depression. Discontent mounted as the economic crisis worsened until, in October 1930, Vargas's forces in league with key military commanders rose up, overthrew the Old Republic, and prodded Brazil into a new era.

Under the Old Republic, foreign control over Brazil changed hands and ceased to be as absolute as under the empire. The United States had become a major industrial, trading, and shipping nation with a recently expanded navy. Not only did it replace Britain as the dominant Caribbean military power around the turn of the century, but U.S. policymakers sought to displace Britain as top trading partner of the South American countries.

The opportunity for an assault on Britain's preeminent position in Brazil came with World War I, when the British economy and that of Germany, Britain's closest trade rival, directed their production toward the war effort and thus could not supply their Latin American markets. The United States moved into the breach, quintupling in dollar amounts its sales to Brazil between 1913 and 1920. The U.S. share in total Brazilian imports rose from 16 percent in 1913 to nearly 50 percent in 1919. This percentage fell off after the war as the European countries struggled to recover their lost markets, but the United States never again relinquished its primary position. In 1929, the U.S. share of Brazilian imports stood at 30 percent.

Competition between the major industrial nations in this period gave the Brazilians new leverage to defend their economy against the impositions of outsiders. In 1925, for example, U.S. officials tried to bring down the world price of coffee by cutting off U.S. bank credit for Brazil's coffee warehousing scheme. The Brazilians thwarted this U.S. attempt to dictate economic policy to them by floating the necessary loan in London.[8]

MODERN BRAZIL: 1930 TO THE PRESENT

Authoritarian Brazil, 1930–1945

Brazil entered the modern era with the Revolution of 1930. Led by Getúlio Vargas, who ruled as president and dictator until 1945, this civil-military movement overthrew the nominally democratic Old Republic and replaced it with an authoritarian regime. The principal figures who seized power in 1930 and spent fifteen years shaping the institutions of modern Brazil harshly attacked the corrupt, selfish policies of the old landed ruling class, disapproved of their decentralized polity, and rejected the liberal ideology on which the old system was based. Seeing themselves as modernizing nation builders, they proclaimed the establishment of a new political system characterized by administrative efficiency, governmental probity, social responsibility, and—above all—effective, centralized national authority. In designing policies to serve the national interest rather than one special landed interest, they promised governmental responsiveness toward the rapidly growing urban working class and middle sectors. To achieve their goals, Vargas and his authoritarian modernizers enacted a corporative labor code and set up a system of *sindicatos* to represent and control workers and employers.

By the early 1930s, corporatism was for many Brazilians an idea whose time had come. Throughout the Western world, the three major ideologies of liberalism, Marxism, and corporatism were engaged in a struggle to the death, with liberalism the apparent loser to the other two. Vargas and his advisers were well aware of the contemporary international ideological conflict, but it was not a simple shopping trip to the international marketplace of ideas that led them to opt for corporative institutions. Certain underlying values in Brazil's political culture supported this form of organization. Because Brazil achieved independence without having to break with the past, the Thomistic, natural-law world view, with its emphasis on the functional, organic, hierarchical ordering of society, shaped and was perpetuated by Brazil's political systems from the colonial era through the empire.

The Roman law foundations of Brazil's legal system perpetuated a legal tradition that condones and encourages state formation, regulation, and supervision of interest groups. In the 1920s, Brazilian Catholic lay associations, taking their cue from the Thomistic, corporative writings of Popes Leo XIII and Pius XI, urged national restructuring along corporative lines. Finally, an increasingly articulate nationalist current among intellectuals dismissed liberal democracy as a foreign import that ill suited Brazil's social, economic, and political heritage and reality. Stimulated between 1907 and 1916 by the nationalist teachings and writings of Alberto Torres, a prominent politician and jurist, this current captured increasing national attention in the decade after Torres's death in 1917. In the 1930s Torres's theories quite literally helped shape the

Brazilian political system when Francisco José de Oliveira Vianna, one of Torres's students, became adviser to Vargas and a key figure in the just-created ministry of labor, industry, and commerce.[9]

It is in the role attributed to the state that the thinking of Oliveira Vianna and Vargas's other advisers distinguishes itself. They were alarmed at the increasing ideological polarization of the 1930s, which threatened the government. Both the Communist-led National Liberation Alliance and the fascist Integralist movement attempted armed insurrections during the decade, lending weight to calls by Vargas's advisers for a strong state that would play an activist role in representing and promoting the national interest. The state was to pursue its own interest, superior to that of class, party, or faction. Vargas's advisers thus rejected the decentralizing, liberal concept under which the federal government played a passive, minimal role while strong state governments merely served the class interests of the landowners controlling them. Vargas graphically symbolized the new relationship between state and federal governments when, in 1937, he burned the state flags at a public ceremony.

A modern society requires modern social organization and a true sense of nationality, items in short supply in Brazil prior to the 1930s. Oliveira Vianna pointed out that complex, formal social organizations and interest groups were essential to political communication and to the development of national identity in modern Brazil. Given their absence, he argued in elitist and paternalistic terms that the state should create them. The organizations he proposed reflected organic-state thought, for they followed the lines of the principal sectors of Brazil's economy. Specifically, there was one hierarchy of organizations—*sindicatos* at the local level, federations at the state level, and confederations at the national level—for workers and another for employers.

These organizations were, in the words of Estado Novo (New State) publicist Azevedo Amaral, "the authentic representative forces in the State." This phrasing might imply a democratic responsiveness, but in reality Vargas and his aides controlled the state and shaped the *sindicato* system to conform to their views of the national will and national interest. Azevedo Amaral made this abundantly clear: "Docile submission to the authority of the State is not repugnant and cannot be repugnant to normal individuals, for they intuitively understand that in order for a people to transform itself into a nation, it must organize itself into a hierarchical structure."

These nation builders justified the imposition of authoritarian corporative institutions in two ways. First, they pointed to the positive contributions these institutions would make in creating a sense of Brazilian political identity and in coordinating and channeling worker and employer energies into greater national economic productivity. Second, in addressing Brazil's ruling class, they stressed the negative aspects of the alternatives to their authoritarian state. The alternatives, as Francisco Campos, author of the Estado Novo constitution, drew them, were both totalitarian: communism or fascism. Liberal democracy, he believed, had been viable when there were property restrictions upon suffrage, but it could not cope with mass political participation in the modern era. Campos stressed that the principal activity in modern society is economic, so enfranchisement of the working class meant that the ultimate prize of political competition would be control of the national economy. By virtue of their numbers, workers would at last win the class struggle at the ballot box and would then establish a Communist regime.

The bourgeoisie, however, could not be expected simply to sit back and watch this process. Rather, argued Campos, the ruling class would tailor the agenda of legitimate discussion to exclude issues damaging to their class interest. The logical consequence of this path of action, given the predictable resistance of workers and others, was the degeneration of the liberal democratic regime into a totalitarian, fascist state.

Authoritarian corporatism, therefore, offered the golden mean, a solution that would avoid either extreme. At a time when rising industrialization had greatly expanded the ranks of the working class and a surge of militant labor activity seemed imminent, corporatism promised to do away with class conflict and replace it with class harmony. The state, because it sat above and supervised the corporative institutions of both employers and workers, would thus assure that the national interest would prevail over specific class interests.

Vargas's pragmatic notion of the national interest included revitalizing the depression-stricken economy by finding new foreign markets, by expanding old ones that had sharply constricted after the 1929 crash, and by building up domestic industry. In pursuing these goals, Vargas struggled to increase Brazil's leverage vis-à-vis the great powers— particularly the dominant power, the United States. Great-power trade and political rivalry during the 1930s and the first years of World War II may have caused dislocations and problems, but they also presented the Brazilians with unparalleled opportunities for renegotiating the terms of Brazil's dependency. One study describes Vargas as "an opportunist *par excellence*," who "played the great powers off against each other, utilizing pressure or alleged pressure from one as a lever to pry concessions from the other."[10] Brazilian negotiators, against the desires of Washington, developed barter-type arrangements with the Third Reich that enabled Germany to replace Britain as Brazil's second most important trading partner. Brazil thus disposed of products that would otherwise have gone unsold in the moribund world market, and in return it obtained many manufactured goods at prices lower than those of U.S. or British competitors. Germany demanded a more diversified range of raw materials than the United States and Great Britain, so Brazil reduced somewhat its dependence on coffee. Sales to Germany of cotton, tobacco, rubber, meats, hides, fruits, and nuts stimulated local economies from the Amazon to the Uruguayan border.

Vargas, by dangling before U.S. eyes the willingness of a German firm to set up a steel industry in Brazil, obtained a U.S. loan to finance the establishment of the National Steel Company. Finally, Vargas obtained from the United States the military training and weapons that transformed Brazil from a very weak nation into a major South American military power.

The fifteen years of the Vargas regime left a major mark on Brazil, one that cannot be diminished by pointing to certain incompetent or corrupt individuals and agencies or to some ill-considered, unsuccessful, or objectionable policies. Vargas's policies deepened the sense of Brazilian nationality, giving the lower social strata a sense of sharing in the republic, while integrating ethnic minorities (such as German-speaking groups of the south) into the national culture. The government stimulated recovery from the 1929 depression, promoted industrialization, and undertook a vast interventionist role in the economy from which it has never since retired. It created a career civil service with admission based on merit rather than party or family connections; it expanded a few rudimentary social-insurance and pension programs into a broad welfare and health-delivery system for urban workers; and, not least, it left the legacy of corporative organizations to represent (and control!) workers and employers. The civil-military movement that overthrew Vargas in 1945 inherited a much-modernized Brazil.

Populist Democracy, 1946–1964

Vargas, promising to end authoritarian rule in 1945, called presidential elections in which he would not be a candidate. As the election date grew near, however, a mass movement, organized by the dictator's followers in the working class and the bureaucracy and by leaders of the recently legalized Communist party, called upon him to remain in office or at least to be a candidate. When he decreed modifications in the electoral regulations, many in the opposition felt he was preparing to continue in office, and his war minister overthrew him so the democratization would continue.

A broad spectrum of political parties arose, with three major ones dominating Brazilian politics for the entire democratic period through 1964. Two of the three perpetuated Vargas's corporative legacy. Created by his supporters in government bureaucracies and in rural areas, these two parties readily accepted the corporative concept. The third, which claimed to be the liberal democratic opposition party, never expressly challenged the corporative principle or moved to liberate the worker and employer organizations from state tutelage and control. Throughout this democratic interlude, therefore, the corporative system remained intact—a separate nondemocratic set of institutions parallel to the elective offices established by the constitution of 1946.

The coup of 1945 did not end Vargas's political career. He had so successfully cultivated a following in the working class and in the political clienteles of Estado Novo bureaucrats and politicians that, in the free elections of 1946, he was elected senator in two states and deputy in six states and the Federal District. He ultimately accepted a Senate seat from his home state of Rio Grande do Sul. Vargas went on to win the presidency in the democratic election of 1950. His two political parties controlled national politics from 1946 through the coup of 1964, with the exception of the eight months Jânio Quadros spent as president in 1961.

Throughout the period 1946–1964, therefore, the major dividing line between parties and politicians remained the one drawn between the Vargas and the anti-Vargas forces. The principal issues separating them grew out of the ability of Vargas and his allies to mobilize politically the newly enfranchised urban workers—an ability that led the elitist, conservative opposition sneeringly to denounce Vargas as a demagogue and a populist (from the Portuguese term for lower classes: *massas* or *classes populares*).

The concept of populism is critical to an understanding of Brazilian politics in the democratic period. Populism refers to nationalist political movements that arise when incipient industrialization brings on rapid social change. Populist movements generate broad mass support in the working class and certain middle strata, and they proclaim apparently antiestablishment policies. At base, these are cross-class rather than proletarian movements. Populist leaders come not from the proletariat but rather from the ruling class, and they mediate between industrialists and workers.

Populist politicians cannot achieve importance until the working class has begun to count politically. This occurred in Brazil only after the Revolution of 1930. Although Brazilian workers had staged impressive general strikes in 1917 and 1919, government repression had broken their organizations, jailed or deported their leaders, and denied them political significance for most of the 1920s. By 1930, however, industrialization and Brazil's growing foreign trade had expanded the work force, and labor organizations appeared on the verge of a new wave of militant action. Vargas took power at this moment and during the next fifteen years won working-class support. Indeed, Vargas was a prototypical populist politician. He was a large landowner, a member of the pre-1930 political elite, and a nationalist. His policies to provide social insurance and health care, to recognize labor organizations, and to require workplace safety standards earned him the enduring nickname Father of the Common People. Because he provided favorable credit, tariff, and investment policies, he enjoyed substantial backing from the industrial bourgeoisie.

Particularly after Vargas returned to the presidential palace in 1951, the populist movement appealed to both workers and industrialists. To win working-class support, populist politicians like Vargas and his political heirs promised periodic raises in the minimum wage, improve-

ments in the social-insurance systems, and subsidies for public transportation and basic foodstuffs like wheat and black beans. Blaming
foreign capital for exploiting workers and the nation, the politicians
promised stricter supervision of foreign investors.

The anti-Vargas coalition deplored the populist appeal to the lower
classes, calling it demagogy. The coalition's members came from social
sectors that had lost prestige or power under Vargas or had other
grievances. Included were landed interests linked to the opposition
during the dictatorship, middle-sector professionals and technicians (particularly those in the service of foreign firms), and some industrialists
who believed the government's role in the economy had hurt their firms
or had done little to help them. The rhetoric of the principal opposition
party, the National Democratic Union (UDN), included a strong component of classical liberal economic and political ideology.

Regarding the interests of the working class, some serious shortcomings
balanced populism's positive aspects. The term *populism* refers to the
lower classes and suggests that these lower sectors make an important
policy input. It thus masks the fact that populist movements are led
and controlled by politicians from the ruling class, who use them for
their own purposes. They do not welcome workers into the policymaking
process, and this generates tensions within the movement. Nonetheless,
labor leaders achieved some leverage in Brazil by the late 1950s because
they served as intermediaries between the politicians and the rank-and-
file workers who made up the politicians' electoral base.

Corporatism and populism have fundamentally contradictory political
consequences. Corporatism limits and controls political mobilization and
participation; populism increases them. Populist politics, by the late
1950s and early 1960s, began chipping away at the strict controls of
the corporative system.

To reward the labor leaders who helped them build and control their
political clienteles, populist politicians gave them patronage jobs in
government bureaucracies, usually in the ministry of labor, the social
insurance agencies, and the labor courts. These positions, particularly
in the insurance bureaucracies, put the labor leaders in a position to
indulge or deprive workers and, hence, to obtain large worker turnouts
for political strikes or mass demonstrations. This occurred because these
bureaucracies were chronically underfunded, leading to slow and inadequate service for many insured workers. Thus many union members,
hoping that good relations with their officers would cut red tape and
improve access to medical or other services in moments of need, willingly
accompanied them to rallies and strikes. These usually promoted a cause
or career of a populist politician.

As populist politicians became increasingly indebted to labor leaders,
they allowed these union officers growing participation in policymaking.
Perhaps the clearest example of this occurred at a famous mass rally
in March 1964. Osvaldo Pacheco, leader of the militant port workers,

shared the dais with President João Goulart and whispered suggestions to him. The president then incorporated the suggestions, which were audible over the public-address system, into the major policy outlines that he was announcing. This incident increased right-wing alarm about the growing power of radical labor leaders, and it served to activate the conspiracy that overthrew Goulart and repressed militant labor leaders a few weeks later.

The populist relationship not only catalyzed right-wing opposition. Paradoxically, it also contributed to the weakness of the labor movement. Corporative organization had already made labor leaders dependent on the state, and populism reinforced this dependency by providing them with political leverage in state agencies, thus deflecting their attention from organizing the rank and file. Hence, the labor leaders possessed no independent means to resist when, in 1964, the new government ousted them from their patronage jobs and repressed their politician allies. Populism helped create a euphoria about rising labor power in Brazil while perpetuating labor's organizational weakness.

Brazil's dependency upon outside powers played an important role in the destruction of populist democracy in 1964. This occurred because Brazil's pattern of dependent capitalist industrialization exacerbated social and political tensions. Up to the early 1950s, Brazil's pattern of dependency—described by one of Brazil's foremost political sociologists as "national dependency"—was rooted in the markets in which Brazil sold coffee, sugar, cacao, and other primary products to the world's industrial nations. As early as the mid-1950s, the pattern shifted to "structural dependency."

The two patterns can be contrasted as follows: In the national-dependency model, Brazilians, even though subject to the vagaries of the international commodities markets, controlled the capital generated by their primary products and invested it in domestic activities, which by the twentieth century included industries owned principally by Brazilian nationals or permanent immigrants. Most investment and production decisions were still made in Brazil. With economic growth, the manufacturing base shifted from light industry (textiles, apparel, shoes, and processed foods) to heavy industry (capital goods and complex consumer durables such as automobiles). Foreign manufacturing firms began operations in Brazil, marking the shift to structural dependency. Since these firms are foreign owned, the ultimate decisions on investment and production take place outside Brazil. Moreover, Brazilian industrialists began entering into agreements or partnerships with foreign firms to obtain capital and technology. Foreign influence, formerly felt through international markets and through diplomatic channels, thus became integrated into the very structure of the economy and society.[11]

The process of dependent capitalist development broke up the populist coalition, isolating workers and peasants from their former allies in the industrial bourgeoisie and the middle strata. In the national-dependency phase of industrialization, the faction of the ruling class in favor of industrialization sought to place workers' electoral support behind populist candidates who promised beneficial economic development policies. Even industrialists stood to gain from distributive measures given to workers in exchange for their support: Minimum-wage hikes, for example, helped the traditional industries expand their markets for textiles, processed foods, and other basic consumer goods.

Once Brazilian firms had developed structurally dependent ties with foreign companies—particularly after President Juscelino Kubitschek attracted great quantities of foreign capital for development projects between 1956 and 1960—they no longer needed to cooperate politically with workers. The firms received capital and technology from abroad. Moreover, most Brazilian industrialists who entered into structurally dependent relationships with foreign firms produced expensive consumer durables or capital goods—products so expensive that workers earning the minimum wage would be unable to purchase them. In other words, the product structure of the modern industries undermined the shared interest that had made populist political collaboration appealing to both the working class and the industrial bourgeoisie.

Structural dependency had two other effects. First, it aggravated social tensions, leading many industrialists to fear the workers. As real wages declined, workers responded by calling increasingly frequent and militant strikes and demonstrations. The industrialists, no longer needing worker support for industrial development, greeted the coup of 1964 with relief. Second, structural dependency severed the links between workers and the technocratic middle strata. With the growing sophistication of the Brazilian economy, technocratic roles—roles that originated in the already industrialized countries and that involved application of modern technology—spread through the economy, public bureaucracies, media, and military.[12] The technocrats expressed frustration with the disruptive strikes and inefficient patronage practices of the populists, and they contrasted Brazil with the efficient systems idealistically depicted in foreign casebooks of management science and business administration.

Particularly as their numbers increased and they developed a sense of solidarity, the technocrats came to believe that their skills gave them the capacity to govern effectively without the disruptive encumbrance of democratic procedures. To reinforce their discontent with populism, the technocrats—along with most of the less technologically skilled middle sectors—believed that populist welfare programs and labor unrest had caused their standard of living to decline. They therefore welcomed the 1964 coup that put an end to populist politics, fettered the working class, and gave these technocrats the freedom to reshape the economy, society, and polity to conform to their own version of the good society.

Military coups both ushered in and closed Brazil's turbulent democratic period, and it was a coup in 1954 that led then popularly elected President Vargas to commit suicide in the presidential palace. Attempted coups nearly blocked President Kubitschek's inauguration in 1956 and Vice President Goulart's accession to the presidency when President Quadros resigned in 1961. Other lesser military uprisings punctuated the period. Quadros quit his office out of frustration after only eight months. Goulart proved unable to obtain congressional passage of fundamental reforms, to dynamize the flagging economy, or to prevent snowballing national breakdown. These failures led many observers in the early 1960s to claim that Brazil was ungovernable.

If Brazil proved ungovernable in these years, it was because of contradictions among the principles and interests shaping the national political processs. Corporatism, an elitist principle, limited political participation, while populism expanded it. Structural dependency aggravated class conflict. Major sectors of the population sought to change the rules of the game, in effect to make Brazil governable on a new basis. Left-wing groups hoped to establish some form of socialism, but they lacked effective power because both corporatism and populism had undermined their institutional autonomy. When a real confrontation came in 1964, the forces of the right easily seized power, ended the populist era, and shaped the Brazilian polity so it would serve their interests.

Authoritarian Brazil Since 1964

To justify their coup, the new rulers pointed to economic decline, runaway inflation, capital flight, political instability, corruption, and "Communist" subversion. They promised to restore both economic dynamism and democracy.

The anti-Vargas forces, who claimed to be Brazil's liberal democrats, played a major role in ousting Vargas's political heirs from the government. Although they professed to have democratic intentions, the political system they established turned out to be as authoritarian and corporative as was Vargas's Estado Novo. That should not be surprising, for Brazil's historical experience shaped the institutional forms of this new authoritarian period. Throughout Brazil's history, nearly every one of its various political systems has been authoritarian. Even the Old Republic, despite its veneer of liberal democracy, was at base an authoritarian regime. Only the eighteen years between 1946 and 1964 contained significant elements of genuine liberal democracy. Yet in that regime, the parties and politicians calling themselves liberal democrats usually lost elections to the populist politicians who came out of Vargas's corporative tradition.

Harking back to the Vargas dictatorship of the 1930s, Brazil's new rulers in 1964 drew Francisco Campos, author of the Estado Novo constitution, out of retirement to amend the 1946 constitution with the First Institutional Act. This act and subsequent ones granted authoritarian legislative and executive powers to the president and permitted the executive to purge politicians and civil servants without any obligation to comply with due-process laws. Also reminiscent of the 1930s, the new rulers vigorously applied the corporative labor laws to subject worker organizations to strict state control and to oust the most militant labor leaders from union office.

During its first year in power, the military claimed that it would rule briefly—only long enough to remove "corrupt" and "subversive" individuals from public elective and appointive offices. But when populist politicians won several key gubernatorial elections in 1965, the hard liners within the military pushed aside the ruling moderates and decreed the Second Institutional Act. This act brought a new wave of purges, tightened social and political controls, and proclaimed indefinite military rule in order to rid the nation of the vices of its past. In 1968, when civilian forces challenged military rule with strikes, street demonstrations, and even armed resistance, the military closed the Congress, purged politicians, tightened censorship, and began widespread imprisonment and torture of suspected dissidents.

With the inauguration of President Ernesto Geisel in 1974, the military moderates replaced the hard liners. The worst abuses of human rights soon decreased in frequency and finally ended altogether before Geisel transferred the presidential sash to General João Baptista Figueiredo in 1979. Figueiredo was another military president committed to gradual liberalization and ultimate redemocratization. Controls over the press and public debate had relaxed enough by 1980 to permit marked advances toward redemocratization, not only in the form of widespread and intensifying opposition to continued military rule, but more importantly in increasingly institutionalized civilian political organizations and practices. In 1982, for the first time since 1965, Brazilian voters were permitted to elect state governors, and opposition parties won the statehouses of ten of Brazil's twenty-four states. Significantly, these ten states constitute the heart of Brazil's modern economy, accounting for 75 percent of the nation's economic output.

In the first four months of 1984, mass opposition to military rule expressed itself in the largest, best-disciplined political demonstrations in Brazil's history. Over a million citizens massed in the streets of Rio and São Paulo, and correspondingly impressive crowds turned out in other cities to demand that direct presidential elections be restored in place of the present indirect system in which the president is selected by an electoral college skewed toward the governing party. In mid-1984, the government succeeded in blocking a constitutional amendment to restore direct elections. Nevertheless, in early 1985 a democratic government under oppositionist Tancredo Neves was elected amid much hope and euphoria.

SOCIAL AND POLITICAL GROUPS AND INTERESTS

Corporatism is basically a special institutional arrangement linking interest associations and the state. The state lays down the rules governing the activities of these bodies and, when it legally recognizes them, grants them monopoly rights in representing their socioeconomic categories. Corporative controls have conditioned the political activity and limited the autonomy of every major associational interest group in Brazil. The controls have correspondingly increased the autonomy of state policy-making elites.

Urban Workers

Brazil's present system of labor organizations has remained virtually unchanged since Vargas decreed the corporative labor laws in the 1930s. The first duty of the *sindicatos*, as spelled out in the labor code, is "to collaborate with the public authorities in the development of social solidarity." The state possesses strict statutory controls over union activities, finances, and leadership. A trade-union tax, equivalent to one day's pay per year and levied on all workers, provides 60 percent of the *sindicatos'* revenues. Though membership dues are nominal, many workers simply neglect to pay them, depriving the unions of financial independence.

Unions may spend trade-union tax revenues only on certain delineated activities: primary and vocational schools; libraries; maternity, medical, dental, and legal assistance; placement services; credit and consumer cooperatives; and holiday camps and sporting activities. These activities provide social-welfare benefits; they are deliberately not activities to develop a militant working-class consciousness. Because strike activity tends to raise that consciousness, union budgets, whatever their origin, may not be used for strike funds. Finally, the labor ministry and the police screen candidates for union office, and the ministry may oust elected union officers and replace them with interventors (federally appointed officials charged with correcting the alleged violation of law or financial or administrative mismanagement that led to intervention).

Populist politics enabled labor leaders to escape the restrictions of these laws. Union heads promised to deliver working-class votes to populist politicians in return for lax law enforcement along with patronage appointments. The labor leaders drove ever harder bargains with the populist politicians, until they ultimately came to exercise real leverage over decisions on policy matters and over the president's choices for certain cabinet posts. However, the labor leaders built their political influence over President Goulart upon the illusion of power, and this proved their undoing in 1964. Their power was illusory because it did not flow from strong, direct, autonomous, and highly institutionalized links between themselves and the rank-and-file workers in the *sindicatos*. Many Brazilians believed the labor leaders possessed great power because of their success in getting workers to participate in "political" strikes or mass demonstrations and rallies. Even the name of the central labor organization they founded in 1962, the General Labor Command (CGT), added to the illusion that the labor leaders could direct the entire working class.

Large turnouts at strikes and demonstrations, however, did not result from class consciousness or the peer pressure of disciplined, autonomous labor organizations. As already noted, many workers participated in rallies or strikes on the basis of a narrow calculation of self-interest, hoping that being in favor with their union heads would mean improved access to social-insurance services. And in the case of a series of politically important strikes between 1960 and 1964, labor leaders did not get workers into the streets for political ends despite the political demands they included in their lists of grievances. Successful work stoppages occurred because the workers were feeling an economic pinch: Nearly all the successful political strikes occurred in the troughs of the saw-toothed curve of *real* minimum wages, when Brazil's runaway inflation had eaten up between a quarter and a half of most workers' paychecks, creating generalized and intense discontent. Rather than leading the workers into the streets, union heads were, more accurately, following them. Labor leaders lacked the organizational structure and control necessary to call workers off the job in the absence of economic discontent.

Contemporary observers believed that, because of their ability to paralyze the economy, unionized workers possessed power comparable to that of the military. This opinion overlooked evidence that the military, even between 1960 and 1964, set limits upon the activities of labor leaders. Of the seventeen major political strikes and strike threats in the period, for example, a unified officer corps opposed ten. Six of them never went beyond the level of threat, and the military undermined, crushed, or ended three others by forcing an unfavorable settlement upon the workers. In only one of the ten cases did the workers attain their demands, and in this one, too, the military shaped the outcome.

In the wake of the coup of 1964, the new government moved decisively to curtail workers' political and economic leverage. During 1964 and 1965, the labor ministry purged the elected officers in 4 out of 7 worker confederations and in 532 *sindicatos* and federations (nearly one-third of all such bodies), replacing them with interventors. This done, it enforced the laws described earlier. The government quickly eliminated the two principal sources of political leverage for labor leaders. It purged radical workers from their positions in the social-insurance and welfare bureaucracies and then restructured those bureaucracies to reduce the number and power of worker representatives on their administrative boards. The unions lost two functions that can raise working-class consciousness: the power to bargain collectively and the power to call strikes. The government enacted a technocratic formula to raise workers' wages automatically each year (theoretically by slightly more than the increase in the cost of living, though in practice by a good deal less), and it passed a law forbidding most strikes, including any calling for wage readjustments above those determined by the formula. When workers sought to resist, as in two major metalworkers' strikes in 1968, the government crushed them forcefully.

Only after 1977 did a new generation of labor leaders, based principally in such new or newly modernized activities as the automotive and chemical industries, begin developing successful strategies to assert their interests in the gradually liberalizing political and economic system. Strike activity and union organizational efforts increased dramatically from 1978 through 1980. Even though the government has repressed some major strikes since then, it is no longer capable of completely suppressing working-class activism.

In one of the many contradictions that characterize Brazil in this dynamic period of transition, the nation's best-known labor leader— whom the government removed from the presidency of the São Bernardo Metalworkers' Union and barred from further trade-union activity after he directed a major strike in 1980—is now head of the Workers' party (Partido dos Trabalhadores), a new party formed to defend workers' interests in the liberalizing political system. One of its main goals is to repeal the antistrike laws and to remove the corporative controls over workers' union organizations. Although it is impossible to predict the exact nature of the institutions that will emerge from the present transition, many observers note that the working class cannot be effectively woven into the fabric of a stable democracy if continued corporative controls prevent workers from autonomously managing their own institutions.

The Military

Military officers, because they control the state's ultimate instruments of coercion, constitute a major political factor in any nation. In today's Brazil, where officers hold the presidency, some cabinet posts, and the security and intelligence apparatus, they are the undisputed top political force. Even if the prodemocracy movement succeeds in restoring civilian rule, military wishes cannot be ignored.

Observers in the early 1960s underrated the political power of the military because the officers had not, in this century, attempted to run a frankly military government and because a number of well-known officers were known as *constitutionalists*—that is, supporters of the existing democratic constitutional order. Nevertheless, the military has always played a critical role in moments of transition in Brazil. Military officers overthrew the empire in 1889 and replaced it with a republic; they conspired with Getúlio Vargas to carry out the Revolution of 1930; they worked with Vargas to establish the Estado Novo in 1937; they overthrew him in 1945 and allowed a democratic constitution to be written; and they brought down that democracy in 1964 and replaced it with an authoritarian regime.

It is tempting to describe this pattern of political intervention as militarism, but this term obscures the important fact that military intervention in Brazil has always resulted from a dynamic process of civil-military relations. In each of the five cases mentioned, civilian groups helped politicize the officers and bring them into the conflict.

In a sense, civilians have tended to endow the military with the moderating power once possessed by the emperor. In all three constituent assemblies (1889, 1934, and 1946), each time over the objections of the military, civilian delegates wrote constitutional provisions making the military the ultimate guardians of the nation's political institutions and specifying that, in pursuit of this goal, the military should obey the president *only* "within the limits of the law."

The military coup, therefore, is not a pathology but rather a pattern rooted in the political behavior of the principal civilian groups. Prior to 1964, the president regularly sought to win military support for his programs and objectives, and nearly all organized civilian groups, from bankers to trade-union leaders, did likewise. At moments of great tension, civilian appeals for military action ceased to be discreet; they appeared on the editorial pages of the nation's leading newspapers. Take, for example, the following passage from the *Diário de Notícias* of March 23, 1964, a week before the military ousted President Goulart: "If the highest executive is opposed to the constitution, condemns the regime, and does not comply with the laws, he automatically loses the right to be obeyed. . . . The armed forces are charged by Article 177 of the Constitution to defend the country and to guarantee the constitutional institutions, law, and order."[13]

Before 1964, the Brazilian military's role fit the *moderator model.* Military officers, heeding the arguments of opposition politicians, overthrew the existing government, allowed the opposition faction to take office, and then withdrew from the active exercise of political power. After 1964, the pattern changed, for the officers who overthrew Goulart did not turn power back to the civilians. Since the coup, military officers have dominated the polity and reserved for themselves the key positions. They debate and take stands on policies from agrarian reform to national integration and economic development. For fifteen years after 1964, the top two hundred generals and admirals made up an informal electoral college that selected the governing party's candidate for the presidency.

What accounts for the shift from the moderator model to one of direct, long-term exercise of political power? Two decades ago, students of military behavior argued that the more professionalized the military of any nation became, the less likely it was to intervene in politics. This argument, based on European experience, held that professionalized military officers would accept civilian control of the political system because the system itself enjoyed general legitimacy and because the officers had no time for politics while they were developing the highly specialized skills necessary to defend their nation from external attack.

By the 1960s, the nature of professionalization had changed. The new professionalism, fostered by U.S. military assistance programs in the 1950s, emphasized internal security. It had emerged because some civilian groups had challenged Brazil's capitalist economic order and hence, the legitimacy of the polity. For Brazilian officers, therefore, national security could not be separated from the complex issues of social, economic, and political development.

The internal-security vocation is institutionalized and emphasized in the publications and curricula of Brazil's military schools. The three-year Army General Staff School, for example, changed its focus to the new professionalism in the late 1950s and early 1960s. In 1956, its curriculum devoted no class hours to internal security, counterguerrilla warfare, or communism. Ten years later, its students spent 351 hours on these topics and only 24 hours on territorial warfare, a major topic of the old professionalism. In earlier years, the officers' education and training had isolated their activities from civilian political activities. Expansion of training in the social, economic, psychological, and political aspects of internal security gave military officers a new confidence in themselves and their ability to rule. In 1964, equipped now with confidence, with a doctrine for national security and national development, with the trained middle-level personnel to implement these doctrines, and with the armed force necessary to impose them, the military put an end to the populist democratic era and returned Brazil to centralized authoritarian rule.

For high Brazilian officers, the exercise of political power has well served their personal and institutional interests. Not only do they have the prestige that comes with high office, but they have rewarded themselves with exceedingly generous increases in pay and fringe benefits and in some cases graft. They chose economic advisers whose successful policies for economic expansion in the late 1960s and 1970s nurtured their dream of great-power status by the end of this century.

The possession of political power has been a mixed blessing, however. If military officers boast that their rule created the "economic miracle," then they must likewise bear responsibility for the catastrophic economic crisis of the early 1980s. One reason the officers overthrew Goulart was to safeguard their institutional integrity from internal political division. In particular, they were responding to the success of left-wing groups who were building a following among enlisted personnel and noncommissioned officers. Paradoxically, military rule, now that the bloom is off the economic "miracle," has brought out new and very serious divisions within the military. The tugging and hauling of differing military factions have prevented each of the post-1964 presidents from imposing his first choice for a successor. Tensions increased so dramatically in mid-1977, as various factions jockeyed for position, that President Geisel ousted his war minister, Gen. Sylvio Frota. According to some observers, Geisel's action narrowly averted a coup by Frota, who belonged to a hard-line, authoritarian faction of the military. In January 1978, Geisel named Frota's rival, Gen. João Baptista Figueiredo, as his preferred successor.

Tensions of this sort, combined with the onus for the economic crisis of the 1980s, have made the notion of extrication from direct rule all the more attractive to many officers. The transition process remains fraught with tensions and uncertainty, however. No easy and guaranteed plan or timetable exists, so the transition has consisted of ad hoc moves by the civilian opposition and countermoves by the government. In the ten years since 1974, the opposition has made successive electoral gains and then has used these gains to extract concessions from the government that progressively strengthen and institutionalize the rule of law and democratic procedure. Significant among these were the elimination of the government's power to oust legislators from political office and to annul the political rights of citizens; the establishment of political amnesty and the concomitant restoration of political rights to those who had lost them; and the reestablishment of direct elections for governor.

Although some military officers still believe military rule is necessary to protect the nation from "subversion," many others have contributed to the gradual liberalization and redemocratization. Indeed, President Geisel quite consciously broke an important "tradition" by selecting Figueiredo without first consulting the informal electoral college of top-ranking officers, thereby establishing the precedent that those officers cannot by right expect to control access to the presidency. The moves toward redemocratization necessarily weaken the very foundations of military rule. A measure of success of the opposition movement is that, by 1984, Figueiredo had clearly lost control of the selection of his successor.

Industrialists

Among the principal beneficiaries of military rule have been the industrialists, for industrial output boomed at more than 10 percent per year from 1968 through 1974, leading to record profits and opportunities for expansion. Yet industrialists as a class have exercised relatively little political power in this period. It cannot be said that they forced the state to establish policies favorable to them. Rather, technocrats occupying high positions in the state bureaucracy made and implemented policies beneficial to industrialists because these technocrats themselves wished to promote Brazil's industrialization and economic modernization. In effect, Brazil's industrialists have "exchanged the right to rule for the right to make money."[14]

The sociopolitical context of industrialization in Brazil differs markedly from the British-based model of economic growth often taught in U.S. universities. Industrial expansion did not result from a conscious, concerted effort by industrialists *as a class* in opposition to the landed gentry. From the beginning of this century, it was common for the elites in agriculture and industry to merge, often through marriages that infused the new wealth controlled by immigrant industrialists with the old wealth of the landed class.

When Getúlio Vargas, who came from a southern ranching family, took power during the Great Depression, he adopted policies designed both to revive Brazil's export agriculture and to promote local industrialization. The industrial bourgeoisie, which had assumed the anti-egalitarian values of the traditional landed elites, manifested no conviction or sentiment that political democracy would help industrialists pursue their goals. Indeed, industrialization advanced as well in the authoritarian years as in the populist democratic years.

Industrialists, of course, wanted to expand Brazil's manufacturing sector. But the point is that they did not possess the political leverage to impose a policy of industrial development. Other factors led to such a policy. First, Vargas wished to enhance Brazil's power, and industrialization was essential to that goal. Second, the Great Depression and World War II made domestic industrialization an imperative. The depression drastically reduced Brazil's foreign-exchange earnings and its ability to import essential manufactured goods. The war, although increasing Brazil's sales to the belligerents, restricted imports because the major industrial economies were producing for the war effort. Vargas's advisers thus devised industrial plans on their own initiative and in response to the world situation. They consulted with, but took no orders from, the industrialists. After 1947, Brazil's chronic acute foreign-exchange shortages left state policymakers with no alternative save to favor domestic industrialization if they wanted to keep Brazil from being a poor agrarian backwater.

Vargas achieved institutional leverage over industrialists in the same way that he did over workers—through corporative organizations. The labor code established parallel *sindicato* organizations for employers and workers, with the same state controls. State technocrats, by selectively distributing patronage (contracts, tariff exemptions, tax benefits, and the like) to member firms of these organizations, have maintained enough allies within them to prevent significant opposition to official policies. At the same time, these organizations provide structured access to state policymakers. Since these policymakers are themselves interested in promoting industrialization, they pay serious attention to industrialists' messages and information. Lastly, industrialists have established a number of autonomous organizations outside and often parallel to the official corporative bodies. These unmonitored organizations proved useful vehicles in the conspiracy against President Goulart, and during the succession process in 1977–1978, they mobilized public opinion to influence the policies of the new government.

The Catholic Church

During the heady days of the 1960s, scholars, journalists, and lay people believed that the Catholic Church was abandoning its traditional, conservative political role and that it would now support an egalitarian social transformation in nations such as Brazil. These optimistic evaluations proved unfounded because of the Church's close corporative relationship with the state.

During the 1930s, the Church built a close relationship with the Vargas government—a relationship that has endured—and thus secured state financing for Catholic schools, seminaries, hospitals, and other related activities. The history of Catholic political activity from that period shows that at no time did the hierarchy act contrary to the interests of the leaders or parties in charge of the state. After all, the state provided a major portion of Church revenues. When the state, during the radical populist years, permitted and even encouraged political mobilization, the Church did likewise. An extensive network of Catholic student, worker, and peasant organizations appeared and began to take stands favoring progressive and even radical social transformation. When, after 1964, the state sought to turn back the mobilization of the populist era, the hierarchy—frightened by the forces it had let loose—followed suit, disbanding the radical organizations. Since 1964, some significant Church voices have denounced the worsening poverty of the lower classes and the systematic abuse of human rights, and in 1977 and 1978, Cardinal Arns of São Paulo became one of the leading voices in the movement seeking redemocratization. During the 1970s, however, the repressive authoritarian regime limited the opportunities for concrete action in favor of a more egalitarian society, so activist priests worked to help the poor with individual rather than collective solutions, through more purely pastoral activities.[15]

These pastoral activities nevertheless have contributed significantly to building civilian grass-roots political institutions that will serve and help support a democratic political order. Priests, other religious personnel, and Catholic lay activists address critical social problems through a variety of agencies and institutions established or authorized by the National Conference of Brazilian Bishops. Specific pastoral agencies now exist to serve slum dwellers, peasants, urban industrial workers, abandoned children, and such oppressed minorities as blacks and Indians, as well as to secure and uphold human rights. Alongside these socially oriented pastoral activities has arisen a network of Christian Base Communities, groups of lay people who together study the Bible, pray, and analyze and address neighborhood and social problems. These grass-roots organizations of Catholics, which constitute one institutional response by the Church to a serious shortage of priests, were thought by the early 1980s to number some eighty thousand.

Not only do these bodies provide an opportunity for citizens to address local problems, but they necessarily give those citizens important experience in political participation and organization. The very nature of this joint religious and secular experience at the grass roots nurtures and reinforces democratic values, for it leads many participants to a new sense of political efficacy as they exchange their formerly passive social and political roles for active participatory ones. Consider the political implications of the following observation by a long-time student of the Brazilian Church: "Once the process of decentralization is initiated and the people at the grass-roots level are defined as being the church, then the whole system of authority is inverted and the laity no longer has to wait for word from above but can assume responsibility on its own."[16]

Indeed, many in the new generation of labor leaders have had contact with or experience in the Christian Base Communities or in pastoral agencies for workers. The major São Bernardo metalworkers' strike of 1980 demonstrated this relationship. Churches opened their doors as meeting halls after the government seized and closed the union head-quarters, ousted the union officers, and denied workers the use of the local stadium. Catholic organizations helped raise funds, supplies of food, and other necessities for the strikers. Subsequently, members of Catholic organizations have been among the most enthusiastic supporters and activists in the Workers' party.

Students

In Brazil, students emerged as an active political force later than in neighboring countries because the student population was minuscule and the medical, law, and other faculties were only consolidated into universities after the Revolution of 1930. The Vargas government created and subsidized corporative student organizations in order to prevent students from opposing the interests of the state. Students, nevertheless, have proved difficult to control.

Student groups, from the founding of the National Union of Students (UNE) in 1938 until its closure in 1964 (and underground since then), have taken an active stand on critical issues or transitions in Brazil. In 1945, for example, UNE leaders joined the movement that brought Vargas down. In the early 1950s, they worked with nationalist military groups in calling for the creation of a national petroleum corporation (Petróleo Brasileiro, S.A.—Petrobrás). In the early 1960s, they demanded radical social and economic reforms. In none of these cases did they act alone; they had the support of politicians who were in or soon would be in power. After 1964, however, the UNE wound up on the side of the outs. Brazil's military rulers, in the name of rooting out subversion, eliminated the UNE and replaced it with the National Directorate of Students, whose activities were narrowly circumscribed to professional, cultural, or recreational pursuits.

The government's prohibition did not stem student protest. UNE leaders continued to enjoy widespread backing, despite the loss of their subsidies and legally protected status. And until 1968, with military rule becoming harsher and the technocrats seemingly unable to get the economy back on its feet, UNE leaders catalyzed many mass protest demonstrations. The street-demonstration phase ended that year when military and police forces killed a number of students during nationwide protests and then instituted systematic torture of dissidents. With all peaceful avenues of protest closed off, student militants turned to the simplistic lessons that Regis Debray drew from the Cuban Revolution and published in his widely read *Revolution in the Revolution?* Although their rural and urban guerrilla activities failed to shake the regime, they dramatically focused world attention on repression in Brazil when they kidnapped the U.S. ambassador in 1969. The student movement then became quiescent until the mid-1970s, when a number of student activists began trying to reconstruct the UNE and succeeded in holding several clandestine national student meetings. With the revitalization of election campaigns and political activity, students have worked most prominently for opposition parties.

Large Landholders

A landed elite dominated Brazilian politics from independence through the Revolution of 1930, and since then the landholders have retained enough power to prevent the ascendant urban forces from fundamentally violating their interests. Vargas, for example, did not extend the reach of the labor code to the rural areas, in order to avoid provoking the landholders.

Consistent with corporatist logic, a decree by Vargas in 1945 created representative organizations for rural interests, the Brazilian Rural Confederation and its member associations at the county level. Unlike the other corporative organizations, which separated owners and employees, these subsidized bodies included all persons who "practice rural activities." Given the landlords' wealth, political connections, and historical use of force, these organizations naturally offered no influence to small landholders, sharecroppers, and rural workers. Only in 1963, during the radical populist period, was the law changed so that rural workers could organize *sindicatos* independent of the large landowners.

Like other corporative interest associations covered here, the Brazilian Rural Confederation's links to the government undermined the confederation's autonomy and, hence, its ability to oppose the agrarian-reform bills submitted by President Goulart before 1964. The landowners, therefore, relied on independent parallel organizations that they funded with their own money, such as the Brazilian Rural Society in São Paulo. Rather than fight Goulart's bills in Congress, these parallel organizations established contacts with military officers and with parallel industrialist and merchant organizations in order to build an ultimately successful movement to overthrow the president. Ironically, soon after the coup President Humberto Castello Branco proposed an agrarian-reform bill in many ways similar to Goulart's, and the landed elites were powerless to stop its passage. When implemented, however, it served rather than damaged their interests. In the 1970s, technocratic measures to increase agricultural exports and produce fuel alcohol greatly benefited the landholders, for loan programs at low or negative real interest rates enabled them to expand their domains and wealth.

Peasants

Brazilian peasants—here broadly defined to include landless rural workers, poor tenants, and owners of tiny plots (minifúndios)—have, with a few notable exceptions, lacked autonomous organization. This situation is a reflection of the power of the large landholders, who usually control local water supplies, credit, marketing, and feed and seed distributors, as well as the police force (and sometimes hired gunmen). Peasant protest, therefore, has usually occurred only when forces from outside the locality did the organizing and offered some countervailing authority to that of the landlord.

In the early 1960s, for example, influence over state politics began to slip from the landlords' hands in a number of states, including such major ones as Pernambuco and Rio Grande do Sul. The nationally prominent governors in these two states and some other rising politicians supported rural organizers who built up impressive followings in the few years before the military smothered most independent rural organizations. These organizers represented diverse interests, from the Communist party to the Catholic hierarchy, and they fought perhaps as much against each other as against the landlords. The military intervened before any one of these groups triumphed in the infighting, so time did not permit the newly awakened peasant consciousness to institutionalize itself in organizations capable of defending peasant interests in the hostile climate after 1964.

Because the labor code allowed the organization of worker *sindicatos* in the countryside only after 1963, many of the peasant leagues created earlier were originally civil associations and, hence, outside the reaches of the ministry of labor. The post-1964 government closed down the majority of these and intervened in most of the official rural *sindicatos* formed after 1963. The government then fostered in most counties the creation of official *sindicatos* under approved leadership, provoking one analyst to comment: "The last remaining uncorporatized arena that caused so much anxiety during the Goulart regime will then have been preempted and, presumably, placed beyond the reach of any future mobilization."[17]

In the political effervescence of the late 1970s and 1980s, however, such government goals proved illusory. Rural workers developed increasingly able and articulate leadership, and in 1980 a vast array of peasant-union and Catholic organizations called an effective strike of some 250,000 sugarcane workers.

The United States and Brazilian Politics

No discussion of political actors in Brazil would be complete without including the role of the United States. As Brazil's principal trading partner, moneylender, foreign investor, military adviser, trade-union tutor, and general role model as a New World great power, the United States is an overwhelming presence.

Space does not permit a cataloging of the ways in which the United States creates and maintains an infrastructure of dependency (that is, a network of local individuals and institutions supporting U.S. interests) in Brazil. Let us simply examine the U.S. role in a watershed event: the coup of 1964. By late 1963, President Goulart was clearly in trouble, particularly as skyrocketing inflation combined with recession. While domestic groups were deciding whether to support him or those seeking to overthrow him, the U.S. government made its position clear. It cut off economic aid to the federal government at the same time that it approved big, showy projects for state governors who opposed Goulart and sought to bring him down. U.S. military aid helped set the stage for the coup, according to testimony by a U.S. army general. Brazilian officers kept the U.S. military attaché's office informed of their plans, and the attaché offered material help. In case heavy assistance was needed, the U.S. ambassador had a naval task force, including an aircraft carrier, a helicopter carrier, six destroyers, and four oil tankers, move into position off the coast.[18] The publicly funded American Institute for Free Labor Development trained a special all-Brazilian class of labor leaders shortly before the coup, and the institute's director claimed that its alumni actively assisted in preventing labor unrest during the coup. To conclude, U.S. public and private agencies played no small role in setting the stage for the coup, in training labor leaders to control working-class protest, and in providing weapons, planes, and fuel to back up the Brazilian military in the event of a long struggle or civil war.

U.S. public and private agencies welcomed the coup, which brought an aggressively pro-capitalist government to power. In the 1970s, however, serious friction arose between the two countries over U.S. import restrictions on Brazilian manufactures, Carter administration investigations into human-rights abuses by Brazilian security forces, and an unsuccessful U.S. attempt to scuttle Brazil's nuclear-energy agreement with West Germany. During the boom years, Brazil could afford to ignore U.S. pressures, as it did in the case of the nuclear agreement. Now, with Brazil the leading debtor in the world debt crisis, U.S. leverage has increased. Officials in the Reagan administration offered some help, with hopes that Brazil in return would permit the entry of U.S. multinational corporations into activities reserved for Brazilian companies, the most sought after being personal computers.

STATE INSTITUTIONS

Branches of Government

The first constitution of republican Brazil, that of 1891, borrowed heavily from the constitution of the United States. Some of its enduring organizational forms—such as a system of checks and balances among executive, legislative, and judicial branches, a presidential rather than a parliamentary system, and separation of powers through federalism—sound familiar to North Americans. Equally familiar is the fact that in modern Brazil the executive has become the most powerful branch and that the federal government dominates state and local levels.

These parallels, however, may mislead the North American reader, for the degree of centralized control in today's authoritarian Brazil goes far beyond that in the United States. Strong executive control has characterized Brazil from the nineteenth century to the present. During the Old Republic, when the federal government was formally weak in relation to the states, the strength of the presidential role derived not from the authority attributed to the office by the constitution but rather from the power inherent in controlling at least one and usually both of the two most powerful state political machines. The other state machines were in no position to oppose the two big ones, so their deputies and senators conformed to the wishes of the president. Vargas strengthened the presidency during his rule from 1930 to 1945. Indeed, he acted as both legislature and executive from 1930 to 1934 and again from 1937 to 1945.

Only from 1946 to 1964 did some semblance of balance exist between the president and the legislature. The degree of democracy introduced by the constitution of 1946 led to political conflict in the late 1950s and early 1960s, culminating in the coup of 1964. The chief constituency for the popularly elected president lay in the expanding urban areas, particularly among the growing ranks of urban workers. The chief constituency for the legislature, on the other hand, lay in the rural areas. Because an apportionment formula overrepresented rural areas in the Chamber of Deputies, as did the three-seat allotment for each state in the Senate, conservative landed interests dominated the legislature.

At the height of the populist era, therefore, the president represented industrialization, urban improvement, and social change, and the legislature, with its rural bias, showed little enthusiasm for the legislative programs of the president. Anathema to the rural legislators, of course, was the notion of agrarian reform. At a mass rally in March 1964, President Goulart used a constitutional loophole to defy the legislature and decree an agrarian reform on a 6 mile (10-kilometer) strip of land on each side of federal highways and waterways. He also used his decree power to bring under government ownership most of the (few) remaining private oil refineries in Brazil. Conservative forces, rising to defend the principle of private ownership of the means of production in industry and in the countryside, overthrew Goulart less than three weeks later, claiming the president was violating the constitutional balance among the branches of government.

It is ironic that the movement that sought to safeguard legislative and executive equality paved the way for the total subordination of the Congress to the president. Indeed, the military made very clear their future relationship with the legislature in the First Institutional Act: "This revolution does not seek to legitimize itself through the Congress. It is the Congress, rather, which receives its legitimacy through this Institutional Act, as a result of the constituent power inherent in all revolutions."

The new rulers (who included both military and civilian figures, though the military officers held veto power) used two methods to subject the legislature to absolute executive domination. First, they purged the radical populist politicians. A series of institutional acts enabled the rulers to fire or retire civil servants and professors whom they labeled "corrupt" or "subversive." In the legislatures at federal, state, and local levels, they purged the elected representatives who had been most closely associated with the radical populist movement or who protested the arbitrary measures. To consolidate their power, they quickly purged over one-fifth of the 409 federal deputies elected in 1962, and in a political crisis in late 1968 and 1969, they purged one-fifth of the deputies elected in 1966.

Through the new constitution of 1967 and the military-imposed amendments to it in 1969, the new leaders altered the legislative process so that the executive could easily dominate it. Now all bills submitted by the president become law automatically after ninety days (a hundred days in certain cases), unless Congress rejects them. If the president designates a bill as urgent, Congress has only forty days to reject it. Congress has not yet blocked a bill labeled urgent. When, in March and April 1977 the opposition party found itself in a position to reject a government bill to revise the criminal code, President Geisel closed the Congress and decreed a constitutional amendment implementing the new code. The amendment divided one conservative state (Mato Grosso) in two to create three more conservative senators, and it altered the electoral law to prevent the increasingly popular opposition party from achieving real power.

In the transition since the mid-1970s, Brazil's military rulers have recognized that growing civilian opposition effectively puts limits upon their ability to rule arbitrarily. In response, they have regularly adjusted rules and regulations governing the political process in order to permit growing opposition while at the same time retaining (though by dwindling margins) the upper hand. Policies establishing political amnesty, permitting a multiparty system, and reestablishing direct elections for governor constitute part of this strategic retreat, and the ultimate return to a directly elected president will end military rule and permit consolidation of democratic institutions. Because Congress has served as a critical forum in the struggle to open the system, it is likely, as an institution, to build upon this recent experience by fashioning an assertive role in a democratic Brazil.

Brazilian Federalism

In colonial times and during the empire, Brazil's continental dimensions compelled the central government to tolerate a great degree of decentralization. The constitution of 1891 reflected that reality by giving Brazil a federal system. The height of state autonomy came under the Old Republic, when states could contract foreign loans and apply export taxes to interstate commerce and when dynamic states like São Paulo fostered immigration, organized the coffee-valorization project, and created economic infrastructure, particularly in transportation. The wealthiest states possessed both economic resources and the political support of the federal government, so they had the greatest autonomy. For the lesser states, resistance to federal desires brought the removal of governors and their replacement by federally appointed interventors.

In the 1930s, Vargas ruled all states but one through interventors. With the establishment of a democratic system in 1946, the federal government respected state autonomy, and intervention became a thing of the past. After the military ousted Goulart in 1964, however, it removed radical populist governors in three states, though without declaring formal intervention.

The strongest states safeguarded their autonomy with their own armies or militias. When São Paulo seceded in 1932, for example, its militia resisted the federal army for two months before surrendering. After the coup of 1964, the federal government placed federal army officers in command of the militias. Today the states are still viable political entities, although they dare not defy the federal government on major policy matters, because the federal government transfers significant resources to them. They control large budgets and have major responsibility for delivering critical services such as health care and education. In the late 1940s, they spent slightly more than the federal government on these services, about twice as much in the early 1960s, and over three times as much by the mid-1970s.

The *municípios* (local government units roughly analogous to U.S. counties or townships) are weak, underfunded, and almost irrelevant to the majority of citizens. The *municípios* account for only 10 to 15 percent of total public expenditures, as opposed to the states' 40 percent and the federal government's 45 to 50 percent. Since the states provide the essential services, ordinary citizens do not identify with their *município* government or see its officers as particularly important, an attitude that, although not unfounded, helps perpetuate control by local elites—usually landowners—in most *municípios* outside the major cities.[19]

A federal system, in any complex and populous nation, serves to stablize the polity, because it decentralizes decisions and responsibility and hence disperses tensions. This function diminished in Brazil after 1965, when the military rulers put an end to direct elections for state governors and stipulated that they be elected indirectly by the state legislatures—a process less likely to escape the control of the central government. In 1982, however, the federal government responded to pressures for redemocratization as well as to its own mounting economic problems by reestablishing direct elections for governor. While campaigning that year, the opposition parties condemned federal policies for causing the severe economic crisis. Ironically, directly elected opposition-party governors are now in charge of controlling the social tensions born of that crisis in ten of the nation's most important states. Federalism, therefore, is once again performing a stabilizing function in Brazil, a constructive factor in the transition toward full democracy.

State and Society: Means of Domination

Even during the most repressive years of military rule in the early 1970s, the Brazilian political system was authoritarian, not totalitarian. The government did not enforce conformity of thought on all citizens, though it did exercise a variety of controls over their actions, ranging from censorship to outright repression and systematic torture. The film *Pra Frente Brasil* graphically depicted torture by security forces and the surge of armed opposition that it fed. President Geisel succeeded in putting an end to systematic torture in the late 1970s.

Censorship over the print media has been almost completely lifted, and political debate is now wide open and free of all formal fetters. State controls over the electronic media have been relaxed but not ended. It is perhaps symbolic of Brazil's expanded "political space" and the contradictions it has fostered that the aforementioned film, a national box-office success in 1983, was made in Brazil with public funds, though its director secured its commercial release only after a long battle with the film censors.

Military forces nevertheless maintain a pervasive intelligence system for keeping tabs on Brazilian citizens, a system they expanded and sharpened during the years of authoritarian rule. One often hears reference to the political power of the military-run National Information Service (SNI), a kind of Federal Bureau of Investigation (FBI) and Central Intelligence Agency (CIA) rolled into one that Figueiredo headed before becoming president. The reach of what Brazilians refer to euphemistically as the "security community" goes far beyond the visible SNI bureaucracy, for it involves a vast network, some 250,000 strong, of commissarlike military and police agents assigned to each important agency of all civilian ministries, as well as to state and many local agencies. The security community gained considerable public attention during a debate over Brazilian nuclear power plants in 1980, when it leaked a report to the press demonstrating that security agents had meticulously monitored all antinuclear activity and built up detailed dossiers on the participants.[20]

BRAZIL   197

State and Economy: Means of Direction

Ever since the 1930s, the state has been an aggressive economic actor in Brazil. Yet the industrial bourgeoisie, a sector most North Americans would expect to resent and resist an active role by the state, has generally welcomed state intervention, despite some grumbling about specific policies. The explanation is simple: Intervention has greatly enriched the industrialists and dramatically increased Brazil's industrial production over the last three decades.

The technocrats who have made economic policy are few in number. One study of economic policymaking from 1947 to 1964 claimed that the technocratic elite consisted of fewer than forty individuals occupying key roles in the finance and planning ministries, state banks, and the like. Even after the dramatic economic expansion of the 1970s, this elite remains small, estimated in 1977 at fewer than eighty.[21]

The state uses both indirect and direct means to foster and shape economic development. Indirectly, the technocrats attract and guide foreign and domestic investment through tax incentives and preferential interest and exchange rates. They not only protect domestic industry with tariffs and import restrictions, but in some instances they create new industries. Brazil's automotive industry consisted merely of assembly lines using imported parts until the government established carrot-and-stick incentives and sanctions to force the auto firms to manufacture in Brazil. By the late 1970s, with annual output around 1 million vehicles, Brazil's auto industry ranked tenth in the world. Brazilian automobile engines are now exported for installation in cars produced in the United States and West Germany. Many other industries, from shipbuilding and aircraft manufacture to petrochemicals, have similar histories.

Directly, the technocrats also spur industrialization by becoming industrialists themselves. A respected annual ranking of Brazil's top 500 corporations found that, in 1981, 10 of the top 25 firms were owned by the federal government, 8 belonged to state governments, and only 7 represented private capital. Of the top 50 firms, 26 were publicly owned and 24 came from the private sector. These state firms include steel, petroleum, aluminum, chemical, electric power, and iron-mining companies. The economic weight of the state sector has grown progressively. Between 1947 and 1964, public expenditure as a share of gross domestic product increased from 16 to 27 percent, and by 1969 it exceeded 32 percent and was still growing. This is a far higher percentage than in any other Latin American country except Cuba. The state's role in productive investment has evolved similarly. In 1966, the share of assets of state, local private, and foreign private capital in Brazil's three hundred largest industrial firms was as follows: 16, 36, and 47 percent, respectively. By 1974, these figures had changed to 32, 28, and 40 percent.

State economic elites have entrepreneurial ability and the opportunity to apply it. A subsidiary of the state oil company (Petrobrás), for example, recently put together a giant petrochemical complex in the state of Bahia. This complex, which will double Brazil's petrochemical production, consists of eleven three-cornered enterprises combining local private, foreign private (multinational corporations), and state capital; five joint enterprises combining foreign private capital with local private or state capital; one wholly local private firm; and one enterprise owned by the state alone. This arrangement brings together a dozen different multinational corporations from a half dozen industrial nations; through licensing agreements, it draws on technology from fourteen more. Private investors, deciding on their own without the incentives and prods of the state, surely would not have located a petrochemical complex in an area so remote from the industrial South and Southeast. The technocrats, however, resolved to spur industrial development in the Northeast, and they succeeded in setting up this "growth pole."

As a result of policies such as these, Brazil's economic performance was truly impressive from 1947 through 1980. Total economic output grew by an annual average of 7 percent, one of the highest sustained growth rates recorded anywhere. After 1980, however, the boom collapsed, and output suffered an average decline of 1.3 percent per year from 1981 through 1983. Crisis indicators in recent years include record numbers of bankruptcies, aggravated unemployment and underemployment, and spreading despair that has manifested itself in rising crime rates and riots with looting in areas with highest unemployment.

The technocrats who took responsibility for the outstanding growth of recent decades must share responsibility for the crisis, for their policies raised Brazil's foreign debt from $3.3 billion in 1967 to about $100 billion in 1984. The variable-rate loans they took out in the 1970s at low or negative real interest rates now are carrying record high rates, forcing Brazil to take out ever larger loans just to service the past debt. Further aggravating the situation is the world economic recession of the early 1980s that has slowed the growth of markets where Brazil could earn foreign exchange.

Economic Policy and Dependency

From the 1930s through the 1950s, it was commonly believed that if developing nations substituted locally manufactured goods for imports, they would reduce their need for foreign currency and, hence, their dependency on industrial nations. In Brazil as elsewhere, however, this belief proved false. Economic development decreased Brazil's need for finished products but more than offset the savings by increasing the need for imported capital goods, industrial inputs, and fuel. Foreign trade thus remains essential to the Brazilian development model.

Brazilian policymakers have consciously worked to lower their historical reliance on one dominant trading partner, so that no single foreign government would be in a position to strangle Brazil economically. In 1960, the United States absorbed 39 percent of Brazil's exports, but by the early 1980s, this share had dropped to 18 percent. The next six biggest trading partners range from 4 to 7 percent of the total and, together with the United States, consume less than half of Brazil's exports.

Brazil diversified its sources of foreign investment and credit, but these measures were not sufficient to prevent bankers based in the industrial capitalist world from bending Brazilian social and economic policies to their will during the debt crisis of the early 1980s. Brazilian policymakers had clearly lost control of the geometrically ballooning debt by 1983, and they turned to the International Monetary Fund for assistance in order to stave off default and the costly disruption of trading relations that default would provoke. The bitter medicine prescribed by the IMF as a condition for aid—wage reductions, credit curtailments, price increases, and import restrictions—exacerbated the already severe social costs of Brazil's recession.

Brazil's postwar economic model had simply taken abundant supplies of cheap imported oil for granted, and after the oil shocks of the 1970s, this form of petroleum dependency greatly aggravated Brazil's debt. Indeed, Brazil is the Third World's largest oil importer, and the OPEC shocks caused its oil-import bill to increase twenty times, from $.5 billion in 1972 to $10.6 billion in 1981. Policymakers reacted with a variety of innovative measures. They intensified Petrobrás's domestic exploration, fostered conversion from petroleum to other fuels, and facilitated conservation, so that the ratio of imports to total petroleum consumption fell from 85 percent in the late 1970s to about 50 percent in 1984. By 1983, they had brought the oil-import bill down by nearly one-third from its 1981 peak.

Petrobrás also has exploration contracts with ten foreign countries, mostly in the Middle East, and it has several relatively small strikes there. The oil company has created a trading company to set up exchanges of Brazilian products for fuels and minerals. Its large-scale sales include multiple-year contracts to deliver Brazilian iron ore and iron and steel products, manufactured goods including weapons, construction technology and services, and traditional agricultural products, mostly in trade for oil or coal. Its major partners in barter-type deals have included Mexico, Poland, China, the USSR, Nigeria, and several Middle Eastern oil exporters. Such aggressive sales efforts almost sextupled the value of Brazil's exports, from $4.0 billion in 1972 to $23.3 billion in 1981, but the increased revenues have nevertheless failed to keep pace with the import and debt-service bills, leaving a bigger debt each year.

Many dependency analysts argue that the only way for a dependent nation to become independent is to overturn capitalism and replace it with socialism. Brazil's technocrats, reasoning differently, have chosen the (dependent) capitalist route to economic development. They have sought national autonomy not by replacing capitalism with socialism but by seeking to make Brazil a major capitalist industrial nation by the year 2000. The economic reverses of the early 1980s have merely set their timetable behind, but their long-term goal itself is threatened by the current debt crisis that enables foreign bankers to shape Brazilian economic policy.

During the expansive 1970s, Brazil's neighbors came to view with alarm the modernization of Brazil's armed forces, Brazilian purchases of coffee lands in Paraguay and cattle lands in Uruguay, Brazilian plans to exploit natural gas and iron ore in Bolivia, and Brazil's alleged role in Hugo Banzer Suárez's 1971 military coup there. Moreover, in 1975 Brazil and West Germany signed a controversial agreement under which Brazil would take possession of two to eight nuclear power plants, a uranium-enrichment plant, and a fuel reprocessing plant. Because the last facility may be used to extract plutonium, the critical explosive in atom bombs, U.S. officials and many of Brazil's neighbors fear that this deal, despite its contractual safeguards on paper, will put nuclear weapons in Brazilian hands. The debt crisis and the declining fortunes of nuclear power everywhere have stalled the implementation of the agreement, but it is not officially dead.

If other South Americans had reason to be alarmed by the successes of the Brazilian development model in the 1970s, many Brazilians were also alarmed; the economic achievements were made at great cost to them, as the following section shows.

PUBLIC POLICY: THE COSTS OF THE BRAZILIAN DEVELOPMENT MODEL

After considering Brazil's truly remarkable economic growth record, at least through 1980, it is necessary to examine the other side of the coin: the social costs of the Brazilian development model. It would be an understatement to say that the fruits of the economic miracle have been unequally divided; not only have the majority of Brazilians failed to receive a share in the economic increment since 1964, but they have even lost a substantial part of what they had in the early 1960s.

Income Distribution and Working-Class Well-Being

Brazil's structurally dependent pattern of industrialization has caused income distribution to shift dramatically, increasingly favoring the rich. The very product structure of the economy requires this. For example, in 1970 no market for automobiles would have existed in Brazil, whose per capita income that year was about US$400, if income had been equally divided. Yet private passenger-car production, which began only in 1958, passed the half million mark in the 1970s, because the rich got considerably richer at the expense of the poor.

Brazilian census data illustrate the dramatic shift in income distribution during the 1960s and 1970s. The wealthiest 10 percent of the economically active population earned 27 percent of total income in 1960; by 1980, they had increased their share to 51 percent. The bottom 50 percent saw their share shrink from 17 to 13 percent over the two decades, and one source calculates that by 1980 the poorest 50 percent earned less than the richest 1 percent.[22] Most beneficiaries of the economic "miracle" were from the middle sectors and above—particularly aggressive business people and university-trained, salaried managerial and technical employees. Their economic ascent co-opted them into supporting the system during the early boom years, but a variety of reasons led most of them to oppose continued arbitrary rule by the early 1980s. They wanted to participate meaningfully in the political process; to end torture and other abuses of arbitrary rule; to stem or reverse the expansion of the state sector of the economy, which many entrepreneurs and business people saw as a threat; and, after 1980, to reinvigorate the economy and forcefully defend Brazil's national interest in the debt crisis, policy areas where the authoritarian regime was almost universally judged a failure.

Industrial modernization has made the class structure increasingly complex; some groups of workers have done well, most notably the skilled workers in modern industries. Because their skills were in short supply during the boom years, they successfully pressured their employers to raise their wages. One survey of a modern auto-parts factory, for example, found that two-thirds of the skilled workers owned their own cars.[23]

For the much larger working-class stratum earning the minimum wage, however, the squeeze has been extremely painful. To illustrate, consider the labor necessary to buy a market basket with a month's essential nutritive requirements for one person. In December 1965, a worker earning the minimum wage had to work 87 hours and 20 minutes; in December 1973, this same market basket required 158 hours and 42 minutes! To compound worker misfortune, the government also eliminated the pre-1964 job-security law, paving the way for massive involuntary turnover.

For workers and the poor, diminishing family incomes mean worsening nutrition. It is quite probable that poor nutrition, combined with fatigue caused by excessive overtime in the boom years, led to the rise in workplace accident rates in the late 1960s and early 1970s. One study estimates that Brazilian workplace injury rates are at least five times those in the United States.[24]

Public-Health Policies

No comprehensive study of the political and social effects of Brazil's health policies presently exists. The national accounts reveal, however that the authoritarian government cut back spending on health in its first decade. The share of public expenditures devoted to health ranged between 4.5 and 5.0 percent in the late 1950s and early 1960s, but by the early 1970s, this proportion had fallen to between 3.0 and 3.5 percent.

This cutback in public-health activity, in an era when runaway urbanization was causing the near collapse of urban water and sewer systems, carried a high cost for the poor. Epidemic diseases, such as meningitis, encephalitis, and polio, ravaged Brazil in the mid-1970s. Infant mortality rates, which had been declining in the 1950s and early 1960s, were reversed. In São Paulo, Brazil's industrial capital, 63 out of every 1,000 infants born live died in their first year in 1960; by 1970, 90 out of every 1,000 died. In Belo Horizonte, the infant mortality rates went from 74 to 125 per 1,000 between 1960 and 1973. In Recife, these rates climbed from 126 in 1964 to 174 in 1973.[25] Also contributing to these worsening health indices was the strain placed on all services by the population explosion. Brazil's population doubled between 1949 and 1972, and the government gave no real support to family planning during the 1970s. Finally, the basic approach to public health since World War II has stressed curative programs that treat sick individuals rather than preventive programs aimed at protecting society collectively from disease.

The epidemics of the mid-1970s not only sparked successful crash vaccination campaigns, but they also led the government to return public-health spending to its former share of public expenditures. After the notably successful vaccination programs, which were by definition preventive rather than curative, the government launched two major long-term preventive programs, one to establish a system of rural health posts in the Northeast and the other to control the debilitating parisitic disease, schistosomiasis. Significant resources were invested, and early results were promising. In the early 1980s, the government took steps toward support of family planning. Despite these positive developments, the short-term impact of sharply reduced income during the economic crisis is likely to worsen the health of many Brazilians.

Housing Policy

To tackle Brazil's long-standing urban housing shortage, the new government created the National Housing Bank (BNH) in 1964. About 80 percent of the bank's funds come from the working class through two channels: One is a compulsory savings plan linked to a severance-pay program. The other is a system of voluntary passbook accounts, protected from inflationary erosion by *monetary correction*, a cost-of-living escalator that regularly raises the principal by the increase in the wholesale price index.

The BNH has so successfully captured savings that the United Nations Committee on Housing, Building, and Planning called it "the most advanced system of housing finance in Latin America."[26] In its first ten years, it financed over 1 million dwelling units, compared to a total of only 120,000 financed in Brazil during the preceding twenty-five years. Originally intended as an institution to build low-income housing, the bank in its first ten years did relatively little to help workers and the

Table 9.1 Enrollment in Primary, Secondary and Vocational, and University
Levels in Brazil, 1960–1980

Year	Primary	Secondary and Vocational	University
1960	7,458,000	1,137,000	97,000
1964	10,217,000	1,819,000	138,000
1980	22,149,000	2,824,000	1,407,000

Source: Anuário Estatístico do Brasil, various years.

poor, except that it provided a secure place for them to store their meager savings. One study of the BNH reported in 1975 that "the majority of funds in the program to date is used to finance middle- and upper-income housing, other urban construction, and works of urban infrastructure, rather than subsidized housing for the poor, and that this trend has been increasing."[27]

In 1973, President Emílio Garrastazú Médici, responding to criticism that working-class savings were serving almost exclusively to build homes for the better-off, inaugurated the National Low Cost Housing Plan. Under President Geisel, whose liberalization program presupposed policies more responsive to the needs of the broader electorate, the low-cost housing program picked up speed, so that after 1975 about 30 percent of its loans went to this sector. Low-cost houses are affordable only by skilled workers and others with family incomes at least five times the minimum wage. Recognizing that the very poor often build their own homes, the government devised for them a loan program to cover urban lots and building materials. By 1984, however, the economic crisis—in the form of bank failures, defaults on loans by recipients whose income had fallen, and large net withdrawals from the severance-pay scheme by the unemployed—seriously jeopardized the housing program.

Education Policy

One of the achievements to which post-1964 governments point with pride is the expansion of education. Federal, state, and local government spending on education rose from 1.6 percent of gross domestic product in 1960 to 2.8 percent in 1974. Enrollments increased dramatically, as the data in Table 9.1 illustrate. The goal is to create the human resources necessary for continued rapid economic growth, developing literacy and manual skills in workers as well as research and managerial talents among middle- and higher-level personnel. Despite the impressive statistics, the quality of instruction, particularly at the primary level, is deficient in most rural and poor areas. In the countryside, for example, most children attend a one-room schoolhouse supplied with few books or teaching materials.

To raise the enrollment of higher education the government expanded existing universities and relaxed the rules that formerly held back private institutions in this field. State dominance of higher education ended quickly. In 1964, state institutions enrolled 62 percent of all students in higher education; by 1973, that figure had dropped to 39 percent. The flood of new students caused a sharp increase in the student-faculty ratio, from 4:1 in 1960 to 13:1 in 1973. The government claimed that its educational policies would provide the technical skills necessary for a developing economy, and indeed the number of students in engineering and the exact sciences has risen. Their relative weight in the national student body, however, has not risen, because the new private institutions have concentrated on areas that have the lowest start-up and capital costs—the humanities and social sciences.[28]

Finally, such a fast upsurge in enrollment carries serious political implications. Graduates will surely expect to enjoy middle-class living standards. Should the graduates emerge more quickly than the economy can absorb them, particularly in the context of the economic slowdown, a potentially explosive situation could result. One need only recall the abortive French revolution of 1968. It occurred at a time of massive unemployment among university graduates following a fourfold increase in French university enrollment, from 170,000 in 1958 to 600,000 in 1968.

Land and Agricultural Policies

Agrarian reform was one of the most hotly debated topics in the early 1960s. Radical populists like President Goulart, sympathizing with the poor, powerless, and usually landless peasants, sought vainly to get legislative passage of a redistributive agrarian reform. Finally, Goulart decreed a limited agrarian reform three weeks before he was overthrown, but the new government voided the measure.

Ironically, Goulart's successor, President Castello Branco, also favored rural social justice. He used his authoritarian powers to force legislative passage of an agrarian-reform bill. Before the drafting was completed, however, conservatives deleted the term *social justice* from the bill. Indeed, the final bill merely seeks to enhance rural productivity. Rather than give land to the landless, it creates tax incentives and punishments to get present landowners to turn their *fazendas* into modern, capitalist "rural enterprises." It also attempts to induce owners of small, inefficient *minifúndios* to sell them so that their parcels can be consolidated into commercially viable units. The law permits expropriation, but with so many restrictions as to render it inoperative. From 1967 to 1969, the two most successful years of the Brazilian Institute of Agrarian Reform (IBRA), only two thousand families received land. In 1969, President Arthur da Costa e Silva reorganized the IBRA and cut its budget expressly to prevent it from expropriating and distributing land; following this act, the IBRA's most able officials quit in frustration.[29]

The agrarian reform's "punitive" taxes are so low that they are ineffective. Only its positive inducements—such as credit; extension, technological, and marketing services; and warehousing facilities—serve to guide landowner behavior. Since over 90 percent of Brazil's 3.5 million rural properties do not meet the criteria of rural enterprise, the government could not possibly modernize rural Brazil in less than a generation. Therefore, the government has focused on certain priority sectors that will either generate or save foreign currency. Among the chief beneficiaries are sugarcane farmers in the Northeast and São Paulo, soybean growers in the South, and truck farmers near major cities. As a result, Brazil has gone from soybean importer to the world's second largest soybean exporter (after the United States), and from a large importer of wheat to near self-sufficiency.

In social terms, the chief rural beneficiaries have been middle-size and large farm owners, technicians, and middlemen. By most accounts, the lives of farm laborers and peasants have not improved.

PROSPECTS FOR THE FUTURE

The political institutions of modern Brazil, more than those of any other Latin American nation except Mexico, are built upon and reflect the corporative legacy of the Iberian heritage. Corporative controls over socioeconomic groups secured autonomy for government policymakers as they guided Brazil's outstanding postwar economic growth. Backed up with authoritarian force in the late 1960s and 1970s, these controls enabled the economic planners to impose great hardship on the poor while transferring resources to the rich. Finally these controls served Brazil's technocrats in their bid to end Brazil's historical dependency on the world's dominant capitalist nations—not by breaking with capitalism as Cuba did, but rather by trying to make Brazil a major capitalist industrial power in its own right. The debt crisis has at least temporarily set back this goal. Dependency thus remains a critical variable in any analysis of the Brazilian political process.

Alongside and in direct conflict with the corporative values and institutions is a new, competing set of participatory values that underlies the contemporary movement for democratization. Over the last decade, significant numbers of Brazilians (but by no means all of them) from virtually every socioeconomic niche have developed political demands and a sense of political efficacy and, hence, have begun to claim for themselves the right to decide their own destinies. Students and most intellectuals, of course, have opposed military rule from the very beginning. Prominent lawyers were among the first to make a major issue of human-rights abuses and to call for a return to the rule of law. Many business people, feeling threatened by the growth of the state sector or by the pressures of the economic decline, came to believe a democratically elected government would be more responsive to their interests. Labor leaders and many union members, at least in the most dynamic industrial sectors and in key agricultural activities such as sugar, recognize that the elimination of corporative controls over their organizations would allow them to bargain from strength with employers. Indeed, they have already tested their leadership and organization in numerous strikes since 1978. Even many military officers have supported the movement, some out of democratic conviction and others simply because they want to pass the burden of manifest economic failure from the armed forces to some other group.

Critical to this transformation in value structure has been the Catholic Church. Prominent Church officials like Cardinal Arns of São Paulo publicly put their prestige behind the campaign to end torture and reestablish the rule of law. More important, however, has been the reorientation of the Church's pastoral work toward Brazil's poor majority, especially through the work of the Christian Base Communities. Serving in a sense as action-oriented encounter groups, these bodies have transformed previously passive or alienated persons, particularly in the humbler strata, into confident citizens with participatory values.

Parallel to this growth in values supporting democratization has been the development and strengthening of the institutions and practices of democracy. At no time did the military rulers abolish such democratic institutions as political parties, elections, and representative parliamentary bodies, though in practice they handicapped, muzzled, purged, or gutted them, particularly in the ten years from 1964 to 1974. Because these institutions continued to exist, they could later become autonomous vehicles. After the government banned the pre-1964 parties and stipulated that there be only one official government party and one official opposition party, for example, the wags claimed that the only difference between the two was that one said, "Yes," and the other said, "Yes, sir!" By the 1974 congressional elections, however, the opposition party had become a *real* opposition party, so much so that the government later rewrote the party law to permit a multiparty system in hopes of dividing the opposition and thus prolonging control by the governing party, now called the Democratic Social party (PDS).

Paradoxes and apparently contradictory half measures abound in this period of transition, yet perhaps the process has come as far as it has because participants were willing to compromise and settle for small, gradual concessions instead of demanding immediate and thorough redemocratization. Each step in the process was small enough that by itself it did not constitute a threat to specific officers or to the military as institution. Civilian proponents of amnesty, for example, recognized that the military would surely not support an amnesty for political prisoners or exiles charged with subversion if military and police officials were not absolved of charges of torture and abuse of human rights. The amnesty movement thus linked the two and negotiated the measure that allowed exiles such as Leonel Brizola, now governor of the state of Rio de Janeiro, to return.

No democratic system can function without a good measure of tolerance, compromise, and mutual respect to facilitate bargaining. The gradual process after 1974, through which civilian groups took advantage of small increments in "political space" to organize further and bargain for more, surely provided an education in politics as the art of the possible. Other examples of this process are bargaining after 1983 in the federal Chamber of Deputies (where neither the government's PDS nor the leading opposition party, the Brazilian Democratic Movement party, has a majority without some votes from the three minor opposition parties) and bargaining between the ten opposition-party governors and the federal government that controls many of their purse strings.

The current process of democratization in Brazil is one of the most exciting national-level political experiments in the contemporary world. It remains unfinished at this writing, making it impossible to describe its final outcome or even its timetable. Given Brazil's corporative heritage and the gradualist approach of the democratization movement, it seems certain that many of the corporative institutions and practices will endure long after a directly elected president takes office. Brazil is a complex nation, full of apparent contradictions, so the dynamic contradiction between democratic and authoritarian corporative principles would accurately reflect one of the fundamental paradoxes of national reality.

NOTES

1. Ray S. Cline, *World Power Assessment 1977: A Calculus of Strategic Drift* (Westview Press, Boulder, Colo., 1977), pp. 173–174.

2. Richard L. Camp, *The Papal Ideology of Social Reform: A Study in Historical Development, 1878–1967* (E. J. Brill, Leyden, Holland, 1969), pp. 30–31.

3. Barbara H. Stein and Stanley J. Stein, *The Colonial Heritage of Latin America: Essays on Economic Dependence in Perspective* (Oxford University Press, New York, 1970), pp. 3–26, quotes from pp. 7, 23.

4. Richard M. Morse, "Some Sources of Brazilian Unity," *South Atlantic Quarterly* 61 (Spring 1962):159–182. See also Thomas Flory, "Judicial Politics in Nineteenth-Century Brazil," *Hispanic American Historical Review* 55 (November 1975):664–692.

5. Laura Randall, *A Comparative Economic History of Latin America, 1500–1914*, vol. 3, *Brazil* (University Microfilms International, Ann Arbor, Mich., 1977), p. 90.

6. Cited in Arturo Frondizi, *Industria argentina y desarrollo nacional* (Ediciones Qué, Buenos Aires, 1957), p. 27.

7. E. Bradford Burns, *The Unwritten Alliance: Rio Branco and Brazilian-American Relations* (Columbia University Press, New York, 1966), pp. 40–49.

8. Robert Neal Seidel, *Progressive Pan Americanism: Development and United States Policy Toward South America*, Cornell University Dissertation Series, Latin American Studies Program, no. 45, (Cornell University Press, Ithaca, N.Y., 1973), pp. 422, 418–499 passim.

9. A more detailed discussion of this period, as well as of Brazilian corporatism in theory and practice, appears in Kenneth Paul Erickson, *The Brazilian Corporative*

State and Working-Class Politics (University of California Press, Berkeley, 1977), pp. 15–26 and passim. The following citations to Azevedo Amaral and Francisco Campos may be found on pp. 16–18.

10. Stanley E. Hilton, *Brazil and the Great Powers, 1930–1939: The Politics of Trade Rivalry* (University of Texas Press, Austin, 1975), pp. 212–228, quote from p. 225.

11. Fernando Henrique Cardoso, *Ideologías de la burguesía industrial en sociedades dependientes (Argentina y Brasil)* (Siglo Veintiuno, Mexico, 1971), p. 75.

12. Guillermo A. O'Donnell, *Modernization and Bureaucratic-Authoritarianism* (Institute of International Studies, University of California, Berkeley, 1973), p. 82.

13. This section draws from Alfred Stepan, *The Military in Politics: Changing Patterns in Brazil* (Princeton University Press, Princeton, N.J., 1971), quote from p. 104; and Alfred Stepan, "The New Professionalism of Internal Warfare and Military Role Expansion," in *Authoritarian Brazil: Origins, Policies, and Future,* ed. Alfred Stepan (Yale University Press, New Haven, Conn., 1973), pp. 47–65.

14. Barrington Moore, Jr., *Social Origins of Dictatorship and Democracy: Lord and Peasant in the Making of the Modern World* (Beacon, Boston, 1966), p. 437.

15. The preceding section draws from Ralph Della Cava, "Catholicism and Society in Twentieth-Century Brazil," *Latin American Research Review* 9 (1976):7–50; and Thomas C. Bruneau, *The Political Transformation of the Brazilian Catholic Church,* (Cambridge University Press, New York, 1974); the materials that follow on recent Catholic activities are drawn from Maria Helena Moreira Alves, "Grassroots Organization, Trade Unions, and the Church: A Challenge to the Controlled *Abertura* in Brazil," *Latin American Perspectives* 11 (Winter 1984):73–102; and Thomas C. Bruneau, *The Church in Brazil: The Politics of Religion* (University of Texas Press, Austin, 1982), quote from p. 130.

16. Bruneau, *The Church in Brazil,* p. 130.

17. Philippe C. Schmitter, "The 'Portugalization' of Brazil?" in Stepan, *Authoritarian Brazil,* p. 209.

18. Kenneth Paul Erickson and Patrick V. Peppe, "Dependent Capitalist Development, U.S. Foreign Policy, and Repression of the Working Class in Chile and Brazil," *Latin American Perspectives* 3 (Winter 1976):39–40; *Washington Post,* December 29, 1976, pp. A-1, A-16; Moniz Bandeira, *O governo João Goulart; As lutas sociais no Brasil, 1961–1964* (Civilização Brasileira, Rio de Janeiro, 1977), pp. 126–186.

19. Ana Maria Brasileiro, *O município como sistema político,* (Fundação Getúlio Vargas, Rio de Janeiro, 1973), pp. 103–107.

20. Kenneth Paul Erickson, "State Entrepreneurship, Energy Policy, and the Political Order in Brazil," in *Authoritarian Capitalism: Brazil's Contemporary Economic and Political Development,* ed. Thomas C. Bruneau and Philippe Faucher (Westview Press, Boulder, Colo., 1981), pp. 151–152, 174.

21. See, for pre-1964 figures, Nathaniel H. Leff, *Economic Policy-Making and Development in Brazil, 1947–1964* (Wiley, New York, 1968), pp. 143–145. For 1977 figures, see "Os mandarins da República," *Jornal do Brasil* (December 11, 1977). This and the following sections rely on Leff for pre-1964 material and, for the post-1964 period, on Peter Evans, *Dependent Development: The Alliance of Multinational, State, and Local Capital in Brazil* (Princeton University Press, Princeton, N.J., 1979), and Ronald M. Schneider, *Brazil: Foreign Policy of a Future World Power* (Westview Press, Boulder, Colo., 1976); data on corporations in

1981 from *Conjuntura Econômica,* "Suplemento especial: As 500 maiores em 1981," September 1983.

22. Eduardo Matarazzo Suplicy, "Os dados da distribuição," *Folha de São Paulo,* May 16, 1982, p. 36, as cited in Alves, "Grassroots Organization," pp. 74, 102.

23. J. Sérgio R. C. Gonçalves, "Perfil do operariado numa empresa da indústria automobilística de São Paulo," *Contexto,* no. 3 (July 1977):44.

24. Richard Ginnold, "Job Hazards in the U.S. and Brazil—How Do They Compare?" typescript, School for Workers, University of Wisconsin Extension, Madison, 1977, pp. 1–3.

25. Charles H. Wood, "Infant Mortality Trends and Capitalist Development in Brazil," *Latin American Perspectives* 4 (Fall 1977):58; *Anuário Estatístico do Brasil,* 1967, p. 40; *Latin America* 9 (October 24, 1975):330; materials that follow on population are from Peter McDonough and Amaury de Souza, *The Politics of Population in Brazil: Elite Ambivalence and Public Demand* (University of Texas Press, Austin, 1981); and on health from Peter Knight and Ricardo Moran, *Brasil: Pobreza e necessidades básicas* (Editora Zahar, Rio de Janeiro, 1981), pp. 35–40, 57–64.

26. This section relies on Janice Perlman, *The Myth of Marginality: Urban Poverty and Politics in Rio de Janeiro* (University of California Press, Berkeley, 1976), pp. 195–241, quote from p. 204; Clark W. Reynolds and Robert T. Carpenter, "Housing Finance in Brazil: Toward a New Distribution of Wealth," *Latin American Urban Research* 5 (1975): 147–174, and Knight and Moran, *Brasil,* pp. 77–86.

27. Reynolds and Carpenter, "Housing Finance in Brazil," p. 170.

28. This section draws from Knight and Moran, *Brasil,* pp. 67–77; and from Rui Mauro Marini, Paulo Speller, and Ana Rius, "The Brazilian University," Brazilian Studies/Latin American Research Unit Working Paper 21, Toronto, June 1977, pp. 16–23.

29. Marta Cehelsky, *Land Reform in Brazil: The Management of Social Change* (Westview Press, Boulder, Colo., 1979); and Armin K. Ludwig and Harry W. Taylor, *Brazil's New Agrarian Reform* (Praeger, New York, 1969).

SUGGESTIONS FOR FURTHER READING

Alves, Maria Helena Moreira. *State and Opposition in Military Brazil.* University of Texas Press, Austin, forthcoming 1985.

Baer, Werner. *The Brazilian Economy: Growth and Development.* 2d ed. Praeger Publishers, New York, 1983.

Barzelay, Michael. *The Politicized Market Economy: Alcohol in the Brazilian Energy Strategy.* University of California Press, Berkeley, forthcoming.

Batley, Richard. *Power Through Bureaucracy: Urban Political Analysis in Brazil.* St. Martin's, New York, 1983.

Black, Jan K. *U.S. Penetration of Brazil.* University of Pennsylvania Press, Philadelphia, 1977.

Brazil in Crisis. Special issue of *Latin American Perspectives* 11, no. 1 (Winter 1984).

Bruneau, Thomas C.. *The Political Transformation of the Brazilian Catholic Church.* Cambridge University Press, New York, 1974.

————. *The Church in Brazil: The Politics of Religion.* University of Texas Press, Austin, 1982.

Bruneau, Thomas C., and Philippe Faucher, eds. *Authoritarian Capitalism: Brazil's Contemporary Economic and Political Development.* Westview Press, Boulder, Colo., 1981.

Cehelsky, Marta. *Land Reform in Brazil: The Management of Social Change.* Westview Press, Boulder, Colo., 1979.

Davis, Shelton H. *Victims of the Miracle: Development and the Indians of Brazil.* Cambridge University Press, New York, 1977.

Dean, Warren. *The Industrialization of São Paulo, 1880–1945.* University of Texas Press, Austin, 1969.

Degler, Carl N. *Neither Black nor White: Slavery and Race Relations in Brazil and the United States.* Macmillan, New York, 1971.

Della Cava, Ralph. "Catholicism and Society in Twentieth-Century Brazil." *Latin American Research Review,* 9 (1976):7–50.

Erickson, Kenneth Paul. *The Brazilian Corporative State and Working-Class Politics.* University of California Press, Berkeley, 1977.

————. "Populism and Political Control of the Working Class in Brazil." In *Ideology and Social Change in Latin America,* edited by June Nash, Juan Corradi, and Hobart A. Spalding, Jr. Gordon and Breach, New York, 1977, pp. 200–236.

————. "State Entrepreneurship, Energy Policy, and the Political Order in Brazil." In *Authoritarian Capitalism; Brazil's Contemporary Economic and Political Development,* edited by Thomas C. Bruneau and Philippe Faucher. Westview Press, Boulder, Colo., 1981, pp. 141–177.

Erickson, Kenneth Paul, and Kevin J. Middlebrook. "The State and Organized Labor in Brazil and Mexico." In *Brazil and Mexico: Patterns in Late Development,* edited by Sylvia Ann Hewlett and Richard S. Weinert. Institute for the Study of Human Issues, Philadelphia, 1982, pp. 213–263.

Erickson, Kenneth Paul, and Patrick V. Peppe. "Dependent Capitalist Development, U.S. Foreign Policy, and Repression of the Working Class in Chile and Brazil." *Latin American Perspectives* 3 (Winter 1976):19–44.

Evans, Peter. *Dependent Development: The Alliance of Multinational, State, and Local Capital in Brazil.* Princeton University Press, Princeton, N.J., 1979.

Flynn, Peter. *Brazil: A Political Analysis.* Westview Press, Boulder, Colo., 1978.

Gall, Norman. "Atoms for Brazil: Dangers for All." *Foreign Policy,* no. 23 (Summer 1976):155–201.

Graham, Richard. *Britain and the Onset of Modernization in Brazil, 1850–1914.* Cambridge University Press, London, 1968.

Hewlett, Sylvia Ann, and Richard S. Weinert, eds. *Brazil and Mexico: Patterns in Late Development.* Institute for the Study of Human Issues, Philadelphia, 1982.

Hilton, Stanley E. *Brazil and the Great Powers, 1930–1939: The Politics of Trade Rivalry.* University of Texas Press, Austin, 1975.

Jaguaribe, Hélio. *Economic and Political Development: A Theoretical Approach and a Brazilian Case Study.* Harvard University Press, Cambridge, 1968.

Leeds, Anthony. "Brazilian Careers and Social Structures: A Case History and Model." In *Contemporary Cultures and Societies of Latin America,* edited by Dwight B. Heath and Richard N. Adams. Random, New York, 1965, pp. 379–404.

Leff, Nathaniel H. *Economic Policy-Making and Development in Brazil, 1947–1964.* Wiley, New York, 1968.

Levine, Robert M. *Brazil Since 1930: An Annotated Bibliography for Social Historians.* Garland Publishing, New York, 1980.

Love, Joseph L. "Political Participation in Brazil, 1881–1969." *Luso-Brazilian Review* 7 (December 1970):3–24.

McDonough, Peter. *Power and Ideology in Brazil.* Princeton University Press, Princeton, N.J., 1981.

Malloy, James M. *The Politics of Social Security in Brazil.* University of Pittsburgh Press, Pittsburgh, 1979.

Manchester, Alan K. *British Preeminence in Brazil: Its Rise and Decline.* University of North Carolina Press, Chapel Hill, 1933.

Morley, Samuel. *Labor Markets and Inequitable Growth: The Case of Authoritarian Capitalism in Brazil.* Cambridge University Press, New York, 1983.

Parker, Phyllis R. *Brazil and the Quiet Intervention, 1964.* University of Texas Press, Austin, 1979.

Pereira, Luis Carlos Bresser. *Development and Crisis in Brazil.* Westview Press, Boulder, Colo., 1983.

Perlman, Janice. *The Myth of Marginality: Urban Poverty and Politics in Rio de Janeiro.* University of California Press, Berkeley, 1976.

Roett, Riordan, ed. *Brazil in the Seventies.* American Enterprise Institute for Public Policy Research, Washington, D.C., 1976.

————. *Brazil in the Sixties.* Vanderbilt University Press, Nashville, Tenn., 1972.

Schmitter, Philippe C. *Interest Conflict and Political Change in Brazil.* Stanford University Press, Stanford, Calif., 1971.

Schneider, Ronald M. *The Political System of Brazil: Emergence of a "Modernizing" Authoritarian Regime.* Columbia University Press, New York, 1971.

————. *Brazil: Foreign Policy of a Future World Power.* Westview Press, Boulder, Colo., 1976.

Skidmore, Thomas E. *Politics in Brazil, 1930–1964: An Experiment in Democracy.* Oxford, New York, 1967.

————. "The Historiography of Brazil, 1889–1964," Parts 1 and 2. *Hispanic American Historical Review* 55 (November 1975):716–748, and 56 (February 1976):81–109.

Stein, Stanley J. "The Historiography of Brazil, 1808–1889," *Hispanic American Historical Review* 40 (May 1960):234–278.

Stepan, Alfred. *The Military in Politics: Changing Patterns in Brazil.* Princeton University Press, Princeton, N.J., 1971.

Stepan, Alfred, ed. *Authoritarian Brazil: Origins, Policies, and Future.* Yale University Press, New Haven, Conn., 1973.

Wesson, Robert, and David U. Fleischer, eds. *Brazil in Transition.* Praeger, New York, 1983.

10
Chile and the Breakdown of Democracy

J. SAMUEL VALENZUELA
ARTURO VALENZUELA

Chile, a country of 11.4 million people isolated by sea and geography on a narrow and elongated strip of land running 2,650 miles (4,265 kilometers), has often been the subject of headline writers and political commentators. In the 1960s the discussion centered on the reformist policies of President Eduardo Frei (1964–1970), widely touted as an alternative to the Cuban model for Latin American development. From 1970 to 1973 scores of reporters flocked to Santiago to observe the elected Socialist government attempt an untried form of transition to socialism, one that would take place without violence or disruption of democratic procedures. The bloody military coup that put an end to that experiment has led to a widespread debate on the viability of such a democratic path to socialism, particularly in countries such as France, Italy, Portugal, and Spain, which have large Marxist parties. The brutal repression of both actual and presumed political dissidence by the present military government has placed Chile among the world's most notorious human-rights violators.

The attention Chile has received is partly due to the fact that the nation developed a very distinctive political system, one more akin to certain European patterns than to its counterparts in Latin America. The present military government thus represents a sharp departure from Chile's past. Only once before, in 1924, and then for less than five months, was the country governed by a strictly military junta. The crisis years of 1891 and 1932 produced juntas, composed of military as well as civilian figures, that lasted only a few weeks. Furthermore, from 1830 on, only in the period 1924–1932 did military elements have any real influence on the formation of governments. The majority of Chilean presidents were replaced by their constitutionally designated successors. And suffrage, though limited, was the accepted mechanism for selecting national and local leaders. This chapter examines the origins, evolution,

Chile

characteristics, and subsequent breakdown of Chile's political system. It concludes with an overview of the present military regime.

CHILEAN POLITICS AND POLITICAL CULTURE IN HISTORICAL PERSPECTIVE

Phase 1: The Consolidation of Oligarchical Democracy (1830–1850)

As elsewhere on the continent, the defeat of Spanish and Chilean royalist forces after the long wars of independence (1810–1818) did not open the way to an easy transition toward autonomous rule. The break with Spain did not alter the socioeconomic order. The predominantly rural population, located mainly between San Felipe and Concepción, continued to live on large estates without sharing the fruits of a weak economy based on exports of animal products, grain, and copper. The break, however, clearly disrupted the political system. Gone was the omnipresent and complex bureaucracy of the colonial administration as well as the legitimating power of the Crown, the final arbiter of all conflicts. Chile was left with no political institutions that could easily be adapted to the new situation. It is not surprising that the nation became engulfed in political anarchy as different family, regional, and ideological groups fought each other only to produce unsuccessful dictatorial governments and a series of paper constitutions.

Political anarchy ended in the early 1830s, but it is a mistake, often made in Chilean historiography, to look to those years for an explanation of the consolidation of stable government. Surely the defeat of what were viewed later in the nineteenth century as the liberal factions in the Battle of Lircay (1830), the skillful political and financial maneuvers of ministers Diego Portales and Manuel Rengifo in the administration of President Joaquín Prieto (1831–1841), and the adoption of a centralizing constitution in 1833 were important steps in establishing new authority structures. But there is a difference between *establishment* of such structures and their *consolidation*. Consolidation involves the acceptance of the viability and legitimacy of new institutions by the political elites. It is a lengthy process, subject to continuous challenges and reversals. The actual consolidation of the limited democracy took many years and was aided by several factors.

The first was the victory of Chilean forces over those of the Peru-Bolivia Confederation. Though the confederation led by General Andrés Santa Cruz had sought to extend its dominion southward, the real spark that ignited the Chilean war effort was the assassination of Portales in 1837. Portales's policies, repressive measures, and advocacy of the war had made him the target of great enmity in Chile. Ironically, because it was rumored that he had been assassinated by agents of Santa Cruz, his death stirred a wave of patriotic emotions that were channeled to military preparations. For the first time Chilean elites mounted a joint endeavor to fight a common enemy, since the war of independence had been as much a civil war as a struggle against colonialism. Plots against the government were forgotten, and victory led to internal amnesty and to a restitution of pensions and ranks for the defeated forces of the 1829–1830 civil war. It also led to the election of the first truly national hero, Manuel Bulnes, to the presidency in 1841. The victorious general's election was facilitated by his control of most of the armed forces and by the fact that he was Prieto's nephew and, like his uncle, was supported by the important regional center of Concepción with its large military detachments deployed on the frontier of hostile Indian territories. Bulnes also married the daughter of the prominent Liberal leader who had opposed him in the presidential election. A Chilean defeat in the war would have magnified factional disputes and threatened the stability of fragile institutions. The clear-cut victory, with no parallel in Latin America, created common symbols and a new sense of unity and led to the inauguration of an elected government with unprecedented support.

The second factor was the decisive control of the military by civilian authorities. As leader of the victorious army, Bulnes did not experience much opposition from the military in his first years in office. However, under his leadership the government deliberately reduced support for the regular army, so that by the end of Bulnes's term there were fewer soldiers than at the beginning and the budget for the regular military was severely curtailed. In place of the regular army, the executive encouraged the development of a highly politicized National Guard. Led by loyal government supporters (leadership positions became patronage devices for the president), the part-time guard was composed mainly of lower-middle-class civilians such as artisans, shopkeepers, and small proprietors. It numbered ten to twenty-five times the size of the peacetime army. The outbreak of a revolt against the government in 1851 was partly the reflection of the discontent of regular army officers, based in Concepción, with military policy. Bulnes himself led National Guard forces to suppress the uprising aimed at preventing his elected successor from taking office, even though his cousin was the rival leader. A similar revolt in 1859 was put down by mobilizing loyal army and National Guard forces.

As illustrated by Bulnes's decisive 1851 action, the third factor in the consolidation of the regime was the deliberate support he gave to the fledgling institutional system during his two five-year terms in office (1841–1851). Indeed, Bulnes's role in the consolidation process was, contrary to assertions in Chilean historiography, much greater than that of Portales, whose actual ministerial tenure was short. It is important to stress that a written constitution, fixed terms of office, and impersonal authority based on suffrage, however limited, were revolutionary precepts at the time. Bulnes was certainly in a position to ignore those precepts and draw on his prestige and military strength to impose personal rule as did his counterparts in Argentina, Mexico, and Venezuela. Instead, under his leadership the broad outlines of the formal rules of the Republican Constitution of 1833, with its separation of powers between the executive, the Congress, and the courts, became a reality.

The most important single factor contributing to this process was the president's refusal to rule autocratically. Following the example of his predecessor, he relied on a strong collegial body, the cabinet, to carry out the main tasks of government. But, unlike those of his predecessor, Bulnes's cabinets drew from different sectors of public opinion, and its members were periodically changed to reflect new pressures and interests.

Though the executive took the initiative, Congress had to approve all legislation. The legislature was initially docile, but it gradually became more assertive and a platform for dissenting views. As early as the 1840s the Congress resorted to delaying approval of the budget law in order to extract government concessions. Rather than defying this challenge to his authority, Bulnes sought compromise with the legislature. The legitimacy of Congress was therefore not questioned, even if cabinet officials manipulated the electoral process in favor of the official list of congressional candidates. This set the rudiments of the political game for the rest of the century. Given the government's control of the votes of national guardsmen and public employees (which constituted large but decreasing percentages of the electorate, that is, 65 percent in 1850 and 25 percent in the late 1880s), as well as its occasional resort to arbitrary procedures, the cabinets could forge favorable majorities in Congress. However, when the coalitions supporting the presidency broke down or when political opposition from important sectors became obvious, the president would change the cabinet. This often left a new cabinet with a Congress elected by its predecessor, thus reinforcing the role of the legislature as an arena of opposition.

Throughout the nineteenth century all relevant factions gained representation in the cabinet or in the legislature and diverse opposition groups had to learn to collaborate within the shared institutional base to further their interests. It is noteworthy that every nineteenth-century head of state, with the exception of Jorge Montt, who became president after the 1891 civil war, had extensive prior experience as an elected representative in Congress. And the five presidents who succeeded Bulnes, that is, until 1886, began government service as young men in the Bulnes administration.

The fourth factor contributing to regime consolidation was the impressive economic prosperity that accompanied political stability. The break with the colonial trade limitations opened the country up to the international market, and Chilean exports throve. Mining, primarily of silver and copper, was expanded with the opening of new mines, and the new markets of California (after the gold rush), Europe, and Australia led to a boom in agricultural sales, mainly of wheat. The state played an important role in encouraging economic development based on external markets: It obtained foreign credit, improved dock facilities, opened new ports, began railway lines, and established a merchant marine. From 1844 to 1864 Chilean exports increased five times, and foreign creditors were quick to take note as Chilean issues brought higher prices on the London market than those of any other Latin American country.

Underlying the success of the government in promoting economic growth, and indirectly the success of the consolidation process itself, was the broad elite consensus on the merits of an "outward-oriented" development policy. Landowners in the central valley, miners in the north, and merchants in Santiago and in port cities all benefited from and promoted an economy based on the export of raw materials and the import of manufactured goods. There was no industrially oriented bourgeoisie pressing for effective protectionist policies to develop a large-scale domestic manufacturing sector, although limited protectionist policies were followed in some areas. An incipient industrialization did not take hold until the 1880s.

In sum, by midcentury Chile had experienced a full decade of relatively peaceful rule. Victory in an international war had contributed to a previously elusive elite unity, and under the leadership of the war's hero, republican political institutions established in the 1830s attained considerable legitimacy. The tradition of an independent Congress as an arena for accommodation, compromise, and opposition had taken root. Though the franchise was limited and subject to intervention, it became the principal mechanism for leadership selection. The control of the military and the healthy state of the economy contributed further to setting Chile on a unique course in Latin America.

Phase 2: State Expansion and Elite Reaction (1850–1890)

The sharp political differences of the nineteenth century should be viewed as resulting from the reaction of local and national notables, particularly those close to the Church, to the expansion of the state, which resulted from the very success of regime consolidation. As long as the government obtained foreign credits, improved port facilities, and guaranteed order it did not impinge on vested interests. But when state institutions began to expand into the local level, rationalize taxes and duties, invest in public-work projects, and foment secular education and civil registries, they generated bitter opposition. Our perspective is different from that of many historians, who have interpreted nineteenth-century controversies as a struggle between a Conservative rural aristocracy with a firm grip on the state and a rising group of miners, bankers, merchants, and professionals seeking political control. That view presupposes that political differences were the product of a fundamental, economically based cleavage among the elite. In fact, as already suggested, there was broad consensus on the merits of free-trade policies and on the pursuit of a development model based on raw material exports. Moreover, socioeconomic divisions among the dominant sectors were not so clear-cut: The wealthiest families often had cross-investments in all areas of the economy. It is also clear that the Conservatives, whose political bases were in fact largely among landed elites (although not all landed elites were Conservative), were far from controlling the government. Quite to the contrary, they were driven into opposition at an early date and remained so for most of the century.

It is important to stress that by midcentury the state was not simply a tool of economic elites but had in fact attained a considerable degree of autonomy. An entirely new profession of urban-based government officials and politicians had appeared on the political scene. Like President Manuel Montt (1851–1861) himself, they relied on the state for their positions and had a real stake in the expansion of governmental authority. By 1860 over twenty-five hundred persons worked for the state, not counting thousands of workers hired by municipalities and government-financed public-works projects or the many individuals associated with the National Guard and the armed forces.

State autonomy was in part a function of growing governmental institutionalization and of the ability of state officials to manipulate the verdict of the electorate. But ultimately it was the product of a system of revenue collection tied to an export economy. Reliance on customs revenues in a time of export expansion meant an incremental and automatic infusion of larger and larger sums of money into state coffers. By tapping trade, and particularly imports, to finance the national budget, the government avoided the politically difficult choices involved in imposing large-scale domestic taxation. Ironically, had the Chilean economy been more balanced and less dependent on external trade, the state would have been much more vulnerable to the immediate and direct pressures of economic elites. The very dependence of the economy on international market forces provided the state with significant resources for autonomous action. From 1830 to 1860 government revenues from customs duties, representing about 60 percent of all revenue, increased seven times. State revenues enabled the construction of numerous public-works projects, including the second railroad system of Latin America and the first to be operated by a government. In the fifteen-year period 1845–1860, expenditures on education alone quadrupled.

Given the encroachment of the state on the localities, it is not surprising that control of the state and its expenditures became the most important political issue of the time. Were urban or rural areas to be favored by state resources? Which port facilities should be improved? Where were the railroad lines to be built? Should local officials remain subordinated to the national government's decisions and largess, or should they be autonomous from it? And most importantly, should the state or the Church control the expanding educational system, civil registry, cemeteries, and hospitals?

The Conservative party became the foremost expression of elite discontent over the decreasing autonomy of rural areas and the challenge to the Church's monopoly over educational, cultural, and family life, the maintenance of which was viewed as essential to the preservation of the traditional social order and thus of elite privilege. The party was originally formed by a group that split away from the Montt government as Manuel Montt pressed further to enhance the role of the state. In opposition, the Conservatives soon made alliances of convenience with some ideological Liberals who, while supporting the concept of a secular state, wanted more decentralization of political authority and an expansion of electoral participation. The unsuccessful 1859 uprising reflected the seriousness of the political controversies as a few Liberal, Conservative, and regional elements attempted to prevent Manuel Montt's closest associate from succeeding him to the presidency. Though the government forces, known as the Nationals, controlled the rebellion, Montt's associate wisely withdrew his candidacy. The new National president, José Joaquín Pérez (1861–1871), saw the political wisdom of granting amnesty to the rebels and, following the Bulnes precedents, of incorporating both Conservatives and Liberals into cabinets of national unity in what became known as the Liberal-Conservative Fusion.

A few measures were adopted during the Pérez administrations to curb the power of executive authority. The president was restricted to one term, armed personnel were barred from voting booths, and other electoral reforms were made. However, the basic character of the state remained unchanged. With Pérez's support, the Liberals outmaneuvered their Conservative allies and continued the basic policies of the preceding National governments. State power transformed the Liberals, not vice versa. State authority expanded further, state-sponsored projects increased, and the secularization of public institutions continued. The Liberals were not about to dismantle a state structure they now controlled. They appreciated the political value of using its resources to create public works, parks, and monuments in urban areas and to foster programs designed to create a larger group of urban-based middle sectors dependent on the state. However, because of their laissez-faire and free-trade ideology, the Liberals did not channel state resources to directly productive investments or use state authority to foster internal industrialization.

By the midpoint of the administration of Liberal president Federico Errázuriz (1871–1876), the Conservatives had had enough. They left the government determined to oppose the drift toward a secular society and the continued encroachment of the state over national life. Ironically, the Conservatives once again made an alliance of convenience with another opposition group, the anticlerical Radical party, which upheld the Liberal principles its government colleagues had seemingly abandoned. This unlikely alliance held a majority in Congress, since the Conservatives had formed part of the official candidate lists in the 1872 election. The Conservatives took advantage of this majority to press for a dramatic liberalization of the electoral system in 1874. As a result the electorate tripled from 50,000 to 150,000 by 1878, as suffrage was extended to all literate males. The changes in the electoral system would have been more far-reaching had the government not persuaded the Radicals, in exchange for a seat in the cabinet, to vote against some Conservative proposals.

In fact the 1874 reforms were not sufficient to counteract the strong intervention of local agents of the executive in the electoral process, an intervention that became more blatant and violent as the government's control over the electorate diminished. Hence, the Conservatives demanded genuine local autonomy, in which full control of elections (going beyond certain 1874 provisions) would be given to elected local governments independent of the executive. To electoral reforms was added the cry for municipal reform.

The Conservatives were not behaving irrationally. Given their lack of penetration in state structures and the failure of armed conspiracies, their only hope of curbing state authority and of gaining control of government resources lay in the expansion of suffrage and in the reduction of government manipulation of the voting process. Like their counterparts in northern European countries, the Conservatives knew that their dominant position in small towns and in rural areas gave them the upper hand in capturing the ballot box. The more urban-based Liberals and Radicals stood to lose, since only 12 percent of the population lived in cities over twenty thousand and 26 percent in towns over two thousand. The key role played by the Conservatives in suffrage expansion (which, surprisingly, has been attributed to the Liberals and Radicals by most historians) meant that the principal party of the Chilean right became committed to expressing its power capabilities *through the electoral system*, not, as in other countries, through conspiracies within the armed forces or by gaining the allegiance of the central bureaucracy. It also meant that Church opposition to republican electoral democracy, typical of Latin Europe until at least the 1890s, would not develop in Chile. The strength of the Chilean electoral system as a mechanism for national leadership selection was largely due to these circumstances.

The stakes involved in the control of the executive increased dramatically with the Chilean victory in the War of the Pacific (1879–1883), again against Peru and Bolivia. In the 1860s and 1870s customs duties as a percentage of government revenue had declined to as low as 40 percent. After the war, with the incorporation of Peruvian and Bolivian land with enormous nitrate wealth into Chilean territory, customs duties once again climbed to over 70 percent of government income, eventually eliminating the need for internal property taxes. Though a majority of nitrate fields fell into the hands of foreign interests, the Chilean state was able to retain close to 50 percent of all profits through taxation. From 1870 to 1890 government revenues climbed over 150 percent, leading to a new wave of public-works projects and other government expenditures.

The struggle over the role of the state in society finally resulted in the brief civil war of 1891, during the closing months of José Manuel Balmaceda's government (1886–1891). With burgeoning nitrate wealth, his administration embarked on the most ambitious effort yet to channel governmental resources into massive public-works projects. Though some of his detractors objected to his hostile attitude toward British nitrate interests, opposition to Balmaceda crystallized over the perennial issue of the nineteenth century: control over state resources. The president refused to yield to mounting pressures in the Congress to liberalize the system and approve far-reaching electoral and local government measures. When his cabinet was censured, he departed from the traditional practice of attempting to broaden the government's political base. Congress responded by refusing to approve the budget; the president retaliated by approving it by decree. As the armed conflict broke out, congressional forces were backed by the navy, the president retaining the loyalty of much of the army. The anti-Balmaceda forces included a wide spectrum of political opinion ranging from dissident Liberals to Conservatives and Radicals, not to mention the British nitrate entrepreneurs. The defeat of Balmaceda led to the long-awaited liberalization of electoral registration and counting processes and to a significant change in the character of the political system.

Phase 3: The Party System and
Incipient Participation (1890–1925)

After 1891 the center of gravity of the Chilean political system shifted dramatically from the center to the locality. Municipal autonomy and electoral reform finally gave local notables control over suffrage and, therefore, over congressmen and senators. Acting as agents of their local sponsors, the legislators sharply reduced the role of the executive and of the cabinet through constitutional reforms. Politics in the so-called Parliamentary Republic (1891–1925) became an elaborate logrolling game in which legislative factions jockeyed for influence. Budget laws were carved up to please local supporters, and public employment became a primary source for congressional and party patronage. Central government employees increased from 3,048 in 1880 to 13,119 in 1900 and 27,479 in 1919, and the monolithic character of the state changed as its structures were permeated by different political elites. The incredible ministerial instability of the period, with its constant coalition shifts and complex electoral pacts, must be seen in this light.

A key organization of twentieth-century politics, the political party with extensive local bases, developed principally during the Parliamentary Republic. An unanticipated consequence of the liberalization of suffrage was the transformation of elite factions and protoparties into largescale party organizations and networks. Buying of votes and the manipulation of the electorate became a complex and demanding job, and much of the day-to-day party activities shifted from the hands of notables to those of professional politicians and brokers of lesser status. A new political class began to take shape.

The Conservative rural notables clearly gained influence with local suffrage control. But other forces were not left out of the political game. This resulted partly from the profound socioeconomic transformations set in motion by nitrate production, which gave political groups new potential electoral clienteles. Nitrate fields soon employed 10 to 15 percent of the active population and by expanding the internal market generated a host of other activities, including metallurgical works, clothing industries, and transportation. Rural areas and their commercial networks also experienced changes, as agriculture sought to meet the demand for food in the arid north. The urban population increased dramatically from 26 percent of the total in 1875 to close to 45 percent by the early 1900s, and the Radicals as well as a new group of Social Democrats assured themselves an increased role in the system with their skillful organizational efforts in the changing cities, towns, and nitrate areas.

It is important to stress that in Chile viable political parties with direct access to the legislative process developed simultaneously with the establishment of a large-scale government bureaucracy. The growth of the public sector in this period was thus shaped by organizations whose primary goal was electoral success and accountability, organizations that continued to exert a major influence over state institutions and the policy process until the military coup of 1973. Where, as in Brazil or Argentina, the bureaucracy emerged before the structuring of strong party networks as the fundamental linkage mechanisms between society and the state, alternative informal or officially sponsored networks with access to the bureaucracy became the norm.

Parties were not the only important organizations with local bases to appear in this period. Labor unions mushroomed, as nitrate, dock, railway, and industrial workers and artisans sought to improve their lot. However, whereas parties were legitimate actors, labor unions were restricted and repressed. Industrial militancy presented a real threat not only to dominant economic groups but also to the viability of the whole system. Since nitrate revenues were the lifeline of the state and of the rest of the economy, any cut in export revenues because of strikes would have devastating repercussions. The army was repeatedly used to put down strikes, often with great brutality, as in the Iquique massacre of 1907 when (depending on the account) between five hundred and two thousand workers were killed. Repression of labor-union activities created a radical union leadership, since radical workers were more likely to assume the great personal risks involved. Moreover, moderate individuals had difficulty in maintaining leadership positions, since they could obtain few concessions from recalcitrant employers and did not have the persuasive ideological framework of their radical counterparts to explain their lack of success.

Ironically, the openness of the political system, a product of the intense conflict among established elites, meant that industrial repression was not accompanied systematically by political repression. Working-class leaders were allowed to publish newspapers, create cultural associations, lobby Congress, and create political parties. Despite their intensely radical outlooks, they soon realized that their cause could best be advanced politically through alliances of convenience with traditional parties eager to maximize their fortunes. Thus in 1921 the founding father of the labor movement and of the Communist party, Luis Emilio Recabarren, and one of his comrades were elected to Congress through an electoral pact with the Radical party. This repeated earlier successes in local elections in which pacts had been forged with either Radicals or Democrats. The repression of the working class therefore contributed to the formation of a Marxist labor union and party leadership, and the relatively open and representative character of the political system meant that the Marxist parties soon turned to traditional political strategies to advance their positions.

The freewheeling and free-spending Parliamentary Republic could not survive the decline in nitrate exports with the discovery of synthetic nitrate during World War I and the inability of the complex logrolling process to come up with solutions to many of the social pressures spawned by a changing society. The challenge from reform sectors was matched by a challenge from more traditional groups, which resented excessive democratization. President Arturo Alessandri's (1920–1924) populist politics violated many of the norms of political accommodation and led to demands to do away with politics and to obtain order. Though young army officers had reformist objectives in mind, their intervention in politics in late 1924 marked the end of the Parliamentary Republic and opened the way for the election of a "nonpolitical" figure, Col. Carlos Ibáñez. During his government (1927–1931), Congress lost influence and the president resorted to heavy-handed tactics in an attempt to reduce the role of parties and the strength of the Communist-controlled labor federations, which represented a majority of organized workers.

Ibáñez expanded the bureaucracy, revised the budgetary system, and "purified" the civil service. Liberal parliamentary politics were to be replaced by a more corporatist conception of the state. Interpreting the comprehensive labor laws approved in 1924 to suit his own end, Ibáñez established legal unionism only where his agents could find leaders who agreed to support his government. But the military president failed. Party politics were too entrenched to be easily purged or manipulated from above. His use of the 1924 labor laws only delayed their full and correct implementation until the late 1930s. With the catastrophic effects of the Great Depression (in which Chilean exports dropped to less than a fifth of their value by 1931), a political crisis erupted, forcing Ibáñez to resign. And after a short interval of unrest, Arturo Alessandri was reelected president by a large margin.

Phase 4: Polarization and
Mass Participation (1925–1970)

The collapse of the Parliamentary Republic produced constitutional reforms that strengthened the presidency and established the separation of Church and state. However, the so-called 1925 Constitution does not represent the most important political change of the 1920s, which is surely the rise of the left. The Communist party was officially founded when the Socialist Workers' party convention of December 1921 voted to adhere to the Third International. By the end of the decade, a Trotskyite splinter had been expelled from the party, and various Socialist groups had been created. After Ibáñez's resignation, all these organizations emerged from their underground work to produce a confusing array of political groups on the left with few well-known figures. The ill-fated Socialist Republic of June 1932 was, however, to change this. It created, if little else, a core of highly popular leaders who proceeded, in April 1933, to form the Socialist party of Chile by bringing together some of the preexisting Socialist and Trotskyite organizations. The new Socialist party quickly gained significant working-class bases by attracting the support of the country's legal unions, with which the Communists had refused to collaborate because of their origins. Thus by the early 1930s two major parties claiming to represent the workers had emerged on the political landscape, leading to a complex relationship of competition and/or cooperation between them that continues to this day. And with the rise of the Marxist left, the party system became highly polarized, covering the full range of the ideological spectrum.

Following the Popular Front strategy adopted in late 1934 by the Third International, the Communist party agreed to a previous Socialist initiative designed to unite the labor movement and to coordinate political strategies. With an eye on the next presidential elections, the by then historical Radical party decided to withdraw its support of the conservative second Alessandri administration (1932–1938) and to join the left's discussions. These resulted in the merger of the labor movement into a single federation in 1936 and in the creation of a Popular Front coalition that elected the Radical Pedro Aguirre Cerda to the presidency in December 1938. This electoral victory over the candidate of Liberals and Conservatives marked the success, for the first time, of a center-to–Marxist left coalition, which would govern the country until 1947. The coalition government expanded state social services in areas such as health, education, and social security. It also encouraged the rise of legal unionism, including Communist-led unions, within the framework of the 1924 labor laws that shaped Chile's elaborate industrial-relations system. And, just as significantly, the Popular Front government created a State Development Corporation (CORFO) in order to plan and direct an industrialization process aimed at substituting imported consumer goods with locally produced articles.

Table 10.1 Distribution of the Labor Force and Gross Domestic Product (at Market Prices), 1940, 1955, 1970 (Rounded to Nearest Percentage)

	1940		1955		1970	
	Labor Force	GDP	Labor Force	GDP	Labor Force	GDP
Primary Sector	35	15	29	14	24	7
Secondary Sector	30	38	33	39	33	48
Service Sector	35	47	38	47	43	45

Source: Estimated from Instituto de Economía de la Universidad de Chile, *La Economía de Chile en el Período 1950–1963*, and ODEPLAN figures.

The creation of CORFO was symptomatic of a profound change of direction in the Chilean economy and economic policy, the repercussions of which are still felt today. The depression had dealt the final blow to the crippled nitrate industry, and by the late 1930s copper had become Chile's principal export, representing roughly 55 percent of export earnings in the 1940s and 80 percent by 1970. With the drastic decline of the capacity to import in the early 1930s, policymakers became convinced that the nation should not rely on imported consumer goods to satisfy most of its needs. They sought to encourage industrial growth by establishing new lines of credit, protectionism, direct and indirect subsidies, price controls, and state investments in key areas such as steel and energy, which required large capital outlays. As a result, by the late 1960s Chile's industrial sector produced a broad range of consumer goods, if not always at internationally competitive levels of efficiency.

One of the Popular Front government's objectives in fostering industrialization was the creation of jobs in urban areas, which were urgently required because of the decline of the labor-intensive nitrate industry and of the influx of new migrants into the cities. By 1940, 53 percent of the population lived in urban areas, a figure that increased to 76 percent by 1970. The population in cities with more than twenty thousand people increased at an even faster rate. The new industrialization, however, in the long run did not generate employment at a faster rate than the increase in urban population. The secondary sector (mining, construction, transport, and particularly manufacturing) absorbed roughly the same proportion of the economically active population in 1970 as it had in 1940, even though its proportion of the gross domestic product increased from 38 percent in 1940 to 48 percent in 1970. As illustrated in Table 10.1, it was the service sector that absorbed increasing shares of total employment while contributing a smaller share of the GDP, while the primary sector (agriculture, forestry, and fishing) declined on both counts.

The Popular Front coalition broke down in part because of bitter internecine squabbles among Socialists and between Socialists and Communists and in part because of the fear of both Socialists and Radicals (particularly after the 1947 municipal election) that the Communists with their strong organizational base were making too much electoral progress. The onset of the cold war and U.S. pressures also played a role in the Radicals' decision to not only expel the Communists from the cabinet but also to declare the party illegal in 1948. The disarray of the left and the unpopularity of the Radicals after so many years of opportunistic bargaining with both the left and the right finally led the electorate (including women for the first time in a presidential election) to turn to an old stalwart of Chilean politics, who once again promised progress at the margin of party politics. Gen. Carlos Ibáñez (1952–1958) was easily elected to the presidency by a surge movement ranging from the far right to the Socialist left.

Ibáñez's heterogeneous movement did not become a durable political force. As he began his term, the economy entered a recession and inflation increased sharply, finally reaching a high of 86 percent in 1955. Ibáñez abandoned the populist appeal of his campaign and early programs and attempted to apply an austerity economic program, which led to a wave of protest demonstrations and an increase in the number of strikers. In the face of this opposition, the austerity program was not fully implemented, although it did lead to a reduction in the earning power of wages and salaries. One of Ibáñez's last measures was the legalization, once again, of the Communist party, thereby fulfilling a campaign promise.

The disintegration of the Ibáñez movement might have allowed the Radicals to move once again to fill the center of Chilean politics. However, they were challenged in that role by the emerging Christian Democratic (DC) party, whose candidate, Eduardo Frei, outpolled the Radicals in the 1958 presidential contest. But the real surprise of that election was the showing of Salvador Allende, the candidate of the Communist and Socialist parties. With 28.9 percent of the vote in the sharply divided contest, he failed by a fraction (2.7 percent) to defeat the winner, Jorge Alessandri.

In office, Alessandri (1958–1964), a businessman supported by the right and occasionally by the peripatetic Radicals, applied a new set of austerity measures and obtained increased foreign aid to attempt economic stabilization. In the wake of the Cuban Revolution, the United States became determined to prevent a growth of leftist influence in the rest of the hemisphere. Chile, with its large Marxist parties, became a priority of the Kennedy and Johnson administrations' foreign-aid programs and covert intelligence operations.

During the 1964 presidential election, the Chilean center and right as well as the U.S. government sought to prevent what almost occurred in 1958—an Allende victory. As a result the right decided to support the centrist Frei candidacy, which promised a "Revolution in Liberty," and the CIA contributed $1.20 per Chilean voter to the antileft propaganda effort, over twice as much as the $.54 per U.S. voter that Lyndon Johnson and Barry Goldwater jointly spent in their own presidential campaigns that year. Frei was elected with an absolute majority of the votes. His government, that of his successor, and the breakdown of democracy will be discussed after reviewing the principal aspects and actors of the political game of twentieth-century Chilean politics.

POLITICAL GROUPS AND THE STATE:
THE POLITICAL SYSTEM AT MIDCENTURY

By midcentury the Chilean state had evolved into a large and complex set of institutions. Even before the election of Salvador Allende to the presidency in 1970, the state played a greater role in the economy than was the case in other Latin American nations, with the exception of Cuba and possibly Brazil. Total state expenditures represented about 24 percent of the GDP. The state also generated over 55 percent of gross investment and roughly 50 percent of all available credit. About 13 percent of the active population worked for the state, not counting the employees of the thirty-nine key corporations in which CORFO owned majority shares or the forty-one other enterprises where its participation was substantial. Government agencies were responsible for health care and social-security benefits, for the regulation of prices and wages, and for the settlement of labor disputes. Indeed, the dominant role of government in regulatory, distributive, and redistributive policies meant that private groups were constantly turning to state agencies and to the legislature, at times through elected local government officials, to gain favorable rulings and dispensations.

Over the years, myriad interest groups developed, closely paralleling the expansion of the state. They ranged from professional societies and business organizations to student unions, trade and pensioners' associations, youth and church groups, mothers' clubs, and neighborhood councils. Workers were represented by industrial, craft, and peasant unions (the latter legalized only in 1967), which were subjected to a series of state regulations and restrictions, although their leadership was democratically chosen by the rank and file. Civil servants were organized into a series of associations that, though acting as unions, were never officially recognized as such. Most groups sought to maximize their political clout before the state by organizing national associations with national headquarters. Large industrial, agricultural, and commercial interests were, for example, respectively organized into the Society for Industrial Advancement (SOFOFA), the National Agricultural Society (SNA), and the Central Chamber of Commerce. Professional societies were grouped in the Confederation of Professional Associations. Roughly 60 percent of all unionists were affiliated directly or indirectly with the Central Labor Federation (CUT). Some categories of specialized workers, small industrialists and retail merchants, truck owners, and so on also had national confederation offices.

Following the 1925 Constitution, the president—elected for a six-year term—was clearly the source of major initiatives in the political process. And yet the president was far from an all-powerful figure, and the state was certainly not a monolithic institution. The most important checks on executive authority came from the competitive party system, which will be described in the next section. But presidential authority was also checked by the differentiation of governmental institutions and the marked autonomy of agencies even within the executive chain of command.

The legislature was no longer the focal point of the system, as it had been in the Parliamentary Republic. Nevertheless, the Chilean Congress remained the most powerful in Latin America, with the ability to modify and reject executive proposals. The Congress was the main arena for discussion and approval of budgetary matters as well as for the all-important issue of wage readjustments for public and even private employees.

In the final analysis, legislative politics was party politics, and presidents could cajole and bargain with allied as well as with adversary political groups for mutual advantage. By contrast the two other branches of government, the court system and the comptroller general (Contraloría), were well insulated from both presidential and legislative scrutiny. Judicial promotions were determined by seniority and merit, and though the president retained some power of appointment, his candidates had to come from lists prepared by the judges themselves. Equally independent was the comptroller general, who, like the Supreme Court judges, was appointed for life. His agency was charged with auditing public accounts and ruling on the legality of executive decrees. The comptroller's rulings on financial matters were final; on other matters, the president could, with the concurrence of his cabinet, overrule the comptroller. However, because of the prestige of the latter's office, this could be done only at the risk of considerable controversy, and until the Allende years presidents rarely overruled the comptroller.

Even within the executive branch presidential authority was circumscribed. The president was the head of the armed forces, but the military establishment was in fact quite autonomous, controlling much of its own budget, training programs, and external linkages. Presidents would generally promote senior officers following seniority lines. Allende, for one, scrupulously followed this rule.

Forty percent of public employees worked for over fifty semiautonomous agencies that, though nominally under government ministries, enjoyed significant managerial and even budgetary autonomy. As elsewhere, the web of private interests affected by a particular agency soon learned to develop more or less workable relationships of mutual benefits with it. Vested interests often made it difficult for a new administration to abolish old programs and bureaus, and innovations often required the creation of new agencies to administer the new projects, thus contributing to the progressive expansion of the state apparatus. Civil-service organizations and professional associations anxious to place their members in the expanding state sector further complicated the picture. Some state agencies became virtual fiefdoms of architects, civil engineers, lawyers, or doctors.

Though many agencies actually had formal interest-group representation on managing councils, it is important to stress that such representation never became as important as the more informal and more fluid constituency ties. Chilean politics never became corporative politics. Most private groups did obtain legal recognition. But that was a routine procedure and hardly meant that the government was officially sanctioning particular associations with exclusive rights to represent functional segments of society before the state. Indeed, most claims on the state were made by highly competitive groups, often representing interests drawn from the same horizontal or class lines.

If Chilean politics was not corporative, neither was it praetorian. Despite the vast and disarticulated state apparatus and the claims of a multiplicity of interests jockeying for advantage, Chilean politics did not involve the naked confrontation of political forces each seeking to maximize its interests through direct action in the face of weak or transitory authority structures. The key to the Chilean system, which discouraged both corporatist and praetorian tendencies, was the continuing importance of political parties and a party system tied to the legislature, the principal arena for political give-and-take. From the turn of the century on, the norm in Chile was not the direct link between government agencies and interest associations or the unmediated clash of organized social forces. Rather, party structures, permeating all levels of society, served as crucial linkage mechanisms binding organizations, institutions, groups, and individuals to the political center. Local units of competing parties were active within each level of the bureaucracy, each labor union, each student federation. Parties often succeeded in capturing particular organizations or in setting up rival ones. Once an issue affecting the organization arose, party structures were instrumental in conveying the organization's demands to the nucleus of the policy-making process or in acting as brokers before the ubiquitous bureaucracy.

As the historical discussion noted, the Chilean party system was fragmented and very competitive. With the exception of the Christian Democrats in the mid-1960s, no single party received more than 30 percent of the votes in congressional or municipal elections from 1925 to 1973. The party system was also highly polarized. During the 1937–1973 period, the vote for the left (Socialists and Communists) averaged 21.5 percent (or 25.7 percent if one excludes the 1949, 1953, and 1957 elections in which the Communists were banned from participation), and the vote for the right averaged 30.1 percent. Since neither the right nor the left could obtain an effective majority on its own, center groups, especially the Radical party, played a very important if little-appreciated

Table 10.2 Percentage of the Vote Received by Parties on the Right, Center, and
           Left in Chilean Congressional Elections, 1937–1973

	1937	1941	1945	1949	1953	1957	1961	1965	1969	1973	Mean
Right[a]	42.0	31.2	43.7	42.0	25.3	33.0	30.4	12.5	20.0	21.3	30.1
Center[b]	28.1	32.1	27.9	46.7	43.0	44.3	43.7	55.6	42.8	32.8	39.7
Left[c]	15.4	33.9	23.1	9.4	14.2	10.7	22.1	22.7	28.1	34.9	21.5
Other	14.5	2.8	5.3	1.9	17.5	12.0	3.8	9.2	9.1	11.0	8.7

[a]Conservative, Liberal, and National parties after 1965
[b]Radical, Falangist, Christian Democratic, and Agrarian Laborist parties
[c]Socialist and Communist parties
Source: Dirección del Registro Electoral, Santiago, Chile.

role in the polarized system: By dealing with both extremes, they were
essential elements in most legislative majorities or in winning presidential
coalitions—all of which permitted the political system to muddle through
despite the sharp ideological divergences. And yet the center movements
could not succeed in establishing themselves as a majority force, although
they occasionally eroded the strength of either the left or the right. For
example, supported by voters on the right, the Christian Democrats
scored a dramatic gain in the 1965 congressional election, obtaining
42.3 percent of the vote. But the Liberals and Conservatives, having
merged to form the National party in 1966, regained much of their
historical strength by 1969, and their candidate outpolled the Christian
Democratic nominee in the 1970 presidential election. Table 10.2 sum-
marizes the electoral strength of the three tendencies in the 1937–1973
period.

Given the fact that no single party or tendency could capture the
presidency alone, coalitions were necessary. These were either formed
before the election and resulted in winning an absolute majority, as
was the case in 1964, or they had to be put together after the election
in order to obtain the constitutionally mandated congressional approval
of a candidate receiving only a plurality of the vote, as occurred in
most cases. But, invariably, coalitions tended to disintegrate shortly after
the election. The president could not succeed himself, and party leaders
scrambled to disassociate themselves from the difficulties of incumbency
in order to maximize electoral fortunes in succeeding contests. This
meant that presidents had to compromise often with new supporters
in the legislature, to salvage part of their programs and to govern.

Despite the polarization of the party system, politics did not revolve
around only ideological and programmatic discussions. Obtaining benefits
for groups and even favors for individuals, the essence of politics during
the Parliamentary Republic, continued to be an important part of party
activities. In fact, officials from all parties spent most of their time acting
as political brokers—processing pensions for widows, helping Protestant
ministers qualify for the white-collar social-security fund, interviewing

the labor minister on behalf of a union leadership, seeking a job for a young schoolteacher, obtaining bridges and sewer systems for communities, and so forth. Legislators had particular access to state agencies because of congressional influence over purse strings, promotions, and programs affecting the bureaucracy.

An important political issue that led to extended bargaining in the legislature and to a flurry of demands and pressures from organized groups was the yearly discussion of the wage readjustment law. The law was intimately related to the budgetary approval process and gave the legislators (and therefore the parties) an input into the economic policy planning process. The state-controlled wage scales in the public sector were used as guidelines for the private sector, and therefore the readjustment laws, which also regulated social-security benefits, were of direct concern to the various party constituencies. In an economy averaging over 25 percent inflation with sharp yearly variations, a fundamental demand would be readjustments that would exceed, or at least match, the rate of inflation. Occasionally, amendments favoring specific groups or unions, but not all in the same category, would be approved as the legislators in the majority group sought to pay off political debts or favor their party comrades in positions of leadership. And yet the political ramifications of class cleavages in the society would become apparent as the left would, in the middle of dense and legalistic discussions over specifics, normally press for higher wages and benefits for working-class sectors, and the right would generally favor the restrictive readjustments tied to fiscal and economic austerity policies.

There were no giants in the Chilean political system. No single group could win a complete majority or totally impose its will on the others. In fact, since there was no ideological or programmatic consensus among the polarized political forces, the Chilean polity was in many respects a stalemated one, in which each decision led to extensive debates and long processes of political accommodation—or to lengthy protests by the dissatisfied groups. In such a setting, change could only be incremental, not revolutionary. Though upper-class sectors were favored by existing arrangements, the intricate stalemate reflected a situation in which each group derived real benefits from participating in the system and thus had real stakes in its preservation. It is therefore not surprising that there was such a strong consensus over procedure, over the expression of power capabilities through elections. But as the left gained positions through the commonly shared political process, the right and the sectors it represented began to question the validity of the process itself.

THE BREAKDOWN OF DEMOCRACY

Chile Under Eduardo Frei

The election of Eduardo Frei to the presidency in 1964 marked a significant change in Chilean politics. Unlike the Radical party or the

Ibáñez movement, the Christian Democrats claimed to be a new and cohesive ideological center, intent on breaking the political stalemate. They argued that their reformist strategy would lead to genuine economic and social progress and that it represented a viable third way between the right and the Marxist left. The Christian Democrats therefore ignored the facts that they had achieved the presidency with official endorsement from the rightist parties and that their unprecedented 1965 majority in the Chamber of Deputies was obtained with the support of traditionally right-wing portions of the electorate. They tried to govern as if they had become a majority party that would monopolize the presidency without coalition support for decades to come. Thus they refused to "lower themselves" to share in the distribution of patronage to satisfy electoral clienteles. The Radicals, rather than being cultivated as a potential ally in the political center, were maligned as pragmatic opportunists and were forced to relinquish some of their hold over the state bureaucracy. With the exercise of rigid party discipline in the Chamber of Deputies, which prevented the legislature from overruling presidential initiatives, the lower house became more and more a rubber stamp and the Senate a negative force. The bitterness against the president was illustrated by the Senate's unprecedented step of refusing to permit Frei to go on a state visit to the United States in 1967.

The animosities created by the DC's disdain for coalition politics were compounded by the reforms they set in motion. These were ostensibly designed to raise the living standards and political participation of lower-class sectors as well as to modernize the social and economic systems. Two new groups, in particular, were mobilized as never before: the urban shantytown dwellers and the peasants. The first were encouraged to set up neighborhood councils and a variety of self-help organizations with cultural and community-development ends. The second rapidly became unionized once the peasant unionization law was approved in 1967 or were included in the peasant cooperatives that were set up in the lands expropriated under the government's new agrarian-reform program. Small landholding peasants were also encouraged to form cooperatives. As a result, roughly half the peasant labor force had become organized one way or another by 1970. Many new (particularly craft) unions were also formed among urban workers, and consequently the urban labor movement recovered from the numerical losses of the 1950s. Training programs were begun for both workers and peasants to increase their skills, and an educational reform increased the minimum number of mandatory schooling years.

The reforms, especially those in the countryside, engendered great opposition on the right, which traditionally had a strong political base among the landowners, who were now threatened with expropriations and peasant unionization. The reforms also caused resentment and bitterness on the left. As the many young Christian Democrats in charge of the new programs spread throughout the country using modern techniques and displaying new equipment, it became clear that the DC was in effect attempting to build a strong political base among popular sectors, precisely those sectors that Communists and Socialists considered their own natural base of support. This led to an intense effort by the left to compete with the DC in the creation of the new popular organizations. As a result sharp party conflicts were extended to broader sections of the population, creating sectarian divisions and feelings at the grass roots as never before. The threat to the left and the overall party competition for popular support were enhanced by the rise of an extreme left movement that also sought to organize its following.

The popular mobilization of the 1960s should therefore be seen as the result of party competition, with primarily political consequences. It cannot be said that the process got out of hand, either in terms of the capacity of party elites to control it or in terms of its having overburdened the nation's economy. In fact, during the Frei administration the general economic situation improved and state income increased, thereby generating greater economic capacity to increase the income of the newly mobilized popular sectors as well as a larger government capability to finance new programs. Though state income rose with better tax collection, it must be noted that the economic and fiscal improvements of the period were largely due to a rise in the price of copper during the Vietnam War and to a massive inflow of foreign credit, mainly from U.S. government and private sources. The latter caused an increase in Chilean external debt to US$3 billion by the end of Frei's term and debt-service payments equivalent to roughly a third of export earnings. This would not in itself cause economic dislocations, that is, as long as export income continued to rise and as long as new loans could be obtained to help pay for the old ones. Thus the increasing indebtedness of the Frei period led to a much higher dependence on international markets and financial sources for the proper functioning of the economy.

Despite all their efforts, the DC vote in the 1969 congressional elections was reduced to 29.8 percent. And given the events of the previous six years, it proved impossible to have anything but a three-way race in the 1970 presidential elections. The right would have nothing to do with the Christian Democrats and decided to rally behind the candidacy of former president Jorge Alessandri. The Radicals and other small centrist and leftist groups joined the Socialists and Communists in forming the Popular Unity (UP) coalition, which presented Salvador Allende as candidate. Allende obtained 36.2 percent of the vote, Alessandri came in a close second with 34.9 percent, and the Christian Democratic nominee trailed with 27.8 percent. It must be noted that the result was not the expression of heightened electoral radicalism. Allende, in fact, received a smaller percentage of the vote than in 1964, when he was supported by only Socialists and Communists, and fewer new voters than his conservative adversary. Moreover, although the

Christian Democratic candidate ran on a leftist platform, it is clear from survey and electoral data that his voters would have gone to the right rather than the left.

Following constitutional procedure, the Congress had to elect the president from the two front runners, since none of the candidates received an absolute majority of the vote. In the most flagrant foreign intervention in Chilean history, U.S. President Richard Nixon ordered the CIA to do everything necessary to prevent Allende from coming to power, including economic sabotage and provoking a military coup. The Christian Democrats, unable to vote for their own candidate, held the key swing votes in the legislature, and President Frei and his colleagues were subjected to numerous internal and external pressures to get them to vote for Alessandri. When it appeared that they would reluctantly honor tradition by selecting the front runner, the CIA helped to organize an attempt to kidnap the chief of staff of the armed forces to provoke a military coup. Gen. René Schneider was killed and the coup attempt backfired. It was the first assassination of a major Chilean leader since that of Portales in 1837.

The Allende Years

Allende's inauguration as president represented the first time that a coalition dominated by the Marxist parties took control of the executive. The coalition had campaigned on a program designed to initiate a transition to socialism while preserving Chile's traditional democratic freedoms and constitutional procedures, and the new administration moved swiftly to implement it. With the unanimous consent of the Congress, U.S. interests in the copper mines were nationalized. Resorting to executive powers, some of which were based on admittedly obscure though never repealed legal statutes, the government purchased or took over a broad range of industries as well as the private banking sector and, using Frei's agrarian-reform law, accelerated expropriations of farmland. It should be noted that some industry and land takeovers were instigated by their workers or peasants, led in most cases by leftist or extreme leftist militants, who began sit-in strikes demanding the expropriations. This phenomenon was aided by the overall political climate created by the Allende inauguration, one that favored rather than repressed working-class actions, even when they contradicted government policies.

The government also quickly set in motion a plan to raise wages, salaries, and benefits, particularly for the lowest-paid workers, and to increase the social services in poor communities. These measures were taken in part to stimulate the economy by increasing demand and in part as an attempt to strengthen the government's electoral support as well as to satisfy the expectations of the left's working-class bases, for whom socialism principally meant a better standard of living. The policies were apparently successful, as the economic growth rate during

1971 was the best in decades, and the Popular Unity obtained roughly 50 percent of the vote in the 1971 municipal elections.

The initially favorable economic trends were, however, quickly reversed. Reflecting the poor's needs, the rising demand was disproportionately channeled to a greater consumption of basic consumer items such as food and clothing, areas of the economy that were least able to respond with rapid production increases. Inflationary pressures were therefore strengthened, particularly since government spending increased without a proportional rise in tax receipts, partly as a result of greater tax evasion. By the end of 1972 inflation had reached 164 percent and currency emissions accounted for over 40 percent of the fiscal budget. Moreover, the economy was clearly hurt by politically motivated cutbacks in credits and spare parts from the usual U.S. private or governmental sources. Foreign-exchange reserves dwindled rapidly as Chile imported more food and equipment with less recourse to credit and as it sought to meet payments, though partly rescheduled, on the large foreign debt inherited from the Frei administration. The greater financial dependence of the economy began to take its toll. The price of copper dropped to record lows, adding to the difficulties.

Early political success also proved short-lived. In 1972 the UP suffered reverses in key by-elections as well as in important institutional elections, such as those of the University of Chile or of labor federations. The courts, Contraloría, and Congress also objected increasingly to government initiatives. And most importantly, the early tacit support of the Christian Democrats turned into active opposition, leading to congressional censorship of ministers and to attempts to limit presidential authority.

The process that led to the brutal 1973 military coup that ended the Allende experiment is a highly complex, multidimensional, and dialectical one. It cannot be reduced to a simple set of causes that are easily construed with the benefits of hindsight. Surely the government made many erroneous decisions or proved indecisive at important turning points. The sabotage and conspiracies of foreign and domestic interests seeking to preserve privilege at all costs helped to create an acute economic and political crisis; the actions of revolutionary groups both within and without the government coalition contributed to the exacerbation of an atmosphere of extreme confrontation that strengthened the disloyal and reactionary opposition; elements in the armed forces proved to be less than totally committed to the constitution and the democratic system; the capacity of the state to control and direct civil society disintegrated; taking a longer view, the dependency of the economy made the Allende experiment excessively vulnerable. All these are important factors, but they are not sufficient to explain the final result if viewed apart from a historical process in which contingent events played an important role. The breakdown of the regime was not preordained. It is a mistake to view the middle sectors as hopelessly reactionary, the workers as so radicalized that they would not stop short of total revolution, the army so antidemocratic that it was only waiting for its opportunity, the economy so dependent and the United States so single-handedly powerful and intransigent that the only possible denouement was full-fledged authoritarianism. There was room for choice, but with each unfolding event in the historical process that choice was markedly reduced.

If a single factor must be highlighted, the breakdown of Chilean democracy should be viewed as the result of the inability and unwillingness of moderate forces on both sides of the political dividing line to forge center agreements on programs and policies as well as on regime-saving compromises. The UP could not obtain a workable majority on its own, and the option of arming the workers as demanded by revolutionary groups was not a realistic alternative. The Chilean left was organized to compete in elections, not fight in battles; to change strategy would not have been easy, and any attempt to do so would have provoked an even earlier coup d'état. Without support from centrist forces, principally from the Christian Democrats who had made Allende's election possible in the first place, the UP government would remain a minority government without sufficient power to carry out programs, given the vast and unwieldy character of the Chilean institutional system.

The failure of center agreements resulted from political pressures originating in the extremes of both sides of the polarized party system. The government coalition was in fact sharply divided, the basic disagreements being those separating the Communists from the majority faction in the Socialist party. The latter wanted to press as fast as possible to institute the UP program and felt that support for the government would increase only insofar as it took decisive action to implement a socialist system. Compromise with the DC would, in the Socialists' view, only divert revolutionary objectives and confuse the working class. They therefore sought to undermine UP-DC collaboration and agreements. The Communists were much more willing to moderate the course of government policies in order to consolidate a narrower range of changes and to broaden the government's legislative base by resolving differences with the Christian Democrats. Both Socialists and Communists were pressured by the non-UP extreme left, which sought to accelerate changes through direct action outside constitutional procedures. Their influence in the UP coalition was magnified by the proximity of their positions with those of elements in the Socialist party majority; therefore, the extreme left was not marginalized at the fringe of the political process.

Allende shared the Communists' position but did not wish to cause a break with his own Socialist party. He therefore projected an ambivalent image and at times failed to take decisive action—for fear of alienating his party—without the certainty of receiving consistent support from the center forces in exchange. These political differences affected the daily operations of government agencies; employees, for example, often would not take orders from superiors belonging to other parties. The president and the ministers were so often involved in tending to these daily crises that they had little time to structure long-term policies, analyze the consequences of short-term ones, or develop a coherent strategy to deal with the moderate opposition.

The Christian Democrats were also torn by internal differences: The party was divided into left- and right-leaning factions of approximately equal strength. The 1971 party leadership came from the left-leaning group, and it sought to maintain a working relationship with the government, while the right-wing faction pressed for the adoption of a tougher opposition stand. However, the party leadership was at first rebuffed by an overly confident UP government exhibiting the same arrogance the DC had shown previously, a situation that only strengthened the position of the right-wing sector within the party. Ironically, constitutional reforms adopted in 1970 by the DC and the right had diminished the role of the legislature, thus reducing the executive's need to reach agreements with the opposition. The right-wing faction was also strengthened by the vehement attacks on prominent DC leaders in the leftist media and by the assassination of a former Frei cabinet minister. Though this killing was the action of a small leftist fringe, the DC blamed the government for tolerating a climate of violence that, it argued, led to such incidents.

As a centrist opposition force, the DC was also extremely vulnerable to pressures from the right of the party system. If the DC leadership could not show that its tacit support for the government had resulted in moderating UP policies, the party stood to lose the anti-UP vote to the right without gaining greater support from the left. Therefore, the DC was soon forced to work with the right in opposition. The turning point came in mid-1971 with the first special by-election to fill a vacant congressional seat in which, given the winner-take-all nature of the contest, a UP victory was certain if the opposition fielded separate candidates. Consequently, the DC approached the government suggesting an agreement that would have led to a joint UP-DC candidacy, an offer that Allende accepted but the Socialist party vetoed. In view of this rejection, the DC turned to the right, and the joint opposition candidate won decisively. As a result of this experience, a leftist splinter group decided to leave the Christian Democratic party, which strengthened further the right wing within it. The DC alliance with the right-wing National party continued in future elections, adding to the polarization of forces.

In February 1972 the DC obtained congressional approval of legislation severely limiting the president's ability to intervene in the economy, thereby challenging the essence of the government's program and marking the beginning of a fundamental constitutional confrontation between the president and the Congress. Interpreting 1970 constitutional amendments differently from the president, the opposition argued that Congress required only a simple majority to override a presidential veto of the new legislation, while the UP maintained, in fact more correctly, that a two-thirds majority was needed. It then became clear to moderates on both sides that accommodation was essential. On two separate occasions government and DC representatives met in an attempt to reach a compromise that would have allowed the government to keep a substantial public sector of the economy while giving the private sector certain guarantees. But the talks collapsed. The Nationals suggested a DC sellout, while the Socialists and other leftist groups stepped up factory expropriations in order to present the DC with a *fait accompli*. They thus undermined the negotiating position of the moderate Radical splinter group entrusted by Allende with conducting the discussion, and as a result this group left the UP coalition to join the opposition. Again, this only polarized the political forces further, reducing the potential success of a center agreement.

By mid-1972, the critical situation of the economy and the growing aggressiveness of the opposition led the government to try once again to hold talks with the Christian Democrats. This time Allende was strongly committed to reaching a compromise, and the UP made substantial concessions leading to agreement on a broad range of issues. However, the more conservative faction within the Christian Democratic party maneuvered successfully to prevent the negotiators from finishing their work. By that point, most sectors within the DC felt that the government was clearly on the defensive and thought that by concluding an agreement with it the party would surely lose support among the increasingly discontented middle sectors, thereby running the risk of being routed by the Nationals in the March 1973 congressional elections. Considerations of short-term party interest thus carried the day.

Toward the end of 1972, qualitative changes had begun to take place in Chilean politics. The parties had repeatedly called the mass rallies that characterized the Allende years not only to increase their bargaining stakes but also to prove actual power capabilities. Nonetheless, the nature of this mobilization soon changed. Business and professional associations increasingly took matters into their own hands, and before long the DC and the Nationals were falling over each other not to direct but to pledge support for the independent action of a whole range of groups. These demonstrations culminated in the massive October 1972 strike and lockout by hundreds of truck owners, merchants, industrialists, and professionals. The government parties countered by mobilizing their own supporters, also engendering a significant organizational infrastructure that could operate at the margin of party leadership directives. These demonstrations and counterdemonstrations by a vast array of groups, the numbers of which had continued to increase during the Allende years, were partly stimulated by a vitriolic mass media giving at least two totally different interpretations of every event, generating a dynamic in which the symbolic became the real, falsehoods turned into hysterically believed truths, and perceived threats were taken as imminent. The climate of agitation was also increased by the CIA funds that flowed to opposition groups, strengthening them significantly as political actors independent of party control. For government leaders the decreased capacity of party elites to control group mobilization and confrontation was more serious than for the opposition. It meant that the government lost an important measure of authority over the society, that the state itself would be bypassed as the central arena for political confrontation, and that the legitimacy of the regular processes of bargaining was undermined. In this crisis atmosphere, Allende turned to a presumably neutral referee who would ensure institutional order until the March 1973 congressional elections could clear the political air. Military men were brought into the cabinet, and the chief of staff was made the minister of the interior.

The incorporation of the military into the government ended the strikes of October 1972 and freed the political forces to concentrate on the congressional elections, which party leaders saw as the decisive confrontation. But in serving as a buffer between contending forces, the military itself became the object of intense political pressures. The left within the UP criticized it for slowing down government programs and initiatives, while the more strident elements on the right accused it of helping a government that would otherwise fall. Other sectors went out of their way to praise the military, a tacit recognition that they were the only force with real power. These pressures politicized an institution that had largely remained at the margin of political events. Though it was hardly perceived at the time, a cleavage began to appear within the military between officers supporting the government because they saw it as the constitutional government and those more receptive to the increasingly louder voices of opposition elements calling for the government's downfall.

The March 1973 elections symbolized the final polarization of Chilean politics as the government and the opposition faced each other as two electoral blocs. Not surprisingly, the elections did not help resolve the political crisis. The opposition failed to gain the two-thirds majority it needed to impeach Allende, and the government failed to obtain majority control in either house of Congress. Given the massive inflation and serious shortages of basic goods as well as the climate of political uncertainty, the government's showing was commendable since it managed to win seats at the expense of the opposition. And yet the final results were not dramatically different from those that the two blocs had obtained as separate parties in the previous congressional contest. The electorate did not provide the magic solution. Their task done, the military left the cabinet.

Soon after, a decisive event initiated the final stage in the breakdown of the regime. On June 29, 1973, a military garrison revolted. Though the uprising was quickly put down, President Allende and his advisers realized that it was only a matter of time before the *golpista* (pro-coup) faction of the armed forces consolidated its strength. They again dismissed the far left's counsel to arm the workers. The creation of a parallel army would only accelerate the coup, and it would have been impossible, in any event, to organize a significant counterpower. Ironically, military officers were quicker to believe, or to make believe, not only that the workers could be a potent force but that sectors of the left had already structured a viable military force. But the well-publicized efforts of military commanders to find secret arms caches uncovered nothing of importance, although they attempted to convey the impression that they had.

To the consternation of the leadership of his own Socialist party, Allende once again called for talks with the Christian Democrats. And despite the vocal opposition of many of their followers, the Christian Democratic leaders, urged to do so by the cardinal, agreed to the new negotiations. However, an agreement at that point was unlikely. The hard-line faction of the Christian Democrats had replaced the more moderate leadership, and Allende was thus obliged to deal with the group most hostile to his government and policies. Moreover, the country was once again in the throes of massive lockouts, strikes, and civil disobedience campaigns led by business and professional associations (with considerable CIA funding), all demanding the president's resignation. By that time significant working-class groups, such as the copper miners, had also staged strikes to express their discontent with specific government policies, which only reenforced the confidence of the opposition. Any form of support for the government by the Christian Democrats would therefore have been seen as a sellout by the opposition. The political arena had been reduced to a few men attempting to negotiate a settlement. Even though these men no longer had the kind of control over social forces they once had, a dramatic announcement from the talks would still have placed the nation's largest parties and most respected leaders on the side of a peaceful solution and would have seriously undermined the subversive plans of military officers.

But agreement was not forthcoming. The Christian Democrats did not trust Allende's word that he really wanted a settlement, believing instead that he merely sought to buy time in order to force an armed confrontation. However, it is clear from the president's actions that he sought an agreement. He kept moderate leaders in his cabinets, even though they were severely attacked by the left within and outside the UP, and he virtually broke with his own party. Furthermore, Allende finally did agree to the Christian Democratic demand of bringing the military back into the government. In combating to the end the dubious prospect of "Marxist totalitarianism" and in constantly increasing bargaining demands, the DC leaders failed to realize how much stake they had in the political order they thought they were defending. By not moving forcefully to structure a political solution, they undermined the fragile position of the president and his advisers, who were clearly seeking accommodation. Instead the DC supported a Chamber of Deputies declaration calling on the military to safeguard the constitution and declaring that the government had lost its legitimacy.

Two weeks later, prominently displaying the chamber's resolution as evidence of the legality and broad-based support for their action, the top military leadership led the brutal revolt against the government. Air force jets bombed and strafed the presidential palace, in which Allende himself died fighting, officially a suicide. Thousands of government supporters, or presumed government supporters, were arrested, mistreated, tortured, or killed in the months that followed.

Some prominent Christian Democrats condemned the coup in the initial moments. But others, including the leadership, welcomed it as inevitable and blamed the government for all that had transpired. Little did they realize what the "saving" action of the military would mean for the country's and their own future.

THE MILITARY IN GOVERNMENT

The September 11, 1973, coup marked the most dramatic political change in Chilean history. Though in 1891, 1924, and 1932 elements of the armed forces played a role in the formation of governments, never before had the military ruled on its own. And, whereas the unelected governments that came to power in those years lasted for only a few weeks, the military junta would become the longest lasting government in the nation's history.

At first the military junta, constituted by the commanders of each of the services and the national police, argued that they had overthrown the Allende government in order to protect democracy and that their aim was to restore constitutional government. But the new authorities soon defined the Chilean crisis as one of regime rather than of government. They placed the blame for the breakdown of Chile's institutions not only on the Popular Unity government, but on liberal democracy itself. Democracy had permitted divisive party competition and the rise of Marxist political leaders intent on defining the nation's cleavages in class terms. In their view, demogogic politicians, responding to narrow group interests, contributed to economic mismanagement by not permitting "technicians" to formulate the "best" policy choices with administrative efficiency.

The goal of the new junta thus became one of transforming the Chilean system, creating a "new" democracy and a "new" citizen, devoid of the "vices" of the past. The Congress was closed, local governments disbanded, and elections banned. Newspapers, radio stations, and magazines were shut down, and those allowed to publish were subjected to varying degrees of censorship. Officials and leaders of the Popular

Unity government and parties were arrested, exiled, and in some cases killed. Within months of the coup, Christian Democratic leaders, unwilling to accept an indefinite military regime, saw their activities severely curbed as well.

Although the military authorities sharply restricted the activities of traditional political parties, they ignored the strong pressure of right-wing supporters to create a massive progovernment party or "civic-military movement." For this reason it is inappropriate to label the Chilean regime as fascist.

Neither is it appropriate to view the regime as corporatist. Despite early pronouncements that the junta intended to draw on Catholic integralist doctrine to structure corporative institutions, all of the countries' major interest groups, including employers and professional associations and trade organizations (many of which had supported the coup with enthusiasm), saw their influence markedly diminished. The new authorities were simply not interested in bringing into the decision-making process any expression of societal interests. They were convinced that through disciplined administrative management and the advice of qualified experts they would be able to govern and modernize the country without the advice of "interested" or "partisan" groups. They thus sought to replace party politics and interest-group politics with technoadministrative solutions imposed by fiat. The governing style for the country as a whole paralleled the internal governing style of the military institution itself.

It is important to stress that these fundamental policy decisions were made by the leadership of the armed forces, acting with considerable autonomy from their institutions. Although in the early moments there was some consultation among higher-ranking officers, the junta soon established itself as the government to which the armed forces were supposed to relate, in very much the same way that they had related historically to civilian governments. In this sense, the Chilean military government is of the armed forces, but not by the armed forces. Policy decisions are formulated by the government and do not originate with, nor are they reviewed formally by, military officers within the institution. Military officers assigned to the government report to their superiors, civilian or military, in the government, not in the military.

The separation of the military in government from the military in the institution has been reenforced by the "apolitical" character of the Chilean military. It has also been reenforced by the ascendancy of Gen. Augusto Pinochet as Chile's strong man. Pinochet, who joined the coup effort late, made skillful use of his position as commander in chief of the army to outmaneuver his colleagues on the junta and to have himself designated as president. Although the junta retains important legislative functions, it lost executive authority to Pinochet. By virtue of his ability to appoint government officials, as well as to control the military promotion system, he has become the locus of power, accountable to no other institution or group.

It was not until 1980, however, that Pinochet was able to consolidate his position juridically. Key provisions in the 1980 constitution, which was submitted to popular referendum, designate Pinochet as president until 1989 and permit the four commanders of the armed forces to reappoint him to an additional eight-year term. The Chilean regime thus evolved into a dictatorship based on the unconditional support of the armed forces, particularly the army, who see the government as their government, even though there are no institutional mechanisms for military influence in day-to-day policymaking matters.

Junta Policy Initiatives

The policy initiatives of the Pinochet government have been more far-reaching than those of any other Chilean government, including the Popular Unity government. All elected public officials have been eliminated, and the government has instituted a wide-ranging security apparatus that deals harshly with opponents and restricts fundamental liberties including habeas corpus.

Even though the repressive apparatus of the state has increased enormously, in other respects the role of the state in national life has been severely reduced. Productive enterprises, including many created with public funds, were sold to private firms. This led to a significant transformation in the physiognomy of the private sector. Economic power became more concentrated behind bank-based conglomerates able to purchase enterprises at bargain prices, often making use of funds borrowed from abroad. Although the state continues to own the large copper mines and most utilities and railroads, the authorities have encouraged new private investments in these categories. The junta also turned over to the private sector many programs dealing with social security, health, and welfare. New labor legislation was adopted aimed at atomizing the union movement by encouraging a proliferation of unions at the plant level.

The "privatization" initiatives were part of a broad set of policy measures introduced by a team of young economists. These economists soon came to be known as the Chicago Boys because many either studied at the University of Chicago or were followers of the free-market and monetarist economic doctrines identified with the economics department at that university. The Chicago Boys appealed to junta members, and to Pinochet in particular, because of their apolitical status, their high level of technical competence, and their strongly held beliefs that Chilean underdevelopment was a product of an overbloated state, one that the military leaders identified so closely with the parties and groups they wished to eradicate from Chilean society. The Chicago Boys, in fact, held out a promise of a substantially changed political system, by way of significant transformations in the economic and social sphere. Through free market policies that encouraged economic growth and a higher standard of living and social policies that encouraged private initiative, they hoped to do away with parties and groups identified with the political ideologies of the past.

By 1980, the economic team seemed to be meeting with substantial success. Inflation had been brought down from over 500 percent to manageable levels, the government deficit had been wiped out, and large reserves were accumulated in the foreign account. Government officials pointed to a substantial rise in new exports of Chilean agricultural products and semiprocessed goods as evidence of the wisdom of drastically reduced tariff barriers that pitted local companies against foreign competitors. By following the doctrine of comparative advantage, the Chicago Boys felt that Chile could modernize by selling to the world what it could do best while importing products made more cheaply elsewhere.

In 1981, however, the economic model of the Chilean military regime came to a resounding end. Despite lower wages and sharp restrictions on union activity that initially protected domestic firms from the full impact of lower tariff barriers, massive imports of foreign goods soon undermined even the strongest national industries. Unemployment skyrocketed to over 20 percent as local firms went bankrupt in increasing numbers. Large capital inflows into the country, which helped improve the balance of payments, did not translate into higher investment. Instead, foreign funds were used to finance speculative ventures and the massive purchase of imported consumer items. Although the international recession added to Chile's woes, Chile's fate was much worse than that of other Latin American countries. In 1982 the gross national product fell 14 percent, by comparison to a drop of about 1 percent for Latin America as a whole.

Rather than modernizing Chilean industry, the Chicago Boys' policies dealt a severe blow even to the country's most efficient corporations. In less than a decade the percentage of the population employed in the industrial sector had diminished significantly. In agriculture, where reform initiatives were reversed, government economic policies had an equally devastating effect. Farmers became hopelessly indebted in a futile attempt to compete with imported products. Whole industries, like the sugar beet industry, which had been designed to give Chile self-sufficiency, were allowed to languish so that Chilean agriculture could concentrate on producing only those goods that Chile could produce efficiently for international trade. While Chile found new export markets in fruits and forest products (the latter the result of massive state investment in prejunta years) the net effect was to drive countless agricultural businesses into bankruptcy and to make the country more dependent on imported foodstuff. Agricultural leaders, particularly in the southern wheat-producing areas, were arguing by 1981 that the Pinochet government's free market policies had damaged their interests far more than the socialist policies of the Allende government.

Political Opposition and the Prospects
for a Return to Democracy

When Pinochet celebrated the tenth anniversary of the military coup that overthrew Chile's constitutional government, it was clear that the military regime had failed in its cardinal objective to transform the underlying nature of the Chilean political system. Political parties, which were supposed to disappear as irrelevant relics of the past, were able, despite severe repression, to maintain organizational presence and continuity. The labor movement, which was supposed to become depoliticized and oriented toward bread-and-butter issues, survived and gained in militancy. Labor leaders, including many who initially supported the coup, took the initiative in organizing the first massive protests against the government in mid-1983. By that year most professional and trade associations had elected slates of officers either closely identified with political parties or openly hostile to the government. Joining the chorus of opposition were large numbers of business people devastated by the economic recession.

The survival of opposition elements in Chile was aided by the stand taken by the Chilean Catholic Church. The Church, by continuing its call for the reestablishment of liberal democracy, refused to lend legitimacy to some of the junta's earlier declarations based on integralist Catholic doctrine. What is more, the Church actively championed the cause of human rights, helping to check some of the most flagrant abuses of the regime. Church leaders, both at the national and local level, provided meeting grounds and institutional protection for community groups, labor organizations, political parties, and intellectuals. Under Church auspices magazines and books were published exposing government abuses and maintaining a measure of open discourse.

Widespread dissatisfaction with the regime, leading to mass protest rallies, placed the Pinochet government on the defensive. In an attempt to stave off growing demands for his resignation or removal from office, Pinochet reluctantly removed the last advocates of free market economic policies, bringing into his cabinet individuals closely associated with Chile's beleaguered business elite. He also turned to elements of Chile's traditional rightist party, the National party, to help cope with the opposition. While arguing that Pinochet should complete his term in office, they sought to accelerate the timetable for a transition back to civilian rule, proposing the legalization of political parties and the holding of congressional elections before 1989, the date specified in the constitution.

These measures gave Pinochet some breathing room, defusing somewhat the open opposition to the regime. Pinochet also benefited from the sharp disagreements over strategy among opposition elements. Although the centrist Christian Democrats repudiated any understanding with the regime and the right (with whom they had allied against Allende) and gradually developed a working relationship with elements of the left, these understandings were tenuous and fragile. A central issue was the role of the Communist party. Christian Democrats argued that an alliance with the Communists was impossible so long as that party called for an insurrectionary strategy in seeking the downfall of the regime. The Communists, in turn, condemned any form of dialogue with regime spokesmen. Center-left forces were caught in the middle, with the Socialists badly split on whether to side with the Christian Democrats or the Communists. Center party officials argued further that violent demonstrations against the regime only antagonized Chile's large middle classes, thus strengthening Pinochet's hand. Leaders on the left argued, in turn, that accommodation with the authorities would only demoralize popular protest and reduce the pressure on the military to force Pinochet out.

Because military support is the fundamental pillar of the Chilean regime, the position of the military is the key to any early transition back to democracy. Continued economic difficulties and mounting social unrest might force high-ranking commanders to remove Pinochet in order to prevent political chaos. However, three factors contribute to the reluctance of the military to intervene even under difficult circumstances. In the first place, the Chilean armed forces are highly disciplined institutions, and Pinochet maintains firm control. It is very difficult for conspiracies to develop in a climate where discussions about politics in the officer corps are strongly discouraged. Second, any violation of the 1980 constitution is in fact a violation of the very legality the military has supported, reenforcing the claims of opposition elements that the institutional system set up by the Pinochet regime with the support of the military is in fact illegitimate. Third, military officers fear that the removal of Pinochet might lead to a great deal of uncertainty, ushering in a government dominated by political parties that have opposed the military regime. Officers fear that they will lose some of the many privileges, in status and in material rewards, that they have gained under military rule, They also fear that they could be blamed for economic failures and human-rights violations.

And yet the fact remains that as long as Pinochet remains in office, Chile is out of step with the growing trend to redemocratization in the mid-1980s. Unless he is able to move in a genuine fashion to an earlier transition than the one envisioned in the 1980 constitution, it is difficult to envision Pinochet's being able to maintain a highly personal style of authoritarian rule in a country so used to democratic institutions and procedures. Despite enormous obstacles, it is likely that opposition forces will find common strategies for regime opposition and regime transition. Some sectors of the right are likely to join the opposition unless they can persuade Pinochet to accelerate the liberalization process. And, ironically, the military may move against Pinochet not because of broad-scale societal opposition, but because of growing allegations of personal corruption, a factor that might convince even the most loyal officers that their institutional interests can be served best by forcing a return to civilian rule.

SUGGESTIONS FOR FURTHER READING

Angell, Alan. *Politics and the Labour Movement in Chile.* Oxford University Press, London, 1972.

Bauer, Robert J. *Chilean Rural Society from the Spanish Conquest to 1930.* Cambridge University Press, London, 1975.

Blakemore, Harold. *British Nitrates and Chilean Politics, 1886–1896: Balmaceda and North.* Athlone Press, London, 1974.

Boorstein, Edward. *Allende's Chile: An Inside View.* International Publishers, New York, 1977.

DeShazo, Peter. *Urban Workers and Labor Unions in Chile, 1902–1927.* University of Wisconsin Press, Madison, 1983.

Drake, Paul W. *Socialism and Populism in Chile, 1932–52.* University of Illinois, Urbana, 1978.

Foxley, Alejandro. *Latin American Experiments in Neoconservative Economics.* University of California, Berkeley, 1983.

Galdames, Luis. *A History of Chile.* Translated and edited by Issac J. Cox. University of North Carolina Press, Chapel Hill, 1941.

Gil, Federico. *The Political System of Chile.* Houghton Mifflin, Boston, 1966.

Gil, Federico, Ricardo Lagos E., and H. A. Landsberger, eds. *Chile at the Turning Point: Lessons of the Socialist Years, 1970–73.* Institute for the Study of Human Issues (ISHI), Philadelphia, 1979.

Kaufman, Robert R. *The Politics of Land Reform in Chile 1950–1970: Public Policy, Political Institutions, and Social Change.* Harvard University Press, Cambridge, 1972.

Mamalakis, Markos J. *The Growth and Structure of the Chilean Economy: From Independence to Allende.* Yale University Press, New Haven, Conn., 1976.

Moran, Theodore. *Multinational Corporations and the Politics of Dependence: Copper in Chile.* Princeton University Press, Princeton, N.J., 1974.

Petras, James, and Morris Morley. *The United States and Chile: Imperialism and the Overthrow of the Allende Government.* Monthly Review Press, New York, 1975.

Pike, Fredrick. *Chile and the United States.* University of Notre Dame Press, Notre Dame, Ind., 1963.

Roxborough, Ian, Philip O'Brien, and Jackie Roddick. *Chile: The State and Revolution.* Holmes & Meier Publishers, New York, 1977.

Sigmund, Paul E. *The Overthrow of Allende and the Politics of Chile, 1964–76.* University of Pittsburgh, Pittsburgh, 1977.

Smith, Brian H. *The Church and Politics in Chile: Challenges to Modern Catholicism.* Princeton University Press, Princeton, N.J., 1982.

Stallings, Barbara. *Class Conflict and Economic Development in Chile, 1958–1973.* Stanford University Press, Stanford, Calif., 1978.

United States Senate. *Staff Report of the Select Committee to Study Governmental Operations with Respect to United States Intelligence. Covert Action in Chile.* U.S. Government Printing Office, Washington, D.C., December 18, 1975.

Valenzuela, Arturo. *Political Brokers in Chile: Local Politics in a Centralized Polity.* Duke University Press, Durham, N.C., 1977.

_____ . *The Breakdown of Democratic Regimes: Chile.* Johns Hopkins University Press, Baltimore, 1978.

Valenzuela, Arturo, and J. Samuel Valenzuela, eds. *Chile: Politics and Society.* Transaction Books, New Brunswick, N.J., 1976.

_____ . *Chile Under Military Rule.* Johns Hopkins University Press, Baltimore, forthcoming 1985.

Zammit, Ann, ed. *The Chilean Way to Socialism.* University of Texas Press, Austin, 1973.

11
Colombia: Modified Two-Party and Elitist Politics

HARVEY F. KLINE

The Colombian presidential campaign of 1974 demonstrated, more graphically than usual, the basic characteristics of that country's politics. There was little doubt that the winner of the election would be the next president; though there have been certain military rumblings in recent years, Colombia in its own way has a liberal democratic record equaled by few other countries in Latin America (there has been only one military dictatorship in this century and only two successful military coups d'état). Two major parties were involved in the election, but there was a third candidate from a splinter party. The existence of a party other than the historical Conservatives and Liberals was unusual; that once again there was no simple contest between two candidates for the presidency was typical. Although the country is termed one of the few two-party systems in Latin America, only one presidential election in this century has been contested by one representative of each of the two parties.

Finally, the parentage of the three major candidates illustrates the continued domination of the nation's politics by the same families. The winner, Alfonso López Michelsen, was the son of former president Alfonso López Pumarejo. Coming in second was Alvaro Gómez, son of former president Laureano Gómez. And finishing third was María Eugenia Rojas de Moreno Díaz, daughter of the only military dictator of the century. This election thus demonstrated that democratic Colombia, albeit in a different way than in other Latin American countries, has a stable and very small group of people at the very top, who monopolize meaningful political power and produce children who follow their fathers' careers.

Since that symbolic election of 1974, some apparent changes have taken place. The third party has disappeared; only one of the presidential

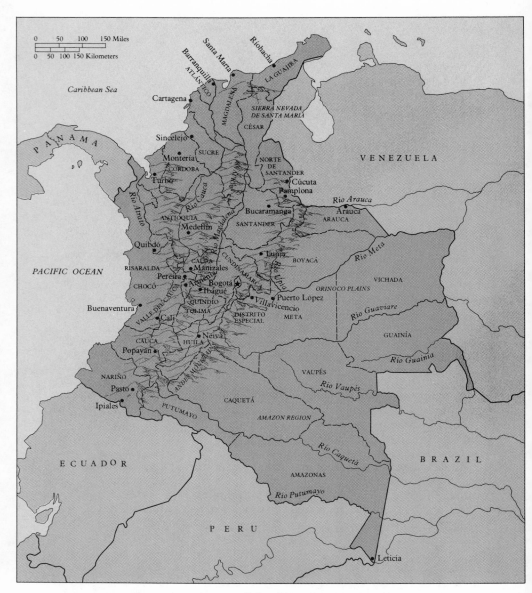

Colombia

candidates has been the son or daughter of a former chief executive—
Alfonso López Michelsen when he sought reelection in 1982. The basic
Colombian state structure has remained the same.

BACKGROUND

Colombia is a country of great geographic diversity. It is crossed by
three ranges of the Andes Mountains and includes a part of the plains
of the Orinoco River and seemingly limitless expanses of Amazonian
jungle, as well as coasts on the Atlantic and Pacific oceans. Of the
national territory, the fifth largest in Latin America, the one-third made
up by the Andean region contains 75 percent of the population and all
major centers of economic and political activity, with the exceptions of
Barranquilla and Cartagena on the Atlantic Coast.

Yet the Andean region itself demonstrates much regional diversity.
Transportation difficulties led to little interaction between the areas
before the advent of the airplane. There is a great diversity of climate,
based on altitude. Bogotá at 8,530 feet (2,600 meters) has cold nights,
brisk days, and seemingly endless rain. Medellín, at 4,852 feet (1,479
meters) calls itself the "city of eternal spring," with temperatures the
year round in the sixties at night and low eighties during the daytime.
Cali and Bucaramanga, being slightly lower, have warmer climates.
Agricultural pursuits tend to be different at different elevations, the
highest areas being most productive in the cultivation of grains and
potatoes, medium altitudes in coffee, and the low altitudes in the tropical
crops, such as sugarcane and bananas. These tropical products are also
common in the lowlands of the coasts, whereas the llanos of the Orinoco
River are most suitable to ranching. The Amazon region, formerly a
center of rubber production, is now economically important only insofar
as tourists can be convinced to visit it.

The diversity of Colombian geography is matched by the diversity
of its people, who number 30 million, making the country the third
largest in population in Latin America. The chief Indian group at the
arrival of the Spanish, the Chibchas, had reached a level of civilization
that was relatively high but below that of the Aztecs of Mexico or the
Incas of Peru. As a result, Spanish colonization led to a nearly complete
incorporation of the Chibchas, although more so culturally than racially.
One still sees in the highlands of central Colombia individuals who
must be direct descendants of the Chibchas. However, unlike their
counterparts in Ecuador and Peru, they dress no differently from people
of Spanish or mixed background of the same social standing and they
speak Spanish. Only in the southernmost *departamentos* (provinces) of
Nariño and Cauca, to which the Incan empire reached, and in certain
parts of the isolated areas of the country, such as the Amazon jungles
and the Guajiran peninsula, are there sizable groups of people of Indian
background whose spoken language is other than Spanish.

In other parts of Colombia, especially the coastal areas and the Cauca Valley region, large numbers of slaves were brought in to work on sugarcane plantations. In the areas of Antioquia and Chocó, the slaves came for mining because of the small number of Indians. These regions are characterized by societies quite different from those in the Spanish-Indian areas. Not only is race visibly different but so are social relations, religion, and indeed, politics.

Today Colombian society demonstrates a great racial diversity. One meets in the "right circles" Colombians of pure Spanish ancestry speaking what is reputed to be the best Spanish of the hemisphere and taking great pride in their *abolengo* (pedigree). Quite often they have social prominence, economic wealth, and political power. On the other end of the racial spectrum are those individuals of pure Indian or black descent, speaking a Spanish not so technically proficient (but at least speaking Spanish, as is not the case in some other Latin American countries). Most often they have neither social, political, nor economic wherewithal. In the middle are the majority (although it is difficult to be more precise, since no recent Colombian census has included "race" as a question) of individuals who are a mixture of white and Indian (*mestizo*), white and black (mulatto), black and Indian (*zambo*), or of all three great racial currents. Race is not the salient issue that it is in the United States, but clearly it is better to be white, and there is a great correlation between race and socioeconomic status.

The country is marked by strict stratification along class lines. The most basic division is between those who have manual jobs and those who have nonmanual (or mental) occupations. Within the nonmanual groups, further stratification is decided by the criteria of wealth, race, and *abolengo*. At the very top are those with the "best" of all three criteria, although there are notable cases of "fallen aristocrats," who no longer have the extensive wealth of the past, and of the *nuevos ricos*, without pedigree but with much wealth. Within the manual group, stratification follows the same criteria (it's better to be a fairly white individual with a relatively high degree of income), but *abolengo* does not enter into the equation, and there appears to be much less stability in the social orderings. Yet there are notable differences, in the cities, for example, between the members of a labor union and a *marginal* living in a hut illegally constructed on someone else's land.

In foreign trade Colombia is still a one-crop economy, although the degree to which coffee dominates export earnings has fluctuated in recent years. In 1964 coffee contributed 79 percent of the export earnings, a figure that had decreased, in part because of governmental policies favoring other exports, to 42 percent by 1975. Then due to a frost in Brazil, coffee prices and the Colombian share of the world market increased. By 1978 the percentage of export earnings coming from coffee reached a zenith of 66 percent, afterward declining as Brazilian production recovered. A coffee "bonanza," such as that of the 1970s, is not an unmixed blessing. The increased foreign exchange led to a higher value for the Colombian peso, making it easier for foreign imports to enter, thus damaging local industry, and making it more difficult for exports other than coffee to be sold, also damaging local industry. This was particularly the case in the 1970s when a new illegal commerce began, especially of marijuana and cocaine. It was estimated that by 1979 the illicit drug trade plus other contraband brought some US$3.2 billion into the country, greater than all legal export earnings combined.[1]

The nature of coffee production has affected the kind of dependency in which Colombia lives. Although it is certain that the country suffers from the vagaries of world market prices for coffee and that the buyer of the product has predominantly been the United States, there is one characteristic of some dependent agricultural economies that does not pertain in Colombia: the presence of foreign owners of the lands. Colombian coffee has traditionally been shade-grown (although this is changing) on lands owned by the Colombians themselves. The popular myth (as seen in the Juan Valdez commercial) of the independent family farmer working his own land may be the case in some instances, but evidence suggests that family-size farms are not the norm. Even though Colombian coffee cannot be harvested mechanically, probably most of the product is picked by tenant farmers who own little or no land of their own. Indeed, the issue of land reform, both in the coffee areas and elsewhere, has been a salient one for decades, but one largely unsolved.

Colombia has chronically suffered from a negative balance-of-payments problem. It appeared in the mid-1970s that the problem would become worse, when the country stopped being an exporter of petroleum and became an importer of that essential product of increasing price. Government policymakers, projecting growing consumption and prices as well as declining production trends, concluded that by the mid-1980s the country would import about US$1.5 billion worth of petroleum a year, more than twice the value of the unusually high coffee exports of the coffee bonanza years. Such a crisis did not eventuate, because of the coffee and drug bonanzas and because more favorable terms for the foreign multinational corporations resulted in the discovery of new oil fields.

Before the bonanzas, one of the strategies to meet the trade imbalance was import-substitution industrialization (ISI). Many manufactured goods, especially food products and clothing and even some consumer durables such as cars, stoves, and refrigerators, are now produced in Colombia. Some are produced by purely Colombian industry; others are produced by U.S. and European-based multinational corporations. The "cheap" dollar that came with the bonanzas dealt a serious blow to such ISI. Added to this mixed economic picture is the problem of inflation. By the mid-1970s, the consumer price index was in the low thousands (1954 = 100). The bonanzas increased the inflation rates. Between 1976 and

1981 the yearly inflation rate was between a low of 17.8 percent and a high of 26.5 percent. By the end of 1982 the consumer price index (1970 = 100) was at 1,122.

In conclusion, the Colombian economy is an intermediate one in Latin American terms. Gross domestic product per capita is estimated at US$922 per year. The country's GDP grew at an average of 6 percent a year between 1970 and 1979, before slowing down in the early 1980s. Although surely not an "economic miracle" such as that of Brazil, Colombian growth was sound.

The basis for many of the problems is the growth of the Colombian population at 2.3 percent per annum since 1973, down from about 3 percent a year in the previous two decades. This rate makes Colombia one of the fastest-growing countries in the world, with its population increasing from 17.5 million in 1964 to 27.3 million in 1980. This growth, as well as massive urban inmigration, has led to the meteoric growth of the cities. Bogotá's population has increased from 1.5 million in 1968 to 5 million in 1980. Other major cities, especcially Medellín and Cali, have had similar growth. This has led to a whole series of new problems and political issues.

HISTORY TO 1930

During the Spanish colonial period, Colombia was neither a backwater nor a center as important as Mexico or Peru. The quantity of precious metals was less, although there was a substantial amount of gold. For most of the period Colombia was part of the viceroyalty of Peru, but in 1739 Bogotá became the center of a new viceroyalty, which also included the present countries of Venezuela, Panama, and Ecuador.

The struggle for independence in Colombia came from those *criollos* (creoles) of the very highest standing. The battles were fierce, highlighted by various reversals and historic treks through the rugged mountains on horseback. Independence finally came through the Battle of Boyacá (1819) and the victorious army, led by Simón Bolívar, continued to the south, where it played instrumental roles in the liberation of Ecuador, Peru, and Bolivia.

The first ten years of national independence were ones of confederation with Venezuela and Ecuador in Gran Colombia. Yet regional differences among the three countries had already appeared. Bolívar himself once remarked that Venezuela was a military garrison, Ecuador a convent, and Colombia a debating society—a prophesy of "national character" that demonstrated certain validity in the following years. In 1830 the countries went their own ways, and Colombia (called Nueva Granada and including a distant province that later became Panama) was alone.

Although the first years showed the chaos so prevalent in newly independent Latin America, by 1850 the new country settled into patterns that, in large part, continue today. For some reason, about which historians disagree, the norm became civilian, partisan politics, a sharp departure from the experiences of most other Latin American countries. By 1849 there were two political parties, one calling itself Liberal and the other Conservative, both with public programs that were not dramatically different. These were elite-instigated parties (as most in Latin America were at that time), rather than ones coming from popular demands. Ideological differences soon developed between the two parties, at least at the leadership level. The Liberals favored federalism, free trade, and a restricted role for the Church in politics. The Conservatives favored centralism and protectionism for nascent industries and were proclerical.

During the nineteenth century, constitutional structure changed when one party replaced the other. Other public policies, most obviously in the realm of trade and the position of the Church, were altered with change of the majority party. Furthermore, competition was not restricted to the ballot boxes; there were six civil wars between the two parties, some of which were lengthy and led to many deaths. In these wars the elites of the parties mobilized as their troops the people who were economically and socially dependent on them—largely the peasants. A *campesino* became a Liberal or Conservative because of the affiliations of his *patrón*, not because of his "own" interests. Due to the many civil wars, the peasants developed strong, intense loyalties to their parties. The wars left "martyrs" in many peasant families—relatives who were killed by members of the other party. As a result, Colombians began to be born "with party identification cards attached to the umbilical cord," as one Colombian sociologist has expressed it.[2] But not only were they born into the party of their parents, they learned to hate the other party. This socialization, combined with the religious nature of the conflicts—the Conservatives using the Catholic religion to mobilize its followers against the "atheist liberals"—led to a division of the Colombian population into two closed worlds—one Liberal and the other Conservative.

The results of this intense party socialization have been numerous, beginning in the nineteenth century and continuing into this one. Other cleavages—occurring in social class, the economy, and region—have been placed in a secondary importance to the overwhelming importance of political party. Third-party movements were difficult, and later socioeconomic changes did not lead to new parties.

The peasant and lower-class masses took these party differences seriously. The elite elements of the parties gained the benefits and governed. In some cases there were periods of hegemony of the parties, the Liberals monopolizing power from 1861 to 1886 and the Conservatives from 1886 to 1930. In some cases the two elites of the parties disagreed violently, leading to civil wars. But in nine instances before 1930 (and three other instances afterward), all or part of the elite of one party formed electoral and/or governing coalitions with part of the elite of the other party. Roughly twenty-eight of the eighty years between 1850 and 1930 showed such a coalition,[3] which usually came in response to a strong, antiparty executive, after a civil war, or at the end of a party hegemony.

Before 1930 Colombian economic development was slow, leading to few new social groups seeking entry into the political system. The few new middle-income people, who came with the growth of government and private industry, never banded together into a group leading to new political parties. Rather, the importance of the party cleavage continued; new middle-income sectors were first Liberal or Conservative in identification, based on family loyalties, and only secondly members of the middle sector. Their political importance came to be through the traditional parties, not by forming parties of their own.

POLITICAL HISTORY SINCE 1930

Toward the end of the 1930s, the Conservative party hegemony ran into difficulties, in part caused by the Great Depression, in part by the apparent bankruptcy of the party itself, and in part by its repressive tactics in relation to a growing labor-union movement. The Conservative hegemony was replaced by a Liberal one in 1930, with many of the themes the same as before, although with new variants. The new Liberal president, Enrique Olaya Herrera, was elected by a coalition of Liberals and Conservatives. A civil war that broke out between Liberal and Conservative peasants was only in part called for by elite elements of the party, also being caused by the increasing land pressures on the *campesinos*.

Yet there were important contrasts with the previous period. A significant faction of the Liberal party had become identified with a new liberalism, in which the state was to take an active role in social reform (including agrarian reform). This group of Liberals held most of the power during Alfonso López Pumarejo's Revolution on the March (1934–1938), when various reform programs were attempted, albeit most unsuccessfully. In response to this new thrust in Liberalism, one part of the Conservative party, led by Laureano Gómez, took a reactionary stance, evoking as a model the Spain of Ferdinand and Isabella, that is, of traditional Spanish corporativism. The "middle" part of the spectrum, made up of both "moderate" Liberals and Conservatives, wanted to maintain the status quo. The coalition of moderates of both parties and Gómez Conservatives was successful in delaying social legislation of the López Liberals, finally leading to López's early retirement during his second term (1942–1945).

Yet neither party could or was willing to stop social change. An organized labor movement was first made legal by López, who was also instrumental in the creation of the first national labor federation, the Confederation of Colombian Workers (CTC), in 1935. The Conservatives, in 1946, reacted favorably when the Church formed the Union of

Colombian Workers (UTC). Hence, in the normal way of politics in Colombia, organized labor entered the political scene in two groups, one basically Liberal and the other predisposed to the Conservatives.

An important chapter of modern Colombian history began with the election of 1946, in which two Liberals were opposed by a single Conservative, Mariano Ospina Pérez. Following Ospina's election, rural violence began between the followers of the two parties. In large part it was elite instigated: by the Conservatives to consolidate their new presidential power and to win a majority in the congressional elections of 1948 and by the Liberals to avoid the same things. At the same time, Conservative peasants took over land that had been taken from them by the Liberals sixteen years earlier, now believing correctly that the government in Bogotá would support them. Nineteen forty-six was the beginning of a civil war so dramatic that Colombians call it *la violencia*, well indicating its scope and intensity. Aggravated by the April 9, 1948, assassination of Jorge Gaitán—a populist Liberal who had lost the 1946 election but later became head of the party and odds-on favorite to win the 1950 presidential election—the violence covered the entire Andean region (save southernmost Nariño) and the llanos of the Orinoco region. It was less intense but existed in the Atlantic Coast region. In the next ten years *at least* 200,000 Colombians (in a country of some 10 million) lost their lives fighting in the name of party loyalty. The war largely began as Liberal versus Conservative, apparently was most grave in those areas of land pressures, and eventually disintegrated into banditry and some leftist movements. In the final analysis, an entire generation of Colombian peasants grew up thinking that violence was the *normal* way of life.

One result of the violence was the only military dictatorship of the century, that of Gustavo Rojas Pinilla from 1953 to 1957. Rojas came to power promising to end the violence and with support from all major factions of the two traditional parties, except the Gómez Conservatives. It was the presidency of Laureano Gómez (1950–1953) that the coup d'état ended. The Rojas government was only partially successful in ending the violence for a time, and, although Rojas talked of social reform and carried out a good deal of economic infrastructure improvements, he began to show signs of wanting to continue in power and grew increasingly repressive.

Two motivations—the "nontraditional" group in power and the continuing violence in the countryside—led leaders of the two historic parties to plan a coalition to replace Rojas and to institutionalize bipartisan government. Rojas also lost the support of various other power groups, including the Church, the students, and, most importantly, the military itself. In 1957 he was overthrown and replaced by a caretaker military regime for a year. This was followed by the most dramatic case of bipartisan coalition government in Colombian history—the National Front.

The National Front, approved by the people of Colombia in a plebiscite and by the National Congress as a constitutional amendment, was basically the creation of two men—Alberto Lleras Camargo, a Liberal who had been president during 1946, completing López's second term, and Conservative ex-president Laureano Gómez (1950–1953). The basic stipulations of the National Front amendments for the sixteen-year period from 1958 to 1974 were the following:

1. The presidency would alternate every four years between the two traditional parties (*alternación*).
2. All legislative bodies (National Congress, departmental assemblies, municipal councils) would be divided equally between the Liberals and Conservatives regardless of the electoral results within a district (*paridad*, or parity). Within each of the traditional parties, seats would be assigned by a list form of proportional representation.
3. This same rule of party parity would apply to all high administrative appointments, such as the president's cabinet, governors' cabinets, governors, and mayors.
4. No new political parties could participate in elections during the period, only the Liberal and Conservative parties.
5. The lower-level, nonappointive bureaucrats would not be chosen on the basis of partisan affiliation but rather on merit in a proposed civil-service system. This was to end the pre–National Front practice of complete changes of bureaucrats with changes of the party in power.
6. All legislation had to be passed by a two-thirds majority in the National Congress.

In sum, the National Front was a legal mechanism designed to divide political power equally between the two traditional parties. In doing so it established a limited democracy. Political competition was legally restricted to the two traditional parties, and indeed they would not compete with each other in elections.

Although many thought that the National Front would not run its course, in the final analysis it did. Two Liberals were president (Alberto Lleras Camarago, 1958–1962; his cousin, Carlos Lleras Restrepo, 1966–1970) and so were two Conservatives (Guillermo León Valencia, 1962–1966); Misael Pastrana, 1970–1974). New groups entered elections, but did not call themselves "political parties" until after a constitutional reform in 1968 made it possible for them to do so. Parity prevailed, until the same constitutional amendment reopened competitive elections for departmental assemblies (roughly the equivalent of state legislatures in the United States, but with considerably less power) and town councils in 1970. The violence was ended, but it took at least six years for the governments to accomplish this.

On August 7, 1974, the National Front ended with the inauguration of freely elected Alfonso López Michelsen, who gained 56 percent of the popular vote. Yet this Liberal was restrained by certain aspects of the "dismantling" (*desmonte*) of the National Front, as contained in the constitutional reform of 1968. During López Michelsen's entire four-year term, all cabinet ministries, governors, mayors, and other administrative positions not part of civil service were divided equally between Liberals and Conservatives, a continuation of parity.

After the end of López's term, the same offices were divided between the parties "in such a way that gives adequate and equitable participation to the major party distinct from that of the president," as called for in the constitution. However, if that party had decided not to participate in the executive, the president would have been free to name the officials in any way that he chose.

To this point, the major party other than that of the president has chosen to participate in the executive. After the 1978 election of Liberal Julio César Turbay Ayala, the Conservatives joined the executive. Likewise, after Conservative Belisario Betancur defeated two Liberal opponents in 1982 some Liberals were members of his executive, although former President López Michelsen took exception that he was not consulted by the newly elected Conservative president.

In the years of the National Front and since, new socioeconomic groups have appeared. But basically the Colombian system remains the same as before, with two predominant (and factionalized) political parties most important. Large landowners, industrialists, and other upper-income groups are very organized and effective. Labor unions are organized in both political parties (and elsewhere), while the *campesinos* and urban poor are only in the process of being organized.

SOCIAL AND POLITICAL GROUPS

Political Parties

The most important power contenders in Colombia are the political parties, especially the Liberals and Conservatives. Going back over a century, these traditional parties are strong in emotional terms, if not organizational ones. Organization includes directorates at the national, regional, and city levels, as well as youth organizations. Yet the parties do not approach the "mass party" model, nor indeed do they need such structure to mobilize votes.

But one should not be overwhelmed by the appearance of a two-party system. Colombian parties at the leadership level have most commonly been split into various factions, sometimes along ideological lines, other times on more personalistic lines. The majority of Colombian voters, however, remain identified with the party only and apparently not with the various factions.

Today the ideological differences of the party elites are about as great (or meager) as those of the Democratic and Republican parties in the

United States. The Liberals have their internal divisions but *as a whole* they tend to be more welfare state oriented, more anticlerical, and less private property oriented than the Conservatives. The latter, although having their own internal divisions, tend to take opposite positions on these ideological dimensions.

One key fact of present Colombian partisan life is that the Liberal party is the majority one. All public opinion polls indicate a majority of the electorate identified psychologically with this party. Throughout the National Front, more people voted for Liberals for Congress than for Conservatives (although of course parity meant that each of the parties received 50 percent of the seats). López Michelsen, in his successful 1974 presidential campaign, received 56 percent of the vote in a contest against two principal opponents and several minor ones. Turbay Ayala received a smaller majority over Belisario Betancur in 1978.

Although a Conservative president was elected in 1982, the election seems to reinforce the conclusion that the Liberal party is the majority one. In a three-man race, the congressional elections of March showed lists identified with Alfonso López Michelsen as a near majority, with 46.9 percent of the votes, followed by those of fellow Liberal Luis Carlos Galán (11.5 percent) and those of Conservative Belisario Betancur (41.7 percent). After none of the candidates dropped out of the presidential election, and compromise between López and Galán proved impossible, Betancur won the presidential election of May with 46.6 percent, followed by López with 40.9 percent and Galán with 10.9 percent. Betancur thus became the first Conservative elected in a competitive election since 1946, and in so doing reinforced the historical tradition of a minority party winning when the majority party split between two candidates.

Furthermore, third-party movements of the early 1970s have now failed. In 1961 ex-dictator Gustavo Rojas Pinilla founded a National Popular Alliance (ANAPO) in an attempt to vindicate himself. ANAPO did not declare itself to be a new political party; that would have made it ineligible for elections before the constitutional reform of 1968. Rather it was a "movement" that offered both Liberal and Conservative candidates for Congress, departmental assemblies, and town councils. Since the electoral system *within* parties was one of proportional representation, Anapistas (members of ANAPO) were elected at those three levels. The movement had its greatest success in 1970 when the Liberal Anapistas garnered 14 percent of the national Liberal vote, while the Conservative Anapistas collected 21 percent of the national Conservative vote. The same year, Rojas lost the presidential election by about 3 percent to Misael Pastrana, a coalition candidate agreed to by the Liberals and a significant group of the Conservative party.

Since then ANAPO's fortunes have declined. In 1971 the movement dramatically declared itself a party, which was perhaps a logical step since the parity restrictions no longer pertained in town council and assembly elections, but ill considered since all evidence suggests that

Colombian voters still predominantly considered themselves to be Liberals or Conservatives. In addition, with the end of the National Front, votes once again became more meaningful. Although in 1970 a Liberal might vote for Conservative Rojas since all the candidates for president *had* to be Conservatives, this situation was no longer relevant in 1974 when once again Liberals and Conservatives (and additionally Anapistas) were contesting the elections. In addition, ANAPO had always been a personalistic party, with little organization or leadership from outside the Rojas family. As Rojas's health declined, leadership was more and more centered in his forceful daughter, María Eugenia Rojas de Moreno Díaz, who was a presidential candidate in 1974. Hampered by the return of partisan conflict between Liberals and Conservatives, as well as by being a woman in male-dominated politics, María Eugenia received only 9.4 percent of the popular vote, finishing a poor third to both López and the Conservative Alvaro Gómez.

There are a few minor parties, of various gradations of leftism, none of which is important. Colombia remains a two-party system, in which the two parties are factionalized, in part because of an electoral system that does not discourage it.

Other Groups

There are a variety of other political groups of importance in Colombia, the most powerful of which tend to be those representing or allied to the upper classes. A study of the Colombian Congress in 1970 found that congresspersons themselves ranked the top groups in the following order:

- National Association of (Large) Industrialists (ANDI)
- National Federation of Coffee Growers
- the clergy
- Union of Colombian Workers (UTC)
- Confederation of Colombian Workers (CTC)
- the military

Although there are scores of groups within the upper- and middle-income sectors in Colombia, I will limit myself to descriptions of these six.

Founded in 1944, ANDI has become the leading advocate of free enterprise among the Colombian organizations. ANDI counts more than five hundred of the largest industrial enterprises affiliated with it throughout the entire country. Its power in Colombian politics is due to the wealth of its members, the social prestige they have, and the common overlapping of this group with the agrarian interests. Furthermore, industrialization has been a goal of half a century of Colombian presidents, especially those of the National Front and since.

If Colombian development in one part depends on industrialization, it also depends on exporting coffee to earn foreign exchange to purchase capital and other goods. Therefore it is not surprising that another important group is the National Federation of Coffee Growers. Founded in 1927, this private association is open to those interested in developing the coffee industry. However, the association tends to be dominated by the larger coffee producers and/or exporters. The relations between the Coffee Growers and the government are close, as we shall see.

The Roman Catholic Church of Colombia is probably the strongest politically in Latin America. This is in part because of the religious fervor of the Colombian people and in part because of Church land-holdings in the past century and alliances with other upper-class groups.

During the nineteenth century, there was a close relationship between the Church and the Conservative party. At various times, even quite recently, bishops have threatened to excommunicate anyone who voted Liberal, and during *la violencia* some parish priests refused sacraments, including burial, to Liberals. Perhaps this attitude is best seen by a quote from some bishops in 1949 prohibiting the faithful from voting for Liberal candidates who might "wish to implant civil marriage, divorce, and co-education, which would open the doors to immorality and Communism."[4]

With the coming of the National Front, partisan politics of the Church ended. The Church hierarchy strongly supported the concept of the Front and in doing so embraced Liberal presidents as well as Conservative ones. In turn, Liberal presidents treated the Church well.

Today the Church still has many functions and much power. Until the early 1970s the majority of secondary schools were parochial. Although government efforts have led to a majority of state schools, even in them (and in public universities as well) a course of religious instruction is required. In addition the Church must approve textbooks. No major governmental project is opened without a bishop to bless it; no divorce legislation is introduced without the Church mobilizing to fight it.

The Church hierarchy is no longer a unified, monolithic friend of the status quo (if indeed it ever was). Although growing numbers of priests come from the middle-income sectors, the upper level of the hierarchy is still dominated by sons of the upper classes. But even these upper- and middle-class priests differ, often not along class lines. In recent years there have been cases of priests who are anything but status quo oriented. The most dramatic one was Camilo Torres, son of the Bogotá upper middle class and sociologist as well as priest, who concluded that to be Christian in Colombia was to be a revolutionary. After his failure to change society as a priest, Camilo left the clergy and went to the guerrilla wars, where he was killed.

The two major labor federations are each connected to one of the traditional political parties. The CTC was founded in 1935, during the first presidency of Alfonso López Pumarejo, and flourished during the rest of the Liberal hegemony. The UTC was founded in 1946, during the presidency of Mariano Ospina, and by the late 1950s had become the largest labor federation, a status it maintains to date. But not all of the local labor unions in Colombia are organized into one of these national federations. There are several other national federations, as well as locals with no affiliation. Although the CTC and UTC owe much to respective parties, neither is *formally* a part of the parties, as membership is prohibited by law. Members of the CTC leadership, for example, are also leaders of the Liberal party but chosen *as individuals* and not *ex officio* as leaders of the union.

Labor legislation has generally been unrestrictive. However, labor leaders are still required to be full-time workers in their industries, a requirement that if enforced (and it isn't) would mitigate against labor unions. At present, Colombian political leaders are pleased to have active unions (at least usually, if they are CTC or UTC) but are not reluctant to have the law enforced more rigorously when the union is allied with Communist elements.

The military has been one of the least interventionist in Latin America. Before the turn of the century there was little professionalism, with a "national army" supporting the party in power, but another "army" of the party not in power. Only in 1907 were the Escuela Militar de Cadetes and the Escuela Naval founded, with the Escuela Superior de Guerra following two years later.

Colombian presidents cannot, of course, ignore the military, which jealously guards its share of the governmental pie (although it is one of the lowest per capita in Latin America) and the integrity of the military institution. Moreover, the Colombian president must take care that the military does not oppose him for reasons of national politics. López Pumarejo, during his first term, transferred military officers who opposed him to remote posts and promoted his supporters. During his second term, López Pumarejo was captured in a coup attempt in the southern town of Pasto, but the rest of the military supported him. During the Conservative years 1946–1953, both presidents Ospina and Gómez took steps toward making the army an arm of the Conservative party, a process that politicized the military more than ever before (and was very likely a precipitant of the military coup of 1953).

One cannot categorically ignore the possibility of military rule in a future Colombia. The National Front went a long way toward ending the *partisan* identification of the military, but beginning in about 1962, with the aid of the U.S. government, the army began a program of civil-military action in which the army's personnel, equipment, and skills are used in social and economic projects. Furthermore, the military has developed expertise in a number of developmental areas, and in some cases it is greater than that of the civilian bureaucrats. Evidence is slight and speculative, but it appears that the military has certan "moderating power predispositions," shown clearly in the case of the 1953–1957 government of Rojas, which came in a most dramatic instance of the civilians not being able to rule. If civilian governments fail to carry out what leading military officers feel are necessary reforms, it seems quite possible that the officers might take over, in spite of the civilian mystique of 150 years, and adopt something similar to the Peruvian experiment.

The groups discussed above, while likely the most powerful in Colombia, are surely not the only ones. The society is replete with groups at the upper- and middle-income levels—merchants, large land-owners, teachers (at all levels), doctors, and so forth. It is no exaggeration to state that anyone of middle or upper income fits into an occupational group that is organized (within limits stated by the laws), has *personería jurídica*, or a license to exist, and has at least some power in the political process. However, the great majority of the Colombia people—especially peasants and the urban poor—are not organized into such groups. There is some peasant organization through the National Association of Land Users (including about half a million small farmers who use the services of governmental organizations) and in the National Agrarian Association, an affiliate of the UTC claiming to represent 100,000 peasants. Some of the urban poor fall under Communal Action. But in both cases the organizations are incomplete, elite instigated, and divided along traditional party lines.

The nature of group relations, with that middle- and upper-class bias, is the subject of some academic debate. Surely Colombia is not a purely corporativist society, with every group controlled by the political elite. But neither is it the "pure" pluralistic system in which groups are formed and operate almost completely free of government control. Rather, Colombia is somewhere in between.[5] The National Federation of Coffee Growers, for example, is quite tied to the government: Of the eleven members of the national committee, five are *ex officio* ministers of foreign relations, finance, development, and agriculture and the government-appointed manager of the Agrarian Credit Bank. The superintendent of banking supervises the financial transactions of the federation; the manager of the federation is appointed by the president of the republic from a list of three names submitted by the federation, and the manager in turn acts as Colombia's representative in international negotiations pertaining to coffee. Although this is the extreme case, other economic associations have government-appointed members, usually cabinet ministers, on their boards, with the concurrent influence of the government over internal policy. In addition many groups receive moneys from the government, sometimes even in the millions of pesos. At the other extreme, some groups, such as ANDI, receive no moneys from the government and have no government members in their leadership groups. But ANDI, by law, does have representatives on a half-dozen boards of governmental agencies, a situation very common in Colombian group behavior.

Government Machinery

Colombia's national government is one very similar, in appearance at least, to that of the United States: three branches of government with separation of powers and checks and balances. There are some important differences, however. The executive is clearly the most powerful branch of government, with that power centered in the president, who is elected for a four-year term with no immediate reelection allowed. Congress is bicameral, with both chambers elected on the basis of population, and is clearly secondary in power. Legislation is rarely written by the Congress, but it is not merely a rubber stamp—projects initiated in the executive are often dramatically changed, or indeed blocked altogether, by the Congress. In comparative terms, probably only the congresses of Venezuela and Costa Rica have more power than the Colombian one. The Supreme Court has the right of judicial review. Its members are appointed by the president, with approval of Congress, for fixed terms.

The Colombian system is an extremely centralized one. *Departmentos* have only slight independent taxation abilities; the governors are appointed by the president. *Municipios* (townships) have even lower taxation abilities, and the mayors (with the exception of Bogotá) are appointed by the governors. Although *departmentos* might have some of their own bureaucracy, most bureaucrats are *national* employees, reporting back to officials in Bogotá.

The machinery of government has been purposefully manipulated by the party elites, as in the National Front, for certain goals. The same is true of the form of elections, so important in democratic Colombia. The electoral system (for both houses of Congress, departmental assemblies, and town councils) is a list system of proportional representation. Although this is not uncommon in Latin America and elsewhere, there is a particular Colombian variant, which encourages factionalism in the parties. If a list does not receive one-half of the electoral quotient (which is equal to the total number of votes in a district divided by the total number of seats to be filled), then the votes of that list go to the list with the same label with the most votes. Thus a party (or a group within a party) can safely offer more than one list of candidates in a legislative election with the security that there will be no "wasted" votes, since they will revert back to the list with the same label and the most votes. The results of this system have been a multiplicity of lists in most elections, both during and since the National Front. For example, in the 1966 election for the lower house from Nariño, there were ten different lists of the Liberal party, not to mention various lists of factions of the Conservative and ANAPO parties. This makes the individual voting choice a difficult one for the average Colombian.

Colombians take pride in having a "mixed" economy—one that is not purely capitalist or socialist. This means that certain industries, especially heavy ones, are government owned and run: communications, railroads, the national airlines. Others are purely private capital, either Colombian or foreign: consumer goods, especially. In still others the government is one of several stockholders. The end result is a society in which the government plays a much larger part in the economy than it does in the United States, and government spending represents a larger percentage of the GNP.

One result of this government role is a large bureaucracy. Before the National Front governments, bureaucratic posts were one of the chief spoils of the political system, with the changing of the party in the presidency leading to a nearly complete bottom-to-top turnover in the bureaucracy. This ended with the National Front, but the principle of spoils did not and the civil service grew rapidly. Bureaucratic posts are sought after, as they give a decent salary, the chance not to work with one's hands, and the concurrent social prestige. However, the technical training of government bureaucrats is not one of the high points of Colombian government. The major purpose of the bureaucracy, still today, often is to give nice jobs to bright young people rather than to develop bureaucratic expertise. One study in 1969 concluded that of the 100,000 civilian employees of the national government, only 3,000 were part of the civil service. Seven years later, the number had increased only to 13,000.[6] Whether or not to have a real *carrera administrativa* is still the subject of lively debate.

One way to avoid the spoils problem was through the *institutos descentralizados* (decentralized institutes), which have been set up to administer certain specialized programs and governmental industries. This form of bureaucracy has become predominant. In 1976 36 percent of the government employees fell into this category, as compared to 26 percent who were teachers and 8 percent who were in agencies directly under the cabinet ministries. In 1975 fully 59.5 percent of the national budget was spent by the decentralized institutes. It is not at all clear if these decentralized institutes have been more immune than the regular bureaucracy to the politics of spoils or have developed more bureaucratic expertise.

PUBLIC POLICY

The Colombian public policy process is conditioned by a number of characteristics discussed in the preceding paragraphs. Bureaucracies are not very efficient in carrying out laws as proposed by the president and passed by Congress (a situation not uniformly condemned); certain numerically large groups of peasants and urban poor are not yet among the major power contenders and hence do not have the power that their numbers would indicate. The political elite is far from being a microcosm of the society as a whole: a 1970 study showed that 87 percent of the congresspersons had some university education, in a society in which only two out of every hundred university-aged individuals pursue post-secondary-school education.

In addition, the National Front system (and the *desmonte* that followed) was not conducive to strong, innovative policies. National Front presidents had to preside over the policymaking process with half of their cabinets from the other party, half of the Congress from the other party as well as the governors and mayors—and with politicians constantly looking for the next president, who could not be the current one or even someone from his party. All of this was worsened by the existence of personalistic factions within the parties, especially the Conservative one. As a result, presidents found it increasingly difficult to form a majority around any policy.

Yet the National Front presidents tried. Even before the United States started the Alliance for Progress, the Alberto Lleras administration had started a Colombian Agrarian Reform Institute (INCORA). Later a national development plan was written. Many new governmental agencies, both within the ministries and as decentralized institutes, were formed. The verdict is still out on some of these. Others have had mixed results, but many appear to have been just paper agencies, the true purpose of which was to furnish white-collar jobs for the middle sectors and to comply with the stipulations for U.S. aid.

Yet it would be unfair categorically to condemn the Colombian government. Agrarian reform has been a modest success, especially since most of the good lands were already occupied at the time of the initiation of the program. Redistribution was slight, most of the reform taking place on public lands. Land titles were handed out to tens of thousands of families, but many more did not receive land. Schools and classrooms were built, with the result that the state now enrolls more secondary students in public education than does the Church in higher-priced parochial education. Health programs led to more physicians and nurses and to lower death and infant mortality rates, and as a result average life expectancy has increased. Public housing was constructed, but not nearly enough for the masses of urban migrants. Roads were built and kilowatt hours of electricity increased. But in this process the foreign debt doubled in size.

But much remains to be done to integrate fully the lower classes into national society, especially those in rural areas. Land reform still remains an issue, although one probably should not look for very rapid reform given the power of the large landowners. Urban reform—housing and public services—is becoming more and more of an issue as the size of the cities increases dramatically every year.

Difficulties of an international nature continue. Although the Colombian economy is healthier than it was a decade and a half ago, since the dependence on coffee exports has declined, balance of payments have typically been negative and inflation has been rapid, at least in terms we are used to in the United States. Various sets of policies have been used to meet this problem. During times of foreign-exchange shortages, policies include taxes on consumer imports, tighter control of dollar exchanges, control of tourism, and encouragement of domestic manufacturing industries, for both export and internal consumption. During times of foreign-exchange excesses, policies have been quite different: a loosening up of consumer imports, lighter dollar-exchange regulations, and discouragement of domestic industry.

One hope for Colombian economic stability that is about to appear is coal. In 1982 the first coal was exported from the central area of the El Cerrejón coal fields in the department of La Guajira. Although most of the central area coal will be used in domestic thermoelectrical generation, the larger northern area of El Cerrejón will begin production for export in 1985. This production, which will reach a minimum of 15 million tonnes (16.5 million tons) annually, comes from a joint venture between the Colombian state coal company (Carbones de Colombia, CARBOCOL) and International Colombia Resources Corporation (INTERCOR), a wholly owned subsidiary of Exxon. Whether this new resource will be another "bonanza" and whether the new foreign exchange will be used for the benefit of the economy are questions that cannot be answered at this writing.

Another policy of the Colombian government—to meet many of these foreign-trade policies as well as the problem of the multinational corporation (MNC)—has been the Andean Pact. This pact, dating from 1969, is a cooperative effort of Colombia, Venezuela, Ecuador, Peru, Bolivia, and Chile. The six countries agreed (1) to eliminate all trade barriers among the member countries by 1980, (2) to establish a common external tariff on imports from outside the subregion by 1980, (3) to develop a mechanism to coordinate investment and encourage specialization rather than duplication of industry, and (4) to have a common foreign (non-Andean) investment code. The last was intended to place limitations on MNCs, requiring them to sell some of their stocks to Andeans if they wanted to enjoy the benefits of the lower intraregion tariffs, prohibiting MNCs from buying existent companies, and not allowing additional investments of MNCs in public services and insurance. To date the Andean Pact has had mixed results, complicated among other things by the abrupt change of governments in Chile.

PROSPECTS FOR THE FUTURE

The resiliency of the Colombian system has been remarkable. Party hegemonies have come and gone; civil wars, including the dramatic *la violencia*, have appeared about to tear the social fabric apart, leftist guerrillas have called for Cuban-like revolution, and university students have literally fought battles between Fidelist and Maoist groups. The Colombian population was doubling every twenty-four years or so; this has now "slowed" to every thirty. Thousands of landless peasants have left the countryside for a life no better in the urban slums. Yet at its very essence Colombian politics has remained the same: elitist, patrimonial, civilian, modified two-party, classist.

The irony of Colombia is that, while being one of the most "liberal democratic" of Latin American countries—albeit in its own way, it has actually done less for the masses than many of the other countries. In part this is because of the great problems and complexities of the country. But in another way this irony is due to the political system, which, whether by design or accident, has been and continues to be one favoring nondecisions. Of course, not making a decision favors the current situation, one that gives the Colombians the "human rights" of being able to vote every four years for unlimited numbers of candidates but does not give all Colombians the "human rights" of *pan, techo, y tierra*—bread, a roof, and land.

Most probably Colombia will continue with its only kind of liberal democracy, making the country a fine place for the middle and upper classes to live. Although "new" natural resources, such as coal, might become economically important, it seems unlikely that their value will be such that it will be possible for politics to become significantly more distributive rather than redistributive. The current elite system will surely continue its attempts to co-opt emerging groups and individuals, with all the benefits and liabilities of that strategy. However, any elite has a limited potential for co-optation. A continuation of this approach will likely lead to either revolution or a stalemate such as that in Argentina. Yet if anyone in Latin America is likely to come up with a viable alternative to these two extremes, it is very apt to be that same Colombian elite (or its sons and daughters) that gave birth to the National Front.

NOTES

1. "Análisis del sector externo colombiano," *Revista ANDI* 48 (1980):55.

2. Eduardo Santa, *Sociología Política de Colombia* (Ediciones Tercer Mundo, Bogotá, 1964), p. 37.

3. Harvey F. Kline, "The National Front: Historical Perspective and Overview," in *Politics of Compromise: Coalition Government in Colombia*, ed. R. Albert Berry, Ronald G. Hellman, and Mauricio Solaún (Transaction Books, New Brunswick, N.J., 1980), pp. 59–83.

4. Quoted in John D. Martz, *Colombia: A Contemporary Political Survey* (University of North Carolina Press, Chapel Hill, 1962), p. 84.

5. John Bailey, "Pluralist and Corporatist Dimensions of Interest Representation in Colombia," in *Authoritarism and Corporatism in Latin America*, ed. James Malloy (University of Pittsburgh Press, Pittsburgh, 1977), pp. 259–302.

6. Jonathan Hartlyn, "Consociational Politics in Colombia: Confrontation and Accommodation in Comparative Perspective," Ph.D. dissertation, Yale University, 1981, p. 338.

SUGGESTIONS FOR FURTHER READING

Berry, R. Albert, Ronald G. Hellman, and Mauricio Solaún. *Politics of Compromise: Coalition Government in Colombia.* Transaction Books, New Brunswick, N.J., 1980.

Berry, R. Albert, and Ronald Soligo, eds. *Economic Policy and Income Distribution in Colombia.* Westview Press, Boulder, Colo., 1980.

Dix, Robert. *Colombia: The Political Dimensions of Change.* Yale University Press, New Haven, Conn., 1967.

Fals Borda, Orlando. *Peasant Society in the Colombian Andes: A Sociological Study of Saucio,* University of Florida Press, Gainesville, 1955.

Fluharty, Vernon Lee. *Dance of the Millions: Military Rule and the Social Revolution in Colombia, 1930–1956.* University of Pittsburgh Press, Pittsburgh, 1957.

Hoskin, Gary, Francisco Leal, and Harvey Kline. *Legislative Behavior in Colombia.* 2 vols. International Studies Series, Buffalo, N.Y., 1976.

Kline, Harvey F. *Colombia: Portrait of Unity and Diversity.* Westview Press, Boulder, Colo., 1983.

Lombard, Francis J. *The Foreign Investment Screening Process in LDCs: The Case of Colombia, 1967–1975.* Westview Press, Boulder, Colo., 1979.

Martz, John D. *Colombia: A Contemporary Political Survey.* University of North Carolina Press, Chapel Hill, 1962.

Morawetz, David. *Why the Emperor's New Clothes Are Not Made in Colombia.* Oxford University Press, New York, 1981.

Oquist, Paul. *Violence, Conflict, and Politics in Colombia.* Academic Press, New York, 1980.

Payne, James. *Patterns of Conflict in Colombia.* Yale University Press, New Haven, Conn., 1968.

Urrutia, Miguel. *The Development of the Colombia Labor Movement.* Yale University Press, New Haven, Conn., 1969.

12
Peru:
The Authoritarian Legacy

DAVID SCOTT PALMER

Peru is a study in contrasts. A coastal desert gives way inland to imposing peaks of the Andes, which in turn fall off to the dense tropical rain forest of the Amazon Basin. The bustling, aggressively cosmopolitan coastal capital of Lima contains over a quarter of Peru's 19 million people, over half of its government employees, and at least two-thirds of the nation's manufacturing and commerce. It seems worlds away from the many villages and communities of the *sierra*, where most modern conveniences are absent and centuries-old traditions still thrive. Irrigated coastal valleys cultivated in sugarcane, cotton, and rice with the latest equipment and technology coexist with small family plots and communally held lands, where a base subsistence is eked out in most years using the implements and practices of Indian ancestors. Institutions and practices dating from the Spanish conquest of 1532 still predominate over 160 years after Peru's independence in 1824.

Such continued predominance is largely the result of the importance the colonizing country attached to Peru because of the enormous wealth and large numbers of Indians its conquerors found there. As a result Spain became more concerned with the Peruvian part of its empire and worked more diligently to impose a political and administrative apparatus that would endure. This institutional framework was fundamentally and unequivocally authoritarian in nature. Peru as an independent nation has never overcome its tradition. Even the reformist military government that was in power from 1968 to 1980, dedicated to transforming Peru's underdeveloped economy and unstable politics, was in many ways a late-twentieth-century version of this authoritarian legacy.

BACKGROUND AND POLITICAL CULTURE

The basic elements of Peruvian political culture through history include persistent authoritarianism and regular military intervention, the con-

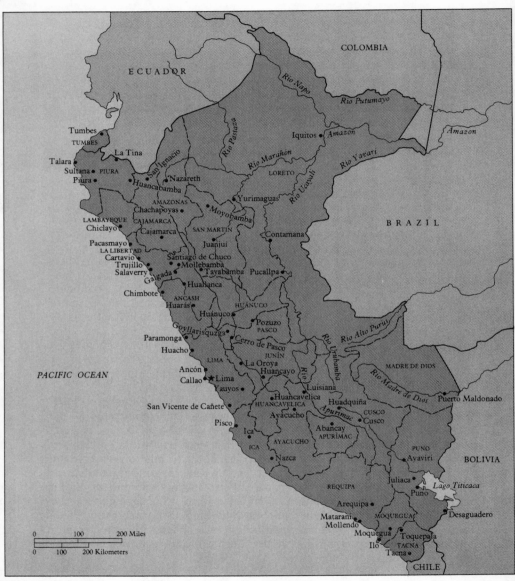

Peru

centration of resources in the capital city, dependence on foreign markets and capital, a dependent economic elite, a personalistic leadership style, and a largely isolated Indian subculture.

The political culture has been shaped by a number of factors, of which the most important is close to three hundred years of Spanish colonial presence. The main elements of Spanish control included authoritarian political institutions and mercantilist economic institutions, both of which provided most colonists with little experience in handling their own affairs. The carryover into the postcolonial period was greater in Peru than in other Latin American countries not only because control had been imposed more consistently but also because of the nature of the independence movement itself.

The belated struggle for independence in this part of the empire was more a conservative reaction to liberalizing forces in Spain and elsewhere than a genuine revolution. As a result there was no real break in Peru with the colonial past after 1824, even though some liberal organizations and procedures were introduced at that time.

Not surprisingly, therefore, authoritarian rule continued long after independence. There was no elected civilian president until Manuel Pardo in 1872, although there were some enlightened military leaders such as Ramón Castilla (1845–1851, 1854–1862). Also continuing were neomercantilist economic policies, as Great Britain replaced Spain as Peru's major trading partner and the source of most capital and investment. Few local entrepreneurs emerged in this context, and most who did acted as agents for British interests. Peru did experience its first economic boom during this period, based on the rich deposits of bird droppings, or guano, from islands off the coast. The economic benefits were short-lived, however, due to the outbreak of the War of the Pacific (1879–1883).

The war forced a partial break with Peru's past. Chile wrested from Peru at this time the coastal department of Tarapacá with its immense nitrate deposits and occupied a large portion of the country, including Lima. Politically this disaster demonstrated the weakness of existing institutions and contributed to the emergence of Peru's only sustained period of limited liberal democracy (1895 to 1919). Economically the war left the country bankrupt and, by mortgaging many of the country's basic resources, required Peru to become even more dependent on British interests.

This coincidence of sharply increased economic dependence and liberal democracy set the pattern of a limited state and free foreign enterprise that most governments tried to follow until the institutional military coup of 1968. With few exceptions the Peruvian economic elite was dependent for its well-being on foreign trade and investment, predominantly British until the 1920s, largely U.S. since. It did not advance, by and large, on the basis of its own innovations and risk taking in productive domestic investment.

In addition most of Peru's independent political life has been marked by a flamboyant leadership style that has tended to garner support on the basis of personal appeal rather than institutional loyalties and obligations. Many leaders have tended to place personal interests above obligation to any political party organization or even to the nation. As a result, most parties have been personalist vehicles and most presidencies tumultuous struggles among contending personalities, usually ending in a military coup.

Furthermore, throughout the postindependence period a large percentage of the national population has not been integrated into national economic, political, or cultural life. The Indian subculture of Peru, though in numbers predominant until very recently, has participated in national society only in the most subordinate of roles, such as peon, day laborer, or maid. The only way open for Indians to escape repudiation by the dominant society has been to abandon their own heritage and work their way into that of the Spanish. One of the most important changes occurring in contemporary Peru is large-scale Indian immigration to towns and cities, where Indians feel they—or their children—can become a part of the dominant culture: Catholic, Hispanic, Spanish speaking.

HISTORY TO 1968

For most of Latin America, traditional domestic politics were challenged in fundamental ways between 1900 and 1930 by the emergence of new social and political groups within the countries, and by the effect of such outside international economic forces as post–World War I and depression price declines and such outside political forces as the Russian Revolution and Mussolini's corporatist state. Peru, of course, did not escape the effects of these various factors. However, politics did not change in any basic way until 1968, when a military coup ushered in a period of unprecedented reform under the improbable auspices of the military itself.

This transformation of Peruvian politics was delayed for a number of reasons: Domestic elites were willing to retain strong foreign economic control; the military was largely under elite dominance; political leadership retained a personalist and populist character; a non-Communist, mass-based political party absorbed most of the emerging social forces; and the Indian cultural "barrier" slowed the flow of new elements into national society. As a result the liberal model of the limited state and the open economy was retained with few modifications right up to 1968.

Peruvian political history before 1968 may be divided into three main periods: consolidation (1824–1895), civilian democracy (1895–1919), and populism–mass parties (1919–1968).

Consolidation (1824–1895)

Peru took much longer than most Latin American countries to evolve a reasonably stable political and economic system. Because Peru had been a core part of a larger viceroyalty during the colonial period, it took some time just to define its national territory. The boundaries were roughly hewn out in 1829 (by the failure of Augustín Gamarra and José de la Mar to capture Ecuador for Peru), in 1839 (by the Battle of Yungay in which Andrés Santa Cruz lost his post as protector of the Peru-Bolivia confederation when defeated by a Chilean army), and in 1841 (by the Battle of Ingavi when Gamarra was killed in his attempt to annex Bolivia to Peru).

Once the boundaries were more or less settled, there remained the key problem of establishing reasonable procedures for attaining and succeeding to political office. Peru had at least fifteen constitutions in its first forty years as an independent country, but force remained the normal route to political power. Of the thirty-five presidents during this period, only four were indirectly elected according to constitutional procedures and no civilians held power for more than a few months. Regional caudillos often attempted to impose themselves on the government, which by the 1840s was becoming an important source of revenue with the income from guano.

Unlike much of Latin America during the nineteenth century, politically Peru was less divided into Liberals and Conservatives and more over the issue of military or civilian rule. By the 1860s a clearly discernible political movement was emerging called *civilistas*, or partisans of civilian rule. The War of the Pacific eventually confirmed this trend by dramatically demonstrating the need for professionalization of the Peruvian military establishment. The *civilista* trend was to result in the formal establishment of the Civilista party, as well as a number of more personalistic party rivals, and eventually brought about an extended period of civilian rule starting in 1895.

The War of the Pacific also more firmly embedded the tendency to depend on foreign markets, foreign entrepreneurship, and foreign loans. The debts of more than $200 million, accumulated by the war, were canceled in 1889 by British interests in exchange for Peru's railroads and Lake Titicaca steamship line, a large tract of jungle land, free use of major ports, a Peruvian government subsidy, and large quantities of guano.

The Civilian Democratic Interlude (1895–1919)

Peru's one period of sustained civilian rule emerged from the War of the Pacific debacle. While the military reorganized itself under the guidance of a French mission, a coalition of forces from the new commercial elite succeeded in bringing about a period of civilian dominance of government. Embracing neopositivist ideals of renovation, modernization, and innovation, the civilians also advanced the classic liberal precept of a government that would serve to enhance the capacity of the private sector. Their main political objective was the very modest one of keeping civilians in power. This implied the fostering of a civilian state and a civilian society and led to substantially increased government expenditures on communications, education, and health. Such improvements were financed by the rapid expansion of exports during this period, by encouragement given to new foreign investment, particularly from the United States, and by new foreign loans after Peru's international credit was restored in 1907.

Civilian rule, although long-lived by Peruvian standards, was nevertheless somewhat tenuous even at its height. The Civilista was the only reasonably well organized party, but even it suffered periodic severe internal divisions. Other parties, such as the Liberal, the Democratic, and the Conservative, were largely personalistic agglomerations that rose and fell with the fortunes of their individual leaders.

The civilian democratic interlude, ensured when Nicolás de Piérola (1895–1899) provided for the direct election of his successors, was undone by three major factors. First, because the regime's economic foundations had been built arouund the international economy, the international economic crisis accompanying World War I precipitated a severe domestic inflation if not a dramatic decline in exports.

Second, the efforts made by the *civilista* administrations to improve commerce and industry, communications, education and health, and urban conditions increased substantially the number of people within the effective national system in a position to make demands on government. As this occurred, the elite-oriented parties became less willing to accommodate to these demands. Although the electoral mechanism could still be manipulated, elites were increasingly divided on the issue of how to deal with the demands of the newly mobilized population. To a certain degree, then, the civilian regimes failed politically because of their own economic success.

Third, the actions of some of the leaders themselves eroded the fragile bases of the civilian political edifice. In particular Presidents Augusto B. Leguía (1908–1912, 1919–1930) and Guillermo Billinghurst (1912–1914) operated in ways that seemed self-serving and personalistic and actually helped to bring down the very civilian democratic order to which they had ostensibly been committed.

Billinghurst, once elected, eschewed Civilista party support to make populist appeals to the Lima "masses." Though he was beholden to the commercial elite, Billinghurst did not try to work within the party or the club to try to bring about some quiet accommodation that might have avoided a confrontation. Elite dismay eventually drew that group to the military, which intervened in 1914 just long enough to remove Billinghurst.

Leguía, after ruling constitutionally during his first presidency, ended once and for all the shaky civilian democracy in 1919. Rather than work out a behind-the-scenes accommodation with opposition elements in 1919 after he had won an open and democratic election, he led a successful coup of his own and ruled without open elections until being ousted himself in 1930.

Certainly a different perception of reality and a different set of priorities guide such individuals to contribute to the discrediting of the set of political institutions and procedures that have facilitated their rise to political prominence. Among these must be a sense that the individual is more important than institutions, a distrust of organizations, and a reluctance to compromise a position or accommodate oneself to the view of others. These differences, although not unique to Peru, suggest the tension between some Latin American leadership styles and a well-institutionalized, routinized political system.

Populism, Parties, and Coups (1919–1968)

The populism of this period took two forms: civilian, of which Leguía (1919–1930) is perhaps the best example, and military, best illustrated by Gen. Manuel Odría (1948–1956). Both forms were characterized by efforts to discourage the development of political organizations and to encourage loyalty to the person of the president through favored treatment within elites and by the distribution of goods, jobs, and services to politically aware segments of nonelites. Both were also marked by very favorable treatment for the foreign investor and lender; thus they maintained long-standing external-dependence relationships.

The great advantage of the populist alternative is that it gains popular loyalty to government at very low cost. The great disadvantage is that it operates best in an organizational vacuum and thus does not provide a long-term solution to relating citizen to system.

Civilian and military populism both had a number of important effects on the Peruvian political system. They permitted elites to retain control through their narrowly based interest-group organizations, the National Agrarian Society (SNA), the National Mining Society (SNM), and the National Industrial Society (SNI), or their clubs, Nacional and La Unión. When confronted after 1930 with Peru's first mass-based political party, the American Popular Revolutionary Alliance (APRA), the elites were forced to rely on the military to carry out their political will because they had no comparable party to turn to. The military, in turn, found it could accomplish its own objectives by direct intervention in the political system rather than by working through organized intermediaries. Thus populism, by discouraging political parties, contributed significantly to continued political instability.

Between 1914 and 1984 Manuel Prado, whose first term began in 1939, was the only civilian elected in reasonably open fashion to complete his term. Why he did so is instructive: (1) he was of the elite and accepted by it, (2) he did not try to upset the status quo, (3) he reached an accommodation with the military and supported its material and budget requirements, (4) he reached an implicit *modus vivendi* with APRA, (5) he happened to be president during a period when foreign market prices for Peruvian primary-product exports were relatively high and stable.

Perhaps the most important political event in pre-1968 Peru was the organization of APRA. Although founded in Mexico by exiled student leader Víctor Raúl Haya de la Torre in 1924, APRA soon became a genuinely mass-based political party in Peru with a fully articulated if not completely coherent ideology. By most accounts APRA was strong enough to win or determine the outcome of all open elections held in Peru after 1931. The military ensured, however, that the party would never rule directly.

Although APRA has had through the years a strong populist appeal, the party's importance for Peruvian politics rests on its reformist ideology and its organizational capacity. APRA absorbed most of the newly emerging social forces in the more integrated parts of the country outside of Lima between the 1920s and the 1950s, most particularly labor, students, and the more marginal middle sectors. The party's ideology and organization helped prevent the emergence of a more radical alternative with wide popular appeal. Many elements of the ideology have been adopted by subsequent governments and other parties. However, even though APRA was an outsider for most of the period from its founding to 1956, it never overthrew the system so allied against it. At key junctures the party leadership searched for accommodation and compromise to gain entry even while resorting simultaneously to such extreme measures as assassinations and abortive putsches in trying to impress political insiders of its capacity.

Between 1956 and 1982 APRA was a center-conservative party willing to make almost any compromise to gain greater formal political power. In 1956 APRA supported the conservative Manuel Prado in his successful bid for a second term as president (1956–1962) and worked with him through his administration in what was called in Peru *la convivencia* ("living together"). When APRA won open elections in 1962 but was just shy of the constitutionally required one-third, the party made a pact with its former archenemy Odría to govern together—at which point the military intervened. During the Belaúnde administration (1963–1968), APRA formed an alliance with Odría forces in Congress to attain a majority and blocked or watered down many of Belaúnde's reforms. Although such actions discredited the party to many during this period, APRA remained the best organized and most unified political force in the country.

The Popular Action party (AP) founded by Fernando Belaúnde Terry in 1956 brought the reformist elements of its generation into the system just as APRA had done before. AP's appeal was greater in the *sierra* and south, where APRA was weak. Thus the two parties complemented each other by region, and over time they began to channel newly articulate elements of the population into the national political system. AP also had the advantage of being acceptable to the military in the early 1960s, so when Belaúnde won the 1963 presidential elections held under the auspices of the progressive 1962–1963 military junta, he took office amid high expectations.

Important reforms were carried out between 1963 and 1968, including establishment of various new agricultural programs; expansion of secondary and university education, cooperatives, and development corporations; and reinstitution of municipal elections. For all intents and purposes the extremist threat to Peruvian institutions remained stillborn. But Belaúnde and AP were confronted by an obstructionist APRA-Odría opposition in Congress, which blunted initiatives or refused to fund them. And the U.S. government, anxious to assist Standard Oil Company's settlement of the investment-expropriation dispute between its Peruvian subsidiary (International Petroleum Company, IPC) and the Peruvian government, withheld for more than two years Alliance for Progress funds badly needed by the Belaúnde administration to help finance its reforms. Growing economic difficulties in 1967 and 1968 eroded public confidence, and a badly handled IPC nationalization agreement sealed Belaúnde's fate. On October 3, 1968, the military once again took over the reins of government.

HISTORY SINCE 1968

From the day of the bloodless 1968 coup, the Peruvian military declared its determination to make fundamental changes in all areas of Peruvian life. "The time has come," stated the October 3 manifesto of the new government, "to dedicate our national energies to the transformation of the economic, social and cultural structures of Peru." The underlying themes of the major statements of the military regime between 1968 and 1980 included a commitment to change, national pride, social solidarity, the end of dependency, a worker-managed economy, and "a fully participatory social democracy which is neither capitalistic nor communistic but humanistic."

Past governments had declared their intention to change Peru, but this one was prepared to act significantly on its rhetoric. In so doing the military regime altered substantially past practices, procedures, and organizations in the country. True enough, the civilian government from 1963 to 1968 was also a reformist one, and in many ways it set the stage for continued change after the takeover. But what was so surprising in the Peruvian context, given the past history of military involvement in politics primarily to protect elites, was that the 1968 military coup was prompted more by the failure of the reformist civilian government to carry out its plan than by its success.

An explanation for this surprising development is found in a cumulative pattern of changes going on within the military over a period of time.

Much of the military leadership had concluded (through a combination of educational experiences in the Center for Higher Military Studies—CAEM, a small antiguerrilla campaign, U.S. military training, and a vigorous civic-action program) that the best protection for national security was national development. In the eyes of many officers, political parties and civilian politicians demonstrated their inability to meet the development-security challenge in the 1960s. This led many in the military to conclude that only their institution, with its monopoly of legitimate force, was capable of leading the country toward this goal.

Although often couched in revolutionary rhetoric, the government's major policy initiatives between 1968 and 1975 were reformist. This is because they were based almost without exception on improving the distribution of increments in the nation's total resource pie rather than on redistributing the existing pie. Even so, the accomplishments of the Peruvian military regime were quite significant.

One of the most important changes was the rapid extension of state influence and control. New ministries, agencies, and banks were established. Basic services were expropriated, as were some large foreign companies in mining, fishing, and agriculture, and state enterprises or cooperatives were established in their place. Important areas of heavy industry were reserved for the state. New investment laws placed various controls on the private sector. Government employment mushroomed. In the international arena, Peru rapidly established itself under the military as a leader of Third World causes and concerns and pursued at the same time its objective of becoming more diversified in its economic and political relationships with the countries of the world. Another significant initiative was a large-scale agrarian-reform program, which effectively eliminated the hacienda system. About 360,000 farm families received land between 1969 and 1980, most as members of farm cooperatives. Commitment to such cooperative farms illustrated the military regime's concern for popular participation at various levels. Neighborhood organizations, worker communities, and cooperatives of several types proliferated after 1970, as did various coordinating bodies.

By 1971 an official model of the future political system of Peru had emerged in more or less coherent form; subsequent government rhetoric, decrees, and practices tended to flesh out the model until an August 1975 coup led by General Francisco Morales Bermúdez brought Peru to a consolidating phase of the "revolution." The official model was essentially corporativist in nature. It perceived Peruvian social and political reality in terms of an organic whole, organized naturally by functional sectors, and within each sector by a natural hierarchy. Government was to serve as the overarching body to initiate, coordinate, and resolve disputes within or among sectors. In this context, established political parties and unions were perceived as disruptive forces, and numerous decrees before 1975 were designed either to marginalize such groups or to provide them with competitors.

Although military government after 1968 broke with Peru's past in several ways, three major factors led to the regime's undoing. Economic difficulties multiplied rapidly after 1974. In part these were caused by resource-availability miscalculations, in part by the military's own felt needs for perquisites and equipment. In addition, those in power failed to consult openly and as equals with those who were the intended beneficiaries of the new participatory modes, and this contributed to popular resentment and mistrust. Third, the illness of Gen. Juan Velasco Alvarado after 1973 contributed to the loss of institutional unity of the armed forces themselves that his dynamic and forceful leadership had helped to instill. The eventual result was a continued mix of old and new in yet another overlay.

In 1977 the Morales Bermúdez regime, under pressure, decided to initiate a gradual return to civilian rule. The resulting constituent assembly elections in 1978 were won by APRA, and the assembly itself was led by Haya de la Torre. It produced the Constitution of 1979, which set up national elections in 1980 and municipal elections in 1981 and 1984. The irony of the 1980 and 1981 elections was that they returned to the presidency the same Fernando Belaúnde Terry (and to many local mayoralties his same party colleagues) so unceremoniously unseated in 1968.

This time Belaúnde's Popular Action party (AP) was able to forge a majority in Congress in coalition with the small Popular Christian party (PPC) and won the first plurality in the 1981 municipal elections as well. But events conspired once again to make life difficult for the governing authorities. Inflation continued to increase well into 1984 at record levels of over 100 percent annually. The recession deepened so that in 1983 GNP actually declined by over 10 percent. World market prices for Peru's exports remained low, and devastating weather accompanying the arrival of the El Niño–caused ocean current in 1982 destroyed crops and communications networks in the northern half of Peru with rain and flood and withered crops in the south as a result of drought.

Another unanticipated problem for the second Belaúnde administration was the growing violence associated with the activities of the radical political group known as Shining Path (Sendero Luminoso). Based on the isolated south-central *sierra* provinces of Ayacucho and headed by university professors and students from the local University of Huamanga, Shining Path advocated a peasant-based republic forged through revolution on the principles of Mao and José Carlos Mariátegui. After more than fifteen years of theorizing at the university and praxis in the Indian peasant-dominated countryside of Ayacucho, the group's leaders moved to increasingly violent confrontations, first against symbols of authority and then against authorities themselves. By early 1984 over one thousand deaths, substantial property destruction, and the militarization of twelve provinces in the Ayacucho area were associated with both Shining Path and the military's response. Although it appeared unlikely that such a radical group and such violent tactics could gain power in Peru, the government's inability to end the threat further weakened its legitimacy. This was reflected in AP's poor showing in the 1983 municipal elections, in which its candidates ran behind both APRA and the United Left (IU) in many parts of the country.

SOCIAL AND POLITICAL GROUPS

Organized social and political groups have played less of a role in Peruvian affairs than in most Latin American countries. The reasons for this may be traced in part to the strong patterns of Spanish domination that inhibited growth long after the formal Spanish presence was removed. What emerged instead was a strong sense of individualism within the context of region and family for that small portion of the total population that was actually included within the nation's political system. In the decades following independence, governments were made and unmade by regional caudillos or officials whose power was based on control of arms, personal appeal, and family or regional ties. The best lands were increasingly controlled by non-Indians, who took advantage of postindependence decrees and constitutions that removed Indians and their preserves from state protection. The Church also lost some of its land-based financial strength, and private beneficent societies (*beneficencias*) took over the ownership and administration of many Church properties. Thus political and economic power was quite fragmented in nineteenth-century Peru.

With the consolidation of a limited civilian democracy in the 1890s, some of what were to become the country's most important interest groups were founded, including SNA, SNM, and SNI. However, it was long remarked that the important decisions affecting the country were usually made in the Club Nacional, formed much earlier (1855) and the lone survivor of post-1968 reforms. Even the military operated between 1914 and 1962 largely as the "watchdog of the oligarchy." Thus elites could determine policy outside the electoral arena and had limited incentives to operate within any party system.

Elections themselves have been intermittent and tentative, and electoral restrictions historically kept most Peruvians out of the national political arena.

Property ownership requirements were not lifted until 1931, when the secret ballot was also introduced. Women were not enfranchised until 1956. Literacy and age requirements remained in effect until the advent of universal suffrage in the 1980s.

The political party scene in Peru is quite fragmented. AP split into pro- and anti-Belaúnde factions, though it came back together with the Belaúnde victory in 1980. APRA divided after the death of Haya de la Torre in 1979, but the dominant progressive faction regained legitimacy and dynamism with the election of youthful Haya protégé Alan García as party head in 1982. A small but influential Christian-Democratic party (DC) also divided into a tiny leftist faction and a larger conservative group (PPC). A Marxist political movement (founded by the intellectual José Carlos Mariátegui in 1928) that emerged as the Communist party has retained its Moscow-oriented core while fragmenting almost endlessly into Maoist, Castroite, and Trotskyite splinters. All share pieces of equally divided urban and rural union movements. The military government's efforts between 1968 and 1975 to build a new corporativist structure of political participation compounded the confusion.

The emergence of Shining Path to public prominence beginning in 1980 and its recourse to guerrilla tactics evoked an almost universally negative response by Peru's Marxist left, suggesting that the core of the Communist movement is not inclined at this time to pursue its goals through violence. With most of its members now joined loosely in the IU, they have found that they can fare quite well in elections, with about ten senators and congressmen and the key mayorship of Lima, among others, to the party's credit. Some would maintain that the rise of an organized and largely responsible left is one of the positive legacies of the *docenio* (twelve-year period) of military rule.

The role of U.S. public and private actors has also been quite complex. Private investment in Peru grew rapidly in the early twentieth century but was almost exclusively in isolated enclaves on the North Coast (oil and sugar, later cotton and fishmeal) and in the *sierra* (copper, mixed minerals, later iron). Most governments encouraged such investment. Even during the *docenio*, in spite of some expropriations and a conscious attempt to diversify sources of foreign investment, substantial new U.S. investment took place, particularly in copper (Southern Peru Copper Company) and oil exploration and production (Occidental Petroleum Company). Since 1980, the Belaúnde government's policy toward private investment has been more open but only partly successful as a result of international and domestic economic problems.

However one may debate the issue of foreign dependence, in a very real sense U.S. investment and loans served in predepression Peru to balance the country's extreme reliance on Great Britain. Their enclave nature had a multiple impact: reduction of economic ripple effects on the rest of the Peruvian economy, provision of islands of relative economic privilege for workers in which unions could become established and creation of small areas of virtual foreign hegemony within Peruvian territory.

With growing economic nationalism in Peru in the 1960s, the U.S. government collaborated closely with U.S. businesses to try to work out solutions satisfactory to "U.S. interests." The International Petroleum Company case between 1963 and 1968 illustrates this policy in the extreme. One basis for Peru's desire to expropriate IPC rested on well-founded claims that the concessions giving Standard Oil of New Jersey subsoil rights in La Brea y Pariñas in 1921 and 1922 were illegal. The

U.S. government supported Standard Oil's position; when negotiations bogged down periodically, U.S. government foreign assistance and loans under the Alliance for Progress were interrupted. The Belaúnde government, under duress, finally struck a bargain with the company. The controversial terms generated public debate and turmoil and provided the immediate precipitant for the 1968 coup: Within a week after taking power, the military intervened in IPC. This and subsequent periodic expropriations kept most new official aid suspended between 1968 and 1972 except for earthquake relief and rehabilitation assistance after 1970. Eventually the military government found itself obliged to resolve expropriations with financial settlements that companies considered fair, in part as a result of U.S. government pressure but also because the Peruvian regime wanted and needed continued foreign private investment and loans.

Historically the U.S. government presence in Peru has not been a large one. Starting in 1938, however, with heightened U.S. concern for the threat within the hemisphere of international fascism, and continuing after World War II with the perceived menace of international communism, the U.S. government must be considered a major actor. Between 1945 and 1975 grants and loans to Peru totaled $1.107 billion, of which $194 million was military assistance. Aid funds during the Belaúnde years, when available, went primarily for projects in marginal sectors the Peruvian Congress was unwilling to fund. A large-scale civic-action program for the military in the 1960s helped shape officers' views on the national development mission of the Peruvian armed forces. The U.S. government's refusal to permit the sale of jet fighters to Peru in 1966 and 1967 also shaped the armed forces' perspectives—helping officers realize that their own welfare, as well as their country's, would be enhanced by diversifying their sources of supply and, hence, their dependence. Actions and reactions by both the Peruvian and U.S. government since 1968—including aid and loan cutoffs, the expulsion of most of the large U.S. military mission, and the end of the Peace Corps presence—have lowered considerably the U.S. official profile in the country. Since 1973, Peru has had a substantial military sales and assistance relationship with the Soviet Union—in excess of $1 billion— that involves the training of several hundred Peruvian army and air force personnel.

GOVERNMENT MACHINERY

The Peruvian government, like many of its Latin American counterparts, may be characterized through most of its history as limited, centralized, and personalistic. Until the 1960s government employees constituted a very small proportion of the work force and at all levels were usually selected on the basis of party affiliation, family ties, or friendship. Most ministry bureaucracies were concentrated in Lima. For all practical purposes, government presence in the provinces was limited to prefects and their staffs, military garrisons in border areas, small detachments of national police, local teachers, and a few judges. All of these were appointed by the appropriate ministry in the capital.

A government monopoly of the guano industry and of tobacco, matches, and salt marketing were among the few official ventures before 1960. Until the 1960s the Central Bank was privately controlled, and even government taxes were collected by private agencies. Within the government the executive branch predominated. During periods when Congress was functioning, however, the executive's authority was subject to numerous checks, including Congress's power to interrogate and censure ministers and to appropriate the budget.

The government's size and scope increased considerably during the Belaúnde administration (1963–1968), largely in the number of semiautonomous government agencies: for example, provincial development corporations, a national housing agency, a domestic peace corps (Cooperación Popular), a national planning institute, a cooperative organization, and squatter settlement organizations. Total government employment increased from 179,000 in 1960 (6 percent of the work force) to 270,000 in 1967 (7 percent of the work force) and the public sector's share of gross domestic product grew from 8 percent to 11 percent during the same period.

However, the most dramatic changes in the size and scope of the state occured between 1968 and 1980, within an official ideological context of "statism." This ideology advanced the virtue of government involvement to accelerate development along nationalistic lines. Most existing ministries were reorganized, and numerous new ministries and autonomous agencies were created. By 1973 total government employment had increased by almost 50 percent over 1967 figures to 401,000 (9 percent of the work force) and by 1975 to an estimated 450,000 (11 percent of the work force). The public-sector share of gross domestic product doubled between 1967 and 1975 to 22 percent.

Although a great deal of attention was given to the need to decentralize government activities to make them more accessible to a larger share of the population, in practice central government activities remained as concentrated in Lima as they had been historically. Much of the increase in government budget went toward construction, equipment, and white-collar employment in the capital rather than toward activities in marginal areas.

The political and financial crises of 1975 and the change of government brought to an end the dynamic phase of public-sector reforms. After that, source limitations, financial and human; the continuance of prior modes of party, union, and interest-group activity; and the practical inability of the military regime to effectively act upon all decrees prevented the full implementation of the corporativist model articulated between 1971 and 1975. The second Belaúnde administration (1980–1985) has announced its intention to restore the dynamism of the private sector and to reduce the role of government. Continuing economic problems and substantial public resistance have made these changes difficult to carry out.

PUBLIC POLICY

Historically, public policy in Peru may be characterized as limited. Laissez-faire liberalism applied from consolidation in the 1890s up to 1968 with few exceptions. Most services were privately owned. The government's role was normally that of facilitator or expeditor for the private sector, including foreign enterprises.

Unlike many Latin American countries, Peru did not respond to the challenge of the world depression after 1929 by sharp increases in public services and enterprise. This may have resulted in part from the simultaneous domestic challenge to the elites posed by APRA, with its advocacy of sharply expanded state control. By successfully keeping APRA from gaining control of the political system in the 1930s, the elites also retained the limited state. By the time APRA was finally permitted to enter the political arena as a legitimate force in 1956, its position on the role of the state was much more accommodating to elite interests.

The electoral campaigns of 1961-1962 and 1962-1963 raised more explicitly the need for a greater public-sector role. The ultimate winners, AP and Belaúnde, worked actively to make the state a more dynamic force between 1963 and 1968 with numerous public initiatives. Some redistribution of income in favor of the less-privileged sectors did occur in the 1960s, although it is not clear just how much of the change was the result of government polities. Perhaps the most important legacy of the Belaúnde administration was to break down the long-standing aversion in Peru to the state as a dynamic force and to create a climate of increased popular expectations regarding what the state could and should do.

The military government between 1968 and 1980 served as the motor force for unprecedented expansion in the size of the state and in the sheer number of policies flowing therefrom, in a country with what was hitherto one of the weaker state apparatuses in Latin America. There were, nevertheless, serious problems associated with rapid state expansion. In trying to do so much so quickly, government spread itself too thin. Though providing new job opportunities for the middle class, the rapidly expanding bureaucracy often had difficulty delivering promised goods and services, especially in outlying provinces. Official announcements and periodic flurries of activity raised expectations and often turned government offices into "lightning rods" for popular demands that could not be met. Growing economic resource limitations compounded the problems.

The expropriation of IPC a week after the 1968 coup set the nation and the world on notice that the new military government was serious in its reform objectives. The action served simultaneously to unite the armed forces around the realization of a long-held aspiration: to establish the legitimacy of the new regime with the citizenry and to demonstrate to the U.S. government and foreign investors that the Peruvian government would no longer tolerate the degree of foreign-actor influence heretofore prevalent within the country. Several subsequent expropriations of foreign enterprises have taken place, but with compensation generally believed to be fair. New foreign investment was welcomed under stricter regulation and has occurred principally in copper mining and oil exploration. Foreign loans were avidly sought and were acquired at levels approaching a total of $9 billion by 1980, far in excess of that received by any previous government.

Thus, even while adopting a radical posture in its foreign economic relations, the military government recognized the necessity of continued foreign loans and investments to help accomplish national development goals. However, such heavy international borrowing after 1971, in part the result of the reluctance of the domestic private sector to invest in spite of generous incentives, came back to haunt the government. Prices for some Peruvian exports declined markedly, domestic production of others also declined, and optimistic forecasts on probable oil exports proved erroneous. A severe financial crisis resulted in 1978 and 1979. Consequently many development objectives were compromised and the very legitimacy of the regime came into question.

The subsequent civilian government had to face many of the same problems. Although no new nationalizations occurred, efforts to sell some enterprises back into private hands and to encourage new foreign investment were largely thwarted by domestic depression, international recession, and large debt-repayment responsibilities.

The agrarian reform of 1969 was the revolutionary military government's first major domestic policy initiative. Agricultural land throughout the country in excess of relatively modest maximum holdings was expropriated and turned over, at nominal prices, to those who actually tilled the soil. Some 360,000 farm families received land under the reform, over 90 percent in cooperative enterprises of one sort or another. In spite of numerous problems, the agrarian reform was the most far-reaching of all the military government's policy initiatives.

One difficulty with the reform is that there is not enough arable land, so that about 70 percent of the farmers estimated to need land did not receive it. Another is that the land is most scarce in the *sierra*, where most needy farmers are located. Farmers who were already relatively better off, mainly on the coast, have received most of the redistributive benefits of the reform. Furthermore, the government did not mount a major effort in the more isolated *sierra* to overcome deficiencies there until 1975, as consolidation and retrenchment began. In addition the central government is limited in its capability to control peripheral areas in a country as geographically and culturally diverse as Peru, however good its intentions. As a result many cooperative enterprises in the *sierra* did not operate effectively. Finally, one by-product of the reform was a serious decline in agricultural production, which was overcome only partially by the civilian government's sharp reduction in food subsidies and the resulting increase in food prices after 1980.

Another important area of reform by the military involved the rapid expansion of various types of "local units of participation." These included various cooperative forms in agriculture, neighborhood associations in the squatter settlements, and worker self-management communities in industry and mining. In the agricultural sector, one cooperative form was the Agrarian Social Interest Society (SAIS), which combined expropriated haciendas with adjoining peasant communities. Others included the agrarian production cooperative, which pooled land, labor, and capital, and agrarian service cooperatives, which pooled some capital and some labor.

In the urban squatter settlements, including people in Lima and in the provincial cities, the government continued to encourage neighborhood associations. In these areas, the self-help and community-action concepts the government wanted to encourage elsewhere are already quite well rooted. With the return to civilian government in 1980, initial optimism and support in the squatter settlements gave way to growing cynicism and distrust. In the 1983 municipal elections, the victory of the IU candidate Alfonso Barrantes depended on the plurality he received from every major squatter settlement in Lima. The vote for the Belaúnde government's candidate was less than 13 percent of the total.

Worker self-management communities in the industrial sector were first introduced in 1970. They involved the sharing of profits and management of the enterprise by all full-time members of the firm. The worker's management role was to increase over time, originally up to 50 percent, but was modified first by the Morales Bermúdez military government and then by the Belaúnde civilian administration. As of 1984, ownership was restricted to one-third, and workers' shares were individual rather than held collectively.

State enterprises (25 percent or more government control) share profits with the community but not with management beyond the initial two community representatives placed on the firm's board of directors. By 1977 there were about thirty-four hundred industrial communities with some 200,000 members and an average worker ownership of about 15 percent. Membership remained fairly static into the 1980s, but efforts by the Belaúnde government in 1982 to phase out the industrial community were overwhelmingly voted down by the membership.

Such proliferation of various kinds of local units of participation had for the military government the advantage of providing an alternative for citizen participation at the level of workplace and residence at a time when routinized participation by party at the national level was cut off. Although the benefits of local-participation unit membership are often significant to members, most worker members are by and large from the working-class elite. Furthermore, growth of the units is predicated on the generation of future profits or surpluses that can be more equitably distributed to members. Since 1974 economic conditions have not favored such growth.

The restoration of civilian rule in 1980 did give back to parties and unions their power as transmitters of their memberships' concerns to government authorities. However, the continuing economic crisis severely limited their ability to reap many benefits. As of early 1984 unemployment and underemployment affected over 55 percent of the economically active population.

Some initiatives concerning citizen participation at other than local levels have been legislated and have at times played an important role in aggregating and articulating popular concerns. The National Agrarian Confederation (CNA), established in 1972 as the sole legitimate organization for all farmers, has local, regional, and national boards made up of representatives selected on the principle of democratic centralism. The National Industrial Community Commission (CONACI) performs much the same function. Although officially abolished in 1978, the CNA continues to operate with the support of much of the citizenry of the sector it represents.

Responsibility for organizing, coordinating, and controlling citizen participation was entrusted after 1971 to SINAMOS, the National Social Mobilization Support System. SINAMOS was essentially an "umbrella" agency incorporating several older government agencies, most of whose top leadership positions had been held by military officers.

As SINAMOS became operative after 1972, regional offices became a focal point of opposition to government policies, and some were sacked and burned in 1973 and 1975. These disturbances showed the limits of popular support for the government. Originating as a conflict between national police and the military, large groups of citizens took to the streets of Lima and several provincial capitals on a massive looting and burning spree with antigovernment overtones. These events were a key precipitant of the August 1975 coup, which replaced the original military leadership, headed by Gen. Juan Velasco Alvarado, with another military group led by Gen. Francisco Morales Bermúdez. SINAMOS itself was phased out in 1978.

The stated objective of the military regime in international affairs was the elimination of dependence. Peru took some rather dramatic steps between 1968 and 1975 to alter its international position and to diversify, if not end, its dependence. Several East European countries were recognized, as were some Arab oil states, China, and Cuba. Trade and barter arrangements and some loans were worked out with numerous countries of the socialist bloc. Important trade and loan agreements were arranged with such countries as Japan, Belgium, Holland, Italy, and Spain. Foreign investment and loans continued to be avidly sought from individual countries and international institutions. But rather than depend on a few sources, as in the past, the government consciously diversified Peru's trade, investment, and loan assistance. These policies continued in the Belaúnde administration and may have helped to keep the severe economic problems from being even worse.

At the same time, Peru attempted to strengthen its position as a developing nation vis-à-vis developed nations. It took on an important leadership role among the Third World nonaligned countries, hosting conferences, serving as a leading spokesperson at others, and generally asserting an independent position. Unfortunately, Peru's struggle to diversify its dependence and to achieve a position of Third World leadership was seriously compromised by the country's growing economic difficulties after 1974. In 1978, 1982, and 1984, Peruvian governments were forced to accept stringent IMF conditions for the continuance of economic and loan assistance.

Most assessments of the post-1968 period in Peru conclude that military leaders erred in expanding public policy as quickly and across as many areas as they did. In attempting to do too much, government resources were stretched too thin and quality of delivery suffered at the same time that public expectations were being raised. The post-1975 consolidation phase of the military government was an acknowledgment of failure. The election of Belaúnde in 1980 with over 45 percent of the vote in a multicandidate race demonstrated the level of popular dissatisfaction with the policies of the military *docenio*. However, the civilian government proved equally unable to sustain economic growth and to ensure domestic tranquility. Even so, a new round of military government is unlikely in the near future. In part this is because of the armed forces' recent difficult experience with long-term rule.

PROSPECTS FOR THE FUTURE

Peru as an independent nation never overcame its authoritarian legacy. The Spanish authoritarian heritage was an important factor impeding the evolution of liberal democratic institutions in the nineteenth century. Other considerations, including international market forces, the incorporation of more and more of the national population into the national political and economic system, and political leadership perceptions, have prevented the emergence of a stable institutional structure in the twentieth.

Peru's economic and political crises of 1975–1979 are evidence of the failure of the reformist military government. They demonstrated the boundaries within which reformers must operate to accomplish national political and economic development objectives. In particular the crises illustrate the degree to which policymakers in a middle-sized Third

World country, with a long dependent tradition, are hemmed in by forces essentially beyond their control. Under the circumstances what is remarkable is that the military reformers accomplished as much as they did in an authoritarian but essentially nonrepressive context, not that they failed to achieve all they set out to.

Some of the difficulties of the succeeding civilian government may be traced to policies of its military predecessors. The civilians have made their own share of mistakes as well, however, in addition to being similarly constrained by factors beyond their control. Perhaps the most important long-term legacy of reformist military rule in Peru between 1968 and 1980 is the articulation of concerns by a new generation of Peruvians, mostly on the left and mostly within the political system. Union movements and political parties alike are now highly pluralistic and highly competitive and offer the possibility that civilian government might continue for some time in Peru.

SUGGESTIONS FOR FURTHER READING

Astiz, Carlos A. *Pressure Groups and Power Elites in Peruvian Politics.* Cornell University Press, Ithaca, N.Y., 1969.

Becker, David G. *The New Bourgeoisie and the Limits of Dependency: Mining, Class, and Power in "Revolutionary" Peru.* Princeton University Press, Princeton, N.J., 1983.

Bourque, Susan C., and Kay Barbara Warren. *Women of the Andes: Patriarchy and Social Change in Two Peruvian Towns.* University of Michigan Press, Ann Arbor, 1981.

Bourricaud, Francois. *Power and Society in Contemporary Peru.* Praeger, New York, 1970.

Chaplin, David, ed. *Peruvian Nationalism: A Corporatist Revolution.* Transaction Books, New Brunswick, N.J., 1976.

Collier, David. *Squatters and Oligarchs: Authoritarian Rule and Policy Change in Peru.* Johns Hopkins University Press, Baltimore, 1975.

Dew, Edward. *Politics in the Altiplano: The Dynamics of Change in Rural Peru.* University of Texas Press, Austin, 1969.

Dietz, Henry A. *Poverty and Problem-Solving Under Military Rule: The Urban Poor in Lima, Peru.* University of Texas Press, Austin, 1980.

Dobyns, Henry F., and Paul L. Doughty. *Peru: A Cultural History.* Cambridge University Press, New York, 1977.

FitzGerald, E.V.K. *The Political Economy of Peru 1956–1978: Economic Development and the Restructuring of Capital.* Cambridge University Press, Cambridge, 1979.

Goodsell, Charles T. *American Corporations and Peruvian Politics.* Harvard University Press, Cambridge, 1974.

Handleman, Howard. *Struggle in the Andes.* University of Texas Press, Austin, 1974.

Hilliker, Grant. *The Politics of Reform in Peru: The Aprista and Other Mass Parties of Latin America.* Johns Hopkins University Press, Baltimore, 1971.

Kantor, Harry. *The Ideology and Program of the Peruvian Aprista Movement.* Octagon Books, New York, 1966.

Klarén, Peter F. *Modernization, Dislocation, and Aprismo: Origins of the Peruvian Aprista Party, 1933–1970*. University of Texas Press, Austin, 1973.

Kuczynski, Pedro-Pablo. *Peruvian Democracy Under Economic Stress: An Account of the Belaúnde Administration, 1963–1968*. Princeton University Press, Princeton, N.J., 1977.

Larson, Magali Sarfatti, and Arlene Eisen Bergman. *Social Stratification in Peru*. Institute of International Studies, University of California, Berkeley, 1969.

Lowenthal, Abraham F., ed. *The Peruvian Experiment: Continuity and Change Under Military Rule*. Princeton University Press, Princeton, N.J., 1975.

McClintock, Cynthia. *Peasant Cooperatives and Political Change in Peru*. Princeton University Press, Princeton, N.J., 1981.

McClintock, Cynthia, and Abraham F. Lowenthal, eds. *The Peruvian Experiment Reconsidered*. Princeton University Press, Princeton, N.J., 1983.

North, Liisa, and Tanya Korovkin. *The Peruvian Revolution and the Officers in Power, 1967–1976*. Occasional Monograph Series no. 15, Centre for Developing-Area Studies, McGill University, Montreal, 1981.

Palmer, David Scott. *Peru: The Authoritarian Tradition*. Praeger, New York, 1980.

Palmer, David Scott, and Kevin J. Middlebrook. *Military Government and Political Development: Lessons From Peru*. Comparative Politics series no. 01-054. Sage Publications, Beverly Hills, Calif., 1975.

Philip, George D. E. *The Rise and Fall of the Peruvian Military Radicals, 1968–1976*. University of London Institute of Latin American Studies Monographs no. 9. The Athlone Press, London, 1978.

Pike, Frederick B. *The Modern History of Peru*. Praeger, New York, 1967.

———. *The United States and the Andean Republics*. Harvard University Press, Cambridge, 1977.

Sharp, Daniel A., ed. *U.S. Foreign Policy and Peru*. University of Texas Press, Austin, 1972.

Stepan, Alfred. *The State and Society: Peru in Comparative Perspective*. Princeton University Press, Princeton, N.J., 1978.

Thorp, Rosemary, and Geoffrey Bertram. *Peru 1890–1977: Growth and Policy in an Open Economy*. Columbia University Press, New York, 1978.

Werlich, David P. *Peru: A Short History*. Southern Illinois University Press, Carbondale, 1978.

13
Venezuela:
The Politics
of Democratic
Developmentalism

IÊDA SIQUEIRA WIARDA

For nearly three decades, Venezuela has been one of the few bright spots in the Latin American political panorama. Those who have studied the country extensively are virtually unanimous in this appraisal, and the statistics are there to back their assessment: years of life expectancy at birth, 67, one of the highest in the Americas; illiteracy down to 14 percent; foreign-exchange reserves the equivalent of those of all the rest of Latin America; per capita income, $4,051, the highest in South America. Moreover, development and affluence have taken place within a generally free and democratic context.

Since 1958 the constitutional system has been stable, there has been minimal tampering with the constitution, a vigorous series of electoral campaigns has been waged, and—rare in Latin American politics—the government in office has three times handed over power to the opposition. Students, peasants, labor, professionals—in fact, nearly all sectors of society—seem involved in the political process, electing their own leaders, competing for party positions, bargaining with the government for their share of the huge spoils brought in by immense oil revenues. There are problems—inflation, a burdensome foreign debt, lethargic agriculture in spite of a far-ranging agrarian-reform law, shantytowns, and a million abandoned children in a country that boasts it is the world's leading per capita champagne consumer. But in spite of these problems, Venezuelans are fairly optimistic about their country's present and future prospects, so much so that they are convinced their own experience can be replicated and that Venezuela can serve as a model for underdeveloped countries as well as a bridge between the "rich" countries and the vast Third World.

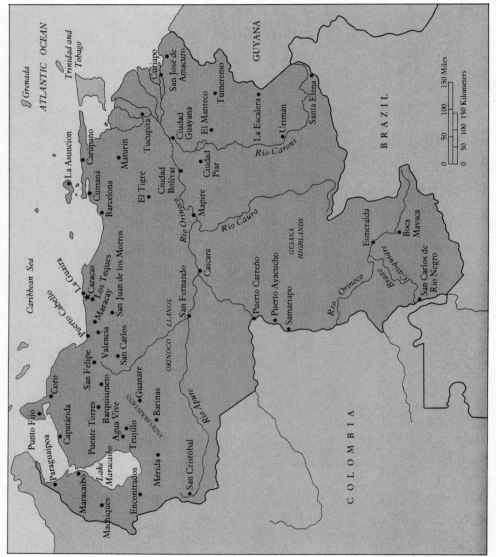

Venezuela

Venezuela has gained international stature through its leading participation in the Organization of Petroleum Exporting Countries (OPEC), the International Monetary Fund, the North-South Conference in Paris, the Contadora Group, and its own program of cultural exchanges and foreign-aid programs. Venezuela has used its economic power to forge a foreign policy that both supports those human rights Venezuelans themselves enjoy and seeks a more equitable economic relationship among the highly industrialized countries and those, like Venezuela, that are primarily exporters of raw materials.

The success of democratic development in Venezuela has not been achieved easily—and one cannot discount the possibility of future disruptions in the present democratic course. A great deal of effort has been involved—and also considerable luck, for Venezuela almost literally floats on oil and has vast quantities of other natural resources. To achieve its present enviable position, Venezuela has had to overcome a particularly turbulent past, which has seen the enactment of more constitutions than in any other Latin American country and a steady succession of dictators. Yet since 1958 Venezuela has demonstrated that modernity and traditionalism can coexist in a dynamic symbiosis and that democracy, albeit with a peculiarly Latin American style and structure, can be made to function effectively. In spite of severe tensions, the governmental process has functioned efficiently and without breakdowns; there has been an open and democratic flow of communication between the government and the governed; and a number of well-organized political parties have not only facilitated democratic development but have helped institutionalize the democratic process itself.

Whether, as slowly but inexorably Venezuela's oil reserves dwindle, the country will be able to maintain its present position and its democratic processes is an open question and one that has preoccupied a succession of governments. Since the 1930s, a major national goal has been to "sow the petroleum"—to use oil revenues to establish a stable economy, with a secure future in the form of profitable agriculture and dynamic and powerful industry. Although this goal has been pursued for decades, it is still far from achieved, for the fact remains that a considerable proportion of food has to be imported. Industrial diversification has grown apace, with massive investments in transportation, power, mining, and steel. Yet Venezuela remains highly dependent upon oil. The petroleum sector still accounts for over 90 percent of foreign-exchange earnings and over 80 percent of revenues for a government that plays the dominant role in the economy. The adverse impact of the drop in oil prices in the late 1970s has been devastating. With the downturn in world demand for oil and an OPEC-dictated decrease in prices and production, Venezuela was forced to carry out a 40 percent devaluation of the bolívar in 1983 and to declare a temporary moratorium on much of its heavy foreign debt, estimated at $36 billion in 1984, half of it short-term.

Another question is whether, as the oil reserves dwindle, Venezuela will be able to maintain its spectrum of costly social programs, such as those in education and health. Much has been achieved, but even when the oil profits were coming in and the myriad of ambitious programs were being attempted, Venezuelans, in the words of former President Carlos Andrés Pérez, were still plagued by a "monstrous inequality" in terms of income and life-style.

Finally, with such an overwhelming share of its revenues tied to international markets and with seemingly chronic internal problems, the ultimate question remains whether Venezuela will be able to retain its present international preeminence and its system of democratic problem solving at home. Although none of these nagging questions will be put to rest in the course of this chapter, some clues and possible answers may evolve.

BACKGROUND AND POLITICAL CULTURE

The present enviable political position was not always held by Venezuela, and it would be impossible to understand the country's odyssey from a turbulent past into a promising present without taking into account the types of limitations—and possibilities—the land and history have imposed on it. Venezuela's 14.6 million people (1981 census) live in an area the size of Texas and Oklahoma combined (352,150 square miles—912,050 square kilometers), stretching for some 1,750 miles (2,816 kilometers) along the Caribbean Sea and Atlantic Ocean. The country extends southward into the South American continent, crossing snow-covered mountains and broad plains (the Llanos), and reaches into the Amazonian jungle. Some 3,000 miles (4,800 kilometers) of continental border form the frontiers with Colombia, Brazil, and Guyana. Four-fifths of the country is drained by the Orinoco River, one of the largest and most navigable rivers in the world. But it has been the mountains and not the river that have historically been the most influential geographical feature. The mountains that rise in the north have been the site of most of Venezuela's first colonial settlements, agricultural estates, and urban centers, and this area has remained the administrative, economic, and social heartland of the country.

The customary geographic divisions of the country are the Guayana Highlands, the Orinoco Lowlands, the Northern Mountains, and the Maracaibo Basin and Coastal Lowlands, in addition to the numerous small islands near the Caribbean coast. These regions show immense variations in size, resources, climate, population, and historical input.

The Guayana Highlands is the largest region (45 percent of the national territory) and traditionally poor, remote, and sparsely populated. Here one finds steep plateaus rising out of the dense Amazonian forest and the highest waterfall in the world, fabled Angel Falls. Traditionally, this region has had the least influence in national affairs.

Although much of the Guayana is still unexplored and covered by forest, the Venezuelan government is determined to make it a tropical Ruhr, and steel mills, aluminum-processing plants, and the huge Guri Dam are already functioning. The Guayana Project has effectively changed the economic and political identity of the region. Where, until as recently as twenty years ago, primitive rafts carried bush cattle and gold and diamond prospectors tried their luck, the industrial center of eastern Venezuela is taking hold. Ciudad Guayana, with a population of around 400,000, is the industrial hub and the most vivid example of "sowing the petroleum." Development has made the Guayana Highlands one of the most rapidly growing regions in Latin America and easily one of the most productive and influential areas in Venezuela. But the recent emergence of the Guayana has brought to the fore old border conflicts with the countries of Guyana and Brazil.

The Orinoco Lowlands, commonly called Llanos (plains), has traditionally been the great ranching region. In the nineteenth century it was here that a series of future Venezuelan presidents first tested their leadership capabilities as chieftains of illiterate but loyal and fierce horsemen and cattle hands. The climate alternates between equally long periods of rain and dry, dusty heat. Open range is unbroken by fences, and cattle ranches reach as many as 1 million acres (400,000 hectares) each. Some rice is grown. More recently oil has been found, and now this region supplies close to a fourth of the total Venezuelan crude oil production.

The third major geographic region is made up by the Northern Mountains. The principal mountain chain consists of the Sierra Nevada and the coastal range. The Sierra Nevada, a branch of the Andes, is high and rugged, reaching 16,411 feet (49,233 meters). The coastal range is lower and less rugged but still reaches 9,000 feet (27,000 meters) east of Caracas. This region encompasses only 12 percent of Venezuela's land area, but it supports about two-thirds of the country's population. The cool, healthy highlands provide for intensive farming, but the geographic isolation has traditionally made it a seat of strong regionalism.

In the Sierra, Mérida has long considered itself a traditional and aristocratic center, and its university has long rivaled the one in Caracas. This is also the "whitest" region of Venezuela, as the culture and the language are close to the Spanish roots. Religion and family are strong, as are the traditional values of Hispanic civilization. There is a tradition of personalism and military leadership. This, in part, explains why so many Venezuelan presidents have come from this region, from corrupt Cipriano Castro, the "lion of the Andes," to powerful and seemingly indestructible Juan Vicente Gómez, to Andrés Pérez.

The area made up by the Maracaibo Basin and Coastal Lowlands is where most of the Venezuelan oil is found. It is also rich in agricultural lands and cattle ranches. The swampy flatlands, mosquito infested and famed as a fever-ridden backwater, were largely ignored until the industrial exploitation of oil in the 1920s. Maracaibo, Venezuela's second city, is a thriving commercial, industrial, and educational center. The basin and the lowlands have over 3 million people, over 80 percent of whom are classified as urban. Black influence is stronger here than anywhere else in Venezuela. On this Caribbean coast are the best beaches; the climate is clear and dry, and the area is famous for tourism and resorts.

In addition to the mainland, there are seventy-two islands of varied size and description. The most important and best known is Margarita, the site of some of the oldest Spanish settlements in Latin America and today a thriving tourist center.

Although the country lies wholly within the tropics, and its southern extremity is less than one degree north of the equator, its climate varies considerably. The variations are determined first by elevation and second by topography and the direction and intensity of the prevailing winds. Seasonal variations in temperature are small, but rainfall is subject to changes so pronounced that the rainier months are called "winter" and the remainder of the year is considered summer.

The great majority of the population is an amalgam of white, black, and Indian, but it shares a common culture based on the Hispanic traditions described in Part 1, and it is enriched by African and Indian contributions. Most people belong to the Roman Catholic Church, speak Spanish, and consider themselves *venezolanos*, members of essentially the same ethnic mix. Since no national census has classified these *venezolanos* according to ethnic or racial groups since 1926, we can only make educated guesses. Thus, it is estimated that between 10 and 25 percent are white, between 3 and 10 percent black, between 4 and 17 percent mulatto, between 2 and 5 percent Indian, and between 40 and 80 percent mestizo or persons of mixed ancestry. Ethnic mixing has occurred at all social levels, and ethnicity does not serve to distinguish either separate groups or classes. Venezuela does boast of a few old, proud white families who trace their ancestry to renowned Spanish names, but of greater significance is the large number of people of various ethnic shades and social backgrounds who have "made it" in Venezuelan society and polity. Former President Rómulo Betancourt used to refer to his rather dark shade of skin as showing how close he was to the man on the street; another presidential candidate was affectionately known as El Indio; and such un-Spanish names as Ravard, Boulton, Ball, Marshall, Burelli, Petkoff, Vollmer, Pietri, Greaves, Lander, and Guden are familiar in Venezuelan economic and political circles.

In a very rough way, we can say that whites predominate in the largest cities of the highlands, blacks and mulattos in the Coastal Lowlands, and pure Indians in the back country near the Colombian and Brazilian frontiers. The end of World War II and especially the Pérez Jiménez years in the 1950s saw an influx of Spanish, Italian, and Portuguese, many of them lured by new economic opportunities and the booming construction industry. In 1981 estimates showed that 6 percent of the population was foreign born. A substantial addition to the population has been the *indocumentados* (literally "undocumented," illegal), Colombian immigrants who have crossed the border in search of better jobs and living conditions.

Less difficult to estimate, and certainly more visible, has been the massive movement of people from rural to urban areas, especially since World War II. This has transformed the country from a rural, sleepy society into a highly urbanized one. In spite of governmental efforts to implement agrarian-reform laws and better conditions in the countryside, this mass movement continues unabated. The 1950 census showed that about 19 percent of native-born Venezuelans lived in a state other than that of their birth. By 1980, conservative estimates put the urban population at 75 percent of the total.

The rapid urbanization has brought increasing pressure to provide adequate services and housing. Schools, medical facilities, and public services have expanded at rates faster than the rate of population increase, but urban housing has not kept pace and this represents a major problem. The high birthrate, coupled with increased life expectancy, has been reflected in the progressive decline in the size of the labor force as a proportion of the total population. Thus, Venezuela's population is so young that more than half are under age eighteen, not unusual in developing and Latin countries. What is unusual is that the government is taking notice not only of the urban housing and economic problems directly attributable to this situation but also of the social and family problems involved. Former President Pérez expressed alarm that 52 percent of the children are born out of wedlock and that a large number of these children are abandoned. To face this problem, Pérez called for family planning, and in this predominantly Catholic country contraceptives are being distributed through public-health centers, and a campaign for responsible parenthood has been launched.

The Catholic Church has not actively opposed a program of family planning. In fact, it has followed a generally moderate course on most issues for a number of years. Some attribute this moderation to the weakness of the Church, for Venezuelans, although overwhelmingly Catholic, are generally indifferent toward all religion. Protestantism has had little success, in spite of a free religious climate. It is estimated that less than 1 percent of the population considers itself Protestant. Protestants have had some of their greatest success in the barrios, which often lack Catholic priests. The Jewish population is estimated at around fifteen thousand and is located mostly in the major cities.

HISTORY TO 1908

Mainland Venezuela was discovered by Columbus on his third voyage in 1498. The Venezuelan region, the first on the South American mainland to be explored by Spain, proved an early disappointment. In spite of the legend of El Dorado, little gold was found. Pearl fisheries enticed some Spaniards, but the fisheries soon became unprofitable and the first settlements were abandoned. A distant dependency of Santo Domingo, after 1550 Venezuela became an unimportant part of Nueva Granada. Black, sulfurous tar oozed from the ground in various sites, but it was gold the Spaniards sought and not tar, the "devil's excrement," which yielded only a few coins when bottled and shipped to Spain as a gout cure. After the conquests of Mexico and Peru, far richer in gold, silver and Indians to be enslaved, Spain had so little faith in Venezuela's prospects that it was willing to "rent" that colony to a German banking house.

This pattern of colonial neglect persisted. Finally, in 1730, a group of Basque merchants were granted an agricultural monopoly in Venezuela. Their Royal Guipuzcoa Company was an unexpected success. The production of tobacco, cacao, sugar, and indigo was vastly expanded. Black slaves had to be imported in large numbers. New schools were created, and the University of Caracas dates from this period.

The increased economic and cultural pace entailed new tensions. During the long years of neglect, Venezuelans had for the most part run their own affairs. With the advent of the Guipuzcoa, Venezuelans were confronted with hitherto unknown regulations and competition. Resentment festered, and in 1749 an abortive revolt against the Spanish governor was led by a *criollo*. The revolt was suppressed in 1752, but the fact that it had occurred and the extent of its popular support led to a number of reforms. These reforms limited the freedom of the Guipuzcoa Company, and in a few more years it failed. The colony was authorized free trade with other Spanish possessions—the last colony to obtain this privilege. Actually, free trade was received with mixed emotions—landowners rejoiced because their products would now have a bigger market, but some merchants feared the increased competition and decreased profits free trade would bring. Both groups felt complete domination by Spain in their everyday affairs.

Independence itself had as its immediate cause the international events occurring in Europe. With the 1808 invasion of Spain by Napoleon Bonaparte and the subsequent usurpation of the throne by his brother Joseph, events were set in motion that soon made obvious the weakness of the "legitimate" Spanish crown. Venezuela and Argentina were the first to claim the right to govern themselves in the absence of a legitimate authority in Spain.

Venezuelans are proud that they were among the first in Latin America to declare independence, in 1810, and that during the long wars that followed they furnished some of the most outstanding leaders in the struggle. Indeed, Venezuelans claim a rich heritage—most of their heroes battled not only for the freedom of Venezuela but for the freedom of all South America. This sense of pride in the nation's heritage has given

Venezuelans, throughout their sometimes chaotic history, a common bond and mystique, which has helped form the nationalistic cement of a genuine, integrated nation-state.

The Wars of Independence cost the country dearly, and such natural disasters as the 1812 cataclysmic earthquake cost the lives of one-fourth of the population. On July 5, 1811, seven eastern provinces promulgated a constitution that provided for a federal government, a recognition of the strong attachment to regionalism. The three western provinces remained aloof. Above and beyond regional differences were those of race and class. Not only were the lower classes of mulattos, blacks, and mestizos—the majority of the population—against the new regime devised and controlled by rich, well-educated, white *criollos*, but the *criollos* themselves were bitterly divided between royalists and rebels. The Church was likewise split, and independence soon degenerated into civil war. The struggle went on for nearly a decade.

The Battle of Carabobo in 1821 marked the end of the protracted struggle, but by then the idealism of Simón Bolívar, Venezuela's greatest national hero, had become only that—an ideal. Bolívar's vision of a Gran Colombian confederation, encompassing not only Venezuela but Ecuador and Colombia as well, soon lay shattered beyond repair. This untenable arrangement lasted until 1830, the year of Bolívar's death, when the Venezuelan popular hero—mestizo general José Antonio Páez—took Venezuela out of the confederation. The new constitution proclaimed that same year marked the beginning of a truly independent Venezuela.

For the next sixteen years, Páez controlled political life as president or president maker. His main support came from the fierce *llaneros*, who had rallied for the independence battles under the war cry "Death to the wealthy and the whites." For these *llaneros* independence meant a war between classes and a search for social justice. Páez, once he became president, gained the support of the conservative oligarchy. For one who had gained the loyalty of his men under the banner of class war and social justice, this abandonment of his earlier position and his new friendship with the privileged classes he had promised to vanquish created new disaffections. Not surprisingly, at least five major rebellions took place against Páez.

But this semiliterate man of the plains gave Venezuela better government than it would experience for nearly a century. He sought to reform the tax structure, rebuild the economy, stimulate agriculture, attract foreign investments, create a governmental bureaucracy. Schools were built, some slaves freed.

A series of more or less corrupt strong men and wealthy autocrats followed Páez. Brief periods of anarchy and chaos were followed by longer periods of authoritarian rule by strong men, or caudillos. The best known of these, Antonio Guzmán Blanco, remained in power from 1870 to 1888. With intellectual and messianic pretensions, he liked to be called The Illustrious American and The Regenerator of Venezuela.

Guzmán Blanco presided over a period of anticlericalism, and he took great pride and pleasure in persecuting the Catholic Church, threatening to create a national Venezuelan Church, and closing monasteries and churches. After Guzmán Blanco another series of minor figures emerged, enriched themselves, and were thrown out of office by other greedy men. This phase of caudillo politics was brought to a close by that powerful and enduring strong man, Juan Vicente Gómez, who ruled with near absolute power for almost thirty years. He came to power in 1908 and died peacefully in bed in 1935.

MODERN POLITICAL HISTORY AND THE EMERGENCE OF NEW POLITICAL GROUPS

Though oppressive and traditional, Gómez's rule marked the beginning of the emergence of a more modern Venezuela. In contrast to previous caudillos, Gómez strove to rule effectively over all Venezuela and emerged as the *national* caudillo. As power was increasingly centralized, Caracas became in deed, as well as in name, the capital of the country. Gómez made an early decision to fashion a modern national army that would be more loyal and efficient than the previous ragtag bands of local chieftains and personal bodyguards that had surrounded former presidents. All opposition was silenced, but the intermittent terror wielded by bandits and scores of strong men in the incipient civil wars that had plagued Venezuela for nearly a century was no longer experienced. Terror continued to exist, but like all else it emanated from Caracas and not from the provinces.

Gómez became an embodiment of the legendary Latin dictator: Venezuela was his personal possession, and he strove to make it prosper because he, too, would prosper even more in the process. El Benemérito ("the well-deserving") was the center and the only real power behind all Venezuelan events for nearly three decades. His well-trained and loyal army and an efficient spy system kept opposition at a minimum. Political parties disappeared, and all branches of the government became arms of the federal government, that is, Gómez. A semiliterate *andino*, Gómez was extremely cunning in his use of other ambitious men and even of the few Venezuelan intellectuals. Potential rivals were isolated, made utterly dependent on him, and, if recalcitrant, "disappeared." Intellectuals were flattered when Gómez called on their talents, and one of the most brilliant of his collaborators, Laureano Vallenílla Lanz, wrote a classic work, *Ceasarismo Democrático*, in which he applied social Darwinism to Venezuelan history. As a result of the factors of race, climate, and Hispanic culture, he said, Venezuelan society was inherently unstable and unsuitable for representative democracy. By the process of natural selection, the strongest emerged to become the necessary dictators. Gómez—and everybody else—saw Vallenílla Lanz's conclusions as a justification and/or an apology for authoritarian rule.

During the early years, Gómez presided over the country as a master over his hacienda, in almost classic patrimonialist fashion, disposing of his subjects' lives and fortunes, as well as the national wealth, with nearly absolute authority. But oil exploration, which got into full swing in the 1920s, began to change the whole pattern of life. Low taxes and wages, oil, and the enforced order attracted much foreign capital. The economic boom accelerated, with social and political ramifications that would soon undermine the system on which dictatorial regimes like Gómez's depended.

From the Maracaibo Basin, oil revenues poured into the treasury at the "center" and into the pockets of Gómez, his cronies and family, his army and bureaucracy, and eventually even into the pockets of those not directly linked to the dictator. The profits were enormous. Gómez and his supporters became extremely rich, but the flood of money also benefited the economy as a whole. A chronic debtor nation, Venezuela became solvent, and its currency, the bolívar, long a source of jokes, became a respected strong coin in international markets. Oil created a powerful new industry directly and a myriad of others indirectly. It stimulated urbanization, gave rise to a paid laboring class, and accelerated the emergence of a middle class.

The rate of Venezuela's economic growth has been phenomenal, so much so that a respected social scientist remarked that "in the history of the entire Western world there has been no similar experience."[1] In the early 1920s, when the process began, Venezuela was one of the poorest, most backward, and most isolated countries in Latin America. Its social structure was traditional and relatively simple; the economy was almost completely agricultural. A small ruling group of agrarian property owners controlled the exports, provided the governing personnel, accepted the protection granted it by the current dictator and his friends, and at the same time helped prop up the regime.

Oil changed the pattern of life and of the economy. Agriculture declined; abundant money was available to import foodstuffs and even luxuries. Peasants migrated to the cities: Caracas quintupled in size, and Maracaibo became a bustling cosmopolitan center. The landed aristocracy was replaced by industrialists, both native and foreign. A new generation began to show little patience with the old ways and even less respect for the aging dictator.

By the end of the 1920s, university students and intellectuals became openly critical of the rampant nepotism, corruption, and pervasive repression. In 1928 students at the Central University in Caracas began to agitate for an end of the dictatorship and for political freedom. A student strike was called. Because the students had managed to gain some support among the people, including some elite elements, the government's response was less harsh than it might otherwise have been. The university was closed and some students were sent to jail, but others were allowed to go into exile. Among those arrested were

Rómulo Betancourt, Raúl Leoni, Jóvito Villalba, and a host of others who came to play a prominent role in politics for years to come. The students' rebellion of 1928 is taken as the year in which the Venezuelan social revolution began.

The death of Gómez in 1935 signaled the emergence of a number of underground political leaders. In spite of his identification as a Gómez man, Gen. Eleazar López Contreras, the new president, allowed parties to be organized, permitted a measure of debate, and initiated a series of programs aimed at improving the living conditions of the majority of the population. Gen. Isaías Medina Angarita, who followed, broke even more sharply with the past. He was deeply influenced by reformist currents and the general liberalizing trends ushered in during World War II. Some economic reforms were undertaken, and a vigorous political opposition was permitted. Betancourt, Villalba, and even the Communists had a chance to form political groupings, and the president himself saw the need to build up popular political support. Acción Democrática (AD), Betancourt's party, organized a large political machine encompassing members of the middle class, students, intellectuals, workers, and peasants.

Just as López Contreras had chosen Medina Angarita as his successor, the latter now prepared to impose his choice. But this time, with active opposition parties and with López Contreras himself wanting to return to the presidency, the outcome of the scheduled 1945 elections was in doubt. Medina's first choice suffered a breakdown, López Contreras's friends were incensed, and the whole political scene was in disarray.

Acción Democrática accepted the invitation of a group of young army officers to participate in a coup against the Medina government. These officers were unhappy with the turn of events and their meager chances for advancement as long as the entrenched old guard and *andino* oligarchy dominated the services. Once these military officers were on the Acción Democrática bandwagon, the days of Medina were numbered. The revolution of 1945 came about through an alliance of hitherto contradictory elements—leftist political leaders with a large poor and middle-class following, intellectuals, and impatient young officers.

Following the Medina overthrow, Betancourt became the president of the governing junta, made up mostly of AD members, two officers, and one "independent." For the next three years, the conservative elite continued to be unalterably opposed to AD's moves and policies, which it interpreted as being directed toward undermining their privileged status.

AD undertook a massive politicization campaign aimed at organizing workers and peasants. For all practical purposes, the new peasant and worker unions were arms of AD, but at the same time AD sought to advance not only its own goals but also those of Venezuelan working people through the implementation of legislation directly beneficial to the less-privileged classes. A new constitution, with many provisions for human and social rights, was drafted, and since AD was sure of its popular support, the new basic law called for direct elections. Acción Democrática selected distinguished novelist Rómulo Gallegos as its candidate and he was overwhelmingly elected, but his tenure was to last less than a year. Lacking Betancourt's political skills, Gallegos soon found himself embroiled in controversy and at odds with the military. When Gallegos reduced the number of military officers in his cabinet, advocated a reduction in the size and budget of the military, and hinted at the possible formation of popular militias, the military could not wait any longer. When AD called a general strike to show its support for Gallegos, the military staged a coup. Accusing the government of disrupting the social and economic life, incompetence, collusion with subversives, and corruption, the same military leaders who had ushered in the AD *trienio* closed it in 1948.

For the next ten years, Venezuela was dominated by the military, most specifically by Marcos Pérez Jiménez. Acción Democrática and one of the Communist factions went underground. When controlled elections were permitted in 1952, the early tabulations showed the Republican Democratic Union (URD) candidate Jóvito Villalba, with AD's support, as the clear winner over Pérez Jiménez. The counting was stopped, emergency conferences among military leaders were held, and Pérez Jiménez declared himself president. He remained in office until January 1958.

During those ten years, Pérez Jiménez surrounded himself with a small group of loyal men, developed a modern and extensive secret police system, and was not above using the country's large oil revenues for his and his friends' private gain. Because he presided over a regime of "law and order" and outlawed one of the Communist parties, and also because, with its large oil potential and huge U.S. investments, Venezuela was a strategically and economically important country, the U.S. government supported Pérez for most of this period. The majority of Venezuelans grew disenchanted with the dictator, but they were keenly aware of his U.S. support. Many were dismayed when the United States conferred the Legion of Merit award on their unpopular dictator. Shortly after Peréz fell, Vice President Nixon visited Caracas. His motorcade was set upon by mobs, and he had reason to fear for his life.

During the Pérez Jiménez decade, general prosperity prevailed as superhighways and huge construction projects were undertaken. To help in the construction, Pérez Jiménez facilitated the large-scale immigration of Europeans and thus further exacerbated the enmity of labor toward him, especially after labor had experienced a position of privilege during the AD years. The Church became increasingly vocal in its denunciation of the regime. Students were involved in the opposition underground and became more hostile after the closing of the central university. Peasants, who had made significant gains and become organized during the AD period, were again relegated to the traditional position of neglect by the government. A cross section of Venezuelans were incensed by the fact that the dictator seemed to favor foreign enterprises over national ones. Nearly everybody resented the predominance of military elements and the use of government funds for private gain. Within the military itself, some officers began to feel uncomfortable with the whole tone of corruption and resentful that the bad reputation of Pérez Jiménez was reflecting on them also. They resented even further the fact that the secret police seemed to get more of the spoils and the power than they themselves did.

This was the situation at the end of 1957, when the dictator decided to bypass his own constitution's electoral requirements and call for a plebiscite. The people were called to vote either yes or no for a continuation of his administration for the next five years. The vote came in "yes," but this brazenly manipulated "election" proved to be the last straw. Weeks of agitation by students and workers, a general strike, and finally support from elements of the armed forces and the business community brought the dictatorship to an end in January 1958.

THE CONTEMPORARY POLITICAL SCENE:
TOWARD A NEW POLITICAL ORDER

Fair and honest elections were held at the end of 1958, and the reform-oriented Betancourt was elected with over a million votes, just short of 50 percent. The URD, whose leader for decades had been Villalba, this time backed Adm. Wolfgang Larrázabal, who had acted as provisional president after Pérez Jiménez's fall. Larrázabal, with unsolicited support from the Communists, came in second, and Rafael Caldera, the Social Christian (COPEI) candidate, received a disappointing vote of less than 15 percent. The balance was divided up among a number of small parties.

Since 1958 AD, COPEI, and URD have remained the largest and most durable parties, although URD membership has steadily decreased and other parties have emerged. Without question Venezuela has one of the broadest-based electorates anywhere—close to 40 percent of the total population. All Venezuelans eighteen years of age or older have the right to vote, regardless of literacy, sex, or property. The only limitation is the denial of the right to vote to those subject to prison sentences that carry the loss of political rights and to personnel of the armed forces on active duty. Voting is a right and also a compulsory duty for eligible voters.

The democratic spirit prevailing since 1958 is a distinct break with the past. Other than earlier, short-lived attempts, the Betancourt administration represented the first determined and continuing effort toward solving the country's problems in the context of a representative democratic system. From that time to the present, Venezuelan history has been characterized by the effort to bring more and more people into the economic and political life of the nation, by implementing goals implied in an ideology devoted to development *and* social justice, and by the conviction on the part of the government and governed alike that at long last Venezuela is on the threshold of putting its great reserves of natural resources and its vast potential to work for the benefit of the nation as a whole. Betancourt's major accomplishment was that he not only survived the crosscurrents of opposition to his rule—both from within and from without—but that he also succeeded in carrying out a wide range of democratizing and development programs.

Betancourt was one of the ablest and most skilled politicians ever to come to power in Latin America, and he personified a neat blend of the old and new caudillo traditions. His capacity for charisma, personal leadership, and assertion of his own power placed him in the mold of a traditional caudillo, but the way he exerted these characteristics placed him among the most effective democratic leaders. His mastery of reducing complex problems to simple, understandable language, his gift of iden-tification with the common person, and his brilliant organizational strategies in building up a mass political party that cut across ideologies and classes made him a caudillo attuned to new, democratizing currents. He worked through and with the emerging "brokerage" groups—the political parties, the labor unions, the armed forces, the ever more powerful entrepreneurial groups and peak organizations, even the Cath-olic Church. He persuaded his own AD party to work in a necessary coalition with other parties, most prominently the COPEI. He shrewdly handled the military—on the one hand, they continued to receive the accustomed favors and perquisites and were allowed leeway to combat "subversives," while on the other hand, he made sure they accepted his preeminence as their ultimate boss.

Betancourt was equally successful in isolating and discrediting the Communists and the Fidelistas, and his popularity with the peasants made them hostile to guerrillas. The costs were at times high—recalcitrant congressmen were stripped of their rights when Betancourt became convinced they were linked to subversion, demonstrations were broken up, student leaders imprisoned. Betancourt took Fidel Castro's subversive attempts against his government to the Organization of American States and liked to boast that he, perhaps even more than the Americans, had isolated Cuba from inter-American councils and trade links. But to show that he was concerned with *all* types of subversion and all types of undemocratic regimes, he launched the so-called Betancourt Doctrine, which denied Venezuelan recognition to *any* regime that had come to power by force and not by elections.

Raúl Leoni, elected in 1963 by a much smaller percentage than his eminent predecessor, was able to consolidate and implement much that had still remained in the planning stage under Betancourt. This was possible, at least in part, because he could govern with far fewer attempts at subversion and violent confrontation. The economy was booming again, and by now AD's programs had acquired considerable legitimacy. Social welfare, industrialization, agrarian reform, education, transportation, and a variety of other social and development programs continued to be stressed, and in most of these policy areas more was accomplished quietly during Leoni's term of office than had been possible under Betancourt.

With the radical left isolated and the guerrillas unable to gain a base in the countryside, restrictions on political activities relaxed. But personal and ideological differences racked the high command of Acción Democrática, and the party split before the 1968 elections. The presidential victory went to the COPEI candidate, university professor and lawyer-sociologist Rafael Caldera.

To Leoni's credit, the elections went off peacefully, and the opposition was allowed to succeed to power. Caldera, for the fourth time the candidate of the Social Christians and an articulate ideologist who had been involved in politics since his student days, presided over a government that was not unlike its predecessor. Agrarian reform, social and welfare services, expansion and diversification of industry, further steps toward the nationalization of the petroleum industry, and negotiations over regional arrangements within South America occupied Caldera as they had Leoni and Betancourt. In spite of these common denominators, Caldera was almost from the beginning faced with the hostility of an opposition-dominated Congress that sought to embarrass and slow down the president's initiatives. Coalitions were shaky, and only through much compromise and his adept use of his popularity and the media was Caldera able to govern for the next five years.

In foreign relations, Caldera continued the inconclusive negotiations with Colombia over the problems of *indocumentados* and border disputes with Colombia and Guyana. The Betancourt Doctrine was laid aside, and Caldera sought a "positive" foreign policy that, instead of isolating undemocratic regimes, sought through cooperative relations to make them less likely to emerge in the first place.[2]

Caldera's party suffered a painful blow when the socialist Allende was overthrown in Chile in 1973. President Allende had been preceded by Frei, like Caldera a long-time Social Christian. To some Venezuelans it seemed as though Frei's tenure had opened the door to the "Communist" Allende, with the inevitable consequence of the armed forces taking over the government. This fear was cleverly exploited by Acción Democrática as new elections approached. AD was further aided by the fact that this time it was united and that many who had earlier abandoned it were back in the fold. Betancourt campaigned effectively for his longtime protégé, Andrés Pérez, who proved a formidable and indefatigable campaigner. Unlike COPEI's Lorenzo Fernández, Andrés Pérez was at ease with shantytown dwellers and peasants, and although he did not have a university degree, he had a sharp mind and an effective campaign style.

When the 1973 voting was over, Andrés Pérez had received 48.77 percent of the votes; Lorenzo Fernández, 36.74 percent. Jesús Angel Paz Galarraga of the Nueva Fuerza party, with some Communist support, came in with 5.09 percent of the total. José Vicente Rangel of the Movimiento al Socialismo–Movimiento de Izquierda Revolucionaria (MAS-MIR), with the support of some defectors of the Venezuela Communist party (PCV) and other defectors from the AD, received 4.21 percent. Old-time political leader Jóvito Villalba received 3.05 percent. Not only did Andres Pérez far outdistance his opponents, but his party captured an absolute majority in both houses of Congress.

The administration of Andrés Pérez will probably be best remembered for its successful nationalization of the iron and the petroleum industries. However, in the short run it became tarnished in the eyes of many Venezuelans who perceived a lack of probity and of even simple technical competence among many who had been appointed by the president to run the vast state economic machine. Many were also less than sanguine about Andrés Pérez's penchant for the grandiose gesture and his liberal aid to Caribbean countries when Venezuela itself was beginning to feel the predictable pinch generated by lessened oil revenues.

Luís Herrera Campíns, the 1978 COPEI candidate, capitalized on the popular disenchantment and won the presidency with 46 percent of the vote. His victory was further consolidated when his party won 50 percent of the votes in the 1979 municipal elections. But Herrera Campíns himself was to fall victim to the people's disenchantment even faster than his predecessor. In spite of his easygoing manner and good nature, his administration was politically bland and economically disastrous. The failure of the huge Workers' Bank seemed to be symptomatic of the president's inability to act swiftly to shore up one of the government's own agencies.

The Venezuela elections of 1983 resulted in a landslide for Acción Democrática. Jaime Lusinchi won the presidency with 56.8 percent of the valid votes cast. Former President Caldera, although still admired and respected, was unable to disassociate himself from COPEI's bungling administration. He managed to receive 29 percent of the vote. In addition, Acción Democrática won just under two-thirds of the senate seats and nearly a three-to-two majority of deputies over all opposition parties combined, as well as control of the legislatures of every state and territory except one. AD won every Caracas precinct. To this should be added the governorships, which are filled by the president.

Almost as striking as the dimensions of the AD triumph is the moribund state of the left in Venezuela. AD and COPEI together obtained 78.6 percent of the valid votes for the legislature, and their presidential candidates received 91.3 percent of the total. MAS won 5.7 percent of the legislative vote; MIR (separated from MAS in 1983) received less than 1.6 percent; the PCV garnered only 1.7 percent. Other minor parties fared worse.

Lusinchi's impressive victory should give him the necessary mandate to reorganize the discredited bureaucracy and the weakened economy. The latter task is likely to demand most of the new president's energies; restoring confidence at home and abroad in the basic soundness of the Venezuelan economy may be a far more difficult task than obtaining an electoral mandate. Until 1980, petroleum had been the primary mechanism for creating surplus revenues that could be disbursed as social programs. With both the price and the quantity of petroleum declining, Venezuelans are faced with the unaccustomed need for controls and restricted government programs. At the same time, because the government has always been so deeply involved in the economy, any default by a big or a small state enterprise means that the whole investment worthiness of the country is affected.

There are studies by the Venezuelan government itself that predict the possibility of a prolonged recession or depression beginning in 1980 and lasting from four to fifteen years before a full recovery. These same studies show that the key to recovery is the trade-off between consumption and investment for both public and private sectors. The fact that Venezuela is viewed as a stable, moderately developed capitalist democracy, as well as the usual expectation that a richly endowed country such as Venezuela should be able to work itself out of an economic morass, should help the possibility of keeping up the new traditional political consensus.

PARTIES, POLITICS, AND PUBLIC POLICY: NEW TRADITIONS AND PROSPECTS

AD and COPEI share the vision of a democratic, development-oriented society in which the state plays a major direct and indirect role. By "state," in Venezuela one means the national government and preeminently the executive, because state and local units of government have meager powers. State governors are appointed by the president and may be removed by him, and the judicial power is equally national in scope. With this much power in the hands of the executive, it is surprising that it has been used with considerable moderation by six elected presidents. One explanation is that the large political parties have shared a generally reformist orientation and that politically powerful groups such as industry and commerce, labor, the military, and the bureaucracy have not sought (or, cynics may say, been able) to monopolize for themselves alone the spoils of this rich nation. Each of the recent presidents has owed his victory to a cross section of societal groups, which has enabled him to pursue policies that are not always those most desired by each of these groups.

Finally, the consensus on national goals that has been achieved among the major parties goes a long way toward explaining the failure of the Communists as well as of the extreme right to exercise any more influence than they have in recent years. AD and COPEI have successfully articulated a democratic, development-oriented social program in such ways as to occupy the broad middle of the road in the Venezuelan political system.

The Venezuelan consensus and the political party system as a whole lie considerably farther left than would be the case in older and more established nations of North America and West Europe. Thus, the two largest parties, AD and COPEI, both considered basically democratic-left but occupying the middle of the Venezuelan party spectrum, would in the U.S. context probably be labeled socialist or social democratic. Both parties have always had a strong youth sector, which has, almost without exception, been farther left than the overall party ideology and thus more vocal in its demands for greater state control of the economy, income redistribution, nationalization of key industries, and so forth.

Until now, Venezuela's democratic environment has permitted a high degree of participation and competition. Even the isolated farmer and the marginalized rancho dweller have been able to exert pressure and generally to obtain some response to their most pressing demands. This is because every party has realized the intrinsic value of each vote and, given the openness and competition of the system, that one of the few ways of assuring a vote is to provide a service or at least a hearing.

Going beyond these links between local *político* and individual, the groups that are most important in the policymaking process in Venezuela include the parties, the armed forces, the industrialists, the bureaucracy, labor, and the new urban middle class; of perhaps lesser importance (but not so much as to be ignored) are the Catholic Church, the peasants, and the university students. Although all these groups have their own interests to protect, they also, for the most part, share the values of a democratic, development-oriented society. Venezuela has not deeply fragmented and polarized the way other Latin American countries have. Instead its major groups have generally been brought in or come to share the national consensus. Again it is the political parties—and prosperity—that have served as the agents of this remarkable trans-formation.

So far the Venezuelan political system has been able to blunt the major challenges and to answer, in the form of expanded services, the demands of its people. Unlike the situation found in many Latin American countries, the Venezuelan political system has been fairly stable, durable, and relatively free of the worst excesses of *personalismo*. Many small political parties have appeared sporadically on the political scene, forming at election time and folding or merging with other groupings shortly thereafter. The system of proportional representation has helped the proliferation of small parties, but the steeply escalating costs of the political campaigns are now discouraging the emergence of many new parties. AD and COPEI have proved more durable, retaining their followings over the course of the years, and so far have been able to

survive divisive internal splits, persecution by the Pérez Jiménez dictatorship, and more recently the challenges of both Fidelista and other
revolutionary groups and intermittent efforts on behalf of Pérez Jiménez.

AD and COPEI, which have been in existence for the longest time
as major parties, have extensive and dynamic organizational networks
throughout the country. They operate basically within a liberal-democratic
framework but there is something of a corporatist influence also. By
having special "sectors" for each particular group in the society and
by incorporating these diverse elements into their party ranks, they have
proved to be unifying and integrating forces in the community. These
corporate sectors are often tied in closely with government agencies..
This has enabled them to absorb and assimilate a variety of viewpoints,
to provide access to government decision making, and to maintain an
openness to new and fresh ideas and people.

Thus, for example, the labor unions; such professional groups as
doctors, teachers, and engineers; the youth (even as far down as high
schools and junior high schools); the industrialists; the peasants; the
landholders; and many others all have their own party unit within
which they can work that, in turn, forms a portion of the greater party
whole. Each sector has its own interests that it seeks to articulate and
present; at the same time, each unit provides opportunities for its
members in partisan and leadership activities. When a law or policy is
being considered or when a position is to be filled, those affected by
it are consulted so they too have a chance for participation and say in
policy implementation. There is a great deal of two-way flow and
interaction between the society at large—represented by these various
groups—and the parties. The parties, in turn, are bound up with the
government and serve as transmission belts to it. They help articulate
issues; bring them to the attention of the national leadership in the
executive, in the Congress, and at the local levels; and, finally, help
people and carry out the policies that emanate from the government.

In the realm of public policy enactment and implementation, Venezuela
has made some of its most significant advances. The Venezuelan government has not only demonstrated an awareness of such issue areas
as agrarian reform, economic development, education, health, family
planning, and industrial diversification, but it has organized itself to do
something about them. It has sought to discuss these issues intelligently
and openly, to relate them to the needs of the country and its people,
to devise programs for carrying out its ambitious development goals,
and to utilize new as well as existing institutions in implementing these
policies.

A case in point is the way Venezuela undertook the nationalization
of its most important industry. Almost from the earliest stages of oil
exploration in the 1920s, the government was aware of the need to
keep tabs on the multinational companies in order to make sure that
Venezuela would receive a fair share of the profits upon which so much

of its development depended. For a long time, the government had to take the multinationals' statements on faith because it had neither the resources nor the trained personnel to develop its own methods of assessment. Beginning in the 1940s, a determined effort was made to evolve a concession system that would give the government a greater measure of control.

Slowly but steadily new controls were placed in effect. During the AD *trienio* of 1945–1948, under the able leadership of Minister of Development Juan Pablo Pérez Alfonso, one of the most outspoken critics of the oil policy of previous years, profits were declared to belong to Venezuela on a fifty-fifty basis, a revolutionary concept at the time and one eagerly copied by other producing countries. The cozy *modus vivendi* between the multinationals and the Pérez Jiménez dictatorship made them more vulnerable to criticism once the democratic Betancourt government came into power in 1959. The Venezuelans were not deaf to appeals of nationalism and the feeling that the multinationals, while obeying the letter of the law, had violated the spirit of the regulations. AD and COPEI usually worked in concert in fashioning new controls: more taxes, the creation of a national petroleum company, and a variety of other schemes. Pérez Alfonso lobbied with other producers and managed to bring them around to his idea of OPEC, an organization that would emulate the system of Venezuelan controls but at the international level and that would bring a further measure of "order" to the international market and "profits" to the individual countries. Also, in Venezuela itself, private entrepreneurs no longer felt kinship with foreign oilmen, whom they now viewed with growing suspicion after the bitter experience in which they had joined with multinationals to oppose new taxes, only to be left stranded, with their taxes increased, when the companies negotiated a separate and less onerous arrangement with the government.

After the oil crisis of the early 1970s, the accommodation of the oil companies' threats was no longer seriously contemplated. At the same time, the government engaged the public in a purposeful and long educational campaign on the merits of a variety of nationalization plans. The national debate preceding nationalization involved the various political sectors, the professional middle class, labor, academia, and the oil technocrats themselves. This dialogue between the government and the public enabled Andrés Pérez to proclaim the January 1, 1976, nationalization decree as the outcome of a wide-ranging consensus.

Once Venezuela had nationalized its $5 billion oil industry, the process of Venezuelanization went on—smoothly at first, but increasingly subjected to political interference. The multinationals, which had for years been sharing their skills and even some management with Venezuelans, adjusted fairly well to the new regime. At the time of the nationalization, the industry's twenty-three thousand workers were ready to handle their jobs without the foreigners. Venezuela agreed to fair compensation settlements, and the multinationals, under contract, continued to participate in several technical aspects of the industry.

To manage the nationalized enterprise, the government tapped retired army general Alfonso Ravard, an able administrator who had proved his skills as the developer of the Guayana industrial complex and who enjoyed good working relationships with the private and public sectors and with the military. Petróleos de Venezuela (PDVSA) became the holding company that supervised the activities of an already extensively structured oil sector. Fourteen nationalized concerns replaced some forty foreign companies; eventually these were consolidated into four major companies.

Although the nationalization scheme worked surprisingly well initially, it was almost inevitable that it would become increasingly a prey to issues more political than purely technical. In the words of Coronel, who was initimately involved in the industry, "before [,] the oil industry had been a rather isolated sector, going its own way without being an integral part of Venezuelan life. Now it was part of it, and everyone in the country suddenly felt that they had a voice on how it should be run."[3] Among the voices that eventually prevailed were those that insisted that funds previously earmarked for the strengthening and modernizing of the oil industry were now to be used for expanded social services, for other sectors of the economy, and even for the bailing out of mismanaged state enterprises.

Whether this shift represents a definitive and permanent reorientation of the nationalized industry remains to be seen. However, even those who are critical of the shift do not deny that it is an expected feature of an open and democratic system. In fact, if this shift results in a more effective "sowing of the petroleum" than has occurred to date, it may pave the way for bridging the huge income gap, for providing more services to all Venezuelans, and for reenergizing the whole economy of the country. Thus, a convergence of political decisions, abundant resources, and capable and imaginative human resources may help cement Venezuela's commitment to democratic developmentalism.

The short-term prospects are not, however, without problems. Venezuela has not resolved its debt problem. For nationalistic as well as political reasons, it has insisted on not accepting various plans put forward by the international banking community. At the same time, the transition from Herrera Campíns to Lusinchi provided the opportunity for a euphoria that had been absent in Caracas for most of the previous five years. Furthermore, Venezuela in 1984 celebrated twenty-five years of democracy, a proud reminder to all that the turbulent era of coups had been left safely behind. Finally, the new president had taken over the political and economic reins with an impressive electoral mandate and much experience. If Lusinchi can effectively use all these assets to keep labor's demands in check and to reassure the international community that Venezuela remains an attractive investment haven in Latin America, then the short-term prospects will brighten considerably.

In any case, the overall picture of the last quarter century gives cause for guarded optimism. Venezuela has been fortunate in that it has had the resources, both material and human, to move ahead, to foster a sense of pride and involvement among its citizens, and to pursue a nationalistic but not xenophobic foreign and economic policy. Its riches have assured the wherewithal to pursue ambitious programs and imaginative goals. Its political leadership, seasoned by years in exile and in the give-and-take of national politics, has been uncommonly willing to work in coalitions and to grant legitimacy to those who have been chosen in broadly based and honest elections. For nearly thirty years, major problems and ambitious programs have been pursued and handled within a democratic context. Although the cult of the individual leader— a Betancourt, a Caldera, for example—is by no means dead, and each party stresses that its own position is distinct from all others, there has been room for compromise and a faith that the political system is open enough that even the losers will be granted another chance within a constitutionally prescribed electoral calendar. It may be that Venezuela, at long last, has found its true El Dorado: the physical, human, and political resources to achieve Bolívar's great dream of national integration.

NOTES

1. Jorge Ahumada, "Hypotheses for the Diagnosis of a Situation of Social Change: The Case of Venezuela," in *Studying the Venezuelan Polity,* ed. Frank Bonilla and José A. Silva Michelena (Center for International Studies, MIT Press, Cambridge, Mass., 1966), p. 34.

2. Rafael Caldera, *El Bloque Latinoamericano* (Oficina Central de Información, Caracas, 1970), p. 166.

3. Gustavo Coronel, *The Nationalization of the Venezuelan Oil Industry* (Lexington Books, Lexington, Mass., 1983), p. 121.

SUGGESTIONS FOR FURTHER READING

Alexander, Robert J. *The Venezuelan Democratic Revolution.* Rutgers University Press, New Brunswick, N.J., 1964.

Arnove, Robert F. *Student Alienation: A Venezuelan Study.* Praeger, New York, 1971.

Betancourt, Rómulo. *Venezuela: Oil and Politics.* Houghton Mifflin, Boston, 1979.

Blank, David Eugene. *Politics in Venezuela.* Little, Brown, Boston, 1973.

Blutstein, Howard I., et al. *Area Handbook for Venezuela.* Government Printing Office, Washington, D.C., 1977.

Bonilla, Frank, and José A. Silva Michelena, eds. *A Strategy for Research on Social Policy.* Vol. 1 of *The Politics of Change in Venezuela* (3 vols.). MIT Press, Cambridge, Mass., 1967.

Coronel, Gustavo. *The Nationalization of the Venezuelan Oil Industry.* Lexington Books, Lexington, Mass., 1983.

Levine, Daniel H. *Conflict and Political Change in Venezuela.* Princeton University Press, Princeton, N.J., 1973.

Lombardi, John V. *Venezuela: The Search for Order, the Dream of Progress.* Oxford University Press, New York, 1982.

Martz, John D., and David J. Meyers, eds. *Venezuela: The Democratic Experience.* Praeger, New York, 1977.

Powell, John D. *Political Mobilization of the Venezuelan Peasant.* Harvard University Press, Cambridge, 1971.

Ray, Talton F. *The Politics of the Barrios in Venezuela.* University of California Press, Berkeley, 1969.

Taylor, Philip B., Jr., ed. *Venezuela: 1969.* University of Houston, Office of International Affairs, Houston, 1971.

14
Uruguay:
The Costs of Inept
Political Corporatism

PHILIP B. TAYLOR, JR.

Uruguay is the smallest Spanish-speaking country of South America, in both area and population. It was considered by Latin Americans and outside observers for nearly half a century to be the most democratic, progressive, and constitution-observing state of the entire region. Its people were, as late as the early 1950s, on the average among the most comfortable in the world. And its society had developed a tone of felicity and mutual confidence seldom seen in any part of the world. To be a Uruguayan was to be privileged; *"como Uruguay no hay"* ("there is none like Uruguay") was less boast than statement of fact. Nationalism did not need to be obvious.

In the 1970s all of this was reversed. At least forty persons are known to have been tortured to death by the authorities since 1972. In April 1983 over two thousand political prisoners were being held, and torture was still in steady use. The private property of dissidents, including former government officials, has been confiscated. Life had become so unrewarding economically that in the thirty-month period ending in November 1974 about 400,000 people had emigrated to Argentina alone, and 41 percent of those remaining in the country replied to pollsters that they also would leave if they had the chance.[1] The country has become a harshly authoritarian, military-fascist regime. Politicians, academicians, and private-opinion leaders have been deprived of political rights, and the constitution has been set aside while substitute institutions have been decreed into being. The president elected in 1970 became a puppet of the armed forces in February 1973. A second civilian puppet served from 1976 to 1981, and in September 1981 Lt. Gen. Gregorio Alvarez, who headed the 1973 *golpe de estado*, retired from active duty and became president.

Uruguay's modernization began about 1870, when neighboring Argentina and Brazil finally ceased meddling in its internal affairs. The

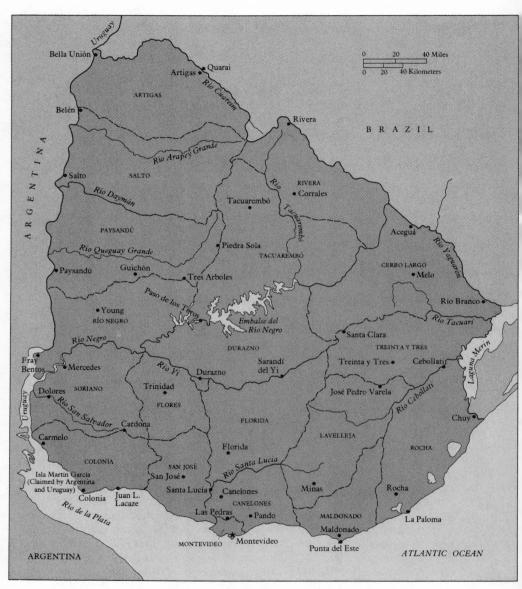

Uruguay

goals of state and nation building were being approached by that time. These goals implied the creation of a single political authority and the establishment of the country's political and cultural identity. Uruguay was essentially a traditionally Iberian society; it was controlled by a landowning oligarchy in this early period.

Massive working-class European immigration began to change the country after 1860. Politics adjusted to the new urban population base, and a commitment to pluralism and to social democracy had begun to appear by 1904, when the last civil war ended. The state began to manage selected segments of the economy. The result ultimately resembled pragmatic socialism, and ideological liberal critics have used this simplistic analogy in assigning blame for the country's economic collapse. In fact this state activity was an expression of inherited corporatist/authoritative tradition from Spain. Since the country's concentrated growth was in the capital, Montevideo, and in its suburbs, the social effect was to create in the short term a relatively undifferentiated substate urban dominance, a nascent bureaucratic and welfare-based professional middle class, and a modified but nevertheless very strong neocorporatist system.

Later political system changes led to enhanced popular political participation and distribution of services and social goods such as education, subsidized or controlled basic food prices, job tenure, and retirement privileges. Beginning in the 1930s these policies were endangered by the passing of the long-term political leader, José Batlle y Ordóñez, who was most responsible for their establishment, and by the effects of the world depression. Under new leaders a "political class" of political brokers emerged; their services in obtaining benefits led to their gradual entrenchment, and the universalized corporate relationship that had been established under Batlle began to break down. Loyalties were created between these broker-politicians and their clients. An almost Byzantine restructuring of the major parties abetted this development. Clientele relationships firmed, and vertical segments within the parties separated from each other. Eventually these relationships rigidified and tended to override loyalty to the nation.

Bureaucratic demands on the economy, coupled with the middle class's ever increasing appetite for imported goods, outran the country's productive capability by the late 1940s. The expansion of services, and especially the availability of generous early retirement opportunities within the enlarging bureaucracy, created disincentives to invest. Uruguay remained a distinctively nontechnological society. This was compounded by severe errors in economic management in the 1950s. When agriculture's export capability fell below the need for foreign-exchange earnings after the Korean War, the economy's decline accelerated. Although this decline was occasionally checked during the 1960s and 1970s, world recession in the 1980s only confirmed the trend.[2]

While these events were occurring, political happenings worsened the country's problems. The aggrandized political class became increasing

self-indulgent. The decision process became unresponsive to client demands, and system efficiency fell notably. Although the average citizen
felt frustrated, the economic elites reacted more vigorously. They had
long felt irritation at the high costs of government and in the 1960s
began to penetrate the political class in order to gain control. By the
1970s they had gained dominance. The voters continued, unperceptively,
to support the parties as well as the overall system, for they had been
socialized to accept appearances with confidence. Stability thus continued
despite growing popular concern and disaffection until the *golpe* of 1973
cut off political freedoms, but by that time state services had lost much
value for the middle class.[3]

The decay and collapse of the system thus became inevitable. Uruguay's
tragedy lies not only in the collapse and the gratuitous violence imposed
by the widely propagandized urban guerrillas, the Tupamaros, but in
the revelation that the continent's most experienced social democracy
was in fact a defective corporate society and that its system characteristics
would preclude finding means to resolve its internal differences and to
discover an acceptable political solution. In 1972 the armed forces were
ordered to destroy the "unmentionable" Tupamaros (even the name of
the group was then censored from the press). The military continued
on to become a suppressive influence in the nation. A return to
constitutionalism is scheduled for May 1, 1985, after a presidential and
plebiscitary election in November 1984, but this will depend on the
wish of the soldiers. In late 1984 the process seemed to be continuing
on schedule.

HISTORICAL BACKGROUND
AND POLITICAL CULTURE

Uruguay is a geographically modest and gentle land. Sixteenth-century
Spanish explorers did not find significant mineral resources, nor did the
area have enough indigenous population to justify an *encomienda* system.
These characteristics have changed very little; persistent search for
minerals has revealed little of marketable value. The population is now
more than 95 percent Caucasian. In 1603 Hernando Arias, governor of
the plata estuary region, released one hundred cattle and one hundred
horses in the Banda Oriental, the eastern shore, to run wild. Occasional
bands of gauchos from Buenos Aires crossed the river to capture these
animals in later years, but there was no permanent Spanish settlement.
Portuguese, with British support, began to smuggle goods into Argentina
from what is now Uruguay in the mid-seventeenth century and in 1680
founded Colonia do Sacramento as a base of operations, opposite Buenos
Aires. Spain responded with an attack, but Montevideo was not built
as a permanent settlement until 1726.

Well into the nineteenth century Uruguay remained a ranching frontier.
It sought independence in 1811, under the leadership of José Gervasio

Artigas, a rancher and regional caudillo. Artigas's efforts were frustrated by the larger power conflict between Spain and Portugal and, later, between Argentina and Brazil as successor states. In 1828 Juan Lavalleja succeeded Artigas and embroiled the neighboring states in unresolvable conflict. Great Britain finally intervened to make Uruguay's independence good. Politics soon centered around the conflicts of two bands—the Nacional or Blanco led by Manuel Oribe, and the Colorado led by Fructuoso Rivera. Although most of the armed struggles between these two groups were in some way related to continuing international pressures, in the later nineteenth century their civil wars were generated by Uruguayan internal concerns. Some of the later fights grew out of resentment at central government efforts to impose national policies in the interior through departmental chiefs or *jefes políticos*. The last civil war between the two bands, which now had become de facto political parties, ended in 1904. In the meantime other interests and influences had made their warfare moot.

From the ranching-gaucho experience come popular and historic values. The pastoral life was harsh, but it bred self-reliance and pride. The diet was freshly killed meat roasted over an open fire and yerba maté drunk bitter from a pipestem gourd. Families and family life were informal. The gaucho was a centaur, an indigent, and a mystic, as well as a democrat, an individualist, and an occasional gangster. He gave little loyalty to institutions, and his fighting was often for personal reasons. He began to disappear in the 1860s as foreign interventions decreased and his life-style was restrained by fences, railroads, and the extension of national law to the interior. Newly established modern ranches introduced more systematic commercial practices as the meat-packing industry was revolutionized by freezing.

The gaucho still lives as a self-conscious theatricality; wealthy Uruguayans often play at being gauchos on their weekends. The gaucho's intense claim for personal liberty commands the popular imagination. Uruguay is the world's largest importer of yerba, and per capita meat consumption is among the highest in the world. The land-distribution pattern reflects the reality of the ranch as the principal primary products–producing sector. The agricultural census of 1956 showed that 7,133 properties (8.01 percent of registered agricultural properties) of 500 or more hectares (1,236 acres) contained 11,829,000 hectares (29,229,459 acres) or 70.59 percent of land used. No land reform or distribution policy has ever been embraced fully by the government, although such a policy was legislated in the 1940s.

As the interior changed the cities grew. Montevideo offered the attractions of a provincial European town and at first did not approach the rural economy in importance. Its architecture and university were modeled on French patterns, and the intellectual environment tended to parallel French thought. By the 1880s the first effects of European investment and management were being felt and a bourgeois class that regarded the Colorado-Blanco warfare as a nuisance was gaining influence. In contrast to Buenos Aires, Montevideo seemed more modest and family oriented. In later years its miles of excellent beaches tended to make personal behavior relatively informal during many months of the year.

Beginning in the 1860s lower- and lower-middle-class immigration began from southern Europe. As early as 1852 the census reported 28 percent of the country's population was foreign born. By 1860 the figure was about 33 percent, and in 1880 it was reported at 40 percent. The majority of immigrants settled in the capital and in neighboring Canelones Department. Many garden farms and orchards appeared, although many newcomers were skilled artisans and industrial workers. Coming from regions already influenced by anarchist and some Marxist thought, they were prepared for class struggle for the rights of labor and for access to the political process. The elites resisted, and bitter strikes in the 1890s were often fought over both issues. Immigrants became a potential clientele for political leaders able to perceive the advantages of worker support. José Batlle y Ordóñez elected to play that role. In doing so he won a principal place in his country's political pantheon. It has been said that subsequent history has displayed "the lengthened shadow" of this man.[4]

Batlle entered Colorado party politics in the 1880s. As the son of a former Colorado president of the republic, he was attuned to partisanship and policy. He attended the university in Montevideo but did not graduate; an eighteen-month period at the University of Paris followed. On his return he plotted unsuccessfully against the military dictatorship of Máximo Santos and then began his rise within party and elective office from a power base implemented by a newspaper, El Día, which he founded. As president in 1903, he led the government to a victory over the Blancos in the civil war of 1904, which ended when the Blanco caudillo Aparacio Saravia was killed. Batlle imposed a benign settlement, allowing Blancos to retain control of some departments in the interior. Ignoring the fact that not all ranchers were Blancos, that party claimed to represent "the gentlemanly, pure-blooded and patrician tradition of Uruguay." It continued, pejoratively, "The Colorados are the party of immigrants."[5] Batlle welcomed the comment; his strategy denied the new urban mass to Luis Alberto de Herrera, who had succeeded Saravia, and Herrera never made up the numerical disadvantage while Batlle lived.

Foreign—principally British—involvement in the Uruguayan capital market was a necessity for Uruguay's growth. Batlle recognized this, although his nationalist sense was offended. He also understood that his political goal of improved working and wage conditions for his clients could not be achieved while large earnings were transmitted abroad. Pragmatically, he organized autonomous state enterprises (entes autónomos) for essential services, sought to exempt them from partisan influence, and required that they earn profits. He thus retained much capital in the country. He expanded the existing welfare and retirement system, for which the first laws had been enacted in the 1830s. He opposed creating sinecures, however, and although civil employee ranks grew the growth was not disproportionate to the country's population or its needs.

Batlle's scheme was pragmatic rather than ideological. Private funds, largely foreign, created banks, export-import houses, shipping firms, agricultural processing firms, railroads, and the elements of social overhead capital; these fell within the approved opportunities. The state was freed to direct its budget surpluses to modernizing such social functions as education, health, and communications. Although his commitments were humanistic, Batlle also believed in ethical values supportive of principled fulfillment of personal and national obligations, and within demarcated areas capital could feel secure. Batlle thus emerged as a skillful and pragmatic politician with unusual philosophical and innovative depths. The success of his policies is shown in the growth of the economy's capital value while services were expanding. By the 1940s a British economist judged that Uruguay shared sixth place in the world in per capita national stock.[6]

Many writers have described a model of Latin America based on a nascent developmental middle class, or sector, with unique values and expectations. The Uruguayan experience resembles this model. It includes commitment to upward mobility through merit, usually acquired through state-supported education; the growth of a commercial, banking, and industrial sector that would create jobs and products; the encouragement of autonomous labor organizations with access to bargaining rights so that labor would seek autonomous political action rather than be captured by a directive political party or a class-deterministic ideology; a demand for equality of civil rights and the possibilities of upward mobility, with implications for both social and political access; a demand for free flow of ideas and information; a demand for legal and political respect for personal and private property; and a demand for constitutional, republican, and democratic institutions of government that would support all of these goals but also remain adaptable to change over time.[7]

All of these goals were achieved by the 1920s. To them was added, by later events, a marked commitment to consumption, with a reduction of commitment to political choice. As late as 1970 at least half of the respondents in Montevideo behavioral surveys considered themselves to be middle class, with all the inference of material possessions and of social and psychological support for the current system. A Uruguayan socialist at that time believed at least 65 percent were middle class in objective terms.[8] Eventually, this introduced rigidity to the system and contributed to its decline.

Batlle's libertarian and populist blueprint, based on state involvement in the economy, has been criticized as enduring and ultimately harmful. The comment greatly oversimplifies. Batlle died in 1929, and the system began to change almost at once, not necessarily for reasons intrinsic to the plan. There was a fundamental change in the nature and intention of leadership, for Batlle's heirs were often not as committed to democratic-constitutional principles as he. The inner balances of his plan were more sophisticated than most observers realized. Batlle built a staunch arrangement; Gabriel Terra, who gained the presidency in 1930, seemed devoted to distorting the system to his own benefit. Terra ruled only briefly, but his distortions, combined with other changes, began the slow collapse of the Batllista system. Yet that collapse took at least forty years to occur.

The world depression of the 1930s and its aftermath changed Uruguay greatly. The economy had been founded on a world-competitive commercial ranch and farm sector, which underwrote other aspects of national growth. The depression's curtailment of foreign trade, and the consequent depression of prices, changed the country's mood from the ebullient optimism of the Batlle era. Ranchers' surpluses were increasingly diverted to the national market; this, combined with tax disincentives and smaller world markets, reduced permanently the country's ability to export. But at the same time national industry grew substantially, from about 7,000 establishments of all sizes in 1930 to 27,000 in 1960; industrial employment grew from about 77,000 to 207,000 in this period. Batlle's successors in office perceived the depression as an incentive to begin subsidies to workers and the lower middle class. State employment rolls grew rapidly in the *entes*. Private industry was given protective tariff legislation, and labor and managerial efficiency decreased. The country became a much higher cost producer than its neighbors, and its ability to compete in world commerce decreased. The spiral of dependence on the state grew ever tighter, and the system began to stagnate by the 1950s. As conditions worsened, and the political system lost its responsiveness, rising criticism drove the political class to serious errors of judgment. After 1952, with the end of the Korean War, inflation grew exponentially and endangered the living levels of all but the elite.

By the 1960s the Tupamaros epitomized a rising tide of criticism of the system, initially from within it. The elite oligarchy was increasingly discredited as the urban guerrillas uncovered evidence of their malfeasance. The Tupamaros could not win; the disbelieving majority of Uruguayans felt themselves attacked individually—not surprising in view of the increasing incidence of terrorist acts, since violence had all but disappeared from the country's political life by the 1920s under Batlle's influence. The Tupamaros were, in Chalmers Johnson's model of revolutionary change, the "accelerator" that demonstrated the decaying political system's real incompetence either to solve problems or to maintain the peace, and loss of legitimacy followed inevitably.[9]

Some of the army officers now in power claim to be restoring the country's lost values.[10] News reports cite their puritanical, nationalist, moralist, and anti-Communist mood. They seek to redirect the country toward what they perceive as capitalist conservatism, with reduced service and bureaucratic goals. But they also have imitated the former political class's self-indulgences. By mid-1984 the armed forces' government had accomplished some economic recovery, however, and had substantially reoriented the society away from the goals of the Batllista system.

Uruguay's political culture will always be conditioned in some degree by its unique Batllista experience. To those who know the country well—or thought they did—events have been most saddening.

POLITICAL HISTORY
INTO THE MIDDLE 1930s

The timing of Uruguay's development differs from that of most of its neighbors. Few Latin American countries have fully experienced development, and even fewer have suffered decay.[11] Despite the recency of its political collapse, the breaking point for analysis is the early 1930s. We must examine the presidency of Terra, and to evaluate it properly we must review the Batllista system.

Given the country's lack of mineral resources, Batlle's post-1904 system was based on the continuing strength of the farm and ranch sector. "Smokestack industry" has never been possible. Batlle's pragmatic settlement after the 1904 civil war gave all sectors the necessary incentives; it contributed to system legitimacy and capability, and the country's reputation was enhanced abroad.

Batlle's mixed economy worked well. The state enterprises created a state-dependent semiprofessional middle class, which, immune from partisan pressures, could be notably efficient. In the early years these enterprises earned profits that were divided among the central treasury, capital reinvestment, and worker benefits. They contributed toward the political socialization of the workers. At the same time, small and medium national industry in private hands grew to meet domestic needs. Legislation established some quasimonopolies, required the employment of substantial numbers of Uruguayan employees, and established the eight-hour day. The bases for a diversified, skilled, and competitive socioeconomic system were laid.[12]

The success of this system made Batlle unchallenged political boss for many years. He held the presidency from 1903 to 1907 and from 1911 to 1915; during the constitutionally required interim period he left the country. The Blanco opposition, unable to win elections, campaigned for "coparticipation," seeking the apportionment of elective positions by means of quotas in the electoral law among the parties offering candidates. Batlle rejected the idea, since he was determined that power and responsibility would be held by a single party. If the Blancos could win constituencies, well and good.[13]

In 1913 Batlle announced a new constitution that would feature a nine-member Executive Council elected in a seven-year cycle in place of the president. This proved costly to his political control. The Blancos fought back obdurately, fearing the plan would confirm the Colorados in power forever, since Batlle would maintain his charismatic hold on the working-class voters. They claimed it was a Swiss conception, since Batlle had spent part of 1907 in Switzerland, where a council executive was used. This incorrectly simplified the matter, for there had been a long experience in the Río de la Plata region with plural executives or juntas in earlier years.

Batlle's opponents within his own party joined the Blancos to win a majority in the special 1916 election for a constitutional convention. The majority forced an impossibly awkward executive compromise on the strangely stubborn Batlle. The product included a nine-member Council elected by thirds every two years, split two to one between the two leading parties, and a president with a four-year term. The Council controlled all internal issues save maintenance of order, and the president controlled this function plus war and foreign policy. The cabinet therefore was divided, and the president had to negotiate the budget with the councilors. The Blancos had achieved coparticipation. The new constitution contained one Batllista goal, article 100, which tried to guarantee even more firmly the managerial autonomy of the *entes*.

In 1921 Batlle prepared a party platform that was adopted as the Colorado Convention and remained in force until 1931. While Batlle lived the arrangement retained a certain coherence. But the system began to decay soon after his death, and Terra played a principal role. Most tragically, the precedent of seemingly facetious tampering with the fundamental document had been set, and it remained an unsettling phantom in the political system ever afterward.

Both the traditional parties had begun a Byzantine splintering in 1916. In part this was a reflection of Batlle's failure to convince the political groups of the integrity of his constitutional proposals. Although Herrera's conservative and authoritarian control of the Blanco majority remained firm, the moderates of that party opposed him. Similarly, Colorado conservatives rebelled at Batlle's control; after his death they captured control of the Batllista faction convention and nominated Terra. Terra won the presidency in the 1930 election as the "most-voted candidate of the most-voted party" (to adapt the language of the 1925 election law). Batlle had distrusted Terra, and the reasons soon became apparent. Within a few months after the March 1931 inaugural, Herrera's Blanco critics began to leave him. Terra and Herrera made common cause, and their coalition enabled them to enact a law establishing the conglomerate state petroleum company, ANCAP (Administración Nacional de Combustibles, Alcohol y Portland—the latter for cement). Terra sneaked in a rider depriving all the *entes* of their autonomy and opening their budgets and staffs to partisan raids and spoils appointments. The law ultimately was known as the Pacto del Chinchulín, the pork-barrel agreement.[14]

The two men also made explicit their wish to change the constitution; each had earlier demanded a return to a single presidency. They attacked by speeches, in their personal newspapers, and by plans for subversion. Terra made use of the presidency, juggling cabinet posts, shuffling the duty assignment of army officers to separate them from troop units loyal to the constitution, and frustrating the legislature as well as the national executive councilors by interdicting their preventive efforts. Herrera's preparations were like those used by earlier Blanco caudillo-plotters: the marshaling of forces in southern Brazil while seeking a propitious moment. The two met privately in January 1933; the details never have been made public, but it must be supposed they exchanged support while still competing to see who would strike the first blow. On March 31, 1933, the *golpe de estado* occurred. Terra sent the legislators home with the help of an infantry platoon and dissolved the Council. His planning had been so thorough that the Montevideo Fire Department was used as the headquarters.[15] In 1934 Terra and Herrera joined to rewrite the constitution to formalize the event and to lock their sharing of power into the country's legal system—but their agreement had broken down by 1936.

The new regime gave a mixed impression. A lack of toughness with opponents led to jokes of its being a *dictablanda*, a soft dictatorship, rather than a *dictadura*, or hard one. Although institutional violence had occurred, no persons had been harmed in the *golpe*. Terra balanced the national budget by firing government employees and cutting salaries on a short-term basis; the bureaucracy was later greatly expanded. New tax incentives for industrialization were adopted, as well as measures to control available foreign exchange and reduce outward capital flows. Taxes were imposed on agricultural exports to fund increased public-welfare benefits and subsidies for basic food. Although there was constant talk of national economic planning, little occurred. The country suffered substantial foreign disinvestment, especially of British interests; this principally harmed large agriculture and began the decrease of exports of meat. On the whole the country turned inward and began to abandon the finely tuned balance of national and foreign linkages that had served so well.

In the political arena the personal interests of Terra and Herrera redirected the state away from policies intended to benefit the whole public and toward particularistic patronage distribution. This was an explicit step toward corporatism (Terra and Herrera had both expressed admiration for Benito Mussolini), and personalistic fiefdoms began to emerge. Batlle explicitly had believed an open political system would tend to preclude class struggle and end pseudostruggle among party organizations, and this belief had had some validity. But he also had assumed that competitive and open elections would occur and that decisions, once made, would be respected. The insertion of coparticipation into almost all levels of government, electoral or appointive, by the 1934 constitution blurred responsibility, heightened conscious partisanship, and reduced responsiveness. Decisions now inherently required negotiations and biparty support. Since policies increasingly had selectively beneficial outcomes, class tensions rose. Since the state became a dispenser of patronage, as distinct from increased and equal opportunities, efficiency became undesirable; historical indifference to forward planning based on accurate data now found its logical and lowest level, and already unreliable statistical and economic data became, at times, fantasies. Finally, since Uruguay never had been notably nationalist the sense of nation weakened.

Many voters, offended by the 1933 *golpe*, refused to legitimate it by voting. Amendments to the 1934 constitution in 1936 gave control of the Senate to Herrerista senators, as Terra deferred to Blanco demands for influence. Terra's picked successor, Alfredo Baldomir, refused to accept this outcome after winning the 1938 election, and solicited public support for a new constitution. He was able to bring back the abstaining parties and factions to participation by this means. A second *golpe* on February 21, 1942, brought down the 1934 document, but coparticipation was little changed and the *entes* did not regain their lost autonomy. The president never regained full control of the government.[16]

There was much apparent continuity in events as late as the 1960s. The "conventional wisdom" of the era held that nearly all the necessary administrative and political solutions to problems had already been devised. Batllismo became a kind of mythical Uruguayan scholasticism. When an issue became difficult a relatively mechanical modification would be used: reintroduction of a plural executive body. The *golpe* of 1933 had announced the primacy of political over integrative policymaking, and this remained the keynote for the indefinite future. In the short run, changes came with glacial slowness. Comparisons over longer periods of time allow the conclusion that the quality of life for the working class was falling, especially after the later 1950s, but the middle class became larger and more affluent, supported by government loans and subsidies of imported articles. The system's costs rose, but its efficiency fell. Interclass cleavages widened, and politics became even more Byzantine and corporatist as ever increasing effort was expended on manipulation. Ultimately, there was a tyranny of all by all; people and leaders were frozen in place, unwilling to risk personal positions for the benefit of society.

GOVERNMENT AND CONSTITUTIONAL MACHINERY

In the first constitution (1830), the presidency was modeled partially on that of the United States. Presidents were powerful and, occasionally, tyrannical. Batlle made full use of the attributes of the position, but he was less arbitrary than some of his predecessors; it was the modernizing thrust of his policies that had aroused hostility, but he was also envied for his charisma. His implacable commitment to the Executive Council was inexplicable, but this has been worsened by the automatonlike devotion of his sons and disciples to the concept ever since. Finally, the authority of the presidency was damaged by others' commitment to coparticipation, even after the council form was terminated.

In the 1830 constitution the president controlled all his ministers of government. In the 1918 document he controlled only three of nine, while the Council controlled the six concerned with internal affairs save for policing. In 1934 the president named six of nine (without reference to portfolio), but three were named by the second party. In the 1942 constitution the president could name only four of nine from among his own party faction without constraint; the other five required the "confidence" of the legislature, the two chambers voting separately. In the later constitutions of 1952 and 1966, ministers were appointed without reference to party affiliation but had to be supported by an absolute majority of each of the two legislative chambers. Once they were seated, the ministers were *directed* by the president or the Council; the Council briefly was reestablished by the 1952 document in possibly even more counterproductive form than before.[17] The president's authority was always subject to challenge; he thus did not *control* ministers.

All constitutions have provided for a General Assembly or parliament, composed of a Senate elected nationally and a Chamber of Representatives elected from the departments. In later constitutions the Senate has had thirty-one members and the Chamber ninety-nine. The 1830 constitution said nothing of parliamentary confidence, but the 1934 document referred to *juicio político* or impeachment of the ministers for their "conduct." In the 1942 document and in later ones "censure" is referred to for ministers, and the 1942 constitution even provides a procedure for parliamentary removal of the president. The document bears an unmistakable imprint of French Third Republic practice. Fulfilled formal censure seldom occurred up to the 1960s, although interpellations, questions, and motions of censure were common enough. Parliamentary debates only infrequently reflected the substance of issues confronting Uruguay, however, until the country entered an irretrievable crisis in the 1960s.

The electoral laws contributed greatly to the system's complexity. The "double simultaneous vote" was legislated in the election law of 1925. The various parties (Colorado, Blanco, Unión Cívica [Catholic] or Christian Democrat, Socialist, Communist, and [in 1971] Frente Amplio or Broad Front) were known as *lemas*, literally, "slogan." A *lema* might have any number of *sublemas* or factions, and a *sublema* any number of *fracciones*. The fractions normally appeared only for a single election, but the *sublemas* and *lemas* proved virtually permanent. The double simultaneous vote occurred when the voter selected both *sublema* and *lema* by a single vote. In the vote computation, votes were accumulated by *sublemas* and then by *lemas*. The "most-voted *sublema* of the most-voted *lema*" obtained the presidency (as did Terra in 1930). *Sublemas* were allowed to receive parliamentary seats in their own right in proportion to votes cast. When the 1952 constitution reestablished the Executive Council, six seats were assigned the most-voted *lema* (by prior arrangement one seat could be given to that *lema*'s second most-voted *sublema*) and three to the second *lema*. But since, given the corporatist clientele pattern, each councillor commanded the support of his own parliamentary members, the Executive Council's majority was seldom united. Granted the 1966 constitution's requirement of an absolute majority of chamber votes for ministerial appointment, and an absolute 60 percent for membership in a board of directors of an *ente*, all significant issues had to be negotiated.

Uruguay is a unitary state. It is divided into nineteen departments. Under the 1966 constitution, each department elected its own thirty-one-member unicameral junta, or legislature, and its *intendente*, or executive officer. Elections were direct, popular, and similar in procedure to national elections. Each department had at least two members in the national Chamber of Representatives and might have more depending on its population. These territorial governments enforced national laws and administered national social and educational policies and institutions within their territories. These territories had limited taxing powers, might borrow funds, and might acquire property. They also had the power to establish unpaid five-member local juntas, or town councils, in municipalities other than the departmental capital, if the population was large enough to warrant such a body.

The 1966 constitution was overthrown by the 1973 *golpe*; no elections for public office were held until 1984. In November 1980 the military government submitted a constitution to the voters for ratification by plebiscite; it would have ratified the existing dictatorship and barred competitive party activity. Of 1.6 million voters, 57.1 percent rejected the proposal. In consequence there was no constitution until late 1984.

SOCIAL AND POLITICAL GROUPS AMID INNOVATIVE SECULAR CORPORATISM

Prior to 1900 Uruguay was a quasi colony in many respects. The foreign sector, which included both resident foreign nationals and Uruguayan nationals oriented toward investment, management of enterprises and ranches, and the brokerage of international trade, was important in the society. Whatever self-governing corporate characteristics this sector might have acquired were never dominant prior to the surge of immigration in the last decades of the nineteenth century, and immigration reduced them to nullity for practical purposes.

By 1900 the bases were being laid for a pluralistic secular society and economy. Catholicism remained the nominal official doctrine until the 1918 constitution, but it had lost its predominant and acknowledged role several decades previously, and official separation was only confirmation of this fact. Uruguay is today the Latin American country most open to competing sects.

Private enterprise had enjoyed legal freedom from restraints before Batlle's presidency but had constantly fretted because of the instability caused by Colorado-Blanco clash and warfare. Batlle's 1904 victory brought relief from civil strife, but his proreform attitudes, when linked to the gradual demarcation of functional areas for the *entes*, led to ever increasing entrepreneurial complaint. Batlle encouraged the growth of national enterprise, however, and although foreign firms often felt that they suffered discrimination in tax or profits transmission policies, there was little evidence that they had better treatment in other South American countries. No restraints were placed on the private sector's freedom to organize its representatives or to lobby the government for acceptable laws and decrees, and complaints were belied by the data of industrial and agricultural production, which reached their highest points in the country's entire history in the 1920s. Education at public expense, through the university, nourished the professions and trained professionals; these, and intellectuals and students, took their places in this pluralism as well.

Nascent labor unions appeared in the 1860s. Discriminated against in law and politics, with their laborer-members disadvantaged by the traditional Euro-Latin disrespect for hand labor, unions found the Batllista era attractive. Early unions had often had radical doctrinal bases derived from European experience. Batlle's decision to support labor's goals for upward mobility, and its strikes, reduced the influence of those doctrines and led workers' views toward moderation. Consequently, labor supported the Colorado left—which was led by Batlle during his life—and only in the late 1950s could claims of union radicalism begin to gain credibility.[18] After 1965 allegations by authoritarian civilian and military leaders—most of them nominally Colorados—that labor's peak organization, the National Confederation of Workers (CNT), was Communist-influenced could not be ignored, but neither could they be taken entirely seriously.

The Batllista policies allowed labor organizations to be free of party domination. This was and is in marked contrast to nearly all other Latin American countries, in which unions often are auxiliaries of dominant parties. Before Terra's reforms, workers were able to respond to parties' brokerage proposals while still regarding their unions as serviceable instruments for economic and social gain. The growth of new bureaucratic jobs and favors, under the control of politicians, tended to reorient individuals toward the nascent corporate fiefdoms and away from the unions, which became both weaker and more radical. Government employees were unionized; in 1984 they constituted at least 20 percent of the working population. In general, however, private-firm unions were the only ones to retain real autonomy after the mid-1960s.

The "traditional" parties also suffered under this readjustment. No longer required to compete with each other for votes, because both the new corporatism and the baroque electoral laws assured them their positions in power, they deteriorated organizationally. Elections became exercises that fascinated by their spectacularity but resolved few issues; the voters were intellectually inert, precluded after the mid-1960s by a rising torrent of anti-Communist propaganda from considering if the nontraditional parties or nonparty reform movements, such as the Frente Amplio in 1970, might offer useful channels toward the resolution of conflicts and crisis. Even the plebiscitary campaign of 1980, when the country's reputation and past practices of personal liberty were at stake, featured media jingles more suited to selling patent medicines than a constitution.[19]

Throughout the country's history, until the late 1960s, the armed forces seldom played the "typical" Latin American roles of quasi party or autonomous power behind the throne. During the decade of "military dictatorship" (1876–1886) caudillo-generals had held the presidency, but the scanty precedent was soon forgotten. The success of the Tupamaros in destroying the credibility of the government's civilian police as a law-enforcement agency led to the calling-up of troops for this purpose toward the end of the 1960s. The officer corps changed quickly from a civilian-oriented and apolitical group, passing through the stage of uniformed interest group to an armed bureaucracy with specific political goals. Essentially naive at the outset, prepared to believe in the legitimacy of the decaying political class and later of the nascent oligarchic-financial elite, the soldiers quickly allowed themselves to be convinced by documents seized in Tupamaro raids on the archives of Montevideo businesses. The documents, which told of elite financial manipulations, stripped the officers of their mistaken loyalties but did not, simultaneously, offer them guidelines for resolving the country's crisis. As of this writing the armed forces are still not decided, although they hold decisive power. They are not interest group, political party, or armed bureaucracy. They are internally split. In March 1983 General Alvarez bid for continued power, possibly into 1987. Within days, navy and air force leaders began to negotiate privately with Colorado and Blanco leaders, to weaken Alvarez. Other army officers, farther to the right, sought common cause with ultra-right Blanco factions.

As the army has moved toward more authoritarian practices, the interest groups have lost the ability to contribute to policy. The CNT organized a general strike in 1966 over the erosion of political and economic rights; many workers were mobilized, as army reservists, into active duty, and the strike was broken. By 1973 another general strike failed, not because it was crushed by the army but because it was so successful that it brought the workers to literal starvation while the army closed shops that had not been struck. All religious sects have been harassed, and Catholic pastoral letters have been published only in censored versions. The Federación Rural, the large ranchers' organization, was barred in 1975 from discussing demands with the president—although this had been his own primary base group during his political rise. Even academic and scholarly analyses of economic issues and procedures have been denied publication, and the leaders of all parties have been jailed and even murdered, and "hard-line" officers have removed "soft-line," or procivilian, officers from active duty.

The struggle for expression has continued by civilians, often at great personal cost. Major strikes and demonstrations occurred frequently in 1983. In May 1983 the outlawed CNT was replaced by the Plenario Inter-Sindical de Trabajadores (PIT), which organized a highly successful country-wide general strike on January 19, 1984. The "dependency" interpretation of Latin America's economic and political problems is today much in style among both political and academic specialists. Marxist in its inspiration, it holds that the United States, as the most wealthy and influential country in the hemisphere, has imposed underdevelopment and poverty on the Latin American countries. Since the agents of this imperialism within the individual countries usually are upper-class nationals, they constitute a unique, occasionally corporate, and potentially subversive interest within the countries' policies. But in Uruguay, although spokesmen for the dependency view do exist, and indeed U.S. (as well as many other foreign) investments and firms can be found, the most perceptive and ideologically committed criticisms of the country's current regime and crisis tend not to subscribe to such a "devil" theory. Rather, the position clearly taken is that the current problems are largely the product of intrasystem deficiencies, by which the government and society have been rendered unable to deal with the crisis of decay.[20]

RECENT POLITICAL HISTORY AND CURRENT CRITICAL POLICY ISSUES

The intentional focus of the political system on distribution, with its designed inefficiencies, had several logical consequences. Uruguayan voters were dutiful in supporting the system and generally reluctant to change partisan affiliation. The parties tended to seek noninnovative leaders. Public policies, especially in the vitally important areas of fiscal policies and international trade and financial matters, were clumsy and were logical extensions of the propensity to internal inefficiency. Events since 1976, when the constitutional president was finally removed by military decision, have changed this fundamentally.

Under the pre-1970s sociopolitical pattern, voter loyalties in urban areas—and Uruguay is now heavily urban—were maintained by a system of party clubs and clubhouses, especially in working-class sections. These clubs performed the same functions associated with the machines of U.S. politics. The local party leader was a part of the "political class," and personalism contributed at both local and regional levels to maintenance of the national *lemas* and *sublemas*. Voter loyalty followed the heirs of deceased leaders. After Herrera's death some of his *sublemas* passed to his grandson, and Batlle's mantle was contested by his family successors into the mid-1970s.

There was some "floating" vote, amounting up to 20 percent in normal elections. During the 1940s at least half of this went to minor parties; the Communist party seldom received more than 2 to 5 percent of the total. In the late 1960s, as the corporate political class gradually lost effectiveness in serving its clientele and as average annual inflation in excess of 75 percent reduced the usefulness of services, the floating vote moved to a more focused opposition. In 1958 the floating vote gave the victory to the Blancos for the first time in nearly a century, but there was little change in the behavior of the system, and the deterioration of the position of both workers and the middle class continued. By 1966 the small parties began to coalesce to the left, but power returned to the Colorados. By the 1971 election, rejection of growing fascism led to the Frente Amplio, yet only 18 percent of the voters nationwide supported this left-of-center coalition. The Montevideo vote was much more revealing, however; the Blanco vote fell from 32 percent in 1966 to 29 percent in 1971, but the Colorado vote fell from 51 to 39 percent. The total of the minor parties' vote in 1966 was 17 percent, but in 1971 the Frente received 31 percent. Furthermore, preelection polling had shown the Frente markedly supported by young adults and by groups that, for professional or personal reasons, were developmentally oriented or otherwise disaffected from the stagnant traditional parties. The Colorado candidate won the presidency by a margin of .3 percent. No basis for policy change necessarily was suggested by this outcome.

The 1971 vote was accompanied by a constitutional reform proposal, however, and this was rejected. It would have allowed the incumbent, Jorge Pacheco Areco, to retain the presidency by direct reelection; no such provision had ever existed previously. Pacheco's reply to the Tupamaros and to union unrest had been to introduce totally unfamiliar official violence into the country in the name of law and order. He also had substantially furthered the displacement of the then stabilized corporate political system by a rising oligarchic system of great corruption. The armed forces, which now comprise the real government, turned against him after they took power in 1976, although they had supported him within the constitutional framework during his incumbency.

Before the disintegration of the party and constitutional system, exceptions to the clearly manifested preference for journeyman presidents were interdicted by the system: Luis Batlle Berres, nephew of José Batlle, was contained by his own party as well as by electoral defeat. Benito Nardone, a nonaffiliated but highly manipulative man of fascist preferences who was president in 1960, was contained by the traditional parties working together and by a campaign of ridicule of his personal characteristics. Even Luis Herrera, the Blanco caudillo from 1904 until 1958, was contained by dissenters within his own party and by Colorado opposition. In each of these cases, the rules of the game, as developed by the political class, controlled until the 1970s, when their incompetence had been demonstrated and the country was sliding into the chaos of dictatorship.

The collapse of economic policy has been the fundamental demonstration of system decay. Beginning in the 1930s, international trade and finance patterns changed. Respites occurred, especially during international crises: Uruguay's economy emerged strengthened from the World War II period, and this stability was momentarily heightened by a flow of flight capital from Europe in the later 1940s and by the effects of the Korean War. But by the middle 1950s the downward turn had begun, and alleviations have been short-term. After the 1960s the failure of policy was little short of catastrophic; in 1981 the external public debt was $1,464 million, 34 percent of the gross national product of $4,224 million that year, and private international debts were $1,665 million additional (39.4 percent).

The collapse of international economic standing was furthered by world finance policy. The Bretton Woods decisions of 1944, which founded the International Monetary Fund (IMF) and the World Bank, sought to integrate all countries into the gold-based capital system of the victorious and developed Allied powers. This was to be achieved by markedly more liberal access to international credits and capital funds for countries in development and by the creation of an international climate conducive to private overseas investments in those countries. Shortly afterward the argument for major new import-substitution policies within Latin America was advanced. Almost heedlessly Uruguay subscribed to this strategy (ignoring the fact that much of the industrialization possibility of the country had already been taken up) and made use of the IMF and World Bank to borrow to balance its chronic internal budget balances (since the mid-1950s, the budgets seldom have shown balances, due largely to reluctance to tax business and private wealth). Despite the international incentives, since the late 1950s Uruguay's gross domestic investment rate has been so low as scarcely to maintain the physical plant; 10–12 percent is considered necessary for simple maintenance. In the 1965–1975 period Uruguay's rate was 11.7 percent, although it rose to 15.5 percent in 1979–1981.

Study groups in the university sought to analyze the problem in the late 1960s. In the meantime the government was under very heavy pressure from the IMF to achieve balanced budgets and reduce the social commitments that provided the base for the political class. But since the 1920s, budgeting procedures in Uruguay had demonstrated an indifference (if not hostility) to statistical data, and each presidential term had allowed constitutionally for only one budget built alluvially on the expenditures of preceding presidencies. In effect, conventional budgeting criteria would have been radical restructuring for Uruguay.

The Tupamaro attack on Pacheco in the late 1960s and early 1970s, and on his successor, Juan María Bordaberry, protested the incompetence of the political class. Their few comments on the economy were, in general, uninformed Marxist slogans, and their early raids seemed to be sporadic mischief and Robin Hood acts. Increasingly, however, they scooped up documentary evidence of elite-oligarchic manipulations, flagrant raids on the treasury, and violation of public trust, and they gave their findings full publicity. They were romanticized in film, books, and poems, but ultimately the armed forces took the evidence seriously. The first overt army defiance of the political class and the elite-oligarchy occurred in August 1969, when the defense minister bluntly warned the General Assembly that the soldiers were better qualified to defend the constitution than was the government. In progressive steps the army warned of its intentions. A National Security Council, COSENA, was established in February 1973 to "advise" the president. In June 1973 the president dissolved the General Assembly on the advice of COSENA, and the Council of State was organized. Finally, in July 1976, the president was removed and a puppet imposed.

PROSPECTS FOR THE FUTURE: A CIVILIAN PUPPET GOVERNMENT?

The Council of the Nation is now the supreme governmental body. Composed of the twenty-five civilian members of the Council of State and twenty-five officers of the armed forces, it holds executive and legislative functions. Eight institutional acts, which replace many of the functional provisions and guarantees of the 1966 constitution, are in force. Some are frank adaptations of similar provisions employed by the Brazilian military government established in 1964. Act 3 deprived hundreds of persons of political rights; it nearly wipes out the active roles of former members of both the political class and the elite-oligarchic elements that will open the country's political future, should this ever actually occur. Acts 4, 6, and 8 intervened in all courts and restricted the judicial function. Act 7 began the process of reducing administrative staffs.

The most difficult problem will be the recovery of international economic standing. Internal changes cannot eliminate the foreign debt. Herculean changes in life-styles for all Uruguayans will be necessary if a purely economic solution, involving turning to a more conservative and private-enterprise mode, is undertaken. World recession and the growing world awareness that Latin American countries have severely overborrowed in international banks have created for Uruguay a severe problem of economic recovery. U.S. internal fiscal and monetary policies, which have caused exaggerated world interest rates and slackening world trade exchanges, have contributed to the country's problems as well. Without short-term stabilization and longer-term recovery, political solutions will be difficult for Uruguayans to find.

The rejection by voters of a new constitution in 1980 forced the military to offer a new scheme in November 1982. At that time about five hundred party convention delegates were elected to internal restructuring conventions of the three legalized parties (Blancos, Colorados, and Unión Cívica) by 1,260,000 voters (53 percent of eligible voters). Only 15 percent of the votes cast were for delegate lists promoted by the military, and 12 percent of the ballots were purposely spoiled. The three conventions elected delegates to participate in negotiations with a newly created military body, the Committee for Political Affairs. These negotiations were to create a political settlement and to prepare a new constitutional draft. In turn an election-plebiscite in November 1984 created a new government headed by Colorado Julio Sanguinetti, which was to be inaugurated in March 1985.

The negotiating group held only a few meetings from May to July 1983, however. Civilians insisted on a return to some degree of respect for civil rights and the right of political action. The military responded with suppression; it also insisted that the forthcoming government effectively ratify all the repressive acts of the military during the past fifteen years and accept a military supervisory body during the new governmental period. In July the negotiations broke down. Although in early 1984 the military continued to insist that the scheduled elections would be held, their obvious expectation was that a puppet government would be created.

The central weakness of the military's perception of itself and its power appears to rest with its inability to understand the country's historical commitment to pluralism on the political surface, undergirded by corporatism based on a complex socioeconomic structure. The armed forces have demanded quiescent obedience from the public, whatever might be its class and economic level, and have sought, unsuccessfully, to quash the interests of even the economically advantaged, liberal, private sector that might have underwritten a more sensibly conservative regime. The prime leaders of all three parties have moved substantially to the ideological right in their policy expectations during these years of trauma, so there is little likelihood either that the socially benign-to-generous policies of the Batllista era will be renewed or that the destructive aspects of corporatism that had emerged in the years after José Batlle's death will recur. But the political insensitivity of the officers appears, at this time, to make all but impossible any chances for political redevelopment.[21]

The conclusions in the first edition of this book are as valid in 1984 as in 1977: "The future of the country is literally as unpredictable as

tomorrow's news dispatches . . . , and those dispatches are contradictory
. . . as to whether the official terror and violation of civil rights is
diminishing or increasing, whether the parties are enjoying restored
activity, and whether the economy is being set on the first tiny steps
toward recovery." Uruguay, once the most respected country of Latin
America, has become hostage to its own military; the apparent progress
in 1983 and 1984 in neighboring Argentina, where the military now
appears to be starting to pay for its malicious mischief, has only made
the Uruguayan armed forces dig in their heels.

NOTES

1. Juan Martín de Posadas, "Why Do Uruguayans Emigrate?" republished
in translation from *Perspectivas de Diálogo*, Montevideo (September 1974) in
Ladoc (May-June 1976):32–34. Also, *Latin America* (London), May 28, 1976.

2. Herman E. Daly, "The Uruguayan Economy: Its Basic Nature and Current
Problems," *Journal of Inter-American Studies and World Affairs* 7 (July 1965):316–
330; Eric N. Baklanoff, "Notes on the Pathology of Uruguay's Welfare State,"
Mississippi Valley Journal of Business and Economics (Spring 1967):63–69; Economic
Commission for Latin America, *Economic Survey of Latin America, 1981* (United
Nations, Santiago, Chile, 1983), pp. 741–753.

3. Robert E. Biles, "Patronage Politics: Electoral Behavior in Uruguay," Ph.D.
dissertation in political science, Johns Hopkins University, Baltimore, 1972, pp.
355–369. This paper is the source of current behavioral data used elsewhere
as well.

4. Russell H. Fitzgibbon, *Uruguay, Portrait of a Democracy* (Rutgers University
Press, New Brunswick, N.J., 1954), p. 122.

5. Alberto Zum Felde, *Evolución histórica del Uruguay* (Editorial Maximino
García, Montevideo, 1945), pp. 224–225.

6. Colin Clark, *The Economies of 1960* (Macmillan, London, 1962), p. 80.
Clark's "national stock" is weighted by what other, more recent authors call
"economic infrastructure." Also see M.H.J. Finch, "Three Perspectives on the
Crisis in Uruguay," *Journal of Latin American Studies* 3 (November 1971):173–
190.

7. John J. Johnson, *Political Change in Latin America: The Emergence of the
Middle Sectors* (Stanford University Press, Stanford, Calif., 1958), pp. 1–14; Aldo
Solari, "The New Urban Groups: The Middle Classes," in *Elites in Latin America*,
ed. Seymour Martin Lipset and Aldo Solari (Oxford University Press, New York,
1967), pp. 61–93.

8. Biles, "Patronage Politics," p. 307. At pp. 484–485 Biles presents Ulises
Graceras's social stratum index. Also see Aldo Solari, *El desarrollo social del
Uruguay en la postguerra* (Editorial Alfa, Montevideo, 1967), pp. 58–60.

9. Chalmers Johnson, *Revolutionary Change* (Little, Brown, Boston, 1966), pp.
99–106.

10. See General Alvarez's speech to the nation on the tenth anniversary of
the 1973 *golpe de estado*, February 8, 1983.

11. Ronald H. McDonald, "Electoral Politics and Uruguayan Political Decay,"
Inter-American Economic Affairs 26 (Summer 1972):24–45; and McDonald, "The
Rise of Military Politics in Uruguay," *Inter-American Economic Affairs* 28 (Spring
1975):25–43.

12. Luis A. Faroppa, *El desarrollo económico del Uruguay: Tentativa de la explicación* (Centro de Estudiantes de Ciencias Económicas y de Administración, Montevideo, 1965); Julio Millot, Carlos Silva, and Lindor Silva, *El desarrollo industrial del Uruguay de la crisis de 1929 a la postguerra* (Universidad de la República, Montevideo, 1972).

13. Philip B. Taylor, Jr., "The Electoral System of Uruguay," *Journal of Politics* 17 (February 1955):19–42.

14. Roberto M. Giudici and Efraín González Conzi, *Batlle y el batllismo*, 2d ed. (Editorial Medina, Montevideo, 1959).

15. Philip B. Taylor, Jr., "The Uruguayan Coup d'Etat of 1933," *Hispanic American Historical Review* 32 (August 1952):301–320.

16. Milton I. Vanger, "Uruguay Introduces Government by Committee," *American Political Science Review* 48 (June 1954):500–5123; Philip B. Taylor, Jr., "Inter-party Cooperation and Uruguay's 1952 Constitution," *Western Political Science Quarterly* 7 (September 1954):391–400.

17. Philip B. Taylor, Jr., "Interests and Dysfunction in Uruguay," *American Political Science Review* 57 (March 1963):62–74; Ronald H. McDonald, "Legislative Politics in Uruguay: A Preliminary Statement," in *Latin American Legislatures: Their Role and Influence*, ed. W. A. Agor (Praeger, New York, 1971), pp. 113–135.

18. Hugo Fernández, "Parties and Labor Unions: Uruguay, a Case Study," *King's Crown Essays* 15 (Spring 1968):12–15.

19. *Washington Post*, February 9, 1981.

20. Vivian Trias, *Uruguay hoy: Crisis económica, crisis política* (Ediciones de la Banda Oriental, Montevideo, 1973).

21. See Carlos Abalo, "Un largo viaje hacia la sombra," *Comercio Exterior* 32 (May and June 1982):518–525, 621–630, for a comprehensive examination of recent economic policy and its political effects in Uruguay.

SUGGESTIONS FOR FURTHER READING

Ardao, Arturo. *Espiritualismo y positivismo en el Uruguay.* Fondo de Cultura Económica, Mexico, 1950.

Brannon, Russell H. *The Agricultural Development of Uruguay: Problems of Government Policy.* Praeger Special Studies in International Economics and Development, New York, 1968.

Fitzgibbon, Russell H. *Uruguay, Portrait of a Democracy.* Rutgers University Press, New Brunswick, N.J., 1954.

Gilio, María Esther. *The Tupamaro Guerrillas: The Structure and Strategy of the Urban Guerrilla Movement.* Saturday Review Press, New York, 1972.

Hanson, Simon G. *Utopia in Uruguay: Chapters in the Economic History of Uruguay.* Oxford University Press, New York, 1938.

Johnson, John J. *Political Change in Latin America: The Emergence of the Middle Sectors.* Stanford University Press, Stanford, Calif., 1958.

Kaufman, Edy. *Uruguay in Transition: From Civilian to Military Rule.* Transaction Books, New Brunswick, N.J., 1979.

Lindahl, Goran G. *Uruguay's New Path: A Study of Politics During the First Colegiado, 1919–1933.* Institute of Ibero-American Studies, Stockholm, 1962.

Porzecanski, Arturo C. *Uruguay's Tupamaros: The Urban Guerrillas.* Praeger Special Studies in International Politics and Government, New York, 1973.

Solari, Aldo E. *Sociologia rural nacional.* Universidad de Montevideo, Montevideo, 1953.

———. *El desarrollo social del Uruguay en la postguerra.* Editorial Alfa, Montevideo, 1967.

Street, John. *Artigas and the Emancipation of Uruguay.* Cambridge University Press, Cambridge, 1959.

Taylor, Philip B., Jr. *Government and Politics of Uruguay.* Tulane Studies in Political Science, New Orleans, 1962.

Vanger, Milton I. *José Batlle y Ordóñez, The Creator of His Times, 1902–1907.* Harvard University Press, Cambridge, 1963.

Weinstein, Martin. *Uruguay: The Politics of Failure.* Greenwood Press, Westport, Conn., 1975.

15
Authoritarian Paraguay: The Personalist Tradition

RIORDAN ROETT
AMPARO MENÉNDEZ-CARRIÓN

Since Paraguay achieved independence in 1811, its political history has been marked by short periods of turmoil followed by long ones of authoritarian rule.[1] This study will attempt to analyze Paraguay's authoritarian tradition, seeking to reach a preliminary understanding of its origins, development, and consequences.

A nation under attack since its inception, Paraguay has suffered recurring threats to its territorial, political, and economic integrity with devastating results. Whenever an authoritarian ruler—José Gaspar Rodríguez de Francia, Carlos Antonio López, Francisco Solano López, José Félix Estigarribia, Higinio Morínigo—has exercised power, the nation has prospered. In turn, when attempts were made to open up the system, the state ceased to function and anarchy prevailed (1870–1936). Paraguayans have thus learned to equate open politics with weakness and authoritarian politics with strength. This personalism, understood as a tendency to emphasize the individual qualities of the leader and to stress interpersonal trust over ideology or adherence to specific doctrines, fostered the continuation of authoritarian rule and reinforced the idea that the national interest is best served by paternalistic leadership.

BACKGROUND AND POLITICAL CULTURE

Paraguay is a country about the size of California (157,047 square miles—406,752 square kilometers) with a population of 3.4 million. Surrounded by Brazil, Argentina, and Bolivia, the country has access to the Atlantic Ocean by way of the Paraná-Paraguay river system, which flows south to Argentina through the Río de la Plata. Its capital and principal commercial center—Asunción—is 1,000 miles (1,600 kilometers) from the ocean.

Paraguay

Racially and culturally, Paraguayans are among the most homogeneous people in Latin America: About 95 percent of the population is of mixed descent and almost all are bilingual. Guaraní is understood by 90 percent of the population, and 80 percent speak Spanish, the country's official language. Given Paraguay's peripheral position geographically and economically within the Spanish empire, only a few of the early Spaniards settled in Paraguay, which remained outside the stream of European immigration for a long time.

In the 1814–1840 era, Francia's isolationist policies prohibited European immigration. Government policies of confiscation and forced austerity eliminated accumulation of wealth, and many upper-class families were imprisoned or driven into exile. By the end of the Triple Alliance War (1865–1870), the white male population had been either exiled or killed, and the pattern of marriage between white women and Indian or mestizo males had been firmly established. Unable to preserve their racial identity, the Spaniards failed to evolve into a privileged socioeconomic class with a monopoly over the positions of power and influence, as was the situation in other parts of Latin America.

In today's Paraguay, upper, middle, and lower classes are identifiable, but for the most part differences in income and cultural levels are not as extreme as in other parts of Latin America. The country's elite is made up of a small, tightly knit group, most of whom owe their position to association with the chief executive and the ruling party. The middle class contains professionals, intermediate-level government officials, and a few who have achieved a modest degree of prosperity as administrators or business people. Almost 80 percent of the population of Asunción is lower class.

Paraguay is a rural society. Productive land is concentrated in the hands of relatively few owners, and the ower class constitutes practically the entire rural population: small farm owners, tenant farmers, sharecroppers, squatters, and wage laborers. The land provides subsistence but little monetary return. Traditionally, events in the capital have had little impact on the countryside.

Economic development has been hindered by lack of adequate transportation facilities, continuing budgetary deficits, and inflation. Cattle raising, agriculture, and lumbering have traditionally been the basis of the economy, and agricultural commodities normally account for a large percentage of the country's exports. Industry is characterized by many small factories and handicraft workshops, and most manufacturing consists of processing agricultural raw materials. Major imports include foodstuffs, machinery, transportation, equipment, fuel, and lubricants. Paraguay's leading trading partners are Argentina and Brazil, followed by the European Economic Community, the United States, and Japan.

Paraguay has suffered an almost continuous drain in human resources through emigration. According to informed estimates, more than 500,000 Paraguayans are living abroad, for political or economic reasons. The first great exodus occurred during the Triple Alliance War; since then, the outflow of people has been an irregular but recurrent historical phenomenon. The most recent wave of departures started after the 1947 civil war.

The national self-image is that of an ethnically and culturally distinct people characterized by long-suffering resignation and austerity. Most of the nation's values are rooted in a self-reliant nationalism that resulted from isolated development throughout the colonial period. As a remote outpost of the Spanish empire, forced to rely on its own resources, Paraguay developed an ingrained self-sufficiency that remains characteristic of the national ethos. This nationalism has been bolstered by repeated threats to its territorial integrity and by devastating wars.

HISTORY TO THE 1930s

Early in the sixteenth century, European explorers in search of El Dorado discovered the territory that is now Paraguay. Asunción was founded in 1537 and remained the seat of Spanish authority in southern South America until power was transferred to Buenos Aires in 1616.

Because Paraguay did not harbor the fabled treasures of El Dorado after all, it soon became little more than a zone of transit between the silver mines of Bolivia and Peru and the port of Buenos Aires at the mouth of the Paraguay River, serving also as buffer province against the Portuguese in neighboring Brazil. Its struggle to fend off the Brazilian advance was largely futile: By 1811, as much as two-thirds of Paraguay was effectively claimed and occupied by Brzail. In the south, the increasing influence of Buenos Aires during the seventeenth and eighteenth centuries caused a constant erosion of territorial jurisdiction over lands long administered from Asunción.

The Comunero revolt (1720–1735), a special source of pride for Paraguayan nationalists, was the first major rebellion against royal authority in the New World. Jesuit missionaries had organized a series of communities in which the majority of the Guaraní Indians lived and worked. They cultivated yerba maté (Paraguayan tea), the colony's major export. In an attempt to break the Jesuits' power and to free the Indians for other work, the Paraguayan colonists attacked the missions and defied royal authority. The Paraguayans successfully fought off a coalition of royal forces and Jesuit-led Indian armies for fifteen years, finally defeating them in 1735.

The role and impact of the Jesuits in colonial Paraguay remain controversial. There is little doubt about their effectiveness in creating a series of self-sustaining, productive communities that were hierarchically organized. In the missions, the Jesuits successfully established a state within a state. The political philosophy of the Jesuits combined elements of paternalism and entrepreneurship similar to other forms of organization in colonial Spanish America.

In Buenos Aires in 1811, a new junta of radical creole leaders came to power and invited Asunción to join in a new political union. Paraguay refused. The junta responded by sending an army of liberation into Paraguay. Led by Gen. Manuel Belgrano, the army was defeated. That event signified Paraguay's cry for independence from Spain and a rejection of Buenos Aires.

Dr. José Gaspar Rodríguez de Francia, a theologian-lawyer, emerged as the dominant personality in the revolutionary junta in Asunción. In 1816, a congress designated Francia absolute ruler for life, and he remained in power until his death in 1840. Thus the personalist tradition accompanied the creation of the Paraguayan state.

With Francia, Paraguay became a nation characterized by incipient state socialism and paternal rule, prospering quietly despite lack of recognition as an independent state. Today, more than a century after his death, Francia remains a controversial figure; but there is little question that he was an agent of social change, who worked to make Paraguay an egalitarian society. He successfully pursued a policy of isolating the country from its unfriendly neighbors and from the anarchy that dominated the other emerging nations of the continent. With Francia, all potential power contenders were eliminated: The creole elite was financially destroyed and most of its adult males executed or driven into exile and their haciendas confiscated. The Church was brought under total control, and an army established answerable only to him. By 1840, Paraguay was "a rustic, inner directed, self sufficient and reasonably prosperous society, more racially homogeneous and linguistically standardized than ever."[2]

In 1844, a congress met and promulgated Paraguay's first constitution, which provided for a ten-year presidential term and a republican form of government. Carlos Antonio López, a mestizo, was chosen president and ruled until his death in 1862. Opposition was out of the question, and virtually every aspect of the society came under some form of state regulation. National defense was strengthened, Paraguay's independence was recognized internationally, and social and economic development were stimulated. At López's death, Paraguay was a unified, militarily strong, prospering nation, keenly aware of its regional vulnerability despite treaties of friendship and navigation with its neighbors.

In spite of a constitutional provision that "the government of the Republic will not be the patrimony of one family," a unanimous congress elected Carlos Antonio López's son, Francisco Solano, to succeed him. Francisco Solano inherited a powerful state machinery, and solidly backed by the army, the police, and the masses, he determined to make Paraguay a great power in the Plata region. In 1865, Francisco Solano sent an army into Uruguay to prevent a Brazilian-inspired coup. The objective was to preserve Uruguayan independence and to forge a third force to counterbalance Brazil and Argentina, but instead he provoked a disastrous war with both countries and the puppet government of Uruguay. In

1870, Francisco Solano was killed on the battlefield, and the War of the Triple Alliance came to an end. Paraguay's population had been reduced from an estimated 525,000 in 1865 to about 220,000 in 1871; furthermore, it was stripped of over 60,000 square miles (156,415 square kilometers) of territory and forced to pay a war debt of nearly 19 million gold pesos; only Uruguay eventually renounced any intention of collecting its debt.

With the death of Francisco Solano López, the first chapter of the nation's history came to a close. It had been a period of authoritarian rule, paternalism, and state omnipotence, a response to the turbulent conditions under which independent Paraguay—peripheral, landlocked, with vulnerable borders, surrounded by anarchy and civil strife—was forced to survive. The next historical phase opened under conditions of defeat, devastation, and foreign domination.

Allied armies occupied Asunción and installed a provisional government, which promulgated the 1870 constitution. The new document remained in effect until 1940 and provided for a liberal, democratic government. It forced a clearly artificial structure alien to Paraguay's tradition on the defeated nation. The document did nothing to make elections less of a farce, to diminish the imposition of *oficialismo* (government retaliation) against opponents through fraud or violence, or to preclude caudillos from using the military as a private army.

When the occupation forces withdrew in 1876, the politically articulate coalesced into two parties, the Colorados and the Liberals. The Colorados claimed to be the political heirs of Solano López and ridiculed their opponents for being legionnaires: educated, liberal Paraguayans who had left the country before the war and collaborated with the enemy. The Liberals professed to believe in free elections, representative government, the rights of private property, and minimum state intervention. These differences, however, should not be taken too seriously. There were legionnaires in the directorate of the Colorado party, and former López officers in that of the Liberal party. Futhermore, Colorados in power followed economic policies just as liberal as those advocated by the Liberals themselves. In reality, both were personalist parties, given to violence, electoral manipulation, and opportunism. Politics became simply a case of the ins versus the outs.

The founder of the Colorado party, war hero Gen. Bernardino Caballero, dominated the country for thirty years (1874–1904), making and unmaking presidents, supported by Brazil. With the backing of Argentina, in 1904 the Liberals took over and retained power until 1936. International meddling in Paraguayan politics was characteristic of the period. Argentina and Brazil attempted to influence internal politics so that Paraguayan foreign-policy decisions would favor their respective positions.

The 1870–1936 period was one of economic collapse and financial fraud. After 1870, the country was opened to foreign speculators. In addition to the heavy war debt, a number of dubious financial machinations plunged the country even deeper into the red. Liberal and Colorado rulers alike proceeded to sell the public patrimony as a means of raising needed capital. In 1874, the railroad built by Carlos Antonio López was sold to an Argentine-Brazilian company. Between 1883 and 1887, vast quantities of state-owned lands were sold in large parcels at extremely low prices to Argentines and Brazilians. The prices were too high for the Paraguayan peasants, who were driven from land many had occupied for generations. For the first time, appreciable numbers of Paraguayans began to emigrate.

Foreign companies subsequently formed huge domains in these cheap fertile lands, and by 1935 it was estimated that the nineteen largest companies owned over half of the country's territory. The revenue from the sale of the public land was either stolen or squandered. Every year the country fell further into debt, while large corporations organized by Argentine, British, North American, French, and Italian capitalists began to control important segments of manufacturing and processing industries, transportation, stock raising, and agricultural production.

By the first decades of the twentieth century, however, some prosperity had returned to Paraguay. Small middle and working classes existed in Asunción. Intellectual ferment was prevalent during the period. Normal trade relations were reestablished with the outside world. Communications within the country improved.

MODERN POLITICAL HISTORY

War with Bolivia—the Chaco War—erupted in 1932. Efforts by Bolivia to secure an outlet to the sea through the Paraguay-Paraná river system were largely responsible for the outbreak. Bolivia's territorial losses in the War of the Pacific (1879–1883) had left the country landlocked. Inevitably, successive Bolivian governments looked east to the Paraguay-Paraná rivers as an alternative sea route. Access to that route was possible only through the Chaco region. The alleged participation of international oil companies in financing the war to gain advantage in petroleum speculation in the Chaco remains a controversial issue.

Paraguayans saw the war as a defense of their homeland. Disease and the brutal climatic conditions of jungle warfare may have killed more men than actual combat. A truce was signed in 1935 and the peace treaty in 1938. Paraguay gained some 20,000 square miles (51,800 square kilometers) of territory, which represented most of the contested area, and Bolivia, in compensation for the loss, received access to the upper Paraguay River and the free use of Puerto Casado in the Chaco.

The 1930s were a time of unprecedented social ferment and political mobilization directly traceable to the Chaco episode, which strengthened the solidarity of the masses, stimulated ideological ferment and debate, and inspired discussion of a New Paraguay among groups of war veterans, students, intellectuals, and workers. They perceived themselves as a new force capable of responding effectively to the needs of the nation and demanded recognition in the political system as new contenders for power. This new force overthrew the government of President Eusebio Ayala in February 1936. Col. Rafael Franco became president, and his Febrerista movement assumed power. The 1870 constitution was abrogated, all political activities were banned, and any syndicalist or interest group activity that did not emanate from the state was prohibited.

A newly created department of labor briefly exercised great power. Labor unions and business associations were required to register with the department which was authorized to study, revise, and approve their statutes. Deprived of much of their freedom of action, they were forced to accept a paternalistic, corporative framework. Franco gave the country its first social legislation, including a labor code progressive for its time and place.

To restructure the land tenure system, almost 8,000 square miles (20,700 square kilometers) of land were expropriated. By August 1937, some one thousand families had received title to about 800 square miles (2,070 square kilometers).

The actions of the Febrerista government antagonized the very beneficiaries of the reforms, whose expectations had now been raised without being entirely satisfied. Stimulated by government reform efforts, organized labor increased its demands, creating a period of agitation and confrontation. Radical elements accused the government of vacillating and being pseudorevolutionary, while old power contenders felt their position in the political structure was threatened by Franco's program. The heterogeneity of Franco's support weakened the administration's capacity to face attacks from all sides. Some of Franco's original army supporters who regarded his program as too radical unseated him in August 1937—ostensibly because of his diplomatic failure at the Chaco Peace Conference but actually because Franco had violated the old rules of the game. The February Revolution was over; Franco was arrested and sent into exile; the 1870 constitution was reestablished.

Elections were scheduled for 1939. The Liberals, realizing they needed a prestigious figure who could stand above factionalism, reunite the party, and win at the polls, drafted Marshal José Félix Estigarribia, the hero of the Chaco War. For the 1939 elections, the Colorados returned to their old policy of electoral abstention. The Liberals won without opposition.

From the beginning, Estigarribia was caught between two violently opposed forces: the traditional elements within the Liberal party, who wanted a return to the *status quo ante;* and the new forces—students, labor, and war veterans—who favored the continuance of the social changes initiated by Franco. Faced with discordant elements that had to be reconciled, strikes that threatened to paralyze the economy, and discontent among the military, Estigarribia assumed dictatorial powers in February 1940, six months after his election. Estigarribia's views, reflected in a new constitution, were a rejection of the 1870 document. The new document attempted to mirror the basic economic, social, and political realities of the country, with the state at the apex of the system, generating, regulating, controlling, penetrating, distributing. It abandoned the pretense that the legislative or the judicial branches were coequal with the executive—never the case in Paraguay, the 1870 constitution notwithstanding.

Estigarribia's attempts to structure representation along corporatist lines were embodied in a new Council of State, composed of the cabinet ministers, the rector of the National University, the archbishop of Asunción, a representative of business, two representatives from agriculture and industries, one from processing industries, the president of the Central Bank, and two retired officers of the armed forces.

In September 1940, three weeks after the new constitution went into effect, Estigarribia was killed in an airplane crash. Upon his death, the war minister, Gen. Higinio Morínigo, became provisional president. Morínigo was quick to replace the Liberal members of his cabinet with military men, dissolve the legislature, and exile Febrerista leaders. Morínigo suppressed the Liberal party altogether, charging it with subversion. Elected in 1943 in a one-candidate election in which all citizens were for the first time compelled by law to vote, Morínigo said:

> We reject liberalism, a product of the nineteenth century, because it does not admit of the positive intervention of the State in satisfying human needs. . . . We propose interventionist methods, above all in the field of economics and especially in the relations between capital and labor, in order to rectify social injustices. The inertia of the liberal State must give way to the dynamism of the State as protector and leader.[3]

Although these were Morínigo's words, they could have been those of Francia, the Lópezes, Franco, or Estigarribia, whose authoritarian tradition he followed. Morínigo assumed complete control of the state. Labor unions were brought under state control and all social organizations, student groups, and even entertainment were subject to state supervision. Morínigo ruled without a congress, and political parties had little impact for the duration of World War II. Press and radio were censored. This total control was endorsed by the military, who received about 50 percent of the national budget in exchange for their support.

In July 1946, Morínigo experimented with a coalition government of independents, Colorados, and Febreristas. The cabinet collapsed in January 1947, and a civil war erupted three months later. In six months, Morínigo, supported by the Colorados, defeated the Febrerista-Liberal coalition. Strengthened politically, the Colorados overthrew Morínigo in 1948 and elected one of their own as president the same year.

During the Morínigo years (1940–1948) the country made considerable economic progress, aided by the demand for Paraguayan exports during

World War II, by foreign loans and gifts, and by skilled immigrant labor from Europe, which he encouraged. Morínigo also showed great skill in dealing with Paraguay's powerful neighbors, playing upon their mutual jealousies and ambitions.

The Morínigo era was followed by a struggle for power among factions of the Colorados that resulted in a series of short-lived governments, elevated to power through coups and confirmed in single-ticket elections. Any attempt to form an effective opposition was precluded by the prohibition of party activities and the severe repression of Liberals and Febreristas, many of whom went into exile in neighboring countries. In September 1949, Federico Chaves came to power. Chaves was named constitutional president in 1953 for a five-year term but served only one year. Gen. Alfredo Stroessner, commander in chief of the armed forces, backed by a faction of the Colorado party, unseated Chaves in 1954.

After a brief provisional presidency under Tomás Romero Pereira, Stroessner was subsequently elected president in a single-ticket election and inaugurated on August 15, 1954. He has remained in power since then, proving more durable than any Paraguayan ruler since Francia, in what constitutes the longest rule of any political leader in the Western Hemisphere.

Backed by a large and privileged military establishment and the secret police, Stroessner has silenced most of the outspoken critics of his regime within the country and has suppressed more than two dozen internal revolts as well as attacks organized by Paraguayan exiles based in Brazil and Argentina. Stroessner has eliminated many of the traditional leaders of the Colorado party; those who remain are expected to give their undivided loyalty to the president. The constitutional system functions with the Colorado party at its center and the armed forces as its guarantor.

In 1963, despite a constitutional provision forbidding more than two presidential terms, Stroessner ran for reelection and won again. The president persuaded the Renovación faction of the Liberal party, which consisted of about one hundred expelled younger members, to participate in the election. It was the second time in the history of Paraguay that two candidates appeared on the ballot for the presidency. The majority of the Liberal party did not support the other candidate and accused the Renovacionistas of cooperating with Stroessner to make the elections appear democratic. Stroessner was reelected by an overwhelming majority and the "opponents" rewarded with twenty seats in the sixty-member Congress. The party's presidential candidate was appointed ambassador to Great Britain.[4]

From 1963 to 1969, there was some relaxation fo regime controls. Elections were called in 1967 to choose delegates for a National Constituent Convention, and the Liberal party accepted the legal status offered by the government—as the new Radical Liberal party (PLR)—

in time to participate in the elections. The Colorados received 68.7 percent of the vote. The new constitution replaced the unicameral legislature with a bicameral one and ruled that Stroessner could serve two additional five-year presidential terms.

In the 1968 election, Stroessner received 490,000 of the approximately 635,000 votes cast. Radical Liberals charged that one-third of their registered voters were turned away from the polls. Predictably, given the nature of the electoral process in contemporary Paraguay, Stroessner has been reelected three times since (in 1973, 1978, and 1983) by wide margins. In the latest count he was confirmed in office by more than 90 percent of the approximately 1.02 million votes cast.

Opposition party members permitted to serve in Congress since 1968 have directed much of their energy toward criticizing and competing against one another and, overall, have avoided offending the president.

The "process of democratization" begun in 1963 has worked to Stroessner's advantage. The aging general still holds all the cards; no fundamental change in the nature of power or in the political system as a whole has been effected, and participation in electoral politics remains a futile exercise for the opposition.

POLITICAL AND SOCIAL GROUPS

Any discussion of political and social groups should be prefaced by noting that organized, structured, institutionalized pressure groups do not exist in Paraguay. The military and Church provide the only two exceptions to this rule. "Structured participation," "strong mass-based organization," "instruments for collective action" are concepts alien to the nature of politics in Paraguay, where patronage, paternalism, and clientelism have prevailed from the start.

The two traditional parties, the Liberal and the Colorado, are patronage organizations that have consistently restricted political participation when in power. Membership in one of the two parties is not based on ideology as much as on family ties and interpersonal relationships. The differences that developed as the parties evolved were often as great among factions within each party as between the two parties; occasional temporary coalitions were formed at the leadership level when party interests appeared threatened by other groups or factions.

Colorado party members are the direct beneficiaries of the political system. Civilian employees of the central and local governments are recruited from within the ranks of the party, and party dues are deducted from their salaries.

The Colorado party was the only legal party in Paraguay from 1947 to 1962. Since 1962, a very small group of Liberals, formally designated the Liberal Renovation Movement (MLR), has served as the president's loyal opposition and as such has enjoyed some of the privileges formerly reserved for the Colorados. After two decades in exile, in 1967 the old

Liberal party accepted the president's offer of legal participation and returned to the country, renamed the Radical Liberal party (PLR). In 1976, the two factions of the Liberal party united to form the United Liberal party (PLU). Shortly thereafter, the electoral board declared the PLU had no legal existence. That decision, made at the request of a minority faction of the Radical Liberal party that had rejected unification, appeared to many observers as an *oficialista* maneuver to dispose of a united Liberal opposition. The electoral board subsequently recognized new directories for the Liberal party and the Radical Liberal party that were composed of a minority of dissident Liberals, thereby sanctioning a token opposition. Both parties were granted parliamentary seats in return for taking part in the 1978 and 1983 elections.

The only other legally recognized party is the Febrerista Revolutionary party (PFR). It does not hold any parliamentary seats. Although such diverse influences as liberalism, Marxism, and fascism have been noted in party pronouncements and activities, Febrerismo is generally considered to be an indigenous adaptation of socialist currents, comparable to Aprismo in Peru and other democratic-left parties in Latin America. The revolt of February 17, 1936, resulted in the National Revolutionary Union (UNR). After 1937, Febrerista clubs developed in exile separately from the original revolutionaries. The Febrerista party was established in 1951 in exile. Since 1965, the party has accepted the government's conditions for recognition of its legality. The reformist youth to whom Febrerismo has traditionally appealed are drawn increasingly to the newer and still illegal Christian-Democratic party. The Febrerista party is isolated, small, and racked by internal differences.

The Christian-Democratic movement launched in 1960 was converted into a political party in 1965. It identifies with the international Christian-Democratic movement, and its goals include genuine agrarian reform, liberation of the universities and labor unions from government control, and comprehensive national planning in agriculture, education, and administration. The leadership of the party is drawn largely from among the young professional and intellectual elites. The organization maintains close ties with the Church, which it has helped to organize agrarian leagues in the countryside as part of a program of developing the political consciousness of the masses.

Parties without legal recognition are the Authentic Radical Liberal Party (PLRA)—another splinter group of the Liberals—and the Colorado Popular Movement (MOPOCO), set up by dissident Colorados after Stroessner took over the party in the 1950s. Though most of their leadership is in exile, they have managed to keep some presence inside Paraguay. Along with Christian Democrats and Febreristas they form a loose opposition grouping called the Acuerdo Nacional, which grew increasingly vocal during the Carter years. With the exception of the Christian Democrats, the Acuerdo Nacional parties appeal to the emergent middle sectors rather than to the *campesinado* (or peasant groups), which represent over 60 percent of the population. In the months preceding the 1983 election their discourse concentrated on political rights rather than on social and economic issues.

The other illegal party is the Communist party founded in the 1930s with student and labor support. It has only been legal for nine months of its existence (in 1946 and 1947). Its membership was estimated in 1984 at approximately thirty-five hundred people, many of whom were exiled in various Latin American and European countries. Its action within Paraguay is minimal.[5]

Paraguay's low level of industrialization has traditionally limited the political roles of both labor and capital. Labor is not an organized, tightly knit, autonomous force in Paraguay. Economic enterprises are small, workers' politicization is low, and personal (not professional) relationships between employers and workers prevail. Labor benefits such as shorter working hours and minimum wages, rather than being conquests of organized labor, were preemptively granted by the paternal state. Anticipating the demands of an incipient labor force, the state acted first and thus precluded the formation of strong labor organizations with the capacity to pressure for workers' rights. Furthermore, every attempt to mobilize the workers from below has been severely repressed. The Paraguayan Workers' Confederation (CPT) is the only legally recognized large labor organization. It is under strict government control.

The CPT probably represents over 90 percent of Paraguay's organized labor. Through the CPT, labor has direct access to the government, and frequent meetings are held with the government and the labor section of the governing council of the Colorado party. The 40.4 percent of the labor force engaged in agriculture has enjoyed few of the benefits given urban labor.[6] Attempts by a group known as the Christian Confederation of Workers (CCT) to organize peasant leagues in collaboration with the Christian Democrats and the Catholic Church have encountered government repression.

The alienation of about half of the national territory in the public land sales of the late nineteenth century resulted in the concentration of land in the hands of a few families, mainly Argentines, a situation in effect today. Foreign absentee landlords, like the wealthier local landlords, have consistently favored the Colorado party and have supported Stroessner since 1954.

Business as a corporate group is also weak. Many of the country's financial institutions and industries are foreign owned. Furthermore, local business people have found political and monetary stability profitable and cooperate closely with the government.[7] The incentives are clear: Benefits accrue from supporting the government; being uncooperative places business in jeopardy.

University students have traditionally been among the most outspoken critics of the government. In general, the student body is politically oriented but not affiliated with any party. Various nonpartisan student associations have issued publications, held seminars on social issues, and engaged in demonstrations and other activities considered subversive, often working directly with the Church. However, they have found it difficult to maintain an effective organizational structure because they are subject to constant police surveillance, and student leadership is continually depleted through arrest and banishment.

No Paraguayan president has remained in power without the support of the military, which constitutes the dominant force in the country. Senior members of the officer corps occupy cabinet positions, administer some of the major national autonomous government agencies, and have been appointed to positions of national importance in the political and economic fields.

In the absence of a genuine aristocracy of wealth and birth, the military has emerged as both the economic and the status elite of the nation. The officer class exercises great influence in securing positions in the government for friends and relations. The army is well looked after and thus loyal.

Just as the most essential element of the president's power base lies outside the party system, so does the focal point of opposition, the Catholic Church. Until recent years, the Church either supported the government in power or assumed political neutrality. Since the late 1960s, however, it has played an increasingly activist role, raising its voice in defense of social reform and against violations of human rights, the inequitable distribution of the benefits of economic growth, smuggling, bribery, the present land tenure system and so forth. Government officials accused of engaging in torture and corruption have been excommunicated. The Church has not been immune from official retribution, but its cohesion, from the village priest to the archbishop, has strengthened its position. With the military, as one of the only two firmly entrenched institutions in the country with a nationwide network of personnel, the Church remains the chief center of opposition. Eventually, it will face the reality that without party support it cannot continue to confront the regime effectively. A single institution, even one as influential as the Roman Catholic Church, would be unable successfully to challenge the Colorado party and the Stroessner regime without the support of a broad spectrum of political opinion.

A discussion of actual or would-be pressure groups in Paraguay is not complete without mentioning the role of outside forces that do, or seek to, influence the nature of political events. Traditionally Paraguay has been unduly dependent on its powerful neighbors, Argentina and Brazil. Until the late 1950s, Argentina's influence prevailed over that of Brazil. Argentina's good will has been essential to Paraguay's viability as a result of Argentine control of Asunción's links with the outside world by road, rail, and river. This in turn has determined the direction of Paraguayan trade, which throughout this century has depended heavily on Argentina.

Beginning in the 1960s, Brazil began to court the Stroessner government in a variety of ways that included new buildings for the National University of Asunción, the granting of Paraguay's request to build a bridge between the two countries across the Paraná River, and the creation of free-port privileges on the Brazilian coast. The port at Paranaguá offered an alternative export route.

With the signing of the Itaipú hydroelectric power agreement in 1973, it became increasingly clear that the Brasília-Asunción relationship had replaced the Buenos Aires–Asunción axis, at least temporarily. During 1973 separate agreements were signed with Brazil and Argentina for the joint construction of the huge Itaipú and Yaciretá hydroelectric projects. Itaipú is the largest dam in the world, with 12.6 million kilowatts of installed capacity. (Yaciretá is 3.3 million kilowatts). The dam's major benefits to Paraguay are large supplies of low-cost power and the foreign-exchange earnings from sales of energy to Brazil. The Itaipú treaty is highly controversial even among Colorado leaders and sectors of the military, some of whom have expressed concerns about the effects the project may have on national sovereignty.

The Brazilian presence in the border areas is a reality, and Paraguayans watch with alarm the colonization of the Alto Paraná in northeastern Paraguay. There, Portuguese has replaced Guaraní, and transactions increasingly take place in cruzeiros rather than guaranies. It is estimated that approximately three hundred thousand Brazilians have settled in the area, outnumbering by far the native Paraguayans.

The Itaipú treaty links Paraguay to Brazilian industrial growth, and some fear it will lead to Brazilian hegemony over the entire Paraguayan economy. There are those who see Paraguay following the Puerto Rican example, becoming a country vertically integrated with a more powerful one and the recipient, due to Brazil's investment in the economy, of a reasonable standard of living for its middle, technical, and upper classes at the price of its autonomy.[8] In the future, Paraguay will have an opportunity to play one side against the other in the increasingly dynamic and complex geopolitics of the Río de la Plata subsystem.

Relations between Paraguay and the United States since World War II have been largely conditioned by a complementarity of security interests, U.S. interest in trade and investment, and Paraguay's desire for military and development assistance. On security issues in the Organization of American States and the United Nations, Paraguay has voted with the United States more consistently than any other South American country. The United States has given generous military aid, police training and matériel, and economic and technical assistance. Paraguay has proved a safe and generous market for U.S. foreign investment.

There are those who regard the elections held in Paraguay since 1963 as a plan imposed on Stroessner by the United States to formally institutionalize a democratic facade in order to justify economic assistance to Paraguay. But Stroessner remains indifferent to democratic niceties and is not easily threatened. Stroessner made a token gesture to the Carter administration by releasing political prisoners who had languished in jail for almost twenty years, but at the same time he unleashed a new wave of political repression that included the closure of the head-quarters of the Radical Liberal party, the freezing of its bank account, the confiscation of its records, and forceful repression of the agrarian peasant leagues, all just a few months before the February 1978 elections. Itaipú, and therefore Brazil, have become Stroessner's primary concern.

GOVERNMENT MACHINERY AND PUBLIC POLICY

Under the present constitution, the president, elected by popular vote for a five-year term and assisted by an appointed cabinet, stands at the apex of the system. Broad powers are given to the executive: The president prepares annual budgets, conducts foreign relations, appoints government officials, commands the armed forces, and in times of emergency can declare a state of siege, giving the president virtually limitless authority. Paraguay has been under a state of siege virtually continuously since 1954.

Following the corporatist elements of the 1940 constitution, the 1967 constitution provides for a Council of State.[9] The function of the council is to render opinions on matters submitted to it by the executive, such as decrees, laws, and matters of economic, financial, or international policy. However, the council is not taken into account in major policy decisions.

The 1967 constitution provides for a bicameral Congress consisting of a thirty-member Senate and a sixty-member Chamber of Deputies. This structure, however, is largely alien to the realities of politics in Paraguay, where there is little legislative power and the Congress is an appendix of the executive. The same holds true for the judiciary. For administrative purposes, Paraguay is divided into sixteen departments, each headed by a government delegate appointed by the president. There is little local government in Paraguay. The central government exercises complete control over local administration.

Paraguay has a centralized economy in which the government plays a strong role. Economic controls cover prices, wages, banking, and insurance. Certain farm products receive price supports; subsidies and marketing quotas exist for others, primarily sugar and meat.[10] The state is directly involved in banking, electricity, telecommunications, trans-portation, and industry as well as in overall economic planning. Priority is given to investments in infrastructure—such as the Trans-Chaco highway, modernization of the river fleet, and telecommunications—over social programs.

The state is engaged in some business activities. The Paraguayan Alcohol Administration is the only wholesaler of domestic alcoholic beverages. The Paraguayan Meat Corporation, jointly owned by the government and private interests, has a monopoly on providing meat to the Asunción area. The government also involves itself in ship repairing, furniture making, and quarrying and owns sawmills and cattle ranches.

Unable to finance its investment in the economy from domestic sources, the state has more and more resorted to foreign sources. Paraguay treats domestic and foreign investment equally and no restrictions are placed on foreign capital, which is actively encouraged with liberal tax benefits. This has led to the increasing denationalization of the economy through such measures as the 1975 Investment Promotion Law 550, which provides fiscal incentives and other benefits to national and foreign investors supporting priority areas such as energy-intensive industries, forest-related activities, agri-industries, and programs in the less-developed departments of Alto Paraná, Nueva Asunción, Chaco, and Boquerón. Large-scale foreign investment in aluminum smelting, cement, cellulose, and fertilizers is, currently under way. This is bound to increase the outflow of capital in the form of profits and remittances.[11]

During the mid 1970s, under the driving force of an expanding agricultural frontier and the growth of construction due to the implementation of various infrastructure projects (most notably the Itaipú dam), employment increased rapidly, with GDP expanding at annual rates exceeding 7 percent in the 1972–1975 period, approaching 5 percent in 1975, and reaching more than 6 percent in 1976, one of the highest rates of Latin America. In the late 1970s the government created the National Employment Service (SENADE) and the National Service for Professional Promotion (SNPP) to identify the areas requiring skilled workers and to implement labor development and training programs. These services have had little impact so far, under changing economic conditions. As of 1983 open unemployment affected about 10 to 12 percent of the economically active population, or about three times the average of the preceding decade, as economic growth decelerated, the construction activity of Itaipú wound down, and the building of the Yaciretá dam was delayed. Gross domestic product fell by 2.5 percent in 1982 and by 5 percent in 1983.[12]

In spite of some improvements in education—the latest literacy figure for Paraguay is reported as 80.5 percent—and life expectancy, which increased from fifty-six years in 1960 to sixty-five years in 1980, economic growth has not translated itself into significant changes in the continuing low standard of living of the bulk of the population. The basic-needs problem is particularly acute in the areas of health and sanitation—as evidenced by the fact that as of 1980 indoor water supplies and sewerage services covered 18.4 percent and 6.5 percent of the population, respectively.[13]

PROSPECTS FOR THE FUTURE

Until recently, Paraguay's economic prospects were viewed as promising because of the continued development of the country's intensive primary sector resources, the construction of the Itaipú and Yaciretá dams, and the country's potential for becoming one of the world's largest exporters of hydroelectric energy in the near future. Despite present recessionary strains, linked in great measure to Argentina and Brazil's economic downturn, such medium- to longer-term prospects remain unchanged. However, present economic conditions, coupled with the increasing salience of the issue of succession as the general grows old, have provided a context favorable to the emergence of some strains in autocratic politics, Stroessner-style. The business sector is beginning to distance itself from the government for the first time, as evidenced by the respectful, but public, expression of disenchantment with government economic policies on the part of the two leading business associations—the Federation of Production, Industry, and Commerce (FEPRINCO) and the Industrial Union. In turn, the anti-Stroessner faction in the Colorado party appears to be slowly reemerging. Encouraged by signals of intraestablishment dissent, the press has grown somewhat more vocal, and trade unions have begun to call for the formation of a movement free of the tutelage of the government, the political parties, and the Church.

These novel features of Paraguay's recent political dynamics do not mean, however, that Stroessner's command has weakened or that substantial changes in the nature of the political system are in the offing. That system has evidenced, throughout the country's history, a remarkable capacity to deal with potential or new power contenders effectively, either through incorporation or repression. An example of recent incorporation is the return to Paraguay of the MOPOCO faction leadership and its absorption by the governing Colorado party. Unwilling to accept even mild criticism, the regime in 1984 closed one of Paraguay's two major daily newspapers, *ABC Color*, and arrested the editor. The alleged reason for the action against *ABC Color* was its overly frank criticism of government policies.

Paraguayan development is a response to the political and economic dynamics of the Rió de la Plata region. The flexibility that Itaipú—and, eventually, Yaciretá—will give Paraguay is a novel component in the country's dealings with its neighbors. Historical alliances are being reconsidered, and new commitments are begin made. However, it is unlikely that the economic wealth that Itaipú and Yaciretá represent will substantially modify the nature of politics within Paraguay. Even if new social forces—such as new middle-class groups seeking a wider representational role in decision making—emerge with the willingness to restructure the distribution of power, it is unlikely that the pattern of authoritarian rule will change very much.

Given the basic themes discussed in this chapter, there is little likelihood that the stability of the Colorado-military regime will be seriously upset. The continuity of personalist leadership throughout Paraguay's history is a recurring and dominant theme, from Francia to Stroessner. Personalist politics define the authoritarian tradition. A nation-state that has perceived itself under siege for centuries, Paraguay has turned time and again to the strong man who represents order and predictability in public affairs.

It is clear that Stroessner will remain in power for as long as he wishes, eventually presiding over the transition to a post-Stroessner era that will not alter the basic features of the authoritarian state. Although Itaipú and Yaciretá represent new resources, they also signify a new threat and challenge. Paraguay's characteristic response when confronted with any challenge is to turn to a strong leader. The combined forces of the opposition appear unable to change that historical inevitability in the foreseeable future.

NOTES

1. During Paraguay's first sixty years of independence there were three rulers: José Gaspar Rodríguez de Francia (1814–1840); Carlos Antonio López (1842–1862); and Francisco Solano López (1862–1870). In contrast, in the eighty years between 1870 and 1950 there were fifty rulers, six of whom completed their terms. The rest (with the exception of Higinio Morínigo, who was reelected) were deposed or did not finish their terms.

2. John Hoyt Williams, "Política Paranoica: Paraguay, 1800–1870," unpublished paper, p. 4.

3. Morínigo quoted in Harris Gaylord Warren, *Paraguay, An Information History* (University of Oklahoma Press, Norman, 1949), pp. 338–339.

4. In the 1963 elections, women were allowed to vote for the first time. They made up half of the registered electorate of 710,000.

5. Richard F. Staar, ed., *Yearbook on International Communist Affairs* (Hoover Institute Press, Stanford University, Stanford, Calif., 1984), pp. 162–163.

6. As of 1981 the distribution of the Paraguayan labor force by sector of the economy was as follows: mining, .2 percent; manufacturing, 18.7 percent; construction, 8 percent; others, 32.7 percent. See Interamerican Development Bank, *Economic and Social Progress in Latin America* (Washington, D.C., Interamerican Development Bank, 1983), p. 290.

7. Paraguay's exchange rate was fixed at 126 guaranies to the U.S. dollar in 1961 and was not altered until the 1980s.

8. Daniel Fretes Ventres, "Evolución y Perspectivas de la Estructura Social y Económica en Paraguay," *Estudios Paraguayos* 3 (October 1975):5–30.

9. In the 1967 constitution the Council of State is composed of the archbishop of Asunción, the rector of the National University, the president of the Central Bank, cabinet members, retired members of the three branches of the armed forces, and representatives of corporate groups such as farmers, stock raisers, manufacturers, and commercial and labor leaders. The two representatives from the agricultural sector (one for farmers and one for stock raisers) and the three representing manufacturing, commerce, and labor are selected from slates pre-

pared by the three trade organizations and submitted to the president for consideration.

10. Between 1967 and 1973, under a program carried out by the Rural Institute (IBR), over 4,000 square miles (6,436 square kilometers) of arable land were given out to Paraguayan farmers. Evidence suggests that only a small percentage of this land was actually exploited since little was made available in terms of credit or technical assistance. With nothing in the law to prevent Paraguayan beneficiaries from selling the land and with many of them forced to do so, the actual result of this program was to transfer land to those who could afford it—namely, the Brazilian settlers. According to a Catholic group's 1971 unpublished survey of thirteen rural settlements in the Alto Paraná region, Paraguayans were in control only of the smaller and poorer farms. Four colonies comprising about 600 square miles (965 square kilometers) were run predominately by Brazilians; the largest unit run by Paraguayans was only one-seventh the size of the smallest Brazilian settlement. *Latin America* 9 (August 1, 1975).

11. It is estimated that "for each dollar invested three went abroad" between 1970 and 1973. Aníbal Miranda. "Efecto de las Inversiones Extranjeras en la Economía Paraguaya," *Estudios Paraguayos* 4 (December 1976):136.

12. During the 1970s the Paraguayan economy exhibited high and steadily increasing growth rates, especially from 1977 to 1980 when real domestic product expanded at an unprecedented average annual rate of 11.4 percent. The 1983 fall to 2.5 percent was the worst performance in GDP in thirty years. Per capita GDP declined by 5.4 percent in 1982, after almost twenty years of steady growth. It should be noted, in addition, that even though Paraguay's debt-service ratio has risen steadily in recent years, it remains one of the lowest in Latin America. Moreover, as of 1982 the share of international agencies and governments in total indebtedness was slightly over 40 percent and 20 percent, respectively: High ratios compared with most non-oil-producing less developed countries (LDCs) that have been increasingly forced to borrow from private sources on less-favorable terms. See Interamerican Development Bank, *Economic and Social Progress in Latin America* (Washington, D.C., Interamerican Development Bank, 1982 and 1983).

13. Anibal Miranda, *Desarrollo y Pobreza en Paraguay* (Inter-American Foundation, Rosslyn, Va., and Comité de Iglesias para Ayudas de Emergencia, Asunción, 1982), p. 156.

SUGGESTIONS FOR FURTHER READING

Agarwal, Manmohan, and Hugo Zea-Barriga. *Paraguay, Economic Memorandum.* World Bank, Latin America and the Caribbean Regional Office, Washington, D.C., 1979.

American University. *Area Handbook for Paraguay.* Government Printing Office, Washington, D.C., 1972.

Corvalán, Grazziella. *Paraguay: Nación bilingüe.* Centro Paraguayo de Estudios Sociológicos, Asunción, 1981.

Latin American Bureau. *Paraguay Power Game.* Latin American Bureau, Nottingham, England, 1980.

Lewis, Paul H. *Politics of Exile: Paraguay's Febrerista Party.* University of North Carolina Press, Chapel Hill, 1968.

_____ . *Paraguay Under Stroessner*. University of North Carolina Press, Chapel Hill, 1980.

_____ . *Socialism, Liberalism, and Dictatorship in Paraguay*. Praeger, New York, 1982.

Miranda, Anibal. *Apuntes sobre el desarrollo paraguayo 1940–1973*. Universidad Católica "Nuestra Señora de la Asunción," Asunción, 1980.

_____ . *Desarrollo y pobreza en Paraguay*. Inter-American Foundation, Rosslyn, Va., and Comité de Iglesias para Ayudas de Emergencia, Asunción, 1982.

Pastore, Carlos. *La Lucha por la Tierra en el Paraguay*. Editorial Antequera, Montevideo, Uruguay, 1972.

Pelham-Box, H. *The Origins of the Paraguay War*. Russell & Russell, New York, 1967.

Rivarola, Domingo M., et al. *La Población del Paraguay*. Centro Paraguayo de Estudios Sociológicos, Asunción, 1974.

Rout, Leslie B., Jr. *Politics of the Chaco Peace Conference, 1935–1939*. Latin American Monographs, no. 19. Institute of Latin American Studies, University of Texas, Austin, 1970.

Warren, Harris Gaylord. *Paraguay and the Triple Alliance: The Postwar Decade*. Institute of Latin American Studies, University of Texas, Austin, 1978.

Ynsfran, Pablo Max, ed. *The Epic of the Chaco: Marshal Estigarribia's Memoirs of the Chaco War, 1932–1935*. Greenwood Press, New York, 1969.

Zook, David H., Jr. *The Conduct of the Chaco War*. Bookman, New Haven, Conn., 1960.

16
Bolivia:
An Incomplete Revolution

JAMES M. MALLOY

Bolivia stands out as one of only four Latin American nations (with Mexico, Cuba, and Nicaragua) to have sustained a popularly based revolution. During Easter week of 1952, an urban uprising carried a political group known as the Movimiento Nacionalista Revolucionario (MNR) to formal governmental power. In little more than a year, the new government sponsored a number of structural changes that profoundly altered the social, economic, and political reality of the country. The two most important measures were the nationalization of some 80 percent of the nation's key industry, tin, and broad agrarian reform, which broke up the old hacienda system and distributed land to the Indian peasant masses. In addition the regime sharply curtailed the power of the official armed forces and mobilized worker and peasant groups, which rapidly formed their own armed militia units.

Revolutions, however, entail not only the forceful destruction of an old order but also the definition and imposition of a new order upon society. Although the MNR accomplished the first task, it proved incapable of achieving the second. In November 1964 the MNR was overthrown by a revived military. Since the fall of the MNR, Bolivian political life has been basically dominated by the nation's armed forces. Under the military the autonomous armed power of the worker and peasant organizations has been dismantled, and a fairly coherent economic structure has begun to emerge. However, the military, like the MNR, has been unable to create a self-sustaining national political order. At the moment it is mainly the guns of the soldiers that guarantee the stability of the central government. In this political sense the Bolivian national revolution has yet to be completed.

BACKGROUND

The theme of incompleteness actually goes much deeper. In fact Bolivia has yet to complete the task of establishing a viable nation-state within its territorial confines.

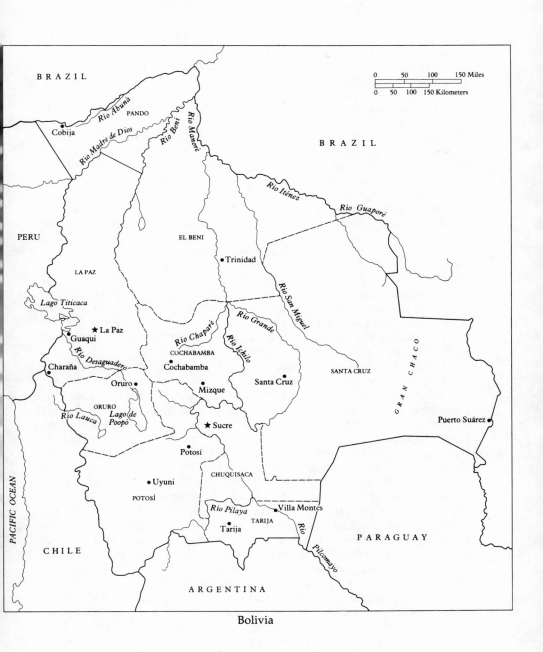

Bolivia

The Bolivia of today, like the other nations of the region, is based on an administrative fragment of the Spanish colonial system. Alto Peru, as it was known then, was part of the larger colonial entity of Peru, which spawned the contemporary nations of Bolivia and Peru. Like Africa today, nineteenth-century Latin America was dominated by a struggle to convert the administrative fragments of a previous colonial empire into viable nation-states. And as in Africa today, this generated a great deal of conflict both within and among the new fledgling nations of the region.

Because it shares borders with five other nations (Peru, Brazil, Paraguay, Argentina, and Chile), Bolivia's problem of external sovereignty was severe and the source of numerous major and minor international conflicts. In these border disputes Bolivia was singularly unsuccessful in defending its national integrity. With 424,000 square miles—1,098,160 square kilometers (about the size of Texas and California)—Bolivia is the fifth largest country in South America, yet Bolivia today is roughly one-half the size it was when it gained independence. Behind this dismal reality lies the fact that Bolivia has lost every major and minor test of arms with its neighbors. As a result of its defeat in the War of the Pacific, 1879–1882 (Peru and Bolivia versus Chile), Bolivia lost its seacoast and is now a landlocked country. A later and even more humiliating defeat in the Chaco War with Paraguay (1932–1935) played an important role in preparing the ground for the revolution of 1952. The present outlook of the nation's elite groups (especially the military) has been shaped by this history of territorial contraction and defeat.

Internal sovereignty (the effective authority of the national state) has been even more problematic. At the formal level the constitutional structures of Bolivia have clearly reflected the Spanish tradition of bureaucratic patrimonialism, in which the bulk of political power inheres in the chief executive and the administrative apparatus of the state. Since the economic crisis of the 1930s, numerous Bolivian constitutions have juridically expanded the tutelary role of the state in guiding the nation's social and economic development. This was particularly true after 1952. At the formal level one can see in post-1930 Bolivia the general regional trend toward a kind of neomercantilism in which capitalist economic growth is directed by a modernized version of the traditional patrimonial state. Until most recently, however, there has been a great disparity between the patrimonial pretensions of the formal state and its effective power over the disparate substantive reality that is Bolivia. In fact, for most of its modern existence Bolivia has been characterized by a formally strong but practically weak state structure.

The fundamental historical weakness of the central government in Bolivia can be attributed to many factors. Relative to its geographic size, Bolivia has a very small population (in 1979, 5.4 milllion). His-torically the bulk of this population has been rural (still 67 percent) and concentrated in the Andean Highlands and adjacent valleys. Vast portions of the eastern interior are largely unpopulated; indeed, as late as the 1950s less than 2 percent of the arable land was under cultivation. In 1976 only three cities had a population of over 200,000, and only the population of the capital city, La Paz, surpassed .5 million (La Paz, 695,566; Santa Cruz, 255,568; Cochabamba, 204,414).

The relatively small population has been fragmented along myriad racial, ethnic, and cultural lines. Some 60 percent of the population are racially and culturally Indian, and these in turn are divided into 60 percent Quechua speakers and 40 percent Aymara speakers. Until 1952 the bulk of the Indian people were locked into the hacienda system of landholdings, and the only authority they knew was that of their *patrón* (landowner). Around 30 percent of the population are racially mixed (mestizos) and less than 10 percent are of white extraction. Historically the whites dominated the social, economic, and political life of the country, with the mestizos in the middle and the Indians at the bottom. These groups have always maintained different and mutually hostile racial and cultural identities, which have undercut any sense of a common national identity.

Racial and cultural diversity has been exacerbated by geographic and regional diversity. Bolivia is divided into three distinct topographical regions. The core region is the high plain (*altiplano*) situated within the Andes Mountains at heights of over 12,000 feet (3,657 meters). Traveling east over the Andean chain, one descends into another region of semitropical valleys call *yungas*. Continuing east and descending, Bolivia spreads out into the *llanos*, or lowlands, of the Amazon Basin. Rail and road links between these regions are minimal, and vast stretches of the country are accessible only by air.

Topographic diversity and economic realities have contributed to a strong sense of regional identity and interregional rivalry in Bolivia. Since the colonial period (1550–1820) the economy of Bolivia has been based on the export of minerals to foreign powers. From the conquest until the mid-nineteenth century, silver was the main export. Since the 1880s tin has been the main export, but in the last decade there has been a steady rise in the importance of oil and natural gas. The political life of the country has reflected this underlying economic structure. Silver was extracted from the southern mountains of Potosí, and during that period the capital was located in the nearby city of Sucre. Tin, on the other hand, has been drawn from the more northern districts of Oruro and La Paz, and with its rise to importance the capital shifted to its present location in La Paz. Thus far the bulk of the oil and gas has come from the eastern regions, especially Santa Cruz, with the result that that city has begun to challenge La Paz both economically and politically.

Historically the residents of provincial cities such as Cochabamba (valley region) and Santa Cruz (*llanos* region) have viewed the capital city, La Paz (*altiplano*), as an alien force hostile to their regional interests.

Thus regionalists have resisted or tried to dominate the national government, and this regionalism has often been tinged with racial animosity. The people from Santa Cruz, for example, consider themselves to be white and proudly refer to themselves as Cambas. They look upon the Indian and mixed populations of the mountains and valleys with a mixture of fear and disdain and refer to them derisively as Collas. This particular mode of regional-racial tension has been a crucial political factor in the last fifteen years and has helped to undermine the effectiveness of the national government as well as a sense of national identity. Moreover, political conflict in Bolivia cannot be reduced to a simplistic model of class conflict. Regional, cultural, and racial divisions cross class lines and make for a much more complex pattern of political conflict.

Perhaps the most crucial factor in understanding political development in Bolivia, however, is the nature of its economic links to the international capitalist system. Bolivia is one of the most extreme cases of the phenomenon of dependence in all of Latin America. At the end of the nineteenth century, Bolivia was integrated into the international system as a supplier of minerals to, and a consumer of goods made in, the advanced capitalist countries. Until recently Bolivia relied almost exclusively on the export of tin to underwrite its local economic health. Bolivia, therefore, has been more vulnerable than most to fluctuations in the levels of international demand. As a result, Bolivia is also a classic case of a dual society: a relatively small modern urban sector (historically less than 30 percent of the population) based on the exportation of tin, differentiated from a large rural sector (over 70 percent of the population) structured within the traditional mode of organizing people and land known as the hacienda. As in other Latin American countries, the more modern urban sector achieved dominance over the traditional sector at the expense of the latter.

The extremity of Bolivia's economic dependence contributed greatly to the essential weakness of the national government. Since early in the century, Bolivia has relied on foreign powers, especially the United States, to consume its minerals and provide needed capital to underwrite government spending, thereby providing foreigners with important levers to influence government policy. Internally over 80 percent of tin production fell under the control of three giant corporations: Patiño, Aramayo, and Hochschild. The "big three" parlayed their control of tin into substantial control of banking, commerce, and transport, acquiring in the process a power base that dwarfed all other opponents, including the state. Under internal and external pressures Bolivian governments followed policies that tied the relatively small modern export sector more tightly to the international system, while permitting the vast rural sector to languish in backwardness. It was against this basic reality of a weak state presiding precariously over a fragmented and backward nation that the revolution of 1952 was directed.

POLITICAL HISTORY TO 1930

Aside from a lack of national integration and an extremely weak central state, Bolivia has been characterized politically by the extremely unstable tenure of incumbent governments. Since its independence in 1825, Bolivia has experienced no fewer than 186 irregular changes of government. With the exception of the uprising of 1952, these abrupt changes of government involved mainly the circulation of governing personnel and had little or no impact on the underlying patterns of the distribution of wealth, power, and prestige among groups. In essence they were the result of struggles among rival elite factions to control the central government and the largess that lay therein. Prior to 1930 this process of intraelite factional struggles passed through two distinct stages.

Between 1825 and approximately 1880, Bolivian public life, like that of most of the new Latin American states, was dominated by a series of quasi-military strong men known as caudillos. Caudillo politics was a particular mode of organizing power that emerged with the collapse of the central patrimonial institutions of the Spanish empire. In Bolivia the collapse was particularly severe due to the exhaustion of silver and the country's subsequent lapse into economic stagnation and isolation. As a result of these two factors, effective power reverted to the fragmented and dispersed creole landed elite, which had led the fight against the Spanish. The semifeudal hacienda thus became the key economic, political, and social unit of the new nation. Indeed the creole elite seized the opportunity to despoil most of the remaining free Indian communities and convert their lands into haciendas upon which the Indians now labored in semiservitude for their white or mestizo masters.

In that context the new republican constitution, copied largely from those of France and the United States, was a piece of paper without effect, and the national government was little more than a prize to be captured by one or another regionally based alliance led by a prominent caudillo. These alliances in turn were based on personal loyalties to specific leaders and the patriarachal family structure of the creole landed elite. In fact the patriarchal family structure, in which all power and authority inhere in the dominant male of the family, rapidly became the primary model of all authority relationships in the society. The overall pattern was similar to the warlordism that has cropped up in other historical and cultural situations following the collapse of a highly organized imperial system, such as early medieval Europe, Renaissance Italy, post-Imperial China, and parts of contemporary Africa.

In an era when caudilloism was rampant in most of Latin America, Bolivia again stands out for the degree to which this primitive form of dictatorship gripped its national life. By far the most colorful and at the same time horrific of these strong men was Mariano Melgarejo (1862–1871), who, among other depredations, abrogated the land titles of some

100,000 Indian peasants and occasionally sold off large slices of the national territory to Bolivia's neighbors as if it were his own personal property. The parallel to some areas of contemporary Africa is again compelling, and one cannot resist pointing out the stylistic similarities between a Melgarejo and contemporary leaders like Idi Amin of Uganda.

In the 1870s there was a revival of *altiplano* mining activities because of a partial recovery in the silver industry and the first stirrings of the new giant, tin. At the same time Bolivia began to be integrated into what was fast becoming an international capitalist trading system. Bolivia's period of isolation was coming to an end, and the coutnry began to experience a new process of externally stimulated economic development and modernization. Within the traditional oligarchy a new mining elite made its appearance. Oriented to a stable and predictable environment that would assure the outward flow of minerals, the new elite supported by external capitalist interests struggled to suppress the unstable caudillo pattern of rule and, in the rhetoric of the day, sought to impose a new civilian regime of "order and progress." They were aided in this task by the complete discrediting of the Bolivian armed forces in the War of the Pacific of 1879.

In the 1880s the civil forces oriented to the unfettered development of the private sector, especially mining, gained the upper hand and ushered in a brief era of relative political stability and social peace. More importantly, Bolivia began to take on the outward accoutrements of a typical Western democratic political system, for example, a functioning constitutional order, programmatically oriented political parties, interest groups, and so forth. At the same time, new social groups such as entrepreneurial and commerical elites, a new urban middle class, and an embryonic working class made their appearance.

At the elite level the civil groups quickly split into two party formations, Conservative and Liberal, which reflected competing regional and economic interests. The Conservatives were more identified with southern silver-mining interests, the traditional landed elite, and the claim of the city of Sucre to continue as the capital. The Liberals, on the other hand, were associated with the tin interests, the emerging urban middle class, and the regional claims of La Paz. In 1898 the two clashed in a civil war that was won by the Liberals.

The Liberals rewrote the constitution and established a centralized unitary political order based on a standard Western separation-of-powers system, that is, executive, legislative, judiciary, in which the office of the presidency was dominant. Bolivia entered a new era of political peace, rapid economic development based on the tin industry, and considerable modernization in the urban-based mining sector. Development and modernization had no positive effects on the rural sector, where the mass of the Indian populace remained locked as *colonos* in the hacienda system. The new elites that emerged with tin quickly merged with the more traditional landed elite to form a relatively coherent oligarchy that dominated the nation's political and economic life until the 1930s.

At that point Bolivia was a good example of a formal democracy with legally limited participation. Literacy and property requirements excluded the Indian masses and most of the urban working class from participation in politics; formal political life was the preserve of a tiny upper class and a relatively small urban middle class. Public policy in turn reflected this fact; it was aimed at maintaining a stable rural order and pushing the growth of the export sector.

Superficially Bolivia settled into a stable two-party political system in which the Liberals and a new Republican party did electoral battle. Behind the facade, however, was a new mode of intraelite factional politics in which personalistic cliques formed around dominant person- alities who stood a chance to win the presidential chair and the store of patronage jobs it controlled. Thus, although the armed caudillo bands had been supplanted by an ostensibly institutionalized political order, the essential reality of job- and office-oriented personalistic factional politics remained. Party labels and programs meant little. The real game was one of "ins" and "outs," with the latter, regardless of party affiliation, forming coalitions to harass and unseat the former.

This dynamic, in turn, was rooted in Bolivia's extremely skewed pattern of dependent, outwardly oriented economic development and in the fact that in the 1920s growth began to sputter to a halt. In that type of economic and political order (common to a number of Latin American countries) sources of hard wealth were limited mainly to landholding and control of export enterprises. By the 1920s both were monopolized by a very small elite and not available to other social groups, especially the new urban middle class. The urban middle class was a very dependent group in the sense that it relied on salaries and fees paid by the elite, which controlled hard wealth. The major sources of employment for the middle class were the liberal professions (par- ticularly law and medicine) and public jobs. As growth leveled off, competition for a limited number of positions increased, and control of the executive branch of government became the key mechanism for distributing the coveted positions and contacts: A lawyer with no political contacts was of little use to fee-paying clients. Government, in effect, became a prized commodity to be struggled over by factions made up of leaders drawn from the elite and ambitious personal followers drawn from the middle class. In Bolivia there is a saying that captures this point well: *La industria mayor de este pais es la política* ("The major industry of this country is politics").

This underlying dynamic of job politics necessitated by a skewed and dependent economic structure proved to be one of the key structural weaknesses of the old order and contributed directly to the revolution of 1952. As the middle class grew in size, the static economic base could not generate sufficient jobs to absorb all of this important social stratum into the system. Hence sectors of the middle class, especially the young, began to question the system.

Another key group that developed in this period was an urban working class drawn mainly from railroad workers, miners, commercial workers, and a few factory workers. The working class was a small (never more than 100,000) but strategic force in the economy. By and large workers were excluded from the political process, their demands for better conditions ignored, and their organizations suppressed. Not surprisingly these groups began to turn toward more radical organizations and ideologies that projected the need to seize political power and destroy the existing order.

Even prior to the 1930s, serious strains and tensions had developed within the more modern urban sector rooted in the mining industry. Structural constraints were generating disaffection with the existing order not only among the working class but also among sections of the urban middle class. However, it was the Great Depression of 1930 and the disastrous Chaco War that bowled the props from under the system and laid the base for sections of the middle class to coalesce with the working class to form a broad revolutionary movement.

MODERN POLITICAL HISTORY SINCE THE 1930s

From the mid-1930s to 1952, Bolivia was in a revolutionary situation in the sense of an almost continual open and violent struggle between groups oriented toward substantial change in the existing order and groups defending the status quo. As in most of Latin America, the most significant challenge to the old regime did not come from the Marxist left but from the MNR, the broad multiclass "populist" party officially formed in 1941. Contrary to the Marxist concept of class conflict, the MNR projected a conflict between the "nation" (middle class, workers, and peasants) and the "antination" (the local oligarchy and its imperialist allies such as the United States). The stated aim of the MNR was to form a multiclass movement of the middle class, workers, and peasants to seize the state and use it to break the external power of the imperialist forces and to destroy the local power of the oligarchy so as to liberate human and natural resources for the purposes of state-sponsored economic development and social justice. Key to these goals was the need to diversify the local economy so as to escape from the national economic dependence on a single export product.

By the late 1940s the MNR had built a fairly broad alliance among sectors of the urban middle class and key sectors of the working class such as railway, mine, and bank workers. Prior to 1952 there was little direct mobilization of the mass of Indian peasants. The leadership of the MNR came overwhelmingly from the youth of the urban middle class. Their ties with the more Marxist-influenced workers' unions were tenuous and based on the pragmatic perception that, working alone, neither had sufficient strength to seize power.

An important factor that paved the way for the revolution of 1952 was the extreme political and economic weakness of Bolivia's old elite, which, in turn, was rooted in the extremity of Bolivia's distorted and dependent economic structure. Some Latin American countries were able to traverse these difficult decades without a revolutionary upheaval because of their ability to generate economic growth within a new framework of import substituting industrialization and subsequent accommodation of their urban middle and working classes. This time-buying strategy was not available to Bolivia, which lacked a substantial internal market. Moreover, the steady exhaustion of the country's tin mines weakened its ability to recoup in the export sector. The economic crises of the 1930s persisted and even worsened in the 1940s.

Other Latin American countries escaped revolution in this period because their incumbent elites had both the will and the means to forcefully suppress opposition. In neighboring Peru, the military remained the implacable foe of the American Popular Revolutionary Alliance (APRA) party, which in many ways was very similar to the MNR. The humiliating defeat of the Chaco War, however, demoralized the Bolivian armed forces, which split into a variety of factions, some of which supported the populists to the extent that three reform-oriented, civil-military regimes were attempted in 1936–1937, 1937–1939, and 1943–1946. Other military factions ousted these regimes, but nonetheless the military could not provide a stable source of power to defend the status quo. The revolution of 1952 was more a result of the internal fragmentation and collapse of the old elite than of the organized and coherent strength of the MNR.

The insurrection of April 9–11, 1952, brought the MNR middle-class elite to power, but almost immediately they lost control of the situation. With the collapse of the old control structure, there was a significant expansion of political mobilization, not only among the working class but now among the peasantry as well. At the same time large numbers of weapons fell into the hands of workers and peasants, who quickly formed autonomous militias only nominally controlled by the party elite. These worker and peasant groups demanded radical structural change and most particularly nationalization of the mines, agrarian reform, universal suffrage, and redistribution of income. The MNR leadership, always more reformist than revolutionary, had little choice but to acquiesce to the demands of their ostensible followers. The question was this: Having transformed the old structures, could the MNR wield its disparate support base of urban middle-class groups, workers, and peasants into a viable coalition to create a new institutional order?

The MNR elite sought to create a new institutional order by following the Mexican example of a formal democratic framework within which the official revolutionary party dominated all of the effective levers of power. The MNR was to be the main mechanism by which all of the key groups of the society were integrated into a centrally controlled corporate political structure. The party was organized along functional lines, like the Mexican PRI (Institutional Revolutionary party), with official party sectors for each key functional group such as labor, peasants, the middle class, the military, and so forth. Theoretically, this all-inclusive party structure would underwrite a strong and autonomous state structure capable of guiding a new process of development and modernization.

In practice, however, the party structure was less a means by which key sectoral organizations were controlled than a means by which essentially autonomous sectoral organizations legitimately pressed their demands on the executive. Prior to the early 1960s, the most powerful sectoral group was labor. Organized in a central labor confederation (Central Obrero Boliviana, COB), labor demanded and received a system of cogovernment, in which it had a veto power over policy decisions and directly named the ministers of mines, labor, public works, and peasant affairs. The system of cogovernment was extended to key industries such as the new Bolivian Mining Corporation—COMIBOL.

Not surprisingly, the disparate revolutionary coalition split into contradictory ideological factions regarding the substantive shape a new Bolivia should take. The old-guard MNR middle-class elite, led by men such as Víctor Paz Estenssoro and Hernán Siles Suazo, pushed for what one might call a state capitalist system of political economy. On the left more radical labor leaders, led by Juan Lechín Oquendo, pushed for the creation of a state socialist system.

Between 1952 and 1956 the labor left faction had the upper hand, and Bolivia began to move in a socialist direction. The public sector expanded, and the state dominated the economic system. There was also a dramatic redistribution of income in favor of the mass of workers and peasants and an increase of state investment in development projects. The government was attempting to follow a dual policy of elevating popular consumption and development investment, which was beyond the capacity of Bolivia's backward economy. The result was a decapitalization of the tin industry, a crisis in the nation's balance of payments, and uncontrolled inflation in which the value of the Bolivian peso plummeted from sixty to the dollar to twelve thousand to the dollar. The brunt of inflation fell on the urban middle class, which quickly turned against the MNR and the revolution.

Although it grew in size and formal powers, the state remained extremely weak in the face of such internal pressure groups as the armed workers and peasants. The same was true at the international level. The revolution did not end Bolivia's external dependence and in many ways actually increased it. Bolivia remained dependent on mineral exports to earn foreign exchange. The dual policy of investment and consumption increased levels of public spending dramatically and hence the government's need for revenue. Unable to control its own support groups, the government could not extract sufficient resources from society at large by means of taxation. Given its weak economic base, the government, of necessity, had to turn to outside sources for economic aid.

The structure of the international economic situation, as well as the cold war, placed narrow limits on the MNR's external options. The facts were that the United States was the major consumer of Bolivian minerals and that in the 1950s the Soviet Union had neither the will nor the means to assume the burden of complete economic and military support for Bolivia as it was to do later for Cuba. Furthermore, the core MNR leaders were anti-Communist and never contemplated a complete break with the Western powers. Hence, Bolivia turned to the United States and U.S.-dominated funding institutions, like the International Monetary Fund (IMF), for the much-needed foreign aid. In short, revolutionary Bolivia became doubly dependent on the United States: to purchase its products and to provide economic aid and investments.

By the mid-1950s both external and internal realities converged to force a significant shift in the entire thrust of the revolution. Internally it was evident that the regime could not continue to follow a simultaneous policy of investment and consumption and that the old populist premise of a community of interests among the middle class, workers, and peasants was illusory. The government had to decide which of its own support groups would bear the costs of the society's advance, a reality that confronts all economically backward countries as they seek to develop and modernize.

The external reality was that strings were firmly attached to the needed assistance. This became clear in 1956 when the IMF forced Bolivia to accept a specific type of monetary stabilization program as the price of aid. The key to the plan was a series of measures to curtail mass consumption in such a way that the continuing costs of the revolution would be transferred directly to the working class and the previous socialist thrust of the revolution would be curtailed. The revolution in effect had to shift gears, a reality that quickly provoked a confrontation between the old-guard MNR elite, backed by the United States, and the labor left. To make the plan stick, President Hernán Siles Suazo, using U.S. aid, began to rebuild and modernize the armed forces as a counterweight to the workers' militias. Under the new course even the tenuous formal unity of the MNR began to fall apart as the government began a concerted effort to bring the labor left to heel.

In the early 1960s, under President Víctor Paz Estenssoro (who was also president from 1952 to 1956), the shift of the revolution toward a mixed-state capitalist economic framework continued. Infused with U.S. economic support under the Alliance for Progress, a two-pronged economic strategy was adopted. First, the public mining sector was to be "rationalized" and put on a profit-earning basis; second, a major effort was made to stimulate large-scale agricultural development in the eastern departments, especially Santa Cruz. Again the key to implementing the policy was the need to break the political power of the labor left, and again U.S. military aid was used to beef up and expand the role of the armed forces. Throughout the period there were a number of open clashes between the armed forces and the labor left, especially in the mines.

By 1964 the MNR was in total disarray, and the military, led by the ambitious air force chief René Barientos Ortuño, found it an easy task to topple the remaining fragments of the MNR. Since November 1964 the military has been the dominant force in Bolivian political life. Under Barientos (1964–1969) the military followed the same state capitalist strategy as the Paz government. To enforce it, the military invaded the mines, destroyed the unions and militias, and completely supplanted the COB. At the same time certain key peasant unions were bought off by the regime, and others were squashed. After the death of Barientos in 1969, there were two brief "leftist" military regimes (General Ovando, 1969–1970, and General Juan José Torres, 1970–1971) under which the labor left appeared to make a dramatic comeback and foreign holdings, such as Gulf Oil, were nationalized.

In August 1971 this brief leftist phase was terminated in a bloody coup that brought Col. Hugo Banzer Suárez to power. Between 1971 and 1977 Banzer and the military ruled Bolivia with an iron hand. At first Banzer tried to rule with a civil-military coalition in which the Paz Estenssoro sector of the MNR was included. This experiment was quickly terminated, and after 1973 the military ruled alone. The Banzer regime followed the same state capitalist strategy based on a rationalized mining sector and eastern agri-industry that was started in the early 1960s. To enforce the strategy the government was draconian in its handling of all opposition forces, especially those associated with the old labor left. Leftist union and political leaders were hunted down and either killed or exiled, and the old union structure was systematically dismantled. After 1974 all unions and political parties, whatever their ideological stripe, were in official recess, and Banzer, backed by the military and the United States, ruled by dictatorial decrees.

In 1977, Banzer, responding to both internal and external pressures, attempted to orchestrate a return to democratic rule, preferably with himself emerging as an elected president. However, things did not work out anything like his implicit plan.

The three years from 1978 to 1981 testify to the sorry state of Bolivian public life. The shattered condition of the civil party system was reflected in the seventy-odd political parties that appeared. The MNR alone had generated around fifteen recognizable factions and parties, some of which claimed ideological positions while others were frankly personalistic cabals. The same tired faces that had dominated the revolution of 1952 were again trotted out to center stage; the now-gray titans like Victor Paz Estenssoro, Hernán Siles Suazo, Juan Lechín Oquendo, and Walter Guevara Arce refused to fade away.

The elections of July 1978 were abrogated by a coup in which the official candidate, Gen. Juan Pereda Asbun, reacting to charges of fraud, simply had himself appointed by the commanders of the armed forces. He, in turn, was overthrown in January 1979 by Gen. David Padilla, who called elections. The voting of July 1979 was inconclusive and as a compromise between Paz and Siles, who were emerging as the major contenders, Guevara was appointed as an interim president. Guevara was overthrown in a bloody coup in November 1979 that led to the appointment of another interim president, Lydia Gueiler, who set elections for June 1980.

By 1980 the boom in export agriculture in Santa Cruz had gone bust, oil production was down, the balance of payments had deteriorated, and the debt was overwhelming. Stiff economic measures were clearly indicated, including devaluation, but since 1977 no government felt it had the political muscle to force such medicine on the country.

Seventy-three parties inscribed for the elections, although only five had any real chance. Personalities were important, but the main division was still ideological: The old left-right struggle that was first articulated in the revolution of 1952 was still the central national issue.

The MNR, itself a welter of factions and personality cliques, was a microcosm of the struggle: Leftist factions clustered around Siles and right-leaning factions around Paz. The Paz coalition contested with a pro-Banzer clique and the old FSB for the leadership of the state capitalist forces; thus the groups that supported the rise of Banzer in 1971 were split into three rival groups. Ten leftist parties formed the Democratic Popular Union (UDP) that supported the Siles candidacy. The flamboyant Marcelo Quiroga led his own Socialist Party Number One (PS-1) into the electoral fray.

The leftist trend evidenced in the two previous elections was confirmed in 1980. The UDP polled 507,173 votes (38 percent), a clear plurality, and the PS-1 garnered 113,959. The main right parties (MNRH—Movimiento Nacionalista Revolucionario Historico, ADN—Acción Democrática Nacionalista, FSB—Falange Socialista Boliviana) polled a total of 505,387. The electorate was almost completely polarized. Failing a majority, the choice of a president was left to the Congress, which was clearly going to elect Siles. But that was not to be.

The military moved on July 17, 1980, overthrew President Gueiler, and installed Gen. Luis García Mesa in the presidency. The resulting military regime turned out to be one of the most brutal and corrupt in Bolivian history. During the García Mesa presidency, the issue of cocaine trafficking came to the fore, and the regime itself up to the president was perceived to be directly involved in the trade that some estimate brings around $2 billion a year into Bolivia. The García Mesa regime was so corrupt, incompetent, and discredited that it was openly opposed by the Bolivian private sector and the U.S. government. By its end, the regime left Bolivia bankrupt with a foreign debt of close to $4 billion, negative growth rates, and rampant inflation.

In 1982, military officers seeking to regain some credibility ousted García Mesa in August and then in October returned power to the Siles-led UDP coalition. Since then, Bolivia has been struggling to reestablish democracy in the midst of an economic crisis that each day has worsened. Moreover, the Bolivian regime in dealing with the crisis has been forced into an austerity policy straitjacket by the International Monetary Fund. By 1984 the country was again in disarray politically as Siles, reliving the days of 1956–1960, struggled to resolve the myriad contradictions pulling Bolivia apart. The outcome is far from clear.

THE MAJOR FORCES
IN THE PRESENT SITUATION

The Bolivian military is the key political force, but unlike the Peruvian and Brazilian regimes, the Bolivian military is fragmented into person-alistic cliques. Banzer's hold on power depended in large part on his proven ability to manipulate the fractious military. Fragmentation in the military is symptomatic of a general fragmentation at the elite level in society. Bolivia remains an export-dependent society in which the bulk of the urban middle sectors rely on public employment. Thus despite the revolution and its intense ideological differences, the old intraelite dynamic of ins and outs continues. Banzer solidifed his control by a masterly manipulation of patronage to build personal support among sectors of the civil elite. This mode of rule, however, was quite unstable and a civil-military factional alliance gathered enough force to unseat the dictator. Even so, such an action probably resulted in little more than a personnel change, with a new dictator drawn from the military playing essentially the same role as Banzer. Siles, although elected, has a similar role and a tenuous tenure.

At its base Bolivia also remains a deeply fragmented society divided along class, regional, and racial lines. The forces mobilized by the revolution of 1952 have been contained and suppressed by a highly repressive state apparatus. With the old parties and unions in abeyance, there exists no institutional infrastructure to link state and society and provide a fundamental structural stability. The regime rules almost exclusively through a mixture of suppression and manipulation and thus is inherently unstable.

The key to Banzer's longevity was the economic success of the state capitalist strategy, which provided the regime with enough surplus to play the manipulative game. This in turn was based on favorable international prices for Bolivian minerals, as well as growth in the oil and natural gas industries. In the mid-1970s the GNP grew at a respectable 7 percent per year and the balance of payments was favorable.

Perhaps the most significant political development has been the emergence of Santa Cruz as a regionally self-conscious national political force. This eastern lowland region is the seat of the nation's agri-industry and the source of the bulk of the oil and natural gas production. The department of Santa Cruz directly receives 11 percent of the taxes on locally produced oil and natural gas, and the city of Santa Cruz has been turned into the fastest-growing and most modern city in Bolivia. Santa Cruz uses its political power to press its regional interests on the national government, and indications are that the region has veto power over who will head the government in La Paz (Banzer was a native of Santa Cruz). This region will clearly resist any government it perceives to be pro-Colla and would not hesitate to provoke a civil war should such a government emerge. Old-fashioned regionalism is very much alive today, and Santa Cruz will play a definite role in shaping any future Bolivian regime.

Since 1952 three politically important groups have been the Indian peasants, labor unions, and university students. Organized into militant armed syndicates, the peasants played a crucial role in radicalizing the revolution in the early 1950s. Since the late 1960s, however, the overall power of the peasantry has declined significantly, and regimes such as Banzer's have been able to garner peasant acquiescence, if not active support, by buying off syndicate leaders and giving symbolic payoffs to selected regional groups. Nonetheless, sporadic protests such as occurred in the Cochabamba Valley in January 1974 indicate that all is not rosy in the countryside and that given the right conditions the peasants of at least certain regions could reemerge as a potent political force.

Despite the systematic repression of the regime, the labor unions remain strong politically. Throughout the twentieth century, governments have used violence in an attempt to crush the labor movement, but the unions have always bounced back. The most important group are the mine workers, who have a long tradition of militant unionism and who work in what is still the nation's most strategic industry. But although labor is able to harass the regime, the organized working class is simply not large enough to threaten it by acting alone. Moreover, the government has had some success in splitting the labor movement by favoring specific groups, such as petroleum workers.

To be really effective, political groups must enter into coalitions. Historically one of the most powerful coalition groups has been university students. In recognition of this, the regime has sought to depoliticize the universities by abrogating university autonomy and imposing a new centrally controlled governance structure on the system of higher education. Although the campuses are quiet now, it would be a mistake to count the students out of the picture. Given a wrong turn on the part of the regime, the students could be back in the streets as the shock troops of the opposition. Should student demonstrations coincide with politically motivated worker protests, the government would be in considerable trouble. Although such a coalition could topple a government, it is doubtful that it could force any significant reorientation in the present thrust of the nation's political economy.

STATE CAPITALISM AND PUBLIC POLICY

Bolivia continues to follow the U.S.-supported state capitalist strategy initiated in the early 1960s. Like any other development model, the strategy carries within it an implicit distribution of costs and benefits among regions and groups. The state is the most powerful force in the model and plays a multifunctional role in stimulating and guiding the development process.

Even though Bolivia remains essentially a capitalist economy, the state has assumed the role of the major entrepreneur and source of economic investment in the nation. Through government agencies, public corporations, and mixed corporations, the state directly controls and manages most of the basic industry and infrastructure; the public sector accounts for more than 70 percent of total investment. In addition the state uses positive and negative incentives to guide growth in the private sector in terms of its overall development priorities. Finally, the state plays the critical role of imposing, through force if necessary, the costs of the strategy.

The state capitalist strategy in Bolivia and other Latin American countries is geared to adapt the local dependent economy to the latest phase of international development led by the advanced capitalist states. Hence the strategy gives priority to modern capital-intensive corporate enterprises in both the public and private sectors and clearly discriminates against traditional, more labor-intensive enterprises. Structurally this means that the agricultural sector, which contains the bulk of the population, bears a significant proportion of the costs of development. In the 1960s less than 3 percent of investment went to agriculture, and future government plans earmark less than 9 percent for it. Moreover, of this investment the vast bulk has gone to support agri-industrial development in Santa Cruz. Hence the costs fall mainly on the mass of Indian peasant small landholders who produce food for the local urban markets, a fact that is aggravated by the government policy of maintaining food prices at an artifically low level.

In Bolivia the strategy also has a regional bias. The two poles of the economy presently are *altiplano* mining, and hydrocarbons and agri-industry in Santa Cruz. Thus La Paz and Santa Cruz, linked by Cochabamba, form a primary investment zone that is designated to receive more than 63 percent of total investment in the next five years.

In addition to the sectoral and regional cost and benefit allocations, the strategy also has a class content within the modern corporate sector. As we saw, the political key to the strategy since the early 1960s was the ability of the state to hold down popular consumption by smashing working-class organizations, especially the miners' federation. This policy continues to be the basis of the strategy. The state has imposed the costs of development on urban workers through wage freezes. To achieve this goal the regime has forcefully repressed all autonomous working-class organizations. Aside from its strict wage policies, the government shifts the costs to worker groups through its investment policies, which invest less than 13 percent for social infrastructure such as sanitation, health, education, and human resources.

Although there is no reliable data on income distribution, most would agree that the major losers in state capitalist strategy are the mass of traditional peasants, urban worker groups, and the urban marginally employed. The major winners are private-sector entrepreneurs, high-level public and private corporate managers, sectors of the urban middle class absorbed in midlevel positions in public and private enterprises, and urban commercial and banking interests. Since the regime still depends heavily on foreign investment, external corporate interests also benefit from a favorable investment climate and a "stable" political order.

THE FUTURE

Bolivia will continue to be a dependent, primary-product, export-oriented country, although the number and types of exports will expand from minerals to hydrocarbons and such agricultural products as cotton. Barring a highly unlikely resurgence of the left, Bolivia will continue to follow a state capitalist development strategy. The inherent need of this model to accumulate investable capital by holding down popular consumption, as well as the need to attract foreign private investment, will in the foreseeable future reinforce the tendency toward an authoritarian, executive-dominant state structure oriented to the forceful repression of popular demands. We can then expect the persistence of a strong patrimonial state overseeing a process of neomercantilistic growth and modernization.

The major weaknesses in the model are the lack of any institutional links between state and society, the fragmentation at the elite level (especially in the armed forces), and the persistent possibility of regional conflict. Hence, although the government is following a very modern economic policy, it must rule through the traditional instrumentalities of personalism, manipulation, and repression. The regime is therefore very vulnerable to fluctuations in the export sector, which generates the necessary resources to keep the personalistic elite factional coalitions intact. Should export earnings drop significantly, renewed political instability is a real possibility. Even in that eventuality, however, it is doubtful that there would be any return to a "populist"-oriented regime, let alone a socialist system. Most probably Bolivia would slip into a modern version of the old intraelite faction struggles of ins and outs, with the military producing the strong men around whom factional alliances would form and reform. From the point of view of Bolivia's laboring mass, the short-run outlook is grim indeed.

SUGGESTIONS FOR FURTHER READING

Alexander, Robert J. *The Bolivian National Revolution.* Rutgers University Press, New Brunswick, N.J., 1958.

Fifer, Valerie. *Bolivia: Land, Location, and Politics Since 1825.* Cambridge University Press, Cambridge, 1972.

Klein, Herbert. *Parties and Political Change in Bolivia, 1880–1952.* Cambridge University Press, Cambridge, 1969.

McEwen, J. William. *Changing Rival Bolivia.* Oxford University Press, London, 1975.

Malloy, James M. *Bolivia: The Uncompleted Revolution.* University of Pittsburgh Press, Pittsburgh, 1970.

Malloy, J., and R. Thorn, eds. *Beyond the Revolution: Bolivia Since 1952.* University of Pittsburgh Press, Pittsburgh, 1971.

Mitchell, Christopher. *The Legacy of Populism in Bolivia: From the MNR to Military Rule.* Praeger Special Studies, New York, 1977.

Osborn, Harold. *Bolivia: A Land Divided.* Oxford University Press, London, 1964.

17
Ecuador: Authoritarianism, Personalism, and Dependency

JOHN D. MARTZ

Ranging from verdant Amazonian jungle to snow-capped Andean mountain peaks and steamy tropical coastlands, Ecuador provides a microcosm of endemic Latin American traditionalism. Deeply penetrated by the values and patterns of Spanish colonialism, Ecuador has remained steeped in authoritarianism and personalism throughout its republican experience. Whatever the constitutional trappings, the country has been dominated by enduring socioeconomic elitism and guided by a long line of forceful, often singular political figures. From such nineteenth-century strong men as Gabriel García Moreno and Eloy Alfaro to the demagogic populism of José María Velasco Ibarra and Assad Bucaram, Ecuador has been accustomed to paternalistic leadership. These men have in turn been heavily committed to or influenced by those controlling national social and economic destinies.

The economy has similarly reflected patterns familiar elsewhere in the hemisphere. During colonial times, crop cultivation and livestock predominated, and the coming of independence led in time to ever greater dependence on foreign trade. Throughout the republican era agricultural exports remained paramount, with periodic economic fluctuations registering an increasing impact on national affairs. Dependency on cacao early in the twentieth century helped determine the configuration of the political system, as was later the case with the banana boom of the 1950s. Since 1972 petroleum has been the product about which the pressures of both domestic and foreign dependency have swirled. Despite the magnitude of its oil income, Ecuador remains traditionalistic in outlook and highly susceptible to political personalism.

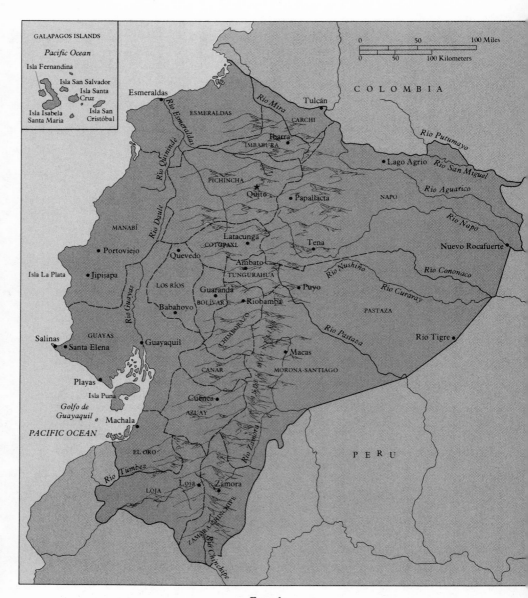

Ecuador

CONFLICTFUL POLITICAL CULTURE

The profound fragmentation of Ecuadorean political culture presents a legacy of disunity that has never been overcome. Its most striking manifestation rests on the foundations of regionalism, identified through the respective traits of the highlands (*sierra*) and the coast (*costa*). Of today's estimated population of 8.5 million, nearly one-half live in the Andean chain bisecting the country. Although ethnic components can only be estimated, the *serranos* are predominantly Indian or mestizo, with no more than 10 percent of pure European ancestry. The Indians live and work in a rural setting, indentured to large landowners and accustomed to economic and social subjugation. Constituting the bulk of the impoverished *serrano* masses, the Indians subsist under a dependency relationship. Largely powerless to achieve upward mobility, they are defensive, suspicious of outsiders, and tied to centuries-old pre-Columbian values and beliefs. In contrast, dominant whites project ideas and attitudes inherited from Hispanic times. Wealth and power, traditionally derived from landownership and the control of rural labor, have only recently been touched by the expansion of light industry in the highlands. Political and social conservatism has been marked, and Church influence has endured.

The highland subculture stands in stark contrast to that of the coast. With a population that has surpassed that of the *sierra* and is increasing more rapidly, the coast presents a very different racial composition and social structure. The African element is found all along the Pacific—especially to the north—and the Indian population is small. The mixed-blood coastal peasant, the *montuvio*, is active, independent, and highly mobile. His cultural outlook is more Western than Indian, and his work often places him in towns and cities rather than in isolated rural areas. The very independence of outlook and a life-style of occupational movement on the part of this lower-class *costeño* also contribute to the quality of volatility and upheaval so characteristic of coastal life and politics. This is particularly noticeable in Guayaquil, Ecuador's most populous city.

Coast-highland subcultural diversity is epitomized by the Quito-Guayaquil rivalry. The port city, some 1 million in population, constitutes the country's major economic center. Since the early twentieth century it has been the primary focus for banking, commercial, and export-import activities. Port facilities on the banks of the Guayas River have made Guayaquil the hub of international trade, as well as a major source of tax revenues for the central government. Bananas, sugar, rice, and similar coastal agricultural products are shipped through Guayaquil; Ecuadorean industry also has established itself on a larger scale than in the highlands. Modernizing elements of the economic elite are evident, representing a clientele linked to the international system as junior partners of external exploitation. Certainly the port city has long since emerged as the locus from which internal dependency has emerged and taken shape. Just as Quito has been historically a Conservative stronghold politically, Guayaquil from the nineteenth century has provided the popular base for the Liberal party and its offshoots. Its people have been susceptible to the populistic appeals and individual charisma of such men as Velasco and Bucaram and periodically provide the inspirational source for rebellion against central authority.

This is not to say that the traditional conflict with Quito is wholly one-sided. The latter retains the advantage of being the national capital, thus exercising ultimate control over Guayaquil's tax revenues. Moreover, the belated creation of industry in the highlands has offset in some part the economic leverage of the coast. There are also coastal rivals to Guayaquil, most notably Esmeraldas to the north, which has often secured plums from the central government as a means of challenging *guayaquileño* ambitions. In 1972 a pipeline was opened from the Amazonian petroleum fields to Esmeraldas, where a refinery and marine terminal have also been constructed. This has slightly shifted the weight of coastal dominance away from Guayaquil, much to the satisfaction of *quiteños*.

In terms of sheer geography, there is a third center of Ecuadorean regionalism: The jungle area to the east of the highlands constitutes virtually half of the national territory. However, its sparse population of primitive Indian tribes is barely 3 percent of the total. This so-called *oriente* is a world of virgin forests and exotic flora and fauna, and its many waterways provide the prime means of transportation and communication. With the 1967 announcement of the discovery of petroleum, oil workers traveled to the region, establishing their camps and beginning the exploitation of subsoil deposits. The *oriente* nonetheless remains a largely unexplored and underpopulated area.

Ecuadorean political culture, then, provides a source of disunity and conflict that casts a giant shadow over the country. It strongly mitigates against development of a true sense of national identity and consequently presents a formidable obstacle to the quest for modernization and progress. An exaggerated degree of regional competition and intense partisanship is thereby infused into both national attitudes and political life. It strengthens internal colonialism, impedes efforts to cope with international dependency, and encourages a continuation of the authoritarian and personalistic legacy traceable to Ecuador's early history.

FORMATION AND CONSOLIDATION OF ECUADOREAN TRADITIONALISM (1532–1944)

Fratricidal wars for control of the Incan empire between the half-brothers Huáscar and Atahualpa were raging when the conquistadores first arrived. Although Atahualpa ultimately prevailed, he was later imprisoned and, in 1532, put to death at the order of Pizarro. Two years later the Spaniards founded San Francisco de Quito; Guayaquil was established in 1537. Centralized colonial rule was exercised through the viceroyalty of Peru after 1544, and in 1563 Quito was designated an *audiencia* by royal decree. Its functions were administrative, judicial, and political; responsibility to the Spanish monarch passed through Lima until 1718, when it was transferred to the viceroyalty of Nueva Granada in Bogotá. Throughout the long colonial period, the *audiencia* stood as the major mechanism of Spanish authority.

Agriculture was the center of economic life, for the limited deposits of gold and silver were soon exhausted. The society that grew up in relative isolation from the outside world was rigid and hierarchical, shaped and controlled by a small upper class of Spanish officials. Material wealth in land and property, social prestige, and political authority remained their exclusive domain. The lower class was composed of Indians, mestizos, black slaves (first introduced in the late sixteenth century), and some poor Spaniards. The *encomienda* system, designed to provide moral and civic education for the Indians, became in practice a form of near slavery. Thus the colonial system cultivated and nurtured the traditions of authoritarian rule, an unbendingly hierarchical and elitist society, and Hispanic attitudes.

By the late 1700s the enfeeblement of the Spanish monarchy was mirrored in the New World. Resentment toward Spanish authorities grew apace with the administrative weakening and relaxation of colonial controls. In 1808 a local junta was created in Quito, and in the following year it ousted the Spanish president of the *audiencia*. Although royalist forces regained power for a time, fighting broke out in Guayaquil in 1820. On May 24, 1822, independence forces won the decisive battle of Pichincha on the mountains overlooking Quito, from which point independence from Spain was assured. From 1822 to 1830 the former Quito *audiencia* formed a part of Gran Colombia in conjunction with Venezuela and Colombia. When Venezuela withdrew in 1830, Ecuador promptly followed suit, naming the Venezuelan-born Gen. Juan José Flores as its president.

The Conservative period thereby introduced was to survive until 1895. Flores dominated national affairs for fifteen years, although strongly mistrusted by the Liberals in Guayaquil, one of whom—Vicente Rocafuerte—occupied the presidency from 1835 to 1839. This early republican period went far to establish the patterns of authoritarianism and disunity, which have parallels in more recent events. The first and subsequent constitutions sketched a system of authority with power resting heavily upon the personal skills of the president. Force was frequently utilized either to preserve or to overthrow governments. The clash of provincial highland and coastal interests, first symbolized by competition between Flores and Rocafuerte, became a fact of life. Public policy was applied at the whim of the chief executive, and attention to socioeconomic needs was ignored in the pursuit of personal ambition.

Quito and Guayaquil emulated the patterns of Spanish elitism, while the status of the masses was one of impoverishment.

Accompanied by both secular and spiritual Church interests, the apotheosis of Conservative rule was introduced in 1861 through the person of Gabriel García Moreno. An austere intellectual of fanatic clericalism, he invited the Jesuits to staff an ambitious education program and purify the morals of the country. Among the measures of his zealotry were the constitutional requirement of Catholicism to enjoy citizenship and in 1873 the dedication of Ecuador to the Sacred Heart of Jesus. In his ardent drive to create an orderly and progressive theocracy, García Moreno spurred business and attempted to diversity the economy. An excellent road was built from Quito to Guayaquil, port facilities were improved, and a railroad begun. Efficiency accompanied the tyrant's organizational ability, as did personal probity. Liberals and anticlericals found his rule stifling, however, and in 1875 García Moreno was assassinated on the steps of the government palace.

His conservatism, implanted on a receptive society, retained power for another twenty years. If personalism was temporarily in eclipse, the traditions of authoritarianism and of elitist society throve. Only slowly did the Liberal party and its spokesmen undermine the prevailing conservatism of the system. The great poet and essayist Juan Montalvo, who had exulted that his pen had killed García Moreno, helped to inspire the movement that led to open rebellion from Guayaquil in 1895. Led by Eloy Alfaro, the Liberals seized power and were to retain it for a half century. With Alfaro, the Old Campaigner, occupying the presidency from 1895 to 1901 and 1906 to 1911, the Liberals sought to curb the power of the Church, promote a respect for civil rights, and establish a fiscal stability attractive to foreign investors. The school system was enlarged, public sanitation improved, a railway constructed linking Quito with Guayaquil, and attention devoted to the plight of the Indian.

Alfaro proved no more willing or capable of abiding by constitutional precepts than his predecessors. In January 1912 he was killed by a proclerical mob in Quito, although the Liberals retained power. They enjoyed a period of uncharacteristic calm until 1925, at which time rampant inflation and a spiraling cost of living led to serious unrest. Commercial banking and financial interests in Guayaquil proved no less adamant than conservative landowners in maintaining their social and economic hegemony, supporting the use of government troops when necessary to suppress dissidence. The rigidity of the system continued, notwithstanding severe economic dislocations through the decline of the cacao industry, which had been the main source of foreign exchange. A series of fiscal reforms under Isidro Ayora (1925–1931) helped to strengthen elitist control, and new forces found themselves largely unable to alter the situation.

Only in 1944 did the long Liberal hegemony draw to a close, effectively marking a watershed in republican history. In that year an improbable coalition including Liberals, Conservatives, and Marxists banded together to oust Carlos Arroyo del Río, already unpopular for his acquiescence to the loss of territory to Peru in the wake of 1941 aggression from the south. Emerging from the scramble was José María Velasco Ibarra, a former president (1934–1935). Supporters of Velasco, who reflected a strange amalgam of populism and conservative authoritarianism, were joined on the political scene by Marxist elements. Fascist and pro-Nazi groups also appeared, nascent labor organizations began to stir, and a minuscule but identifiable middle class emerged in both Quito and Guayaquil. Thus new ingredients had been added to the brew. Moreover, the early experience with a dependency relationship revolving about cacao was to be repeated on a larger scale, first with bananas and then with petroleum.

THE MODERN ERA (SINCE 1944)

During much of this time Velasco either occupied the presidency or plotted his return from exile. Civilian rivals have relied more upon personality and wealthy supporters than upon respective party organizations, while the military has periodically intervened. Although the years 1948–1960 saw three successive elected presidents serve their full constitutional terms, post-1944 politics has generally been no less disorderly than during the earlier period. And despite increased participation and activism on the part of new forces, the traditional elites have survived challenges to their power. The Ecuadorean masses have been kept in a subordinate position, with privilege and power remaining the patrimony of the few.

With the overthrow of Velasco in 1947, a military junta and three provisional presidents followed in swift succession before the election in 1948 of Galo Plaza, son of a former Liberal president. A man of genuine democratic commitment, he viewed the strengthening of representative institutions as a prerequisite to socioeconomic reforms, and much of his attention was necessarily devoted to survival of the constitutional regime. The first man elected president in over a quarter century to serve out his term, Plaza transferred power to his elected successor, José María Velasco Ibarra, in 1952. This, the third of Velasco's five presidencies, proved the only one not to end in mass demonstrations and military intervention; in 1956 he was followed by Camilo Ponce Enríquez, leader of the right. After a sixty-one-year hiatus, conservatism had regained power.

Ponce was driven to stringent austerity in the wake of Velasco's spendthrift policies, and fundamental reforms were again ignored. Pledges to introduce a host of such measures were uttered extravagantly by Velasco in his 1960 campaign, the result of which was his victory with the greatest popular mandate in national history. Entering office with a newly projected image as a leftist reformer, the irrepressible Velasco failed to implement his campaign promises or maintain command of Velasquista forces. Fifteen months later he was deposed, ironically to be replaced by his 1960 vice presidential running mate, Carlos Julio Arosemena Monroy. The resultant administration, scarcely less volatile than that of Velasco, proved mildly leftist within the Ecuadorean context. Relations with revolutionary Cuba were cordial, domestic leftists were permitted to operate, and Arosemena cautiously initiated reformist plans. The rapid decline of popular support, accusations by the right of his encouraging Communist infiltration, and episodes of public drunkenness provoked Arosemena's removal by the military on July 11, 1963.

The military junta broke from earlier practice by announcing its intention to retain power for an indefinite period. Elections and the restablishment of constitutionality were to await the introduction of major reforms. Although the military may have been well intentioned, its capacity to implement policy proved slight. Rent by internal dissension, the junta resigned in disillusionment and frustration on March 28, 1966. Two interim presidents served prior to the elections of June 1968, when by a narrow margin voters opted once more for Velasco, then seventy-five years old. Old habits were not about to be broken. He was soon feuding with Congress, and it was dissolved in June 1970. Repeating past failures to cope with economic questions, deserted by his supporters, and turning instinctively to erratic and arbitrary leadership, he survived only with military acquiescence.

The prospect of impending petroleum riches whetted appetites for their control, however, including those of the armed forces. Moreover, with a host of parties and erstwhile presidential candidates crowding the political landscape, the way appeared open for a 1972 electoral victory by the populist former mayor of Guayaquil, Assad Bucaram. A self-educated son of Lebanese immigrants, who had emerged from the coastal working class and enjoyed magnetic power over its allegiances, he was an anomaly in Ecuadorean politics and decidedly unworthy of trust in the eyes of the elites. After weeks of covert maneuvering, the armed forces under Gen. Guillermo Rodríguez Lara removed Velasco on February 15, 1972, and canceled elections. Proclaiming themselves a "revolutionary nationalist" regime, Rodríguez and his associates arrogated unto themselves the responsibility for introducing structural changes—all to be financed by oil revenues.

From the outset the government suffered problems of self-definition, with its ranks embracing advocates of both Peruvian-style military reforms and of repressive order and economic growth a la Brazil. General Rodríguez himself adopted a centrist orientation that leaned first to one side, then the other. Emerging as fundamentally petit bourgeois, the government favored infrastructural development over social reform, despite periodic rhetorical salvos unleashed on behalf of the oppressed. Rodríguez was skilled at political maneuver and dedicated his talents to the art of survival. They served him well until January 11, 1976, when fellow officers forced his resignation. The subsequent Supreme Council of Government (CSG) eventually if reluctantly opted for a return to civilian rule.

Faced with growing pressures from civilian politicians and latent dissatisfaction with military government, the CSG acquiesced to a torturously slow and complex reestablishment of constitutionalism. Voters chose from alternate constitutions by national referendum, after which presidential elections were convened, with the new schedule calling for inauguration of an elected president in September 1978. As in 1972, fears of a popular victory by Bucaram suggested to opponents the inadvisability of his candidacy, leaving the prospects for competitive elections an open question.

The armed forces attempted to control the outcome through the disqualification of several candidates, most notably Bucaram. However, their efforts were unavailing. Bucaram was replaced by a younger associate, Jaime Roldós Aguilera, who was joined in an electoral alliance by the Christian Democrats and Osvaldo Hurtado. In a six-candidate race, Roldós and Hurtado unexpectedly led the field. In keeping with the new constitution, a subsequent runoff was held between the two leading slates. On April 29, 1979, the reformist coalition rolled to victory over a conservative ticket, with 68.5 percent of the vote. Inaugurated in August, Jaime Roldós, at thirty-eight the youngest president in the hemisphere, soon encountered opposition from the new unicameral Congress.

Although committed to social justice and to structural changes, Roldós was besieged by both political and economic difficulties. In January 1981 there was a renewal of border hostilities with Peru. Nationalistic sentiment temporarily strengthened the president's hand; in May, when his administration was again floundering, Roldós and his wife died in a plane crash. Constitutional order was maintained by the succession of Osvaldo Hurtado to power. However, the successful transition produced a government with even less popular support than Roldós had in 1981. Driven by falling oil revenues, rampant inflation, and a burgeoning foreign debt, Hurtado enacted a series of devaluations in 1982 and 1983. Accompanying austerity measures bought the nation more time, but at a considerable cost in terms of social unrest and hardship for the masses.

Among the effects of the Roldós-Hurtado term was a flourishing of democratic politics and partisanship. Thus the elections of January 29, 1984, were contested by seventeen political parties. Nine presidential candidates were entered, while some twenty thousand Ecuadoreans competed for other offices. Illiterates voted in presidential races for the first time, and a record high of some 2.5 million citizens went to the polls. Unofficial figures gave a narrow victory to Rodrigo Borja of the social democratic Izquierda Democrática (ID), with 28.4 percent of the valid vote. He was followed closely by the candidate of the conservative alliance Frente de Reconstrucción Nacional (FRN), León Febres Cordero, with 27.5 percent.

In the second-round runoff on May 6, 1984, some 2.9 million Ecuadoreans returned to the polls. León Febres Cordero defeated Rodrigo Borja, receiving 52 percent of the valid votes to Borja's 48 percent. This mild upset resulted from a vigorous and effective personal campaign that overcame the combined center-left forces backing Borja. The margin of victory came from Guayaquil, where Febres Cordero won by some 260,000 votes. In a decisive campaign that peaked by election day, Febres Cordero therefore symbolized a determined and lavishly funded effort of the Ecuadorean right to regain power. Once inaugurated on August 10, 1984, he undertook an economic approach frankly derived from Chicago school theories. With center-left representatives controlling the new Congress, however, Febres Cordero confronted a situation that was no easier politically than it was economically.

DOMESTIC AND INTERNATIONAL POLITICAL FORCES

The corporate strength of most domestic groups is relatively limited. Certainly this is true of associational interest groups—political parties, labor, and student organizations. They are capable of periodically disrupting the flow of national affairs but can only infrequently provide positive impetus to meaningful development. Fragmented, diffuse, and motivated primarily by parochial interests, they customarily reflect either personalistic or ideological biases. Among the many political parties, such narrow partisanship is especially characteristic.

Both traditional parties (Liberals and Conservatives) and Marxist groups have divided. In the 1970s the Conservatives split, with one faction more rightist than the other, while the more progressive wing of the Liberals broke away to form the Democratic Left (ID). As early as 1931 the Communist Party of Ecuador (PCE) left the original Socialist party (PSE). Further balkanization of the left saw the frankly Fidelista Revolutionary Socialist Party of Ecuador (PSRE) leave the PSE in 1962; a year later a Maoist group left the pro-Moscow PCE to establish the Marxist-Leninist Communist Party of Ecuador (PCMLE). The panorama has been further complicated by the Ecuadorean Nationalist Revolutionary Action (ARNE), which developed a quasi-Falangist world view upon its 1942 founding in the wake of Peruvian military annexation of Ecuadorean territory.

There is also a bewildering array of personalistic and sometimes populist parties. The two most striking have been those of Velasco and Bucaram, which both recently suffered the deaths of their caudillos, in 1979 and 1981 respectively. Jaime Roldós's death also further shattered the Concentración de Fuerzas Populares (CFP) that Bucaram had headed, and Roldosista loyalists themselves fragmented further. The traditionalist parties, including both the Liberals and Conservatives, have lost the bulk of their support. The national inclination lies clearly toward the center-left, where only the ID currently enjoys anything approaching national appeal and organization. Thus the party system, invigorated by the post-1978 political interplay, is presently in a state of flux. This also is the tendency for organized labor.

None of the three self-styled "national" confederations has systematically or effectively worked for the betterment of the workers. The National Confederation of Ecuadorean Workers (CTE), founded in 1944 under the aegis of the Communists, stands as the most important, numbering an estimated sixty thousand members. Affiliated with the Moscow-controlled World Federation of Trade Unions (WFTU), it was typically opportunistic in following Communist party support for the military regime until November 1976. Competition for the CTE comes from the Ecuadorean Central of Class Organizations (CEOSL) and the Ecuadorean Confederation of Free Labor Organizations (CEDOC).

Where the CTE has been responsive to the Soviets, CEOSL and CEDOC in turn are associated with Christian Democracy and with the U.S.-dominated Inter-American Regional Organization of Workers (ORIT). CEDOC, founded in 1938 but relatively inactive until the 1960s, has benefited from West German support and, according to several sources, that of the Central Intelligence Agency as well. In 1976–1977 CEDOC was severely rent by internal strife between centrist and radical forces, thus adding to its debility. The ORIT-backed CEOSL, founded in 1962, has continued to enjoy Washington's favor, with much of its energy aimed at the recruitment of white-collar associations. The subordinate position of labor is different only in degree from that of the parties, where influence is exercised by domestic elites that finance one or another of them.

Activism by students is qualitatively distinct, in that they constitute the most eloquent and militantly dedicated pressure group in Ecuador. Although the federations of university and of secondary-school students (FEUE—Federation of Ecuadoran University Students and FESE—Federation of Ecuadoran Secondary School Students) are customarily Marxist in outlook, they have stood as two of the few political forces outspokenly opposed to authoritarian government. They have been involved in all but one nonconstitutional change of government, conducting nationwide protests against Velasco in 1961 and 1972, the military regime in 1966, Otto Arosemena's provisional rule in 1968, and the post-1972 authoritarianism. Sensitive to violations of individual rights and to socioeconomic inequities, the highly politicized students have lent an important impetus to change and development. It is the misfortune of the country that this has necessarily been directed more toward unrepresentative governments than to the formulation and implementation of basic policy initiatives. Moreover, the students wield less true power than Ecuador's three major corporate groups—the armed forces, the Church, and socioeconomic elites.

The political role of the military has historically been that of defending the constitutional order when endangered by disorder and chaos. Its preference until the 1960s was that of returning to the barracks at the earliest possible juncture; this obviously changed with those who seized power in 1963 and again in 1972. Stimulated in part by better training and advanced studies, the officer corps has come to believe that its capacity to guide the country is at least equal to that of civilians. However, the sharply differing currents of opinion among military leaders between nationalistic reform and strengthening of the status quo hand-cuffed first General Rodríguez and then the Supreme Council of Government in introducing meaningful change. With the trend toward restoration of civilian government assuming an air of inevitability after the departure of Rodríguez, the armed forces retreated to their former institutional position. This is not, however, to suggest future unwillingness to reassume government responsibility should the armed forces perceive a threat to either corporate or national interests.

The Church, a potent force ever since colonial times, lost many traditional prerogatives during the Liberal incumbency launched by Eloy Alfaro in 1895. In recent times, it has not been wholly immune to broadly reformist papal encyclicals and to contemporary Catholic thought. Modernizing ideas and actions have been best personified in Leonidas Proaño, the bishop of Riobamba, a longtime critic of landowners in his province and an outspoken advocate of agrarian reform. However, his is a minority view, very much at odds with other ranking Church authorities. This was illustrated by a bizarre episode in August 1976, when the government arrested and deported participants in a pastoral conference in Riobamba, including three North American bishops and others from several Latin American countries. Hardened attitudes still prevail in the Ecuadorean Church and dominant spokesmen, especially from the *sierra*, still articulate highly conservatizing and tradition-oriented views.

Perhaps most crucial to the ongoing course of national life, politics, and economic growth is the domestic elite—Ecuador's wealthy and powerful oligarchical sector. Among the large property owners and to a slightly lesser degree the modernizing entrepreneurial sector, the rigidity of class structure and upper-class consciousness of their social heritage endures. Economic and family bonds with most political figures are tightly drawn, and these political figures in turn opt for financial support and social approval from the oligarchy rather than developing mass appeal or a broad political base. Most conservative among the oligarchical sectors are the *serrano* landowners, deeply wedded to the traditions of ancestry, arbitrary control of their property, and alleged racial "purity." Outside Quito they exercise the maximum possible control over local and provincial government, only infrequently being touched by the tentative actions of a remote and weak central government.

On the coast, the oligarchy is chronologically younger and less aristocratic, but wealthier than its highland counterpart. Somewhat more sensitive to pressures from below and generally less insular in outlook, the coastal elites are nonetheless themselves anxious to protect and extend their privileged status. Connections with international trade and commerce and with coastal agricultural activities strengthen the rivalry with Quito and the highlands. The powerful Guayaquil Chamber of Commerce, for instance, is almost continuously complaining about the loss of tax revenues to the central government; certainly the *costeño* elites exert constant leverage on behalf of their own local and regional interests. Projecting a nouveau riche quality, they are especially instrumental in the survival of internal colonialism and, moreover, provide an important link for the transmission of influence from foreign economic interests.

The presence of multinational corporations (MNCs) in Ecuador is less powerful and direct than in many Latin American countries, for the level of industrialization has not yet attracted them in large numbers. The most notable involvement has been that of foreign oil interests, especially Texaco and Gulf. Although the government took over Gulf's holdings in 1977, the petroleum corporations remain powerful. Historically Ecuador's domestic development, based on export commodities, has been conditioned and affected by the demands of world market forces. As the country was first drawn into international trade early in the century, its heavy economic reliance on cacao established a pattern that has survived and expanded. The banana boom of the 1950s, with acreage multiplying tenfold in a half-dozen years, led to Ecuador's emergence as the world's leading exporter. Until the rise of oil in the 1970s it accounted for some two-thirds of the country's foreign exchange. Today it is of course petroleum on which the economy rests.

Both economically and politically, the role of the United States has been writ large as a force in national affairs. An important early manifestation was the 1926 Kemmerer Mission, the recommendations of which led to a major reorganization of the monetary and banking system. U.S. spokespersons have also exerted pressure on behalf of economic interests; prominent examples include quiet intervention on behalf of fishing, banana, and oil interests. The long conflict over 200-mile (320 kilometers) territorial seas and Ecuador's periodic seizures and fines of U.S. tuna boats in support of its claims of sovereignty frequently produced private and public admonitions from the Department of State and the U.S. Embassy. U.S. retaliation in the form of suspending arms sales in 1971 merely provoked greater nationalistic ire. Meanwhile, as recently as 1976 the U.S. ambassador registered protestations on behalf of Gulf Oil during its dispute with the government.

U.S. intervention through the CIA has been described by Philip Agee, who cites involvement in the 1960s in Ecuador, especially in the case of labor. U.S. interference has also stimulated strong protests from Ecuadorean leaders on several occasions. U.S. pressure to recognize territorial losses to Peru through the 1942 Rio Protocol rankles even today, as do covert efforts that helped undermine the government of

Arosemena Monroy in 1963. Four years later his cousin Otto Arosemena Gómez, then provisional president, was the only Latin American chief of state refusing to sign the resolution of hemispheric presidents meeting at Punta del Este. He also ordered the expulsion of U.S. Ambassador Wymberley Coerr when the latter criticized Ecuadorean implementation of the Alliance for Progress.

Among recent irritations was U.S. passage of the Foreign Trade Act of 1974, whereby all OPEC members were denied favorable tariff treatment extended to other nations. Although neither Ecuador nor Venezuela had participated in the 1973 oil boycott, they were included in the punitive measure. This led to hemispheric-wide protests in support of the two countries. Notwithstanding apologies from the Ford administration, the measure was not rescinded until the 1980s. And in February 1977 the United States prohibited Israel from selling twenty-four Kfir fighter-bombers (powered by General Electric engines) to Ecuador for $150 million. This was viewed as but the latest example of Yankee meddling in domestic affairs abroad. The role of the U.S. government and of North American business interests, therefore, cannot be gainsaid even today as an integral component of Ecuadorean national life.

STATE AUTHORITY AND STRUCTURE

The power of the state is characteristically unfettered by and unresponsive to the needs of the majority. Whether a given regime is unconstitutional or not, it operates in authoritarian style, reflecting both personalistic leadership and a faceless, nonresponsible bureaucracy. Constraints on executive power depend more on political dynamics than on formal governmental structures. Even under constitutional rule, a president relies far more on individual prestige, oligarchical approval, and military support than on Congress or the courts. The courts enjoy little political weight, and the customarily obstreperous and obstructionist legislature is occupied with internal politicking and incessant sniping at the executive. Labor unrest, student demonstrations, and popular discontent become factors only if successful in producing a withdrawal of oligarchical and military backing for the incumbent.

If the machinery of Ecuadorean government is dominated by personalism and by narrow sectoral interests, its effective authority is nonetheless weak. For all practical purposes the system is decentralized, with Guayaquil frequently challenging national leadership while small towns and communities lie beyond the effective reach of the Quito government. It is not coincidental that Guayaquil's mayor is the second most powerful elected official in the country; the clash of regional and subregional interests, already outlined, compounds the difficulty. In rural areas political authority is exercised by the *teniente político*, whose responsibilities include arrests, fines, issuing of marriage licenses, and the requisitioning of local labor for community construction projects and public works. Although appointed by the executive and subject to removal at any time, the *teniente* enjoys relative freedom of action. Especially in Indian highland regions, government authority for the ordinary citizen will effectively be embodied in the *teniente*, the local priest, and the large landowner.

Application of presidential authority is also frustrated by the "fourth branch" of government, the bureaucracy. Its genesis stems from the administrative and fiscal reforms of the late 1920s, which marked for Ecuador the advent of modern statism and acceptance of the notion that the role of the state in socioeconomic matters was decisive. A plateau was soon reached that lasted until the armed forces seized power in 1963, when the junta adopted a plan for administrative reform that included creation of a supervisory Technical Secretariat. Bureaucrats, commonly known as *kikuyus*, moved toward a technocratic elite that, considering itself superior to the previous type of civil servant, elaborated complex procedures and mechanisms. Over thirteen hundred organs and agencies existed by the end of the junta's stay in power.

With the 1972 return of the military, a new surge of agencies and personnel took place, stimulated by the increase in petroleum earnings. In three years the government payroll increased from 80,000 to 150,000 employees; of the latter roughly 70,000 worked directly for the central government. With a meaningful centralization of authority rendered impossible—not to mention the concomitant budgetary drain—the independent power of the bureaucracy grew apace. Its importance is further enhanced by the tradition of high ministerial instability. One study showed a total of sixty-nine changes in eight ministries from 1960 to 1967.

The prevalence of *palanqueo* (employment derived through influence and personal connections) and irresponsible bureaucratic autonomy of action further undermines presidential power. Thus Ecuador's governmental machinery combines features of the worst possible worlds: a personalistic chief of state primarily responsive to oligarchical and military elites, simultaneously shackled in his policymaking by diluted authority in the countryside and a swollen, self-indulgent bureaucracy independent of both his will and that of the ordinary citizen. It is scant wonder that problems abound in the capacity and performance of government to undertake measures for collective and individual development.

PUBLIC POLICY

Creation of the framework for a modern state has done little to alter the essentially elitist and discriminatory distribution of benefits. No recent government has failed to articulate a shimmering vision of social reform and equitable treatment for all and, similarly, few have achieved measurable results. Traditional attitudes of dominant social groups, buttressed by time-honored authoritarian patterns and a frequently turbulent political system, have all mitigated against the realization of constructive reforms in such areas as health, housing, and education. Population growth and migration to cities and towns have taxed municipal services, and the central government has been ineffective in taking up the slack. Just as the banana bonanza was of limited benefit to the ordinary citizen, much the same has been true of the contemporary oil era.

The history of Ecuadorean petroleum, now so central to the country, lies beyond the scope of this chapter. Suffice it to say that after four decades of limited production, the March 1964 exploration contract with a Texaco-Gulf consortium led to development of reserves in the northeastern Amazon region. By 1972 production capacity surpassed 200,000 barrels daily. In 1973 the military government created the Ecuadorean State Petroleum Corporation (CEPE), and in November Ecuador became a member of OPEC. A contractual agreement granted Texaco-Gulf equal shares totaling 75 percent of production, with the remaining 25 percent allotted to CEPE. The next few years saw increasing demands by Gulf for more favorable treatment. Eventually Gulf threatened to withdraw from Ecuador, and the government countered by proposing nationalization. In October 1976 Ecuador announced its intention of taking over Gulf's holdings in the country; negotiations over the terms of compensation ran through much of 1977. Texaco remained in the country while CEPE expanded to control 62.5 percent of the *oriente* holdings as a result of Gulf's departure.

Although correctly perceived by the oil multinationals as a weak link in the OPEC chain, Ecuador has met its obligations to the cartel and attempted to withstand international pressures. Facing virtual bankruptcy under Velasco in 1972, Ecuador reestablished international credit, strengthened foreign reserves, and channeled funds into infrastructural expansion, which has stressed public works, expansion of port facilities, and improved transportation and communications. By 1977 the economic growth rate stood at about 8 percent. After Ecuador's half-dozen years as an oil exporter, its economy had been altered in important ways. Currency was relatively stable, and the country was a small-scale producer of capital goods. Some 35 percent of nearly $1 billion in oil revenues was funneled into the national budget. Despite official claims for income redistribution through public investment, however, little has been perceptible.

The anticipated "dance of the millions" has benefited only a minority: large landowners through subsidization of agricultural production, industrialists through preferential contracts and artificial tariff protection, the armed forces by continued purchases of modern military gadgetry, and an increasingly consumer-oriented middle sector capitalizing on the doubling of the bureaucracy. Largely untouched are rural Indian workers, unemployed or underemployed coastal *montuvios*, and residents of the teeming urban slums. Inflation has plagued workers as well as the middle sector while food prices and unemployment have risen.

Economically motivated discontent has therefore been inevitable. In 1976 and 1977 a series of civic regional demonstrations denounced the unresponsiveness of the central government. Despite armed intervention, strikes became more frequent. Industrial expansion did little to alter the central government's characteristic inefficiency and lack of profitability, notwithstanding government incentives; most factories were still working at less than 65 percent capacity. Despite the emphasis placed on industrialization by the 1978–1982 national plan, progress was erratic and halting. A strongly regional orientation to official plans produced a sizable flow of funds to centers other than Quito and Guayaquil, although the capital itself became especially active in the effort to attract new light industry. Much of the necessary infrastructure was absent, and inflation served further to limit the local spending power on which many of the new industries had to rely. The marked increase of foreign investment in the 1970s, while aggravating Ecuador's dependency status, itself has fallen off in the light of political uncertainties and labor unrest.

Agriculture has remained the most depressed sector of the economy. Its growth rate in 1984 was only 3.5 percent, despite increasing infusions of capital from the oil financed National Development Fund (FONADE). Many government-funded rural projects have collapsed or fallen far behind schedule, and long-term credits have been difficult to secure. Most bank loans have gone to the large landowners, while medium and small farmers have suffered in the process. Redistribution of land-ownership, even on a limited scale, has produced constant opposition by the propertied elite, forcing the government to back down on its high-flown rhetorical promises of 1972 and 1973. The regime has therefore directed increasing attention to colonization programs in the *oriente*, none of which are designed to improve basic shortcomings in production.

Coffee, bananas, cacao, and sugar—each with potential as an earner of export dollars—manifested the general malaise. The first of these registered increased earnings in 1976 and 1977 as a product of spiraling international prices, but its long-range future was at best mixed. Bananas were faced with the competition of Central Ameican producers, and the government wavered indecisively over the question of possible membership in the Union of Banana Exporting Countries (UPEB). Milk and corn were two important staples that had to be imported, and by 1977 half of the barley consumed was being obtained from abroad. In short, while petroleum income was being channeled into the agricultural and industrial sectors, population expansion outran the capacity of public policy to meet growing human needs. Thus the avowed effort to "sow the petroleum"—in the famous Venezuelan phrase—had faltered badly and been found wanting.

FUTURE PROSPECTS

The national transformation optimistically heralded as the result of the petroleum windfall has not occurred. Although production has remained at or slightly above 210,000 barrels per day, the decline in world prices in the early 1980s was accompanied by increasing domestic consumption of fuels and other derivatives. As a consequence, the heralded bonanza of 1972–1978 has disappeared. Moreover, although the capacity of CEPE has increased, foreign technology is still necessary if additional reserves are to be located. The government signed new risk contracts with multinationals in early 1984 to promote further exploration. New resources must be located if the nation's reserves are not to be dissipated by the close of the decade.

Petroleum remains the core of economic policy, for in 1983 it constituted 72.2 percent of total exports, the highest in the history of Ecuadorean foreign trade. Traditional exports suffered from a combination of factors, including devastating rains on the coast. Only coffee increased foreign sales in 1983, by some 6.6 percent. However, bananas dropped 28.8 percent and cacao a staggering 71 percent. Fish—excluding shrimp—declined by 65.8 percent. Thus the new government was faced with problems over the future of petroleum, stagnating agriculture, and a drastic fall in traditional exports. The very capacity to feed the populace was deteriorating at a time when the rate of population increase of 2.7 percent was among the highest in Latin America.

Although the incoming administration confronted the need for major new investments in these economic sectors, it was faced with the continuing fiscal and monetary crisis. Short-term debts contracted by the outgoing military regime in 1977–1978 had seriously plagued both Roldós and Hurtado. The manipulative skills of the latter had bought Ecuador some time. However, an estimated 30 percent of export income in 1984 was required merely to service the international debt. The total of some $7 billion was equivalent to three times annual exports. The 1984 budget of $2.115 million required the payment of $480 million solely for interest on the debt. A new round of debt renegotiation loomed ahead, while the International Monetary Fund carefully monitored the situation. The international monetary reserve had continued to fall in 1983, with the 8 percent decline producing the worst year in a full decade.

Amid this discouraging economic panorama, social problems were also aggravated. Although Hurtado was adept in handling fiscal diffi-culties, he paid the price of popular alienation and disapproval of austerity measures. At the same time, traditional Ecuadorean elites continue to accept the perquisites of international and domestic colo-nialism. Their hostility toward the moderate orientation of both Roldós and Hurtado has been marked by venom and irrationality. Character-istically, they explicitly praise the accomplishments of the Chilean model under Augusto Pinochet, despite its evident failure. Moreover, the degree of governmental activism and statism—primarily the doing of the military from 1972 to 1979—also draws oligarchical wrath.

The political scene is perhaps less gloomy. A new generation of political leadership has emerged, reformist organizations are displacing traditionalist images of past decades, and leftist influences probe for more varied approaches to national problems. Yet the degree of immaturity is pronounced. The 1984 electoral campaigns, for example, were virtually bereft of programs and policy proposals, while the mudslinging reached unprecedented heights. The impact of personalism cannot be dismissed, and the authoritarian impulse endures as a societal characteristic. Revolution with a capital R does not appear looming in the wings, although greater discontent and popular alienation is not unlikely. For the majority of Ecuadoreans—among the most captivating and variegated people in Latin America—life will change but slowly and gradually. For its political leaders, as the five-time president Velasco Ibarra remarked more than once, it will remain true that "Ecuador is a very difficult country to govern."

SUGGESTIONS FOR FURTHER READING

Agee, Philip. *Inside the Company: CIA Diary.* Stonehill, New York, 1975.

Blanksten, George I. *Ecuador: Constitutions and Caudillos.* University of California Press, Berkeley, 1951.

Bork, Albert William, and Georg Maier. *Historical Dictionary of Ecuador.* Scarecrow Press, Metuchen, N.J., 1973.

Brooks, Rhoda and Earle. *The Barrios of Manta; A Personal Account of the Peace Corps in Ecuador.* New American Library, New York, 1965.

Fitch, John Samuel. *The Military Coup d'Etat as a Political Process: Ecuador, 1948–1966.* Johns Hopkins University Press, Baltimore, 1977.

Hurtado, Osvaldo. *Political Power in Ecuador.* Translated by Nick D. Mills, Jr., University of New Mexico Press, Albuquerque, 1980.

Icaza, Jorge. *Huasipungo: The Villagers, A Novel.* Translated and with an introduction by Bernard M. Dulsey. Foreward by J. Cary Davis. Southern Illinois University Press, Carbondale, 1964.

Martz, John D. *Ecuador: Conflicting Political Culture and the Quest for Progress.* Allyn and Bacon, Boston, 1972.

Needler, Martin C. *Anatomy of a Coup d'Etat: Ecuador 1963.* Institute for the Comparative Study of Political Systems, Washington, D.C., 1964.

Thomsen, Moritz. *Living Poor: A Peace Corps Chronicle.* University of Washington Press, Seattle, 1969.

Whitten, Norman E., Jr. *Class, Kinship and Power in an Ecuadorean Town: The Negroes of San Lorenzo.* Stanford University Press, Stanford, Calif., 1965.

Part 3

The political systems of Central and Middle America and the Caribbean

18
Mexico in the 1980s: From Authoritarianism to Power Sharing?

EVELYN P. STEVENS

To most U.S. citizens, Mexico is a challenging paradox: We think we know something about it, yet its political and social realities continue to elude us, lost in a glut of information and a cloud of oversimplifying generalizations. More has been written in English about Mexico—in the form of books, articles, reports, doctoral dissertations, masters' theses, and newspaper stories—than about all the other Latin American republics together. Mexico is the nearest of all the republics to the United States, sharing a common border that is crossed from the north by millions of U.S. tourists in search of rest and recreation and from the south by hundreds of thousands of Mexicans in search of jobs. But, as with the author of "Faces and Masks," a much-quoted essay on Mexico, each time the student peels off a layer of appearance in order to uncover the basic reality, she or he encounters another layer.

Each Latin American republic is different from all others, but there are a number of distinctive features about Mexico that place it in a very special category as one of the keys to the entire region. Most important, it was the birthplace of the first—and until 1959 the only—genuine social revolution in the hemisphere. Forty-nine years before the Cuban Revolution, Mexico attempted to restructure the economic basis of social classes, and the reasons for its failure to do so make it as worthy of study as if it had achieved its objective.

Towering above all the facts known and published about Mexico is the fact of the Revolution itself. Mexican authors always capitalize the word to indicate the process that began in 1910 and that government spokesmen insist continues to unfold. At the same time some disillusioned patriots claim that not only is the Revolution dead but Mexico has actually regressed to a stage of economic, social, and political relationships like those that prevailed before 1910. Thus to all Mexicans the Revolution

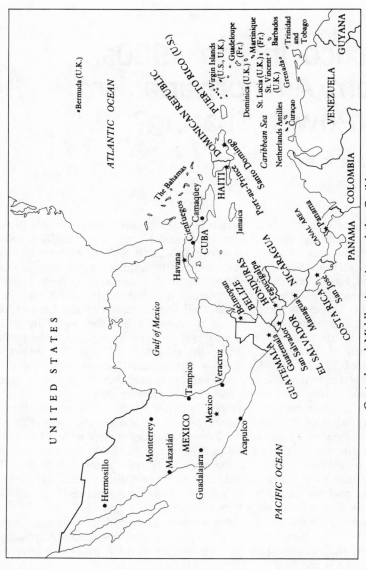

Central and Middle America and the Caribbean

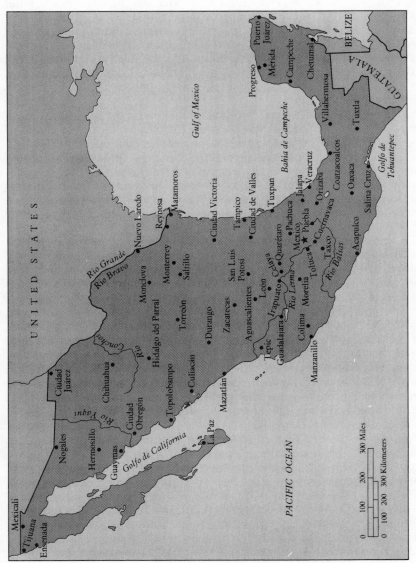

Mexico

is the touchstone of their collective life; to some, it is the symbol of their proud achievements to date and the achievements yet to come. To others—perhaps as many as the first group and possibly even more than those—it is the sorry reminder of what might have been, what still might be if proper leadership could be found. To all it is a record of turmoil and bloodshed, of guerrilla warfare, individual heroism, treacherous assassination, disruption of families, ruined crops, and desolation that started in 1910 and continued for nearly eighteen years. At the end of that period, there was no glorious victory, only exhaustion and a willingness to accept almost any arrangement that would bring peace again to the land.

Just as the United States' war of independence is personified by a picture of a Minuteman, so the Mexican Revolution takes the shape of an embattled peasant with cartridge belt slung over his shoulder and rifle in his hands. The peasant is the concrete embodiment of the Revolution because numerically peasants were the most important element; for most of its history, Mexico has been a predominantly agricultural nation, and for all of the "modern" period, that is, for nearly two hundred years, there has not been enough land to satisfy the needs or wants of the rural population.

The greatest achievement of the Revolution was the adoption in 1917 of a unique constitution that was a radical departure from the eighteenth-century liberal-democratic models provided by the French and U.S. constitutions, which had been widely copied by Latin American nations when they achieved independence from Spain. The new Mexican constitution embodied notions of social and economic justice, proclaimed hostility to organized religion, guaranteed the rights of labor unions, and established the national government's inalienable claim to the land as well as to the subsoil. More will be said about specific provisions of this remarkable document; for the present it is enough to note that it was the first truly modern constitution reflecting an entirely new approach to the philosophy of government, antedating by several years and in some ways foreshadowing the development of the first Soviet constitution.

Another distinctive feature of Mexican politics is the "invention" of the huge, well-organized official party, the Institutional Revolutionary party (PRI), which dominates the electoral process and provides mass support for the government's conduct of national, state, and local affairs. Quite simply, the party, in its present form and previous incarnations, has preempted the field of organized political activity and has redefined the concept of participation, providing a new model for many developing nations throughout the world. It continues to be the subject of fascinated inquiry by native and foreign social scientists. In the pages that follow, much more will be said about this protean phenomenon because it is one of the keys to an understanding of the Mexican political system.

No less a subject of study and speculation is the unusual relationship between state capitalism and private capitalism, which provided the basis for twenty-five years of phenomenal economic growth. A major question concerns the relative power exercised by each of these two elements: Which one calls the tune to which the other dances? In spite of the occasionally inflamed rhetoric of official spokespersons, it is obvious that the government is most anxious to share the burden of entrepreneurship with native and foreign private investors, and in spite of frequent alarms by the latter, they continue to profit from the relationship. Other Latin American nations have tried to copy some of the features of the arrangement, but apparently none to date has found the secret of its success.

In an era of official distrust of U.S. motives and popular accusations of imperialism, Mexico has earned the respect of other Latin American nations for its steadfast resistance to encroachments on its sovereignty. One of the measures of its success in this delicate balancing act is the increasing recognition of its role as one of the leaders in Latin Americans' aspirations for a bigger voice in world affairs. Critics may argue that the area of autonomy of the Mexican government is limited, that U.S. influence on Mexican policy is in fact enormous, but no one disputes that whatever independence it enjoys has been achieved by its own sophisticated diplomacy, without the support of another major world power.

All the achievements just described have taken place against a background of more than fifty years of political stability: regular elections, orderly succession in office, and considerably less civic unrest than in most of the nations of this hemisphere. These are the aspects that make Mexico's past, present, and future the subject of continued interest by students of Latin American politics.

With an estimated 69 million inhabitants in 1981, Mexico is the second most populous nation in Latin America. Its 1970 growth rate, estimated at 3.5 percent per year, later slowed with the introduction in 1974 of a government-sponsored birth-control program; however, even if the rate continues to decline it will be well beyond the year 2000 before population pressures ease noticeably.[1] This inescapable fact is a source of some of Mexico's most serious problems.

Heading the list of these problems is the rate of unemployment and underemployment, which, combined into one figure, is estimated to be as high as 50 percent of the economically active population. Traditional agriculture, which was labor intensive, has declined steadily—from 55 percent of the total labor force in 1960 to 40 percent in 1979—while the number of persons seeking employment has continued to rise. Meanwhile the industrial and service sectors have expanded without generating enough new jobs to take up the slack.[2]

Government agricultural policies favor the large landowners—individuals or agribusinesses that link Mexican nationals with transnational corporations producing for the export market. These large-scale enterprises are located mainly in northern Mexico, where extensive irrigation systems have been installed by the government. The big farmers invest in mechanized equipment, fertilizers, and improved seed that for the most part are unavailable to small farmers because of lack of credit. Mountainous terrain and lack of rainfall in some areas limit Mexico's cultivable territory to about 20 percent of its total 760,373 square miles (nearly 2 million square kilometers), and only about 15 percent is of good quality for farming.

The income of people classified as farmers is less than that of persons employed in manufacturing, service jobs, or commerce. Because it is a losing proposition to try to eke out a living on miniature plots of ground, peasants migrate to towns or cities, with the result that today nearly 75 percent of all Mexicans live in urban areas of fifteen thousand or more population. By 1982 the "urban agglomeration" of Mexico City had more than 16 million inhabitants.

Mexico is usually described as a mestizo society, that is, a human group whose gene pool (genetic heritage) has received contributions from the original Amerindian inhabitants and from the later (since the sixteenth century) Spanish conquerors-colonizers. There were also small genetic contributions from Africa, but these were confined mainly to the coast areas and were statistically unimportant, although the physical traits of the population in those areas still exhibit some features clearly identifiable as of African origin. Mexico's largest ethnic minority, however, is the Indians, often physically indistinguishable from the mestizo population but a culturally separate group. Cultural Indianness is a traditional life-style manifested through dress ("native costume"), diet, place of residence (self-contained ethnically separate villages), and language preference. Over two hundred Indian languages are still spoken in Mexico, and although many Indians are bilingual (preferring to speak an Indian language but able also to communicate in Spanish), approximately 2 percent of Mexico's population is completely monolingual, speaking only an Indian language. Monolingual Indians are unable to communicate with other monolingual Indians who speak a different Indian language.

Over the years the policy of the Mexican government toward the "Indian problem" has varied widely, ranging from official attempts to integrate this group into the mestizo culture to other attempts to protect and nurture the unique values of Indian culture. Unofficially, this ethnic group is widely regarded as an anachronism and an obstacle to national development. The observer cannot fail to note that in spite of protestations to the contrary, many mestizos discriminate against Indians, whom they regard as inferior.

SOCIAL POLICY

"Development" as it is understood in Mexico has come to mean continuing economic growth through industrialization. This goal has been pursued through varying strategies, with the result that from 1946 to the early 1970s and again in the late 1970s the gross national product rose at an average rate of more than 6 percent per year—an achievement described by some observers as the "Mexican miracle." But the benefits of growth did not extend to all sectors of the population; as a matter of fact, the old adage about the rich getting richer and the poor getting poorer is well illustrated by current conditions in Mexico.

Whereas in 1969 the poorest 20 percent of Mexican households received 4 percent of income earned, the same group in 1977 received only 3.3 percent. During the same period the next lowest 30 percent of households increased its share from 11 percent to 13.4 percent, and the next highest 30 percent fared even better, rising from 21 percent to 28.2 percent. Part of those increases came from a decrease in the share received by the highest 20 percent of households, from 64 percent to 55.1 percent, but the biggest losers were the one who could least afford it: those at the bottom of the economic scale. During the present decade, because of inflation and currency devaluation, all but the very rich have felt the sharp bite of lowered living standards.

The rural poor—including the small landholders and seasonal agricultural workers—suffered greater hardships than their urban counterparts, especially with respect to employment opportunities, which accounts to a great extent for the massive migration to the cities. Ironically, it was the rural segment of Mexican society in whose name the Revolution was carried out.

Although educational opportunities in Mexico are among the best in Latin America and this is clearly a result of government commitment to the principle of expanded opportunity, the results have not been as encouraging as might be expected. At present about 98 percent of Mexican children are able to enroll in the elementary school system. However, if recent experience is a guide, it is probable that only about 30 percent of that age group will actually complete the full six grades. At the next step, grades seven through twelve, it is expected that the dropout rate will be nearly as high. Still, this is a great improvement over the situation that existed twenty years ago, when only 56 percent of children reached second grade.

In the opinion of some education specialists, satisfactory completion of the first four grades of elementary school will equip most individuals with the basic skills needed to participate at least minimally in the activities associated with modern social life. For those fortunate enough to complete their secondary education—usually young men and women from the middle- and upper-income strata of society—two roads are open in higher education. The one taken by 85 percent of the secondary-school graduates leads to publicly financed universities and technical institutes; the remaining 15 percent of students enter the more prestigious private institutions. Graduates of these elite schools are far more likely to find employment as professionals in private industry or government, starting in middle-level positions, while most of their public-school cohorts must be content with less-promising opportunities.

Other groups that have benefited from changes in the economic structure are lower-level bureaucrats, office workers, and unionized employees of privately owned commercial or industrial enterprises. Among the advantages they enjoy are medical treatment and hospital care through the government-subsidized social-security system, paid vacations and old-age pensions, and a variety of other social services, including educational extension courses and entertainment programs. Underemployed and unemployed workers remain on the outside looking in at those who enjoy these privileges; the disadvantaged majority have no social-security coverage, no pensions, and no vacations. If they become ill they go to understaffed and crowded government hospitals or dispensaries that operate under the national health program.

Politics and Culture

During the 1960s perceptions about Mexican politics and Mexican citizens were clustered around two themes. The first of these was the proposition that Mexico was the prototype of a new political mutant: the "single-party democracy." Some observers describing the dominant political party, the PRI, saw in its structure a near-perfect vehicle for interest aggregation, and they assumed that it also functioned to articulate the interests of the major social groups of the nation. Other observers studied the activities of groups not included in the party and concluded that they operated under conditions that made them similar to the numerous "interest" or "pressure" groups found in pluralist democracies. Although it was already evident that a small percentage of citizens benefited economically far more than the majority, it was confidently assumed that the time was not far off when the "trickle-down" effect of the nation's economic boom would begin to bring greater prosperity to the disadvantaged classes.

The second view, actually a corollary of the first, was that Mexican citizens had the ability to affect the decisions of their government and that they overwhelmingly supported the government and its policies. Certainly the electoral statistics seemed to confirm this interpretation: Turnout at the polls was high, and PRI candidates at all levels of government—municipal, state, and national—were regularly elected with about 90 percent of the votes cast.

The inevitable conclusion drawn from these two views was that the Mexican political system, while far from perfect, provided a bridge between political and economic underdevelopment to a more perfectly developed pluralistic democracy. One of the difficulties was that most analysts felt that every political system had to be classified either as totalitarian or democratic. To the question "If it isn't either one of these, then what is it?" they felt obliged to answer, "I guess it's a *sort* of democracy." However, there were dissenters who saw the system as a well-oiled machine run by the few for their own benefit.

Other observers who felt uncomfortable with a framework of analysis that excluded more facts than it included were heartened when a new model that relieved them of the necessity of making either-or choices appeared. The model, first elaborated by Juan Linz to describe the political system of Franco's Spain, was given the name of authoritarianism. According to Linz, this system is characterized by the following features:

1. Limited pluralism. In contrast to liberal democracies, which allow almost unlimited pluralism, the authoritarian regime limits, either legally or de facto, the participation of some interest groups. In Mexico the constitution forbids participation by the Church and the clergy; in addition many groups are excluded in actual practice from effective participation, that is, from influencing the choice of policies. In contrast to totalitarian regimes, these groups are never completely suppressed but instead exist in a kind of limbo in which their sporadic protests are heard but not heeded.

2. Lack of ideology. In Mexico there is no organized system of thought that prescribes certain objectives and guides behavior in pursuit of those objectives. Instead there is a distinctive *mentality* or frame of mind that translates into a fairly consistent program of action.

3. Limited mobilization. In liberal democracies, many interest groups are continually mobilizing in order to exert pressure for the adoption of their preferred policies. In totalitarian systems, such groups are completely suppressed. In political systems like that of Mexico, groups that have been organized by the government are occasionally allowed to act, but only to support official policies. At other times groups are expected to remain quiescent, waiting for the government to take the initiative.

4. Decisional elite. Policymaking by a small group to which newcomers can be admitted only by satisfactorily demonstrating that they share the prevalent mentality of the group.

Linz observed correctly that the authoritarian regime is neither an imperfect rendering of the democratic model nor a halfway house between totalitarianism and democracy but rather a fully developed sui generis form of centralized political control. Like totalitarianism it responds to an elitist distrust of popular preferences, but instead of total repression it depends for its effectiveness on systematic discouragement of popular participation. At the same time that the formal structure in Mexico discourages direct participation, the informal structure fosters mediated participation through patron-client relationships.

A number of recent studies of Mexican attitudes toward political participation indicate that most of the individuals interviewed have a relatively low sense of political efficacy and a high degree of dependence on the government to solve their problems for them. The demands of poor people for a larger share of benefits, which was to result from an anticipated "revolution of rising expectations," simply never materialized. Even members of the middle class who tried to organize in order to pressure for reforms became discouraged as a result of a realistic appreciation that structural obstacles defeated individual and group efforts.

Widespread support for the dominant party is still manifested at the polls, but this support is now seen as a passive behavioral characteristic: a belief that there is no viable alternative to the present agreement. This kind of support is most evident among the very groups that know the least about politics and benefit the least from government policies: the urban and rural poor. Opposition to the government as indicated by electoral behavior is manifested almost exclusively by higher income groups, while major protest movements are mobilized by intellectuals or a few militant independent labor unions. What had appeared to earlier investigators as Mexicans' confidence in their individual ability to affect governmental decisions turned out to be an attitude of dependence on some other individual or group to obtain results on their behalf. This type of relationship is more accurately called *mediated efficacy.*

In the cities, hosts of brokers mediate between individuals and the institutions of government, expediting completion of paperwork and distributing payments to bureaucrats to obtain licenses, certificates, permits, and health and welfare benefits for their clients. Urban brokers are of many types, ranging from highly paid lawyers to sleazy operators who haunt the corridors of government buildings, offering their services to bewildered and frustrated citizens. Political folklore has it that if one can just find the right broker with the right connections, almost any concession can be obtained.

To a large extent Latin American politics were historically dominated by caudillos ("men on horseback") and caciques (local strongmen). Both of these types have been absorbed into the hierarchical structures of the Institutional Revolutionary party and have lost the ability to dominate national policy. At the level of regional and local affairs they still control considerable patronage and influence; citizens often turn to them for help in getting favorable official action on some personal matter. However, the myth of omnipotence has now been transferred to the central government. If provincial groups become sufficiently incensed about what they feel are gross abuses of authority by local officials, they feel they can appeal to the *mero mero* (the real top boss) in Mexico City for redress.

A number of cultural traits, most of them shared to some extent with the peoples of other Latin American, Iberian, and Mediterranean societies, operate to produce the attitudes and behavior just described. Most important of these is *personalism:* the persistent tendency to trust certain individuals rather than to expect results to flow from legal rights or impersonal bureaucratic procedures. In Mexico the achievement of a political or economic goal depends very heavily on whom one knows.

The Sacred Triad

To a greater extent than most Western people, Mexicans distrust their fellow citizens unless bound to them by strong personal ties. These ties have their origins in one or another of three lifetime commitments of loyalty:

1. Family. Throughout Latin America, blood relationships and marriage relationships demand the highest form of loyalty, taking precedence over claims arising from any other type of human association. This means that in business organizations as well as in government bureaucracy nepotism is the general rule rather than the exception. Whenever one member of a family succeeds in any kind of enterprise, that person surrounds himself with relatives, partly in order to share his good fortune with those whose welfare most concerns him but also—and this is very important—because these are the persons he can trust completely to defend his interests. They are "persons of [his] confidence." They will not betray him to his business or political rivals because his downfall will also blight their fortunes. Many otherwise opaque situations can be clarified by reference to an individual's double surname, which reveals his connections with his mother's side of the family as well as with his father's.

2. Friendship. Distrust makes it difficult for Mexicans to form deep lasting attachments to persons outside the family. The word *amigo* (friend), as distinguished from *conocido* (acquaintance), is reserved for a very limited number of persons with whom an individual has established bonds of mutual loyalty second only in intensity to those of family. With rare exceptions these friendships are formed in childhood or youth and persist throughout the lifetime of the persons involved. Whenever possible, friends form part of a successful politician's team of trusted subordinates.

3. Ritual coparenthood, known as *compadrazgo* in Latin America, is the third and last source of loyalty-trust relationship, having its historically distant beginnings in the Iberian custom of choosing godparents for one's children. The *padrino*, or godfather, is present at a child's baptism and ritually assumes responsibility for the child's welfare in case of death or disability of the natural parents. From this symbolic sharing of parenthood spring two types of mutual obligations: those between the godfather and godchild and those between the godfather and the natural parents. Any member of this group may make claims on any other member; these claims—ostensibly at least—must be honored in the same way as family relationships, and such members often—but not always—are included in the circle of trusted associates. Successful and prosperous persons are chosen as *compadres* by many persons anxious to establish a bond with them. Although it is difficult to refuse these requests, an anthropologist has shown that godfathers are often able to avoid honoring claims made by some of their *compadres* or

godchildren by pleading higher loyalties to family members. However, the custom of *compadrazgo* often accounts for the presence of otherwise anomalous individuals in a politician's team of associates.

Every Mexican politician sits at the center of a network of relatives, friends, and *compadres* who move with him as a group when he moves up the political ladder or laterally into a new position. Aware that his particular patron may suffer reverses, each member of the team tries to preserve a number of "fallback" relationships with other members of his own personal sacred triad, to whom he may have recourse in case of necessity. Every politician, with the exception of the incumbent and past presidents of the nation, is in a client relationship with some other more powerful politician. An examination of the political biographies of bureaucrats reveals the pervasiveness of this situation. With each six-year change in the presidency, tens of thousands of individuals at all levels of government service move in and out of positions because of their personal relationships.

Demand making as a form of political participation is transmuted by Mexican political culture into petitioning, because a direct demand, that is, a request for benefits from the government based on juridical rights, would be considered a hostile act. In approaching officials, individuals or groups of citizens present themselves figuratively—and often literally—hat in hand to beg favors, often enduring long waits with seemingly inexhaustible patience. But Mexican patience does have its limits, and when frustrations become intolerable, citizens may abandon their humble stance to engage in active, even violent, protest. Such movements have erupted sporadically during the past three hundred years, occasionally spreading to far-reaching rebellions. Land invasions, unauthorized labor strikes, students' and doctors' strikes have been recent manifestations of protest. Government response to these movements has been authoritarian and repressive.

THE REVOLUTION

Modern Mexican history dates from 1910 when, after nearly a century of independence from Spain—a century characterized by foreign invasions, attempts to implant a monarchy, struggles between Liberals and Conservatives, and two long-lived dictators—the Mexican people arose and brought about the first fundamental social revolution of the twentieth century.

The last of the old-style dictators, Porfirio Díaz, gave his name to a thirty-four-year period of Mexican history: the Porfiriato. For much of that time he occupied the presidency, but on occasion he allowed someone else to be elected to that office as long as it was he who actually controlled the affairs of the nation.

Diaz's formula was simple: He set a goal of economic growth whose achievement was guaranteed by an ironhanded maintenance of order and persistent wooing of foreign capital. Peace and prosperity were unfamiliar but welcome conditions to Mexicans. Foreign investors, attracted by the prospect of profits, were reassured by the new atmosphere of political stability that prevailed throughout the country, guaranteed by the government's mounted troops of rural police.

Díaz gathered together a group of very able advisers who, because they were much influenced by Comtean positivism, were called *científicos*. Under the brilliant finance minister José Yves Limantour, the budget was balanced and Mexico's international credit improved remarkably. The nascent rail system was expanded from 287 miles (about 460 kilometers) to a network of 12,000 miles (19,200 kilometers), and many distant parts of the country were linked by telegraph and roads; a few important centers even had telephones. Industry and commerce flourished, giving middle- and upper-class Mexicans a new sense of national pride. The poor, the great majority of the population, remained poor, oppressed, and voiceless, as they had always been.

Time was the great agent of change. As Díaz and his advisers grew older and more conservative, the young intellectuals grew restive and bold. Some were outraged at the ugly contrast between the opulence of the few and the abject poverty of the many; others felt stifled by the repressive atmosphere; and all were indignant about being denied a voice in national affairs. Continuism in office gave a suffocating air of decay to the councils of government.

In 1908 President Díaz granted a widely publicized interview to an American journalist, James Creelman. In the interview, calculated to enhance Mexico's image abroad, Díaz stated that under his long tutelage the Mexican people had been gradually educated to make them fit for democracy. The time was approaching, he said, when real political parties could offer candidates for election, and his firm hand at the helm would no longer be needed to direct the affairs of the country. The effect of these statements in Mexico was electrifying. Although skeptical, rebellious critics began to talk and write about what kind of changes should take place when the hoped-for day arrived. Francisco Madero published a small book titled *La sucesión presidencial en 1910* (The presidential succession in 1910) suggesting the steps that could be taken to open the electoral process to opposition parties. When official silence greeted his efforts, he carried the ideas a step further by declaring himself a candidate for the presidency and campaigning openly. He was jailed for his effrontery, and Díaz was duly reelected. Meanwhile, in widely separated areas of Mexico, quickly suppressed uprisings were evidence that Madero's lonely effort had brought the general discontent to the surface. When Madero was freed on bail, he crossed the border into Texas and from there launched a verbal assault urging the people of Mexico to rebel, with the slogan Effective Suffrage and No Reelection.

The liberal intellectuals of Mexico hesitated, paralyzed by fear of reprisals, which soon began to occur. Accustomed to violence and impatient for action, the caudillos Pascual Orozco and Francisco "Pancho" Villa took maters into their hands by initiating the armed rebellion. Under their urging, Madero reentered national territory to take charge of the Revolution that his ideas had started. Within six months the campaign in the north had evoked uprisings in other parts of the country and finally in Mexico City itself. Díaz was forced to resign and leave the country, and Madero's entrance into Mexico City signaled the triumph of the rebels.

The violent phase of the Revolution continued until about 1920, as caudillos fought and killed each other and plotted to attain undisputed power. Ever the middle-class intellectual, Madero proved a timid, ineffectual leader. While Villa in the north counseled a firm course of action, Madero hesitated long enough to allow his rivals to assassinate him in 1913. Villa himself was tricked into an ambush and killed soon thereafter. In the south the revered peasant leader Emiliano Zapata met a similar fate.

Victoriano Huerta, who had seized power after Madero's death, was ousted in 1914 and replaced by Venustiano Carranza. In an attempt to restore order to the country, Carranza convoked a constitutional convention in 1917, intending that the delegates should produce a mildly liberal amended version of the 1857 reform constitution. Some of the delegates arrived with the conviction that what was needed was a radically different document that would provide a new social and economic structure for modern Mexico.

It was an amazing convention of immense historical importance, reaching far beyond the confines of Mexico itself. Although some of the delegates had only elementary notions of constitutionalism, others were politically sophisticated and able negotiators. The Jacobins in particular were well grounded in theory and won reluctant support for key provisions that set the tone for the entire document.

Article 27 concerned agrarian reform, providing the legal basis for breaking up the huge haciendas and parceling out the land to peasants. Almost incidentally, this article also reaffirmed national ownership not only of the land but of any and all mineral resources in the subsoil. This section, which established the legality of future nationalization of petroleum resources, was based on principles originally enunciated during the colonial era by the Spanish Crown.

Article 123 guaranteed the rights of labor, including the right to organize unions, to engage in collective bargaining, and to strike in support of demands. It anticipated federal labor legislation in the United States.

Article 130 went much farther than provisions of the 1857 constitution in declaring the separation of Church and state and setting the conditions for universal free secular education.

As Mexico entered the 1920s, armed warfare abated among caudillo-led bands, principally because the most powerful leaders had killed each other off. Political power in the hinterlands reverted to the caciques. In Mexico City the national government under Álvaro Obregón continued consolidating its authority over the entire nation. Violence did not completely disappear, as is shown by the assassination of Obregón himself in 1928 when he dared to violate the most sacred principle of the revolution by campaigning for reelection.

Historians who like to divide their subject into neat periods are inclined to view Obregón's death as the event that closed the revolutionary era in Mexico. Mexican politicians, on the other hand, have steadfastly maintained that it merely signaled a transition to a new stage: the institutionalization of the Revolution. From that time forward the word itself would be capitalized by Mexicans to emphasize its permanent significance in the political continuity of the nation.

MODERN POLITICAL HISTORY:
1929 TO THE PRESENT

Peace and Populism

The great innovation that marked the turning point in the nation's political life was the founding in 1929 of a modern mass-based party with a structure radically different from the traditional nineteenth-century parties. In the previous century, party members were an elite of educated middle- or upper-class persons. They sought electoral support from the newly enfranchised masses in order to represent them in legislative bodies, but they did not necessarily consider their supporters as members of the party. In the new type of party organization, the masses were incorporated, directly or indirectly, into the party.

The new Mexican party was conceived by its founder, President Plutarco Elías Calles, as preempting or at least dominating the field of electoral activity by virtue of being identified with the group of leaders already in power. The party was organized not to achieve power but to protect decision makers from challenges. There had been political parties and mass organizations during the 1920s, but they represented regional or special-interest groups. They had no synthesizing vision of Mexican national life as did the Liberal and Conservative leaders of the nineteenth-century reform movement.

Although it has undergone two name changes and several important structural reforms, the National Revolutionary party (PNR), as it was first called, has preserved its original essential features as a virtually monopolistic mass-based organization. Soon after it was established and began to function, there was a marked decrease in overt political conflict in Mexico. The nation was able to turn its attention to repairing the ravages of the prolonged civil disturbances, restoring the communications that had been disrupted, and trying to improve the devastated economy.

What achieved for the party its preemptive position in the Mexican political system was its claim to be the legitimate heir to the revolutionary tradition and to be the defender of the rights guaranteed by the 1917 constitution. An impressive lineup of revolutionary leaders soon associated themselves with the party and lent credence to this image. The violent stage of the Revolution was over, they argued; so also was the formative stage. Now the country was ready to translate the promise of those stages into the reality of a peaceful and good life for all Mexicans—but especially for the workers, who were the majority of the population.

As time went on some of the most revered leaders became disenchanted by what they believed was the betrayal of these lofty ideals and quietly disassociated themselves from party activities, retiring to their homes in the provinces. But by the time the myth would be firmly established, rival claims would be eliminated, and alternative electoral choices would be foreclosed. By getting there first with the most, the party achieved a monopoly of organizational force.

In its original form the party was not intended to be a framework for functional interest groups but an instrument for political control. President Calles apparently deliberately excluded from the constituent assembly representatives of the powerful Mexican Regional Labor Confederation (CROM) and the large peasant organization known as the National Agrarian party. Instead he issued invitations to local and regional leaders whose sphere of influence crossed occupational lines to include a wide network of interpersonal relationships based on the sacred triad. He apparently saw the best chance of success in shaping a national organization that would draw its strength from local leaders whose initial tasks were to eliminate competition in their own area and to deliver votes for party candidates. The first part of their mandate—that of eliminating competition—initially required extensive use of violence and fraud, features of party activity that critics allege still persist. As the party gained strength, largely because of government support, it became possible to use other strategies to neutralize opponents.

From the beginning it was apparent that in the broadest sense political competition could not be eliminated; it could only be contained, and the national party, organized in regional units, was designed as the container. Competition became an internal activity, with the party acting as a clearinghouse for the personal ambitions of leaders whose ideological orientations or lack of them frequently conflicted with each other. In a sense it can be said that the party itself has never had an ideology but that its pragmatic objectives were carried on behind the facade of the revolutionary myth. Since its origin the party has been depicted as the instrument of the Revolution, and this party-Revolution identification has been a constant feature throughout its various reorganizations and name changes. By a process of semantic circularity, the concepts of party, Revolution, national redemption, stability, and progress have become linked, while opposition to the party is associated with counterrevolution, disloyalty, disruption, and regression.

Within a few years of the founding of the PNR, it became apparent that its federal structure was allowing regional strong men to become dangerously powerful. The 1933 reorganization was aimed at restraining them by centralizing authority at the national level and situating the regional leaders in a more dependent position. At the same time the process of candidate selection was removed from the public domain and made the prerogative of nominating conventions. Power contenders advanced their claims clandestinely, and winners were presented as the unanimous choice of the conventions.

In 1938, under President Lázaro Cárdenas, another reorganization gave the party the structure that has persisted until the present. With personal power struggles now ritualized, Cárdenas drew from the then current European models of populist corporatism to create a sectoral— rather than a regional—structure, grouping citizens of similar characteristics into four sectors: peasant, labor, popular, and military. By isolating the military forces in a separate sector, he apparently planned to contain their ambitions and outweigh their influence with the other three groups. (The military sector was abolished in 1940 and military men were absorbed into the popular sector.) The remaining sectors—peasant, labor, and popular—are the components of the Institutional Revolutionary party as it exists at present. Each sector is structured vertically, with city, state, and national offices. Communications between the various levels is represented as originating at the lowest level and proceeding up the hierarchy to the national level; in fact, however, the reverse is usually true. Policy is determined at the national headquarters or in unpublicized meetings elsewhere in the capital, and the decisions are sent down the line for implementation. The three sectors do not interact with each other except at the level of the National Executive Committee of the party, of which the national heads of the sectors are members.

The structure chosen by Cárdenas reflected both his ideological and pragmatic objectives. In the peasant and labor sectors can be seen his conviction that these two groupings encompass the range of socially productive human activities. By including the third grouping, the popular sector, he hoped to gather in all other unclassified workers who might provide support for the government, which under his leadership was identified with populist sympathies.

Other major groupings in Mexican society were intentionally excluded. The clergy, at any rate, were barred by the constitution from political activity. Given the revolutionary rhetoric of the government, it was necessary also to exclude organized business groups from the party structure. But this formal exclusion did not mean that business groups had no voice in the determination of economic policy. In 1936 and 1937

under Cárdenas the government moved to establish the National Confederation of Chambers of Commerce (CONCANACO) and the National
Confederation of Chambers of Industry (CONCAMIN). The laws regulating these groups make it mandatory for all businesses, except firms
employing less than forty people, to belong to one or another of the
two confederations, depending on the nature of their activities. One of
the most disputed questions in analyses of Mexican politics is the extent
to which these business associations are able to influence public policy
in favor of their private objectives. We shall return to this problem in
another part of this chapter; at present it is enough to note that even
though there are both formal and informal links between business groups
and the government, these links are not subject to party control. Businesses
may be regulated, but they are not mobilized.

Cárdenas must be given the credit for being the first Mexican leader
to view the national political system as a whole body of interrelated
components. The party structure that he bequeathed to the nation was
a form of populist corporatism that corresponded to a view of the
working class as the only important element of society. He ignored
many groups that did not fit into the narrowly conceived compartments.
The excluded groups and individuals did not remain silent; from the
sidelines they challenged the underlying assumptions of government
policy. The failure to recognize the legitimacy of such criticisms has
been a persistent weakness of government policymakers and may yet
prove to be the Achilles' heel of Mexico's political system.

Cárdenas was the first—and the only—Mexican president to take
literally the mandate of the 1917 constitution to break up the large
estates (*latifundios*) and to redistribute the land among the peasants.
During his term of office 20 million hectares (49.4 million acres) were
expropriated and parceled out to 776,000 members of *ejidos* (collective
landholdings). This was more than the total amount distributed by all
of his predecessors.

In spite of the danger of retaliation by the U.S. and European
governments, Cárdenas managed successfully in 1938 to nationalize the
Mexican petroleum industry—a step that reconciled economic wisdom
with national pride. Conscious also that technology was the key to
economic growth, he established special schools such as the Polytechnic
Institute and the agricultural training centers.

During the early years of his presidency Cárdenas's apparent radicalism
had made many Mexicans and foreigners apprehensive. Before the end
of his term of office he began quietly to withdraw encouragement from
the radical elements in the party's ranks. The administration of President
Manuel Avila Camacho (1940–1946) was notable chiefly for two developments: the restoration of political respectability to practicing Catholics and the passage of federal legislation outlawing subversive intentions
or behavior. He also continued the process of deradicalizing the official
party.

Mexico's Law of Social Dissolution—actually Articles 145 and 145bis of the National Penal Code—was enacted in 1941 for the expressed purpose of combating subversion by pro-German groups during World War II. It was not actually utilized during the war, but it remained embedded in the penal code and was brought into play during the 1950s and 1960s as part of the government's efforts to repress rebellious labor and intellectual movements.

Unrelated to either of the two major developments of Avila Camacho's presidency was the enactment of legislation that established the Mexican Institute of Social Security. Its original scope was comparatively modest, but in later years it was to grow and assume great importance in the nation's economic and social policies.

The Businessman's President

The administration of Miguel Alemán (1946–1952) did for Mexico's merchants and industrialists what Avila Camacho's had done for the Catholics; it restored them to political respectability. There was no official statement at the beginning of Alemán's term, but the new attitude became apparent almost immediately.

Alemán set out to assure investors that the government's fiscal policy was conservative, that the country was politically stable and to the right of center, and that the government was not hostile to foreigners as long as they brought money into the country. He appears to have succeeded on all counts.

Since 1938 the nationalization of the petroleum industry had been the cause of great bitterness on the part of foreign oil companies, principally U.S. and Dutch firms, whose property had been expropriated. An international arbitration commission had recommended the amount of indemnification, but it was not until Alemán's administration that the Mexican government approved a settlement, which included payment of interest retroactive to 1938.

Foreign investors were openly courted, with encouraging results, and the nation's economy began a period of phenomenal growth that was to continue until the early 1980s, except for one short hiatus in the mid-1970s. Agrarian reform was quietly shelved, and labor unions were exhorted to forgo wage increases in order to underwrite national economic growth. When peasants or union workers tried to organize for protest against these involuntary sacrifices, they were harshly repressed. Agricultural production was stimulated, not by extending the technical and financial assistance to *ejidos* and small farmers, but by amending Article 27 of the constitution to create exempted categories that allowed retention or recovery of land by large-scale farm and cattle enterprises.

Prosperity, Poverty, and Protest

The years 1952–1970, encompassing the administrations of Presidents Adolfo Ruiz Cortines, Adolfo López Mateos, and Gustavo Díaz Ordaz, were characterized by continued economic growth, increasing inflation, widespread unemployment, and a steady deterioration in the standard of living of most peasants and urban workers at the same time that Mexico's middle class was expanding to include certain privileged groups of workers (for example, government employees and members of "captive" unions). The latter were unions headed by long-entrenched leaders who were able to obtain limited concessions for their members from the government in exchange for guaranteeing industrial peace and support of government policies. In effect these leaders agreed not to press for additional benefits unless they had prior permission from the government.

Discontent was reflected in the rising number of large-scale protest movements, which included peasant rebellions such as that led by Rubén Jaramillo, the railroad strike led by Demetrio Vallejo, the doctors' strike led by a coalition of disaffected governmental physicians, and the student strike that spread from the UNAM (National University) and the Polytechnic Institute in Mexico City to include provincial campuses in other parts of the nation.

The total number of people involved in these and other movements reached into the hundreds of thousands; all were suppressed by the government by widespread use of legal and extralegal measures. Jaramillo, together with members of his immediate family, was assassinated in 1962; Vallejo and Valentín Campa were convicted in 1963 under the Law of Social Dissolution and imprisoned for more than eleven years; hundreds of participants in the doctors' strikes were dismissed from their posts in the health services in 1965, and some of the most prominent leaders were later jailed on charges of subversive activity. During the student strike of 1968, the army occupied the UNAM campus in September, and in October army units and police riot squads killed hundreds of students and bystanders in what is now known as the massacre of Tlatelolco. Other hundreds were herded into jails, and dozens were later convicted on various charges and imprisoned for years.

Zigzagging Toward Crisis, 1970–1984

During the first years of President Luis Echeverría's term, aggressions against students continued. Groups attempting to reorganize after the debacle of 1968 were infiltrated by intelligence personnel and attacked by armed street gangs whose actions were tolerated by the police. Charges that these gangs were trained and financed by the government were not convincingly refuted. Prior to his election, Echeverría had served as head of the Ministerio de la Gobernación, which, among other responsibilities, was in charge of internal intelligence and countersubversive operations. Thus he was putatively the director of the repression of the students.

Apparently determined to erase the memory of those events, he embarked on a new course. To cultivate a reputation for populism, he created a host of new government social-welfare agencies that were financed by increased public borrowing. To mollify criticism from the left he waged a war of words against the business community, accused its members of economic disloyalty to the nation, and threatened to impose new controls on them. Opposition leaders, perceiving a lack of concrete action, were unconvinced, while business people became alarmed and hostile.

Echeverría's credibility as a champion of ideological pluralism was seriously eroded in 1976 by his part in ousting the editorial staff of *Excelsior*, an internationally respected newspaper that had been very critical of his administration. Turning his attention outward, the president sought a new role for himself as an internationalist and spokesman for the Third World. Although many Third World nations received his visits and declarations of amity with cordiality, he failed to leave a permanent impression on international organizations.

In 1970, Mexico's economic growth was already threatened by an accumulation of problems. During Echeverría's term these problems worsened and others were added: An unfavorable balance of payments—due to a continued increase of imports in relation to exports—became acute, and inflation rose sharply. Investors began to send their money abroad; in the last year of Echeverría's term the flight of capital became a stampede, reaching a total of about 2 billion dollars withdrawn and invested elsewhere. During the period 1970–1976 the total foreign public debt rose from about 4 billion dollars to nearly 20 billion dollars. During the last few months of the six-year term, two successive devaluations of the peso reduced its value by 37 percent.

In an atmosphere of deepening economic trouble, José López Portillo took office in December 1976. To slow the deterioration, his government curtailed public spending, reduced social services and subsidies to low-income groups, and borrowed more money from the International Monetary Fund and foreign banks. Even so, the peso continued its downward course, dropping to seventy to the dollar by December 1982.

Almost the only bright spot in Mexico's economic picture was the announcement of the discovery of major new petroleum and gas deposits. A brief economic boom in the late 1970s imparted a temporary atmosphere of prosperity, which evaporated as new problems arose. Development of these resources made it necessary to borrow more money from abroad. Furthermore, the decision to accelerate extraction of petroleum and to increase the quantities exported provoked strong criticism from opposition leaders, who warned of rapid depletion of reserves.

Two major events, one political and the other economic, took place during the López Portillo administration. The first was a liberalized electoral law passed in 1977, which will be treated at greater length in "The Institutionalization of Dissent." The second was the nationalization by President López Portillo, three months before the end of his term, of all the private banks in the country, a step seen as necessary to prevent further flight of capital from the country. In spite of a great outcry from the private sector, the transition was accomplished smoothly. Economic growth took an upward turn, and massive public-works programs gave a needed stimulus to employment. Increased oil exports improved the balance of payments.

During the first year of President Miguel de la Madrid's term, further misfortunes beset the nation: The external debt had ballooned to $81 billion, investment shrank by 17 percent, and prices increased by nearly 50 percent. The government announced that it would allow the peso to "slide" in value at the rate of thirteen centavos per day, representing an additional annual devaluation of 32 percent.

The possibility of new price cuts by petroleum-producing nations threatened disaster for Mexico, which would lose 500 million dollars a year in revenue for each dollar of reduction. In the midst of accumulated misfortunes the president projected an image of calm and strength, the citizenry seemed to bear its increasingly heavy burdens with fortitude, and the newly enfranchised political parties offered responsible criticism.

SOCIAL AND POLITICAL GROUPS

Although Mexico does not fit the model of a corporate state and no leader has ever publicly proclaimed an intention to follow such a model, it is apparent that for more than half a century there has been a sustained effort by the political elite to channel the activities of some of the major contending groups into vertically structured hierarchical organizations that are controlled by a powerful centralized authority. The political system resulting from this effort is a fragile equilibrium that has persisted for a remarkably long time. Lately there have been signs that it may have reached the limits of its usefulness.

In trying to enumerate the components of the system and to describe their relationship to each other, it is helpful to divide them into two main classifications: the "insiders," who support the system and benefit from it, and the "outsiders," who are denied benefits from and influence on the system.

"Insiders"

The national decision-making elite (hereafter called simply the elite) is the set of persons who at any given historical moment choose the goals for the nation and decide how these goals shall be achieved. These are the people whom Frank R. Brandenburg referred to as "the inner council of the Revolutionary Family."[3] Among them will be found the president of the nation, his successor (when that person has been designated); former presidents; several important regional and national leaders (among the latter are the secretary of *gobernación*, who is the internal security arm of the executive, and the secretary of the army, who is publicly responsible for external security but who also shares with *gobernación* important aspects of internal security activity); some representatives of important commercial and industrial groups; and often a few labor leaders. These are the persons whose opinions are sought—usually informally and often secretly—before binding decisions are made. They are the most influential persons in Mexico, but the decisions themselves are formally enunciated only by the most powerful member and recognized head of the group; the incumbent president.

It would be unrealistic to expect that members of the inner council always agree on what should be done and how it should be done, but once a decision has been made these persons have always supported it.

Recoiling from the implications of the term "power elite" as used by C. Wright Mills, some analysts insist that there is not one elite in Mexico but actually two distinct elites, one representing the autonomous power of the government and the other articulating the views of business interests. Most analysts agree, however, that in spite of frequently divergent policy preferences of these two groups, major decisons are the product of interaction between the two. Because of this interaction, we shall treat the two groups as one elite, unless otherwise indicated in the text.

The government is the structure that utilizes formal-legal institutions as well as informal and extralegal processes to implement the decisions of the elite. To an extent never fully comprehended outside of Mexico, the only "branch" of government that has any discretionary power is the executive, that is, the various ministries (secretariats, or *secretarías*, as they are called in Mexico) and the numerous autonomous and semiautonomous institutes, boards, and commissions whose heads report directly to the president. At the national level the Congress and the judiciary have been completely subordinate to the president, and at the state level the legislatures and courts are subordinate to some powerful state leader, usually the governor, who in turn is subordinate to the president.

Some high government officials are members of the national elite, but their influence on decision making does not derive from their official position. Rather, the reverse is true: They are appointed to such positions precisely because they are influential, and they have achieved this influence because of their personal relationship to other influentials through one or more aspects of the sacred triad. They are members of a "team," bound together by ties of personal loyalty to a chief. Always subordinate to the chief, the more able members of the team are rewarded, as the chief rises to positions of greater influence, by being appointed to positions of greater responsibility and influence.

As we have seen, the party is the officially designated institution that formally organizes several important functional groups for the purpose of controlling the amount and kind of their participation in the political process and for mobilizing them to support the government. The head of the party is chosen by the president and reports to him;

the national executive committee, whose members include the national heads of the functional sectors, has a very close relationship with the executive branch of the government. Regional (that is, state and municipal) party leaders are subordinate to national party leaders.

Probably the most confusing aspect of the party to foreign observers is the fact that party leaders are very often officials of the executive arm of the government. In this capacity they carry out the day-to-day administrative duties common to such positions, but in the former capacity they control party membership.

Party membership is indirect, that is, most individuals usually belong not to the party itself but to some organization such as a labor union or peasant association that is affiliated with one of the three party sectors. For example, the National Peasant Confederation (CNC), which is the mainstay of the party's peasant sector, is the umbrella for a multitude of organizations, many of whose members may not even be aware that they are counted as members of the party. They exercise little if any control over party activities and receive the least benefit from the government. Nevertheless, at election time they allow themselves to be transported to the polls in party buses and cast their votes for the party.

The different sectors of the party share unequally in the benefits of membership: The popular sector, known as the National Confederation of Popular Organizations (CNOP), most of whose members are government workers, receives the largest share in the form of its own health and pension plans, guaranteed salary increases, job security, and other perquisites. Members of the labor sector, whose largest organizational component is the Confederation of Mexican Workers (CTM), groups together a number of large blue-collar unions whose entrenched leaders (called *charros*) negotiate "sweetheart" contracts with private industry, keeping demands for wage increases and other benefits within the range allowed by the government.

Top party leaders are part of the national political elite. As to their social origins, they spring from the middle class and represent the values of that class. Probably the most important thing to remember about the political elite (in contrast to the economic elite) is that it is not a static group; it changes in size and composition. Individuals experience a wide range of mobility both upward and downward, especially at the time of change from one president to the next. So what we are talking about when we refer to the political elite is not a set of names but a set of roles.

Large formal groupings such as CONCAMIN and the National Chamber of Manufacturing Industries (CANACINTRA), as well as the more informal Monterrey Group (about two hundred powerful entrepreneurial families in northern Mexico), act more like outsiders than insiders. They often oppose government economic policies, and because of their importance they have sometimes been able to influence policy decisions.

It would be a mistake, however, to compare Mexican business groups with their U.S. counterparts; lobbying, as practiced in the United States, is not an effective activity in Mexico. It might be a more accurate analogy to say that the relationship between government and business in Mexico is like that of an estranged couple who have joint custody of their children. Neither can act without the cooperation, or at least the grudging consent, of the other.

The important difference between the Mexican system and the U.S. system with respect to economic policy is that Mexico has a clearly formulated policy with respect to government control of economic activity, whereas in the United States the lack of any clearly articulated doctrine has allowed private business interests to exercise decisive influence on government regulation of their activities. In establishing its moral and legal right to dominate economic activity, the Mexican government relies on two historic sources: the strict regulation exercised by the Spanish Crown during the colonial era and the principles of economic control preempted for the government by the 1917 constitution. In contrast, the whole history of U.S. government-business relationships has pointed in the opposite direction, with only occasional and partial victories for the government.

Whatever the theoretical importance of determining to what extent Mexican business interests are dominated by the government, few observers would dispute that (1) the elite mentality assigns a very high priority to the goal of a resumption of economic growth, (2) the elite recognizes that achievement of this goal requires the continued consent and collaboration of private business, and (3) to assure this consent and collaboration the regulatory process must make sure that private business is allowed to operate profitably.

Since 1940 the military forces have not participated as an organized group in the electoral process. This fact, together with the rarity of military men in government positions, might lead a casual observer to conclude that they are politically irrelevant. Such a conclusion would be a serious error: As insiders, military leaders are important beneficiaries and supporters of the political system. Mexico's universal military service law requires that all young men upon reaching the age of eighteen go on active duty for a year and continue in reserve training status for an additional period, but the regular army is small and the navy and air force much smaller. Owing in part to a tradition opposed to foreign military adventures dating back to the reform movement and in part to Mexico's comparative military weakness vis-à-vis the great world powers, the external role of the armed forces is relatively unimportant. U.S. military power has been a perennial source of apprehension for Mexicans, but the threat has remained latent for the past six decades. The combat role of the military, therefore, has been confined to the control of militant protest groups and guerrilla activities within the national boundaries.

Earlier a few examples of the most widely publicized protest movements were given, but it must now be emphasized that those barely touched on the problem. In addition to other similar movements specifically familiar to most Mexicans (although unknown outside of Mexico), there have been an unspecified number of uprisings in rural areas that have received little or no mention in the national press; often such incidents are reported only as banditry and their political significance obscured.

The division of responsibilities with respect to intelligence gathering and counterinsurgency efforts has been unclear, and much overlapping occurs among the activities of the secretariat of *gobernación*, local police forces, and the army. But the army has more and better weapons and personnel, greater mobility, and superior communications facilities. For this reason, as the level of protest has risen, especially during the past two decades, the importance of the armed forces has grown, evidenced by the greater readiness of the government to resort to suppression rather than try to negotiate with protestors. It has now become commonplace to categorize all evidences of unrest as either banditry or foreign-inspired subversion, thus justifying the use of military force for suppression. As long as such incidents remain relatively small-scale and sporadic, military leaders will probably be satisfied to subordinate their role to civilian leadership, but if widespread and prolonged violence were to occur, the army leaders might step in to control the situation, with or without prior consent of civilian leaders.

The PRI's hegemonic presence in political life should not obscure the emergence and growth of other parties, especially since the major electoral reforms of 1977. Since 1970 new groups have emerged whose opposition to government policies has been more often expressed in closely reasoned criticism than in protest marches.

The Institutionalization of Dissent

Because the old methods of repression would be ineffective under the new circumstances, other means were sought to contain and channel dissent. A reform of the restrictive laws regulating participation of parties in the electoral arena was clearly indicated. The government itself took the lead in drafting new legislation; by encouraging public discussion it gave the appearance of openness while at the same time avoiding an all-out onslaught against its prerogatives.

The resulting legislation enacted in December 1977, the Federal Law of Political Organizations and Electoral Procedures (LOPPE), revises and spells out election procedures; defines the rights of political parties, coalitions, and fronts; and lays down the rules under which they may participate in elections. For the latter purpose, a party must apply for registration by the Federal Electoral Commission and comply with several regulations. In order to obtain or keep its registration it must receive at least 1.5 percent of the total vote in the election for which it has registered.

The Mexican Congress is bicameral, with a Senate and a Chamber of Deputies (corresponding to the U.S. House of Representatives). The sixty-two senators (two from each state and the Federal District) are elected for six-year terms by a simple majority vote. Almost without exception they have been members of the PRI.

Under the previous legislation, enacted in 1963, a number of seats in the Chamber of Deputies were reserved for candidates from minority parties, meted out proportionately to parties obtaining a minimum of 2.5 percent of the total vote. No party could obtain more than twenty seats under that rule. The National Action party (PAN) clearly qualified for the largest share of the so-called party deputy seats, but the rules were bent to allow much smaller parties, such as the Popular Socialist party (PPS) and the Authentic Party of the Mexican Revolution (PARM), to obtain seats. The latter two were "tame" parties that presented no challenge to the PRI, but the PAN was an independent right-of-center party that frequently voiced views critical of government policies.

Under the revised 1977 legislation, the party deputy system was abolished, and membership in the Chamber of Deputies was increased from 250 to 400. One hundred of these seats are reserved for representatives of minority parties, elected for three-year terms by proportional representation from party lists in the four districts into which the nation is divided. Minority candidates may also seek election to one of the 300 seats that are filled by simple majority vote, but to date only one party—the long-established PAN—has been able to get candidates elected by this procedure. In the first election held under the new rules, in 1979, three parties in addition to the previous four obtained a share of the seats. They were the Communist Party of Mexico (PCM), the Socialist Workers' party (PST), and the Mexican Democratic party (PDM).

The New Left and Parliamentary Participation

In 1981 several competing political parties of the left met, settled many of their differences, and merged into a new consolidated party known as the Unified Socialist Party of Mexico (PSUM). The participants in this union were the PCM, the Revolutionary Socialist party (PSR), the Party of the Mexican People (PPM), and a coalition of smaller groups. The new unified party fulfilled all the legal requirements for participating in elections.

The 1982 national election provided the first opportunity for the new party alignment to seek a share of the one hundred Chamber of Deputy seats reserved for the opposition. When all the votes were counted, the biggest winner was still the Catholic middle-class PAN, with fifty-two seats. This was hardly a surprise, as PAN had developed an effective organization during its forty-two years of electoral campaigning. The next largest winner was PSUM, with eighteen seats; other parties that benefited were PDM with eleven seats; PPS with ten seats, and PST with nine.

With the PRI retaining a three-to-one majority over the combined forces of opposition, it might seem that little change would be accomplished. Although it is true that as of summer 1984 no opposition-sponsored bills had been enacted, the new deputies have participated vigorously in the work of the drafting committees and have persuaded the PRI committee members to make significant changes in bills that were later enacted by the chamber. In addition, the reasoned analyses and reasonable arguments presented in particular by the PSUM deputies have won them the respect of the liberal wing of the PRI. A fringe benefit of the new legislative composition is the increased public exposure accorded to the opposition parties by the news media and inclusion of speeches in the official congressional record. These new changes have brought the Mexican electoral system into a closer approximation of West European multiparty representative models reflecting diverse points of view.

How did the PRI achieve its predominance and how has it maintained this position? There is little doubt that in the first years after its founding rival groups were suppressed by a combination of widespread violence and fraud. More important, however, are the following elements:

1. the sectoral organization that mobilizes millions of voters at election time
2. government support and ample financing
3. preferential access to communication media (although opposition parties are now legally guaranteed some public exposure)
4. the "bandwagon" effect (a recent study reveals, for example, that when questioned about why they voted for the PRI, many Mexicans responded that as the PRI was sure to win, they wanted to be on the winning side)
5. fear of change by millions of government employees, middle-class citizens, and wealthy individuals
6. lack of a viable alternative (no existing party offers the citizens any hope of improvement)

There are signs that the PRI may have become too successful. For the past ten years, party theoreticians have lamented the lack of effective opposition and have proposed measures to guarantee effective representation to minority parties. They were increasingly uncomfortable with the possibility of projecting a "totalitarian" image abroad. Some Mexican observers appear to think that the large-scale changes embodied in the new 1977 electoral law may actually oblige the dominant party to relinquish a share of real power to other groups. This is potentially a very important development. Party reform may also have provided the stimulus for the new regional mass associations and nationwide political groups that represent the interests of peasants, farm workers, and low-income urban people.

To summarize: The insiders, that is, the groups that find it advantageous to operate within the formally organized political system, are (1) the leaders and members of the PRI, which is organized into three sectors covering peasants, "captive" labor unions, and middle-class groups such as government employees; (2) organized business groups; (3) leaders of the armed forces; and (4) leaders and members of minority parties. Members of the elite are drawn from the first three groups.

"Outsiders"

With so many insiders, is there any significant number of outsiders? And if so, what are the bases of their discontent with the government? First, it should be remembered that Cárdenas had structured the political system from the viewpoint that the working class was both the subject and the object of the political process, that this class occupied a preferential position with respect to the goals of the entire system. Therefore he advocated a kind of populist corporatism that was reflected in the sectoral organization of the party, and the party itself was seen as occupying almost all of the existing political space. Even before he left office, he saw the need of providing some kind of structure for the business interests, and shortly after he left office the orientation of the political elite underwent an important change, as a result of which the primary goal became the achievement of economic growth. The working class was then seen to be an incidental beneficiary of that goal. In fact, as time went by, even business groups were seen as incidental beneficiaries of economic growth, and growth itself was regarded as too important to be left in the hands of any particular interest or group of interests. In the later stage, the government became the bureaucratized executor of the elite's policy decisions in what some scholars have described as a "bureaucratic-authoritarian state." At that point the party lost its relevance to the policymaking function and became an instrument for mobilization of electoral support, which was seen as periodically necessary for legitimating the exercise of authority.

The efficiency with which the party is utilized is reflected in the fact that in election after election, at the local, state, and national levels, the party "delivers" a mandate for continuity (or "continuism" as some critics call it). Nevertheless, votes for federal deputies in the two elections held since the 1977 reforms reflect a small but perhaps significant change in the pattern of voting. In 1979, for those seats contested under the simple majority balloting, PRI candidates polled 74 percent of the votes, whereas 72.7 percent of the ballots cast under the proportional representation method went to PRI candidates. In 1982, PRI candidates polled respectively 69.11 and 67.95 percent of the two categories. The biggest beneficiary was PAN, with 11.5 and 11.9 percent in 1979 and 17.5 and 17.98 percent in 1982. The Communist party received a greater proportion of the vote (5.5 percent and 5.4 percent) in 1979, when it campaigned under its own name, than in 1982, when PSUM (of which the Communist party formed a part) polled only 4.38 and 4.37 percent of the total.

It may be that middle-class voters have registered their dissatisfaction with economic conditions by increasing their support for PAN, whereas other categories of voters remain unconvinced that PSUM or other parties of the left offer them any hope of improvement. If the nationalization of Mexico's banking system had taken place *before* the 1982 election instead of immediately after it, the middle-class vote for PAN might have drained more votes from the PRI, but support for parties of the left probably would not have been affected.

Of course, long-term trends may show a different pattern, resulting from the changing perceptions of members of different interest groups. For the sake of convenience, we might describe the most important groups in terms of the bases for their disaffection, as follows:

1. Ideological bases. Included here are individuals or groups ranging along the entire spectrum of preferences: (1) socialists who object to the capitalist basis of the system, (2) populists who want a return to the principles expressed in the 1917 constitution, and (3) capitalists who are alarmed at the redistributive implications of the government's social-welfare policies—even though actual redistribution has been negligible.

2. Moral bases. These include (1) those who are critical of the government's failure to extend social-welfare benefits to the neediest part of the population, (2) those who are repelled by the widespread corruption in government, and (3) those who perceive widespread electoral fraud as a mockery of the democratic process.

3. Material bases. Included here are individuals and groups who subjectively perceive themselves as excluded from economic benefits, who see their economic situation as deteriorating under the impact of inflation and unemployment.

These are the categories of recognized outsiders who actively demonstrate their rejection of the status quo by voting for minority candidates. To them we might add at least an equal number of passive individuals who continue to cast their votes for the party simply because it is less inconvenient or risky than taking some positive action.

Extraterritorial Influences on the System

No political system operates in a vacuum, sealed off from international events and influences. This is particularly true of Mexico in the realm of economic affairs. For a brief period during the early 1970s, however, it appeared that the nation might be able to break the pattern of dependence and approach its goal of full development. The basis of this hope was the discovery of new reserves of petroleum, amounting to around 150 billion barrels, at about the same time that the industrialized nations appeared to be facing a possible paralysis of production because of an impending oil shortage. The Organization of Petroleum Exporting Countries (OPEC), of which Mexico was not a member, began the process of successive price raises, making the cost of available oil very high.

To bring Mexico's newly discovered oil fields into rapid production required investments on a scale that even much richer nations would have been unable to mobilize entirely from their own financial resources. But this proved to be no obstacle as international banking firms, sensing an opportunity to reap great profits, hurried to offer their assistance in the form of billions of dollars in loans at high interest rates. The terms did not seem excessive in view of the prospective prosperity for Mexico. As petroleum resources had been nationalized in 1938, it was the responsibility of government planners to devise an energy program for rational exploitation of the resource, coupled with prudent conservation measures. In the haste to take advantage of world market conditions, planning was overlooked and quickly forgotten, except by a few critics on the left of the political spectrum who insisted that the government was squandering the national patrimony.

In an atmosphere of euphoria as money poured in and oil began to pour out, the government borrowed more money to finance programs to create new jobs. Unemployment decreased while the national economy experienced a growth rate of 8 percent. Inflation, however, increased at an even faster rate.

By the end of 1981 the threat of an oil shortage suddenly evaporated as the OPEC countries, having achieved their goal of higher prices, began to offer almost unlimited quantities at the new price levels. Mexico, still in the process of developing its fields, found itself in a difficult position. Economic growth slowed down and eventually reversed itself, reaching a negative rate of minus 4 percent at the end of 1983 while inflation for that year rose to nearly 92 percent. At the same time the total external debt, which included the high-interest loans from international banks, rose to $89 billion. To obtain additional loans in order to make payments on its external debt, the government complied with conditions prescribed by the International Monetary Fund for drastic cuts in internal spending, which again increased unemployment, reduced wages, and extended privation deep into the middle class.

Some years ago the government had adopted legislation known as the Mexicanization of industry, by requiring that in joint business ventures 51 percent of the stock must be owned by Mexican citizens. Although the law has not been repealed, the government announced in 1984 that foreign control would be allowed in thirty-four types of industries, including production of farm machinery, generators, computers, pharmaceuticals, and plastics. The decision was strongly opposed by minority members of the Congress, to no avail.

Thus by the mid-1980s, after a decade characterized by prosperity and optimism followed by a sudden plunge into economic privation, Mexico finds itself in an extremely difficult situation. If it can avoid political turmoil without resorting to repression, it may survive the crisis and resume the process of political and economic development.

Massive migration of workers to the United States has relieved some of the pressures of Mexico's high population growth and unemployment rates. Millions of persons have slipped over the border as "undocumented" (illegal) immigrants, and most probably many more will do so in spite of increased vigilance by U.S. immigration patrols. Money sent by documented and undocumented migrants to their families in Mexico is calculated to amount to at least $300 million a year, which also helps to keep the balance-of-payments deficit from rising even higher. The sheer numerical bulk of this migration has proved a serious problem for the United States and an embarrassment for Mexico, but there is no easy solution. The underlying cause is the sharp contrast between economic opportunity in the two neighboring countries, and the problem will persist until the situation in Mexico improves. Although the United States has recently experienced a rather serious recession, conditions there appear opulent compared with those prevalent in Mexico.

The 2,000-mile (3,218-kilometer) border shared by the two nations has also proved a drain on the Mexican economy in the form of purchases of contraband goods of U.S. manufacture. The government has severely limited the importation of many categories of goods as part of its twin policies to protect and encourage Mexican manufacturing firms and to curtail the outflow of money.

To open more employment opportunities, the Mexican government's Border Industries Program encourages U.S. firms to establish "in bond" assembly plants in Mexican cities along the border, where the cost of manufacturing is kept down by the low wages paid to Mexican workers. The finished products, mainly electronic and textile items, are reexported to the United States. This program provides additional employment opportunities to thousands of Mexicans and adds to the country's GNP. Critics point out that most of the employees are poorly paid, nonunionized young women.

Events in other parts of the world have affected Mexico's internal situation as well as its relationships with other nations. Since the 1910 Revolution, Mexico has consistently given asylum to nonfascist political exiles, including the Russian revolutionary leader Leon Trotsky, who fled from Stalin's persecution, as well as exiles from Spain, German-dominated countries during World War II, and Chile after the anti-Allende military coup of 1973. The Cuban Revolution of 1959 posed special problems, however. Despite pressure by the United States and the Organization of American States, Mexico refused to break off diplomatic and commercial relations with Cuba.

Although Mexico has continued to honor its tradition of affording refuge to individual political exiles, conflicts in the Central American nations have placed great strains on its capacity to accommodate the thousands of refugees who have streamed across its southern borders from nearby Guatemala and more distant El Salvador. The government has set up camps for those people, staffed by military personnel with the dual mission of providing at least minimal living conditions while at the same time assuring that the refugees do not stray farther into the national territory in search of employment. If they were to compete with unemployed Mexicans, an already tense situation might become explosive.

On the international diplomatic scene, Mexico has assumed a leading role in the work of the Contadora Group, whose other members are Colombia, Panama, and Venezuela, in an attempt to mediate the conflicts in the region and to reduce U.S. intervention.

GOVERNMENT MACHINERY

Discussion of how the government is organized and how it operates must center on two key concepts: control, as the principal objective of political organization, and centralization, as the most efficient means of achieving that objective. At this stage of Mexico's history, observers both within and outside the country are almost unanimously agreed that its political system cannot be adequately described in terms of classic liberal-democratic pluralism, in which the government is conceived as an arbitrator of contending interests. Instead, they view it as an updated version of the classic authoritarian model bequeathed by sixteenth-century Spain.

Article 40 of Mexico's constitution provides for a "respresentative, democratic, federal" type of republic composed of states that are "sovereign in all that concerns their internal affairs" but that are federated at the national level. In fact, however, state governments are controlled by the president of the republic. One of the factors that accounts for the relative impotence of the states in the face of central authority is the subordination of governors to the president, who is able to control their nomination and election through his control of the PRI.

Acting through the national Congress, the president can have obstreperous governors dismissed and can name substitutes until new elections are held. President Echeverría made use of this power in 1975 to get rid of the governors of Hidalgo and Guerrero. Because of their weak taxing powers, states are dependent on federal funds for all important projects, and state governors spend about a fourth of their time in Mexico City lobbying for a share of federal funds.

There is none of the tension between the president and the Congress that often characterizes relations in the United States and some other countries. The Mexican national legislature invariably enacts into law all bills proposed by the president, with only minor alterations of details. The federal budget is approved in the same spirit of compliance, and the courts are equally careful to avoid confrontations with the executive.

In fact then, if not always in law, the president's personal power is vitually unchecked. He consolidates this power by controlling the appointment and dismissal of thousands of federal officials, major and minor, who are not protected by a comprehensive civil-service law. He also designates the person who will succeed him as chief executive.

The president derives his enormous power from his control of the PRI, which in turn can guarantee the election of almost all its candidates. But controlling the factional conflicts within the party requires constant vigilance, a strong hand, and much political prudence. In the past few years the facade of party unanimity has been broken several times, as in 1977 when two ex-presidents, Díaz Ordaz and Echeverría, engaged in public acts illustrating lack of discipline by feuding with each other.

Seen in this context, the enormous power of the president can be understood as a measure of the fragility of the entire system. Only by accepting virtual one-man rule for a six-year period can rival factions save themselves and the country from devastating conflict. Disappointed power contenders can console themselves that when the present six-year term (the *sexenio*) comes to an end their fortunes may prosper under the next president. That is why the principle of no reelection, enshrined in the constitution, has been a key element of Mexico's long domestic stability. No matter how powerful a man is as president, he can exercise that power for only six years. Understandably, where party conflict always simmers just below the surface, the post of vice president does not exist.

PUBLIC POLICY

The information that we have surveyed up to this point now makes it possible to state some general propositions about the Mexican state and society. It is apparent, for example, that in spite of revolutionary rhetoric the political system is anything but revolutionary; contrary to protestations of populist sympathizers, leaders continue to support policies that favor a privileged minority; notwithstanding the much-publicized agrarian reform, most peasants are landless; and constitutional guarantees of the rights of labor are scant protection for independent unions. Since 1940 the elite's commitment to economic growth has led to a neglect of major redistributive measures that could have reduced economic inequality. Meanwhile, considerations of political stability are reflected in a corporative structure that marginalizes large segments of the population.

It is true that the Revolution did alter the social structure of the country by eliminating the old oligarchy of large landowners, but what has emerged during the post-1940 years is a new privileged class of industrialists and business people and an expanded stratum of the middle class that includes members of favored blue-collar unions in its lowest level. In a rank-order listing of beneficiaries of the system the next lower groups, separated from the middle class by enormous differences in life-style, are the urban unemployed and squatters, the peasants, and—below all the rest—the nation's sizable Indian population, who are theoretically revered as the "most Mexican of Mexicans" but who in practice are the victims of discrimination and neglect, both deliberate and unintentional.

We have already seen how important elements of political and economic life are incorporated into the structure of the PRI in such a way as to guarantee electoral support for the government. Outside of the party, potential challengers are prevented from building bases of power by a general strategy that includes the tactics described next.

Political Control: Limitations of Alternatives

Most effective is the selective use of violence to suppress attempts to organize opposition groups. Some of this violence is exercised under the sanction of law, as in police or military action to break up strikes and demonstrations or to raid headquarters of alleged subversive groups, but in other cases, as in the kidnapping or assassination of dissidents or attacks on protest groups by paramilitary forces, the government is able to evade responsibility for the actions. Use of all these methods demonstrates a sophisticated discrimination, with no more than the necessary minimum brought to bear to eliminate the challenge to authority.

The new political parties that have been admitted to the electoral process still operate under a number of difficulties. They are poorly financed, compared to the PRI's opulence; some of them are torn by factional disputes; and all of them charge—apparently with justification— that ballot-box fraud is cheating them of a significant number of votes.

When feasible, government leaders prefer to co-opt prominent dissidents by offering them a chance to "work within the system" in salaried posts. When these methods fail, the government resorts to procrastination, appearing to grant protestors' demands but failing to implement concessions or delaying remedial action by legal maneuvers and bureaucratic red tape. Other dissident groups, as they begin to organize, are circumvented by the sudden appearance of hastily formed government-recognized groups that preempt their names and programs. More established groups are infiltrated by government sympathizers who take over the leadership positions by demonstrating to the membership their ability to obtain concessions from the authorities.

Prominent persons who are potentially troublesome are sometimes disarmed by being appointed to prestigious posts outside Mexico. In the late 1960s the internationally known poet and essayist Octavio Paz was named ambassador to India but was recalled when he publicly criticized his government for its conduct during the 1968 student strikes. (Another version of this incident depicts Paz as resigning in protest.)

Social Control

Distribution of token material and symbolic benefits has proved very effective in preventing large sectors of the population from becoming politically active. After the student unrest of the 1960s, for example, the state-supported educational system, which had been accused of elitist tendencies in its admission policies, was enormously expanded to include tens of thousands of new students in what appeared to be a turn toward democratization. Many of these new students were so grateful for the chance to get an education that they became a counterweight to efforts to revive political opposition in the schools.

The social-security system, which offers many more benefits than similarly named systems in other countries, offers coverage to about 25 percent of employed workers in selected industries judged by the government to be most important to the country's economic growth. Government employees are covered by advantageous insurance and pension arrangements, and members of "captive" blue-collar unions are granted favorable contracts. By these means they are given a small "stake in the system" and see their own security as dependent on the continuation of the status quo.

In recent years, as inflation has climbed steeply, the government's CONASUPO (National Popular Subsistence Corporation) marketing system has been swiftly expanded to provide basic foodstuffs to low-income groups at controlled prices. Probably the most beguiling but essentially conservative action of the government is the distribution of small parcels of land to groups of peasants selected from the millions of landless persons. Other basic improvements include street paving, installation of water mains, and so forth in squatter settlements. All of these concessions are widely publicized, leaving large numbers of unaffected persons with the belief that if they have patience their turn to reap benefits will also come. Even the officially sponsored lottery system has the effect of giving hope of prosperity to disadvantaged individuals.

Economic Control

In many of its most significant articles, the 1917 constitution asserts the existence of a state, or public, interest in the nation's economic system that overrides any private interest. Beginning with the presidency of Lázaro Cárdenas, the public interest has been served by a relationship between government and business that is as distinct from socialism as it is from laissez-faire capitalism. Continually evolving since 1940, the Mexican variant, described by some observers as economic nationalism characterized by a "mixed economy" and by others as "state capitalism," has enabled the government to own or control many of the most important industries, including electric power production and distribution and steel, petroleum, natural gas, and petrochemical plants. Essential communications and transportation facilities such as telephone, telegraph, railroads, and aviation are owned and operated by the government, which also participates as sole owner or powerful partner in about four hundred public and mixed public-private enterprises.

Influence over economic policy is further extended by government involvement in credit and financing institutions that control the nature and extent of private business activity. Among these are the central bank (Banco de Mexico) and the central planning agency (Nacional Financiera). Nationalization of the banking system has placed another instrument of control in the hands of the government.

In spite of the massive participation of the government in economic activities, it operates within a capitalist framework that allows a wide scope for profit making by private enterprise. The Mexican government regulates private business to a much greater extent than, for example, the U.S. government, but this regulation is never so oppressive as to squeeze firms out of profitable existence. The goal of government economic policy is continued economic growth, and policymakers accept the necessity of large-scale participation by private enterprise to achieve that goal. The resulting set of arrangements has been called an "alliance for profits."

The long-range objectives of the government are (1) to promote economic growth based on capitalism, (2) to reduce the country's overall dependence on foreign capital, while at the same time encouraging foreign investment in selected fields of activity, and (3) to encourage Mexican business people to invest money in Mexican businesses. In the application of specific measures to implement these objectives, policy-makers have shown a flexible approach. Acting in its regulatory capacity, the government restricts the types of businesses in which foreign capital can be invested. Mexican industries are protected from competition by foreign firms by a combination of high tariffs, import quotas, import licenses, and—most recently—devaluation of the national currency, which has raised the cost of imported goods and made Mexican goods more attractive. A 1973 law also provides for the transfer of technology by requiring that firms taking profits out of Mexico train citizens in the skills required to operate the plants and share information on the equipment and processes employed in the plants. Foreigners are not allowed to invest in certain types of businesses, such as restaurants, food-processing plants, public relations, and publishing, all of which are reserved for exclusive Mexican ownership. Also forbidden is foreign takeover of established business owned by Mexicans; investment must be in new types of business that will expand Mexico's economic base. To assure foreign as well as domestic investors of low operating costs and high profits, the government has kept wages low in certain types of activity (electricity production and distribution, rail and truck freight rates), although inflation recently elicited two general wage-increase decrees.

As long as government rules are complied with, every effort is made to provide the most favorable conditions for both Mexican and foreign investors. Within this framework, the government has demonstrated a continued commitment to the capitalist basis of the economy.

So firm is this commitment and so favorable are the conditions that some critics claim the government has been "captured" by business interests and does their bidding. In support of this view, they point out that the economic areas in which the government is most active, for example, transportation, communications, and energy production, are not only the least profitable but also the most necessary as the supports for profit-bearing enterprises. The tax and wage structures are also seen as supporting the expansion of profits at the expense of the workers' standard of living.

These criticisms, however, are rejected by some of the most knowledgeable observers of Mexican affairs, who insist that the government has consistently kept the upper hand in its relations with both foreign and domestic capital. In support of this view, they point out that it is only after the government has made a decision regarding basic policy that business interests are consulted about details of implementation. They concede, however, that the government has exercised self-restraint in effecting economic reforms that might alienate business interests and that lack of unanimity among government decision makers often leads to compromises that are strongly influenced by private-sector input. They also concede the probability of behind-the-scenes predecision bargaining between representatives of business and government officials concerning the nature and magnitude of proposed policies.

Whether or not the government has been "captured" by business, observers agree that the relationship is one of guarded cooperation rather than hostile confrontation. This combination has stimulated national economic growth, but it has done little to improve conditions for the majority of Mexican citizens.

The Forgotten Ones

Since 1940 there has been a gradual reversal of the agrarian-reform policies carried out by Cárdenas. Successive amendments to Article 27 of the constitution subverted the original intent of the framers so that by 1960 *latifundios*, or big agricultural units, had again become very large and *minifundios*, or small units, were getting smaller.

This is only part of the story. The land distributed to small farmers is the poorest and least productive, lacking in irrigation, fertilizers, and modern equipment. In contrast, the large holdings, often owned and managed by U.S. investors, are well irrigated, well financed, and use the latest agricultural equipment, including small planes for crop dusting. They are capital intensive, which means that they do not absorb very much of the available human labor supply.

Farm families have only about half the income of other workers. Malnutrition is much more prevalent in the rural population than in urban areas, and about two-thirds of the rural population have no access to health services in official institutions. The government has clearly abandoned the revolutionary ideal of a self-reliant independent peasantry in favor of the goal of increased agricultural production to be achieved through capital-intensive methods. Those who defend this policy point out that this has been the trend in the United States, where agribusiness has supplanted the small farmers. However, they fail to take into account the fact that industrial expansion in the United States during the crucial transition period absorbed most of the labor displaced from agriculture.

At present, Mexico's unemployment rate is probably around 50 percent, if the number of underemployed people is included in this category. Underemployed persons, often counted in statistics as employed, actually do not have full-time jobs paying regular wages. Instead, they eke out an existence in the cities by shining shoes, tending parked autos, or peddling chewing gum. The number of persons seeking employment is increasing at the rate of 750,000 a year, and under present conditions the government cannot expand employment opportunities to take care of more than a small fraction of that number, much less reduce the accumulated backlog.

The considerable benefits offered by the Mexican Institute of Social Security (IMSS) and other insurance systems are available only to one-fourth of all employed workers. Government workers and those employed in some of the key industries such as petroleum (Petróleos Mexicanos— PEMEX), railroads, electricity, and sugar have their own pension plans and health-care facilities. For them there is an imposing array of modern, well-equipped hospitals and outpatient clinics, staffed by comparatively well paid physicians; low-cost prescription pharmacies; recreation centers; and other amenities; whereas for the urban unemployed and under-employed there are only crowded hospitals housed in deteriorating buildings staffed by overworked, underpaid physicians. Wage contracts, which cover about the same 25 percent of the work force, have fallen behind the increases that would keep up with the inflation of recent years and would at least have afforded some protection as compared with the rest of the workers.

The picture that emerges from these data is one of enormous economic inequities that not only have persisted but have actually widened the gap between the very rich and the middle class and between the latter and the great bulk of the population, with the poorest 40 percent of Mexicans existing at a very low level of deprivation. The heyday of Mexican economic growth seems to have come and gone without having benefited more than a very small number of citizens; the "trickle" of the trickle-down effect expected from prosperity dried up before reaching the broad lower layers of the economic pyramid. Mexico's planners seem to have forgotten an important element: timing. The capitalist industrial expansion that produced a generally higher standard of living in other parts of the world may have been delayed too long in Mexico to produce similar effects. During the nineteenth century, while North Atlantic nations had been forging ahead economically, Mexico had been busy trying to solve its internal conflicts.

Deflation, recession, and current austerity measures dictated by the international lenders impose severe restraints on the postwar growth model that had produced such encouraging growth in the past.

PROSPECTS FOR THE FUTURE

The reader may now envision the dilemma of the elite, faced at this crucial junction with the problem of reevaluating alternative courses of action. Sketched below are some possible scenarios.

1. A better break for the underdog. The government might confound its populist critics by broadening its program of economic redistribution through extending social-welfare benefits to many more marginal groups, reinforcing the *ejido* structure of agriculture with adequate financing and technical expertise, and providing more employment by means of large-scale public-works programs.

Advantage: Popular unrest would be defused; actual policy would more closely match revolutionary rhetoric.

Disadvantage: Excessive cost. The government is already heavily in debt. Failing that solution the Mexican people might turn to insurrection.

2. Full speed ahead. The policymakers may choose to continue their pursuit of economic growth within the same framework of encouraging private investment, with few additional concessions to outsiders, in the hope that an economic upturn is just around the corner.

Advantage: This policy may avoid the unsettling effects that might accompany a major retooling. It will not provoke alarm in the international lending and investment community. If Mexico can ride out its present difficulties, some of the anticipated new revenues from petroleum resources may be used to finance modest increments of benefits to the urban and rural poor.

Disadvantage: Further delay may place an intolerable burden on the traditional patience of the poor, who might react by engaging in widespread acts of violence.

Note that both the preceding scenarios presuppose a continuation of authoritarian methods of decision making; that is, they assume that the elite will continue to make all the important policy choices without publicly consulting the affected groups. The reader may envisage other alternatives, as follows:

3. A "democratic opening." This would involve a process of meaningful public consultation with outside as well as inside groups, purging the electoral system of fraud, strengthening the national Congress, and accepting the cooperation of the opposition in finding solutions to national problems.

Advantage: After an initial period of confusion involving one or more *sexenios*, the insiders may find that sharing the power to make decisions means that others will have to share the blame for the outcome. Public frustration can no longer vent itself in revolt against a single object.

Disadvantage: The initial confusion might deteriorate into violent conflict among opposing groups, sending the political system back to the 1910–1920 period.

4. A "totalitarian closing." A well-organized and single-minded group convinced of the superiority of either scenario 1 *or* scenario 2 might push aside the existing elite and put an end to the precarious equilibrium by eliminating all opposition to the scenario of its choice.

Advantage: The country would at last have unity of purpose; there would be no more distinction between insiders and outsiders; dissenters would be killed or otherwise eliminated. A clear-cut program could be pursued without necessity of consultation with any group and without possibility of opposition.

Disadvantage: Whichever scenario were chosen—either 1 or 2, modern technology in the service of counterintelligence and violent coercion, such as refined methods of torture and mass extermination, would preclude the possibility of scenario 3 for the foreseeable future.

Our description of Mexico's political dynamics reveals a process of decision making that has been monopolized by a small group of insiders with the acquiescense of a majority of citizens. Most of the people born in poverty since the Revolution—three generations of them—have grown to maturity without perceiving any improvement in the material conditions of their lives. At each election, voters went dutifully—or were transported—to the polls to cast their votes for candidates of the institutionalized party who offered no meaningful alternatives to the policies already in effect.

The patience of the Mexican people in the face of adversity aroused wonder and admiration in many observers. For others, it was a source of frustration and exasperation. Insiders had come to count on it to carry them through a series of setbacks in their pursuit of economic growth that they hoped would eventually produce trickle-down benefits for the masses. But the marginal people, the disadvantaged, had rebelled before, and the result had been bloodshed, death, and destruction. Would their long-suppressed anger boil over again into revolution?

Under these circumstances it might appear that Mexico's insiders must be at the point of deciding whether to act out scenario 2 or scenario 4—or perhaps a combination of the two. Two events—one in the 1960s, one in the 1980s—make that outcome more than a remote possibility. As we have seen, the first event was the violent suppression in 1968 of the student movement, revealing the government's intolerance of dissent and the severity of its reaction. The other was the general collapse of the economy in 1982 that brought millions of people to the brink of desperation.

Until now, one aspect has been omitted from this summing up of the Mexican political culture. Our earlier review of the nation's political history revealed that a continuous process of change has been occurring since the Revolution of 1910. During that time there has never been a prolonged period in which the national leadership cut itself entirely away from its mass base, nor were the Mexican people decimated by the kind of medieval savagery visited upon whole populations to the south of them. In other words, the insiders did everything possible, short of sharing power, to avoid a general insurrection and to secure their monopoly of decision making.

In the late 1970s the decision makers took the first small step toward sharing power. If they can bring themselves to take the next step, they may be well on the way to repeating the experience of such European nations as France, Italy, Spain, and Portugal, where parties of the left have been participating in the formulation and execution of policy for several years. If that occurs, the possibility envisioned in scenario 3 can be said to be well on the way to actualization. Those who admire the Mexican people and wish them well may hope cautiously for that outcome.

NOTES

1. Population figures were drawn from publications of the Population Reference Bureau, Washington, D.C., and from James W. Wilkie, ed., *Statistical Abstract of Latin America* (University of California, Los Angeles, various issues).

2. James W. Wilkie, ed., *Statistical Abstract of Latin America* (University of California, Los Angeles, 1983), table 1310, p. 175.

3. Frank R. Brandenburg, *The Making of Modern Mexico* (Prentice-Hall, Englewood Cliffs, N.J., 1964), p. 4.

SUGGESTIONS FOR FURTHER READING

Brandenburg, Frank R. *The Making of Modern Mexico.* Prentice-Hall, Englewood Cliffs, N.J., 1964.

Brenner, Anita. *The Wind That Swept Mexico.* Harper & Row, New York, 1943.

Camp, Roderic. *Mexican Political Biographies, 1935–1980.* University of Arizona Press, Tucson, 1982.

Cornelius, Wayne A. *Politics and the Migrant Poor in Mexico City.* Stanford University Press, Stanford, Calif., 1975.

Cosío Villegas, Daniel, Ignacio Bernal, Alejandra Morena Toscano, Luis González, and Eduardo Blanquel. *A Compact History of Mexico.* El Colegio de México, México, D.F., 1974.

Eckstein, Susan. *The Poverty of Revolution: The State and the Urban Poor in Mexico.* Princeton University Press, Princeton, N.J., 1977.

Fagen, Richard R., and William S. Tuohy. *Politics and Privilege in a Mexican City.* Stanford University Press, Stanford, Calif., 1972.

González Casanova, Pablo. *Democracy in Mexico.* Oxford University Press, New York, 1970.

Grindle, Merilee S. *Bureaucrats, Politicians, and Peasants in Mexico: A Case Study in Public Policy.* University of California Press, Berkeley, 1977.

Hansen, Roger D. *The Politics of Mexican Development.* Johns Hopkins University Press, Baltimore, 1971.

Levy, Daniel, and Gabriel Székely. *Mexico: Paradoxes of Stability and Change.* Westview Press, Boulder, Colo., 1983.

Montgomery, Tommie Sue, ed. *Mexico Today.* Institute for the Study of Human Issues (ISHI), Philadelphia, 1982.

Paz, Octavio. *The Other Mexico: Critique of the Pyramid.* Grove Press, New York, 1972.

Reyna, José Luis. *An Empirical Analysis of Political Mobilization: The Case of Mexico.* Cornell University Dissertation Series, Latin American Studies Program, Ithaca, N.Y., 1971.

Reyna, José Luis, and Richard S. Weinert, eds. *Authoritarianism in Mexico.* ISHI, Philadelphia, 1977.

Reynolds, Clark. *The Mexican Economy: Twentieth Century Structure and Growth.* Yale University Press, New Haven, Conn., 1970.

Russell, Philip. *Mexico in Transition.* Colorado River Press, Austin, Tex., 1977.

Stevens, Evelyn P. *Protest and Response in Mexico.* MIT Press, Cambridge, Mass., 1974.

Story, Dale. "Industrial Elites in Mexico: Political Ideology and Influence," *Journal of Interamerican Studies and World Affairs* 25, no. 3 (August 1983):351–376.

19
Cuba: The Politics of Socialist Revolution

HARVEY F. KLINE

Cuba is distinctive in Latin America for its socialist revolution, clearly the most thorough in the history of the American continents. Before 1959, Cuba was not unlike some other Latin American countries, although it did have historical and economic peculiarities. Then, in January 1959, a group of guerrillas took power, led by a young son of the upper middle class, Fidel Castro. Fidel (as he is called by Cubans) had appeared as an idealistic revolutionary during the guerrilla days, but few expected that the country would alter radically in the next several years. Within the first two years of the Castro government, there were dramatic changes. By late 1961, Fidel had declared himself a Marxist-Leninist, postponed free elections, begun a sweeping land reform, nationalized the education system, and disbanded the prerevolutionary interest groups. Meanwhile, relations with the Soviet Union became cordial, while the U.S. government and private interests grew alienated, attempting as-sassinations, terrorist tactics, and armed invasion. Although relations between the United States and Cuba might some day be normalized, it seems clear that the island will never be the same again.

BACKGROUND AND POLITICAL CULTURE

Geography and Economy

Cuba is a small island of 44,218 square miles (114,525 square kilo-meters). It contains three major mountain ranges (the Sierra Maestra in the east, the Sierra de los Organos in the west, and the Trinidad range in the central area). These mountainous areas occupy one-quarter of the national territory, with the remainder gentle slopes.

One important feature of Cuba is its location. Situated in the northern part of the Caribbean Sea, it is only 90 miles (145 kilometers) from the Florida Keys, close to the Mississippi Delta, and in a strategic position

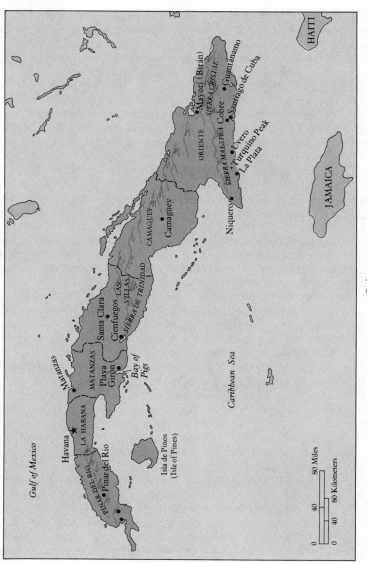

Cuba

between the continental United States and Central America and the Panama Canal. Individuals in the United States have from time to time seen Cuba as crucial to the defense of North America and talked of its annexation.

Another characteristic of the island is its relative homogeneity. This does not mean that all parts of the national territory are exactly alike. Climate does vary and with it the crops grown. But compared to most other Latin American countries, Cuba is a country with few geographic barriers causing problems of transportation and communication, with concurrent political regionalism.

The tropical location of Cuba, along with its soil, makes it ideal for the cultivation of sugarcane. The temperatures are warm, with a mean temperature of 77°F (25°C) in the winter months and 80°F (26.5°C) in the summer. This temperature is fairly uniform across the island, although cooler at higher elevations.

Sugarcane was before Castro and remains the key to the Cuban economy. Its cultivation has typically occupied about one-quarter of the labor force and one-half of the cultivated land. Around 80 percent of Cuban exports, both before and since the Revolution, have been in the form of sugar.

Prior to the Revolution, there were at least three important consequences of the sugar economy. First, while the island did have comparative advantage in the product, this advantage put the economy in a precarious position, booming when sugar prices were up and shrinking when prices were down. The entire economic system depended on world sugar prices, something largely beyond the Cubans' control. Further, Cubans relied on quotas from the industrialized world, particularly at times of world oversupply of sugar. This gave a major source of leverage to the U.S. government, which was the biggest sugar importer.

Second, the sugar economy was concentrated in a few hands, the majority of them foreign. The cane is most economically grown on large plots of land. These plantations were centered around the mills, or *centrales;* there were only a small number of these mills (about 160 for the entire country), and the biggest were owned by U.S. interests.

Third, the sugar economy produced a sizable rural proletariat. Many Cuban *campesinos* (called *guajiros* on the island) were wage laborers, rather than illegal squatters or the more traditional peasants tied to a *patrón* on a hacienda. Although there were both hacienda peasants and squatters in Cuba, no other Latin American country has been so characterized by large numbers of rural wage laborers. The Cuban sugar worker led a precarious existence. Since sugarcane is a crop that requires intensive work only during planting and harvesting, most workers had full-time employment for only four or five months of the year. At harvest, so many workers were needed that cutters were brought in from other Caribbean and Central American countries. For the rest of the year (the dead months), the Cuban sugar worker had to live on the money accumulated during the harvest and quite often went into debt.

Of these three consequences of the sugar economy, Castro's public policy has been successful in changing two. No longer is Cuban sugar owned by foreign or domestic private interests; it belongs to the state. Although work is still most intense during the harvest, the Cuban worker now earns enough for the entire year (although there are fewer consumer goods available than before). But the Cuban economy still booms or busts with the world price of sugar, with the purchaser at preferential rates the Soviet Union rather than the United States.

There are other agricultural ventures in Cuba, none nearly so important as sugar. The country has long been known for its tobacco, cigars, coffee, cocoa, rice, and livestock. A small amount of industry had grown up on the island by the time of the Revolution, most in the hands of U.S. companies. There was also some mining, especially copper and nickel, largely U.S. owned. The Castro government has attempted to increase agricultural production, has nationalized all foreign-owned industries and mines, and has tried to expand industry in Cuba. But the efforts have been only moderately successful. Sugar is still king.

Cuba is a relatively poor country. In 1956, the per capita gross domestic product was only US$415, compared to about US$840 in 1981. Before the Revolution, Cuba was characterized by extreme variations of income, with a few very rich people, a small middle-income sector, and a large number of very poor people. One of the chief policies of the Castro government has been to lessen the great disparities, and in this it has been successful to a degree, making for a higher quality of life on the island.

The People of Cuba

Cuba is a densely populated country of 10 million people. In Latin America, only the Dominican Republic and El Salvador have denser populations. Yet Cuba's population growth rate of 1.4 percent a year is one of the lowest in Latin America.

The people of Cuba have a variety of ethnic backgrounds, reflecting European and African migrations to the island, the native Amerindian population (which was slight and soon decimated by disease), and a very small Asian element. The two predominant racial strains—white and black—have intermarried. It is impossible to state the exact racial makeup of the people of Cuba. Pre-1959 censuses were inaccurate, and racial breakdowns are not considered important by the revolutionary government, as all racial discrimination has, in theory, been ended. A good guess for the racial composition today would be about one-third each for blacks, whites, and mulattos.

Cuba never followed the Latin American pattern of racial relations completely. Due to the great influence of U.S. citizens on the island, racial prejudice resembled that of the North American country. Blacks were discriminated against and not allowed in certain social clubs and exclusive groups; there were some public facilities that did not serve blacks. Race was subsumed into the social stratification system. Basically, the division was between manual and nonmanual workers, but within each of the two strata, race and income determined position. Nonwhites tended to have lower-paying, usually manual jobs, less education, and less social status. There were exceptions, notably Fulgencio Batista y Zaldívar, a man of mixed blood, who reached the presidency. Even so, Batista was not accepted by the social elite of Havana and was rejected for membership in one yacht club while he held the post of chief executive.

There were only two social classes in pre-Castro Cuba. Upward mobility from one to the other was very difficult and, to the degree that it existed, was based on education. Educational institutions, particularly at the secondary level, tended to be private, Church-run ones. The cost—both direct and indirect—of not working during school years effectively excluded the children of the working class, whether rural or urban, from more than several years of education.

Women, like nonwhites and manual laborers, held few important positions before the Cuban Revolution. Although male dominance and *machismo* were probably less extreme in Cuba than elsewhere in Latin America, the women of Cuba were pampered, sheltered, and subordinate to the men.

Race, class, education, and the place of women have all dramatically changed since the Cuban Revolution. Overt racial discrimination has been ended; manual work has been glorified (and salary differentials for different occupations have been lessened, though not eliminated). Education has been made free at all levels, and the illiteracy rate is now one of the lowest in Latin America. Women have been "liberated," although Fidel has had occasion to criticize the women themselves for not leaving the old attitudes behind.

Political Dynamics Before the Castro Revolution

As in the rest of Latin America, there never was a revolution that established the mobilization of votes as the only legitimate political resource. A number of power resources were equal, or nearly equal, in legitimacy—including the ability to obtain votes (political parties); military power; street demonstrations and violence (the labor unions, students, Fidel himself); and economic power (U.S. businesses). The result was a tentative and uneasy situation, and nothing approaching liberal democracy was ever institutionalized.

Cuba's Spanish heritage brought with it a very centralized government, centralized not only in location but also in the hands of one person—the president. Patrimonial relations, also part of this heritage, meant that many individuals of the lower social classes were protected by a *patrón*, but this characteristic was less prevalent in Cuba than elsewhere, given the economic system. Patrimonialism also meant that new groups were organized by the people at the top, in the general co-optive system common to Latin America.

Although in general the Latin American tradition applied in Cuba, the groups in conflict differed from those in most of Latin America for historical and economic reasons. The military was a preeminent group, gaining prestige from the wars of independence and using force as its power resource. But the other two pillars of the nineteenth-century oligarchy in Latin America—the landowners and the Church—were not dominant in Cuba. There was a large Cuban landed elite and it was important politically. However, the situation differed from that of most other Latin American countries because of the substantial amount of land controlled by foreign interests and the market orientation of sugarcane cultivation. Likewise, the Church was not very powerful. The Cubans lacked the religious fervor of most Latin Americans, and the Church was not a large landowner.

Cuba had no powerful group of capitalist entrepreneurs. Industrial and agrarian enterprises tended to be dominated by U.S. interests. Although a Cuban sugar bourgeoisie had emerged and there was also some Cuban industry, the prominence of North American entrepreneurs precluded the locals from gaining the power that they have in some other Latin American countries.

The groups in Cuba—both Cuban and U.S.—operated in an uneasy equilibrium. The president was the one individual who held things together. Groups went along with the president only so long as he could maintain order. Underneath, the Cuban system was a very weak one without a powerful and institutionalized oligarchy.

There were three recurrent themes during Cuba's last forty years as a colony and first half century of independence: violence, radicalism, and a generational aspect. A number of civil wars were necessary before Cuban independence was obtained. Because of this—and for whatever other reasons—Cuban politics was more violent than in most other Latin American countries. The radical tradition was older and stronger than in other countries. Finally, Cuban history has been one of *generations*—groups that have banded together during the great struggles of the nation's short existence. The first was the generation of 1868, which made the first attempt at independence. The second was the generation of 1895, brought together in the war that led to independence. The third was the generation of 1930, gathered against the dictator Gerardo Machado and in favor of revolution. When Castro came to power, he was a representative of the fourth such generation, that of 1953. By that time, the generation of 1930 had been largely discredited as a political class in the eyes of the young. There was no reputable political group that could effectively challenge the new, rebel, Fidelista generation. Nor were there any other institutions that could challenge the new leadership. In a very short time, the new generation had a monopoly of political power.

HISTORY TO 1933

The Colonial Period

Christopher Columbus landed on the island of Cuba during his first voyage in 1492. A few years later a colony was established, beginning a colonial period lasting until 1898. The island was a center of Spanish colonialism for only a brief period in the sixteenth century. Precious metals were scarce, and Indians were few in number and soon succumbed to the abuses of Spanish rule and to the illnesses brought by the new masters. From 1540 to 1800, Cuba was neglected, as Spanish interest turned to the mainland.

This status changed at the beginning of the nineteenth century with the growing significance of tobacco and sugar and with the importation of African slaves. The number of slaves, about 32,000 in 1763, grew dramatically, to 286,942 in 1827.

There was little movement toward independence in Cuba during the first several decades of the nineteenth century. One major reason for Cuba's not participating in movements similar to those going on elsewhere was the number of slaves. Cuban *criollos* felt that any movement begun by them would be taken over by people allied to the large slave population, a result the *criollos* feared would result in a situation comparable to that of Haiti, where whites were eventually expelled from the island. Its sugar had made Cuba too valuable a colony for the Spanish to lose; moreover, Spain felt that Cuba's insular nature worked against a successful independence movement.

As the nineteenth century progressed, there was increasing friction between *criollos* and *peninsulares*. With more conflict came more Spanish repression, which resulted in more conflict. This vicious circle included two early attempts at independence; the bloody Ten Years' War (1868–1878) and the Little War (1880).

A third bid for independence was made in 1895 and lasted until independence three years later. The spiritual leader of the movement was José Martí, an intellectual and writer whose contributions to independence largely came from the United States. Killed soon after his return to Cuba to fight, Martí is still regarded as the father of Cuban independence. Following the outbreak of violence, the Spanish reacted savagely, putting large numbers of noncombatants into concentration camps and using terroristic tactics against the rebels. In spite of these tactics, many historians believe that the rebels were winning when the United States entered the war.

The precipitating factor for U.S. intervention was the sinking of the battleship U.S.S. *Maine* in Havana Harbor on February 15, 1898. Although who sank the ship is still a mystery, the incident was used as a rationale for U.S. entry into a war that lasted only four months but led to the possession of the Philippines and Puerto Rico, as well as to domination over Cuba. After three years of military occupation, Cuban independence came with the strings attached known as the Platt Amendment. Forced into the new Cuban constitution, the amendment included four crucial points:

1. Cuba could enter into no treaty with a foreign power that would impair its independence or permit any foreign power to obtain control over any portion of the island.
2. The Cuban government could incur no foreign debt that ordinary revenues would not cover.
3. The Cuban government consented that the United States could exercise the right to intervene, even militarily, for "the preservation of Cuban independence, the maintenance of a government adequate for the protection of life, property, and individual liberty."
4. For U.S. defense and to protect the people of Cuba, the government of Cuba would sell or lease to the United States lands necessary for coaling or naval stations at certain specified locations.

The Platt Amendment was abrogated in 1934. Before that date, it was the United States that decided on the adequacy of the Cuban government and what amount of debt ordinary revenue would cover (although exception might be made involving debts to U.S. banks). The Guantánamo Naval Base, set up under the stipulations of this treaty on the eastern tip of the island, is still a bone of contention between the governments of Cuba and the United States.

U.S. Private Interests in the Economy of Cuba

The period between independence and the rise of Fidel Castro is an example of a nearly complete convergence of U.S. business and State Department interests. Perhaps no better case of agreement between business and diplomacy can be found in U.S. history. Although different segments of *yanki* business sometimes fought among themselves over Cuban policy, the State Department generally favored those groups that wanted to expand trade with the island.

Likewise, this period marked the development of an economic dependency of Cuba on the United States unmatched by other Latin American countries. Cuban crops were given preferential tariff duties in the United States; in turn, U.S. products were given similar preferential rates on the island. Trade between the two countries quickly increased, and Cuba became a one-crop economy tied to one country.

There were clear economic advantages to Cuba from this relationship, at least in the short run. *Yanki* private enterprise supplied capital and technology for the development of the island, things the Cubans did not possess themselves. Cuba, with its tropical agricultural products, was in many ways a natural trading partner for the industrial United States. Both nations benefited from the relationship, but not equally.

One clear example of this unequal power relationship is seen in the establishment of the International Sugar Committee in 1917. Made up of five men from the United States and Great Britain, this committee limited the Cuban sugar market to those two countries, forcing other nations out of the market. The committee took from the island the power to set the price of sugar and to apportion it between the two countries. When Cuba protested this consumer cartel, the State Department threatened a trade embargo on wheat and coal, for both of which the island depended on the United States.

U.S. private companies were established in Cuba, especially in the cultivation of sugarcane. By 1928, the U.S. groups controlled about 75 percent of the crop. U.S. private investment also dominated rubber, chemicals, pharmaceuticals, communications, and railroads. U.S. banks became so important that the Federal Reserve Banks of Boston and Atlanta opened agencies in Havana. Large loans were granted to the Cuban government, some clearly violating the Platt Amendment. The State Department, far from disapproving the loans from U.S. sources, used the private banks to exert influence on the Cuban government. Such matters as the reduction of the Cuban national budget, tax revision, and even cabinet changes became preconditions to receiving loans from the American bankers. The Cuban government went further and further into debt.

By the 1950s, U.S. capital no longer dominated the sugar industry. Nevertheless, U.S. firms still accounted for 40 percent of the island's sugar production, controlled 40 of the 161 sugar mills, and held 7 of the 10 largest agricultural enterprises. U.S. companies also controlled 2 of the 3 oil refineries, more than 90 percent of the telephone and electric utilities, 50 percent of the public railroads, the mining industry, and a majority of the tourist industry. Overall, the influence of U.S. private investors was increasing. Between 1950 and 1958, U.S. private investments rose over 50 percent on the island, from US$657 million to US$1 billion, with much of the growth in petroleum, mining, and service industries. The per capita book value of U.S. enterprises in Cuba in 1959 was more than three times that of the rest of Latin America: US$143 for every Cuban versus US$39 per Latin American in the rest of the area.[1]

Political Patterns of the New Nation (1901–1930)

The Cuban constitution of 1901 established a liberal-democratic system very similar to that of the United States, with checks and balances and separation of powers. In the first period of independent history, Cubans followed the constitutional pattern, at least in principle, with leadership in government the province of a relatively small group of men who had achieved prominence in the war for independence.

Elections, in which few were allowed to vote, were contests between two parties, the Liberals and the Conservatives. The Liberals had the more critical attitude toward the United States and called explicitly for the abrogation of the Platt Amendment. The Conservatives were the more pro-U.S.-business party and received support from rural interests and Cuban business people, whereas the Liberals tended to get votes from the large cities. At the very foundation of the conflict between the two parties was the struggle to gain and keep the spoils of office. When practical necessity called for it, Liberals and Conservatives could work together.

The presence of the United States was constant during this period, not only in the form of growing private businesses but also through governmental intervention under the Platt Amendment. There were two military interventions, in 1905 and 1917. The 1905 intervention was requested by the first president of the republic, Tomás Estrada Palma, against his Liberal opponents. Later Cubans labeled people like Estrada, who used U.S. businesses and interventions to further their own personal fortunes and careers, *plattistas* or *entreguistas* (from the verb *entregar*, "to hand over"). However, at the time, many Cuban economic and political leaders welcomed the U.S. presence.

The last president of the period was Gerardo Machado, a Liberal elected in 1924 promising honesty and a single term of office. Machado did not live up to either of his promises and in 1927 obtained constitutional amendments that extended the term of the president to six years. After silencing his opposition through deportation and assassination, he was elected to a six-year term in 1928 without opposition.

With the coming of the Great Depression, the price of sugar collapsed on the world market. Cuban domestic politics, already characterized by dissatisfaction, became more acrimonious and violent. Machado responded with repression and terror, and from all of this came the revolution of 1933.

HISTORY SINCE 1933

The Revolution of 1933 and the Batista Years

The revolution of 1933 has been called the "lost opportunity" by some students of Cuban politics. Machado was deposed by a coup d'état, but the events surrounding his fall were much more than a simple palace changing of the guard. Numerous members of the intelligentsia— including professionals, teachers, and students—participated in the rebellion. They called for a new Cuba that would not include the *plattistas* and *entreguistas*. At the same time, there was a popular uprising in Cuba, particularly prevalent on the sugar *centrales*, whose workers had been organized into trade unions. The aims of the workers were revolutionary, calling for redistribution of income. The red flag of communism was allegedly seen flying over some *centrales*.

With the triumph of the coup d'état against Machado, Ramón Grau San Martín, a doctor and professor at the University of Havana, came to the presidency, promising economic reform and social justice. His government was paralyzed by one central factor of Cuban existence: the intervention of U.S. Ambassador Sumner Welles. The New Deal administration of Franklin D. Roosevelt no longer believed in military intervention in Latin America and was to be instrumental in the abrogation of the Platt Amendment the following year. However, this did not prevent Welles and the ambassadors who followed him from using other kinds of influence on the Cuban president. (An ambassador in the 1950s was later to testify that the U.S. ambassador was second in power on the island only to the president of Cuba.) In 1933, Welles thought Grau an unacceptable ruler, probably because of his radical support. On Welles's advice, the U.S. government never extended diplomatic recognition to the Grau government. Welles also apparently encouraged army officers in their coup plans. The coup was led by Fulgencio Batista, who was to dominate Cuban politics for the next twenty-five years.

Batista had been instrumental in the coup that ousted Machado, an overthrow unusual in that it was backed primarily by enlisted men, who began by removing their senior officers. In January 1934, Batista replaced Grau with a colonel and became the power behind the throne until 1940. In 1940, he was elected president for a four-year term and governed in a way quite different from his later dictatorship. Far from exercising repressive tactics, Batista did much in the areas of social reform. A labor ministry was established, and social-security laws were passed. The constitution of 1940, generally accepted as one of the most progressive in Latin America for the time, was adopted. Batista often allied himself with the Communist Popular Socialist party (PSP) and made claims to being a nationalist leader, taking credit for the 1934 abrogation of the Platt Amendment. Batista surprised many when, in 1944, after the defeat of his hand-picked successor in a free election, he voluntarily left the country.

The victor in the 1944 election was Ramón Grau San Martín, who many Cubans hoped would bring about the goals of the 1933 revolution. Grau and his successor, Carlos Prío Soccarrás, were elected by the party of the Cuban Revolution (generally referred to as the Auténticos), which had been founded by Grau in 1936. The platform of the party favored labor, extended social-security benefits, agrarian reform, increased industrialization, expansion of public health and education, more equitable distribution of income, and nationalism. However, the two Auténtico regimes failed to meet those goals. The democrats showed that they could be as corrupt as the strong-man governments of Batista and his puppets had been.

Disillusioned with the Auténticos, a young firebrand named Eduardo Chibás founded the Party of the Cuban People (commonly known as the Ortodoxo). The party called for many programs not unlike those of the Auténticos. Chibás built a popular following through, among other things, his weekly radio program. At the end of one particularly impassioned speech in 1951, disgraced because he had failed to produce promised evidence against a cabinet minister, Chibás shot himself fatally while still on the air. Young Fidel Castro—who, like many of his age group, had been affected by Chibás and his party—rushed Chibás to the hospital.

In the presidential election of 1952, there were three major candidates— one Ortodoxo, who seemed likely to win, one Auténtico, and Fulgencio Batista. On March 10, 1952, supporters of Batista staged a bloodless military coup, toppling President Prío and returning the former strong man. Congress was dismissed and all political parties were dissolved.

Originally welcomed by many as an escape from corruption and ineffective government, the second Batista government was itself an extremely corrupt one, and the dictator left in 1959 with an immense fortune. Batista was indeed more effective than the Auténtico governments, but it was an effectiveness that was repressive and wedded to the status quo. Batista's goals no longer included social and economic change. He encouraged a climate conducive to the growth of U.S. business, which supported him until the very end. U.S. diplomatic representatives were only slightly less enthusiastic about the dictator. Within Cuba, Batista's major organizational strength came from conservative politicians and the armed forces.

By the 1950s, the generation of 1930 had clearly failed. During the previous thirty years, nearly every known mechanism for transferring power had been used. *Personalismo* had proved more important than organized political groups. The strong leader had emerged as the key to the balance between the army, organized labor, university students, professional associations, major business interests, and U.S. diplomatic representatives. The 1933 revolution had brought to center stage a group of left-wing nationalists promising social and economic reforms. However, the nationalists were never united and accomplished little or nothing due to the intervention of U.S. ambassadors, the emergence of Fulgencio Batista as a strong man, and their own corruption and incompetence when they did have power from 1944 to 1952.

Fidel Castro and the Cuban Revolution

Fidel Castro Ruz was born August 13, 1926, on his father's ranch near the town of Birán, Mayarí township, in the Oriente province of Cuba.[2] Although the area was poor, Fidel's family was relatively privileged. His father, Angel, had amassed a considerable amount of land through hard work, illegal movement of boundary lines, and persecution of his political opponents. The Castro estate employed some five hundred workers in growing sugarcane and was worth half a million dollars at the time of Angel's death in 1956.

Fidel was the fourth child of the seven born to Angel and Lina Ruz. There had been two children from Angel's first marriage, which had not been terminated at the time of Fidel's birth. Fidel was the fourth child of the relationship of Angel with his cook, and after the marriage of the two, young Castro grew up in a household with a half brother and half sister, four sisters, two brothers. Family life was filled with tension. The two sets of children did not get along, and Angel was argumentative, strong willed, violent, and authoritarian. Fidel's relations with his father were always bad. At age six Fidel threatened to burn the house if Angel did not allow him to go to school; at age thirteen he tried to organize the sugar workers on the family estate in a strike against Angel. When he was eighteen, Fidel allegedly accused his father of being "one of those who abuse the powers they wrench from the people with deceitful promises."

After completing work at the local rural school, Fidel continued his education at private schools in Santiago and Havana. He is remembered as an excellent though somewhat disruptive student and an outstanding athlete (high school athlete of the year in 1944, with favorable scouting reports from the New York Yankees). In 1945, he entered the law school of the University of Havana and graduated five years later.

During his university years, Fidel became very involved in national politics and in some efforts of an inter-American nature. At the university, there existed a number of "action groups," which had originated as leftist groups during the abortive revolution of 1933. By 1946, they had become little more than opportunist groups in conflict over campus power, favors from the national government, and lecture notes. They were no longer leftist in any meaningful sense. Fidel belonged to one of the two principal action groups, admits to having carried a gun, took part in the armed skirmishes, and was accused of killing several opponents in such activities.

Although he was involved in numerous political activities, both within the action groups and on his own, two incidents of Fidel's university career are particularly noteworthy. In 1947, he was a member of a force that trained on a nearby island to invade the Dominican Republic and overthrow Rafael Leonidas Trujillo. After sixty days of training, this group was disbanded by the Grau government. In 1948, Fidel was in Bogotá, Colombia, during the dramatic April riots. He was there for a meeting of Latin American students sponsored by President Juan Perón of Argentina. The "black legend" about Fidel states that he was there as an instrument of international communism (and might have even been in on the plot to kill the Colombian populist Jorge Gaitán); however, it seems more likely that Fidel had only met with Gaitán and participated in some way in the violence following the assassination of the Liberal party leader.

Some of Fidel's political activities during his university years were of an electoral nature. He was strongly influenced by the reformist ideas of Eduardo Chibás and was one of the founders of the Ortodoxo party. Fidel took an active part in the unsuccessful Ortodoxo presidential campaign of 1948, traveling across the country to arouse mass support for Chibás. Perhaps Fidel, even at the age of twenty-two, did not really believe in the peaceful road to power. Within the Ortodoxo movement he had already created a splinter group, called Orthodox Radical Action (ARO), that favored insurrection.

Fidel Castro continued his political activities after graduating from law school and setting up a small, unprofitable law practice. In 1952, he was nominated as an Ortodoxo candidate for the Chamber of Deputies, the lower house of the national Congress. Once in Congress, he planned to present a revolutionary program. Although he did not expect such a program to be approved, he felt the people could be mobilized on the basis of it. On March 10, 1952, Fidel's candidacy—and everyone else's—was terminated by the pro-Batista military coup d'état.

Castro's first reaction was a legal one. In a brief before the Court of Constitutional Guarantees, he asked that Batista be imprisoned for more than a hundred years for treason and sedition. The court rejected the appeal, on the grounds that "revolution is the fount of law."

Having failed in his legal attempts, Fidel recruited and trained young people who, like himself, abhorred the Batista dictatorship, thought that peaceful means would not be successful in ridding the island of it, and saw a "true revolution" as the way out of the impasse of traditional Cuban politics. The plan was for armed rebels, about 170 in number, to stage a surprise attack on the Moncada army barracks in Santiago. Moncada was the second largest army barracks in the country, with about 1,000 personnel on base. At the same time that the barracks was attacked, there were to be hits at the Bayamo garrison nearby, at a hospital, and at a radio station. A recording of the famous last speech of Chibás was to be broadcast, as well as a call for popular uprising. Despite the use of this recording, the Moncada plan was Fidel's and had no support from the Ortodoxo party.

The attempt was staged at about five o'clock on the morning of July 26, 1953. The plan depended very much on surprise and (since July 26 was the second day of Santiago's traditional summer carnival) on the rebels' finding soldiers who were intoxicated and/or asleep. The element of surprise was lost when a patrol saw the rebels arriving at the barracks. Further, one rebel group failed to arrive on time. A bloody battle lasting about two hours ensued, during which none of the rebel objectives was obtained; it resulted in retreat. The human costs of the two hours were immense. The assailants had 3 killed, 68 summarily executed upon capture, and 46 captured and later tried. The army troops suffered the deaths of 16 enlisted men and 3 officers. Fidel himself escaped to the mountains near Santiago and was captured several days later by government troops. The plans for retreat had been poorly made; the rebels carried no food and did not know the mountains well.

The captured rebels were tried in September and October. Originally Fidel was tried along with the others in open court with press coverage and acting as a lawyer for all. However, when the trial became a cause célèbre, Fidel "took ill," according to the government, and was tried in October in secret in the hospital. He once again defended himself, and that defense has become one of the basic documents of the Cuban Revolution. There was no official transcript of the trial, and Fidel later reconstructed his defense while in prison.

This reconstructed *"History Will Absolve Me!"* speech is a key to understanding the thoughts of Fidel Castro at the beginning of the violent stage of the Revolution. In addition to analyzing the reasons for the attack, the reasons for its failure, and the legal defense of his innocence (rebellion against an illegal government is not a crime), Fidel spent a great part of the discourse telling what the insurgents would have done had they been victorious. He called for the restoration of the liberal and progressive constitution of 1940. Beyond that, Fidel talked about six areas that required immediate attention: the landholding system, industrialization, housing, unemployment, education, and health.

Five revolutionary laws were listed that would have been proclaimed immediately. Besides (1) the reestablishment of the 1940 constitution, they called for (2) granting of property to all planters, lessees, share-croppers, and squatters who worked on small plots; (3) granting workers and employees the right to share 30 percent of the profits of all the large industrial, mercantile, and mining enterprises, including the sugar mills; (4) granting all planters (that is, those working on someone else's land) the right to share 55 percent of the sugar production; and (5) ordering the confiscation of all holdings and ill-gotten gains of those who had committed fraud during the previous regimes. There was nothing extremely radical about these proposals.

The document was more than a legal defense; it was to become the basis for the future organization of Fidel Castro's movement. He never gave up, although the court sentenced him to fifteen years in prison. Dramatically, Fidel concluded:

> As for me, I know that jail will be as hard as it has ever been for anyone, filled with threats, with vileness, and cowardly brutality; but I do not fear this, as I do not fear the fury of the miserable tyrant who snuffed out the life of seventy brothers of mine.
> Condemn me, it does not matter. *History will absolve me!*[3]

Castro spent the following twenty-two months in prison on the Isle of Pines. He spent his time reading, secretly reconstructing and dis-tributing his *"History Will Absolve Me!"* speech, and setting up a school for illiterate inmates using materials that were revolutionary in content. On May 7, 1955, Fulgencio Batista issued a general amnesty for all political prisoners. Castro, far from a repentant former prisoner, returned to Havana to a large, popular welcome. For two months he wrote for newspapers and spoke on radio, while working for the Ortodoxo party. But on July 7 Fidel left Cuba, a voluntary exile, concluding that it was impossible to form a revolutionary movement within the country. Because government resistance and threats prevented his doing so in Cuba, Fidel stated that he was off to the Caribbean to form such a movement and that he would return.

For the next year and a half, Castro planned his revolution from Mexico. One of his first acts was to establish the 26th of July movement (M-26-7), named for the date of the Moncada uprising and open to all Cubans "who sincerely desire to see political democracy reestablished and social justice introduced in Cuba." Other activities were numerous: He kept in contact with Fidelistas in Cuba, encouraging the growth of the organization and continuing opposition to accommodation with Batista; he met with other Cuban revolutionaries, who traveled to Mexico to see him; he went to the United States to build support and raise money. By far the most important task in Mexico was the planning of and training for the Cuban invasion. Troops were taught the art of ambush, hit-and-run tactics, shooting, mountain climbing, and how to make Molotov cocktails, grenades, and booby traps. Ten- to fifteen-mile (16- to 24-kilometer) marches were common, as well as political training based on Castro's statements and letters, Cuban history and sociology, but apparently not on any Marxist or Communist material. During these years he met and recruited a young Argentine named Ernesto "Che" Guevara. Although by training a medical doctor, Che was by desire a soldier of fortune and a revolutionary and by choice a man without nationalistic feelings. He had been a minor functionary in the Guatemalan government during the administration of Jacobo Arbenz Guzmán, and after the overthrow of that regime by Guatemalan elements with the assistance of the CIA, he had gone to Mexico.

In fear of impending arrest, the Cuban revolutionaries hurried to the coast of Mexico and on November 25, 1956, set sail on the yacht *Granma* for Cuba. The crossing was a rough one. Eighty-two individuals crossed on a boat meant for ten, in which the bilge pumps did not work and the lifeboats were unusable.

The Guerrilla War

After landing in Cuba on December 2, 1956, and being ambushed by governmental troops a few days later, the Castro band was reduced to about 20 or 30 men. In the next twenty-five months, the guerrillas never grew to more than about 1,000 in number; nevertheless, they defeated the military dictator Batista, who had about 40,000 troops, well armed by the United States as part of its cold war policy. The military strategy developed through three stages.

During the first stage (January 1957–February 1958), the basic strategy was for the rebels to attack isolated army posts, withdrawing immediately and then preparing ambushes for the pursuing army troops. During this period, the size of the rebel bands grew slowly, most of the new supporters coming from Santiago, where they were recruited by Frank

País. At the same time, the guerrillas cultivated relationships with the local *guajiros*. Peasant support was needed for food and supplies and to assure that the location of the guerrillas not be divulged to the army. Further, the problems of the rural poor had to be solved. In areas controlled by the Castro forces, land reform was initiated, especially in 1958, and legal reforms were made to protect the poor.

Also during the first stage, Cuba and the world learned of the rebel uprising in the eastern mountains of the island. In February 1957, Fidel was interviewed by Herbert Matthews of the *New York Times*, disproving Batista's contention that army troops had killed both Fidel and his brother Raúl two months earlier. In reaction to Castro's attacks, the military dictator became more and more repressive. At one point he ordered the internment of some two thousand peasant families in order to eliminate any possible aid for the guerrillas. This was the beginning of an important theme of the insurrectionary stage: The brutality of Batista and his troops led to increased alienation of the previously neutral Cubans.

Fidel Castro, during the first stage, encountered various problems with fellow revolutionaries who also wanted to rid the island of Batista but disagreed on strategy. One such group was the Revolutionary Directorate, headed by José Antonio Echevarría, who believed that an urban strategy would be more successful than Fidel's rural one. In March 1957, Echevarría was killed following an unsuccessful attempt to assassinate Batista, and other members of the group were exiled. Even within the M-26-7, there were individuals who, without challenging Fidel's leadership, questioned his tactics. These people were referred to as the *llanos* (plains) members, as opposed to the *sierra* (mountain) people. In the first half of 1957, the most outstanding of the *llanos* leaders was Frank País in Santiago, who argued that the emphasis of the struggle should be on urban terrorism, with the guerrillas in the mountains playing a secondary role. Fidel, on the other hand, saw the priorities in the opposite order, with the urban resistance supporting the rural guerrillas through financing, recruitment, and supply. Terrorism on the part of the urban groups was encouraged, but the groups were to play a clearly secondary role. Although País was killed by Batista agents in mid-1957, the basic conflict of strategies continued for the remainder of the insurrection.

By March 1958, there were enough troops to set up a second, more complex military strategy. A guerrilla triangle was established; in addition to the four columns of troops in the Sierra Maestra, Raúl Castro was sent north to set up a new front in the Sierra Cristal, while Juan Almeida went to El Cobre, west of Santiago, to set up another.

The progress of the Castro movement in the Sierra Maestra and environs was due not only to their activities, but to happenings in the outside world. In March 1958 the U.S. government suspended arms shipments to Cuba, as Batista, in clear violation of the statutes of the

United States, had used the arms for internal security matters (fighting the rebels) rather than for defense of the nation against outside attack. This was an important decision of the U.S. government, although the Fidelistas argued that it was a year too late and too little, since the U.S. military mission remained. Cubans were already drawing away from Batista in reaction to his repressive and brutal tactics. The suspension of U.S. arms indicated the Eisenhower administration's disapproval of Batista; a major power contender in the Cuban political process, the U.S. government, had partially withdrawn support from the dictator.

Another event that aided the guerrillas indirectly was the failure of the *llanos* leaders in a general strike called for April 9. This failure discredited the *llanos* leaders of the M-26-7 and helped to consolidate the power of Fidel in the movement, although he had approved and supported the strike.

In May 1958, Batista ordered an offensive, sending 10,000 troops to Oriente, with bombing support, to crush the rebels. Yet various tactics by the leaders of the guerrilla bands led to the defeat of the best armed troops of the Cuban army, which suffered 1,000 casualties, 500 troops captured, and much lost equipment, later to be used by the rebels. Raúl Castro negotiated a nonaggression pact with the 1,000 troops sent to fight him. Fidel eventually arranged a deal with some of the leaders who commanded the troops fighting him. In the meantime, he lectured the opposition troops by loudspeaker and, as the air force bombing was taking its toll, kidnapped some dozen private U.S. citizens residing in Oriente. The U.S. consul in Santiago was told that the citizens would be released when the bombing stopped, and the U.S. government put pressure on Batista to do so, which he reluctantly did.

On August 7, 1958, the Cuban army began a disorderly retreat. The final stage of the insurrection took place between the retreat and the January 1, 1959, victory of the rebels. The approximately eight hundred guerrilla troops were divided into four columns. The first and second, commanded respectively by Fidel and Raúl Castro, stayed where they had been. But the remaining two columns were sent to other parts of the island. One, under Che Guevara, went to the Escambray mountains in Las Villas province in the central part of the island. Another, under Camilo Cienfuegos, was dispatched to the mountains in Piñar del Río province, at the western tip of Cuba, although they never arrived. This detachment ended up working with that of Che in the Escambray.

From a military point of view, this was a new stage for various reasons. For the first time, some of the rebels moved out of the mountains and crossed the lowlands to reach another mountain range. The rebels had near complete control of Oriente. Normal transportation was ended, as were all army troop movements. In November, Fidel left the mountains for the first time in a campaign to lead his forces on the plains of Oriente. Meanwhile, in Las Villas province, Cienfuegos and Guevara were about to cut the island in two. The troops loyal to the government retreated to the capital of Las Villas, Santa Clara, which was besieged by the rebels.

By December 1958, even the U.S. government and the officers of Batista's army realized that the dictator had to go. There was one last attempt to defeat Castro, this time through trickery. General Eulogio Cantillo met with Fidel, promising a coup against Batista that would open power to the rebels. His true intentions were to consolidate power himself, a treachery anticipated by Castro.

On December 31, 1958, Santa Clara fell to the troops of Guevara and Cienfuegos. In Oriente, troops personally commanded by Fidel were laying siege to Santiago; the city could last only a few more days. That night, Fulgencio Batista, dictator for seven years and the most powerful man in Cuba since 1933, fled the island.

Why Did Castro Win?

One of the matters most surrounded by myth and controversy is why the insurrection directed by Fidel Castro was successful. Castro and his followers have muddied the controversy by reconstructing history. Five reasons for the end of the Batista regime have been mentioned, all of which are perhaps correct to a certain degree: (1) military action, (2) the revolutionary potential of the island, (3) the programmatic content of the Castro campaign, (4) Castro's personal characteristics, and (5) the lack of support for Batista.

The military actions, in a conventional sense, were not sufficient in and of themselves for victory. Although after the experience in Vietnam and Cambodia experts give more credibility to a guerrilla strategy as an efficacious way to win a war, even in that sense the Cuban Revolution was not a military victory. The guerrilla strategy of completely controlling the countryside, leaving the cities isolated and surrounded, occurred only in Oriente province, not in the case of the major city of Havana. Further, although Castro later was to give all credit to the people in the hills, the urban terrorism was also crucial, coming from the M-26-7 as well as the Revolutionary Directorate and the Auténtico party.

There is little doubt that the revolutionary potential of the island was important. There were many very poor people on the island with little to lose from a revolution. Although they might have "participated" in the democracy of the Auténtico years, during the Batista years they had no meaningful political rights. Many of the rural Cubans were wage laborers, radicalized as a result of the lack of a patron-clientele relationship and amenable to organization. Later Castro was to term the Revolution a "peasant" one, but the leadership was definitely not from that social level, and it is not even clear that the majority of the combatants were. In short, although the economic structure of great inequality and unemployment contributed to the success of the Castro insurrection, it was not the only cause.

Yet another argument is that the program presented by Fidel Castro was a major reason for his success. During the two years in the Sierra

Maestra, the thoughts of Fidel Castro, as expressed in his private letters and public declarations, had a double thrust and a double appeal. First, Castro's message was libertarian and therefore democratic; second, it was reformist and tending toward socialism. But the program was vague, that of a man with an open rather than closed mind. Some observers of the Cuban Revolution state that Castro purposefully kept his pronouncements vague to hide the fact that he was already a member of the international Communist movement. Other observers state that Castro's program was ambiguous simply because he had no developed ideology at the moment and was too involved in the military campaign to think through another program. Whatever the reasons for its vagueness, the program's effect was positive for the rebels. Most Cubans could agree with what Fidel Castro was saying; few would disagree with such a vague program.

Yet another argument is that Fidel Castro personally was the key factor in the success of the Cuban Revolution. Che Guevara later was to state, "The foremost, most original, and perhaps the most important single factor to render the Cuban Revolution so exceptional was the natural force that goes by the name of Fidel Castro."[4] There is no doubt that Castro was the unchallenged leader of the movement in the Sierra Maestra, although there were urban leaders who questioned his leadership and tactics. The movement was Castro's personal creation, and it was he who brought together people of differing views to risk their lives. From the early days of the movement, Castro was criticized by friends who said that it would be better if more decisions were made collectively. He promised at various times to change his style but in the end never did.

After coming to power, the leader would be called *charismatic*—that is, possessed of a personal magnetism that resulted in the people's following him. This charisma also existed during the years in the mountains. There was something about the man that led some people to fight in the hills with him and others to perform acts of terrorism in the cities in support of him. Yet this factor seems to have been a secondary one during the insurrection, growing much more important during the early years of the Castro government.

A final argument is that the Castro Revolution succeeded because of the weaknesses of the Batista government. Cuba was not a typical Latin American country in that the traditional power groups of the Church and the wealthy landed were relatively unimportant. The governments, including Batista's, depended on the military and police and whatever other groups were willing to give them support. They drifted away from the dictator when he became more brutally repressive in response to the Castro rebellion. In the end, the Batista dictatorship had support only from the two armed groups, and they were not monolithic. In short, the argument states that Castro did not win; Batista lost, due in large part to his overaction to the Castro challenge.

GOVERNMENTAL INSTITUTIONS
OF THE CASTRO REVOLUTION

Before January 1959, the governmental institutions in Cuba were like those of the United States—separation of powers, checks and balances, elections—although these institutions were ignored as much as they were honored. This democratic model has been abandoned by the Castro Revolution, replaced for at least a decade by a "charismatic" stage and increasingly since 1970 by the "formalized" stage.

The Charismatic Stage

From Castro's victory in 1959 until about 1970, the Cuban Revolution was characterized by a lack of institutions other than the personal leadership of Fidel Castro. Castro made promises to become less dominant and to delegate authority, and occasionally groups tried to take more power and reduce Fidel's control. Yet power remained in the hands of the "maximum leader," and the erstwhile pretenders were rudely awakened to the realities of personal leadership on the island.

During this period, Fidel Castro continued to differentiate himself from previous Cuban leaders by adopting a highly egalitarian, populist style of government. He and his followers believed that a more meaningful, direct democracy had been established on the island. The formal democracy of elections was replaced by a face-to-face one, with Fidel traveling throughout the country, talking to people about their problems and trying to solve those he deemed pressing. Fidel was the people's choice, although not by election. The argument was that Fidel would have won any possible election. Equally important, Cuba was a democracy in the sense that the government (Castro) was taking care of the true needs of the Cuban people.

Castro's was a form of rule in which the leader decided what the people's true interests were. In the Latin American tradition, the common good, greater than the sum of individual interests, was perceived and carried out by the leader. As Castro stated,

> The leaders in a revolutionary process are not infallible receptacles of what the people think. . . . One cannot conceive of the leader as a simple carrier of ideas, a simple collector of opinions and impressions. He has to be also a creator of opinions, a creator of points of view; he has to *influence* the masses.[5]

In theory and practice, Fidelismo of this period was premised on the belief that a select core of intellectually superior and proven revolutionaries has to lead the masses. The governing formula was one in which basic policies, and even more mundane ones, were set from above by Fidel and his circle of trusted advisers. These decisions were then communicated to the masses below, who were mobilized by the regime's revolutionary organizations. Castro made an impressive number of decisions himself. At times he made impromptu decisions while talking on national television; at times he imposed his views by fiat although his technical advisers counseled other courses. The small leadership circle around Fidel consisted primarily of his ex-guerrilla comrades from the days in the mountains, who tended to react uncritically and without debate as soldiers obeying their commander.

One of the results of this kind of centralized decision making was that personal access to Fidel was essential. Decisions were made by Fidel and a few others, and there were no normal channels to reach the leader, who might be anywhere on the island. Quite often, no one knew when Fidel would be back in the capital. The informal nature of Castro's government would not have been so important had power been delegated to ministers and heads of departments. But such delegation had not been made.

Edward Gonzalez has called the decision-making process in Cuba during this period the Moncada or Sierra Maestra Complex,[6] since the process shared characteristics with the years of armed struggle. Maximum if not unfeasible objectives were staked out, with a penchant for revolutionary action and elitism. There was a disdain for organization, with Fidel dominating all major decisions and undertaking projects as if they were military adventures, often without adequate preparation. Finally, there was a belief that the will and determination of dedicated revolutionaries (subjective factors) could overcome all obstacles, in spite of the objective reality.

The Formalization of the Revolution Since 1970

Before 1970, institutions had little power. Castro feared that the institutionalization and bureaucratization of the Revolution would take the impetus away from its original goal; lead to a new class governing in its own interests, perhaps not in the best interests of all Cubans; and in the process limit him personally both in freedom of spontaneous informal action and in power. All formal institutionalization before 1970 increased Fidel's power rather than detracted from it. Further, Fidel's distrust of organization included not only any that affected his power directly but also lower-level bureaucracy that might decrease his power indirectly.

The organizational turning point of the Cuban Revolution occurred in 1970. The year was important because it marked the first dramatic failure of Fidel Castro in power: The government failed to achieve the ambitious goal of a 10-million-tonne (11-million-ton) sugarcane harvest, a goal that technical advisers had argued against. What followed after 1970 was an increased formalization of the institutions of the Revolution, both in the government and in the Communist party.

In 1972, there was a reorganization of the top governmental apparatus. An Executive Committee with power above the Council of Ministers was established, composed of ten deputy prime ministers with direct control over agencies or ministries. Fidel Castro became the president of the Executive Committee and retained the premiership of the Council of Ministers, while also maintaining his personal control over several ministries and agencies, most notably those of armed forces and security. However, there was more delegation of authority than before.

The most dramatic institutional change came in 1976, when a new constitution was adopted after a year of discussion of drafts throughout the island. The new document envisioned delegation of authority in Havana, more democracy in the choice of leaders, and a certain decentralization of power away from Havana.

The basic unit of the new governing system is the Municipal Assemblies of Peoples' Power, one for each of the municipalities in Cuba. These municipal assemblies are chosen in free elections for two and one-half years, and all above the age of sixteen have the right to vote. The assemblies are in charge of all purely municipal matters, within the broad guidelines of national policies. The municipal assemblies also elect delegates to the Provincial Assemblies of Peoples' Power (serving for two and one-half years, and with authority for all provincial matters) and members of the National Assembly of Peoples' Power. The National Assembly, with a five-year term, is the law-making body of national scope. In addition to making rules, it elects from its own membership a council of state composed of one president, one first vice president, five vice presidents, and twenty-three other members. The president of the Council of State, thus elected, is the head of state and head of government combined. The duties of the Council of State include bringing legislative projects to the national assembly and serving as an interim law-making body when the National Assembly is not in session.

The highest-ranking part of the executive branch in the new system is the Council of Ministers, composed of the head of the Council of State, the first vice president and five vice presidents from the Council of State, as well as the president of the Central Planning Board, the other ministers, and "others that the law determines." The Council of Ministers "constitutes the Government of the Republic."

Cuba is apparently in a stage of transition from charismatic to more formalized power. What this means for the personal power of Fidel Castro is not at all clear. He is still the most powerful person in Cuba, with great knowledge of many policy fields. In December 1976, Fidel was elected president of the Council of State, hence becoming for the first time both head of state and head of government. He remains first secretary of the Cuban Communist party. It is likely that he will no longer make dramatic decisions without prior consultation with his technical advisers. Perhaps there will be more collegial leadership within the Council of State and the Council of Ministers, although Castro heads both. Fidel will be sixty years old in 1986; he is likely to be at least "first among equals" for some time to come.

As of the early 1980s the formalization of the Revolution had several notable characteristics. In 1979–1980 twenty-three ministers were fired for not doing their jobs well enough. Their functions were given to twelve deputy prime ministers, about 20 percent of whom over a period of time came from the pre-Castro PSP. The National Assembly does modify, and even block, legislation. But the solution in such cases, at times suggested by Fidel Castro himself, is more general "framework laws" to be interpreted by decrees of the deputy prime ministers. The military seem to be growing in importance, as evidenced by the preferred treatment given to military personnel for housing, employment, and other scarce commodities. In general, stratification seems to be increasing. Managers are better trained than before, and members of the Cuban Communist Party (PCC) have higher levels of education than the population in general.[7]

SOCIOPOLITICAL GROUPS IN THE NEW CUBA

By the end of the first two years of the Castro government, it was obvious that a revolution was occurring in government policies and in the elimination of the old groups. The Batista military was replaced by a revolutionary one, commanded by former guerrilla fighters and Fidel Castro. The political parties, including the pro- and anti-Batista ones, were ignored, with the exception of the PSP. The opposition press was first curtailed and later shut down. Labor unions and student movements were purged of dissident elements, in the end becoming instruments of the regime. The Catholic Church was made less powerful by the expulsion of foreign priests and the closing of Catholic schools. The associations of big-business people, landowners, and employers had practically disappeared by mid-1960, with the older professional associations of doctors, lawyers, and architects disappearing as independent entities soon thereafter. At the same time, relations worsened with the United States, culminating in a formal diplomatic break in January 1961. Although the United States as a power contender was not completely removed (as evidenced by the CIA invasion in April 1961 and other military attempts and assassination plots), the main foreign power contender became the Soviet Union. In short, by 1961 the interest-group associations of the prerevolutionary period were either dissolved or incorporated under state control.

Fidel Castro: The Charismatic Leader

No doubt the most important power contender of the first several years of the Cuban Revolution was not a group at all, but one individual, Fidel Castro. He was one of a small number of individuals in recent history who, initially and to some extent to this day, derived authority and legitimacy from their own characteristics and accomplishments. This charisma, literally meaning the "gift of grace," has been more common in Latin America than elsewhere, with various countries following their caudillos or men on horseback. Yet the case of Castro seems to be one in which charisma was remarkably widespread and extremely effective in changing the political system.

Charisma has five important qualities. First, charismatic leaders are the creation of their followers, who expect and reward their leader for superhuman deeds. In Castro's case, he did the impossible by defeating the Batista government and later at the Bay of Pigs by defeating the exiles trained by the CIA. Before his thirty-third birthday, he was a legend. Charismatic leaders are given religious characteristics by their followers. In the early years of the Revolution, many Cuban families had pictures of Castro with his band of "disciples" around him and the slight hint of a halo around his head. Most dramatically, a Cuban Presbyterian minister wrote in 1960: "It is my conviction which I state now with full responsibility for what I am saying, that Fidel Castro is an instrument in the hands of God for the establishment of his reign among us."[8]

A second characteristic of the charismatic leader is contact with the people. In Castro's case, it has been constant and almost complete. He has toured the country, meeting with people and discussing their problems. The now-famous public rallies with speeches by Castro bring large numbers of Cubans in contact with the leader, often more than a million at a time. Further, Castro has effectively used television to talk with the people.

Yet another characteristic of charisma is the leader's self-perception as being elected from above to perform a mission. Castro, even before his conversion to communism, perceived the revolution as part of a greater historical movement against tyranny and oppression. The leader alone retains the right to determine the meaning of the historical movement and the correct behavior within the great historical movement.

The final two characteristics are contradictory. The charismatic leader is against institutions, yet aware of their necessity once the charisma has run its course. In the 1960s, Castro resisted any attempt to bureaucratize the Revolution. In the short run this was a good tactic, since people will follow a charismatic leader regardless of how well the figure governs, particularly if there is an outside threat. In the longer run, the charismatic leader must deliver some of the things that the people want or develop a coercive capability. In the end, charisma is unstable and short-lived simply because the leader is human; this kind of authority cannot be passed on to the next generation. Therefore, the leader must find some way to make the revolution last, most likely through some sort of institutionalization.

Because of his charismatic power, during the 1960s Fidel Castro was able to make nearly all decisions himself, surrounded by his inner circle (particularly his brother Raúl and Che Guevara) from the guerrilla days.

Fidel occupied all of the following posts, sometimes four or five at once: prime minister of the revolutionary government, commander in chief of the armed forces, president of the National Institute of Agrarian Reform (INRA), first secretary of the Communist party (and therefore ranking member of the Politburo and the secretariat of the party), and head of the Economic Group for Special Plans. In 1976, after the formalization of the government, he became for the first time head of state through his election as president of the Council of State. It is not clear that the formalization has taken power away from Fidel, although it might be argued that his power is less due to charisma than to formal position in the government.

The inner circle around Fidel was never completely homogeneous, with subgroups of differing backgrounds, ages, and probably functional interests. At times the disputes within the leadership group have become public. Sometimes individuals and groups of the inner circle have enjoyed sufficient latitude to coalesce around a policy position and to voice their opinions independently of Fidel. But in the long run, any coalition without Fidel has been unstable. If such a coalition is perceived by Fidel to be an opposing faction, it is expelled from the inner circle. He has been known to play off opposing groups to his own advantage. In the end, Fidel has always been pivotal to the outcome of internal power struggles and policy disputes; any coalition ultimately has to group around him if its position is to prevail within the regime.

Popular Organizations

In theory and in practice Fidelismo is premised on the belief that a select core of intellectually superior and proven revolutionaries has to lead the masses. Basic policies are set from above by Fidel and his circle of trusted advisers. These decisions are then communicated to the masses below, who in turn are mobilized by the regime's revolutionary organizations. There is much mass political activity, almost always in compliance with the directives and tasks set by the leadership.

Besides the goal of carrying out revolutionary programs, Fidelismo aims to change individual values and behavior through directed participation in revolutionary institutions. These institutions might be short-lived, like the Literacy Campaign of 1961. The most important institution has been the Committees for the Defense of the Revolution (CDRs). Launched personally by Fidel at the end of 1960, the CDR was to be "a system of revolutionary collective vigilance so that everybody will know everybody else on his block, what they do, what relationship they had with the [Batista] tyranny, what they believe in, what people they meet, what activities they participate in."[9] Besides this vigilance function, the CDRs were to integrate the people, bringing together diverse types to teach them the basics of the ideology of the regime; to mobilize the people in a number of activities such as cane cutting, collecting scrap metal, or enrolling children in school; and to serve as implementors, administering various programs of the Revolution.

The CDRs did give all the people of Cuba a way to participate, within strict limits, in the Revolution. The existence of the CDRs removed any possible excuse for not having an opportunity to demonstrate one's revolutionary fervor. As such they flourished, having some 2 million members by the mid-1960s. Today the CDR still exists, primarily concerned with the function of collective vigilance.

Although the CDR gives everyone an opportunity to belong to a common group, a plethora of other groups have been organized by the Cuban leadership—of peasants, workers, intellectuals, and many others, as well as of women either as part of these or separately. All of these groups are directed by the collective leadership and have little or no independence of their own.

A potentially relevant group, not properly a "popular" one, is the military. With the demise of the old Batista army, a national militia first rose in its place, later to be replaced by a more conventional military, supplemented by the militia. All young Cubans must serve for two years in the military. It has been active in matters of national defense and in assistance to the economy, most notably in its sugarcane-cutting activities. Cuba's military, the largest per capita in all of Latin America, has been controlled carefully by the collective leadership, at times by Fidel himself as commander in chief. It seems unlikely that it will become an independent political force in the near future.

The Party

During the first two years of the Castro government, there was no formal organization of the regime's supporters, only an increasingly uneasy alliance of members of the M-26-7 with members of the pre-Castro Communist PSP. In 1961, these two groups were merged into the Integrated Revolutionary Organization (ORI). During the following two years, the old PSP members became quite powerful, until they were stripped of their authority and the ORI was replaced in 1963 by the Fidelista-dominated Party of the Socialist Revolution (PURS). PURS lasted two years until superseded by the PCC.

On paper, it appeared that Castro had lost power with the creation of the PCC; however, the contrary was the case. An examination of the composition of the PCC at various levels shows that its founding actually guaranteed the continued supremacy of personal rule over institutional authority. At the apex of the party were the one-hundred-member Central Committee, the eight-person Politburo, and the six-member Party Secretariat. Although some ex-PSP members were on the Central Committee, most of its members were former guerrilla fighters with Fidel. The Politburo was entirely of Fidelista background; even though the ex-PSP leadership was allowed representation in the secretariat, it was placed under the control of one of Fidel's most trusted subordinates. Further, Castro himself was named first secretary of the party.

A number of cases from the 1960s show clearly what happened to individuals who thought they could use the party organization to challenge Fidel Castro. The two most notable examples involve one man, Aníbal Escalante, who had been a member of the PSP before the Revolution. Escalante was named the head of ORI in 1961 and during the first year of that organization's existence became quite powerful. In March 1962, Fidel denounced Escalante, saying that he and the ex-PSP members were trying to use ORI to develop their own power on the island.

After several years in East Europe, Escalante returned to the island. He held meetings with former PSP members and others critical of the Fidelista line in foreign and domestic policy, although not critical of the Revolution itself. These dissidents were pro-Soviet in their orientation and loyalty and later established contacts with Soviet-bloc embassy officials. In late 1967, Escalante and thirty-four others were arrested, tried in 1968 by the Central Committee of the PCC, and sentenced to from two to fifteen years for having operated as a subversive "micro-faction" within the regime. What both cases show is that Fidel Castro did not allow organized opposition to his regime or his policies, either within or outside the party apparatus.

For a short time, there were schools to train revolutionaries, presumably to join the party. Called the Schools of Revolutionary Instruction (EIR), they were founded secretly in the latter half of 1960 with the single purpose of the ideological formation of a select group of revolutionaries who would spread their ideas to the people in general. These schools taught Marxism-Leninism as the Cuban leaders understood it. At their high point in 1962, the EIR enrolled approximately ten thousand students. However, in 1965 the schools were discontinued, in part because Soviet teaching materials were not deemed adequate for the Cuban situation, in part because of the shortage of qualified teachers. Even more importantly, Cuban leaders did not believe that revolutionary training could occur in the classroom; one learned from revolutionary activity itself.

During the 1960s, the Cuban Communist party was the smallest per capita of all the Communist countries. As part of the formalization of the 1970s, an effort was made to vitalize the party. In December 1975, the PCC held its first national party congress, adopting a program in keeping both with the thrust of past government policies and with the new constitution. Concurrently, an attempt was made to expand PCC membership and to more thoroughly train its members to perform the PCC's chief function of political guidance.

MAJOR PUBLIC POLICIES
OF THE CASTRO REVOLUTION

No Latin American government or leader has done more in the realm of public policy in the past several decades than Fidel Castro's revolutionary government has since 1959. The pages here are too limited to present more than an overview; the reader is directed to the Suggestions for Further Reading for more extensive research.

The First Major Decisions: The Move to the Left

Within the first three years of the Castro government, three basic and interrelated questions had to be faced if the government was to be more than a repetition of former ones. What was to be the political structure of the Revolution? (Could fundamental revolutionary changes be carried out through the promised liberal democracy, or was a revolutionary dictatorship necessary?) Could a viable revolutionary regime be formed solely with non-Communist elements of the M-26-7, or was it necessary to have the skills and alliance of the PSP? Could the United States be expected to countenance a regime bent on the revolutionary change of Cuba, with its concurrent drawbacks for U.S. business and diplomacy? (If the answer to the third question was negative, could Cuba realign itself with the Soviet Union for support?)

Some scholars see the basic reason for the shift to the left as either Castro's perverse personality or his early clandestine membership in the international Communist movement. Those psychoanalyzing Castro find much in his childhood to suggest a less than normal personality. The proof of this as a motivating factor is lacking and the *ex post facto* reasoning (radicals must be perverse in some way) is subject to challenge. Those who argue that Castro was always a Communist lack any reputable independent sources to that effect. Although these scholars state that the reason there is no evidence is that Castro hid it so well, it is surprising, in this day of clandestine surveillance and dossiers, that no convincing case has been compiled. Indeed, the Eisenhower administration apparently commissioned a study of Castro that found no proof that he was a Communist.

One cannot expect a conclusive statement about why Fidel Castro took his Revolution to the left, particularly given the ideological leanings of scholars for and against the Revolution, the lack of information, and the constant definitional squabbles about such matters as what it really means to be a Communist. Some things, however, do seem to be relatively certain and can be grounded in fairly reliable evidence.

When Fidel Castro came to power, he had been deeply committed to fundamental social change for a number of years, although he had no firm ideological commitment about how to bring about that change. Apparently during his high school days and surely by the time of his allegiance to the Chibás Ortodoxo party in 1947, Castro saw social and economic inequities in Cuba and wanted to abolish them. Soon after taking power, Fidel apparently made two decisions: First, these were not reforms that could be carried out gradually but rather ones that had to be done rapidly; second, it was his personal destiny to bring these changes to Cuba.

From July through November 1959, there was an increased reliance on members of the PSP, who were entrusted with many responsible posts. There is no evidence that the PSP members themselves thought that they were contributing to the birth of a new socialism in Cuba; indeed, they thought Castro was unfit to lead a socialist revolution. Further, there is no evidence that at any time did the PSP attempt to force Castro into a more radical position. Rather, they tried to moderate his reforming zeal lest he come into a direct confrontation with the United States. The PSP did have a number of characteristics that Castro saw as beneficial to his movement: a sense of organization and discipline; a belief in a hierarchical power structure, with leadership centralized at the top; and powerful international allies, specifically the Soviet Union. Although in the first year or so of the Revolution Castro pursued an independent foreign policy under the tutelage of neither superpower, U.S. private interests on the island soon were affected negatively by the Revolution. The Cuban leadership had learned from the experience of the Arbenz government of Guatemala, and the group made two correct assumptions: that no dramatic social and economic reform could be carried out without adversely affecting U.S. business interests and that the U.S. government would take actions against such a revolution, at which time a strong ally was needed.

Yet all of this fundamental change occurred in a very short period. In explaining the rapidity of the changes in Cuba, four factors seem especially relevant. First, there was the nature of the man. When Fidel Castro came to power, large numbers of Cubans were disposed to follow him in whatever direction he took. Second, there was the economic structure of the island itself. Cuban workers had been organized—not only industrial workers, but those of the sugar *centrales*. This gave Fidel the twin advantages of having a more radical and a more organized rural *campesino* population than was true of other Latin American countries.

Third, Castro came to power in a country that had both radical and nationalist traditions. The radical tradition included the PSP and surfaced most dramatically before Castro in the abortive revolution of 1933. The nationalist tradition was older and stronger, having been seen in Martí and later in the entire generation of 1930, which had promised to combat the *entreguismo* of earlier Cuban elites. Although U.S. business had no doubt performed some valuable functions for the island's economy, Cubans in the 1950s had more than sufficient reason to be nationalistic and anti-U.S.

Fourth, Cuban history had been one of *generations*, of groups of people who have banded together during the great struggles of the short national history. When Castro came to power, he was the representative of a fourth such generation, that of 1953. There was no reputable political group that could effectively challenge the new rebel Fidelista generation. Nor were there other institutions (landed, Church, military) capable of challenging that new leadership. In short, the new generation had a monopoly of political power soon after January 1, 1959.

Major Socioeconomic Policies

The new government of Cuba used this near monopoly of power to bring an impressive number of socioeconomic changes to the island. All of these have been interrelated.

Agrarian Reform

Castro's economic program, which took effect immediately after he came to power, combined three goals: income expansion, income redistribution, and structural change. Of these three, income redistribution was the first realized, particularly through an agrarian reform.

The first agrarian reform was decreed by the Castro government in May 1959. It was redistributive in nature, placing a maximum size of 402.6 hectares (994.8 acres) on all holdings. Further, the reform established a "vital minimum" of 27 hectares (66.7 acres), with all holding less than that receiving more land. This first agrarian reform was a reformist one; it did not attempt to suppress private property, although some of the land was to be held collectively in order to benefit from the economies of scale of sugarcane cultivation.

Although the amount of land distributed under the first agrarian reform was considerable (almost 3.8 million hectares—9.4 million acres—by mid-1961), by October 1963 the Cuban leaders had devised a much more radical method. The second reform differed in that the maximum holding was reduced to about 66 hectares (163 acres), which then led to the expropriation of some ten thousand medium-sized farms. The new agriculture was to be neither small bourgeoisie nor cooperative. All of the new land went into state ownership, with the dominant farm organization becoming the state-owned farm, with workers receiving wages.

The first agrarian reform created INRA, which surveyed and divided the lands. INRA later developed a number of other services to the new landowners, such as technical advice, credit, seeds, fertilizers, and rural stores with additional goods available. With the second agrarian reform, INRA's functions grew even more dramatically. The small farms that remained (those under 163 acres—66 hectares, making up some 30 percent of the land area) were closely linked to the government by the National Association of Small Farmers (ANAP), which became the sole disperser of credits, technical assistance, seeds, fertilizer, and other agricultural supplies to its members. INRA determines which crops are to be planted by the private farmers. It also sets production quotas that the farmer is to meet and to deliver to the purchasing agencies of INRA, often at prices below market value.

Agricultural production has decreased since the agrarian reforms. The reasons for the decline have to do primarily with the nature of economic planning in the new Cuba. One result of this lower production, as well as of the increased income of the working classes, has been the necessity of rationing food. This does not mean that the majority of the Cuban people are eating worse than before the Revolution; there were many who barely ate at all during that period. Distribution of food, and of wealth in general, is much more equitable than before.

Because of the agrarian reform, the true winner of the Cuban Revolution has been the agricultural workers. Unemployment has been eliminated; eight-hour working days are now constant; many former agricultural workers have been drained off to other jobs, including those in industry and public works. For the first time, the dwellers of the Cuban countryside have both security and increasing real wages.

Diversification and Industrialization

Two other immediate goals of Fidel Castro were to diversify Cuba's agricultural component and to industrialize the country. The former meant growing things other than sugarcane, and to this end many producing cane fields were dug up and other crops planted. This had a detrimental effect on the Cuban economy.

The industrialization route also met with difficulties. The policy chosen by Fidel and his inner circle was the common one of import substitution. To this end, Cuban leaders started searching for support in the construction of light industries producing consumer goods, hoping later to initiate heavy industry. Support came in the form of loans from the Soviet Union, China, and countries of East Europe. By 1963, however, this policy was largely abandoned; there were critical shortages of skilled workers and of raw materials; planning had been done incorrectly in many cases; the dependency on U.S. industry before the Revolution had resulted in many industries for which replacement parts were unobtainable. Most basically, at that stage of Cuba's development it was more costly to manufacture than it was to import the finished product.

Sugar Policy

Because of difficulties with industrialization and diversification, after 1963 Cuba returned to a dependence on sugar roughly comparable to that before the Revolution. The major difference of the new dependence is that the state is the owner of the sugar lands and mills. Profits from international trade in sugar are not transferred to foreign owners, but instead are funneled primarily into capital goods, research and development, and infrastructure development.

For these purposes, sugar production has been increased, in spite of the lack of foreign cane cutters, who had been called in before the Revolution. The high point of production was 1970, the year for which Fidel had set, against the advice of his technicians, a goal of 10 million tonnes (11 million tons) of sugarcane. During this "sugar obsession," the harvest year was increased from the normal one hundred days to more than a year; workers in other industries (and bureaucrats) took part in the harvesting; and the rest of the economy suffered from neglect. The result was the highest sugarcane harvest in Cuban history—8.5

million tonnes (9.4 million tons)—but a personal failure for Fidel, who had stated, "Ten million less a single pound—we declare it before the world—will be a defeat, not a victory."

The purpose of the large harvest had been to generate more foreign exchange. This goal was achieved to a greater extent three and four years later, when the world price of sugar soared. The price went from about US$.10 per pound (US$.22 per kilogram) to a high of US$.69 per pound (US$1.52 per kilogram) in early 1974. Yet, as is usually the case with primary products, the high prices did not last. By early 1976, the world price was back down to US$.19 per pound (US$.42 per kilogram). To date, even the revolutionary Castro government has been unable to disengage its economy from the sharp discontinuities that come from having comparative advantage in an agricultural product.

Urban Reform

If the true winners of the Cuban Revolution were the agricultural workers, the relative losers have been urban dwellers. The Cuban leaders feel that the real wealth of the country is rural, and they retain the guerrilla feeling that the *campo* has more virtue and worth than the city. The result has been a conscious economic decision to use more investment capital in the country than in the cities; no longer is Havana the glittering capital that it was before the Revolution.

There have been many benefits for the city dwellers in education and health programs. In addition, as early as October 1960, stiff rent controls were decreed. A novel policy of the Castro government has been the *cordón de la Habana*, a ribbon of land around the capital city that is used by the residents of the city to grow crops for personal consumption. For these reasons and others, Havana is not an impoverished city. It is still clearly better to live and work in a large city, especially Havana, but the policies of the Castro government have been successful in narrowing the gap between city and country.

Socialism in Cuba

Several features of Castro's economic policies show their socialist nature. The old capitalist class, both foreign and domestic, is gone. There are a number of collective goods, such as education and health care, that all share equally. Wage differentials still exist to encourage the development of technicians and managerial personnel; dramatically higher wages are paid to those who held upper-level positions before the Revolution. Newer technicians and managers still make more than laborers, but not dramatically so.

As in any socialist society, there is a preponderance of ownership by the state itself. Landownership is about 70 percent in the hands of the government, with the other 30 percent effectively controlled by ANAP and INRA. By 1962, all major industrial and commercial enterprises had been nationalized. In 1968, through a Great Revolutionary Offensive,

Cuba became the socialist country with the highest percentage of public ownership. This offensive had as its goal the elimination of the small capitalists (shops, stalls on the streets, private service establishments).

Also in the socialist mode, economic decisions tend to be made by central planners. In the 1960s, the Cubans adopted a highly centralized and radical model for administering the economy, often referred to as the "mathematical approach to socialism." Central planners fixed production targets in quantitative terms by setting desired goals and matching those with projected resources, without regard to profit or monetary calculations except for bookkeeping purposes.

This system, which gave maximum power to the central elite, was perceived as one that would allow the most rapid radical transformation of Cuba. Nevertheless, it was used by an elite some have termed inexperienced, which often had to rely on faulty data. In the end, the system was replaced, at least in part, by one of market socialism more like that of the Soviet Union. In this transformation, more stress has been placed on price mechanisms, and individual state firms are allowed to make more decisions.

Education

Since 1961, education in Cuba has been free, and students have been given all books and school materials. A system of scholarships, first begun in 1962 and numbering slightly more than a quarter of a million in 1970, pays all expenses, including room and board if the school is away from home. The grand design of this Cuban educational effort has been (1) making education universal from nursery school through the university; (2) developing a Marxist orientation, teaching the children some of the ideology of the regime; (3) combining education with technological principles, productive work, and research, and (4) incorporating the working masses into education.

The educational campaign began in 1961 with The Year of Education, which had as its goal teaching every illiterate to read and write, at the same time "instilling in our children and young people an unbounded love of the Fatherland and a feeling of solidarity with the workers and peoples of all lands in their noble struggle for a free and happy life."[10] During 1961, some 271,000 literacy workers traveled through the island. By the end of the year, the literacy campaign had reached some 979,000 illiterates, of whom 707,000 were claimed as new literates. In this ambitious campaign, Cuba was fortunate to be starting with the relatively low illiteracy rate of about 25 percent.

At higher levels, education has expanded and diversified. The former three faculties at the university have been replaced by eight (technology, agronomy, medicine, sciences, teaching, economy, humanities, and the workers' and peasants' faculty—an adult extension division that prepares its four thousand lower-class students to enter one of the other seven faculties). The largest of these is the faculty of technology; throughout the university, all courses have become more pragmatic, with emphasis on usable skills over basic research. Students in higher education are part of the labor force. Some 60 percent of them are part time, but even the full-time students spend twenty hours a week at work quite often related to their studies. (This rule applies not only in the universities, but all the way down to the junior high school level.) In addition, almost every field of training has a program of preprofessional work, which sends professors and students out into the field together from two weeks to two months a year.

Not all students in higher education are in the universities; another 40,000 are in schools of agronomy and fishing (new since the Revolution), and 30,000 attend industrial schools. In total, there are 133,000 students in postsecondary education, compared to about 22,000 before the Revolution. For these reasons, the educational effort has been called the greatest accomplishment of the Cuban Revolution, although some who disagree with its technological direction and its Marxist content would not concur.

Health and Housing

The first objective of the Castro health policy was to nationalize the health-care system, making it free to all Cubans. By 1969, 93 percent of the medical doctors were working for the state. Health care is free.

The second goal of the health program was to increase the number of doctors; between 2,000 and 4,000 of the 6,000 doctors on the island in 1959 later left as exiles. To replace them, several medical schools were established, and by 1973 there were 8,000 physicians. A related objective was to improve the distribution of medical personnel, who had tended to live and work in Havana. This redistribution has been achieved by assigning doctors to outlying regions and by requiring that all medical students spend two or three years in the countryside.

A third objective of the health policy has been to provide more hospital and clinic space. As a result, today there are about three times more hospitals and four times more hospital beds than before the Revolution, with growth coming most dramatically in the rural areas. Finally, the health policy has sponsored a public-health program that has practically eliminated malaria and polio and dramatically reduced the incidence of gastroenteritis, tuberculosis, and diphtheria.

Yet the ambitious health policy has met snags. Some doctors were trained too rapidly to meet the shortage after the exile wave began. Drugs, which came from U.S. private businesses before the Revolution, are in low supply. The economic difficulties of the Revolution—most specifically the decline in food production—have been translated into health problems: Many Cubans eat too little and do not eat enough of the right kinds of food.

The housing program has been less of a success. Although there has been definite progress in building housing for both rural and urban dwellers, much remains to be done. The problem seems to be one common to underdeveloped countries—a shortage of construction materials, needed for hospitals and schools as well as housing. Within that portion of the materials that go for housing, preference has been given to rural projects.

Minorities: Encouraged and Repressed

Although some individual prejudice remains, the most serious manifestations of racial discrimination (social exclusion and the lack of equal educational and economic opportunities) were terminated by the decrees of Fidel Castro. Today there is more equality, both legal and real, of the races in Cuba than in any other Latin American country.

Likewise, the role of women has been changed by Castro policy. Prostitution has been eliminated, while at the same time civil marriages have been encouraged for those living in common-law relationships. Additionally, the government has urged women to enter the militia and to take other jobs in the economy. To facilitate this, child care centers have been established. This policy has been only partially successful; only one-quarter of the Cuban women were working in 1974, up from about one-fifth before the Revolution. One of the reasons for the slow progress was the "second-shift phenomenon"; working women soon discovered that they spent eight hours on a job, only to return home to do the cooking and cleaning. As a result, the Family Code of 1972 requires that husband and wife, if they both have jobs, share the housework equally.

Yet another problem in the drive for sexual equality has been the long-standing idea of machismo, or male dominance. Some Cuban men have resisted their "disemancipation." In addition, the old attitudes of machismo linger on with some women. In the 1974 election of the Assembly of Peoples' Power in Matanzas, only 3 percent of the delegates chosen were women, although about half of the voters were female. Fidel's conclusion is that women's attitudes have to be changed as well as men's.

Although women and blacks have been beneficiaries of Fidelista public policy, such is not the case with other groups. Those who oppose the Revolution either are allowed to leave the country (750,000 Cubans left during the first twenty years of the Castro government, and another 100,000 left in 1980 during the Mariel boat lift) or are imprisoned (probably between 50,000 and 100,000). The Roman Catholic Church has suffered especially from the policies of the Revolution, since its clergy included a large number of non-Cubans and some priests aided in counterrevolutionary activities. The Church's former monopoly of secondary education has been broken. Today a modus vivendi seems to have been reached with the Church in which the government neither encourages nor discourages Church attendance, and the Church stays completely out of politics.

Another group negatively affected by Castro policy has been the homosexual community. Fidel Castro believes that there is no place for homosexuals in the New Cuba; they are not allowed to be teachers, and in some cases they have been imprisoned.

Intellectuals, writers, and artists have also been a problem for the government. Many left at the beginning of the Revolution. During most of the 1960s the Cuban government's attitude toward the intellectuals who remained was to show a degree of tolerance unsurpassed by other Communist regimes. But the 1971 case of the writer Heberto Padilla demonstrates that there are some limitations. Although Padilla had generally been favorable to the Revolution in his works, he was arrested and charged with talking against the Revolution in conversations with a number of European writers and with writing antirevolutionary poetry. He was subsequently released after confessing to "wrongdoing" and "wrongthinking."

Fidel Castro's approach toward the undesirable minorities—counter-revolutionaries, homosexuals, intellectuals, and priests—is based on two premises. First, he believes that the primary duty of a revolutionary leader is to protect the Revolution. Minorities do not have the right to attempt to destroy, by thought or deed, a Revolution that is aiding the majority of the Cuban people. Second, freedom is defined not as in the United States but in terms of equality. As Fidel has stated,

> I believe that there are two different concepts of freedom. You [the United States] believe that freedom can exist with a class system, and we believe in a system where everyone is equal, where there are no superpowers because there is no pyramid, no millionaires, no multimillionaires, where some don't even have a job. . . . We believe that without equality there is no freedom because you do have to speak about the freedom of the beggar, the prostitute, the exploited, the discriminated, the illiterate.[11]

The Creation of the New Cuban

One of the policies of the Cuban Revolution that has failed to this point is the creation of a New Cuban who would act socially and politically as a member of a society of equals and would act economically by working hard, not for personal reward but for the good of the Revolution. A major problem soon developed: The Cuban leaders learned that in socialist Cuba people worked less than they used to; many goods were collective, available at low prices or for nothing, and other goods were scarce, available to the consumer after working a few days a week.

In the early 1960s, the Cuban leadership went through a "great debate" over the incentives that should be used to get people to work harder. One side, for "material incentives within socialism," argued that there should be more pay for those who worked harder and longer. The other side, led by Che Guevara, argued that people fully liberated from the chains of capitalism would continue to work because work is an integral part of everyone's existence and because there are certain "collective" goods of labor—nonmaterial incentives—that would encourage all to work. By 1965, the great debate was over, with the moral incentive group the victor.

The way to convert people into New Cubans was through social mobilization and a concurrent change of the belief structures, which had begun in 1961 and continues today. Yet the moral incentive approach failed in the short run, and since then other models have been employed. The first was based on coercion and the military model. Although the word *militarization* was never used officially, the whole country was reorganized along those lines in 1968. Command posts led by members of the Politburo of the Communist party were set up in every province to coordinate the great agricultural battle of the 1970 sugarcane harvest. In 1969, these measures were carried even further. It became mandatory for all workers to have a work-force control card on which their productivity, background, political views, and employment history were recorded. Any worker wishing to change jobs needed the permission of a regional officer of the labor ministry.

By 1973, policy shifted toward material incentives for exemplary work. There are no dramatic differences in wages; however, good workers might receive certain nonmonetary rewards, such as preference for new housing or a refrigerator, or a week's vacation for themselves and their families. The idea of moral incentives has not been discarded; the long-term hope is placed on the new generation that has grown up under socialism.

Foreign Policy

The basic foreign policy of Fidel Castro has been one that called for an end to dependence on the United States and for Cuban independence. In the bipolar world of the early 1960s, this meant increased reliance on the Soviet Union. In the 1970s and 1980s, this meant an active role in the Movement of Nonaligned Nations, including a period when Fidel Castro was the elected head of that movement. Yet another goal of Cuban foreign policy has been assistance to other revolutionaries. Although this theme goes back to the very first years of the Revolution, only recently has it been graced by the name *proletarian internationalism*.

The United States and the Inter-American Community

Castro had two goals in his early policy toward the United States: to rid his country of U.S. business interests and to avoid the violent end of his Revolution. The decision makers in Washington had three major objections to the Castro government: its seizure of North American businesses without adequate compensation; its sponsorship of invasions of other Latin American countries; and, later, the military presence of the Soviet Union on the island.

Through the 1960s, the United States employed two basic methods in an unsuccessful attempt to rid the island of Fidel Castro. One was the use of the Organization of American States (OAS), which led eventually to a decision that all governments of the hemisphere should not trade or have diplomatic relations with Cuba and that Cuba should be excluded from the OAS. The second basic method was the support of military and paramilitary efforts on the island. One example of this was the Bay of Pigs invasion in April 1961, a landing of Cuban exiles trained by the CIA. There were, in addition, various smaller attacks by CIA-sponsored troops, efforts to contaminate and/or destroy Cuban sugar, and assassination attempts on Fidel Castro.

One of Castro's responses to U.S. pressure was to form an alternative organization to the OAS, the Organization of Latin American Solidarity (OLAS). Founded in 1967, the OLAS never attained much importance. As the United States failed in its efforts to end the Cuban Revolution, so the Cuban government failed to make the Andes another Sierra Maestra. By the late 1960s, Castro had toned down his support of guerrilla movements; he lent support to some governments that did not meet the guerrilla model, such as Salvador Allende in Chile and, to a much lesser degree, the military revolution in Peru.

In the mid-1970s, for a brief period, the establishment of more normal relations between the United States and Cuba appeared to be a possibility. This was ended, however, by the Cuban intervention in the civil war in Angola. Even afterward the Carter administration began the first steps of normalization through the establishment of "interest sections" in Havana and in Washington, D.C., which still exist at this writing. Yet issues remained during the Carter years. Key for Fidel was the economic embargo of the island, ended collectively by the OAS in 1975, but still part of U.S. law. Public statements from the U.S. government mentioned three important conditions for the normalization of relations: U.S. businesses must be paid for their nationalized property—claims reaching US$1.5 billion with interest; Castro must publicly disavow any intentions of spreading his Revolution; and the Soviet military presence must be removed. Although these conditions might have been opening bargaining positions, little substantive progress in normalizing relations was made by the end of the Carter administration.

Relations between the two countries worsened during the first three years of the Reagan administration. Secretary of State Alexander Haig publicly stated that the source of the Central American crisis lay in Cuba and the Soviet Union. President Reagan accused Cuba of assisting the Sandinista rebels in Nicaragua both before and after their 1979 triumph and of assisting the guerrillas in El Salvador. This assistance was stated to be in weapons and ammunition, as well as political and tactical advice.

Then in October 1983 the United States invaded the small Caribbean island of Grenada, hence entering into combat with Cuban advisers and technicians in the country of 100,000 people and ending a regime that was very close to that of Fidel Castro. By mid-1984 the relations between the United States and Cuba seemed to be no better than they were twenty years previously. Indeed such relations were very acrimonious: Cuba feared a U.S. invasion, while intelligence sources in the United States claimed to have information about a massive, Cuban-supported escalation of the guerrilla warfare in El Salvador by the end of the year.

The Soviet Union and the Communist World

If Cuba was in a dependency relationship with the United States before Castro, it could be argued that it has been in a similar relationship with the Soviet Union since the early 1960s. Most Cuban trade goes to that country; the island receives preferential sugar prices and long-term low-interest or noninterest loans from the Soviet Union; and Cuba has been used at times as a tool of the Soviets in big-power politics, most notably in the missile crisis of 1962 and perhaps in Angola and elsewhere in Africa.

Although there have been clear benefits to the Cubans from this relationship, there have been problems, too. At times Fidel Castro has had philosophical viewpoints that are more radical than the Soviet ones, indeed more in keeping with the Chinese. At times the Cubans have been very uneasy when the Soviets failed to protect other small Communist countries, such as North Vietnam during the 1960s. However, since mid-1968 there has been a honeymoon between the two countries, and Fidel even defended the 1968 intervention of the Soviet Union in Czechoslovakia. At the same time, Cuban communism has been changed into a brand more in keeping with current dogma in the Soviet Union.

There are various theories about this rapprochement. Some argue that Castro is just getting older; he is almost sixty, after all, no longer the young revolutionary. Others see this as a natural process in a revolution—radical at the beginning, becoming more conservative with the years. Yet others argue that the rapprochement between Cuba and the Soviet Union is due to the continued economic difficulties of the island. Cuba, they argue, must do what the Soviet Union wants since the island is in debt to the Communist superpower. Cuba needs, more today than ever, the continued loans and the preferential sugar prices.

PROSPECTS FOR THE FUTURE

Several things seem fairly clear for the future of Cuba, while others are quite uncertain. First, Fidel Castro is likely to be around for a number of years, assuming a natural death for him (perhaps not a realistic assumption if the CIA and exile groups are still attempting assassinations). Fidel will turn sixty in 1986 and, despite rumors in the early 1970s that he was seeing heart specialists in the Soviet Union, seems to be in very good health.

More certain is that socialist Cuba is here to stay. It seems unlikely that the *status quo ante* of 1958 will be seen again. Therefore, if the Cuban exiles ever return to their *patria*, they will find one dramatically different from the one they knew. Although forms of socialism and communism change, as Cuba itself demonstrated in the 1960s, state ownership of the economy will not.

The Cuban Revolution shows that a small nation can break out of its past and establish a new order. Basic rights—to eat, to have housing, to educate one's children—can be made available to all, albeit at the cost of some of those "liberal democratic" rights formerly enjoyed by the upper and middle classes. For these reasons and others, the Cuban Revolution will continue to be an inspiration.

Yet perhaps the greatest irony is that, after more than twenty-five years of the Revolution, Cuba still faces the same fundamental economic difficulties that it did before Castro: dependence on one agricultural crop subject to the vicissitudes of the world market. The Cuban economy boomed from 1973 to 1975, when world prices for sugar were extremely high, and suffered in 1976 and 1977, when prices were low. Granted, there has been some diversification, both in crops and in buyers of the exports, which has lessened the peaks and valleys of the cycles. Further, nationalization of the industry kept more of the profits in Cuba, and the redistributive policies have led to a more equitable distribution of the wealth. All of this said, however, Cuba is still a prisoner of the primary-product monoculture.

The implications of this continual problem form the basis of uncertainty about Cuba's future. There are various policy alternatives that might lessen dependence on one crop but also might bring dramatic changes in the late 1980s. One possibility is a rapprochement with the United States, with increased trade and perhaps a return of U.S. private businesses to the island. This would lead to a Cuba in the late 1980s and beyond different from the island of the 1960s or 1970s. But one might also assume that it will not restore the island either economically or politically to the pre-1959 days. It seems unlikely that U.S. private business will be permitted to dominate the island and even more unlikely that the U.S. ambassador will again be the second most powerful individual in Cuba.

The Cuban revolutionary experience shows that small countries, with few economic resources and with comparative advantage in agricultural projects, exist under certain constraints in the current world economy and polity. No leader—socialist or capitalist, dullard or charismatic—can solve these problems in the short run; maybe not even in the long run.

NOTES

1. Edward Gonzalez, *Cuba Under Castro: The Limits of Charisma* (Houghton Mifflin, Boston, 1974), pp. 62–63.

2. For a more detailed description of Fidel's childhood and youth, early political activities, and the guerrilla war, see Harvey F. Kline, "Fidel Castro and the Cuban Revolution," in *Governments and Leaders*, ed. Edward Feit (Houghton Mifflin, Boston, 1978).

3. *Revolutionary Struggle, 1947–1958*, vol. 1 in *Selected Works of Fidel Castro*, ed. Rolando E. Bonachea and Nelson P. Valdes (MIT Press, Cambridge, Mass., 1972), pp. 220–221.

4. K. S. Karol, *Guerrillas in Power: The Course of the Cuban Revolution* (Hill and Wang, New York, 1970), p. 179.

5. Lee Lockwood, *Castro's Cuba, Cuba's Fidel* (Vintage, New York, 1969), p. 150.

6. Gonzalez, *Cuba Under Castro*, pp. 162–163, 205–206.

7. My notes from a lecture given by Professor Jorge Dominguez at the University of Massachusetts/Amherst on February 18, 1982.

8. Rafael Cepeda, "Fidel Castro y el Reino de Dios," *Bohemia* (July 17, 1960): 110.

9. Richard Fagen, *The Transformation of Political Culture in Cuba* (Stanford University Press, Stanford, Calif., 1969), p. 69.

10. Ibid., p. 37.

11. Frank Mankiewicz and Kirby Jones, *With Fidel: A Portrait of Castro and Cuba* (Playboy Press, Chicago, 1975), p. 93.

SUGGESTIONS FOR FURTHER READING

Bonachea, Rolando E., and Nelson P. Valdes. *Cuba in Revolution*. Doubleday, Garden City, N.Y., 1972.

Draper, Theodore. *Castro's Revolution: Myths and Realities*. Praeger, New York, 1962.

———. *Castroism: Theory and Practice*. Praeger, New York, 1965.

Fagen, Richard. *The Transformation of Political Culture in Cuba*. Stanford University Press, Stanford, Calif., 1969.

Gonzalez, Edward. *Cuba Under Castro: The Limits of Charisma*. Houghton Mifflin, Boston, 1974.

Karol, K. S. *Guerrillas in Power: The Course of the Cuban Revolution*. Hill and Wang, New York, 1970.

Kline, Harvey F. "Fidel Castro and the Cuban Revolution." In *Governments and Leaders*, edited by Edward Feit. Houghton Mifflin, Boston, 1978.

Lockwood, Lee. *Castro's Cuba, Cuba's Fidel*. Vintage, New York, 1969.

Mankiewicz, Frank, and Kirby Jones. *With Fidel: A Portrait of Castro and Cuba*. Playboy Press, Chicago, 1975.

Matthews, Herbert. *Revolution in Cuba*. Scribner's, New York, 1975.

Mesa Lago, Carmelo. *Cuba in the 1970s*. University of New Mexico Press, Albuquerque, 1974.

Weyl, Nathaniel. *Red Star over Cuba*. Devin-Adair, New York, 1962.

Zeitlin, Maurice. *Revolutionary Politics and the Cuban Working Class*. Harper & Row, New York, 1970.

20
Costa Rica:
A Democratic Revolution

CHARLES F. DENTON

Costa Rica's democratic political system sets it apart from the rest of the Central American isthmus. Although the country shares many of the economic problems faced by its neighbors, it has sought to solve these in a different way. Heavy investments have been made over several generations in the educational system—literacy rates are as high as those in the United States—and the educated citizenry and the lack of a standing military force have served as two solid pillars upholding the democratic practices of the country. Lately Costa Rica's economic problems have been exacerbated by a number of external and internal variables that have rocked the foundations of the democratic polity—so far these have withstood the pressures.

In February 1982 Costa Ricans accorded a landslide victory at the polls to Luis Alberto Monge, presidential candidate of the National Liberation party (PLN), which has been setting the political agenda in Costa Rica since 1948. The PLN also obtained a substantial majority in the fifty-seven-seat National Assembly. Monge, longtime party secretary, had been the overwhelming loser in presidential elections just four years earlier, and his victory and the resurgence of the PLN are as much the results of the impact of the worldwide economic crisis on the Central American nation as they are a product of a resurgent popularity.

Monge's predecessor, the charismatic Rodrigo Carazo, and his National Unity party unfortunately presided over the worst debacle in recent Costa Rican economic history, and the voters were not about to continue supporting his party in power. During the 1978–1982 period export prices dropped, import prices rose, and inflation soared, as did unemployment—a phenomenon not unfamiliar to the rest of Latin America. But Costa Ricans were not concerned with the rest of the world, despite Carazo's attempts to draw attention to external factors. The result was the defeat of the National Unity party and its candidate, Rafael Angel Calderón, Jr.

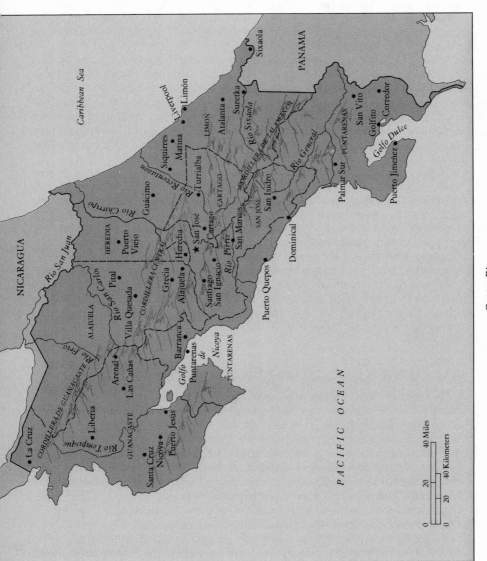

Costa Rica

Prior to the victory in 1982, support for the PLN, which had seized power some thirty-four years earlier in what has been hailed as one of the few democratic revolutions anywhere in the world, had been steadily on the wane. The majority that it had always enjoyed in the National Assembly had been lost in 1978, and it suffered criticism for being corrupt, inefficient, and short of fresh ideas for bringing economic development to the country.

The Costa Rican political system is generally a creation of, or has been molded by, the PLN over more than one generation. After the setback in 1978 the party has now retaken the reins and continues to implement its programs. These programs, which include heavy involvement of the state apparatus in the economy coupled with an aggressive social-welfare policy, are running into strong opposition, as much from external forces such as the International Monetary Fund as from internal ones.

When the PLN took power in 1948 its overall goal was to revolutionize Costa Rican society within the framework of a democratic polity. A significant question for any informed researcher is whether or not the democratic system, processes, and institutions that the PLN created or expanded over more than three decades revolutionized the system or if, in fact, these stabilized society and are now impeding revolutionary change. President Monge, coauthor of his nation's 1949 constitution, since assuming power has found himself facing serious reverses, particularly in terms of his social goals. The long-term impact of these setbacks is difficult to determine, but the carefully built, stable system Costa Rica has enjoyed over the years certainly could be threatened if trends emerging in the early 1980s continue.

BACKGROUND AND POLITICAL CULTURE

Peaceful, small in territory and population, economically weak in comparison to Europe or North America, Costa Rica has always been somewhat isolated from the rest of the world. But in the last five to ten years the world has spilled over into Costa Rica and created new and at times distressing problems for the political system of the tiny former banana republic. So distressing are the problems that President Luis Alberto Monge deemed it necessary in late 1983 to convene the National Assembly, the accredited diplomatic corps and press, and other dignitaries for a solemn ceremony where he announced to the world that henceforth Costa Rica would be a "neutral nation."

Legal authorities will undoubtedly spend the rest of Monge's term of office attempting to juxtapose and reconcile this "neutrality" with Costa Rica's obligations with the Organization of American States, particularly under the provisions of the Inter-American Defense Treaty signed in Rio de Janeiro in 1947. The neutral stance will also have to be assessed within the context of U.S. Agency for International Development (AID) programs for the country, programs that have been stepped up in the early 1980s.

World affairs have affected Costa Rica in a variety of ways over the past decade. Sandinistas, waging their war in 1978–1979 against General Anastasio Somoza Debayle's government in neighboring Nicaragua, used Costa Rica's northern territories as a base of operation with the tacit approval of President Carazo. In the 1980s the so-called contras, guerrillas warring against the Sandinistas, wish to do the same. The wars of Central America have brought refugees and in some cases exiles to Costa Rica. Some live in camps, most attempting to make a living while waiting hopefully for changes back home. Costa Rica has always prided itself on being a political haven, and there are thousands of exiles from non–Central American nations as well—Chileans, Bolivians, Argentines, and others.

The world has also come to Costa Rica as a creditor attempting to collect long overdue and frequently extended loans. By late 1979 this single Central American republic had managed to borrow over $4 billion from official and commercial sources, making it the most heavily indebted per capita of the nations in Latin America. Total Costa Rican exports are worth between $800 and $900 thousand annually, and it appeared unlikely that the heavy international debt would be repaid soon. Austerity in social and government programs has been one of several conditions demanded of the Costa Rican government by international creditors for the opening of negotiations and the extension of further and much more modest credits. Perhaps the rudest awakening to outside world exigencies experienced by Costa Ricans was the abrupt decline of the national currency. In 1980, 8.60 colons equaled US$1. By 1984 the rate was 43.65 colons to the dollar. Prices of virtually everything accommodated themselves to these new relationships.

Costa Rica's population growth rate declined from an estimated 3.8 percent in the 1964–1965 period to 2.4 percent in 1982.[1] The June 1984 national census revealed a Costa Rican population of 2.4 million. Despite the decline in growth rate the population is indeed increasing, and one of the most serious problems facing political decision makers is that of finding employment for an expanding work force. Absorbing new workers is particularly difficult in a country that is still primarily an agricultural one with relatively light investment in industry. The public bureaucracy, which for years was the vehicle for providing employment, has now been frozen as part of the austerity program imposed as a partial solution to the national economic crisis. Between 1963 and 1973 (the last two census dates) there was a 75 percent increase in the number of women in the work force, and as birthrates continue to decline this percentage can be expected to grow.

Most visitors to Costa Rica see only the central plateau region, where San José is located. Regarded by most Costa Ricans as typical of their country, the central plateau is likewise the place where most of them wish to reside. The expanse of some 1,500 square miles (3,900 square kilometers—approximately 8 percent of the total land area) contains more than 64 percent of the population according to latest estimates. It also contains more than two-thirds of the work force, hospital beds, and total capital investment in the country. In the intercensal period 1963–1973 Costa Rica's urban population grew from 460,000 to 760,000, an increase of 65 percent.[2] Most of this growth took place in the central plateau area, heavily taxing urban resources and presenting policymakers with still another significant problem.

Rapid population growth rates in the past have imposed severe penalties on Costa Rican educational facilities in a country that takes pride in boasting one of the highest literacy rates—85 percent—in the hemisphere.[3] Nevertheless, decision makers have not wavered from the long-term commitment to the educational apparatus. In 1982 there were some 35,000 university students registered in the country's universities (four public and one private). High school graduates now constitute 55 percent of Costa Ricans under thirty, and university graduates account for 7 percent of the total adult population.

If the program of absorbing new workers into the economy presents difficulties for political decision makers, the problem is exacerbated in the case of university graduates, 60 percent of whom major in liberal arts, social sciences, and law. There is simply a severe limitation on the ability of a poor country, undergoing an economic crisis, to absorb graduates in fields such as sociology, literature, and political science. If the problem were one involving the fields cited and no others, then one solution could be to stress other fields in higher education curricula. However, slow economic growth has also limited employment prospects for engineers and for business administration and computer science graduates. Some of these have emigrated, permitting other countries to reap the harvest of Costa Rica's heavy investment in the educational area. Others remain in the country in marginal employments and represent a significant potential source of political dissidence.

Despite these problems and others in the educational system, its social impact continues unabated. University graduates continue to represent the elite of the country, and public opinion on principal political issues can be differentiated by educational achievement, whether this achievement took place at home or abroad.

The stratification of Costa Rican society varies in some respects from the patterns in other Latin American countries, principally in the allegiance to democratic norms that persons with more education and economic resources demonstrate. These norms, which have been promoted in the system by the PLN and other organizations, have become thoroughly internalized by the elite. Although the PLN would have the observer believe these norms were not part of the system prior to its appearance in the late 1940s, the fact is that Costa Ricans at least through this century have boasted allegiance to a democratic polity.

This allegiance is held concomitantly with a second trait, an incrementalist attitude toward change. Under the leadership of the elite, a participatory political structure with elaborate checks and balances has been created in Costa Rica, providing for basic freedoms but also hampering broad-scale integrated problem solving.

The agricultural sector of the economy is still of primary importance as job provider for one-third of the work force, as foreign-currency earner, and as a contributor to the gross national product—20 percent in 1975. Of the country's farms, 93 percent are cultivated by the owner of the property, and the average size of these individually owned and operated farms is 24 hectares (10 acres). The average size of the corporate or cooperatively owned farms, which account for the remaining 7 percent of the cultivation, is 250 hectares (100 acres), or more than ten times larger. These figures actually mask a broad range within each category, and it has been estimated by the National Agricultural Institute that 83 percent of the individually owned farms are too small to be economically viable. On these small farms, or *minifundios*, owners are growing just enough staple foodstuffs for their families' needs and in many cases are accepting seasonal employment on neighboring large farms.

Since the large landholdings, which take advantage of the economies of scale, are oriented toward producing cash crops—bananas, coffee, and beef for export—there is a perpetual shortage of staple foodstuffs in the country and a corresponding never-ending price increase in these commodities. For many years the large- and medium-size farmers in Costa Rica devoted all efforts to the production of coffee and bananas. Diversification has been taking place, and beef and sugar have become important exports. Unfortunately, the move to beef production has had a negative impact on the economy except in terms of foreign-exchange earnings, and the drastic drop in world sugar prices has assured that this crop has not brought any benefits. The diversification to beef has actually decreased the demand for agricultural labor at a time when the country faces an employment crisis, leading to an increase in migration to urban centers by job seekers. Since much of the beef is shipped chilled to the East Coast of the United States, its production has not improved the Costa Rican diet. Beef consumption has actually declined since 1949.

The employment situation in agriculture is further revealed when it is pointed out that the sector was expected to absorb only 22,000 new workers in the 1973–1978 period, while the economy as a whole was expected to absorb some 178,000. The Costa Rican agricultural sector is simply not meeting the country's needs. Productivity must improve drastically, and diversification must occur more rapidly if the country's total resources for change are to be increased. But this type of change can only be carried out through the national political arena. Since the very basis of economic position and, indirectly, political power rests on the ownership of land, changes in this area will be difficult and could be expected to cause major social disruption.

The government of Costa Rica has become increasingly involved in the economy in the period since 1948, not only as a consumer but also as a producer and investor. Between 1950 and 1975 the government increased fourfold the percentage of the national work force it employs, a rate of growth unmatched by any other sector of the economy. Since 1955 the government has accounted for at least 20 percent of total annual capital investment. The government's ability to employ more personnel and invest in construction and resource development has primarily resulted from its engaging in a continuous cycle of deficit spending and borrowing abroad.

Although these statistics would seem to belie the fact, Costa Rica is one of the most open nations for private investment in the Western Hemisphere. The free-enterprise model is still honored by the government, and efforts are continuously made to attract new foreign investment. A surge of foreigners into the country during the 1970s has led to varied results. San José now boasts three McDonald's, two Kentucky Fried Chicken outlets, several Pizza Huts, an English-language newspaper, and cable television direct from Atlanta. The lobby of the big Hotel Irazu contains several U.S.-owned realty companies complete with salesmen. A Playboy Hotel is nearing completion. In a different type of development, nonmultinational foreign investors are responsible for the existence of new factories, excellent and modestly priced restaurants and other tourist facilities, and new repair shops and other service industries. Many foreign nationals (German, Swiss, Italian, North American, Spanish) have made major contributions to the development needs of Costa Rica.

As part of the effort to resolve the national economic crisis new efforts have been made to bring investment to Costa Rica. Unfortunately many potential investors, wary about the Costa Rican economy because of the international debt problem, also worry about regional political violence and its spread to all of the countries of the Central American isthmus. The Caribbean Basin Initiative moneys that have been funneled to Costa Rica have been used by a select group of national business leaders to attempt to cope with the image problem abroad while stimulating national entrepreneurs to look abroad for new markets, upping production and employment. In early 1984 it was too soon to render a verdict on this program.

Industry actually declined in terms of its contribution to gross national product in the early 1980s, accounting for 16 percent. Only 12 percent of the work force was employed in this area. The decline in industrial production and employment occurred because of various factors. First, there was a sharp drop in national and international demand for the type of product manufactured in Costa Rica—mostly consumer goods of an import-substitution variety. Second, declines in foreign-exchange earnings or borrowing capacities made raw materials difficult or impossible to obtain. Third, the Central American Common Market (CACM) declined in importance as a selling place for national products. Nicaragua during and after its revolution was left with little or no foreign exchange, and trading with that country reverted to a cash-and-carry basis. Honduras withdrew as an active member of the CACM; trade with El Salvador and Guatemala was made difficult by the prevailing climate of violence.

Commerce, which is oriented to imported commodities, and agriculture are not experiencing real growth nor are those sectors providing enough new jobs to occupy the growing work force. Because of the stagnation in the economy, demand in 1983 dropped. The result was a low 9 percent rate of inflation, a relief from years of rates ranging from 18 to 90 percent.

HISTORY TO 1940

Costa Rica has always been one of the more unobtrusive Latin American nations. It cannot boast of great wars of conquest such as those of Mexico and Peru, wars of independence such as those of Venezuela and Chile, or the many civil wars that have characterized almost all of its neighbors. The most glorious page in the history books of the Costa Rican schoolchild is the defeat of the U.S. filibuster William Walker at the hands of an army of Costa Ricans. The country's only war hero, Juan Santamaría, lost his life in an attack on Walker's headquarters.

Costa Rica administratively belonged to the captaincy general in Guatemala City during the Spanish colonial period but suffered from benign neglect during most of that time. The population of the country never exceeded seventy-five thousand during the entire colonial era. There were no mines for the Spaniards to exploit, no geographic resources, no prime agricultural commodities, and no Indians, and as a result little attention was given to the area by Mexico, Guatemala, or Madrid. When Mexico achieved its independence from Spain in 1821, Costa Rica achieved the same without a drop of blood being shed. When the Central American states seceded from Mexico in 1824 and formed the Federation of Central America, Costa Rica seceded with them without violence. And when in 1838 the various countries went their own way, Costa Rica did not fight hard for federation.

During the nineteenth century the tiny country eked out an international existence marketing coffee in Europe and later bananas in the United States. The coffee-producing families were the elite of the period.[4] They generally elected one of their own to the presidency and operated a legislature and a judiciary little different in scope and operation from those of the United States in the same period. There were two or three extended dictatorships in the late nineteenth and early twentieth centuries, but inevitably the country returned to the participatory practices that have always characterized it.

MODERN POLITICAL HISTORY

The modern period of Costa Rica history begins in 1940, for it is then that personalities still very much in the public eye came to the foreground and the battlelines of modern political conflicts were drawn. In 1940 medical doctor Rafael Angel Calderón Guardia, an immensely popular individual, was elected to the presidency. Calderón and his followers, known as Calderonistas, reestablished the long defunct University of Costa Rica, negotiated a settlement of a long-standing dispute with Panama over the boundaries between the two countries, and with the help and support of the president's personal National Republican party (PRN), put Costa Rica's first labor code into law. The new legislation permitted legal functioning of the only labor movement then in existence, later to be known as Vanguardia Popular, which was Communist-organized and -operated. The movement quickly gained considerable strength, particularly in the North America–owned banana plantations, where organizing efforts and strikes had been occurring for almost a decade.

Calderón Guardia was not a very practical administrator despite his achievements, and it is rumored that during his term in office, 1940–1944, he continued to make house calls and to deliver babies. Because of confusion in the public administration and his prolabor policies, Calderón lost the support of white-collar and private-enterprise groups prior to leaving office. By 1942 the president and his party had to rely more heavily on their Vanguardia Popular supporters led by Manuel Mora Valverde, an outspoken San José lawyer.

Constitutionally prohibited from succeeding himself, Calderón arranged for the election of another capital-city lawyer friend, Teodoro Picado, who assumed the office of chief executive in 1944. During the campaign of that year Picado was opposed by ex-President León Cortés (1936–1940), champion of the right and an avid anti-Communist. Also opposing Picado were two smaller groups, one headed by José (popularly known as "Pepe") Figueres Ferrer and the other by Otilio Ulate Blanco. Figueres represented the interests of small rural groups and to a certain extent some of the more impoverished coffee families; Ulate's group coincided with the same people supporting Cortés. All of the opposition groups campaigned against the PRN's reform legislation, social security, and legalized unions. In 1947 the Picado government, which had to rely on Vanguardia Popular support even more than had its predecessor, announced that its official candidate for the upcoming 1948 election would again be Dr. Rafael Calderón Guardia.

In the face of this announcement and of the drastic financial situation and growing civil unrest, which included a riot on Labor Day and a so-called general strike, the situation was ripe for the civil war that eventually broke out in 1948. The general strike more closely resembled a lockout since unions did not participate; rather, the strike involved the closing of many retail trade establishments, banks, markets, and shops. However, serious violence was averted when on August 1, 1948, a group of women marched on the presidential palace, and the president agreed to listen to their pleas for peace.

In the 1948 election Calderón was opposed by Otilio Ulate, who had the support of Figueres and his followers. When it became apparent that Ulate had won by a small margin, the Calderonistas, who still controlled a majority of the seats in the National Assembly, nullified the results and declared Calderón the winner. Ulate was imprisoned. Armed opposition broke out against Calderón and his followers. Led by Pepe Figueres, who organized the National Liberation Movement with headquarters at his farm, La Lucha, the opposition forces managed to drive back the first government forces sent against them and then rapidly to gain control of key centers surrounding the capital city. Picado quickly surrendered. However, Manuel Mora, leader of the Communist Vanguardia Popular, refused to abide by the Picado-Figueres surrender agreement, and a period of violence settled over San José. The Communist union leader retained control of important areas in the capital, and the fighting between his forces and those of Figueres was particularly bloody. Mora finally surrendered, and a junta, headed by Figueres, by then a popular hero, took over the government.

On December 4, 1948, in an unprecedented action, Figueres disbanded the military forces of his country. Keys to the main military barracks, the scene of heavy fighting and much bloodshed during the violence of revolution, were turned over to the minister of education for the purpose of creating a national museum. At about the same time a new loan was negotiated with the United States, and a constituent assembly was elected to write Costa Rica's sixth constitution. One of the first actions of the new assembly, in which the followers of Calderón had no representation, was to approve the election of Otilio Ulate in the 1948 election. Figueres was determined to permit Ulate to serve a full term in office before moving directly into the limelight himself. The new constitution, finally written and approved, was ratified on November 7, 1949. Ulate took office as president of Costa Rica the following day.

During the time that the Figueres junta ran Costa Rica, the precedents for many future *liberacionista* actions and policies were set. The junta created the first two of the many semiautonomous institutions of public administration still in existence. One of the institutions is made up of the country's entire banking system. Figueres, convinced that the foreign ownership of Costa Rica's banks was detrimental to bringing reform to the country, nationalized and expropriated them all.

Ulate's term in office was uneventful, and as the 1953 election drew closer it became clear that Pepe Figueres would be the next chief executive. On October 12, 1951, Figueres had founded the National Liberation party out of the National Liberation Movement. In the 1953 campaign the PLN was the only party to present a comprehensive program, a pattern that has been repeated in succeeding elections through the early 1980s. Figueres received 65 percent of the presidential vote in the 1953 election and his party an equal percentage of the legislative vote, a high percentage that no party, including the PLN, has managed to match or exceed since. From 1953 to the present Costa Rica has been governed democratically.

After Figueres's first term in office (he was elected a second time in 1970), a pattern was set in which the *liberacionistas* occupied the presidency in alternate periods, and some form of anti-*liberacionista* movement placed its candidate in the chief executive position for four years in the intervening term of office. The only exception to this rule was the election of 1974, when the *liberacionistas* won the presidency for a second consecutive term.

One interesting historical item is that Luis Alberto Monge's opponent in the 1982 campaign, Rafael Angel Calderón, is the son of the former 1940–1944 president, anxious to vindicate the family honor. Calderón, Jr. (known as Junior Calderón around San José), has managed to build up a new political movement made up of the remnants of his father's old organization, many of whose members are elderly; former President Rodrigo Carazo's Unity party; and a small Christian Democratic party. It is widely presumed that the Unity Christian Democratic party will field Calderón in the 1986 presidential elections. Whether or not the practice of alternating in political office will continue remains to be seen.

Recent Costa Rican political and economic history has been dominated by a single political party—the Figueres-founded PLN. Its victory at the polls in 1982 served to confirm this. Recognizing the government as the most likely problem solver for the economically underdeveloped society as a whole, when in power at the presidential level the PLN has undertaken to resolve some of the problems faced by Costa Rica. The PLN has viewed the bureaucracy as the instrumentality of government most likely to be capable of tackling development problems and has strengthened it accordingly. At the same time the PLN has shown a remarkable concern for civil liberties and for all the trappings of democratic government. Since 1948 this party has developed an integrated program of development. For a variety of reasons the PLN's plans and programs have not always been implemented, nor have they consistently been successful in achieving stated goals.

SOCIAL AND POLITICAL GROUPS

The National Liberation Party

The PLN cannot be labeled a strongly ideological organization, although it does espouse an ideology that is vaguely referred to as "social democracy" and that in the past has permitted it to be a member of the League of Social Democratic Parties of Latin America and of the Socialist International. This ideology has been somewhat diluted during the PLN quests for electoral office and by the exigencies of administering the governmental apparatus.

In April 1940 a group of students and professors at the newly founded University of Costa Rica established what became known as the Center for the Study of National Problems. Among the founders of this center were many of the men who later formed part of the PLN leadership. The group published a monthly journal, *Surco*, and tracts and articles that appeared in various local newspapers. As the years progressed and as certain members became dissatisfied with the Calderonista government, the group began to engage in sporadic sabotage. In 1945, during the government of Teodoro Picado, the center merged with a political splinter group known as Acción Democrática, which included Pepe Figueres, Francisco Orlich, and others. The two groups formed the Partido Social Democrático, which stepped up its attack on the Calderonistas. Don Pepe, who was jailed and later deported to Mexico because of a 1942 radio broadcast, had returned to Costa Rica in mid-1944 and was clearly the leader of the organization.

In the basic charter of the party, produced in 1951, a great deal of political doctrine is developed and explained. This document acknowledges the state as the institution charged with promoting the general welfare of the society. This means that each individual has the right to the highest possible standard of living, but that the state must not violate human dignity in attempting to achieve this economic growth. The document is imprecise but provides a framework for later actions.

The PLN left wing, in partial recognition of the modest impact of the basic charter, in 1970 issued the Declaration of Patio de Agua, which at times antagonized the party mainstream. The declaration called for the nationalization of basic industries, large-scale land reform, and severe restrictions on foreign enterprises. In general, the Patio de Agua document has had a minimum impact and party center liners continue to hold the leadership and to believe that democratic liberalism is most likely to achieve the general welfare. Party leaders continue to view the elaborate system of checks and balances and the set of political institutions that the PLN has created in Costa Rica as being a principal catalyst for change.

Still another tenet of the PLN ideology is that full employment and high productivity must be societal goals. Under this principle, if consistently high levels of production are achieved, then everyone in the country will be employed to keep production moving. However, the balance between the two goals is particularly difficult to maintain in Costa Rican society, which faces so many of the change-related problems common to the so-called Third World. The tendency has been to provide all with jobs whether or not they are needed. In the Costa Rican bureaucracy the conflict over the goals of high employment and productivity has been particularly noticeable. Because the educated Costa Rican is the one most capable of placing pressure on decision makers and the government is most capable of providing jobs in its own agencies, the bureaucracy has grown rapidly since the PLN formulated its ideology. Unfortunately, the employment-providing function has interfered with the ability of the administrative apparatus to cope with national development needs. The PLN is still the only major Costa Rican political party with a permanent organizational structure that extends from the national to the local levels of the country. Each regional division of the country boasts a PLN committee, as do the seven provinces and eighty-one cantons.

Other Political Parties

It is still too early to determine what the future holds for the Unity Christian Democratic party (the former National Unity party). There is no doubt that it will be the PLN's chief opponent in the 1986 elections (the name could be modified again prior to that time), but there is no way of telling what will happen after that. After Rodrigo Carazo's substantial victory over the PLN in 1978, analysts hailed the National Unity party as the new and permanent opposition. That party has now disappeared, merged into Junior Calderón's organization. There is little doubt that Calderón has the intention of consolidating his new party on a permanent basis throughout Costa Rica.

The Unified People's party is a coalition of the old Communist Vanguardia Popular, which had been proscribed by the 1949 constitution, and the Socialist Action party (PASO).[5] Unified People's won four seats in the 1982–1986 legislature. The party has undergone a significant leadership crisis, and there is a possibility that it will be divided.

Other Political Groups

In most Latin American countries the most important political group is actually one portion of the bureaucracy: the military. This is not the case in Costa Rica. The reaction against uniformed authority has been so strong that even in the early 1980s, when because of a rising crime rate there has been a demand for more protection for private citizens, this type of demand is directed away from the political system. The relatively inexpert national guard or constabulary, which experiences a major shift in its manpower each time the presidency changes party hands, has served to reinforce the general impression that the government should not be more than minimally involved in the prevention of crime. When a different political party assumes the presidency after an election, it is estimated that within six months after the new chief executive assumes office 90 percent of the men from the previous guard have been removed and replaced by political appointees. Since the abolition of the army in 1948, the presidency has changed political party hands seven times with a similar complete change in civil guard manpower. As can be gathered from this, the constabulary, which in 1983 received less than 3 percent of total government expenditure, is a major source of presidential spoils and has been used by each party to reward its faithful.

The separation of Church and state is not sharply defined in Costa Rica. Although Church attendance is usually reserved for women and children, the influence of the Church is much more far-reaching, particularly as far as rules made by political decision makers pertaining to marriage and the family are concerned. For example, as a result of Church-based influence the government banned the use and importation of intrauterine devices for birth-control purposes, citing them as abortive in function. The Church does not normally participate as an innovator of rules, but it can become actively involved in defending existing ones. According to Ministry of the Treasury figures in 1971, the Costa Rican government paid $38,000 as a contribution to bishops' salaries and $100,000 to Church building funds.[6] Some $150,000 went to Church-related schools, and the cost of religious education, obligatory in Costa Rica, is also supported by the government. Non–Roman Catholics can be excused from these classes.

One of the most important interest groups in Costa Rica is the group owning the nation's largest newspaper, *La Nación*, with a daily circulation of 100,000. Consistently in opposition to the PLN and its policies, the newspaper is generally private enterprise oriented and highly influential in a country with a very literate population.

A number of interest-group organizations are dominated by landowners. Among these are the Chamber of Coffee Growers, powerful because of the important role coffee plays in the export market; the Chamber of Banana Growers; and the Cattleman's Association, which has been most successful in getting the government to press for increases in the U.S. beef quota. Needless to say, the Chamber of Commerce itself is a substantial influence in politics.

The U.S. Agency for International Development can also be termed a Costa Rican political interest group. In return for its assistance, perceived by the government as necessary for achieving certain kinds of developmental goals, AID demands that certain rules and regulations be adopted by the Costa Rican government. AID lobbies both directly and indirectly for its programs through press contacts and by talking to political decision makers. Recently at the behest of AID Costa Rica founded a Ministry of Exports, totally financed by that U.S. government institution. AID director Daniel Chaij was proud to announce that the new ministry was not costing the people of Costa Rica anything, but some analysts wondered about the implications of having an entire ministry financed by an outside power, given the Central American nation's newly declared "neutrality."

GOVERNMENT MACHINERY

In the formal sense, Costa Rican politics resembles that of the United States. The governmental structures are in many ways modeled on those of the North American neighbor. The government is presidential in form; the executive, legislative, and judicial branches are formally separated. This separation actually exists in the informal sense as well as in the formal one, an unusual situation in Latin America. The president of Costa Rica is elected popularly for a term of four years and can occupy this office only once in a lifetime. Although there are two vice presidents, both elected on the same ticket with the president, responsibilities are totally those assigned by the chief executive; in the case of the second vice president there is no salary attached to the position.

The control of the president over the executive branch of the government has been particularly weakened by the National Assembly over the last two decades. This legislative body, under the leadership of the PLN, has created a sizable group of so-called semiautonomous institutions. A recent law gives the president the right to appoint the boards of directors of these institutions, but this has not obviated the fact that the institutions are quite independent of executive controls. Nearly all the organizations of the public adminstration charged with bringing change to Costa Rica are independent of each other and of the chief executive.

The legislature, or National Assembly, is unicameral and in the 1978–1982 term was composed of fifty-seven members. The legislators, or deputies, are elected through a system of proportional representation for terms of four years, and they cannot be reelected unless at least one term intervenes after they have served. Party discipline is not well enforced in the legislature, and issues are sharply debated, but often unresolved.

The Costa Rican Bureau of the Budget falls directly under the supervision of the National Assembly and is entirely independent of the president; the power of the purse strings belongs to the legislature. One of the assembly's six standing committees supervises the bureau. Still another unusual legislative responsibility is the appointment of Costa Rican Supreme Court justices. The National Assembly can also create courts, temporarily cancel civil liberties, and engage in a series of related activities. Despite its apparent powers the National Assembly is as circumscribed as is the president in its ability to carry out its function. The restriction on reelection tends to limit the continuity of the body and discourages specialization in particular policymaking areas. Proportional representation has meant that it is more difficult for any one party to win a substantial majority of the legislative seats.

The judicial branch of the Costa Rican government is less central to decision making than are the other two formal national government branches. This does not mean, however, that the judiciary is any less independent than are those branches already described. The seventeen Supreme Court justices are appointed for terms of eight years and the terms are staggered; few are appointed during any one election period. The court can rule on the constitutionality of executive and legislative actions, including laws passed and presidential vetoes. The Supreme Court is the only court to which a Costa Rican citizen can appeal for a writ of habeas corpus and for the broader writ of *amparo*.

As a result of the 1948 revolution and the attempt by the Calderonistas to introduce a form of *continuismo* into Costa Rican politics, still another institution with autonomy was introduced by the PLN into the machinery of government. The *liberacionistas* in 1949 founded the Supreme Tribunal of Elections (TSE) to ensure that future elections would be honestly and efficiently administered. The TSE is composed of three members elected by the Supreme Court, each of whom serves a six-year term. The justices, who serve staggered terms, enjoy the same status and immunities allotted to Costa Rican Supreme Court judges. The TSE not only supervises the conduct of elections but also exercises exclusive jurisdiction over the interpretation of those constitutional provisions involving voting, party conduct, and elections in general. The TSE, which operates as a fourth branch of government, is responsible for supervising the National Civil Register. It can veto any legislation that applies to voting unless the legislature can muster a two-thirds vote to override the tribunal. Perhaps the most powerful weapon in the hands of the TSE is its responsibility for reimbursing funds to parties for their campaign expenditures. Parties are required to submit expense accounts to the TSE; this institution then decides, according to the votes received by the party, how much each is entitled to get back.

The TSE has three effects on Costa Rican elections. First, it has definitely ensured that elections are among the most honest in the world. Second, it has assured that the chief executive's office has a fair chance of changing hands. Third, it has, through the disbursement of campaign funds, assured the longevity of the larger political parties and made it difficult for the very small parties, to some extent offsetting the natural impact of proportional representation.

The Costa Rican public administration has expanded rapidly in the last two decades, a growth rate unmatched even by the country's population. The growth of the bureaucracy has been neither controlled nor planned, despite the existence of a rapidly growing Ministry of Planning; organizations vary widely even in the regular nonautonomous agencies. There is no career ladder, and a considerable overlapping of function occurs between the various agencies; empire building is a common trait of top administrators. The result of this uncoordinated growth has been a stopgap and piecemeal policymaking process and indirectly a slow evolution toward greater autonomy in all branches of government. Since this growth has been occurring hand-in-hand with a greater emphasis on government as a problem solver for the entire society, a considerable amount of dissatisfaction could be expected both within and without the bureaucracy. Those from whom most dissatisfaction might be expected, members of the better-educated and wealthier groups, are often employed in the public administration, while those most affected by the problems of the bureaucracy are those who are least vocal.

It is possible to argue that there is an excess in the ranks of public employees based on efficiency input-output criteria. However, if the bureaucracy is regarded as a tension-management device for the social system rather than as a problem solver, then the large number of government employees with job security may be desirable.

PUBLIC POLICY AND PROSPECTS FOR CHANGE

Participation in the political decision-making process is easily obtainable for a well-educated Costa Rican. The wide variety of interest groups, the country's many newspapers, and the active if not always well organized political parties are constantly seeking new recruits who are capable of articulating their interests. For the majority of Costa Ricans, however, participation is restricted almost exclusively to the formal act of voting. The well-educated Costa Rican demands and receives health and banking facilities (a minimum deposit of $250 is required to open an account in the nationalized banks), insurance, telephones, refined gasoline, airline service, pensions, white-collar positions in the bureaucracy, and increased salaries for government workers.

The average Costa Rican makes few demands for political resources. He or she does expect adequate health care, and the social-security hospitals have expanded substantially over the past decades. Costa Ricans also demand land, housing, and inexpensive food. In general the system has not been able to meet these demands. The cheapest government-built house in Costa Rica sells for $4,500, which is beyond the reach of 50 percent of rural families, whose incomes average less than $75 monthly.

Notwithstanding limitations on policymaking demands, Costa Rica's high literacy rate, its homogeneous population, and its small size geographically (the last three are factors that considerably facilitate communication), policymakers have nevertheless been faced with numerous demands that limited resources make impossible to meet. As a result they have been forced to control or obliterate certain demands and to produce a great deal of symbolic policy to give the appearance of action. Despite the relatively great amount of political activity in Costa Rica, little of it results in concrete policy. The largest single amount of the government budget each year is spent on education. The law requires every Costa Rican to receive an education through the eighth grade. And yet most do not. Administrative expenses now account for 21 percent of government expenditures because of the practice of using the bureaucracy as a vehicle for employing the well educated.

The Costa Rican political culture has been strongly shaped by the efforts and ideology of a single political party—the PLN. The *liberacionistas* have had the potential to mold the system—most particularly the bureaucracy, the great majority of whose employees are party sympathizers—into an effective policymaking operation. Instead, while the social-welfare system has increased its scope substantially, per capita income ($850 in 1982), industrialization, agricultural diversification, and the nation's position on the world market are relatively little better than when the PLN assumed power for the first time after the violent revolution of 1948. There is some doubt as to whether the weakened economy can support the weight of the highly complex and dependent social-welfare system into which the party has channeled its efforts rather than concentrating on bringing substantial change to the economy. The entire apparatus and its policymakers are liberal, participant, and moderate in orientation. The PLN has become a moderate, well-to-do party with the principal goal of keeping the Costa Rican system stable.

Policymaking capacities have been limited by the formal egalitarianism. Participation in the policymaking process is limited, and a great deal of overlapping responsibility occurs. Moreover, policy can be developed only when problems are perceived, but the Costa Rican political culture tends to shield decision makers from many of the basic problems of the society. No far-reaching efforts are made to solve problems such as overconcentration of the population in one geographical area, dropouts from the education system, land tenure and agricultural production, and the nation's perpetual trade imbalance. Stability, so prized by the PLN and its opposition, would be upset if these problems were to be tackled at all seriously.

The democratic revolution of 1948 has gradually given way to a stable participatory political system deadlocked on crucial economic and social problems. This system, a much-admired democracy, has contributed major stumbling blocks on the country's road to economic and social development. Because of its size and resources—human, economic, and social—the country cannot expect to achieve the levels of prosperity and well-being enjoyed by a larger, better-endowed nation. But Costa Rica, despite its favorable position in the Latin American area, could do much better if policymakers were more capable of controlling the government apparatus and of tackling some of the nation's more basic developmental problems.

NOTES

1. The 1964–1965 figure is from "Población, Fecundidad y Desarrollo en Costa Rica 1950–1970," *Informe de Trabajo*, no. 39 (Institute for Social and Population Studies, National University of Costa Rica), 1984. The 1982 percentage is from Dirección General de Estadística y Censos, *Estadísticas Vitales*.

2. Dirección General de Estadística y Censos, *Censo de Población 1963, 1973*.

3. Dirección General de Estadística y Censos, *Censo de Población, 1973*.

4. Samuel Stone, *La Dinastía de los Conquistadores; La crisis del Poder en la Costa Rica Contemporánea* (EDUCA, San José, 1975).

5. See the Costa Rica chapter by Charles F. Denton in *Yearbook on International Communist Affairs* (Hoover Institution, Stanford, Calif., 1977).

6. Cited in James Backer, *La Iglesia y el Sindicalismo en Costa Rica* (Editorial Costa Rica, San José, 1975).

SUGGESTIONS FOR FURTHER READING

Aguilar Bulgarelli, Oscar. *La Constitución de 1949: Antecedentes y Proyecciones.* Editorial Costa Rica, San José, 1973.

Arias Sánchez, Oscar. *Quiénes Gobiernan en Costa Rica?* EDUCA, San José, 1976.

Bell, John Patrick. *Crisis in Costa Rica: The 1948 Revolution.* University of Texas Press, Austin, 1971.

Biesanz, John and Mavis. *La Vida en Costa Rica.* Ministerio de Cultura, Juventud, y Deportes, San José, 1975.

Denton, Charles F. *Patterns of Costa Rican Politics.* Allyn and Bacon, Boston, 1971.

English, Burt H. *Liberación Nacional in Costa Rica.* University of Florida Press, Gainesville, 1971.

Lizano Fait, Eduardo. *Cambio Social en Costa Rica.* Editorial Costa Rica, San José, 1971.

Stone, Samuel. *La Dinastía de los Conquistadores: La Crisis del Poder en la Costa Rica Contemporánea.* EDUCA, San José, 1975.

21
Nicaragua:
From Dynastic Dictatorship
to Social Revolution

THOMAS W. WALKER

Nicaragua is both typical and remarkably unique. Throughout most of its history, it was very much like many other Latin American countries, having an externally dependent economy run by and for a small privileged elite, which also controlled the apparatus of government and thereby perpetuated its domination over the impoverished majority of the country's citizens. However, in the twentieth century Nicaragua came to stand out from the other countries by producing the longest-lived dynastic dictatorship in the history of the Western Hemisphere, that of the Somoza family (1936–1979), and then giving birth to one of the most thorough-going social revolutions ever to take place in the Americas. What is more, the successful popular insurrection of 1978 and 1979 was unprecedented in Latin America in the degree to which it involved mass mobilization.

BACKGROUND

With a land area of 57,143 square miles (91,943 square kilometers), Nicaragua is the largest Central American country. It can be divided into three regions: the sparsely populated tropical rain forests of the Miskito Coast of the Caribbean, the more populous coffee-growing Central Highlands, and the cotton-producing lowlands of the Pacific Coast. The country also has two large inland lakes, which in combination with the San Juan River present possibilities for the building of a transisthmian waterway. In spite of this potential, Nicaragua remains basically an agricultural country. In 1984, the largest single component of the labor force (42 percent) was employed in agriculture. Coffee, cotton, beef, and sugar are the most important agricultural products.

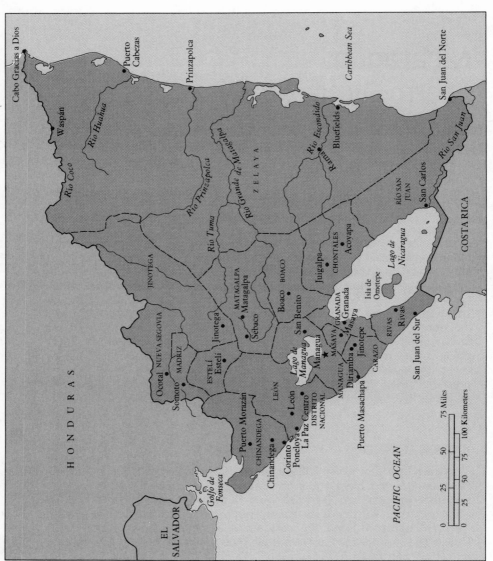

Nicaragua

At first glance Nicaragua would seem to be blessed in a number of ways. Not only is the national territory rich and potentially very productive, but population pressure is relatively low. As of 1982, when the country had a total population of 2,643,000, there were little more than 46 persons per square mile (29 per square kilometer). In addition Nicaragua is an ethnically and culturally integrated country. All but a tiny minority of its citizens speak Spanish. There is little racial tension. Sixty-nine percent of the population is mestizo, another 17 percent is Caucasian, and the remaining 14 percent either black or Indian.

Nevertheless, when the Sandinist Front for National Liberation (FSLN) took power in mid-1979, the average Nicaraguan was leading a stark existence. The annual gross national product per capita was a little over US$800. And that statistic hides the fact that the national income was very poorly distributed. Indeed, the bottom 50 percent of the population had a median income of around US$200 a year. The common citizen, therefore, ate poorly, lived in bad housing, and had little access to medical or educational facilities. Over 50 percent of the population could neither read nor write. Forty-seven percent of the homes had no access to running water, and 80 percent had no sewage system as of 1971. There were only a little over six physicians per ten thousand population in 1973. National life expectancy in 1970–1975 was 52.5 years, which placed Nicaragua seventeenth out of the twenty Latin American republics.

There were those, however, who pointed optimistically to the recent "development" of Nicaragua. They stressed the fact that the national income in the previous several decades had generally grown by respectable yearly percentages. They also pointed to the diversified nature of the national economy, with its commercial, industrial, and service sectors as well as its multifaceted agricultural base. Nicaragua, they noted, was not a one-product "banana republic" in the classic sense. Most of these observations were correct. The conclusion, however, was not. The error lay in the unstated assumption that growth, as measured by increases in the national income, would inevitably "trickle down" to all Nicaraguans. If we look closely at what had actually been happening, we find that quite the opposite was true.

Nicaraguan growth had been based heavily on a dependency relationship with the developed world. The Nicaraguan government and privileged classes depended on U.S. aid, loans, and private investment for much of the capital necessary to built industry, commerce, and agriculture. In addition, the country earned foreign exchange by exporting large quantities of agricultural products. The benefits derived from this dependency relationship were enjoyed by a very small segment of the population—the tiny industrial, commercial, and agricultural elite and the small dependent middle class that served that elite. The most notable beneficiary of all had been the Somoza family itself, which had amassed a fortune well in excess of US$500 million.

The negative impact of dependent "development" on Nicaragua as a whole and on the impoverished majority in particular was quite apparent. First, the production of basic food staples had been downplayed as emphasis on export agriculture increased. The result was that consumer foodstuffs had to be imported in ever increasing quantities and that the price of these staples to the average citizen was painfully high. Another by-product of the dependency relationship was that, as the value of land for commercial export agriculture increased, the temptation for the unscrupulous to buy or swindle the illiterate peasants out of their land, or simply to drive them from it, was increasingly irresistible. In the 1950s, for instance, many peasants in the Pacific Lowlands were dispossessed in order to make way for cotton production.

HISTORY TO 1933

During the colonial period, Nicaragua was a relatively forgotten backwater of the Spanish empire. A hot and humid climate and the lack of easily exploitable mineral wealth discouraged interest in the region. Under these circumstances the principal colonial cities, Granada and León, were allowed to develop essentially on their own. The former derived its income from farming, ranching, and trade with Spain and the Caribbean via the San Juan River, while the latter came to base its economy on commerce with the Spanish colonies of the Pacific Coast. Such limited contact as did occur between the two outposts was tinged with suspicion and mutual mistrust.

Nicaragua became independent in three stages: first as part of the Mexican Empire of Agustín de Iturbide in 1821, then as a member of the Federation of Central America in 1823, and finally as a separate state in 1838. The major effect of independence on Nicaragua was to release such constraints as had previously existed against foreign intervention and internal national conflict. For nearly one hundred years the country was to suffer turmoil of remarkable proportions.

At first regional differences reinforced by Liberal-Conservative partisanship were the major disruptive factor. Armed conflict became endemic. Nicaraguans from the "west" (León) under the Liberal banner clashed repeatedly with their Conservative countrymen from the "east" (Granada). By mid-century, however, meddling by the United States and European powers in Nicaraguan affairs became more frequent. In the late 1840s the British moved to consolidate their control of the Miskito Coast by seizing the mouth of the San Juan River. This brought them into conflict with U.S. interests in the form of Commodore Cornelius Vanderbilt's Accessory Transit Company, which was operating a boat-land transportation route across lower Nicaragua. The United States and Great Britain tried to defuse the situation by agreeing in the Clayton-Bulwer Treaty of 1850 that, henceforth, neither country would embark on the unilateral exploitation of the region.

The treaty failed to bring peace to Nicaragua. In 1855 the Liberals, at the time involved in a losing effort to overthrow a Conservative government, turned for help to William Walker, a U.S. soldier of fortune. Within a short while, Walker assembled a small band of undisciplined but well-armed U.S. mercenaries, sailed to Nicaragua, defeated the Conservative forces, and captured Granada. Then, to the dismay of his Liberal allies, the U.S. filibuster decided to keep the fruits of victory to himself. After ruling for a short while through a Nicaraguan puppet, Walker dropped all pretense and declared himself president of Nicaragua. By September 1856, Nicaraguans were in open revolt against the U.S. intruder. Aided sporadically by troops from other Central American countries and supplied with money and arms from the United States and Great Britain, they achieved final victory in May of the following year.

For the next three and a half decades, the country was ruled by a series of regularly "elected" Conservative governments. On the positive side, a new constitution was adopted in 1858, and Managua, which had become the capital city in 1851, grew and prospered. At the same time, however, stimulated by the growing international demand for coffee, the Conservative rulers of Nicaragua passed a series of laws that dispossessed the peasant and Indian communal landholders of the Central Highlands and forced many of them (under the pretext of control of vagrancy) to work for wealthy coffee growers. This legalized land grab resulted in 1881 in the War of the Comuneros, which was crushed at the cost of thousands of peasant lives.

In 1893, the Liberals under the leadership of José Santos Zelaya joined dissident Conservatives in overthrowing the Conservative government of Roberto Sacasa. Although a dissident Conservative was at first installed as president, Zelaya took control three months later. For the next sixteen years he ruled the country as a firm, yet relatively enlightened, dictator.[1] Zelaya's nationalism appears to have been his undoing, for it brought him increasingly into conflict with the United States. Washington was particularly annoyed by Zelaya's decision to begin negotiating with Japanese and European interests for the construction of a transisthmian waterway through Nicaragua (which would have competed with the U.S. canal at Panama). Responding to this threat, U.S. decision makers encouraged the Conservative opposition to overthrow the dictator. The revolt came in 1909. Four hundred marines under Maj. Smedley D. Butler were then landed in Bluefields to "protect American lives and property"; Zelaya resigned; and in 1910 the Conservatives regained tenuous control of the government. In order to secure their hold on the country, the Conservatives requested and received U.S. advisers and financial help in 1910 and called in the marines in 1912. Thus began a long period of direct U.S. military intervention in Nicaragua.

A variety of motives seem to have been behind the North American interventionist policy. The most important was the gut feeling on the part of Washington that Nicaragua, located as it is in the very heart of the U.S. "sphere of influence" in Middle America, should have a stable, pro-U.S. political apparatus. Instability would, it was feared, lead to financial insolvency, which might give European powers an excuse to meddle in the area. Furthermore, a neutral or anti-U.S. government might negotiate with a third power for the construction of a Nicaraguan canal, which would compete with the U.S.-operated Panama Canal that opened in 1914.

In all, U.S. troops occupied Nicaragua for roughly nineteen years in time segments from 1912 to 1925 and 1927 to 1933. During the first period, the country enjoyed relative peace under U.S.-backed Conservatives. In 1914 the U.S. diplomats negotiated an agreement with Nicaragua, later ratified as the Bryan-Chamorro Treaty, whereby the United States received exclusive rights to construct a Nicaraguan canal in return for payment of US$3 million. In 1925 the United States withdrew its troops from Nicaragua. Civil strife returned almost immediately, and in 1927 the United States again intervened, this time with a contingent of two thousand marines. In the six years before the final departure of the marines, a Nicaraguan constabulary, or National Guard, was created, and supervised elections were held in which more chastened and pliable Liberal caudillos won the presidency. Under their titular rule, Nicaragua ratified the Barcenas Meneses–Esguerra Treaty of 1928 that relinquished the Providencia and San Andres islands off Nicaragua's Atlantic Coast to Colombia. This treaty served U.S. interests by assuaging Colombian resentment over the U.S.-engineered loss of Panama in 1903 and by voiding Colombian claims that clouded the validity of U.S. rights under the Bryan-Chamorro Treaty.

Not all Nicaraguans cooperated with the U.S. occupation. Enraged by U.S. meddling in the affairs of his country, a young man by the name of Augusto César Sandino led a small peasant army in a prolonged war of attrition against the foreign occupiers and their National Guard allies. Through trial and error he became skilled in the standard techniques of guerrilla warfare. The United States responded by employing what have now become familiar counterinsurgency tactics: the aerial bombardment of "enemy" population centers, the forced relocation of populations, and the creation of "free fire" zones. But eventually Sandino was successful; the United States agreed to pull out if the guerrillas would lay down their arms. As they left, however, the Americans placed a pro-American Liberal—Anastasio Somoza García—in command of the guard. In doing so they unwittingly determined the course of Nicaraguan history for the next forty-six years.

HISTORY FROM 1933

Intelligent, persuasive, and crafty, Anastasio "Tacho" Somoza García was an exceptional young man. Educated in Nicaragua at the Instituto Nacional de Oriente, he also obtained a degree from the Pierce School of Business Administration in Philadelphia. Upon his return home, he tried several types of work and, in the mid-1920s, became involved in Liberal politics. During the second U.S. occupation, he served as minister of war, minister of foreign relations, and finally was involved in the creation of the National Guard. A friendly individual with an excellent command of English, he got along well with the North American occupiers.

In the three years following the U.S. withdrawal, Tacho moved adroitly to solidify his command of the guard and, hence, his control of the country. First, on February 21, 1934, he had Sandino seized (as he emerged from a dinner at the Presidential Palace) and executed by the National Guard. This act was followed by "mop-up" operations in which hundreds of people living in villages that had supported Sandino were killed. Somoza also made himself popular with the guard by allowing officers and men to become quite corrupt. Soon Somoza was sufficiently confident of his control over the guard that he staged a coup d'état, oversaw his own "election" as president late in 1936, and assumed office on January 1, 1937.

The Somoza family was to rule Nicaragua until 1979. Old "Tacho" was president or the power behind puppet presidents until he was assassinated on September 21, 1956. Tacho's younger son, Anastasio ("Tachito"), appointed by his father the year before to the key post of commander of the National Guard, then saw to it that power passed uneventfully to his older brother, Luis Somoza Debayle. The latter dominated the country for nearly eleven years, first as president ("elected" in 1957) and then (after 1963) as the power behind two puppet presidents. In 1967, another rigged election brought Tachito himself to the presidency. Though his term was supposed to have ended in 1971, the younger Somoza used various schemes to perpetuate himself in power until he was ousted in 1979.

The three Somozas were by no means identical. Luis, for instance differed from the other two in that he *appeared* to be less personally greedy and more concerned with creating "democracy" and promoting development. This style fit nicely with the stated goals of the Alliance for Progress begun during Luis's presidency. But, in truth, all of the Somozas were dictators who ran the country for personal benefit and to the detriment of the majority of their fellow Nicaraguans.

The Somozas ruled by appeasing and co-opting important domestic power contenders and by cultivating ties with the United States. In prerevolutionary Nicaragua, the principal domestic power contenders were the Catholic Church, the monied elite, the leadership of the traditional parties, and the National Guard. Though originally inclined toward the Conservative party, the Church hierarchy switched its allegiance to the Somozas during Tacho's presidency and continued to back the dynasty until the late 1960s. The monied elite was pleased with the family's laissez-faire, income-concentrating economic policies and the government's lack of interest in protecting the rights of workers.

Most Liberals supported the dynasty because the Somozas were, after all, "Liberals." And, in promoting the image of democracy, the Somozas frequently found it necessary to buy Conservative "opposition" participation in elections by offering the leaders of that party concrete benefits ranging from bribes to minority participation in government.

The National Guard was the most important power contender. To maintain its loyalty the Somoza family employed two tactics. First, they made sure that the top command of the military always remained in the hands of a family member. Second, they isolated the guardsmen psychologically from the people by allowing them to become a thoroughly corrupt sort of Mafia in uniform. Since all classes of Nicaraguans feared and despised the guard, the Somozas could always remind the guardsmen that they would be in serious trouble if the family were ever overthrown.

The second major element of the family's formula for rule was the careful cultivation of the United States through personal as well as political means. At the personal level, all of the Somozas were U.S. educated, spoke fluent English, could affect U.S. mannerisms at will, and were skilled in manipulating Americans. At the same time, in international politics family members were always obsequiously "pro-American." Nicaraguan territory was used by the United States for bases during World War II and for the training of CIA surrogate forces for the invasions of Guatemala (1954) and Cuba (1961). Nicaraguan troops joined those of the United States in the occupation of the Dominican Republic in 1965 and were offered, but politely refused, during the Korean and Vietnam wars. In return, the United States usually assigned ambassadors to Nicaragua who maintained close friendships with the dictators. In addition, U.S. foreign aid was lavished upon the dynasty, and the Somoza National Guard became the most heavily U.S.-trained military establishment in all of Latin America.[2]

Public administration during the Somoza period frequently served ends other than those that were publicly proclaimed. Especially at the time of the Alliance for Progress, the government bureaucracy swelled as agencies were set up ostensibly to administer the various social programs prescribed by Washington. In fact, the large bureaucracy served mainly as a device for channeling funds into the pockets of the politically faithful—corrupt Liberal politicians and national guardsmen to whom the Somozas owed favors. Further, some programs such as the rural literacy campaign and INVIERNO (The Institute for National Rural Welfare, supposedly concerned with agrarian reform) were simply thinly veiled counterinsurgency devices.

The Somoza system finally began to unravel in the 1970s. In part this was because of "accelerators" such as the 1972 earthquake; a changing international environment that included renewed U.S. emphasis on human rights and a more progressive attitude toward social injustice on the part of the Vatican and the Latin American Catholic hierarchy; and the effective strategy of the country's small guerrilla movement, the FSLN. But the intemperate behavior of the last of the Somozas was at least equally important. Tachito's greed and brutality eventually caused virtually all classes and groups—except the National Guard—to oppose him. Soon after his inauguration, abuses by the National Guard—curbed somewhat under Luis—picked up noticeably. Similarly, concern with giving the regime a "democratic" image all but disappeared as the dictator modified the constitution to extend his presidency an additional year after 1971 and then, ruling through a puppet triumvirate, oversaw the writing of a new constitution under which he was "reelected" in 1974.

Tachito Somoza's behavior in the aftermath of the 1972 earthquake (which killed ten to twenty thousand people and destroyed most of Managua) was hardly inspirational, either. While allowing the guard to loot the commercial sector and pilfer and sell relief supplies, he and his associates used their control of the government to pocket a large part of the hundreds of millions of dollars in relief funds sent by the United States and other countries. What is more, the dictator outraged the monied elite by muscling in on segments of the banking, construction, and concrete industries and by levying emergency taxes on the business community while neglecting to tax himself.

In the wake of a spectacular and humiliating kidnap-ransom operation by the FSLN in December 1974, Somoza again behaved intemperately. The enraged dictator imposed martial law and sent the National Guard into the countryside to root out "the terrorists." In acts reminiscent of old Tacho's liquidation of Sandino's sympathizers in 1934, the guard engaged in widespread pillage, torture, rape, summary execution, and arbitrary imprisonment. These excesses brought denunciations from the Catholic hierarchy and were the subject of human-rights hearings in the U.S. Congress.

Removal of the Somozas

By 1977, the stage was set for the overthrow of the dictatorship. In the first place, a significant segment of the Catholic clergy had been working throughout the decade to mobilize poor people. In doing so they were following the directives of the 1968 conference of Latin American bishops that had severely criticized the region's unjust social structures, had urged the clergy to make a "preferential option for the poor," and had specifically suggested that the Church raise the consciousness of the poor by training Lay Delegates of the Word and setting up Christian Base Communities (CEBs) to disseminate the "good news" of the social gospel. By the mid-1970s the progressive clergy, the Lay Delegates, and the CEBs had managed to convince tens of thousands of poor Nicaraguans that they, too, were made in the image of God and therefore had the right to organize and to demand a decent and dignified existence.

Paralleling and often cooperating with the Catholic mobilization drive was a much smaller guerrilla movement, the FSLN. Founded in 1961 by a group of Marxist intellectuals who had become frustrated with the sedentary, antinationalist behavior of the local pro-Soviet Communist party (the Nicaraguan Socialist party—PSN), the FSLN invoked the memory of Sandino and, at first, devoted itself to daring but unsuccessful armed operations. In the 1970s, however, most FSLN military operations were temporarily suspended as guerrilla militants went to live and work with the urban and rural poor. By 1977 the progressive Catholics and the Sandinistas had created a number of mass organizations that were to play a crucial role in the insurrections to come.

The third element that helped create a revolutionary setting was the renewed concern for human rights emanating from Washington. Inaugurated in 1977, the Carter administration saw Nicaragua as the ideal place to demonstrate the viability of its rights policy. Tachito Somoza himself was sure to follow orders, and U.S. "security interests" were not thought to be in danger since, according to U.S. military advisers assigned to the National Guard, the guerrilla threat had been eliminated in the wake of the rural counterinsurgency campaign already described.

In fact, Washington was correct in predicting Somoza's pliability but mistaken about the demise of the guerrilla threat. Under orders from Washington, Somoza not only halted National Guard terrorism against the peasantry (spring 1977) but also lifted martial law and reinstated freedom of the press (fall 1977). The result, however, was like taking the lid off a boiling pressure cooker. In the last three months of 1977 the supposedly extinct FSLN carried out daring raids against National Guard garrisons in several secondary cities; the country's opposition newspaper, *La Prensa*, covered these and other anti-Somoza activities and denounced the crimes of the regime; and a group of twelve prominent Nicaraguans ("los Doce") called for a new government that would include the FSLN.

On January 10, 1978, *La Prensa*'s popular editor, Pedro Joaquín Chamorro, was assassinated by professional hit men. In the ensuing six weeks there were huge demonstrations, Somoza properties were burned, a prolonged and very effective general strike took place, and the prototype of many urban insurrections to follow occurred in the Indian community of Monimbó. Sensing that things were getting out of hand, the Carter administration, according to one State Department insider with whom I spoke at the time, put its human-rights crusade in Nicaragua "on the back burner." U.S. officials urged Nicaraguans to settle their differences peacefully in the next Somoza-run "election" scheduled for 1981. The State Department issued a report noting improvements in Somoza's human-rights performance (which, in fact, was suddenly getting much worse). And, in July, Carter sent Somoza a letter congratulating him for promising to respect human rights.

In August, a small commando unit of the FSLN seized the National Legislative Palace, taking over fifteen hundred hostages and extracting a stinging list of concessions from the beleaguered dictator. This was followed in September by another nationwide strike and spontaneous insurrections in a half dozen of the country's secondary cities. The poorly armed and badly organized insurrectionists were brutally crushed with a loss of about five thousand (mainly civilian) lives.

In the ensuing months of 1978 the United States worked with urgency to promote a "solution" that would preserve the system while jettisoning Somoza himself. From October through January, U.S. diplomats led an Organization of American States (OAS) team in an unsuccessful attempt to mediate an agreement between the dictator and the handful of traditional politicians who were still willing to negotiate with him. The most important aspect of the U.S. position was the insistence that the National Guard—the cornerstone of the Somoza system—be preserved.

Somoza himself was very willing, for a while, to play along with the negotiation process. The tactic bought Tachito time to rearm the guard (with Israeli weapons and Argentine ammunition) and to begin liquidating his immovable assets by mortgaging them at inflated prices to the private and public banks he controlled. The flight of capital from Nicaragua during this period was enormous. Late in January 1979, when he apparently felt the negotiations had served their purpose, Somoza dropped them altogether. Although the United States reduced its embassy staff and withdrew its military attachés, the conventional wisdom in Washington was that Somoza would make it to the 1981 election. Accordingly, the United States approved a large International Monetary Fund loan "for Nicaragua" that May.

Meanwhile the FSLN, the revolutionary Catholics, and various affiliated mass organizations were preparing for the final offensive. The small regular FSLN army was expanded from around three hundred to approximately three thousand. With the assistance of Venezuela, Costa Rica, Panama, and Cuba, weapons were obtained on the international arms market. A coordinated strategy was developed for the final offensive: the country was divided into six fronts; each of the mass organizations had specific assignments and objectives; in March, the FSLN, previously divided into three groups because of disagreements over strategy, announced its reunification.

The final offensive began early that June. One by one National Guard outposts were overcome by civilian insurgents coordinated and backed by the small FSLN army. As city after city was declared "liberated territory," the United States called a special session of the OAS and proposed that a "peacekeeping force" be sent to Nicaragua. However, this thinly veiled attempt to block a popular victory was overwhelmingly rejected by the organization. Then the United States began trying to convince the FSLN-created government in exile to agree to a number of major concessions: the preservation of the guard, the expansion of the new plural executive to include a guard officer and a member of Somoza's Liberal party, and so on. Only on July 17, 1979, after these proposals were rejected, did the Carter administration allow Somoza to fly to Miami. Two days later the FSLN accepted the surrender of the National Guard in Managua.

The removal of the Somozas had cost Nicaragua dearly. The fighting had inflicted about $.5 billion in infrastructural damages. The departing dictator and his associates, while saddling the country with $1.6 billion in foreign debt, had emptied the national treasury of all but about $3 million. And approximately fifty thousand Nicaraguans or about 2 percent of the national population had been killed (an equivalent loss in the United States would be 4.5 million or well over seventy-five times the U.S. death toll in the Vietnam War).

The Sandinista Government

The system of government that replaced the Somoza dynasty was created gradually during the first half decade of Sandinista control. Its informal but central element was the Sandinista Directorate composed of nine individuals drawn in equal numbers from the three former factions of the FSLN. Each branch of the formal government, though by no means powerless, was created by, and existed at the pleasure of, this party Directorate. The Directorate, in turn, drew its strength from its control of the revolutionary armed forces and from the support of hundreds of thousands of civilians who made up the mass organizations that had developed during the insurrection.

The FSLN leadership, however, chose to create formal governmental structures that would encourage the participation not just of Sandinistas but also of all sectors of society. This policy was dictated by practical considerations: The new government needed the cooperation of all groups in the reconstruction process. The executive branch originally consisted of a five-person Junta of National Reconstruction containing two Conservatives, one pro-Sandinista intellectual, and two FSLN guerrilla veterans. Eventually, through resignation and reassignment, the junta was reduced to one Conservative and two Sandinistas. Junta member Daniel Ortega—also a member of the Directorate—became its head. All of the ministries except Interior and Defense were placed under the junta.

The legislative body, or Council of State, which was formally inaugurated in May of 1980, employed a quasi-corporative system of representation. Virtually all political parties (with the exception of the Somoza branch of the Liberal party) and major pro- and anti-Sandinista interest organizations were assigned seats. Each grouping elected or appointed its own representatives. The traditional parties and interest organizations complained, with accuracy, that pro-Sandinista organizations were given a majority of seats. The Sandinistas responded that the traditional parties and organizations were actually overrepresented given the small percentage of the population made up of the classes for which they stood.

In addition, there was a judicial branch comprising regular courts and, at first, some special tribunals designed to try the thousands of national guardsmen and Somocistas taken prisoner as the old system collapsed. The treatment of suspected war criminals created some controversy. As in the Nuremberg trials following World War II, there was an element of *ex post facto* justice. Nevertheless, there were no official executions, the death penalty was abolished, and the maximum sentence was thirty years. Further, those individuals sentenced on the questionable charge of "illicit association" (for instance, being a member of the National Guard) were duly released when their three-year terms were up. The regular courts were fairly independent. Though trials and convictions often tended to be quite speedy, there was an effective appeals process through which convictions were frequently overturned.

The structure of government as it existed in the first five years was avowedly temporary. On August 23, 1980, the Sandinista leadership announced that there would be general elections for national offices in 1985. Early in 1984, they moved the national elections ahead to November 4, 1984. Based on the universal suffrage of all citizens over sixteen years of age, these elections were to produce a president, vice president, and a legislative body chosen on the basis of proportional representation. The latter, in turn, would then write the new constitution.

The conduct of government in the first five years was made easier, less expensive, and more responsive to the people by the existence of a variety of mass organizations. Having a combined membership in the hundreds of thousands, these included the Sandinist Defense Committees (grass-roots neighborhood organizations); the Sandinist women's organization, AMNLAE (the Luisa Amada Espinosa Association of Nicaraguan Women); the Sandinist Youth; the Association of Rural Workers; the National Union of [Small] Farmers and Cattlemen; the Sandinist Workers' Central; and others. Their voluntary involvement in the Literacy Crusade, health and housing programs, the organization of sport and cultural activities, and the reactivation of the economy were indispensable. These grass-roots organizations were integrated into the governmental process through not only their representatives on the Council of State but also institutionalized membership in the local boards of the major ministries concerned with the country's most pressing social problems.

In this same period the new government also faced serious political problems. The smoke of battle had scarcely settled before a process of acute class polarization set in. In general, the middle and upper classes (constituting less than 20 percent of the population) were convinced practically from the start that the Sandinistas—who had never made any effort to conceal their Marxist tendencies—would eventually set up a totalitarian Communist regime. The fact that, contrary to these expectations, the government preserved a mixed economy with a large private sector, gave the Superior Council of Private Enterprise (COSEP) and other opposition groups representation on the Council of State, and encouraged dialogue with and input by the private sector did little to calm the fear that gripped the propertied classes. As a result, a segment of the Church hierarchy became bitterly antirevolutionary; many businesses refused to reinvest their profits, preferring instead to decapitalize and send their money abroad; and *La Prensa*, which was taken over by a conservative faction of the Chamorro family early in 1980, became highly critical of the new government.

Added to the problem of domestic opposition were increasingly tense relations with the United States. The Carter administration at first nervously accepted the new government, offering economic aid with numerous strings attached in order to steer Nicaragua in a "moderate" direction. The Reagan administration, inaugurated in January 1981, had a much less subtle approach. The Republican Platform of 1980 had "abhor[red] the Marxist Sandinist takeover" and had vowed to stop all aid. Campaign advisers close to Reagan had prescribed the removal of the Sandinistas via time-tested devices such as economic destabilization and, if necessary, a CIA-sponsored surrogate exile invasion. The new administration wasted little time in adopting all of these tactics. Aid was immediately terminated on the grounds—essentially unsubstantiated—that Nicaragua was serving as a major conduit for the flow of arms from the Socialist bloc to the Salvadoran rebels. An elaborate plan for CIA surrogate paramilitary activity against Nicaragua was drawn up and signed by the president in December 1981. And in the next two years an army of 10,000 Nicaraguan exiles (the contras or counterrevolutionaries, many of them former national guardsmen) was trained, equipped, and sent into Nicaragua (an equivalent invasion of the United States would number in excess of 840,000).

In the face of these pressures, both internal and external, the revolutionary government restricted some civil liberties—notably freedom of the press and of assembly—and placed heavy emphasis on military preparedness. Helicopters were imported from France and the USSR and tanks, antiaircraft weapons, troop carriers, and light arms were obtained from the Socialist bloc and the Middle East. The number of military and other security advisers from Cuba and the Eastern bloc rose significantly. In addition, a large civilian militia was recruited to complement the Sandinista People's Army. While the Reagan administration pointed to these developments with alarm, well-informed military and intelligence specialists confirmed that this buildup was defensive rather than offensive in nature.[3]

As the fifth anniversary of "the Triumph" drew near, the Sandinista government had managed to deal with internal opposition and the external security threat without massive violations of human rights. The major international human-rights monitoring organizations were frequently invited to visit Nicaragua to examine the local situation. Their report expressed concerns about the curtailment of certain civil rights, the apparent use of short-term imprisonment as a device for political intimidation, and the forced relocation of around ten thousand Miskito Indians from border areas in which CIA-sponsored contras had been active. However, they did not accuse Nicaragua of the extreme abuses (wholesale extralegal executions, torture, and so on) reported for other Latin American countries including Guatemala, El Salvador, Argentina, Chile, and Uruguay.[4] And, thanks especially to the determination of volunteer Sandinista militias, the contras failed to take and hold even one Nicaraguan village.

POWER AND INTERESTS

The Sandinista victory brought a significant redistribution of power in Nicaragua. In the first place, Somoza's National Guard—the cornerstone of the old system—was defeated, disbanded, and replaced by a new revolutionary military establishment. Arguing that all military institutions tend to be the instrument of the ruling class, the FSLN deliberately created a socially conscious, mass-oriented Sandinista armed force to replace the corrupt, elite-oriented National Guard. The young men and women in the Sandinista People's Army (about twenty-four thousand), the Sandinista Police (a few thousand), and the Sandinista People's Militia (over sixty thousand) were trained not just in the skills of their profession but also in the goals of their revolution.

The other major power contenders of the prerevolutionary period—the traditional parties and associated labor unions, the Church, and the monied elite—were significantly reduced in power. After the Sandinista victory several opposition parties emerged, most of them relabeled versions of preexisting organizations. These included the Nicaraguan Social Christian party (PSCN), the Social Democratic party of Nicaragua (PSD), the Liberal Constitutionalist party (PLC), the Democratic Conservative party (PCD), and a couple of small independent Marxist-Leninist or Communist parties. The PSCN, the PSD, and the PLC formed an opposition coalition called the Ramiro Sacasa Democratic Coordinating Committee (CDRS). Two small non-Sandinista labor unions—the Nicaraguan Workers' Confederation (CTN) and the Confederation of Trade Union Unity (CUS)—were also affiliated with the CDRS. It is doubtful, however, that these groups, even in combination, had much public support.

The Church in Sandinista Nicaragua became badly divided. On the one hand, a number of lower-level clergy, taking seriously the idea of a preferential option for the poor, accepted posts in the new government (including the Ministries of Culture and Foreign Affairs and the directorship of the 1980 National Literacy Crusade) or continued to work closely with poor communities. At the same time, most of the hierarchy led by Archbishop Miguel Obando y Bravo, apparently fearing that their authority might be undermined by the mass movement within both the Church and Nicaraguan society, recoiled from the revolutionary process. Although the government guaranteed freedom of religion and even tried to demonstrate its respect for Nicaraguan religiosity by promoting religious celebrations, inviting a visit by the Pope, and retaining In God We Trust on newly minted Sandinista coins, Obando and other bishops moved to separate the Church from the revolution. They attempted unsuccessfully to force all clergy out of public office; they arranged for the removal from the country of many prorevolutionary foreign clergy and for the reassignment of similarly minded native priests; and they denounced popularly oriented church organizations. Given the intense religious identification of the Nicaraguan people, the Church remained an important political factor. Its influence, however, was significantly diminished by its lack of unity.

Yet another important traditional power contender was the private sector. After 1979, its major political instrument was COSEP. The FSLN's decision to preserve a mixed economy in which the bulk of production would remain in the hands of the private sector automatically meant that COSEP and the class it represented retained some political, as well as significant economic, power. This created important political strains in revolutionary Nicaragua. Although the government made significant concessions to the monied elite that included the provision of reactivation loans, an intermittent effort at dialogue, and the inclusion of COSEP in the Council of State, the private sector—convinced from the start that "communism" was just around the corner—was openly hostile in political matters and only grudgingly cooperative in the economic realm. Its political behavior—opposition to the Literacy Crusade, hostility to the mass organizations, and insistence on the "depoliticization" of the military—reflected a desire to return Nicaragua to a prerevolutionary status quo.

While the revolution had eliminated one traditional power contender and somewhat eclipsed several others it had significantly increased the political clout of the masses. The integration and identification of the new revolutionary armed forces with the common people was one aspect of this change. Here the principal vehicle was the Sandinista People's Militia. In no sense a regular army, the militia was composed of civilian volunteers of both sexes and almost all ages. Its members were given enough training to enable them, in times of national emergency, to take up a weapon and defend the country. In practice, high morale made up for scanty training, and the *milicianos* acquitted themselves effectively against the invading contras.

The strength of Nicaragua's impoverished majority was augmented in other ways, too. These included the encouragement of grass-roots organizations, a very significant effort by the government to lift the educational levels—and therefore the social and political awareness— of the masses, an ambitious agrarian-reform program, the imposition of controls on rents charged for urban and rural properties; and the enforcement of rural and urban labor laws.

As a result, many poor Nicaraguans came to feel a new self-worth and confidence, sometimes making demands on the government that significantly altered public policy. One striking example came in 1981, when the Sandinista Rural Workers Association held demonstrations demanding that the government begin to distribute confiscated land rather than put it all into state farms and cooperatives. The government's subsequent acquiescence on this matter, a deviation from Marxist tenets, demonstrated the effectiveness of this pressure.

Therefore, by 1984, nontraditional, mass-oriented organizations seemed to hold a clear and virtually unassailable political advantage. At the heart of the new power configuration was the FSLN, supported by the new armed forces and hundreds of thousands of common citizens mobilized into mass organization. In addition, the FSLN had been joined in a progovernment coalition called the Revolutionary Patriotic Front (FPR) by three small middle-class parties: the old Soviet-oriented Communist PSN, the Popular Social Christian party (PPSC), and the Independent Liberal party (PLI).

PUBLIC POLICY

The programs and policies pursued by the new government during its first half decade were hardly doctrinaire. Indeed the country's new leaders seemed determined to develop and implement a practical Nicaraguan model of revolutionary rule rather than to impose some imported paradigm.

This was true, in the first place, of Sandinista foreign policy. From the start it stressed nonalignment and the maintenance of diplomatic relations with as many countries as possible, regardless of internal ideology. Accordingly, although Nicaragua often voted in the United Nations (UN) with other revolutionary countries, there were also important East-West issues on which its mission either abstained (Afghanistan and the Korean Airlines incident) or sided with the United States against the USSR (the proposal to send a UN peacekeeping force to Lebanon early in 1984). For its part, the FSLN, as a party, had friendly relations not only with the Communist parties of the Socialist bloc, but also with the social democrats of West Europe (through the Socialist International), the Liberal International, and the Permanent Conference of Political Parties of Latin America (COPPRAL). As a result of its diplomatic effort, Nicaragua avoided the international isolation that befell Cuba twenty years earlier. Indeed, in 1982 Nicaragua was chosen by an overwhelming vote to occupy the nonpermanent UN Security Council seat traditionally assigned to Latin America.

Economic policy was also pragmatic. In the international arena Nicaragua chose to honor Somoza's foreign debt as the price for remaining creditworthy in Western financial circles, and it sought and secured trade and aid relations with a variety of countries and blocs ranging from Libya and the USSR to East and West Europe, both Chinas, and such disparate Latin American countries as Cuba, Argentina, Brazil, and

Mexico. In the domestic arena, although the new government did confiscate a large amount of private property—especially that owned by the Somozas and their associates, it left 50–60 percent of the country's productive capacity in private hands and vowed to preserve a mixed economy. Further, the Sandinistas encouraged "patriotic businessmen" to reactivate their enterprises by providing substantial government loans and, in some cases, preferential access to foreign exchange.

At the same time, the Sandinistas consciously sought to employ what they called "the logic of the majority"—to weigh alternative policies against their potential impact on the country's poor. That meant that it was necessary to regulate the economy so that the worst excesses of capitalism could be avoided. Accordingly, banks and insurance companies were nationalized, foreign exchange and international trade were controlled, and a concerted effort was made to stimulate the production of food staples.

The Nicaraguan economy faced very serious obstacles during this period. These included: (1) almost $.5 billion in war damages, (2) the onerous task of paying off Somoza's huge foreign debt, (3) a major decline in the world market value of most of Nicaragua's export commodities beginning in 1980, (4) one of the worst natural disasters in the country's history (flooding followed by drought in 1982), and (5) an elaborate U.S. program of economic destabilization including the severance of economic aid, the restriction of trade, the blocking of loans from international lending agencies, attempts to create an international economic boycott, and the use of the contras to inflict infrastructural and crop damage and to necessitate the diversion of scarce funds into defense. As a result, the country's gross domestic product per capita in 1983 was down significantly from a 1977 prewar high.

Even so, on balance, the new government's economic performance during its first five years had been positive. In part, this was due to the Sandinistas' ability to attract trade and aid from a wide variety of countries. But it is also clear that the revolution had allowed the country's previously stifled human and natural potential to be more fully realized. At any rate, the production of most export commodities and basic consumer staples returned to, or surpassed, prewar levels and, according to United Nations statistics, Nicaragua's real GDP actually grew every year from 1980 through 1983 (except in 1982 when flooding and drought caused short-term setbacks).[5]

Some of the most interesting changes, however, came in the area of social policy. Here, the new government attacked social problems on a number of fronts. Since public revenues were severely limited, the Sandinistas were forced in part to rely on the voluntary participation of the people in the solution of their own problems through activities coordinated by the mass organizations.

In the area of health, government expenditures increased by over 200 percent from 1978 to 1983. The most costly aspect of the program related to the rebuilding, expansion, and staffing of curative facilities such as hospitals and clinics. At the same time heavy emphasis was also placed on primary or preventative health care, and in 1981 the United Nations Children's Fund (UNICEF) chose Nicaragua as a demonstration site for this type of approach to health. Here, voluntary labor was crucial. Within months of the Sandinista victory, innoculation campaigns had been carried out, at low cost, by mass organizations. By 1982, over seventy-eight thousand volunteer health *brigadistas* had been mobilized to work in a variety of preventative projects on designated Popular Health Days. As a result of these efforts, not a single confirmed case of polio occurred in 1982, and by 1983 infant diarrhea, mountain leprosy, and malaria were down 75, 60, and 50 percent, respectively. Infant mortality in general was down from 121 per thousand in 1978 and 1979 to 90.1 per thousand in 1983. Life expectancy had crept up from 52.2 to 57.6 years.

The government was also interested in housing. In addition to controlling rent, outlawing various forms of landlord exploitation, and building some low-income public housing, the Sandinistas also encouraged self-help through a sites and service program called progressive neighborhoods. In these projects the homeless were given title to plots and provided basic utilities and services, but left on their own to build and improve their dwellings and create their own organizations to solve community problems.

There was also an agrarian reform in which about 30 percent of the land was nationalized and subsequently turned into state farms and cooperatives or parceled out to individual farmers. By late 1983, twenty-six thousand families had received 450,000 acres (182,000 hectares). Complementing this reform was a rent-control program that made underutilized privately owned land available to the rural poor at affordable rents. In addition, part of the new agrarian policy focused on the production of inexpensive basic staples. Although the 1982 floods and drought set back the Sandinista goal of food self-sufficiency, the production of basic staples increased markedly in the first half decade, resulting in significant increases in per capita calorie intake and general improvements in nutrition.

The most dramatic social change, however, came in the area of education. By 1982, the total enrollment in all levels of schooling was approximately twice what it had been in 1978. Furthermore, in 1980 the government carried out an adult literacy crusade (relying on almost 100,000 volunteers) that reportedly reduced illiteracy rates from over 50 percent to around 12 percent. This crusade, which won Nicaragua the 1980 award of the United Nations Educational, Scientific, and Cultural Organization (UNESCO) for the best program of its kind, was followed by an ongoing adult education program designed to further erode illiteracy and to raise the schooling of all adults to at least the fourth-year level. By 1983, Nicaragua was claiming an illiteracy rate of only 10 percent— one of the lowest in Latin America.

PROSPECTS FOR THE FUTURE

To predict the future for Nicaragua would be foolish. On the one hand, by 1984 the Reagan administration had already demonstrated that it was prepared to go to some lengths to remove what it viewed as a Communist intrusion into the U.S. sphere of influence. At the same time it was equally apparent that the Sandinista revolution had set down very substantial roots and was capable of withstanding almost anything short of a massive direct invasion by U.S. forces.

NOTES

1. For an excellent examination of Zelaya, see Charles L. Stansifer, "José Santos Zelaya: A New Look at Nicaragua's Liberal Dictator," *Revista/Review Interamericana* 7, no. 3 (Fall 1977):468–485.

2. Richard Millett, *Guardians of the Dynasty: A History of the U.S.-Created Guardia Nacional de Nicaragua and the Somoza Family* (Orbis Books, Maryknoll, N.Y., 1977), p. 252.

3. See Staff Report, Subcommittee on Oversight and Evaluation, Permanent Select Committee on Intelligence, "U.S. Intelligence Performance on Central America: Achievements and Selected Instances of Concern," September 12, 1982 (mimeographed), p. 43; and Lt. Col. John H. Buchanan, USMC (ret.), Prepared Statement before the Subcommittee on Interamerican Affairs, Committee on Foreign Affairs, U.S. House of Representatives, "U.S. Military Aid to Honduras," Washington, D.C., September 21, 1982 (mimeographed).

4. For further information see the various country reports for Nicaragua and other Latin American states issued by Amnesty International, Americas Watch, and the human-rights commissions of the UN and the OAS.

5. From statistics provided me by the Washington office of the United Nations Economic Commission for Latin America (ECLA) in March 1984. See also Michael Conroy, "The Macroeconomics of the Revolution," in *Nicaragua: The First Five Years*, ed. Thomas W. Walker (Praeger Publishers, New York, forthcoming 1985).

SUGGESTIONS FOR FURTHER READING

Black, George. *Triumph of the People: The Sandinista Revolution in Nicaragua.* Zed Press, London, 1981.

Booth, John A. *The End and the Beginning: The Nicaraguan Revolution.* Westview Press, Boulder, Colo., 1982.

Borge, Tomás, et al. *Sandinistas Speak: Speeches, Writings and Interviews with Leaders of Nicaragua's Revolution.* Pathfinder Press, New York, 1982.

Collins, Joseph, et al. *What Difference Could a Revolution Make? Food and Farming in the New Nicaragua.* The Institute for Food and Development Policy, San Francisco, 1982.

Dixon, Marlene, and Susanne Jonas, eds. *Nicaragua Under Siege.* Synthesis Publications, San Francisco, 1984.

Kamman, William. *A Search for Stability: U.S. Diplomacy Toward Nicaragua, 1925–1933.* University of Notre Dame Press, Notre Dame, Ind., 1968.

Macaulay, Neill. *The Sandino Affair.* Quadrangle Books, Chicago, 1967.

Millett, Richard. *Guardians of the Dynasty: A History of the U.S.-Created Guardia Nacional de Nicaragua and the Somoza Family.* Orbis Books, Maryknoll, N.Y., 1977.

O'Shaughnessy, Laura, and Luis H. Serra. *The Church and Revolution in Nicaragua.* Papers in International Studies. Ohio University Press, Athens, 1985.

Randall, Margaret. *Sandino's Daughters: Testimonies of Nicaraguan Women in Struggle.* Crossing Press, Trumansburg, N.Y., 1981.

Rossett, Peter, and John Vandermeer, eds. *The Nicaragua Reader: Documents of a Revolution Under Fire.* Grove Press, New York, 1983.

Rudolph, James D., ed. *Nicaragua: A Country Study.* U.S. Government Printing Office, Washington, D.C., 1982.

Selser, Gregorio. *Sandino.* Monthly Review Press, New York, 1982.

Walker, Thomas W. *Nicaragua: The Land of Sandino.* Westview Press, Boulder, Colo., 1981 (1st ed.), 1985 (second edition).

Walker, Thomas W., ed. *Nicaragua in Revolution.* Praeger Publishers, New York, 1982.

⸺. *Nicaragua: The First Five Years.* Praeger Publishers, New York, forthcoming 1985.

Webre, Henri. *Nicaragua: The Sandinist Revolution.* Verso Editions, London, 1981.

22
El Salvador:
The Politics of Revolution

RONALD H. McDONALD

Over the past decade, Salvadoran politics has become one of revolutionary confrontation, escalating violence, and international intervention. The causes of these changes are complex, deeply rooted in economic, political, and demographic disequilibriums in the society and ignited by the regimes' efforts to induce economic growth and, in a more general sense, "modernization" over the past quarter century. The traditional civilian and military elites, rarely unified among themselves, have increasingly relied on force, violence, and terror to control the processes and the consequences of change, which in turn has promoted increasing violence from those who seek to restructure the traditional society. It is impossible to reconstruct the specific scenario of actions and reactions here, but some of the long-term causes can be identified and placed into a historical and political context.

Historically, El Salvador has been a highly stratified society whose economy and resources were controlled by a small, powerful, upper-class elite, but military leaders have ultimately controlled government institutions and resources for nearly half a century. Fluctuating objectives and personal rivalries among military leaders, and their complex relations with the upper-class elites, were what determined national politics and political conflicts. In recent years, traditional elites have been under siege by a disparate but determined group of reformists and revolutionaries, tenuously united by their commitment to change and their struggle to convince the majority of Salvadorans of the correctness of their cause. The violence of the conflict in El Salvador has brought both international attention and involvement in the struggle, further complicating its resolution. El Salvador has become a political system without viable institutions within the context of escalating demands for change. The resolution of conflict in such a situation has relied on force and intimidation, which is provoking a restructuring, a "reconstituting" of the society and its politics.

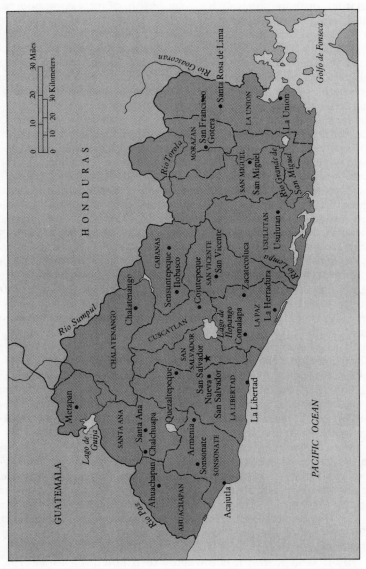

El Salvador

DEMOGRAPHIC, ECONOMIC,
AND SOCIAL BACKGROUND

Population, or more precisely the relationship of increasing population to limited land, created a volatile political context in El Salvador. The smallest of the continental Latin American nations, it has the highest ratio of people to land as well as one of the highest rates of population growth. Combined with this historically has been one of the most unequal patterns of land distribution in Latin America. An agrarian nation, where wealth and even survival have been tied to land, El Salvador has had to cope politically with an aggravated inequality that has worsened at an accelerating rate. Inequality exists elsewhere in Latin America, but in El Salvador it takes on additional meaning since Salvadorans, because of the small size of their national territory, live in unusually close contact with one another. Communications, including transportation and the media, are well developed, enabling people and ideas to circulate around the country in ways not typical elsewhere in the region. The combination of deprivation, inequality, and awareness gradually eroded the traditional politics of the country and brought it to a condition of revolution. The fragile balance between those who have and those who have not was negotiated for three decades by military leaders; when possible the negotiation was political, but ultimately it came to rely on force.

Inequality in El Salvador, unlike that in neighboring Guatemala, is not tied to racial cleavages in the society. El Salvador is a mestizo country, with a smattering of Europeans and other twentieth-century immigrants in the upper classes. About 20 percent of the total population (estimated to be about 5 million in 1984) lives in or around the capital city of San Salvador; the rest is fairly evenly distributed in villages and small cities throughout the nation. What is most important politically about El Salvador's population is the rate of its increase and its relationship to the size of the national territory. The population is increasing at between 3 and 4 percent annually, one of the highest rates in Latin America—indeed in the world. The size of the population and its rate of growth are causing severe pressures on available land, food, resources, and employment. Already there are about 250 persons per square kilometer (380 per square mile) in El Salvador, the highest population density anywhere in noninsular Latin America (over eight times that of neighboring Honduras). The population/land pressure is compounded by the fact that agriculture is so basic to the economy, accounting for about 26 percent of the gross domestic product and 60 percent of the foreign-exchange earnings.

Not only is land scarce, it is unevenly distributed. Historically, about 65 percent of the rural landowners held only 20 percent of the land, in plots averaging less than 10 hectares (25 acres), whereas less than 1 percent of the rural landowners controlled nearly 50 percent of the land in plots averaging over 100 hectares (250 acres). Contrary to official government statistics, probably less than half the population is literate, with male literacy about twice that of females and urban literacy twice rural literacy. Primary education, numbers of teachers, and government expenditures on education have failed to keep pace with population growth, and levels of literacy are falling.

Economic development historically rested on coffee exports. Production of coffee began about a century ago; reliance on it declined somewhat over the past several decades, but was replaced by reliance on other agricultural crops, including sugarcane and cotton. As is often the case, the export agriculture is relatively efficient and productive, but domestic food production is inefficient and unable to keep up with rapidly increasing demand. Nutritional standards have fallen, and malnutrition—especially among children—has increased. Since World War II El Salvador has pursued a policy of import-substitute industrialization, but in so small and poor a country as El Salvador, the results have been ineffective and costly. For a few years El Salvador's comparatively diversified, light industrial economy benefited from trade within the Central American Common Market, which expanded markets and potential demand for Salvadoran products; the decline of that market, however, left the industrial sector stagnant and contributed to widespread unemployment in that sector.

Economic development has been less dependent on foreign capital than has been the case in most Latin American nations. It has, however, been wholly under the control of a cartel of wealthy Salvadorans, organized through the ironically named National Association for Private Enterprise (ANEP), which has been able to allocate sectors of the industrial, financial, and commercial economy to members of the association and, through its political, financial, and institutional influence, control entry and restrain both domestic and international competition. The country has often been described as having been under the control of an oligarchy of "fourteen families," and a century ago this was essentially true. These families controlled the land that produced most of the national economic output and constituted its basic wealth. More recently, the economy has been in the hands of perhaps three or four hundred families, many of them interrelated, which have increasingly shifted their profits and capital into urban industrial, commercial, and financial investments, and over the past decade into investments abroad. With the growing level of revolution, the domestic capital flow out of the Salvadoran economy has exceeded by many times the total international and foreign assistance extended to buttress the failing system.

Although the small size and compactness of El Salvador have posed problems relative to population growth and economic development, they have facilitated the development of communications. El Salvador built an uncommonly efficient road system; before the revolution it was possible to reach any major center of population in less than a day.

Radio stations and newspapers in the capital reach national audiences. These conditions have produced a relatively high level of national awareness and information and a potentially high level of political participation despite economic and social conditions that would otherwise have limited it.

Rapid population growth has produced a society in which well over half of all Salvadorans are under eighteen years of age. Although primary and secondary education have failed to keep pace with this reality, there has been over the past two decades an increase in higher education, although it still is available to a very small percent of the population. Expanding higher education within a condition of economic stagnation has meant that employment opportunities have not kept pace with the growth in educated persons. This disequilibrium is significant; the rate at which young persons enter the labor force is higher than anywhere in Latin America. The inability of the economy to keep up with this by providing new jobs, combined with the increasing levels of education received by a small group of upwardly mobile Salvadorans, has produced a crucial, generally dissatisfied counterelite. It is from this youthful elite that many of the revolutionary leaders in El Salvador have come. Repression of universities, faculty, and students by military governments has increased their alienation and hostility and encouraged their political activism.

HISTORICAL PERSPECTIVE TO 1948

Salvadorans have been conditioned historically to recognize the importance of land in their political culture, for it had assumed unusually explicit importance in national politics long before the present population squeeze and revolutionary confrontation. The pre-Columbian inhabitants of the region, a lesser Indian civilization known as the Pipils, like the neighboring Mayan civilization held their lands communally. Spanish forces conquered the Pipils and regarded El Salvador as an outpost of their headquarters in Guatemala City. Through miscegenation the relatively few Pipils were rapidly absorbed into a new Salvadoran mestizo, but the tradition of publicly held lands continued after independence. Large plots of land held by the government (*ejidos*) were assigned to municipalities and used by peasants until 1882, when—under pressure from wealthy landowners—the courts returned these lands to private ownership. The motivation was to encourage the planting of coffee, which was just being developed as an export crop.

Under the terms of court decisions, lands received from the government had to be planted in coffee or would revert to the government and be assigned to someone else. Although some peasants were allotted land under this policy, over time only the wealthier landowners could cope with the instability of coffee prices on world markets and the fluctuating income derived therefrom. Peasants wanted the land primarily to grow their own food. In a short period of time, poorer farmers either were forced to sell their land to larger landowners or lose it to the government.

The subsequent political consequences of landlessness were dramatized in 1872, 1875, 1885, and 1898, when there were bloody peasant uprisings in El Salvador over the issue of land and the elimination of the *ejidos*. The government ruthlessly put down the rebellions, but in 1898 peasants achieved some retribution on the judges who took their land by cutting off their hands as punishment.

These uprisings had a profound impact on subsequent Salvadoran politics. Land has remained to the present a major source of conflict in the nation, and violence inspired by unequal distribution of land has continued to preoccupy those who own it. The immediate impact was to galvanize the upper class into a pattern of collaboration and pursuit of its own self-interest, which contrasted sharply with the bickering characteristic of the intraelite quarrels of the earlier postindependence period. The uprisings also encouraged wealthy landowners to form and support their own private armies to protect their lands and control the landless; these private militia were slowly merged and ultimately formed the basis of a portion of the present Salvadoran military. In a sense, the upper class formed a gentlemen's agreement to settle its conflicts in private and to present a united front to any who might challenge its interests.

The consolidation of the Salvadoran elite is perhaps best illustrated by the period from 1913 to 1931, when national presidential power literally alternated in a sophisticated fashion between two extended families (Meléndez and Quiñónez). The elite by this time had developed extensive, complex linkages within itself through intermarriage and mutual investments. The period was one of relative stability, with "those who had" conspiring with one another out of a mutual fear that more uprisings could destroy the system that was so beneficial to them. The pattern probably would have continued had not one member of the group elected to the presidency in 1927 been sufficiently naive to take literally the concepts of democracy that shrouded the regime. It had been almost a generation since the last peasant uprising, and a sense of relative security undoubtedly permeated the elite.

In 1925 a Communist party was founded in El Salvador, and by the 1931 elections, pressures for reform had again surfaced. Those elections were the first genuinely competitive ones in Salvadoran history and the first in which party competition for mass support was an important component. The challenge to the regime came from Arturo Araujo, who staged a mass electoral campaign and organized the Labor party, seeking support from the lower and middle classes who found themselves in desperate conditions followng the 1929 world depression. Although Araujo received support from the Communist party, after his election—a close one ultimately decided by the legislature—he found his supporters turning to the streets in demonstrations designed to produce immediate and radical solutions to their problems. Peasants demanded land, workers demanded jobs. Unable to control the situation, President Araujo was summarily deposed in December 1931, less than a year after his election. A junta was established, headed by Gen. Maximiliano Hernández Martínez, who had been Araujo's vice president. The next month, a widespread, Marxist-organized uprising of Indians and peasants occurred, killing between ten and twenty thousand persons and provoking a ruthless response from the government's military forces. Hernández Martínez ruled El Salvador for thirteen years, until his forced resignation in April 1944. He tried to maintain a thin thread of legality, calling for a new constitution and other devices that would allow him to remain in power, and he maintained his regime by controlling the military. His rule was harsh and pathetically irrational. At one time he ordered bottles of colored water dispensed to the public as cures for such things as heart disease, cancer, and arthritis. During a smallpox epidemic he had green lights hung over the streets of the capital to "prevent" the disease from spreading. During his regime, the army dutifully supported him, thanks to the "professionalization" the institution had attained by then, which indoctrinated officers to obey orders. The upper class, for whom Hernández Martínez was little more than a bitter joke, went along out of fear that under a more compliant regime renewed uprisings like those of 1932 (not to mention those of the nineteenth century) might return to challenge their vested interests.

The Hernández Martínez experience was finally ended by a combined if uncoordinated effort by the military and the public. Hernández Martínez had become so ineffective and outrageous that by April 1944 discontent reached the point that a general strike, known as the Huelga de los Brazos Caidos (Folded Arms Strike), was called by workers in both the private and public sectors. The strike was a remarkable, indeed visionary, experience in nonviolent protest. It paralyzed the capital city, as workers marched solemnly past the presidential palace, their arms folded to protest the dictator's policies and regime. So great was the public clamor that military officers ultimately persuaded Hernández Martínez to resign and go into exile. The impact of Hernández Martínez on subsequent politics in El Salvador was substantial, as military leaders who had endured his often degrading leadership reevaluated the responsibilities and objectives of their institution in national development.

MILITARY GOVERNMENT, 1948–1972

Following Hernández Martínez's resignation, elections were held and Gen. Salvador Castañeda Castro won, running on a platform designed to appeal to moderates. But Castañeda, like his predecessor, tried to extend his term beyond its scheduled expiration in 1949; the attempt precipitated a military takeover on December 14, 1948, and initiated a series of events that ultimately produced El Salvador's contemporary political environment. Those who seized power in 1948 described their action as "revolutionary," although it could be argued that the new regime was but a continuation of military control from the Hernández Martínez and Castañeda eras, with different military leaders exercising power.

There was a difference, even if it was not revolutionary. Hernández Martínez was by background a military officer, but his regime had been an old-fashioned personal dictatorship in which he used and controlled the professional military. Castañeda tried unsuccessfully to do the same thing. After 1948, however, the military *as an institution* was firmly into politics on a national scale. Although divisions would break out and leaders would change, the institution as a whole was directly exercising power, for reasons its leaders believed—or rationalized—to be in the general public interest. Some of the subsequent regimes were moderately "reformist," if not radically so, seeing the necessity to address the inequalities of the society and to pursue the obvious benefits of economic development as rapidly as possible.

There has emerged since 1948 an implicit but distinct model and underlying assumptions of political and governmental organization, which the military officers controlling the country have pursued. For many complex reasons (some of which go far back into Salvadoran history) the nation's military leaders have been influenced by Mexico, particularly the Mexican Revolution. Land, historically a critical issue in El Salvador, was one of the rallying points of the Mexican Revolution, and many Salvadoran officers openly admired the success and pragmatism of postrevolutionary Mexican regimes in dealing with that challenge and, more generally, in promoting economic development. They tended to identify themselves more with the Mexicans than with their Central American neighbors. It was the aspiration of an important minority of these post-1948 military leaders to implant in El Salvador an institutional framework of corporate or "controlled democracy" comparable to what they thought existed in Mexico. The government-sponsored political parties were conspicuously modeled after the Mexican Institutional Revolutionary party (PRI), which they conceived as an institution to build support for the regime while tolerating token or moderate opposition from other groups.

The problem with this approach was, of course, that El Salvador was not Mexico, and the events of 1948 were not comparable in any way to the traumatic Mexican Revolution. Nonetheless, many officers aspired to bring a new kind of enlightened administrative technology and planning to their country, pursuant to transforming it into a more modern and gradually a somewhat more egalitarian society, allowing and extending party participation as the society "matured" politically and developed economically. The intervening thirty-five years, however, have shown the military to be unsuccessful at convincing the Salvadoran people of the legitimacy of their plan, inept at dealing with the social and political imbalances provoked by rapid population growth and erratic economic development, and all too willing to use force as required to sustain their rule.

Following the overthrow of General Castañeda, a junta headed by Col. Oscar Osorio took power. Osorio was representative of the younger technocratic military officers who shared a professional commitment to the armed forces and the nation's development. Osorio ran for the presidency in 1950, using as his vehicle a government-created political party, the Revolutionary Party of Democratic Unity (PRUD). There was token opposition from another candidate to make the elections appear democratic and competitive. The opponent was an older, more traditional military officer, General Andrés Menéndez. Osorio tried to build a broadly based coalition stressing economic development and political stability. For economic development he needed the cooperation of the upper-class elite, and so avoided a direct confrontation with them on questions of reform, particularly land reform. He courted the middle class, small as it was, which had consistently been denied access to the political system and was becoming politically restless. He relied on institutional support from the military, specifically a coalition of like-minded officers, pursuing policies designed to maximize stability and generate some public support for the regime. He hoped, like the Mexicans with their PRI, to undercut any possible challenge from the extreme left by appearing to be revolutionary and reformist himself.

It was a difficult if not impossible coalition to build in El Salvador. The election was closer than had been anticipated, even though it is generally known that the government engaged in flagrant fraud during the voting and ballot counting. Osorio had the common sense to realize that his continuation in office would appear suspicious, again perhaps being sensitive to the Mexican rejection of presidential self-succession, but like his Mexican counterparts he was in a position to choose his own successor, Col. José María Lemus. With the help again of government-initiated electoral fraud, Lemus easily won the 1956 election. He also inherited some serious political and economic problems and became increasingly arbitrary in dealing with them, ultimately causing a split with his mentor, former President Osorio, in 1959. PRUD won all the legislative seats in the 1956 election, owing to both fraud and a regressive electoral system under which PRUD could hardly lose even with competition.[1]

By the end of his term, Lemus had lost most of his original support and had undermined the coalition Osorio had tried to build. Lemus alienated the economic elite, since political instability endangered economic growth and threatened their prosperity; he alienated many military officers, since their overwhelming concerns were development and stability; he alienated the middle class, alarmed by the political deterioration and economic stagnation; and he failed to win over the growing urban working classes. On October 26, 1960, Lemus was overthrown in a military coup; the leaders of the coup criticized him personally but openly affirmed their commitment to the "principles" of the 1948 revolution and even urged a quickening of reforms in the nation. The new junta disbanded the discredited PRUD, which had been compromised by Lemus's control over it.

Three months later a military countercoup occurred, organized by more moderate and conservative officers. The new group was concerned particularly by their predecessors' announced intention to allow genuinely free elections and to encourage open party competition. But they too affirmed, like the officers they replaced, their general support of the objectives of the 1948 revolution, and eventually they came to adopt many of the policies announced by the junta they overthrew. The most important consequence of the second coup was the emergence of Col. Julio A. Rivera, whose commitment to reform ran somewhat deeper than that of most of his colleagues.

Rivera was a mix of idealist and pragmatist, a younger military officer who was professional in his behavior and very much aware of, and committed to, what he perceived to be the broad objectives of the 1948 revolution. He ran for the presidency in a largely uncontested race in 1962, and easily won. He created a new government party to replace the extinct PRUD, the National Conciliation party (PCN). He tried to reestablish the fragile coalition that Osorio had fostered and did much to strengthen, at least temporarily, the institutional basis of the regime and to increase its national credibility. Rivera created a Central Council of Elections to supervise elections and guarantee their impartiality. He changed the regressive electoral system to proportional representation, which gave access to national power for the first time to at least some of the small, incipient parties through election to the national legislature.

Rivera was reasonably effective in stimulating economic development, and toward the end of his presidency he began discussing publicly, if not implementing, important reforms, including land reform. There were substantial increases in public services during his administration, particularly health and education. At the end of his presidency in 1967, he left office and became ambassador to the United States, allowing his successors an unencumbered opportunity to exercise national power. Unfortunately for El Salvador, his successors were unable or unwilling to sustain the momentum Rivera had initiated, and a spiral of political and economic degeneration set in that culminated in the revolutionary confrontation.

The electoral reforms, combined with worsening population problems and economic sluggishness, stimulated growing dissent and organized party opposition to the militarily controlled regime in the years followng the election of Col. Fidel Sánchez Hernández in 1967. Population pressures had been responsible for at least 300,000 Salvadorans migrating into border areas in Honduras, looking for land and economic opportunity. Their presence became a source of conflict between the two nations, as

Hondurans resented their presence and Salvadorans claimed they were being persecuted by local Honduran authorities. The tensions finally erupted in 1969 in the so-called soccer war, which followed an assault by Salvadorans on a visiting Honduran soccer team. By July 15, 1969, the two nations were at war, with President Sánchez personally directing Salvadoran troops that occupied Honduran villages in border areas. Honduran planes bombed the Salvadoran airport and port facilities but inflicted little damage. The war temporarily rallied Salvadorans around the military amid nationalistic propaganda and neutralized the growing internal political dissent. The experience was short-lived, however.

By the 1972 elections, the PCN was unable to mobilize a majority of Salvadoran voters behind its candidate for president, Col. Arturo A. Molina. Molina was officially declared the winner "by a few thousand votes," but even government officials have since conceded that the results were fraudulent. The principal opponent to Molina, and probably the winning candidate, was José Napoleón Duarte, three-term former mayor of San Salvador and a leader of the Christian Democratic party (PDC). Within weeks of the election, another presidential candidate, Gen. José Alberto Medrano, tried with Duarte's support to stage a coup. The one-day rebellion failed. Medrano was arrested, and Duarte went into exile.

From 1972 on, armed resistance to the regime spread into rural areas as small guerrilla organizations formed with a broad range of political and ideological orientations. Gradually what had seemed only isolated acts of terrorism became recognized as a full-scale revolution. The historical as well as contemporary social, political, and economic realities of the country made it ripe for a revolution on a scale rarely seen in Latin America.

POLITICS IN A REVOLUTIONARY CONTEXT

Increasing challenges to the military regime were met by escalating violence, repression, and terror by military leaders. It was within this context that a former defense minister, Gen. Carlos Humberto Romero, was elected president in 1977 as the PCN candidate, with constrained opposition by a three-party coalition dominated by the PDC and its presidential candidate, retired Col. Ernesto Claramount. Following the election, disturbances broke out in the capital with supporters of Claramount charging fraud. The government forces dispersed the demonstrators by force, killing many and wounding even more, and then imposed a state of siege that removed the few remaining personal protections for Salvadoran citizens. Landowners and other members of the upper class organized and supported clandestine death squads to intimidate the peasants and the urban poor, trying to prevent them from supporting or aiding the revolutionaries. Some military officers, particularly in the National Guard, privately supported and facilitated these actions. Increasing acts of terrorism and resistance followed as an urban guerrilla movement composed predominantly of youths began to operate in the capital. The military's hopes for an "institutionalized revolution" seemed all but lost.

With the election of General Romero political events began to move very swiftly in El Salvador. In mid-1979, Archbishop Oscar Romero (no relation to General Romero) spoke out against the excesses of the military regime and called for economic justice. A few months later the first of four military juntas was established, and General Romero was deposed. Each of the juntas represented a different balance between military and civilian, between left and right during the period of 1979–1982, but the general drift was unmistakably to the right. In March 1980 the second junta proclaimed a land reform program, and in the same month Archbishop Romero, who supported it, was assassinated by members of a right-wing death squad while he was celebrating mass. Later that year four U.S. churchwomen were assassinated by members of the National Guard, while the death toll for Salvadorans began to be estimated in the tens of thousands. Finally, in December 1980 Duarte agreed to join the fourth junta and was rewarded with the title of "president."

Almost immediately after the inauguration of President Reagan, then Secretary of State Alexander Haig focused public opinion in the United States on the conflict in El Salvador, proclaiming it a crisis and affirming that the United States would increase support and assistance to the junta, which in turn agreed to hold "free elections" in 1982 for a Constituent Assembly that would rule the country until the general elections scheduled for 1984. The junta also appointed an interim president and acted as a legislature during the period. Meanwhile, the civilian politicians opposed to the junta formed the Democratic Revolutionary Front (FDR) in April 1980, representing a broad spectrum of political orientations. In November 1980 the revolutionary organizations combined to form the Farabundo Martí Front for the National Liberation (FMLN) with links to the FDR.

Opponents to the regime refused to participate in the 1982 election, claiming their security would not be protected. Six parties gained representation, but none a majority of the seats. The PDC received 41 percent of the vote; the National Republican Alliance (ARENA), a newly formed right-wing party led by Roberto d'Aubuisson, a former major in the army suspected to have connections with the right-wing death squads, won 29 percent; the PCN won only 18 percent; the remainder was divided among three small, conservative groups. Charges of electoral fraud once again circulated. The total vote reported by the government implied that more than 90 percent of those eligible had voted, an unlikely probability given the context of violence and intimidation.

The Constituent Assembly elected Alvaro Alfredo Magaña as interim president, and Roberto d'Aubuisson as president of the assembly. Meanwhile the revolution took on international dimensions. The United States sent military advisers to El Salvador. Accusations were made that

Nicaragua, Cuba, and perhaps even the Soviet Union were aiding the revolutionaries.

Four moderate Latin American nations known as the Contadora Group (Mexico, Panama, Venezuela, Colombia) called for negotiations between the government and the revolutionaries, as did many European leaders. Honduras began cooperating with the Salvadoran military (and the United States) in the war against the revolutionaries, whereas both the Guatemalan military and that country's revolutionaries took notice of events in El Salvador and stepped up their campaigns against each other. Human-rights violations by the Salvadoran military leaders became a subject of international concern. The human costs for Salvadorans have been enormous from the violence as well as from the economic dislocations caused by it. In the urban areas, industry, commerce, and business declined and unemployment rose sharply; in rural areas, crops often went unharvested. What public services there were deteriorated; prices rose steeply while wages did not; among a people accustomed to deprivation, human misery increased to unprecedented levels. For the elites on both sides of the revolution, the politics of revolution became a struggle to prevail. For the majority of Salvadorans, the politics of revolution became a struggle to survive.

Presidential elections were held in El Salvador on March 25, 1984. The three principal candidates were José Napoleón Duarte of the Christian Democratic party, Roberto d'Aubuisson for ARENA, and José Francisco Guerrero for the National Conciliation party. Several candidates for smaller parties also participated, all of them ideologically on the right. Reformist groups did not participate. Duarte received approximately 45 percent of the vote, a plurality, but less than the 50 percent required to win. A run-off election was held May 6, 1984, between Duarte and d'Aubuisson. Duarte received 54 percent of the vote in that election, and on June 1, 1984, became the first civilian president in El Salvador in fifty-three years. Unfortunately for El Salvador, that has not signaled the end to the civil war or the revolutionary conflict.

MAJOR POLITICAL GROUPS
AND INSTITUTIONS

None of the political parties that have presented candidates in elections have strong roots in Salvadoran politics, nor for that matter extensive organizations. Many small parties have come and gone, and most are visible only at election time. Party identification of voters is weak and transient, often defined by the personality of the specific leaders running for office.

Following the 1982 election, three principal groups emerged in the Constituent Assembly. The strongest was the PDC, particularly in the capital area. It has advocated reforms, often presented itself as the alternative to the military regimes, and tried to generate support from middle and working-class voters. But Duarte, one of its principal leaders, had split the party by his participation in the 1980 junta. A new group, ARENA (formed for the 1982 election and led by Roberto d'Aubuisson), is a personalistic party (at least in terms of its votes) that reflects an extreme right-wing political orientation. The PCN, weakest of the three principal parties, survives after dominating Salvadoran politics from 1962 to 1977 as the "official" government party. It carries the heavy burden of being identified with, and having to defend, the policies of the military regimes of the period.

Of the smaller parties now functioning, Democratic Action (AD) was formed in 1981, representing a moderate group of industrialists and appealing to middle-class business people and professionals. The Popular Salvadoran party (PPS) is a far-right party led by Gen. José Alberto Medrano, founder of the Democratic Nationalist Organization (ORDEN), a paramilitary terrorist group in the country. The illegal Salvadoran Communist party (PCS) is the oldest party in the country, but it has never participated in national elections. It has been active in the labor movement and, after 1972, in the revolutionary movement.

The political movement supporting the revolution, the FDR, is a broad coalition of organizations, including the small Social Democratic party, some elements of the PDC, labor unions, intellectuals, students, and others. Its leaders, in exile, present the case for the revolution abroad and coordiante support within the country. The FMLN is the military arm of the revolutionary movement, coordinated with the FDR, and is also a coalition of organizations, including the Popular Liberation Forces (FPL), the People's Revolutionary Army (ERP), National Resistance (RN), the PCS, and others. Since their formation in 1980 the FDR and the FMLN have become increasingly effective in their struggle with the Salvadoran military.

There are also paramilitary forces on the extreme right, probably the best known being ORDEN. ORDEN was formed in the mid-1960s to recruit peasants in rural areas by offering them benefits from government projects, employment, credit, and other incentives provided by its backers in return for their collaboration as informers and armed militia. It had close contacts with the National Guard and the regimes prior to 1979. There are also an unknown number of "hit squads" supported by the extreme right for selective assassination and terrorist acts against suspected sympathizers of the revolutionaries.

The military is a major political organization in El Salvador. Its organization is very complex, including the regular army, the National Guard, the National Police, the Treasury Police, and the secret police. The total size of the military has about doubled since 1972, but there are still only about six hundred officers, of whom no more than half are field commanders. The military is divided by branch; by ideologies; by personal ambitions, hostilities, and rivalries; by age and generation; and especially by class in that the conscripts who are compelled to serve come from lower socioeconomic origins than the officers, and indeed have more in common with the interests of the revolutionaries than they do with their commanders. Expanding the size of the military has threatened the ability of the officers to control their own troops, perhaps a critical variable in the outcome of the armed conflict. Politics within the military is one of coalition building, a complex and unstable process, which in part accounts for the frequent military coups against military regimes.

The Church in El Salvador has played an increasingly important political role over the past two decades, and a changing one. Once a monolithic and conservative institution, the Church is now divided on ideology, becoming generally more conservative as one moves up in the hierarchy. Archbishop Romero tried to play a role in mediating the conflict by urging an end to the violence and greater social and economic justice for the poor. Many priests in rural areas have openly supported the revolutionaries, as advocates of Liberation Theology. Acting Archbishop Rivera y Damas has taken a moderate position, supporting the regime but criticizing violence from the left and the right.

Within the context of revolution, many organizations have been politicized into the conflict. ANEP, the powerful organization whose members have historically controlled most of the economy, is one. University students, faculty, labor unions, and many other organizations have become involved directly in the political confrontations. For most organizations, political neutrality in a revolutionary situation has ceased to be a viable option.

Many upper-class Salvadorans have left the country, living in self-imposed exile and taking with them what wealth they can. Living in relative security outside the country and having little more to lose, they provide financial resources to their sympathizers inside El Salvador, particularly the right-wing paramilitary forces, in hopes of forestalling a political or military victory by the FDR and the FMLN.

In a country without political institutions, organizations can participate in politics to the extent that they have guns, money, and the ability to persuade large numbers of people to support them. Elections in such a context have little meaning as long as the participants refuse to accept the legitimacy of their outcome.

THE CRISES OF PUBLIC POLICY IN EL SALVADOR

Several long-term trends have emerged in El Salvador that have thrust the country into a revolutionary context. First, the traditional military-civilian alliance that controlled El Salvador from 1948 to 1972 deteriorated and came to rely increasingly on force and fraud to maintain the regime. This deterioration was due partly to the inherent friction between the two elites resulting from their different self-interests and class backgrounds; partly to the inherent conflicts within the military—conflicts based on rank, generation, ideology, personal ambitions and loyalties, and competing self-interests; and partly to the intransigence of the upper class in resisting even modest reforms in the society. Second, economic growth slowed as a result of the exhaustion of the economic policy of import-substitution industrialization and the rigidity and stagnation of the agricultural economy, the collapse of the Central American Common Market that once offered opportunities for continued Salvadoran industrial growth, and the growing malaise worldwide in the 1970s in the economies of developed nations. Rapid population growth during the period produced increasing levels of unemployment and limited prospects for the young, as well as intolerable pressures in rural areas on land that was inequitably distributed. Third, there emerged an articulate and alienated counterelite comprising well-educated youths; professional, intellectual, and religious leaders; as well as political groups, labor organizations, and others willing to support revolutionary activity to change the traditional society. Finally, the Salvadoran conflict became increasingly internationalized, dramatically so as the United States proclaimed a "crisis situation" in the country defined in terms of an East-West confrontation and increased its involvement through military advisers, military aid, and economic assistance.

In such a context, Salvadorans have been so preoccupied with the political and military outcomes of the revolution that all other matters of public policy have been eclipsed. Economic development, employment, improvement of living standards and public services, equalization of wealth or income, even foreign investment—none of these objectives can be met in such a context. Indeed, conditions must inevitably deteriorate further so long as the conflict remains unresolved. In recent years, movements to depose a tyrant or family have produced revolutionary changes afterward, whether or not the majority of those supporting the movements realized during the conflict what the consequences would be. In El Salvador the consequences of the revolutionary conflict are clear before its resolution to all on both sides, for it is in essence a class conflict and not merely an effort to change leadership or regimes. The failure to institutionalize Salvadoran politics over the past thirty years has produced a political vacuum in the country. Power cannot be seized, only created. Military force alone cannot be substituted indefinitely for political institutions. The ability of one side or another to convince the majority of Salvadorans of the legitimacy and correctness of its cause will ultimately determine the outcome of the conflict.

NOTES

1. "Regressive electoral systems," which frequently employ single-member districts and a majority-type representation similar to that used in the United States, assign a greater proportion of legislative representation to larger parties

than their share of the popular vote, while making it difficult for smaller parties to gain legislative representation relative to their proportion of the vote.

SUGGESTIONS FOR FURTHER READING

After years of relative neglect, El Salvador recently has been the subject of many published political analyses. Some of the more useful are listed here.

Anderson, Thomas P. *Mantanza: El Salvador's Communist Revolt of 1932*. University of Nebraska, Lincoln, 1971.
_____ . *The War of the Dispossessed: Honduras and El Salvador 1969*. University of Nebraska, Lincoln, 1981.
Baloyra, Enrique. *El Salvador in Transition*. University of North Carolina, Chapel Hill, 1982.
Browning, David. *El Salvador: Landscape and Society*. Oxford University Prses, London, 1971.
Durham, William H. *Scarcity and Survival in Central America*. Stanford University Press, Stanford, Calif., 1979.
Ebel, Roland H. "The Decision-making Process in San Salvador." In *Latin American Urban Research*, Vol. 1, edited by Francine F. Rabinovitz and Felicity Trueblood. Sage Publications, Beverly Hills, Calif., 1970.
Gallardo, Ricardo. *Las Constituciones de El Salvador*. Vols. 1 and 2. Ediciones de Cultura Hispánica, Madrid, 1961.
Gettleman, Marvin E., Patrick Lacefield, Louis Meashe, David Mermelstein, and Ronald Radosh, eds. *El Salvador: Central America in the New Cold War*. Grove Press, New York, 1981.
LeoGrande, William M., with Carla Robbins. "Oligarchs and Officers: The Crisis in El Salvador." *Foreign Affairs* (Summer 1980):1084–1103.
McDonald, Ronald H. "Electoral Behavior and Political Development in El Salvador." *Journal of Politics* 31, no. 2 (May 1969):397–419.
_____ . "Civil-Military Relations in Central America: The Dilemmas of Political Institutionalization." In *Rift and Revolution: The Central American Imbroglio*, edited by Howard J. Wiarda. American Enterprise Institute, Washington, D.C., 1984.
Montgomery, Tommie Sue. *Revolution in El Salvador: Origins and Evolution*. Westview Press, Boulder, Colo., 1982.
Raynolds, David R. *Rapid Development in Small Economies: The Example of El Salvador*. Praeger, New York, 1967.
Webre, Stephen. *José Napoleón Duarte and the Christian Democratic Party in Salvadoran Politics 1960–1972*. Louisiana State University, Baton Rouge, 1979.
White, Alastair. *El Salvador*. Westview Press, Boulder, Colo., 1973.

23
Guatemala:
The Politics of a
Frustrated Revolution, I

JERRY L. WEAVER

Shortly after 3:00 A.M. on February 4, 1976, a massive earthquake smashed west from Guatemala City into the predominantly Indian highlands and northeast into a region inhabited by subsistence farmers. Over 1 million people were left homeless, 77,000 seriously injured, 23,000 or more killed, and 5,000 children orphaned. Indians and poor farmers traditionally placed their beds beneath the heavy crossbeams that support their roofs; many were crushed by these timbers or were injured or killed by falling adobe blocks. Others died because they could not reach or be reached by medical care. There are few doctors in rural Guatemala, and those who tried to move into the devastated regions were hindered by poor roads made impassable by landslides.

The earthquake produced a massive outpouring of relief assistance from scores of nations and millions of individuals. Yet most who responded to this natural disaster were unaware that during the preceding decade, and continuing to this day, the people of Guatemala have suffered a phenomenon as destructive of life as the earthquake. Since 1965 a wave of political violence has swept the country, killing 50,000 to 100,000 individuals, destroying whole villages, ruining businesses, and forcing thousands to live in terror for their own safety and that of their families. Students, farmers, priests, professors, lawyers, military officers, policemen, politicians, farm laborers, and journalists are victims and perpetrators of assassinations, kidnappings, and torture.

This violence has many origins. Some is purely personal—old scores are settled, debts wiped out. Some is associated with criminal activities such as smuggling, robbery, and extortion. But fundamentally the statistics on violent death reflect a set of historical social and economic processes played out in the political arena. Social and economic institutions have changed enormously over the past century, especially since 1944. A

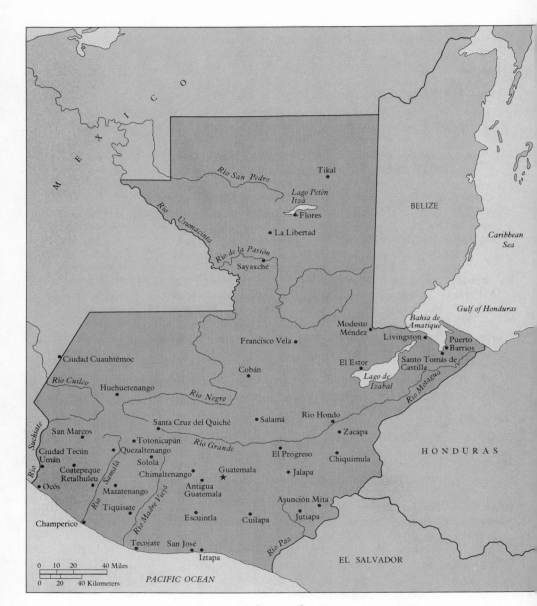

Guatemala

professional army has grown up; roads, education, and mass media have penetrated rural Guatemala; agriculture has changed profoundly and altered the life-styles of millions; manufacturing has developed and drawn peasants to urban areas in search of jobs and better living; and the middle class, small and politically insignificant before World War II, has become the economically and politically dominant stratum of society. For millions these institutional changes brought new experiences, new jobs, even new identities; for many change has meant discomfort and dislocation as traditional patterns crumble and new survival techniques are demanded.

Guatemala is one of a select number of countries, including the Dominican Republic and Chile, in which a constitutional government or movement was overthrown or frustrated through direct U.S. intervention: In 1954 President Jacobo Arbenz Guzmán and his progressive nationalist regime were toppled by a CIA-supported coup. Many observers see this government and its predecessor, that of Juan José Arévalo, as having initiated major changes in the direction of Guatemalan development that might have produced new economic and political institutions capable of meeting basic human needs. It is further argued that the truncation of this incipient revolution destroyed reformist zeal and belief in constitutional politics as a vehicle for peaceful change. The alienation growing from Arbenz's overthrow led directly to the rise of left-wing insurgencies during the early 1960s and the antileft terror and counterinsurgency of the late 1960s, 1970s, and 1980s. Had the revolution been permitted to run its course, reforms and accommodations would have been made to the needs of the peasant, workers, and progressive elements of the middle class, eliminating the conditions that produced the violence of the 1960s and 1970s.

We shall examine the "frustrated revolution" thesis because there is a great deal to support it. Nevertheless, it is clear that the roots of Guatemala's present political violence and the political processes that nurture it reach back beyond 1954. The springs that feed the present political system are found among the social and economic institutions that have developed over the past one hundred years and among the values and attitudes these institutions reinforce. Indeed many of the forces at play in contemporary Guatemala arose in its colonial past.

HISTORY TO 1944

Colonial Origins

A cardinal feature of Guatemalan politics is the presence in the 7.5 million national population of perhaps 3 million Indians. Divided into a score of language groups and well over two hundred distinctive communities, contemporary Indians are the remnants of the Maya-Quiché nation defeated by the Spanish in the 1520s. Today Indians are disproportionately among the poorest, most exploited segments of the society. Unlike North American blacks, for whom racism is associated with physical attributes, Guatemalan Indians remain the target of abuse only while they remain "Indian," that is, speak Indian language, wear Indian clothing, and think of themselves as Indians. Individuals born of Indian parents may discard this identity by learning Spanish, wearing Western clothes, and identifying themselves as Ladinos.

The cultural base of Guatemalan racism originated in its colonial period, when Catholic missionaries who accompanied the conquering Spanish army attempted to destroy all traces of indigenous culture. The Church itself was unsure of the classification of Indians and debated until 1637 whether or not Indians had souls and were human beings. When these questions were answered affirmatively, the institution of *encomienda*, through which "pious" Spanish settlers were given the task of bringing the blessings of Christianity to the pagans in return for free labor, was established.

The Postindependence Period

When Guatemala's colonial epoch ended in 1821, two important institutions were firmly established: the exploitation of Indians and landless Ladinos as cheap seasonal labor and the hegemony of local planters in the rural areas. Government was *of*, *by* and *for* the planters and their associates in the Church and military.

The postindependence period varied little from the colonial era: The national government collected taxes and tariffs and maintained a small army sufficient to crush the periodic Indian rebellions; economically, there was neither diversification nor expansion; socially, the traditional class structure remained static. This stagnant system was challenged energetically by the 1871 Liberal revolution and its first leader, Justo Rufino Barrios.

Unlike his predecessors, Barrios believed in a strong central government, economic development, and European civilization. He began to appoint and supervise provincial governors (*jefes políticos*); to build schools, roads, railroads, telecommunications and postal systems; to stimulate the diversification of agriculture by introducing new plantation cash crops; and to encourage European immigration and the Ladinization of Indians. His goals and methods paralleled those of Mexico's Porfirio Díaz.

As Guatemala entered the international depression of the 1930s, the country's basic economic and social relationships appeared strong and viable. Planters, bankers, owners of commercial houses, and the local representatives of such corporations as the United Fruit Company (UFCO) constituted the political elite. Because this oligarchy was both small and well established, an elaborate network of familial, social, and commercial ties bound its members closely and served as a quick and dependable means for articulating interests and mobilizing support. For the middle class—provincial notables, senior military officers, churchmen, shop-keepers, bureaucrats, professionals, and the technical and managerial personnel of large foreign enterprises—access to political jobs and personal services was obtained either through direct contact with designated official party personnel or with appointed officials such as the *jefes políticos*.

Wage laborers in Guatemala's nascent industries or on UFCO plantations could reach government only through factory owners or their representatives. Labor unions were nonexistent, and anyone who tried to organize workers or remonstrate with management over grievances was subject to dismissal, imprisonment, or death. Rural laborers, landless peasants, or subsistence farmers (*campesinos*) found themselves dependent on the *finquero* (planter), who controlled access to land, health, education, recreational facilities, and even the local church building and priest. In return the *finquero* received work when and under the conditions he established. His will was backed up by the institutions of the state—police, army, and courts. The power and brokerage monopoly of the traditional landed gentry was so complete, so unitary, that it precluded interference from rival brokers because the landlord was virtually the sole source of subsistence, protection, and identification for their dependents.

THE REVOLUTION AND LIBERATION: GUATEMALA'S MODERN POLITICAL HISTORY

At the apex of these pyramids of dependency sat the president of Guatemala. In the 105 years preceding the revolution of 1944, which destroyed it, this system was ruled for a total of 73 years by only four men. The last, Gen. Jorge Ubico, applied the precepts of General Barrios and added to them the fire and ruthlessness of his own personal code of complete rectitude.

After seizing power in 1931, Ubico moved to strengthen his control and enhance his power vis-à-vis the landed gentry by appointing mayors and by outlawing debt peonage. Both reforms reduced the power of the provincial notables while making the administration of local projects *and* access to Indian labor the responsibility of the *intendentes* (appointed mayors) and provincial *jefes políticos*. While in no way improving the lot of the *campesino*, these changes strengthened Ubico's control in rural Guatemala. Traditional Indian leaders, the local upper class, and the *finqueros* lost their regional autonomy and became firmly dependent on the chief executive.

When the United States entered World War II, Ubico was forced to liquidate German coffee, banking, and commercial interests and sit by while hundreds of his staunchest supporters were shipped to U.S. internment camps. Economically and politically the regime was hit a heavy blow. The arrival of thousands of U.S. troops to staff air bases guarding the Panama Canal and the subservience of Guatemalan foreign policy to that of the United States did not generate support for Ubico; rather, these events further antagonized the large profascist segment of the upper class while confirming to nationalists that Ubico was a puppet of the United States.

The Revolutionary Years, 1944–1954

A student strike, a march by teachers and young professionals, and the martyrdom of a young woman by Ubico's bodyguard forced the general's resignation on June 20, 1944. Nine months were required to organize the post-Ubico government, attesting to the low estate to which opposition had fallen during the dictatorship: There were no organized parties, no recognized leaders, and no channels of communication among his opponents.

The coalition that supported liberal Juan José Arévalo's election was led by a generation of nationalistic university students hungry for personal liberty and eager for economic growth and improvement. They were joined by the majority of the middle class and industrial workers, but only a limited number of *campesinos* and very few Indians supported Arévalo's revolutionary regime.

Long on enthusiasm and idealism, short on administrative and political experience, Arévalo and his followers set out to govern Guatemala. Politically, the country had no history of representative politics, no tradition of limited constitutional government, nothing even approximating the free exchange of ideas and political debate that were provided for in the new constitution of 1945.

In 1945 Guatemala was emerging from the depression, but its economic institutions were still very largely colonial. The nation was dependent for most of its consumer goods, investment capital, and technical services on foreign, particularly U.S., sources. Domestic manufacturing was primitive and its products not competitive internationally. In the agricultural sector, commercial production was in its infancy, and local planters showed little interest in converting grazing lands into cotton, sugarcane, and other export crops. Banks were reluctant to lend money for new ventures, in part because many were controlled by coffee-producing families who used their banks as a source of personal credit so that their own capital was not at risk.

Surrounded by these economic problems, Arévalo chose to stimulate and expand the economy by mobilizing investment capital, granting tax holidays to industrialists, and reducing import taxes on capital goods and materials. The government created new institutions to lend money to industrialists and commercial agriculturalists. These and the Industrial Promotion Law were designed to speed diversification and create new jobs.

While attempting to expand the economy, Arévalo moved to regulate foreign enterprises. To this end, he tried to limit the rates charged by the Guatemalan Electric Company, a subsidiary of the U.S.-owned Electric Bond and Share. The United Fruit–owned International Railways of Central America was compelled to submit to the provisions of the newly enacted Law Code and to accept collective bargaining. And UFCO was forced to submit wage disputes with its workers to arbitration. The government further angered U.S. investors by announcing a petroleum law that virtually closed the door to U.S. companies.

Simultaneously, Arévalo offered a broad range of new social services to the urban working and middle classes. One-third of the national budget went to the construction of schools, hospitals, and housing. The educational system was reformed and expanded. A national literacy campaign was mounted, and hundreds of university students went into the countryside to work with *campesinos*. Expanded public-health programs offered sanitation, potable water, health education, and immunization. Hospitals and clinics were integrated into the social-security system, and physicians were required by law to give service in them.

The Arévalo government was surprisingly passive in confronting the major problems of the rural population. Although a National Confederation of Peasants was established and a Law of Forced Rentals was passed requiring landlords to continue to rent to individuals who had previously used the land, virtually nothing was done to attack the land tenure system whereby 2 percent of the landowners held 62 percent of the arable land, 87 percent held 19 percent of the arable land, and medium-sized farms of 17 to 111 acres (7 to 45 hectares) represented only 10 percent of all farms.

Arévalo was succeeded in 1950 by Col. Jacobo Arbenz Guzmán, whose advisers differed from Arévalo's in stressing the necessity of building a strong revolutionary base among *campesinos*. Where Arévalo had eschewed agrarian unionism, the new government pushed it rapidly. By June 1954 at least 533 *campesino* unions and 320 *campesino* leagues were recognized formally, and hundreds of credit and marketing cooperatives had been formed through the help of Ministry of Agriculture personnel. But the keystone of Arbenz's strategy was the 1952 Agrarian Reform Law. In addition to receiving land, 100,000 peasant beneficiaries obtained credit and technical assistance from the National Agrarian Institute and other state agencies.

Of the 1,002 plantations and 2.7 million acres (6.64 million hectares) affected by the agrarian reform, the most significant case was that of the United Fruit Company. The government expropriated 387,000 acres (952,000 hectares) and offered $1,185,115 in compensation based on the company's tax declaration. UFCO, backed by the U.S. State Department, claimed its property was worth $16 million. The ensuing struggle between the government of Guatemala and UFCO led to a swelling chorus of attacks by U.S. politicians, newspersons, and business interests against Arbenz's administration.

In addition to challenging UFCO's interests, the Arbenz government took an independent, often anti-U.S., position in foreign affairs. Guatemalans visited East Europe and China, and spokespersons condemned U.S. imperialism at home and throughout the Third World. Guatemala became an example of nationalism unparalleled in Latin America.

In response, the U.S. government pursued a program of destabilization: Foreign assistance was cut off; international lenders such as the World Bank found Guatemala uncreditworthy; antigovernment subversives received money from the U.S. government and UFCO; U.S. politicians and publications denounced "communism in Guatemala." Encouraged by Washington and its local Embassy, Guatemalan dissidents rallied and demonstrated against the government. And while the archbishop of Guatemala read a pastoral letter condemning communism and calling on all good Catholics to drive it from Guatemala, the CIA was arming a ragtag band of 250 adventurers in Honduras. A counterrevolution was launched on June 18, 1954, when the "Liberation Army" commanded by Col. Carlos Castillo Armas marched into Guatemala with air cover from CIA-provided planes flown by U.S. mercenaries. The Guatemalan army refused to defend Arbenz, and government supporters were unable to arm loyal union members and *campesinos*. Confronted by this crisis, Arbenz raged and wept but offered no personal leadership.

As unexpectedly as it had been born, the Arbenz revolution died. Castillo Armas flew to Guatemala City aboard a U.S. Embassy plane and went quickly about the task of erasing the revolution's programs, policies, and personnel. Arbenz fled to Mexico and later to Fidel Castro's Cuba. Arévalo returned to Guatemala in 1963, and the likelihood of his victory in a forthcoming election convinced the armed forces to seize power. When civilian rule returned in 1966, Arévalo became an ambassador.

Was the revolution Communist? Certainly not in the case of the Arévalo government: Communists were repressed and kept out of office, and the Communist party remained illegal. During Arbenz's administration Communists played an open and occasionally major role in several agencies, most notably the Agrarian Reform Institute. Moreover, the party was legalized under Arbenz. Now, thirty years later, it is clear that the Guatemalan government was surely not Communist in doctrine, program, or personnel.

The 1950s was an era of ideological politics: Neutralism was considered immoral by Calvinist Secretary of State John Foster Dulles—there were only two sides, the United States' and the devil's. Guatemala tried to break the traditional U.S. hold on its foreign policy and domestic economy. In challenging UFCO, it opened itself to the charge that it was anticapitalist and therefore "Communist." In foreign policy Guatemala was vociferously independent and often critical of the United States. Washington branded the revolutionary regime heretical and demanded that it recant. When Arbenz persisted, his government had to be driven out lest it become an example for others.

Perhaps this ideological explanation of U.S. motivation is crude and simplistic. It does not ignore the role played by U.N. Representative

Henry Cabot Lodge, Jr., John Foster Dulles, and Allen Dulles (who was head of the CIA), and other Washington politicians who owned stock in or were associated with law firms that represented UFCO. Indeed, self-interests and a powerful lobby supported by UFCO must have played major parts in setting the disposition to intervene. But the weight of evidence and personalities indicates that the Dulleses, Eisenhower, Nixon, and the others who approved the destabilization of Arbenz and the arming of the Liberation Army genuinely believed Guatemala was a threat. They were right: It was an example of a small nation whose economy and foreign policy were ruled from outside attempting to strike off those chains and chart its own course. In 1954 Washington possessed the reason, the means, and the opportunity to reestablish control—and it did.

Legacy of the Revolution: A Destabilized Political Life

In its ten years of life, the revolution mortally wounded the economic and social institutions passed into its hands almost unchanged after Barrios. By stimulating the growth of local industries and agricultural diversification, the revolution created thousands of new middle-class families. And its programs doubled the public bureaucracy to provide new and expanded social services while creating thousands of additional openings in the middle stratum.

The burgeoning middle class set about quickly organizing itself to negotiate with the government. Dozens of political parties appeared, and a few became important vehicles for meetings between government and clients. Nevertheless, the most important device for collecting and presenting middle-class interests became the industrial or occupational association. Individual entrepreneurs found that associations facilitated private-public intercourse while enabling interested parties to keep abreast of relevant technical and political developments. Where Arévalo's policies encouraged industrialists and business people to organize to seek help from government, Arbenz's programs and public statements frightened them, thus stimulating them to organize for mutual protection. The result was the same: Increasingly the middle class dealt directly with government and made its own political decisions without going to upper-class brokers. The effect was as profound for future politics as it was irreversible: Since 1954 Guatemala has been a middle-class-dominated political system.

The working class was Arévalo's primary target, and he offered its members social security, labor courts, subsidized housing, education, new jobs, health, and other goods and services. These programs mobilized the economic and political potential of this class as the foundation for the nation's economic development and the regime's political survival. To this end the regime employed political parties, unions, prolabor courts, cooperatives, the mass media, and a close identity of the president with the working class.

Although not retreating from these efforts, Arbenz directed more attention and resources to mobilizing Indians and *campesinos*. By providing social services and a sense of political identity for tens of thousands of Guatemalans, the cooperatives, *campesino* leagues, and unions and local agrarian-reform committees undermined the traditional dependency relationship between *patrones* and peasants. Arbenz hoped that the newly freed *campesinos* and Indians would become staunch revolutionaries.

But among traditional Indians there was a good deal of resentment and resistance to Arbenz's programs. Landed Indians feared that their farms might be expropriated; traditional communal leaders saw their years of service in hope of securing leadership positions and prestige threatened by younger, better-educated Indians who dealt directly with representatives of government agencies, political parties, and other service organizations. Where control of traditional and well-to-do Indians was strong, little support went to the revolution. The revolution simply did not offer enough incentives to most Indians to encourage a massive shift of commitment from traditional sources of income, status, legitimacy, and security to the government. Indians might have been mobilized through a widespread land reform, greatly expanded public services, and grants of political autonomy to local communities. But this the revolution was unable to do. Indirectly, however, Indians were affected by the revolution's attacks on the plantation land tenure and utilization systems.

For *campesinos*, agrarian reform, leagues and unions, and cooperatives secured real leverage with *patrones*. When disagreements flared over working conditions, the expropriation of land, or rental agreements, peasants often won. These frequent victories convinced many *finqueros* that their workers were indeed disloyal and ungrateful for the years of care shown them. Other *finqueros*, confronted by uncertain relations with workers and encouraged by government credits, adopted new forms of commercial farming that did not depend on intensive labor. Increasingly, profits meant more to many *finqueros* than the prestige of "owning" *campesinos*. Thus both economic incentives and new social conditions combined to break down generations-old *patrón*-peasant unitary dependencies.

Since the fall of Arbenz, Guatemala has experienced the politics of demobilization: Castillo Armas's government outlawed the parties, unions, leagues, cooperatives, committees, and similar mechanisms through which Arévalo and Arbenz sought to bring the working and peasant classes into national political processes and either assassinated or imprisoned their leaders. A registry of suspected Communists was developed, and secret police and an official Committee of National Defense Against Communism were sent to ferret out sympathizers. "Communist" was applied indiscriminately to anyone who disagreed with the government, even to someone with whom the accuser had only a personal disagreement.

After Castillo Armas's death in 1957, the most repressive features of the demobilization were eased by his successor, a general from the Ubico era, Miguel Ydígoras Fuentes. But Ydígoras Fuentes was unable to provide leadership in solving Guatemala's economic problems, was personally corrupt, and was associated in the minds of many nationalists—including military officers—with an unseemly surrender of sovereignty to the Americans, who used Guatemalan bases from which to launch the Bay of Pigs invasion of Cuba. After two major military revolts, Ydígoras Fuentes was finally toppled on March 30, 1963, by a bloodless coup.

After three years of military rule, the relatively honest 1966 election was won by the civilian candidate of a middle-of-the road Revolutionary party. Hopes for peace and stability were quickly dashed, however, when the government's offer of amnesty to insurgents, who had been fighting the army since 1963, was rejected. When conventional counterinsurgency tactics proved a costly and embarrassing failure, the commander of a northeast military zone located in the center of guerrilla operations, Col. Carlos Arana Osorio, provided arms and hunting licenses to private vigilante groups. As a result, as many as five thousand *campesinos*, students, former revolutionary cadres, members of the Christian Democratic party, and other "suspected leftists" were killed during 1967–1968. The surviving guerrillas moved from the countryside to Guatemala City or to the sparsely settled northern region of the country.

The successes claimed by Colonel Arana plus an effective public relations campaign by the armed forces' military civic-action unit brought him widespread popularity among the former followers of Castillo Armas. In 1970, when the ineffective Revolutionary party split into rival factions, the combined forces of the right elected Arana president. Four years later Arana's handpicked successor, Gen. Kjell Laugerud García, was proclaimed elected after a disputed count. Laugerud followed the rural policy of previous administrations: Build up the counterinsurgency capacity of the armed forces; leave the existing land tenure system untouched; resettle a few *campesinos* in Guatemala's northern wilderness; and tolerate no anti–status quo organizations that could challenge government candidates.

The pattern of repressive military rule continued into the 1980s. In 1978 Gen. Fernando Romero Lucas García was elected president by the congress, since he did not win a majority and most of the electorate had chosen not to vote. In 1982 Gen. Angel Aníbal Guevara was "elected" under similarly fraudulent conditions. However, he never came to power because Gen. José Efraín Ríos Montt, who had lost the fraudulent 1974 election to General Laugerud, staged a bloodless coup. Ríos Montt, an evangelical Protestant, began a program of providing land and security to the peasants as well as honesty in the administration of the public accounts. But he fell out of favor with the Church and his own fellow officers and was replaced in another bloodless coup in 1983 by Gen. Oscar Humberto Mejía Victores.

While this dreary recital of successive military regimes was unfolding the national political scene continued to unravel and polarize. The civilian political institutions have virtually disappeared; the army even more than before is virtually the only power; corruption and brutality are widespread; the guerrilla movements have reappeared. Indian elements have increasingly mobilized. Violence is spreading, while the government seeks to pacify the countryside by turning the clock back to an earlier, "sleepier" era.

The post-1954 regime has followed a parallel policy of depoliticizing workers. Only tame unions are permitted in Guatemala's industries: The labor ministry and courts are openly proemployer. Reinforcing antilabor policies, the cities in which most industries are located have swelled since 1954 with immigrants from the countryside—with an annual population growth rate of 3 percent and no new farmlands being made available, *campesinos* flock to the cities in search of work and provide employers a vast pool of surplus labor that effectively keeps wages low and inhibits strikes.

Castillo Armas came to power on the backs of the U.S. ambassador, the traditional upper class, and much of the middle class. Succeeding governments have continued to rely heavily on these three supports. The Church, *finqueros*, and large firms have been allowed autonomy in their spheres of interest. The middle class has benefited from a wide range of public goods and services: expanding public-sector employment opportunities, strict control of labor, new credit institutions, infrastructure, and subsidies for domestic and foreign industries. And all of this has been done while retaining the lowest property tax rate in Central America.

Castillo Armas showed his gratitude for U.S. support by settling several Guatemala–United States disputes: Labor Code suits against several U.S. firms were canceled; UFCO lands were restored; a new petroleum code that recognized explicitly the rights of foreign companies to Guatemala's oil and to hold it in unused reserve for up to forty years was adopted. In March 1955 Guatemala became the third Latin American nation to sign an Investment Guarantee Agreement, under which U.S. enterprises are ensured against losses from currency inconvertibility or expropriation.

In return the U.S. government demonstrated its pleasure at the restoration of U.S. hegemony by turning on the flow of economic and military assistance. During the revolutionary regime, little aid from either the U.S. government or international lending institutions reached Guatemala: an average per year of only $1.4 million from all sources during the 1946–1953 period. Since 1954 there has been a dramatic upward trend: $16 million annually from 1954 to 1962, $37.4 million annually during the Arana government (1970–1974), and $57.7 million per year during the period 1975–1977. Overall, assistance from the World Bank, United Nations, and other international organizations between 1954 and

1975 amounted to $245.9 million, and combined U.S. military and economic assistance for the same period was $218.4 million. Total foreign assistance since the liberation has been nearly a half billion dollars—$464.3 million.

The importance to the Guatemalan economy of foreign grants and loans is seen in its nearly $100 million annual balance-of-trade deficit and its growing foreign debt. Were it not for the World Bank, the Inter-American Development Bank, and private lenders, the economy would stagnate and perhaps crumble. Given the role of manufacturing, tourism, and commercial agriculture as foundations of middle-class prosperity and as alternative sources of income for thousands of *campesinos* unable to make a living in the prevailing system of land tenure and utilization, a slump in export trade or a reduction of foreign investment would have massive destabilizing consequences for the economy and political system.

Guatemala's post-1954 economic expansion has produced growing contradictions within the middle class. Much of the post-1954 middle class owes its advantageous station to expanding domestic markets for locally produced goods and services. This "new" middle class sees increased minimum wages, land reform, and even tax reform, all of which increase local buying power, as in its self-interest. But support for basic reforms, ones that would incorporate the masses into the economy and political system as full partners, is reserved. The middle class knows that where such reforms have been attempted, in Chile, for example, it has been the middle class that paid the price—through inflation and through increased competition from members of the lower classes for jobs, places in schools, and other prerequisites to continued enjoyment of the good life. Although economic interests may dictate supporting reformists, changes might curtail or even destroy the security and comfort the middle class has built up and wishes to pass along to its children.

Guatemalan managers and executives of international firms are caught in another cross pressure: Their belief in nationalism and social reform must be tempered by a commitment to the interests of their employers. Profits go abroad; decisions are made in distant boardrooms; the resources of giant corporations make them better investment opportunities, so they dry up available local investment capital; technologies that provide foreign firms a competitive advantage are proprietary and are not shared locally—multinational corporations attenuate and contradict local needs and desires. But the election of reformist politicians could lead to a corporate decision to pull out of Guatemala—an option open to corporations but not to their employees.

The traditional middle class—bureaucrats, provincial notables, small-business persons, the semiprofessionals—sees its interests challenged by the numbers, affluence, and influence of the new middle class. Most of the former groups see nothing to be gained personally from improving the conditions of the masses, and, since they will pay for reforms through taxes, inflation, and increased competition, a great deal to be lost. Little wonder that most of the traditional middle class supports conservative law-and-order regimes such as those of Arana, Laugerud, Lucas, and their successors.

Representatives of the major segments of the middle class disagree on how to develop Guatemala and how to direct public resources. Because no consensus has been reached, no political organization, no vision of a future Guatemala, and no effective leadership have come forward. It is little wonder, then, that most of the middle class has accepted the continued political role of the armed forces. Since 1954 the officer corps has repeatedly entered politics to preserve the basic social and economic institutions from which middle-class advantages grow.

THE ARMY AND THE STATE SYSTEM

Establishing a military academy and importing U.S. advisers to teach the art and science of warfare were two of Barrios's major, if unintentional, contributions to the development of Guatemalan politics. Not until the overthrow of Ubico, however, did the officer corps play a decisive role in Guatemalan politics. Since 1954 the military has established and enforced the conditions and selected the major candidates of national politics. This power reflects two factors: the political resources possessed by the military and the cleavages within Guatemalan society. Resources include sophisticated means of violence, organizational unity, past political experience, support from upper- and middle-class notables, and a widespread acquiescence by the civilian population to direct military intervention in politics. Given the economic dependence of Guatemala on the United States, the willingness of Washington to support and assist military-dominated governments is undeniably a major contributor to rule by khaki-coated politicians.

There are reformist and moderate factions within the officer corps, and there is evidence that some commanders, supported by junior officers, are advocating a more vigorous role for government in reforming Guatemalan society, perhaps along the lines of a military-dominated corporate state model. Land reform, tax reform, and basic economic planning initiated and directed by the state are said to be key elements of their strategy for development. To date, however, no redistributive policies have been enacted by the government.

CONFLICT, PUBLIC POLICY, AND THE FUTURE

Crushed in the late 1960s, insurgent bands reappeared during the mid-1970s in at least four areas of Guatemala. It remains to be seen if the counterinsurgency methods of the 1960s plus the continuing effects of the post-1954 regime's demobilization policies will stymie them again. But whether or not the insurgents gain support among *campesinos* and are able to hold off the armed forces, there is a very great likelihood of continued political violence. It is widely accepted in Guatemala that force is an appropriate means of dealing with political opposition. In particular, the National Liberation Movement (MLN), Castillo Armas's party, formed a pact with Colonel Arana during 1967 and 1968 from which party members received weapons for vigilante groups formed by local MLN leaders. In return the party provided the army a ready-made intelligence network, guides for armed patrols, and civilian support for its counterinsurgency activities. After Arana's 1970 election, former vigilantes received police and military positions. Many of these individuals have used their weapons to settle old grudges, eliminate business rivals (especially in the lucrative smuggling trade along the Honduran border), rob payrolls, and kill "Communists." The electoral support given the MLN has in effect legitimated its vigilante elements.

The fundamental cause of Guatemala's violence is the breakdown of old social structures, such as those between *campesinos* and *finqueros* or Indians and their traditional communal hierarchies, which began with Barrios's reforms and accelerated with the mobilization of peasants and workers during the revolution. The coffee economy brought about the consolidation of many small holdings into a few large ones. From their profits, coffee planters bought out holders of noncoffee lands in order to have sites for their workers to live during the off season. Indians were drawn more and more into the cash economy during the nineteenth century until by the twentieth century there were the beginnings of economic differentiation within supposedly traditional communities. At the same time many Indians migrated from place to place for seasonal work and grew more worldly as a result of greater contacts with Ladino society. Into this rapidly changing environment came the health and sanitation programs of the revolution, which reduced infant mortality and extended the rural adult life span—from thirty-seven years in 1964 to fifty-nine in 1981. Thus the rural population more than doubled between 1944 and 1980 while old relationships were being undercut by economic innovations and government programs.

The breakdown of the traditional forms of social control has gone the furthest in areas of small farms (the northeast) and commercial plantation agriculture (the south coast). Here the means of earning a living are now largely free from unitary dependencies on traditional communal leaders or *finqueros*. Small farmers sell their products to middlemen or in local markets; plantation laborers work under contract wages and do not live on *finca* (farm) lands as do traditional *campesinos*. In neither region is there a prevailing system of strong permanent communities; indeed, migration into and movement within both regions is the highest in Guatemala. Thousands of *campesinos* and workers in these regions form a pool of relatively free-floating individuals who, lacking established dependent relationships to constrain them, *may* attach themselves to individuals or organizations that offer them real or imagined benefits. It is noteworthy that Arbenz's rural organizations won the greatest support in the northeast and along the south coast.

In the 1970s pressure on available land, the appearance of better-off Indians who wished to protect their private lands, the impact of education, and the introduction of new technologies weakened traditional Indian communal ties. Traditional forms of exploitation and ruthless suppression of nonconformity at the whim of the *finquero*-dominated rural political system were challenged by progressive priests, cooperative organizers, and Christian Democrats who moved into the countryside. Insurgents operated in El Quiché and other predominantly Indian districts. However, these changes did not succeed in mobilizing much support—thanks largely to the vigilantes and the Indians' pervasive low sense of political efficacy.

Both violence and the potential for violence are created by the combination of loosening social cement and the politics of demobilization. So far the armed forces have successfully contained this volatile mixture while preserving the basic institutions inherited from the Liberal period. If orderly constructive change is to take place, it seems that only the armed forces have the power to bring it about. This would mean an equally basic change in the relationship between the military and the middle class, a partnership that has ruled to the advantage of both since 1954. Hence demands for reform probably shall remain unanswered. Meanwhile, in the 1980s, rising social tension, renewed guerrilla activity, continued military repression, a downward-turning economy, and the general crisis in Central America have combined to make Guatemala a boiling political cauldron.

SUGGESTIONS FOR FURTHER READING

Adams, Richard Newbold. *Crucifixion by Power: Essays on Guatemalan National Social Structure, 1944–1966.* University of Texas Press, Austin, 1970.

Ebel, Roland H. *Political Modernization in Three Guatemalan Indian Communities.* Publication no. 24. Middle American Research Institute, Tulane University, New Orleans, 1969.

Fried, Jonathan L., and Marvin Gettlemen, eds. *Guatemala in Rebellion: Unfinished History.* Latin America Series no. 2. Grove Press, New York, 1983.

Gott, Richard. *Guerrilla Movements in Latin America.* Doubleday, Garden City, N.Y., 1971.

Immerman, Richard H. *The CIA in Guatemala: The Foreign Policy of Intervention.* University of Texas Press, Austin, 1982.

Jonas, Suzanne, and David Tobis, eds. *Guatemala.* North American Congress on Latin America, New York, 1981. (Chapters cover political economy, U.S. intervention, foreign investment, and linkages between business, government, and the agricultural sector.)

Jones, Chester L. *Guatemala: Past and Present*. University of Minnesota Press, Minneapolis, 1940.

Melville, Thomas and Marjorie. *Guatemala: The Politics of Land Ownership*. New York, Free Press, 1971.

Newbold, Stokes. "Receptivity to Communist Fomented Agitation in Rural Guatemala." *Economic Development and Cultural Change* 5 (July 1957):338–361.

Pearson, Neale J. "Guatemala: The Peasant Union Movement, 1944–1954." In *Latin American Peasant Movements*, edited by Henry A. Landsberger. Cornell University Press, Ithaca, N.Y., 1969, pp. 323–373.

Plant, Roger. *Guatemala: Unnatural Disaster*. Latin America Bureau, London, 1978. (Uses the 1976 earthquake as a watershed to today's political repression at the hands of the government.)

Schlesinger, Stephen C., and Stephen Kinzer. *Bitter Fruit: The Untold Story of the American Coup in Guatemala*. Doubleday, Garden City, N.Y., 1982.

Schneider, Ronald M. *Communism in Guatemala: 1944–1954*. Praeger, New York, 1959.

Wasserstrom, Robert. "Revolution in Guatemala: Peasants and Politics Under the Arbenz Government." *Comparative Studies in Society and History* 17 (October 1975):443–478.

Weaver, Jerry L. "Political Style of the Guatemalan Military Elite." In *Militarism in Developing Countries*, edited by Kenneth Fidel. Transaction Books, New Brunswick, N.J., 1975, pp. 59–98.

24
Honduras: Civil-Military Politics and Democracy

JAMES A. MORRIS

Honduras shares certain characteristics with its Central American neighbors: It is a small nation-state with a relatively low level of social and economic development and a high degree of dependence on foreign investments and markets. But considered on its own terms, Honduras presents a distinct pattern of political change, which, since 1950, has been rapid and concentrated. This transformation has yet to reach a definitive plateau, as the balance of old and new political forces remains fluid. As a consequence, the structure of the state, its control, and the pattern of policymaking are only partly institutionalized. Political dynamics in Honduras is perhaps best understood by analyzing the evolving distribution of power among the traditional political elites, the groups that have emerged to challenge the status quo, and the increasingly central role of the Honduran armed forces in politics. Recently Honduras has been thrust into the center of the Central American maelstrom, with the conflictive regional forces further complicating the country's search for political stability and national development.

BACKGROUND AND SETTING

Honduras presented few attractions to the Spanish colonizers, who found neither substantial native population nor extensive mineral wealth. After the capital city of Tegucigalpa was founded in 1524, immigration gradually populated the western and central highlands, where, in addition to the North Coast, most people live today. The population of 4.1 million is 90 percent mestizo, and a growth rate of nearly 3.5 percent a year has complicated the country's development as urbanization, land pressures, and social needs have increased. Honduras is still a rural society, with about 57 percent of the economically active population involved in agriculture. A per capita gross domestic product of $610 a year (1982), a literacy rate of only 60 percent in 1982–1983, and an

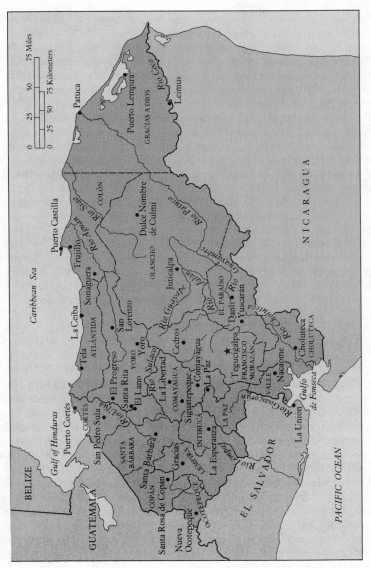

Honduras

infant mortality rate of eighty-seven per thousand live births (1982) rank Honduras below several of its Central American neighbors in terms of wealth and social development. On the other hand, the country has escaped the extremes of political violence that have plagued other Latin American countries, and historically the society has not suffered intolerable excesses on the part of its political elite.

It is the North Coast, including the city of San Pedro Sula, that has been the most dynamic region during the twentieth century. It first attracted the foreign investments that gave rise to the banana industry and more recently has diversified its economic base into manufacturing and processing agricultural products (mainly coffee, meat, sugar, and lumber). The original foreign investments were made in the 1890s, and by 1899 the United Fruit Company (now United Brands) had established its operations. By 1902 bananas represented 53 percent of all Honduran exports. These developments broke the colonial isolation of the nation, whose population had been concentrated in the cooler highlands. Economic opportunities attracted entrepreneurs and workers, and a new source of revenue was created for the state. Though most economic benefits went to the North Coast region, the new revenues did benefit the government and stimulated greater organization of the entire state. The political elites saw their opportunity and facilitated the banana industry by granting favorable concessions on land use, import franchises, and tax exemptions. At the same time an increased dependency on external markets had been created. In 1980 bananas and other fruits still constituted over 30 percent of Honduran export income.

POLITICAL HISTORY TO 1950

The United Provinces of Central America, formed in 1823 in the backwash of the Mexican independence movement, lasted until 1838. A Honduran, Francisco Morazán, was president of the federation from 1830 to 1838, but his dedication to Central American unity was unable to overcome nationalistic rivalries. As the federation broke up, Honduran politics centered on contests among regional caudillos with personal followings who gained power more often than not by force of arms. From 1824 to 1950 the executive in Honduras changed hands over 116 times, with only thirteen leaders serving four or more years in office.

The Liberal-Conservative battles that raged in other Latin American countries were moderated in Honduras. In a sense, the "bucolic" elites conducted political life with less volatility and harshness than in Guatemala or Nicaragua. There were no real political parties until late in the nineteenth century, when the Liberal party (PLH) was first organized under the tutelage of Policarpo Bonilla. The Liberals, though highly factionalized, managed to retain power until 1932. Various political clubs and committees were eventually brought together to form the National party (PNH) in 1916. Among the early *nacionalistas* was Tiburcio Carías

Andino, a self-styled and physically imposing caudillo who, having attracted the favor and support of the United Fruit Company, led his party in the campaigns of 1923 and 1928. In both instances Carías resisted his followers' call to arms in order to reverse their electoral defeats, but in 1932 Liberal disunity and the tenacity of Carías finally brought the Nationals to office with a clear majority vote.

During the next sixteen years, Carías consolidated his power by favoring his supporters as political appointees and by building an extensive party network. Carías was successful in extending his term of office through *continuismo* as the National-dominated legislature created new constitutions and passed amendments allowing Carías to stay in office. Carías was instrumental in introducing basic fiscal controls and establishing a state bureaucracy, but his style of governing, though statesmanlike, brooked little challenge to his authority. He viewed the pre-1932 political chaos as detrimental and justified his *continuismo* as a way to achieve political stability.

Politics until the 1950s was essentially confined to the urban and rural elites, and the rural populace was only peripherally involved, voting Liberal or National in accordance with the loyalties of local landowners and *patrones*. There were few alternative channels of political participation. Most matters were decided within the political parties or through personalistic contacts.

Relative to the rest of Central America, modern political evolution occurred late in Honduras. The era of Carías, though contributing to needed political stability and national institutions, also exacted a price by delaying wider participation and by perpetuating personalistic and authoritarian modes of political control. It was not until after the end of World War II that external and internal factors fully stimulated the processes of modernization in Honduras.

POLITICAL EVOLUTION SINCE 1950

After Carías retired from politics in 1949, a transformation from an elite-dominated system to wider political participation evolved in the wake of an expanding middle class, the organizational success of the working class, and the demands of *campesinos* to be included in the political system. The next two decades saw seven different administrations rise and fall. (For a synopsis of the national executive since 1950, see Table 24.1.)

External factors had a dramatic impact on Honduras during the 1950s and 1960s. Foreign analysts encouraged economic diversification and greater involvement by the state in national planning. Agencies such as the Central Bank, the National Development Bank, the Council of Economic Planning, and later the National Agrarian Institute (INA) and the Ministry of Labor were created in response to demands made by new socioeconomic groups and to facilitate the implementation of de-

Table 24.1 National Executives of Honduras Since 1950

1950–1954	Juan Manuel Gálvez
1954–1956	Julio Lozano Díaz
1956–1957	Military junta
1957–1963	Ramón Villeda Morales
1963–1965	General Oswaldo López Arellano
1965–1971	Oswaldo López Arellano (president)
1971–1972	Ramón Ernesto Cruz
1972–1975	General Oswaldo López Arellano
1975–1978	General Juan Alberto Melgar Castro
1978–1982	General Policarpo Paz García
1982–	Dr. Roberto Suazo Córdova

velopmental programs. Much of the impetus and support for this bureaucratic expansion came from international sources like the World Bank and the Organization of American States and through bilateral aid from the United States.[1] The United States also concluded several agreements to train and equip the loosely organized armed forces of Honduras, and by 1969 over one thousand personnel had taken courses in U.S. facilities.

The successor to Carías, Juan Manuel Gálvez (1950–1954), proved to be less authoritarian than expected, and his broader outlook aided general economic growth and helped set the scene for the arrival of some new political actors. Foreign investments increased and helped to lessen the dependence on banana exports. Industrial expansion continued into the early 1960s, when Honduras joined with its neighbors to form the Central American Common Market (CACM). Intraregional trade rose substantially among the member nations until the trend was interrupted by the 1969 conflict between El Salvador and Honduras.

The Alliance for Progress, launched in 1961, further stimulated Honduran industrial development, which centered around the rapidly growing city of San Pedro Sula. By 1969 nearly 22 percent of the GNP came from industrial production. The demand for agricultural exports and the needs of the expanding urban markets had consequences for the rural society; large landowners began to utilize lands not previously cultivated or those they had formerly leased to sharecroppers. This "enclosure" of lands along with the high birthrate had an evident impact upon the rural sector. The availability of land had never been a real problem for Honduras, but the pressures on the land after 1950 became an important factor in the rise of the Honduran *campesino* movement a decade later.[2]

The increasingly difficult conditions of the countryside also concerned the Catholic Church, whose attention to rural problems had been prodded by the social ferment in Guatemala during the Arbenz regime. The Church's response was an effort to reestablish its roots among the rural parishes by sponsoring literacy programs, community-development activities, and a religious revival movement. The grassroots campaign was timely, as the land enclosures had severed the traditional ties between *campesino* and rural *patrón*. The gradual *concientización* of the rural masses thus enhanced the possibility for new forms of social and political ties.

But political development had not kept pace with economic growth. The period 1954–1957 had been confusing, as the traditional National and Liberal parties became fragmented and the polity was forced to include new social groups. In 1954, over a period of weeks, strikes among banana workers gained national support. The government finally acceded under pressure, granting labor the right to organize. That same year presidential elections failed to produce a clear majority, and Julio Lozano Díaz, vice president under Gálvez, was successful in retaining power until 1956, when he was deposed from office by intervention of the armed forces. The military junta promised new and free elections the following year. The Liberals, long out of power, but now supported by a growing middle class and the newly organized banana-worker unions, won 62 percent of the popular vote for the Constituent Assembly, which proclaimed their 1954 presidential candidate, Ramón Villeda Morales, as president.

Villedismo (1957–1963) was marked by significant legislation in the areas of labor arbitration, social security, and, in 1962, the first comprehensive Agrarian Reform Law. The nationalistic and reformist Villeda Morales was willing to respond to the demands issuing from the labor sector and the mobilizing rural sector. But the Liberal president was caught between the left and the right, and drastic structural reforms were never achieved as he attempted to maintain middle-class support. To counterbalance conservative pressures and a growing sense of independence within the armed forces, Villeda Morales had established a separate Civil Guard. The reaction came just before the scheduled presidential elections and culminated with a second military intervention in 1963, when Col. Oswaldo López Arellano declared himself head of state. Two years later, utilizing the National party political machine, newly promoted Gen. López Arellano became president (1965–1971) via elections characterized by "a brave display of fairness in city elections and high-handed coercion and violence in the rural areas."[3]

The conservative mood of the López Arellano regime was demonstrated by repression of *campesino* activism, neglect of the agrarian-reform program, and coercive action against labor unions participating in a North Coast strike in 1968. Honduras also experienced serious balance-of-trade deficits within the CACM. General economic growth had stagnated, and, for its part, the government failed to expend available funds as called for in a National Development Plan. The 1969 conflict with El Salvador was a further blow to the economy, as Honduras lost one of its major export markets. However, the soccer war (see Chapter 22 on El Salvador) did provide an opportunity for Honduras to withdraw from the CACM. But it also helped to focus attention on rural conditions. The *campesinos* had established an essential "loyalty" to the nation during the conflict, and some military leaders finally perceived that the problem of land availability represented a potential threat to the nation.

The critical nature of such economic and social obstacles to development raised the specter of renewed political violence as the 1971 presidential elections approached. The National and Liberal parties hoped to retain control of the government, but they had yet to propose any comprehensive or viable solution to Honduran national problems. At the same time there was widespread opposition to López Arellano's desire to extend his term of office. The impending political crisis was resolved late in 1970 by a political agreement—the Plan Político de Unidad Nacional. The Pacto, as it came to be called, was proposed to the National and Liberal parties by leaders of some labor, *campesino*, and business groups, and by President López Arellano with support from the armed forces. The Nationals and Liberals reluctantly agreed to the Pacto, which committed the future government to internal reforms and effective action on social and economic programs. The National party won the 1971 elections, contrary to general expectations, which assured it a one-vote congressional majority in accordance with the Pacto.[4]

The political agreement eventually failed, however, as Nationals and President Ramón Ernesto Cruz ignored the policy content of the Pacto and even acted against popular-sector participation. General López Arellano, interest-group leaders, and political party delegations met in mid-1972 in an attempt to revitalize the Pacto, but to no avail. After eighteen months, the experiment ended as the general once again occupied the presidential palace.

The return of the military as governors in December 1972 was achieved with popular-sector support, and the demise of the Pacto regime represented a loss of legitimacy for the traditional political elites, whose dominance was now challenged by organized labor, the restless *campesino* movement, and a growing impatience within the armed forces. López Arellano had recognized this tentative shift in his power base, and he sought to consolidate his position by issuing Decreto 8, which made some private lands available to *campesinos* for a period of two years. This temporary measure was superseded in 1975 by a new Agrarian Reform Law.

Despite the apparent concessions to the *campesino* sector, López Arellano, facing increasing resistance from large landowners and the private sector, never acted forcefully on agrarian reform. Moreover, the general's position within the military was threatened in 1975 when junior officers forced the retirement of forty senior officers. In an effort to stem the erosion of his power base, López Arellano had expanded participation in the command structure with the formation of the Superior Council of the Armed Forces (CONSUFFAA). But conditions deteriorated as the general and members of his cabinet were implicated in the United Brands bribery scandal.[5] Pent-up discontent among *campesinos,* concern within the ranks of the military, and the refusal of López Arellano to cooperate with an investigation led to his removal from office. Col. Juan Alberto Melgar Castro assumed the position of head of state in April 1975, much to the relief of the conservative elements in Honduras.

The question was whether the reformist trend would survive or whether the conservative forces would be able to regain the initiative. The new military leader responded unevenly. Though Melgar Castro expropriated lands from United Brands and other private landowners, he also removed the aggressive director of the INA and jailed several *campesino* leaders in the wake of a series of coordinated land invasions.

Later, in March 1976, Melgar Castro proposed that all sectors should participate in a National Advisory Council (CONASE) to help prepare for elections in 1980. Delegates from labor, *campesino* groups, the Innovation and Unity (PINU) and Christian Democratic (PDCH) parties, and representatives of the armed forces and government participated in the council's deliberations. Conservatives within the Honduran Council of Private Enteprise and the traditional parties refused to participate. Rather, they constantly pressured the head of state for a return to "constitutional order."

In 1978, disputes arose among military officers over issues of new cabinet appointments and military assignments. Published newspaper stories alluded to military involvement in corruption and drug trafficking. Melgar Castro never challenged those allegations; in part, his failure to do so undermined whatever support he had left within CONSUFFAA. Forced to resign in early August, Melgar Castro was replaced by a military triumvirate led by Gen. Policarpo Paz García. The new administration dissolved CONASE, although it did confirm its support for elections and a return to constitutional rule.

This third phase of direct military rule curtailed any further momentum toward popular reforms. Social peace, political order, and consolidation over the expanded state bureaucracy marked a return to conservative policies. The activities of decentralized state agencies and enterprises were coordinated for a time through Regional Development Councils, each headed by respective military zone commanders. State-led development policies meshed with heightened national-security concerns. The Nicaraguan Revolution in 1979, the deteriorating situation in El Salvador, and the steady stream of refugees challenged the sanctity of what some Hondurans viewed as their "oasis of peace." Even so, amid the spreading regional crisis, Honduras prepared for Constituent Assembly elections and the return to a civilian-led government.

Suspicions were prevalent that the elections would favor the National party (PNH). The PINU had gained its legal inscription after a ten-year struggle; however, the PDCH was denied official status. Voter wariness persisted until General Paz García declared to the nation that elections would be open and honest and that no military leader sought the presidency. On April 20, 1980, more than 1 million Hondurans went to the polls, giving the PLH over half the vote.

During the next eighteen months, against the background of regional conflict and a declining national economy, Honduran attentions focused upon new political campaigns. General Paz García remained as provisional president; Liberal party leader Roberto Suazo Córdova was confirmed as president of the Constituent Assembly, which drew up a new constitution, revised the electoral law, and prepared for national and local elections set for November 1981. The National party's presidential candidate, Ricardo Zúñiga, promised voters he would continue the policies of the previous Nationalist administration (1965–1971). Despite intraparty factionalism, Suazo Córdova was able to maintain the Liberals' conservative wing intact. The Christian Democrats, now legally established, argued for basic social and economic transformations. PINU candidates campaigned for honest and efficient government and called for a national dialogue. The militant left decided to participate and to present alternatives to the nation by nominating independent candidates in three departments.

More than 1.2 million voters turned out. With 53 percent of the popular vote, the Liberal party gained firm control of the eighty-two-seat National Congress. PINU maintained its small political base of urban, middle-class supporters while the Christian Democrats' first electoral outing attracted less than 2 percent of the total vote. Independent candidates representing the radical left recorded scarcely less than 1 percent of the popular vote. Significantly, the traditional parties of Honduras, though functioning with outmoded principles and stained reputations and faced with genuine third-party opposition in open elections, together captured almost 93 percent of the popular vote.

In two successive elections, the Honduran public demonstrated its desire to participate in the selection of its political leaders. Disenchanted with military government and with public-sector corruption, Hondurans, with a high degree of civic pride, returned the government to civilian hands. No less important, the electoral results had provided the PLH an absolute majority both in popular votes and in deputies within the National Congress.

The inaugural ceremonies of January 1982 installed Dr. Roberto Suazo Córdova as president, along with three presidential designates (vice presidents), members of the Supreme Court of Justice, and the new head of the armed forces, Col. Gustavo Alvarez Martínez (soon to be promoted to general). The president proclaimed an administration of "revolution, work, and honesty." He indicated that all sectors would participate, alluded to the regional crisis, and urged the international community to recognize Central America as a zone of peace. The new government, however, was faced with serious economic decisions. Budgetary deficits, a mounting external debt, reduced investment levels, capital flight, and rising unemployment all dictated policies that would conflict with popular expectations.

SOCIOPOLITICAL GROUPS

In the evolution from Carías's praetorian rule, through the decade of military governors to the return to constitutional democracy, authoritarian principles of governance were retained. Nonetheless, fundamental socioeconomic changes and the impact of modernizing factors left the Honduran political system in a fluid state. Military rule during the 1970s rested with uncertainty upon political bases characterized by shifting balances of power among older and newer political groups.

The proliferation of organized groups among labor, *campesino*, agribusiness, and commercial sectors created channels of political participation and articulation outside those long maintained within the discredited National and Liberal parties. The organization of the Honduran labor movement, numbering around twenty-five thousand workers, followed the successful 1954 strike. The Honduran Workers' Confederation (CTH), established in 1964, encompasses two labor federations— FESITRANH (the Labor Federation of National Workers of Honduras) and FECESITLIH (Central Federation of Free Worker Unions of Honduras)—and a *campesino* affiliate, the National Association of Honduran Peasants (ANACH). The strength of the CTH rests among the banana-worker unions, and since its inception it has had the support of the U.S.-supported ORIT (Inter-American Regional Organization of Workers). The CTH has maintained close relations with most Honduran governments.

The smaller and rival General Central of Workers (CGT), formed in 1970, combines several labor federations along with a highly active *campesino* organization. The CGT is inspired by social-Christian philosophy, has ties with the PDCH, and perceives the organizations of the CTH and most Honduran governments as "excessively dependent," especially upon the influence of the United States. The CGT's political fortunes have thereby suffered in relation to those of its CTH rival.

The split within the labor movement is also reflected between the major *campesino* organizations. ANACH was legally organized in 1961 and is the largest *campesino* group, claiming about eighty thousand members. It became affiliated with FESITRANH in 1967, and much of its organizational influence is derived from the alliance within the CTH.

The National Union of Peasants (UNC), finally organized in 1964, though lacking the advantages of legal recognition and counting only an estimated twenty thousand members, competes effectively with the ANACH for membership and political influence. The UNC, in fact, is the principal strength of the CGT, although the confederation has suffered internal disagreements between *campesino* and labor leaders over agrarian reform policy.[6]

In 1975 the *campesino* groups were able to overcome their differences temporarily. The immediate cause was General Melgar Castro's repressive actions, but the *campesino* leadership also concluded that more sectoral unity was necessary to stimulate effective land distribution. Since 1979, most *campesino* groups have supported the National Unity Front of Honduran Peasants (FUNACAMPH). It is questionable whether the unity front can meld *campesinos* into a cohesive political force. Besides ideological differences and perspectives, conservative interests and official policy tend to exacerbate divisions within the labor and *campesino* sectors.

Diversification of the economy during the 1960s stimulated private-sector organization beyond the well-established Tegucigalpa Chamber of Commerce (CCIT), first organized in 1918. In response to the growing needs of the expanding business community in San Pedro Sula, the Cortés Chamber of Commerce (CCIC) was formed in 1957, and the following year the National Association of Industrialists (ANDI), headquartered in Tegucigalpa, was created to represent manufacturing interests. Partly in reaction to the rise in *campesino* activity, a national landowners' association, the National Federation of Honduran Agriculturalists and Stockraisers (FENAGH), was chartered in 1966.

As the governmental role in economic policy planning expanded, and along with creation of the CACM, it became imperative for the business community to promote its interests in a more unified manner, but this function was not being served adequately by the Tegucigalpa Chamber of Commerce. Initiatives by business leaders on the North Coast were made to establish an association to represent general business interests and help overcome some of the rivalries within the private sector. Since its founding in 1967, the Honduran Council of Private Enterprise (COHEP) has emerged as a conservative forum articulating opposition to extensive agrarian reform and seeking greater influence over national economic policy. Though COHEP represents organizational unity, private-sector political differences remain, as ties to traditional politics tend to be closer in Tegucigalpa while the business community in San Pedro Sula reflects a more independent attitude.

FORMAL STRUCTURE OF THE POLITY

The Constitution of 1982 provides for a formal division of authority among a president, a unicameral National Congress with eighty-two *diputados*, and a Supreme Court of Justice elected by the congress, all with four-year terms. The presidential appointment of the cabinet, or Council of State, and of all eighteen departmental governors and control over most municipal financial resources connote a system that is highly executive centered. Moreover, except during the Liberal period 1957–1963, and at times during the Pacto regime, the congress has been dominated by the president, and, under the military governors, the legislature was disbanded.

The state's involvement in social services and economic planning has stimulated governmental centralization and resulted in an expanded bureaucracy. It is this bureaucracy, as well as the chief executive, that commands the attention of organized interest groups. Most groups have formed agency-clientele relations; for example, the *campesino* groups support the INA and agrarian-reform efforts, while the labor organizations are regulated by the Ministry of Labor.

Policymaking has also become more centralized, a tendency that originated during the reign of Carías, continued under the military governors, and persisted under the adminstration of Suazo Córdova. The president determines most policy in conjunction with the Council of State, but the head of state is not immune to pressures from organized interest groups. The effect is to focus interest articulation toward the higher levels of policymaking, that is, the chief executive and/or the ministries. Nevertheless, policy shifts often reflect coalitional changes among (1) sectoral organizations, (2) factional struggles within the military, and (3) the fortunes of the traditional political parties.

Political succession has depended more upon the traditional patterns of authority, the impact of evolving sectoral groups, and—since 1963—direct intervention of the military. With few exceptions (1957, 1980, and 1981), Honduran elections have not succinctly represented the popular will. Historically, elections have been excessively manipulated and often accompanied with violence. A national election council (the Tribunal Nacional de Elecciones—TNE), appointed by the president and composed of representatives from each legally recognized political party, has had a checkered past. It has been disbanded from time to time, and its records disappeared after the 1963 *golpe*. In addition, both the National and Liberal parties in the past have protected their electoral dominance with stringent regulations that made it difficult for new political movements to gain a foothold and compete in national elections.

By 1981, two new parties—PINU and PDCH—had been legally recognized and were able to participate in free and open national elections. Despite the challenge, more than 90 percent of the electorate maintained its support of the Liberal and National parties. Analysis of the 1971, 1980, and 1981 electoral returns indicates that most Liberal party support is drawn from urban areas while the National party maintains its rural bases.[7]

In 1983, due to bureaucratic delays and concern over the validity of revised electoral lists, the political parties agreed to postpone midterm municipal elections. All political parties and most sectoral interest groups were maneuvering for position and gauging their prospects for the 1985 elections.

POLITICAL INTEGRATION, REGIONAL CRISIS, AND DEVELOPMENT

The political transformation of Honduras has been characterized by a combination of political decay, emergence, and adaptation. The older, more traditional elements within the National and Liberal parties declined, as they failed to respond to the increased level of demands or to innovate policy in the face of multiple developmental problems.

Nevertheless, the elections of 1980 and 1981 demonstrated that the traditional political parties, despite their staleness, had retained a basic loyalty among the Honduran electorate. The conservatives were able to reformulate linkages with the armed forces. The Association for the Progress of Honduras (APROH), formally recognized in early 1983, included leaders from the political parties, labor federations, the business sector, and government officials. APROH's president was the Honduran head of the armed forces, Gen. Gustavo Alvarez Martínez; and a leading businessman and informal presidential adviser, Miguel Facusse, at one time served as vice president. APROH's objectives were to attract resources that would be invested in Honduras and to win the civic battle against extremism. Critics, including the Catholic Church, were skeptical of the group's early connections with CAUSA International, a branch of the Unity Church (Moonies). APROH's president eventually returned to CAUSA a donation of fifty thousand dollars.[8]

The emergence of new sociopolitical forces was reflected in the proliferation of organized groups, especially among the labor and *campesino* movements. They also served as alternative channels of political access outside the traditional framework of the parties. Despite higher levels of politicization, the new sectors have yet to consolidate political influence beyond an occasional policy concession. Though successful in forcing the 1971–1972 Pacto upon the political parties and though important beneficiaries of the 1972 *golpe*, labor, *campesino*, and other groups experienced internal conflict and suffered setbacks after 1975.

The rate of land distribution dropped sharply until 1982 when the trend was reversed. Teacher organizations, striking over pay and working conditions in 1982, lost the confrontation with the Suazo government. Later, some teacher groups were "intervened," with more amenable officers replacing militant leaders. Critics emphasized that the Liberal government in conjunction with the armed forces was effecting a demobilization of the popular sectors; they pointed to the appearance of human-rights abuses, disappearances, and unexplained deaths of specific leaders.

The military had been drawn into politics as governors, in part by the vacuum of power created by the decay of the old forces and also by heightened concern over the developmental and security problems confronting the Honduran nation. But the military, beset by its own internal factions and limited in its administrative capacities, found itself occupying an unstable point of equilibrium between conservative stand-pattism and demands for basic reforms. By the early 1980s, the reformist elements within the armed forces had been outmaneuvered, and the civilian conservatives had regained their composure, anticipating the return to "constitutional rule."

The Sandinista victory in 1979 and the escalation of civil conflict in El Salvador raised national-security concerns among Honduran military leaders. Aside from the social and economic pressures upon the state and the challenge of integrating the emergent popular sectors, the growing Central American conflict now threatened the Honduran attempt to reestablish democratic institutions and processes.

CIVIL-MILITARY POLITICS AND DEMOCRACY

Two decades after the 1963 military coup that exiled Liberal President Ramón Villeda Morales, the Liberal party under Suazo Córdova returned to power tacitly allied with the military. In an apparent concession to political reality, Suazo Córdova had established positive relations between the Liberals and the now politically dominant armed forces.[9] Shortly after taking office, Col. Gustavo Alvarez Martínez was promoted to brigadier general. Further command changes strengthened Alvarez's control and diluted the "collegial" authority previously exercised by CONSUFFAA. The close relationship between the new president and the head of the armed forces reflected a dramatic shift among the traditional parties and the military institution. Based on its undeniable electoral victories, the PLH had replaced the PNH in the civil-military regime that had evolved since the late 1950s. General Alvarez publicly supported a subordinate role of the armed forces; in return, the president wasted few opportunities to praise the military for its protection of constitutional rule and its defense of Honduran democracy.

The Suazo government faced immense problems of national development, now exacerbated by an economic decline and severe external pressures. The cabinet included many technocrats, and the administration was staffed and being advised by those private-sector elements generally referred to as the Facusse group. Stringent economic measures were required to counter the effects of decapitalization, lowered national income, budgetary deficits, widespread business failures, and rising unemployment. In addition, an attempt was made to recentralize control over the diverse array of semiautonomous agencies created during the 1970s, many of which had failed to fulfill their intended functions and, in some cases, had accumulated international debts eventually assumed by the state.

Tensions in Honduras were heightened by a series of kidnappings, robberies, bombings, and disappearances and by a dramatic hostage incident that took place in San Pedro Sula in 1982. The government responded with increased security measures in an effort to eradicate acts of subversion that were supported by the FMLN of El Salvador and the FSLN of Nicaragua. Both phenomena—subversive activities and government repression—were new for most Hondurans. Inevitably, the governmental actions precipitated claims of human-rights violations.

The perceived threats to Honduran domestic peace and national security effectively drew the United States and Honduras closer together. From 1980 to 1984, U.S. military aid increased tenfold. Airfields were upgraded, seaport facilities were expanded, and a series of joint military exercises was conducted. The ostensible purpose of the exercises was to enhance the defensive capability of the Honduran armed forces, although critics claimed that the United States was "using" the Hondurans and Honduran territory strategically to undermine the Sandinista government of Nicaragua.[10] The political costs of such close cooperation were questioned by dissident Liberals and opponents of the Suazo administration. The establishment near Puerto Castilla on the North Coast of a Regional Military Training Center, to train Honduran troops and troops from other countries of the region, was debated and approved by the National Congress. But this occurred only after the first contingent of U.S. military instructors had arrived.

The Liberal government faced difficult problems, none of which could be resolved immediately. Some, such as the state of the economy and the threat to national security, were long-term issues requiring Honduran patience and international aid. Another persistent pattern has been the inability of the traditional Liberal and National political parties to revitalize their organizational structures and to inculcate a sense of vitality among their rank and file. Despite the high turnouts in 1980 and 1981, the parties have failed to capitalize upon the desire of the citizenry to participate more fully in the political process. Throughout the early 1980s a crisis of generational transition has racked both parties. Old caudillo-style politicians have been reluctant to share power, and aspirant leaders have grown increasingly frustrated. The internal struggles of the parties will no doubt reach their peak prior to the late 1985 elections for president, a congress, and local governments.

The PLH's officially recognized left wing—the Popular Liberal Alliance (ALIPO)—itself was split into two factions. One, led by a coterie of San Pedro Sula businessmen, was granted official status by the PLH leadership; the marginalized faction was composed primarily of those who followed the brothers Carlos Roberto and Jorge Arturo Reina. This latter faction became the Liberal Revolutionary Democratic Movement of Honduras (M-LIDER) early in 1984. President Suazo Córdova's control over the PLH was also challenged by José Azcona de Hoyo, former minister and former head of the party, who campaigned in order to become the Liberal party's presidential candidate in 1985.

The situation within the PNH was similar in that the internal struggle was between old and new leadership. Following two electoral defeats, there were demands to renovate the party's grass roots and to broaden its appeal to the Honduran electorate. The official faction led by Ricardo Zúñiga was challenged by the Movement for Unity and Change (MUC). Former head of state and retired general Juan Alberto Melgar Castro rallied his "independent" followers in support of a bid to become the party's leader. The factional squabbles intensified until February 1984, when a "backroom" slate of candidates for the party's leadership was presented to the Nationalist convention. Zúñiga, Melgar Castro, and Mario Rivera López were among the officers elected by the convention delegates. The essential questions of internal party democracy had been bypassed; the party unity that had been achieved, so necessary in order to effectively oppose the Liberals, was uncertain and tenuous.

Beyond the internal party struggles, political leaders sought to construct broader power bases. For the most part, this involved the calculated risk of soliciting the support of the nation's armed forces. Both Liberal and National party leaders pursued this course. Suazo Córdova had cemented his personal ties with General Alvarez Martínez; and Liberal-military relations were readily apparent under the auspices of the "establishment" APROH organization. On the other hand, political observers noted the efforts of some Nationalists to ingratiate themselves with high-ranking military officers, with the implication that the National party might entertain a military candidate as head of state. This pattern of civil-military relations was not unusual—it had evolved over a period of three decades. The regional crisis of Central America, coming after ten years of direct military rule in Honduras, undergirded the military's role in national policy, especially in matters of national security. U.S. military assistance enhanced this aspect and, at the same time, also helped to maintain the independent central institutional role of the armed forces in national politics. The Honduran military and the political elites grouped around the traditional political parties have been able to interact, engage in dialogue, and form alliances. This factor allowed the political system a degree of flexibility during the 1970s and early 1980s. But the spreading conflict in Central America introduced new burdens to Hondurans and accelerated the forces of social, economic, and political stress. The questions with which Honduras was left were how the country would adapt to those pressures and whether the civil-military regime would evolve toward more authoritarian or more democratic patterns in the process.

Most Hondurans welcome the prospect of elections in 1985, looking back with pride upon their electoral successes in 1980 and 1981. The flurry of political organizing among the political parties indicated that elections were expected. Nevertheless, it was in 1932, when Tiburcio Carías Andino was first elected, that political succession last followed "normal" constitutional electoral procedures. For a new Honduran president to be inaugurated in early 1986 would represent a significant departure from the pattern that has prevailed for more than a half century.

FUTURE PROSPECTS

Contemporary Honduran politics is less simple than during the era of Carías, and any resolution of the political questions raised will have to be based upon the new Honduran realities. Although the older structures of power remain, they function less effectively than in the past. Political integration requires that some provisions eventually be made that will involve new groups and new leaders in policy decisions, yet personalism, authoritarian attitudes, and hierarchical institutions persist. The Honduran polity is thus faced with the dilemma of adapting to expanded participation and at the same time deriving the capacity to fulfill innumerable demands for material development.

Another factor is the country's dependency on transnational economic power and the hegemony of the United States. These influences have stimulated modernization processes and acted as a restraint on the pace and breadth of Honduran development. Some apparent weakening of dependent relations has involved efforts by the state to gain greater control over Honduran resources. But even though the quality of the dependency can change, the Honduran economy and polity remain highly influenced by external factors.

The timing, lateness, and compression of Honduran modernization and concurrent political decay since 1950 have not been dominated by any specific political pattern. Institutionalization of the state has been interspersed with periods of discontinuity and repression, wider sectoral differentiation, and higher levels of political mobilization. The elections of 1980 and 1981 demonstrated that Hondurans support democratic processes, however imperfectly constituted. But given the state of political tensions produced by internal and external conditions, Honduran democratic institutions will be buffeted by the winds of both regional and domestic conflict. Without deeper roots, those institutions are unlikely to survive as Hondurans confront the obstacles to development and challenges to the polity.

NOTES

1. Robert A. White, "Structural Factors in Rural Development: The Church and Peasant in Honduras," Ph.D. dissertation, Cornell University, Ithaca, N.Y., 1977, chap. 4.

2. See J. Mark Ruhl, "Agrarian Structure and Political Stability in Honduras," *Journal of Inter-American Studies and World Affairs* 26, no. 1 (February 1984):33–68.

3. Hubert Herring, *A History of Latin America*, 3d ed. (Knopf, New York, 1968), p. 482.

4. James A. Morris, *The Honduran Plan Político de Unidad Nacional, 1971–1972: Its Origins and Demise*, Occasional Paper, Center for Inter-American Studies, University of Texas at El Paso, El Paso, February 1975.

5. United Brands chairman Eli M. Black committed suicide in 1975. That event led to disclosures that an initial payment of $1.25 million had been made to certain Honduran officials to ensure that a newly created export tax on bananas would be reduced. See the *Wall Street Journal*, April 9, 11, and 14, 1975.

6. In 1968 the Honduran Federation of Agrarian Reform Cooperatives (FECORAH) brought together several producer cooperatives. Though smaller than either ANACH or the UNC, FECORAH is a cohesive organization and constitutes a significant and independent force within the *campesino* movement

7. See James D. Rudolph, ed., *Honduras: A Country Study* (U.S. Government Printing Office, Washington, D.C., 1984), chap. 4.

8. *El Heraldo* (Tegucigalpa), October 4, 1983.

9. Mark B. Rosenberg, "Honduran Scorecard: Military and Democrats in Central America," *Caribbean Review* 12, no. 1 (Winter 1983):12–15, 40–42.

10. E.g., see Juan Ramón Martínez, "Una preliminar evaluación de las maniobras militares," *La Tribuna* (Tegucigalpa), February 16, 1984.

SUGGESTIONS FOR FURTHER READING

Anderson, Thomas P. *Politics in Central America: Guatemala, El Salvador, Honduras, and Nicaragua.* Part 3. Praeger, New York, 1982.

Blutstein, Howard I., et al. *Area Handbook for Honduras.* American University, Washington, D.C., 1971.

Durham, William H. *Scarcity and Survival in Central America: Ecological Origins of the Soccer War.* Stanford University Press, Stanford, Calif., 1979.

Fernández, Arturo. *Partidos políticos y elecciones en Honduras, 1980.* Editorial Guaymuras, Tegucigalpa, D.C., 1981.

Leiva Vivas, Rafael. *Un país en Honduras.* Imprenta Calderón, Tegucigalpa, D.C., 1969.

Meza, Víctor. *Historia del movimiento obrero hondureño.* Editorial Guaymuras, Tegucigalpa, D.C., 1980.

_____ . *Política y sociedad en Honduras.* Editorial Guaymuras, Tegucigalpa, D.C., 1981.

Molina Chocano, Guillermo. "Dependencia y cambio social en la sociedad hondureña." *Estudios sociales centroamericanos* 1, no. 1 (January-April 1972):11–26.

_____ . "Posibilidades y perspectivas del proceso de democratización en Honduras." *Nueva sociedad*, no. 48 (May-June 1980):79ff.

Morris, James A. "Honduras: The Burden of Survival in Central America." In *Central America: Crisis and Adaptation*, edited by Steve C. Ropp and James A. Morris. University of New Mexico Press, Albuquerque, 1984, pp. 189–225.

_____ . *Honduras: Caudillo Politics and Military Rulers.* Westview Press, Boulder, Colo., 1984.

Morris, James A., and Steve C. Ropp. "Corporatism and Dependent Development: A Honduran Case Study." *Latin American Research Review* 12, no. 2 (Summer 1977):27–68.

Pearson, Neale J. "Peasant Pressure Groups and Agrarian Reform in Honduras, 1962–1977." In *Rural Change and Public Policy: Eastern Europe, Latin America, and Australia,* edited by William P. Avery et al. Pergamon Press, New York, 1980, pp. 297–320.

Posas A., Mario. "Política estatal y estructura agraria en Honduras (1950–1978)." *Estudios sociales centroamericanos* 8, no. 24 (September-December 1980):37–116.

Posas A., Mario, and Rafael del Cid. *La construcción del sector público y del estado nacional de Honduras, 1876–1979.* EDUCA, San José, 1981.

Ropp, Steve C. "The Honduran Army in the Sociopolitical Evolution of the Honduran State." *The Americas* 30, no. 4 (April 1974):504–528.

Rosenberg, Mark B. "Honduran Scorecard: Military and Democrats in Central America." *Caribbean Review* 12, no. 1 (Winter 1983):12–15, 40–42.

———. "Honduras: Bastion of Stability or Quagmire?" In *Revolution and Counterrevolution in Central America and the Caribbean,* edited by Donald E. Schulz and Douglas H. Graham. Westview Press, Boulder, Colo., pp. 331–350.

Salamon, Leticia. *Militarismo y reformiso en Honduras.* Editorial Guaymuras, Tegucigalpa, D.C., 1982.

Stokes, William S. *Honduras: An Area Study in Government.* University of Wisconsin Press, Madison, 1950.

25
The Dominican Republic: The Politics of a Frustrated Revolution, II

HOWARD J. WIARDA

The Dominican Republic's history of colonial neglect, wrenching poverty, dictatorship, and dependency is one of the sorriest in all of Latin America. The wheel seemed to be turning when in 1961 Rafael Leonidas Trujillo, one of the bloodiest tyrants ever to come to power in the hemisphere, was killed and his dictatorship dismantled. Elections were held, and in 1963 the country's first democratic government, led by Juan Bosch, took over. But Bosch was opposed by a coalition of reactionary clerics, army officers, and oligarchs; his position was undermined in the United States; and he was overthrown. As the pro-Bosch forces launched an attempt in 1965 to restore constitutional rule, the United States sent in twenty-five thousand marines and paratroopers to quash a democratic rebellion that the United States in its panic thought was under Castro-Communist dominance.

The Dominican invasion served as the prelude to the larger U.S. involvement in Southeast Asia. The Dominican intervention, in which the United States crushed a democratically oriented revolution in the name of fighting communism, gave rise to a credibility gap, helped ruin Lyndon Johnson, and signaled the end of the earlier democratic goals of the Kennedy presidency and the Alliance for Progress. It also helped ruin the Dominican Republic. Not only did the invasion crush the democratic forces and thwart the natural processes of Dominican development, it brought back to power the corrupt and reactionary military officers, oligarchs, and nouveaux riches. By now the Dominican Republic has begun to recover from the intervention and has made considerable economic and political strides with the succession of two democratic governments. But memories are long, and the U.S. intervention is not forgotten.

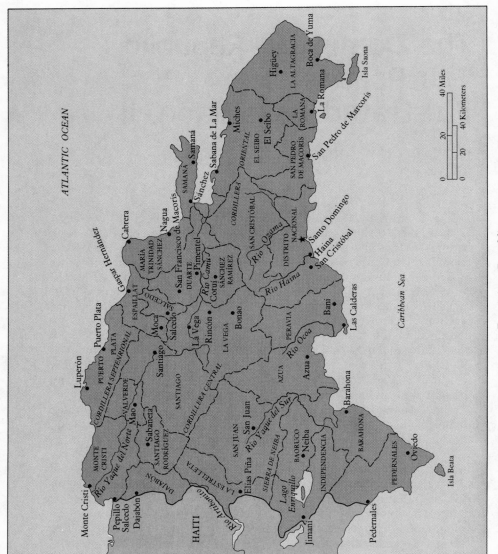

Dominican Republic

BACKGROUND AND POLITICAL CULTURE

The Dominican Republic, up until recently, was one of the poorest and least developed of the Latin American nations. Sharing the island of Hispaniola with impoverished Haiti, it also shared with Haiti a certain "politics of squalor."[1] Its per capita income is about US$1,200 per year, terribly unevenly distributed. Its population remains 50 percent illiterate. Much of the population lives outside the money economy in a pattern of meager subsistence, wretchedly poor, diseased, ill housed, and ill fed. Particularly as one gets closer to the Haitian border, the conditions and culture of poverty seem almost unbelievable.

There are few traces of the island's native Indian population, who were almost completely eliminated by Spanish arms, forced labor, and the diseases brought by the Spaniards, against which the Indians had no immunity. To replace the Indians, the Spanish imported African slaves; henceforth, race and social relations were defined by interaction between African and European rather than Indian and European. Race and class are reinforcing determinants of Dominican social hierarchy: The elite tends to be white, the middle class is usually light mulatto, and the lower classes dark mulatto and black. The best estimates say that 10–15 percent of the population (of over 5 million) is white, 30 percent is black, and the remaining 55–60 percent is mulatto. Although politics and social issues are generally discussed in class terms, and although the country has remained free of racial antagonisms, race is still the great undiscussed issue of Dominican national life.

The Dominican economy is heavily dependent, like neighboring Cuba's, on the export of sugar, and fluctuations in the world market price of sugar or changes in the import quotas given the country by the United States have made and unmade Dominican governments for decades. The country is not rich in mineral resources, although it exports bauxite, manganese, nickel, gold, mercury, and small amounts of other minerals. Its chief resource is an abundance of arable land. Sugarcane is the main crop, but rice, beans, cotton, cacao, tobacco, peanuts, fruits, tomatoes, and beef are also grown or raised for export. Commerce and industry have increased in recent decades: The country is largely self-sufficient in smaller manufactured goods (textiles, shoes, plastics, building materials) and even exports some; it imports cars, appliances, machinery, and oil. The biggest industries, including the critical sugar industry, have been state owned since the government took over the former Trujillo properties after the dictator was assassinated.

The Dominican Republic is surrounded on three sides by water and has made considerable efforts to develop its tourist industry. Its topography is characterized by steep mountain ranges alternating with lush tropical valleys; a broad plain in the east is devoted principally to grazing and sugarcane. The mountains have historically helped preserve regionalism and hindered national integration, although there is now a first-class road system reaching out from the capital city of Santo Domingo on the south coast to the west, north, and east.

The Dominican Republic has a strategic importance out of proportion to its population, size (that of Vermont and New Hampshire combined), and meager natural resources. Hispaniola lies close to Cuba and Puerto Rico and astride all the major trade routes from Europe and the east coast of North America into the Caribbean and the Panama Canal. Historically it has been buffeted about in international crosswinds and battered, manipulated, and occupied by the major powers, of which its large North American neighbor is only the most recent. In this way, a famous quote, variously attributed to a Cuban, Dominican, and Mexican president, applies: "Poor Dominican Republic—so far from God [in terms of its natural resources] and so close to the United States."

THE PATTERN OF DEVELOPMENT: HISTORY TO 1930

The institutional vacuum, lack of development, and dependency that lie at the root of Dominican national frustrations and help produce both repeated revolutionary upheavals and foreign interventions have their origins in the nation's history. The Dominican Republic (or Hispaniola, as the entire island was called in earlier days) was the scene of many New World firsts. It was discovered by Columbus on his first voyage. Santo Domingo, the capital, was the first permanent settlement in the Americas. The first hospital, monastery, and university in the Americas were located here. Santo Domingo was where Spain's first social experiments in the Americas were attempted. The large estate or hacienda was first institutionalized on the island.

The Church served as an agency of conquest, buttressing the civil authority and enforcing religious orthodoxy and scholastic learning. Society was rigidly hierarchical, based on both class and caste considerations. The economic pattern was mercantilist, with the wealth of the colony drained off to Spain or to benefit a small elite. The political authority was hierarchical and absolutist, with power emanating from the king to his local captain-general in Santo Domingo to the local landlords or *patrones*. There was no sense of equality or experience with democratic self-government.

Hispaniola flourished during the first fifty years following the Spanish conquest, but then a centuries-long decline set in. The richer areas of Cuba, Mexico, and Peru lured the most enterprising colonists away. The island's gold and silver were soon depleted and the Indian labor supply decimated. As the population declined, the plantations and mines stopped functioning. Santo Domingo became a bedraggled way station in the Spanish colonial empire. Its military garrison was depleted, and the colony was shelled and occasionally occupied by a succession of Dutch,

British, and French buccaneers. The economy reverted to a more primitive subsistence type and social institutions were in disarray. Although it experienced a brief resurgence in the eighteenth century when cattle raising and trade were revived, the once-proud and premier colony was characterized by woeful poverty and neglect.

It is from this era, however, that the basic drives of Dominican development policy derive. The aim of virtually every government has been to restore the island to its former glory—to revive its industry and trade, populate its empty areas, fill the organizational vacuum, restore society, reassert the island's Hispanic traditions, bring order out of chaos, and recapture international respect. Few Dominican governments have been successful in these quests, although sadly it has often been the authoritarian regimes rather than the democratic ones that have accomplished most.

In the eighteenth century, as Spain's power declined, the French established a rich sugar plantation colony based on slave labor at the western end of Hispaniola. In 1795 the slaves rebelled, and early in the next century Haitian blacks invaded the Spanish colony in the eastern two-thirds of the island, terrorizing the white ruling class. By 1809, however, the Haitians were repelled and Santo Domingo continued as a Spanish colony. In 1821, as a reflection of independence movements throughout Latin America, the Dominicans declared their independence from Spain. But within months the Haitians again overran the entire island, and from 1822 to 1844 the Dominican Republic was occupied by neighboring Haiti.

The Haitian occupation was probably not as cruel as portrayed by most (predominantly white) Dominican historians. Although the Haitians did free the slaves in the former Spanish colony, they also destroyed cattle ranches, disrupted recently revived trade, and drove out many of the white Hispanic ruling elites. These events served to reinforce the historical drives of Dominican development policy and introduced some new ones: spurring population increase to offset Haiti's greater numbers; emphasizing the Dominican Republic's Western and Hispanic traditions in contrast to Haiti's presumed African ones; whitening the Dominican population to stress the differences with the black republic; becoming strong economically, politically, and militarily to check Haitian incursions; and searching for a foreign protector to prevent future Haitian occupations.

Taking advantage of internal divisions in Haiti, the Dominicans were able to reassert their independence in 1844. During the first thirty years of independent life, the new nation was torn by frequent political upheavals. There was little progress. The Dominicans approached various nations with the idea of establishing a protectorate over the country, and from 1861 to 1865 the Dominican Republic was reunited with its former colonial master, Spain.

Beginning in the 1870s, trade increased and some economic progress occurred. During the 1880s and 1890s, under the order-and-progress regime of Ulises Heureaux, these trends were accelerated. Although Heureaux's rule was tyrannous, he presided over a period of economic takeoff. Business and commerce expanded, and new areas were opened to agriculture. Foreign capital flowed in, and in the 1890s the United States, replacing Britain, became the nation's chief foreign investor. Immigration was stimulated, and the population grew. Roads were improved, docks built, communications and trade facilitated. The army and the civil administration were centralized and modernized. Under authoritarian and elitist auspices, the Dominican Republic began to develop.

Following Heureaux's assassination in 1899, political instability returned, but the elite-directed economic growth continued. The period 1899–1930, interrupted by an eight-year period of U.S. Marines occupation (1916–1924), was a heyday of oligarchic rule. More fields were brought into sugarcane production, and coffee and cacao developed as major export crops. A new business elite grew up alongside (and frequently intermarried with) the older landed elite. A new middle class began to emerge.

Heureaux's and his successors' strategy of financing development projects through the printing of paper money and contracting ruinous foreign loans brought the national finances to a perilous state. To avoid the possibility of European intervention to collect on outstanding loans, President Theodore Roosevelt fashioned his famous corollary to the Monroe Doctrine, under which the United States took over the administration of the Dominican customs receipts. To protect the U.S. revenue officials, Roosevelt sent a contingent of marines. The number of marines and U.S. officials gradually increased. Finally, in 1916, President Woodrow Wilson—seeking to stem the continued instability, concerned on the eve of World War I about a potential German threat, and believing he could bring the benefits of U.S. democracy to our "poor little brown brothers"—authorized the marines already on the island to assume full control.

The marines did in the Dominican Republic what the marines have often done. They built roads, a sewer system, and better dock facilities. They installed the first telephone service. They reorganized the national system of land titles, a reform that proved advantageous to large U.S. investors. They sought to pacify the population, an effort that was frequently brutal and capricious and that provoked widespread resentment and a long guerrilla campaign. To preserve order once the occupation ended, in 1924 the marines supervised elections in which the U.S.-favored candidate, not surprisingly, won. A National Guard was set up. But since the more qualified patriotic elements in Dominican society opposed the occupation, the United States could attract only officers of questionable background for the guard. The U.S.-created guard served as the avenue for advancement for a new element in Dominican society, such as Rafael Trujillo.

From 1924 to 1930, the Dominican Republic was governed by Horacio Vásquez, a member of one of the country's elite families. But Vásquez illegally extended his term of office; he was sick and weak; the world market crash of 1929–1930 had devastating effects on the economy. In 1930 Trujillo, the head of the National Guard, stood by while a revolt launched from Santiago, the country's second largest city, toppled the Vásquez government. He then moved to seize power for himself. The Trujillo takeover was more than just another in the long succession of Dominican revolutions: It symbolized the end of oligarchic rule, the coming to power of a new social and racial element, and the beginning of a period of accelerated modernization.

THE TRUJILLO REGIME: MODERNIZATION UNDER AUTHORITARIAN AUSPICES

From 1930 to 1961, Rafael Trujillo dominated the Dominican Republic in a brutal fashion that has seldom been equaled. The entire country was converted into a giant hacienda with Trujillo as the national *patrón*. The dictator so dominated the country that virtually all areas and institutions of national life—army, Church, economy, education, social groups, even personal relations, the family, and sex—came under his control. It could be said that, although on a smaller scale, Trujillo ranked with Stalin and Hitler as one of the most tyrannical rulers of all time.

It would be wrong, however, and would not help explain the longevity of his rule if we thought of Trujillo only as a bloody tyrant. For difficult as it is to comprehend, Trujillo in many ways symbolized the aspirations of the Dominican people. Although the Dominicans did not condone the vicious brutalities of his regime and eventually assassinated him, Trujillo could not have lasted in power for thirty-one years without a large measure of popular support. As one Dominican historian and political leader has said, "You have to remember there is a little of Trujillo in every Dominican."

First, Trujillo was a mulatto and of middle-class origins in a country historically dominated by a white upper-class minority; the ascension to power of Trujillo and his fellow middle-class and mulatto National Guard officers symbolized a class and racial transformation in the highest levels of Dominican society and government with which many lower- and middle-class Dominicans could identify. Second, Trujillo was a powerfully *macho* leader with whose drama and exploits these same elements could sympathize. Third, through his development policies, Trujillo brought the Dominican Republic to a position of parity with Haiti (and eventually of military superiority). The country no longer had to face the threat of a foreign (and black) Haitian invasion.

Under Trujillo, a large number of development projects—docks, roads, public buildings, bridges—were built, which gave a new sense of pride to all Dominicans. Trujillo succeeded in paying off the national debt and in Dominicanizing (although under his own personal ownership) the all-important sugar industry, accomplishments that spoke to the rising sense of Dominican nationalism. Finally, in his construction of a strong state system and a centralized pattern of decision making, Trujillo resurrected some of the glory of the early-sixteenth-century Spanish model. The Dominican Republic thus achieved a great deal of national development under Trujillo, but that development benefited the ruling family as often as it did the nation, and it was achieved under exceedingly authoritarian auspices. In the end, the regime was strongly opposed, and the Trujillo family was driven out.

The Trujillo regime affected all Dominican institutions. The armed forces were strengthened, given modern weapons, and made the nation's most powerful group; but they were cast in the corrupt clan politics of the Trujillo regime. The Church, because of its support of the dictatorship, was discredited and lost influence. The old elites were shoved aside in favor of a new-rich element associated with the Trujillos. The communications media were improved but kept under the regime's thumb.

As the development process went forward, some new social forces appeared that would have major consequences. The economy expanded significantly, and new factories and industries appeared, mostly owned by the first family. After Trujillo's assassination, they were taken over by the government, which gave the Dominican Republic at the time the second largest public sector in Latin America (next to socialist Cuba's) and also immense opportunities for power and enrichment for those in control of the central administration. To run the new enterprises and government agencies under Trujillo, a vast army of civil servants emerged. The middle class grew, but its professional and civic associations were tightly controlled by the regime, and the new middle sectors were not allowed to organize political parties or gain political power. Nor did these emergent middle sectors share a unified sense of class consciousness: They were deeply divided, aped upper-class ways, and thus perpetuated a two-class system in the Dominican Republic rather than laying the basis for a multiclass, pluralistic one. A labor movement also emerged, but like all social groups under the tyranny it was organized as an official trade-union structure subordinate to the regime.

The Trujillo system was patterned on an authoritarian-corporate-patrimonialist structure that the authors of this book have repeatedly found, although under several different forms, to be a favored Latin American response to modernization. Although Trujillo was a man of action and knew little of the new corporatist ideologies, many more well-versed advisers helped fashion both his political ideas and his state system. Furthermore, it was to be expected that the dictator himself would be attracted to the model that Dominican history and his own experience in the streets had taught—the authoritarian-caudillo model of Heureaux and imperial Spain, with all power concentrated in his own hands.

Although Trujillo presided over a period of development unprecedented in Dominican history, that development benefited the Trujillo family's private accounts as much as it did the nation. The development process itself was so perverted and Trujillo's control so total that when the regime fell, a virtual vacuum existed in terms of political leadership, administrative cadres, and political and social institutions uncorrupted by the dictatorship and hence able to fill the void.

By the late 1950s, the pressures on the regime had begun to build. An economic downturn in sugar prices began to hurt the economy and alarmed all groups. Labor was restless and the middle class felt threatened. The Church started to criticize the regime, and some military factions grew impatient at the barriers to advancement and enrichment Trujillo had placed in their way. Trujillo had overreached himself; as his regime became more totalitarian, he exceeded the bounds of permissible caudillo behavior. His own close collaborators and business associates sensed that his time was running out and plotted to rid themselves of Trujillo so they could inherit his power and wealth. The United States, with the Cuban case clearly in mind and fearing that Trujillo might be another Batista, whose rule would be followed by a Communist takeover, launched moves against the dictator aimed at securing a non-Communist government in power. On the night of May 30, 1961, Trujillo was brutally assassinated.

ACCELERATED CHANGE AND THE ROAD TO REVOLUTION

Following the dictator's assassination, the Trujillo family sought to continue the regime under the son and heir, Rafael, Jr. (or Ramfis), just as the Somoza clan had done in Nicaragua. But the Trujillo family was unable to hold the system together, and, in the face of increasing popular pressures and with a nudge from the United States, they fled the country in November 1961.

With the Trujillos finally gone, the people exploded in a frenzy of joy, looting at will and toppling all the Trujillo statues and monuments. The institutional apparatus of the dictatorship was dismantled, except for the powerful Trujillo army. During the next year, under an interim Council of State consisting of business people and new-rich elements, the country experienced a burgeoning of new political associations: thirty-one political parties, seven competing labor federations, and a variety of other new groups. Elections were scheduled. Seeking to make the Dominican Republic a democratic alternative to Castroism, the United States began pouring in assistance. For a time in the 1960s, the Dominican Republic received more aid per capita than any other country.

The winners of the 1962 election were Juan Bosch and the Dominican Revolutionary party (PRD). Bosch was a social democrat and a mercurial leader; his party was fashioned along the lines of the democratic-left Aprista-like parties of Latin America. Together Bosch and the PRD sought to effect a democratic revolution in the Dominican Republic—politically, socially, and economically.

But the Bosch program of democratic reformism encountered the concerted hostility of the Church, the army, and the economic elites. Bosch also faced the seemingly impossible task of constructing an inorganic, individualistic democracy in a country grounded historically on an organic-corporatist-patrimonialist political tradition. In office, Bosch proved an inefficient administrator and let the reins of power get out of his control. The United States helped undermine his rule. In September 1963, the Dominican Republic's first experiment in democratic rule was overthrown.

Following Bosch's ouster, power returned to the same oligarchic and corrupt military elements who had governed before. The political situation degenerated and the economy went downhill. Police repression directed against the pro-Bosch unions, peasant associations, and parties increased. In April 1965, the pro-Bosch forces launched a rebellion aimed at correcting these wrongs and restoring democratic constitutional rule.

As the constitutionalist forces appeared on the verge of triumph, the United States, fearing another Cuba, intervened with a military contingent that numbered over twenty thousand. This was not a Vietnam-type intervention, aimed at suppressing a Communist movement, but an intervention directed against a social-democratic uprising that the U.S. government feared might become Castroist. The nation that thinks of itself as the greatest democracy in the world proceeded to crush a democratic revolution in a small Caribbean neighbor.

After a year of chaos during which U.S. troops disarmed the major opposing camps, "pacified" the population, and installed a moderate oligarch, Héctor García-Godoy, in the presidency, new elections were held. The pro-Bosch forces continued to be harassed by the army, and in elections supervised by the United States the U.S.-favored candidate, Joaquín Balaguer, won. Balaguer also took advantage of the widespread desire for a return to peace and normality after the upheaval of previous years.

Under Balaguer, the Dominican Republic's man-on-horseback tradition was reasserted. Though he appeared a meek and humble man, Balaguer ruled in an imperious, authoritarian manner. His was a one-man government, devoid of parties and checks and balances. Backed by the army, the Church, the financial oligarchy, and the United States, Balaguer remained above the political struggle and was very clever at manipulating the major power groups. While concentrating power in his own hands, Balaguer moved against the opposition democratic forces. He did this by means of repression, co-optation into his regime of numerous PRD leaders, depoliticization of the pro-Bosch peasant and labor groups through major economic programs, and subversion of the PRD through bribery, infiltration, and public relations techniques.

Under Balaguer, a massive amount of U.S. capital, both public and private, flowed into the country. Although it provided some new jobs and an economic stimulus, it also resulted in a selling out of Dominican sovereignty and meant increased power concentrated in the hands of the giant multinationals. Even though Balaguer's economic policies produced new boulevards and showcase public buildings and benefited the elites and middle class, Dominican workers and peasants gained little from the boom and many have experienced declining living standards.

By 1978, after twelve years in office, Balaguer was old and tired and had lost the popularity he had once enjoyed. He lost the 1978 presidential election to Antonio Guzmán of the PRD, a wealthy landowner and representative of the moderate wing of the party. Whereas in the 1965 revolution and the 1966 election the United States had been opposed to Bosch and the PRD, now it helped guarantee Guzmán's victory.

Guzmán brought democracy and human rights to the Dominican Republic, a welcome relief after the repression of the Balaguer era. As a social democrat, he sought to govern fairly and honestly for all groups. But at the end of his term the Dominican poor were as badly off as ever. The world depression had devastated the economy. Corruption reached into high places, including apparently the president's family. Demoralized by this and the fact that he could not control his own party or choose a successor, Guzmán committed suicide in the summer of 1982. The vice president stepped in temporarily until the candidate recently elected, Salvador Jorge Blanco, could be inaugurated.

Jorge Blanco was also from the PRD but its more reformist wing. He had campaigned on a platform of bringing "economic democracy." Like Guzmán, he ruled democratically and respected human rights. But the economic conditions he faced were so severe that he had to instigate a strict austerity program and postpone his reform program.

SOCIAL, POLITICAL, AND ECONOMIC GROUPS

The Dominican Republic lacks a strong institutional infrastructure. Its political parties, interest groups, and government structure are not well established. It has neither the strong institutions of a liberal polity nor the officially directed syndicates of a corporate system. The liberal and pluralist groups have been strengthened in recent years, but they do not enjoy solid legitimacy. With only a weak institutional structure, the Dominican Republic has long been dominated by personalism, caudilloism, and clan politics.

The armed forces and police have grown immensely in strength and influence during the last forty years, bolstering the Trujillo regime, toppling Bosch in 1963, and serving as one of the main props of the Balaguer government. Although there has recently been some increase in professionalism and institutional self-identity, and although some of the younger and more liberal officers sided with the Bosch forces in the 1965 civil war, the majority of the officer corps practices the corrupt caudillistic politics that has long characterized the system more generally. The armed forces provide one of the few avenues in Dominican society for enlisted men and officers to rise in the social hierarchy and to gain wealth and power on a grand scale.

Though the Dominican Republic is a Catholic nation, the Church is not a powerful agency. Although understaffed, the Church can exercise some moral leadership, particularly in such areas as population control; but it does not have a great deal of political influence, and by itself the Church is not a decisive power wielder.

The Dominican oligarchy is concentrated in Santiago, with important branches of the historical families relocated in Santo Domingo, where the money and power lie. The oligarchy is influential, but it has been increasingly superseded by a new-rich element of business people, industrialists, and government officials. Many of these made their money and earned important positions under Trujillo, and they returned to power under Balaguer. Although the military may be the ultimate arbiter of internal Dominican politics, the everyday management of governmental and economic affairs is largely monopolized by these economic elites.

The Federation of University Students contains several diverse factions: Communist, Maoist, Fidelista, PRD, and Christian Democratic. Although the student body is growing and has become predominantly middle class, in national affairs the university students are more a disruptive force than a decisive one. They can embarrass a government but not topple it.

The Dominican trade-union movement is divided among Communist, PRD, Christian Democratic, and U.S. Embassy–sponsored unions. Although strong in the early 1960s, the unions later lost power. The Balaguer government used money and patronage to buy off some leaders, practiced repression against the PRD *sindicatos,* and frustrated an independent unionism by encouraging the foreign-based multinationals to organize docile company unions. Both Guzmán and Jorge Blanco provided a climate more conducive to union activities.

The peasant associations, which enjoyed a brief opportunity under Bosch, were subsequently dismantled. Government paternalism and patronizing handouts were substituted for an independent peasant bargaining force. Under Guzmán and Jorge Blanco the peasants were allowed greated freedom to organize.

The U.S. Embassy and its various arms—military, cultural, CIA, labor, political, commercial—must also be considered one of the most important influences in internal Dominican politics. U.S. influence touches virtually all areas of Dominican life. No prudent Dominican president makes a major decision without checking first with his military chiefs, the economic elites, and the U.S. Embassy—and not necessarily in that order. Although the amount of official U.S. assistance (and hence influence) has diminished in recent years, that gap has been filled by still another arm of the United States, the big multinationals.

The political party system represents the same shifting kaleidoscope, the same lack of institutionalization as the other groups discussed here. The parties tend for the most part to be weakly organized, not very ideological, and based on personalistic followings rather than concrete programs. The alliances are seldom permanent since they derive from personalistic, family, and clan ambitions characteristic of the whole system.

The largest and best organized party is the Dominican Revolutionary party or PRD, the party of Bosch, Guzmán, and Jorge Blanco. It is a social democratic party, a member of the Socialist International, a reformist party with considerable labor, peasant, and middle-class support. With a national organization and a core of able leaders, it is divided into conservative, centrist, and more radical factions.

The second largest group is the Reformist party, which was the personal apparatus of Balaguer. It lacks a clear program and is really a personalist party. Without Balaguer's leadership it has tended to factionalize. It generally represents conservative landowning, business, and government elements as well as the traditional peasantry.

The Christian Democrats have been an important minor party, but they have never lived up to their early promise of providing a strong center and middle way. The several Communist, Maoist, and Fidelista groups are badly splintered; although communism is an important issue in Dominican affairs, the actual Communist groups have not gained a strong organization or following. Most of the other political groups are small and personalistic. They form at election times but usually disappear soon thereafter.

The Dominican Republic is becoming more democratic and pluralist but it is not fully so. The elites enjoy a preponderance of power; the armed forces must always be reckoned with. The mass organizations of peasants and workers are still weak and divided. The PRD has provided a new avenue for mass and middle-class politics, but in many areas of the national life power, influence, and wealth remain highly concentrated. A liberal polity and an authoritarian-conservative one continue to live side by side.

GOVERNMENTAL MACHINERY
AND POLITICAL POWER

The lack of organization and the institutional debility referred to earlier as a historical Dominican dilemma are also manifest at the level of the central state system.

There have never been in all of Dominican history a congress and court system separate from and coequal to the executive. Rather, the courts have traditionally functioned as a subordinate branch, while the role of the Congress is to offer advice and consent (not much dissent) to the president. Power is centralized, not dispersed; it is concentrated in the *organic unity* of the state system, which means in the Dominican case the person of the president.

The Dominican Republic's system of local government is based on a similar tradition of centralized and concentrated authority. Little self-government is afforded the towns and twenty-six provinces; instead, local officials serve at the behest of the central government, and their function is to carry out policies emanating downward from the central ministries.

Power is concentrated in the executive branch, but even here it is not the executive offices that are so important as the person occupying the highest office. The Dominican Republic has all the paraphernalia of a modern executive-centered state system: a planning office, personnel office, budget office, press office, and the like. But few of these agencies have much influence since in most matters it is the president who makes the decisions. Furthermore, in the Dominican case, presidential decisions on policy and appointments to office must often be based on the family, clan, and patronage considerations that dominate the system. Guzmán and Jorge Blanco tried to introduce greater probity into this system.

The cabinet is not a policymaking or even advisory group but a body through which jobs and other favors can be doled out to the rival clans and factions. Cabinet members are not ordinarily allowed to make independent decisions affecting their own agencies; that power is the president's alone.

A special feature of the Dominican system is the array of government agencies and industries, the largest of which is the state-run sugar industry, inherited from the Trujillos. Although supposedly autonomous, these agencies have historically been dominated by the same family, political, and clan considerations as the ministries. They have become vast patronage and sinecure agencies, providing jobs and enrichment opportunities for friends and relatives of those in power. Not surprisingly, virtually all the "autonomous" corporations are losing money.

The president dominates the system. The president makes all the decisions, from those on major policy down to minor appointments. The president is the hub around whom the entire Dominican system circulates. Further, the criteria used in making these decisions (based on the patrimonialist, family, and clan nature of the Dominican system) sometimes seem to run contrary to U.S. AID officials' criteria of "honesty" and "rationality." But that is how the Dominican system works, and in the best of times and with an able president, such a highly centralized system can work very well.

The president is not only the national decision maker to a degree unheard of under U.S. presidentialism, but he is the symbol of the nation and its personification. Presidential values become national values. There can be no sharp separation between the private and the public domains since the president is assumed to have commanding authority over all and to be responsible for the common good. Because of this, and because of the president's monopoly over all jobs, favors, and funds, the president's office and home are always besieged by petitioners, from the highest ranks of society to the humblest, seeking a job here, a favor there, a bicycle for a child, money for an operation, a wheelchair, food, clothing, a lucrative government contract. The president is the source of all power and official funds, and thus the competition for that post is intense and frequently violent. The president rules rather than governs and, in that sense, is a direct descendant of the imperial Hapsburgs, rather than heir to Anglo-American concepts of limited rule and checks and balances.

PUBLIC POLICY

The same characteristics that describe decision making in the state system also determine the policies emanating from the system. The primary consideration in implementing any program is the survival of the government itself. The way the government survives is both by carrying out effective public policies and through awarding jobs, funds, and favors to its followers. Frequently, an entire agency must be turned over to one of the clans or political factions to secure its continued loyalty and support. Only after these priorities have been served can a program be effectively implemented.

There are probably four requirements that a skillful and prudent Dominican president has in mind when implementing public policy. The first is to ensure his own survival in office, implying the jobs and opportunities for enrichment awarded his followers already alluded to. The second is to provide advantages for the groups—principally the army and the economic elites—that have the power to challenge and even to overthrow the president. The third is to keep the U.S. Embassy happy, preoccupied, and distracted. A fourth—new—requirement is to carry out effective social programs. Any Dominican president who can successfully manage these requirements must be very clever.

If these are the president's top priorities, it is understandable that program implementation takes twists in the Dominican Republic that seem strange to North Americans and that sometimes mean little effective program implementation at all. Take, for example, the situation in which fifty-two members of one leading political family were found to be occupying positions in a single branch of the Ministry of Education. Two things are clear: First, that the political loyalty of that family to the government was being secured through a large number of jobs and sinecures (to the extent that the family monopolized the agency); and second, that genuine educational reform was not a high priority and was unlikely to be carried out effectively.

Given the nature of the Dominican system, therefore, it should not be surprising to find that political loyalty given in return for a favor or sinecure is often a more important consideration than program implementation. Nor should one be surprised to find military officers supplementing their incomes through various officially sanctioned opportunities for enrichment at the public trough. It is not considered unusual that the government's development policies sometimes benefit chiefly the wealthy. The same applies to other social and economic programs: Dams and irrigation projects tend to benefit those large owners who already have extensive *latifundia*; extension services benefit those who already own cattle or have large farms; new roads, port facilities, bridges, and highways increase the opportunities for wealth of those who already possess it. Some programs, such as recent efforts at family planning, are designed specifically to keep the Americans busy and to keep the foreign-assistance funds flowing, at the same time providing more sinecure positions for the president to hand out and ensuring that the program is not so successful that it antagonizes an important power like the Church.

Although such politics and priorities may seem Byzantine, bizarre, and in need of reversal, these are the historical realities of the Dominican system and should be understood in terms of Dominican priorities and methods rather than through North American perceptions. Effective program implementation is frequently only a by-product of policy in the Dominican system; and despite the overwhelming need for them, many social programs to alleviate the hardship of the poor and the downtrodden may never be carried out at all.

Any realistic Dominican president now knows, however, that in order to last in office one must not only satisfy the elites but labor and the peasants as well. Hence, there is a new emphasis on public low-cost housing, water supplies, health care, agrarian reform, and educational and social programs. But even here, the other priorities of favoritism and payoffs must necessarily come into play. As former U.S. Ambassador John Bartlow Martin once remarked, concerning his pet plan of providing water for the arid Dominican southwest: "The project was a failure, lost in the jungle of political pressures. I could name a dozen projects like it."

RETROSPECT AND PROSPECT

Over the centuries, the Dominican Republic and its people have struggled heroically for a measure of dignity, a certain respect, a place, however small, in the sun. They have sought to overcome their historical poverty, lack of resources, underpopulation, and lack of organization. They have labored to maintain their traditions and autonomy in the face of repeated foreign invasions and the overwhelming presence of, as well as their own dependency on, their large North American neighbor. Their efforts, despite domestic tyrants and foreign foes, have been heroic. That they have achieved any development at all given their lack of resources, that they have survived as a sovereign nation, that they have built and modernized and achieved some measure of importance in the Caribbean, is nothing short of miraculous.

That is why the revolution of 1965 and the U.S. response to it were so critical. Here was a small nation, finally breaking out of the bondage of elitist, oligarchic rule and seeking to establish a more democratic system, whose revolution was crushed by the United States. Restoring to power the same corrupt and oppressive elements that had long dominated the Dominican Republic, the United States sought to turn the clock back. In the process the United States not only frustrated and perverted the natural course of Dominican development but also insulted the nation's dignity and ran roughshod over its historic and national ambitions. The Dominicans have suffered such reverses and humiliations before, but they have always managed to keep intact their goals and their determination.

Under Balaguer from 1966 to 1978 the country enjoyed stability and considerable economic progress, but at the cost of widespread human-rights violations, a rapacious military again running rampant, a lack of reform, widespread corruption, and a return to the politics of the past. But beginning in 1978 with Guzmán and then from 1982 under Jorge Blanco the country enjoyed a new democratic opening. Human rights were respected, moderate but reform-oriented governments were returned to power, democracy was restored, and efforts were made to achieve a measure of social justice for the poor. These hopeful tendencies, however, ran up against the realities of severe depression and a downward-turning economy. The outcome remains in doubt.

NOTES

1. After the title of the book on Haiti by Robert Rotberg.

SUGGESTIONS FOR FURTHER READING

Atkins, G. Pope. *Arms and Politics in the Dominican Republic.* Westview Press, Boulder, Colo., 1981.

Bosch, Juan. *The Unfinished Experiment: Democracy in the Dominican Republic.* Praeger, New York, 1964.

Crassweller, Robert D. *Trujillo: The Life and Times of a Caribbean Dictator.* Macmillan, New York, 1966.

Gleijeses, Piero. *The Dominican Crisis.* Johns Hopkins University Press, Baltimore, 1978.

Kryzanek, Michael J. "Political Party Decline and the Failure of Liberal Democracy: The PRD in Dominican Politics." *Journal of Latin American Studies* 9, no. 1 (1977):115–143. (On the Balaguer regime.)

Lowenthal, Abraham. *The Dominican Intervention.* Harvard University Press, Cambridge, 1971.

Martin, John Bartlow. *Overtaken by Events: The Dominican Crisis—from the Fall of Trujillo to the Civil War.* Doubleday, Garden City, N.Y., 1966.

Rodman, Selden. *Quisqueya: A History of the Dominican Republic.* University of Washington Press, Seattle, 1964.

Sharpe, Kenneth. *Peasant Politics: Life in a Dominican Village.* Johns Hopkins University Press, Baltimore, 1977.

Slater, Jerome. *Intervention and Negotiation: The United States and the Dominican Republic.* Harper & Row, New York, 1970.

Szulc, Tad. *Dominican Diary.* Delacorte, New York, 1965.

U.S. Army. *Area Handbook for the Dominican Republic.* Government Printing Office, Washington, D.C., 1973.

Wiarda, Howard J. *The Dominican Republic: Nation in Transition.* Praeger, New York, 1968.

_____. *Dictatorship and Development: The Methods of Control in Trujillo's Dominican Republic.* University of Florida Press, Gainesville, 1970.

_____. *Dictatorship, Development, and Disintegration: Politics and Social Change in the Dominican Republic.* 3 vols. Published for the Program in Latin American Studies of the University of Massachusetts. Xerox University Microfilms Monograph Series, Ann Arbor, Mich., 1975.

Wiarda, Howard J., and Michael J. Kryzanek, *The Dominican Republic: Caribbean Crucible.* Westview Press, Boulder, Colo., 1982.

26
Panama's Domestic Power Structure and the Canal: History and Future

STEVE C. ROPP

Panama is a long, narrow country joining Central and South America. By either Central or South American standards, its population is small (2 million) and consists primarily of mestizos and mulattos. The most critical element in determining Panama's distinct course of national development has been its central geographic location and utility as a transit point from the Atlantic to the Pacific. Commerce has been critical to Panama's economic well-being through a series of historical stages, culminating in the construction of the Panama Canal by the United States after Panama gained independence from Colombia in 1903.

A central premise of this chapter is that the country of Panama and the U.S.-controlled Canal Zone have historically constituted a single political and economic system. The system of highly regularized relationships between elite groups in the two constituent units ensured that a new social order did not emerge to challenge the existing order in Panama.

To some extent it can be argued that the government of Gen. Omar Torrijos (1968–1981) challenged this traditional dual system of control through its tentative support of nationalist and development-oriented policies. However, it would seem that the most significant and potentially radical changes in the Panamanian social order have yet to occur and may result from the ratification on April 18, 1978, of the most recent canal treaties. For a variety of reasons that will be detailed in this chapter, the ratification of these treaties may eventually fracture the system of social control.

For the United States, the fracturing of this system and the possible radicalization of Panamanian politics may create major new problems in an area of the world that is already troubled by the ongoing Central American crisis. And in Panama elites and masses would be presented

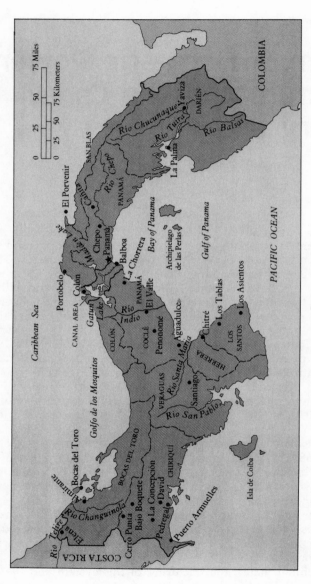

Panama

with a host of new problems and opportunities with regard to the structuring of a new social order. From this perspective, the canal negotiations completed in 1978 can be viewed as a prelude to new and significant changes in the structure and the composition of the Panamanian state.

HISTORY BEFORE 1903

Because of some of the peculiarities of its historical development, Panama has on occasion been referred to as a "nondescript state."[1] But Panama is not so much nondescript as simply nondescribed. For some reason, although considerable attention has been devoted to the study of the canal and related issues, little has been directed toward the study of Panama itself.

To understand the current nature of the Panamanian state, we have first to look at its historical roots and evolution. This is especially necessary because some of the traditional interpretations concerning the evolution of states in Latin America do not seem appropriate in this particular case. Many of the peculiarities of Panamanian history are perhaps best understood in terms of what did *not* happen on the isthmus during the course of the late eighteenth and nineteenth centuries. In most areas of Latin America, this two-hundred-year period saw the emergence of new classes that gradually began to assert themselves against the dominance and control of Spanish mercantile elites. However, in Panama the trend was not nearly so uniform with regard to increased independence.

One difference in Panama's situation was that Spain's relaxation of control over trade in the New World during the late eighteenth century did not serve to strengthen local nationalist sentiment and autonomy as it did in much of the rest of Latin America. In fact, the effect of trade liberalization in Panama was precisely the opposite in that the decline in trade transiting the isthmus drastically weakened the economic and political position of local commercial groups. This situation of economic stagnation forced local elites into an even heavier reliance on the mother country at a time when most of Latin America was moving toward greater independence.

A second difference in these formative years was that Panama did not produce a landed aristocracy. Throughout most of Latin America, the process of creating independent states was linked to a certain extent to the growth of landed elements several steps removed from the direct control of the Spanish Crown. In Panama the lure of trade and commerce and the relative unattractiveness of agriculture tied the state from its very beginnings to urban commercial elements in Panamanian society.

Finally, the character of the Panamanian state was strongly influenced by Panama's experience during the nineteenth century as a province of Colombia. During this formative period, the most vital element in

Panamanian politics was the Liberal party, and it was this party that contributed heavily to the philosophical underpinnings of twentieth-century Panamanian governments. Liberalism had a strong appeal in Panama because it was the ideological voice of new urban commercial classes and of outlying regions vis-à-vis the power of central governments.

Panamanian scholar Ricuarte Soler has argued that the contemporary character of the state is best explained in terms of the failure during the late nineteenth century of Colombian, and hence Panamanian, liberalism. He argues that the Liberals (the "true" nationalists) were terribly weakened by various Colombian civil wars to the point that by the late nineteenth century they were in no position to challenge major outside forces. This situation, Soler argues, created a political vacuum in Panama that was eventually filled by the United States "bearing gifts" of independence and a canal to an *entreguista* (sellout) class of pseudonationalist merchants whose only real interest was profits.[2]

Although it is probably true that the state created in 1903 was to some extent the product of the failure of liberalism, it would be a mistake to assume that liberalism left no mark on contemporary Panamanian politics. Its imprint remains visible in the form of a general absence of corporate philosophy or practice. Historically the development of corporatism has been linked to rural religious values most often expressed through the Conservative party. Panama did not fit this corporate bill of particulars in that it was a relatively open urban society in which commercial Liberal values thrived.[3]

EVOLUTION OF THE STATE: 1903–1968

Put in simplest terms, the new Panamanian state created in 1903 resulted from the convergence of the interests of U.S. and Panamanian elites. President Theodore Roosevelt wanted to build a canal through Central America. Panamanian elites, located primarily in the two terminal cities along the canal route (Panamá and Colón), sought new financial opportunities and also protection from the laboring classes brought in to construct the canal.

What emerged during the early twentieth century was a new alliance of Panamanian elites and zone officials, whose interests converged around the need for stability in Panama. This development was partially obscured because Panamanian political leaders would often lobby for the use of U.S. troops in Panama against dissident members of their own class. Perhaps the best example of the new alliance against the urban working class came during the 1925 renters' strike that took place in Panamá and Colón. The Panamanian elite, many of whom had made considerable sums in supplying cheap housing for canal workers, called in six hundred U.S. troops to suppress the rioting.

To a considerable extent, the peculiarities of the twentieth-century Panamanian state can be attributed to this tacit alliance, which has not substantially changed in over fifty years despite numerous subtle changes in the social composition of the two allies and in their tactics. This system allows Panamanian elites to "farm out" certain traditional functions of the state to their U.S. allies. For example, Panama is one of only five countries in the world that does not have its own currency. Since Panama uses the U.S. dollar, the state has in effect sacrificed control over monetary policy in return for relative economic stability. This relative stability results from the fact that Panama cannot increase the supply of money in circulation, as often happens in other Latin American countries, and thus has seldom suffered from high rates of inflation.

Within this framework of constrained sovereignty, a central government evolved in Panama that has been noted for its corruption. The state came to be controlled by a small group of families who treated the national treasury as their personal preserve. A strangely inverted "democratic" system developed in which those who controlled the state administrative bureaucracy used that control to manipulate the national legislature. This was done through the parceling out of administrative jobs, called *botellas*, to various legislative candidates who could then use these jobs to purchase votes.

Numerous examples can be cited from Panamanian history of high government officials using public office for private gain. José Antonio Remón, while president during the 1950s, was able to amass a fortune through control of houses of prostitution and of drug traffic across the isthmus. Not infrequently, high government officials have used their diplomatic immunity to smuggle drugs into other countries, and there is strong evidence to suggest that this practice still continues.

One noteworthy development related to the evolution of the Panamanian state is that the central government apparatus has expanded tremendously during the past thirty years. This development has been quite similar to that experienced in most other Latin American countries since World War II. Prior to the 1940s the purpose of the state had been conceived in relatively narrow terms related to the maintenance of internal order. During the late 1940s and early 1950s the perception of the legitimate functions of the state expanded to include a new concern for providing services to increasingly broader classes of Panamanians. Particularly during the 1950s and 1960s, the Panamanian government grew tremendously through a rapid proliferation of "alphabet agencies" that increased the number of people working for the central government by more than 60 percent between 1960 and 1969.

It is within this context of a weak and corrupt but nevertheless expanding state that we begin to see the emergence of the Panamanian police force as a participant in politics. During the 1930s a split developed between the political faction led by Harmodio and Arnulfo Arias and the police force, which increasingly fell under the control of José Antonio Remón. Remón is an important figure in Panamanian history because, despite his personal venality, he succeeded in carving out a political role for the police as an arbiter in feuds among the elite. Even more important, he began the process of professionalizing the police force and succeeded in transforming it into a quasi-military unit (the National Guard). This restructuring and redefinition of the role of the police is particularly important because it created a new military organization during the 1950s that was much closer in outlook to military organizations in the rest of Latin America.[4]

It was this process of military institutional development that made possible the coup that brought the Torrijos regime to power. On October 11, 1968, President Arnulfo Arias was removed from office and replaced by a provisional junta composed of senior officers within the National Guard. During the next few months, there was some question as to which faction within the National Guard controlled the junta and what specific policy directions that faction would pursue. Eventually, Gen. Omar Torrijos achieved a dominant position through advocacy of a continued military presence in politics for the purpose of implementing long-range plans for social reform.

THE TORRIJOS YEARS: 1968–1981

The Panamanian government under Torrijos could be described as outwardly civilian but with the eight-thousand-strong National Guard constituting its central core. The fundamental document with regard to the political structure was the 1972 constitution, which granted extraordinary powers to General Torrijos for a period of six years. Under Article 277 the "Maximum Leader of the Panamanian Revolution" could appoint ministers of state, appoint officers to the National Guard, and direct foreign affairs.

The 1972 constitution did create an elected legislature (the Assembly of National Representatives) to replace the old National Assembly. However, this body met only once a year for one month to ratify legislation passed down by a National Legislative Council, which was controlled by General Torrijos. The reality of the situation was that although Panama had a civilian president, civilian ministers, and a civilian legislature, the real control was in the hands of a small circle of military officers.

Since Panama is a relatively small country, it was possible for General Torrijos and his military comrades to keep in close daily contact. When important decisions were made, they were most likely the result of recent conversations between a handful of colonels. Various families and individuals attached themselves to specific colonels in the hopes that their interests would be protected. Thus an understanding of the formal machinery of government is less important than knowledge of the linkages that existed between various high-ranking officers and their respective political clientele.

The fact that all real power was concentrated in the hands of one man and that personal contacts meant more than formal legal rights produced a political system that was often highly authoritarian and arbitrary in its judgments and directions. Political parties were banned, and newspapers were either directly controlled by the government or operated under policies of strict self-censorship. Often military officers and high government officials took advantage of their positions to enrich themselves in much the same manner as had prevailed in the past. The bureaucracy was overwhelmed by the incompetent relatives of powerful military officers. Corruption in government extended from the lowest public official accepting a small bribe to the very top, with the Maximum Leader enriching himself through numerous joint business ventures at home and abroad.

There is a story to the effect that a high-ranking officer in the Panamanian National Guard was once asked whether he considered himself a "rightist" or a "leftist." He responded that "a rightist grabs money with the right hand and a leftist with the left. I consider myself a centrist because I grab money with both hands."

Whether apocryphal or not, this story raises the issue of whether the Torrijos regime is best characterized as conservative, reformist, revolutionary, or simply corrupt. There is no question that General Torrijos attempted to maintain the general image of a forward-looking or perhaps even revolutionary administration. However, "revolution" is a slippery term as applied to Latin America, and thus we must closely examine the policies of his regime in order to see if the label actually applied.

To understand the nature of the Torrijos regime, it is necessary to recall that Panamanian governments have traditionally had no base in rural areas. The state had always been managed by and for interests of commercial elites in the terminal cities. Capital generated in these cities was then used to establish commercial agricultural estates in rural areas, but these estates were quite different from the traditional *latifundia* found in much of the rest of Latin America.

In his search for political support outside of the elite-dominated urban centers, Torrijos found a large rural population that had been virtually ignored since the founding of the republic. This attitude was reflected in the fact that the area removed from the Canal Zone had always been referred to in national censuses as simply the "rest of the country." To some extent, Torrijos's concern for these areas was grounded in the fact that he himself was a product of rural Panama. Raised as the son of a poor rural schoolteacher, he was considered something of a country bumpkin by the urban elites.

Torrijos's search for support among Panama's *campesinos* took the form of frequent trips with his closest advisers into remote interior villages. The style is reminiscent of Fidel Castro's in that Torrijos's appeal was physical and personal and he dealt with problems on the spot. However, the style derived not as Castro's did from the guerrilla experience but from the antiguerrilla civic-action campaigns in which Torrijos participated during the 1960s.

There can be little doubt that General Torrijos's government directed more attention toward rural Panama than had been the case under previous administrations. However, the Torrijos regime seems to have stood in an *evolutionary* rather than a revolutionary relationship to previous Panamanian governments with regard to rural policies. If we look at Torrijos's agrarian programs, we find that most of the central ideas were formulated as five-year plans during the two preceding civilian administrations. Under President Roberto Chiari, a central planning agency was created within the Office of the Presidency. All of the plans that Torrijos eventually implemented were drawn up during the 1960s, but few were implemented due to the indifference or active opposition of the elite. Clearly, with regard to agricultural policy, General Torrijos grafted a new political style onto a set of plans and a planning mechanism that he inherited. To the extent that Torrijos's agrarian policy could be considered "revolutionary," it was because he took plans off the drawing board and into the implementation phase.

Furthermore, if one looks specifically at the land reform effort of the Torrijos government, there is considerable reason to question its revolutionary nature. Since over 90 percent of all land was state owned, the government could distribute acreage without having to expropriate private holdings. Part of the problem in Panama was that many *campesinos* apparently did not want title to a particular parcel of land. The majority of them had been practicing slash-and-burn agriculture on state land for years and felt that the only "benefit" of landownership would be the payment of survey fees and taxes to the government.

Looking closely at the agrarian policies of the Torrijos regime, it might be easy for some to cynically conclude that the general stood to lose little by appearing revolutionary in the countryside. Given the highly urbanized nature of the elite, he avoided confronting it with serious structural changes on its own ground. Even in the countryside he was not forced to battle the elite because of the availability of state land. However, such a conclusion would not seem totally warranted in light of the amount of personal attention and state resources that Torrijos devoted to solving the problems of the rural poor.

Given that the rural areas of Panama have always been marginal in terms of the power structure, the more critical question is the extent to which Torrijos's policies affected urban commercial elites. Here we find little to indicate that anything remotely approximating a revolutionary process took place. The basic problem that Torrijos faced in changing the structure of power in the terminal cities was that he could not gain control over the labor movement. There is little doubt that Torrijos had this in mind in 1969 when he proposed a new party that would be similar to the Mexican PRI in that it would bring all the major sectors in Panamanian society under one umbrella political organization. However, this proposal met with very strong opposition from the elite and had to be abandoned.

There are numerous reasons why Torrijos was not able to base the policies of his government upon a strong and united labor movement. One, the majority of Panamanian blue-collar workers were employed in the Canal Zone. These workers had little interest in the issues concerning Panamanian labor because their working conditions and wage rates were determined not in Panama but in the United States.

A second reason for the weakness of organized labor was that the labor movement traditionally included considerable numbers of black Panamanians who were brought from the West Indies during the period of canal construction and remained to take jobs servicing the canal. These black Panamanians were resented by the "native Panamanians" because their English-speaking ability allowed them to compete effectively for the relatively high paying jobs in the Canal Zone. The result was a highly anomalous situation in which 40 percent of the Panamanians who worked for the Panama Canal Company were in the top 10 percent of all income recipients, even though their jobs were considered relatively menial by U.S. standards.

For these reasons the labor movement was viewed by many Panamanians not so much as an integral sector of national society but as a foreign enclave. Thus the problem any reformist politician faced was not just one of gaining control over the labor movement but also one of giving that movement some legitimacy and standing in the eyes of the nation as a whole.

A final reason for the weakness of organized labor was that commercial and industrial elites remained highly organized and intent upon preserving their control over workers. During the early post–World War II period, unions in both Panama and the Canal Zone had been heavily influenced by left-leaning elements. The dual power structure responded with a strategy that aimed at control of the labor movement through the selective application of "corporatist" regulations and practice. Since the mid-1950s, the state has had the power to determine whether a union has the right to strike, and strikes were frequently declared illegal by the courts. The state could withhold juridical recognition (*personería jurídica*), as was done in the case of the Isthmian Federation of Christian Workers (FITC). Secessionist movements from the major labor federations have been declared illegal as in 1963 when a secessionist movement by four member unions from the Confederation of Workers of the Republic of Panama (CTRP) was prevented.

The situation in Panama with respect to organized labor could be likened to a tug of war in which the labor movement, already vastly weakened by the dual structure of power, was pulled one way and then the other between the regime and big business. General Torrijos wanted to use the labor movement as a political base and did much after 1968 to court its leaders. However, the powerful National Council of Private

Enterprise (CONEP), which represented business interests, would not allow him to implement the changes in the political structure that would make this possible.

In addition to the Torrijos regime's relationship to rural and urban segments of society, it is also important to examine relationships with outside forces. By far the most important structural development affecting the evolution of the Panamanian state that occurred during the Torrijos years was the growing role of banks and multinational corporations in the Panamanian economy. During the past two decades, Panama has become the center of a rapidly expanding "Latindollar" market that services multinational corporations operating throughout Latin America. In the 1960s banks in the advanced capitalist countries began to open branches around the world. Such branches located in Panama have attracted huge deposits of U.S. dollars.

Panama also attracted a large number of multinational subsidiaries due to its highly favorable laws of incorporation. Such subsidiaries were not required to have Panamanian citizens as directors, have Panamanian capital invested, or pay income taxes in Panama if no business was done there. Additionally, financial reports did not have to be filed in Panama, and the subsidiary could keep its books of account anywhere and in any manner it chose.

As more and more Latin American countries attempted to strictly regulate the behavior of multinationals, these companies gravitated toward Panama, where they could still perform financial juggling acts that allowed them to maintain high profit levels. Thus this shift in the role Panama plays in the international community is important not only for an understanding of Panama's internal politics but for developments in Latin America as well.

Looking at the sum total of the Torrijos regime's policies, they might best be described as having been mildly reformist, particularly with respect to rural workers and urban labor. An important reason for the relatively slow pace of reform would seem to be that Torrijos had no real control over urban labor because of the traditional dual system of power that effectively divided and controlled this sector. Given the constraints that were imposed upon his regime from the very beginning, it is difficult to tell how far Torrijos himself would have been willing to carry reformist policies if completely free to do so.

Although the Torrijos government has sometimes been described as "leftist" or "Communist," this was clearly not the case. Torrijos needed international support from leaders such as Fidel Castro to keep pressure on the United States with regard to the canal negotiations and also to satisfy the symbolic needs of left-leaning groups within Panama. Perhaps the clearest indications that the Torrijos regime was not Communist were his open-door policy toward multinational corporations and the large amounts of financial aid he received from the United States.

PANAMA AND THE CANAL AFTER TORRIJOS

On July 31, 1981, Gen. Omar Torrijos was killed when his light plane crashed into a mountainside in western Panama. With a barely audible whimper, thirteen years of uninterrupted one-man rule came to an end, and the political structure that he had so carefully constructed began slowly to crumble. Since the death of Torrijos, Panama has been experiencing a number of serious and mutually reinforcing crises that threaten to tear apart the social fabric.

Perhaps most visible has been the crisis of leadership. In the wake of Torrijos's death, a number of military and civilian contenders sought to replace him as political strong man. Competition became particularly intense as the country moved closer to the May 1984 elections, the first direct elections of a Panamanian president in fifteen years. Between 1982 and 1984, two presidents resigned, and the political party that had been formed to carry on the Torrijos banner disintegrated as a result of political infighting. In addition, the legislature that had been created by the 1972 constitution was disbanded in preparation for 1984. The election of 1984 was won by Nicolás Ardito Barletta, a centrist economist who had formerly served in the Torrijos cabinet. Its results were disputed, which did not augur well for future stability.

Several other factors underlie and compound this crisis of leadership. For one thing, Panama is a quite different country in terms of its economic and social structure from the one that existed when Torrijos came to power in 1968. The service sector has grown substantially through the activities of multinational corporations, and the urban middle class has expanded, becoming increasingly diverse and sophisticated. In a sense, the old style of populist military leadership is no longer compatible with this new urban economic base. Another underlying dimension of crisis relates to the regional context. Torrijos's death coincided with growing ideological polarization and military conflict in Central America. As Panamanians became increasingly worried about the influence of the left in the region and attendant problems such as the influx of refugees, the government took a more conservative stance.

From the perspective of the United States, the enduring central concern as these multiple crises unfolded has been security of the Panama Canal. The canal had been a vital issue in U.S. and Panamanian politics ever since Panama's representatives returned from Washington, D.C., with the 1903 treaty. Major complaints over the years centered around matters such as inadequate annual compensation paid Panama, the operation of commercial enterprises by the United States within the Canal Zone, and U.S. use of the zone for military purposes having little to do with the protection of the canal. However, for Panamanians, such issues had always been secondary to the question of sovereignty over the Canal Zone.

The lack of clarity in the original treaty with regard to this issue contributed to fierce debate, sometimes ending in violence. Various groups in the United States, including conservative members of Congress, retired military personnel, and concerned citizens, traditionally claimed that the 1903 treaty granted the United States full sovereign powers in the zone forever. Panamanians argued that the stipulation in the treaty that the United States could only act in the zone "as if it were sovereign" indicated that sovereignty was never transferred.

In the aftermath of the 1964 confrontation that left twenty-four Panamanians and four U.S. servicemen dead, efforts were initiated to conclude a new treaty that would satisfy the needs of both parties. Although these negotiations were not always smooth, progress over the years established an increasingly broad consensus on the issue of eventual Panamanian control of the zone. The issue came to be not whether a new treaty would be ratified but when. In 1978 agreement was reached.

The canal continues to have a number of important present and future implications for Panamanian politics. Perhaps the most significant way in which the Canal Zone historically affected politics was to prevent the development of alternative configurations of political power based on the labor movement. In this regard, it is important to note that Panama is one of the most highly developed states in Latin America in terms of indicators of economic development and mobilization. However, this level of development has not found expression in strong labor-based political movements as has been the case in numerous other Latin American countries, a situation partially related to the historically overwhelming U.S. military and economic presence that could supply support for Panamanian urban elites when they found themselves seriously challenged as they were in the late 1940s.

The fact that a major segment of the Panamanian blue-collar work force was employed in the Canal Zone effectively prevented the mobilization of this base of support for developmentally oriented regimes. The lack of availability of such traditional bases of support meant that would-be reformists were forced to put together weak populist coalitions composed of marginal groups that had little in the way of a solid organizational base. This in turn left these regimes vulnerable to the pressures of the dual alliance of Canal Zone officials and Panamanian elites.

The real significance of the 1978 treaties is that they are slowly altering this traditional structure of power. Implementation of the treaties will eventually "free" the Canal Zone (called Canal Area since 1978) segment of the Panamanian labor sector from U.S. control, and this development in turn will have multiple consequences for the political system. Most important, the labor movement will become available for mobilization by new political leaders. The Panamanian work force associated with the canal will itself become a new potential source of leadership now that workers previously unable, because of employment restrictions, to hold appointed or elected positions in Panama will be able to do so.

From this perspective, the Torrijos regime may have been one of the last in a long line of Panamanian governments to have been constrained by the historical power of the dual alliance. However, what is not clear is whether successor regimes will be able to take advantage of this fact in the context of the ongoing Central American and global economic crises. The incipient populist coalition that supported Torrijos's nationalist policies and that might have been reinforced by a labor movement strengthened as a result of the 1978 treaties is now in disarray. It remains to be seen whether it can be reassembled.

NOTES

1. Hubert Herring, *A History of Latin America* (Knopf, New York, 1968), p. 502.
2. Ricuarte Soler, "La Independencia de Panamá de Colombia," in *Dependencia y Liberación*, ed. Ricuarte Soler (Editorial Universitaria Centroamericana, San José, Costa Rica, 1974), pp. 25–28.
3. Certainly manifestations of corporate organizing principles can be found in contemporary Panamanian society. However, where these techniques have been used, they have been the result of expediency and have generally proven quite ephemeral. From a historical perspective, John Bailey observes that Colombia itself produced little in the way of corporate thought or practice during the nineteenth century. Hence it is illogical to expect to find such manifestations in Panama. See "Dimensions of Interest Representation in Colombia," in *Authoritarianism and Corporatism in Latin America*, ed. James Malloy (University of Pittsburgh Press, Pittsburgh, 1977), pp. 267–270.
4. Steve C. Ropp, "Military Reformism in Panama: New Directions or Old Inclinations," *Caribbean Studies* 12 (October 1972):50–54.

SUGGESTIONS FOR FURTHER READING

Augelli, John P. *The Panama Canal Area in Transition.* American Universities Field Staff Reports, pts. 1 and 2. Hanover, N.H., American Universities Field Staff International, 1981.

Jaén Suárez, Omar. *La población del Istmo de Panamá del siglo XVI al siglo XX.* Impresora de la Nación, Panamá, 1978.

LaFeber, Walter. *The Panama Canal: The Crisis in Historical Perspective.* Oxford University Press, New York, 1978.

McCullough, David. *The Path Between the Seas: The Creation of the Panama Canal, 1870–1914.* Simon and Schuster, New York, 1977.

Nyrop, Richard F., ed. *Panama: A Country Study.* U.S. Government Printing Office, Washington, D.C., 1981.

Pereira, Renato. *Panamá: Fuerzas armadas y política.* Ediciones Nueva Universidad, Panamá, 1979.

Pippin, Larry LaRae. *The Remón Era.* Institute of Hispanic American and Luso-Brazilian Studies, Stanford, Calif., 1964.

Ropp, Steve C. *Panamanian Politics: From Guarded Nation to National Guard.* Hoover Institution, Stanford, Calif.; Praeger, New York, 1982.

Ryan, Paul B. *The Panama Canal Controversy: U.S. Diplomacy and Defense Interests.*
  Hoover Institution, Stanford, Calif., 1977.
Soler, Ricuarte. *Formas ideológicas de la nación Panameña.* Editorial Universitaria
  Centroamericana, San José, Costa Rica, 1972.
Torrijos, Omar. *La batalla de Panamá.* Editorial Universitaria de Buenos Aires,
  Buenos Aires, 1973.

27
Puerto Rico:
The Question of Statehood, Commonwealth, or Nation

HENRY WELLS

Puerto Rico is an anomaly in the Americas for several reasons. Culturally it is neither truly Latin American nor truly North American. It is a place where Spanish is nearly everyone's native tongue, where Roman Catholicism is at least nominally the religion of about 80 percent of the adult population, and where other cultural legacies of the island's four centuries as a colony of Spain are still clearly discernible. Having been part of the United States since 1898, on the other hand, Puerto Rico has become a place where the inhabitants are U.S. citizens, where nearly half of them can speak English, and where the media, the educational system, and most political and economic institutions are modeled on those of the United States.

Puerto Rico is also anomalous economically. Per capita income is lower there than in any state of the union but higher than in all but two of the twenty Latin American nations. In 1980, for example (according to the United Nations *1981 Statistical Yearbook*), Puerto Rico's per capita income of US$3,157 was exceeded in Latin America only by that of Venezuela ($4,051) and Uruguay ($3,176). It was, however, less than half the 1980 per capita income of Mississippi (US$6,557), which ranked last among the fifty states.

Demographically, Puerto Rico's rate of population growth—3.3 percent a year for the period 1975–1980—was higher than that of Latin America as a whole during that period (2.5 percent a year) and far higher than that of the United States, 1.1 percent a year. The racial composition of the island's 3.2 million people (1980 census) has not been studied in recent years; in the mid-1950s, however, 55 percent was classified as white, 40 percent as mulatto, and 5 percent as black—a configuration typical of neither the United States nor Latin America, though somewhat similar to that of Cuba and the Dominican Republic.

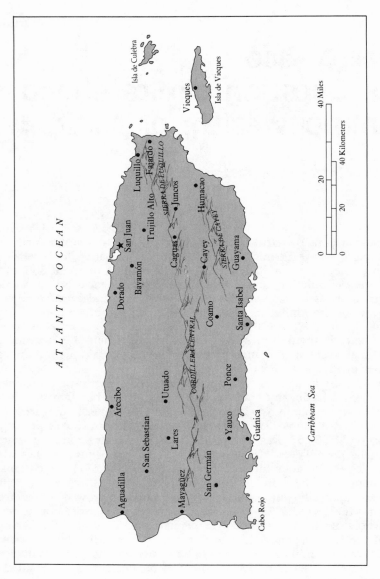

Puerto Rico

Politically Puerto Rico is anomalous because it is neither a state of the union nor an independent republic but a largely self-governing commonwealth within the U.S. political system. Since 1972 two major parties and two small but vocal minor parties have reflected that anomaly. The Popular Democratic party (PPD), which has been a major party since 1940, supports the continuation and improvement of commonwealth status. Its major rival since 1968, the New Progressive party (PNP), advocates the admittance of Puerto Rico to the union as the fifty-first state. Both of the minor parties, the Puerto Rican Independence party (PIP) and the Puerto Rican Socialist party (PSP), favor the separation of Puerto Rico from the United States and its establishment as an independent nation.

Since 1952, when the Commonwealth of Puerto Rico came into being, the principal controversy in insular politics has been the question of whether statehood, commonwealth status, or independence would be the relationship with the United States best suited to Puerto Rico's needs and interests. But the history of what is known in Puerto Rico as the "status" issue goes much further back than that. As early as the 1820s each of the three alternatives had its partisans in the island's small political community. From time to time until 1898, assimilation, autonomy, and separation were each put forward as the most desirable solution to the problem of Puerto Rico's political relations with Spain.

At no time in over a century and a half of preoccupation with the status issue has independence been the solution preferred by most Puerto Ricans. Since 1900, on the contrary, all available evidence indicates that independence is the one alternative toward which a majority of the Puerto Rican people have developed a strong aversion. In the 1980 election, for example, the New Progressive and Popular Democratic candidates together polled 94.2 percent of the votes cast for the office of governor. The Independence party's candidate, on the other hand, received only 5.4 percent, despite his great familiarity to the electorate as one of the most talented and attractive figures in public life. The Socialist candidate, also an *independista*, received only .3 percent of the votes.

It is only in this negative sense that the average Puerto Rican has been concerned with the status issue. Most adult inhabitants of the island do not feel strongly about either statehood or commonwealth status, for they have never had much interest in such concepts as sovereignty, colonialism, autonomy, self-government, and political *dignidad*. Their principal concern has always been economic security and physical well-being, values that they associate with a close relationship between Puerto Rico and the United States. Independence, on the other hand, they have identified with poverty and disorder. Either statehood or commonwealth would presumably suit a great many Puerto Ricans, as long as ties with the United States remained firm.

The Puerto Ricans for whom status controversies are a matter of interest and a constant topic of conversation are understandably a

minority of the adult population. Such members of the political community are, for the most part, persons of middle-class occupations and
income who can afford to concern themselves with more than material
values. The elite of that community, those who have made the status
alternatives the central issue of Puerto Rican politics, have tended to
come from the ranks of teachers, lawyers, journalists, and other professionals, many of them motivated by a keen appreciation of democratic
values.

Puerto Rico's status-oriented political elite and popular responses to
its contemporary views and activities will therefore be a major focus
of the following analysis. If the significance of recent trends is to be
understood, however, it is necessary to have some acquaintance with
two earlier facets of Puerto Rico's development: the patterns of Spanish
and U.S. colonialism in Puerto Rico to about 1950 and the political and
economic innovations of Luis Muñoz Marín, whose Popular Democratic
party controlled the government from 1941 through 1968.

THE POLITICAL BACKGROUND:
SPANISH AND U.S. COLONIALISM

Discovered by Columbus in 1493 and settled by Ponce de León in
1508, Puerto Rico remained a Spanish possession until 1898. From the
sixteenth through the eighteenth century it was ruled by autocratic
governors-general, usually high-ranking military officers. As agents of
the Crown they exercised wide authority over civil government, the
armed forces and police, the economy, and the Church. Puerto Ricans
neither participated in public affairs nor enjoyed any civil rights. The
same pattern prevailed during the nineteenth century except for brief
periods when relatively liberal groups gained power in Spain and allowed
male members of the Puerto Rican elite some freedom of expression
and the right to vote.

During those interludes small groups of Puerto Ricans formulated
demands for independence, for integration into the Spanish realm with
the same status as that of the peninsular provinces, and for self-
government within the kingdom. In 1868, for example, an armed uprising
of *independentistas* occurred in Lares, a town in the west-central mountains, but Spanish troops stationed nearby crushed it within twenty-
four hours. In 1870 the Spanish *cortes* authorized the formation of
political parties, whereupon Puerto Rican assimilationists organized the
Liberal Reformist party. By 1884, however, autonomists had gained
control of it, and in 1887 they changed its name to the Puerto Rican
Autonomist party.

In November 1897, thanks in part to the shrewd politics of Luis
Muñoz Rivera, a prominent Puerto Rican autonomist, the Spanish
government issued the Autonomic Charter of the Antilles, which granted
a good deal of self-government to Puerto Rico. It established a parliament

of broad but not unlimited powers, a cabinet responsible to it, and a governor-general rather ambivalently empowered to act as both representative of the home government and "representative and chief of the colony." But the reforms could not be carried out. On July 25, 1898, eight days after the newly elected parliament had convened and Muñoz Rivera had taken office as prime minister, U.S. troops invaded the island. By July 28, when the parliament disbanded, Puerto Rico's first exposure to political autonomy was at an end.

Having long regarded the United States as a model of freedom, self-government, and economic progress, the political leaders of the island were surprised and disappointed to learn that Congress was prepared to grant the Puerto Rican people hardly any control over their internal affairs. The Organic Act that it adopted in 1900 allowed them to elect only members of the lower house of the legislature and a resident commissioner to represent the island in Washington, D.C., where he could speak but not vote in the House of Representatives. The governor, members of the upper chamber, and other top officials, including the justices of the Supreme Court, were made presidential appointees. The act exempted Puerto Rico from federal tax laws but declared that other "statutory laws of the United States" would have "the same force and effect in Puerto Rico as in the United States." It also reserved to Congress the right to annul insular legislation, but Congress never used that power.

The main reason Congress was unwilling to grant Puerto Rico powers of self-rule comparable to those authorized by the Autonomic Charter of 1897 was that Senate and House committees had received reports and other testimony to the effect that about 85 percent of the adult population was poverty stricken, illiterate, and wholly inexperienced in self-government. The two chambers therefore decided to limit the Puerto Ricans' participation in politics until economic and social conditions had improved and the people of the island had gained some experience with voting and with the functioning of U.S. institutions. Hoping to stimulate economic development, Congress included in the Organic Act a provision for free trade between Puerto Rico and the United States.

The leaders who dominated Puerto Rican politics until the adoption of a new Organic Act in 1917 were Muñoz Rivera and Dr. José C. Barbosa. They had headed rival wings of the Autonomist party until the change of sovereignty and headed rival parties thereafter until Muñoz Rivera's death in 1916. Barbosa founded the Republican party, which endorsed the goal of statehood in 1899 and has consistently held to it, through several changes of party name, down to the present day. The New Progressive party is its lineal descendant. In 1899 Muñoz Rivera founded the Federalist party, which also endorsed statehood, but in 1904 its name was changed to the Union party and its platform broadened to include autonomy and independence, along with statehood, as equally satisfactory forms of self-government. The Unionists thereafter included advocates of all three status alternatives. Muñoz Rivera, still basically an autonomist, remained their leader and, beginning in 1911, also served as Puerto Rico's resident commissioner in Washington.

The Organic Act that Congress adopted in 1917 contained few changes—little more than a popularly elected Senate and a bill of rights. It did, however, confer U.S. citizenship upon the people of the island, a measure that certain Unionist leaders opposed during congressional committee hearings on the grounds that the granting of citizenship would run counter to their aspirations for Puerto Rico's eventual independence. Thirty years were to elapse before Congress again heeded Puerto Rican pleas for political reform. In 1947 it amended the Organic Act to permit the people to elect their own governor and to allow the governor to appoint all the department heads. The auditor and the Supreme Court justices still remained presidential appointees.

In the meantime U.S. corporate interests had turned the coastal plains into vast sugarcane plantations and begun to dominate the production of tobacco and other export crops. Over the years the economy of the island became closely integrated into that of the mainland, but the living conditions of the great mass of Puerto Ricans remained near the subsistence level. Although the plight of the rural and urban poor worsened during the depression, when the gainfully employed dropped to only 35 percent of the labor force, most members of the Puerto Rican political elite showed little concern. They were too preoccupied with corporate payoffs and other spoils of office to pay much attention. The prostatehood coalition that ran the legislature from 1933 to 1940 actually resisted New Deal efforts to provide emergency relief and revive the island's moribund economy.

RAPID ECONOMIC AND POLITICAL CHANGE: THE ERA OF LUIS MUÑOZ MARÍN

One of the few leaders who took a constructive approach to Puerto Rico's problems was Luis Muñoz Marín, the only son of Muñoz Rivera. As a leading *independentista* he had long attacked the island's dependence on absentee U.S. corporations and the subservience of the legislature to their interests. In 1938, at the age of forty, he organized the Popular Democratic party as a vehicle for achieving socioeconomic reforms as well as independence. During the 1940 campaign, however, he found that he and the other PPD candidates could not expect to win the votes of the countryfolk, who accounted for at least 70 percent of the electorate, if they persisted in advocating independence. The *campesinos* welcomed their reform proposals but flatly rejected their goal of separating Puerto Rico from the United States. The Popular Democrats then began campaigning on the slogan Political Status Is Not at Issue and won enough seats to control both houses of the legislature. Their land reform programs and other social-welfare accomplishments gained them an overwhelming endorsement in the 1944 election. They won 65 percent of the votes and all but two seats in each house.

In 1946 Muñoz Marín made two momentous decisions, one economic and the other political. The economic decision was that the achievement of a high standard of living for all Puerto Ricans, as called for by the PPD program, required the industrialization of Puerto Rico's economy, which until then had been predominantly agricultural. The political decision was that both statehood and independence must be rejected and that a third alternative must be developed—one that would greatly improve Puerto Rico's existing political relationship with the United States, which Muñoz described as "highly undesirable," and yet preserve the existing economic relationship, which he called "absolutely necessary to the survival of the people."[1] The two decisions were closely related. Muñoz and his advisers had come to the conclusion that the most effective way to achieve industrialization was to induce large numbers of U.S. industrialists to establish factories on the island and that they could be persuaded to invest in Puerto Rico if the unique advantages of the island's economic relationship with the United States under the Organic Act were made clear to them.

Under the leadership of Teodoro Moscoso, one of Muñoz Marín's closest associates, the economic development agency, known as Fomento, had remarkable success during the 1950s and 1960s in attracting industries to the island. Offering such inducements as loans, subsidies, employee recruitment and training, and other technical services under its Operation Bootstrap program, Fomento also stressed the opportunities for profit afforded by the absence of tariff barriers between the island and the mainland, the abundance of relatively low priced labor (in 1940 Congress had exempted Puerto Rico from full compliance with federal minimum-wage laws), and, most important of all, Puerto Rico's exemption from all federal taxes. After the adoption of the Puerto Rican Industrial Incentives Act of 1947, new industries could obtain exemption from all Puerto Rican taxes also, originally for ten years and later for up to thirty.

These and other incentives led to the establishment of many labor-intensive industries that produced or assembled consumer goods for sale in the United States. By the 1960s a wide variety of manufactures, including capital-intensive industries, were to be found throughout the island. By 1967 Fomento had helped some fifteen hundred factories begin operations. In 1970 manufacturing was employing 141,000 persons and producing 25 percent of net income, whereas in 1948 it had employed only 58,000 and contributed only 12 percent of net income.[2] Industry was the major catalyst of the expansion that had taken place in all sectors of the economy except agriculture by the end of the 1960s. It led also to a general rise in personal incomes, a more equitable distribution of wealth, increased government revenues and hence more public services, and the emergence of a large and ever expanding middle class. The expansion of capital-intensive oil refineries and petrochemical plants, on the other hand, did little to reduce unemployment but a great deal to befoul the environment.

What Muñoz attempted to arrive at after 1946 as a remedy for the political deficiencies of the Organic Act was home rule or autonomy, the solution to the status problem sought for so many years by his father, Luis Muñoz Rivera. Muñoz Marín's strategy for achieving it involved four interrelated actions on the part of Congress and the Puerto Rican people, all of which were accomplished between 1950 and 1952. The first was Congress's 1950 enactment of Public Law 600, which (1) authorized the Puerto Rican people to draft and adopt their own constitution, (2) repealed the internal-government provisions of the Organic Act, and (3) kept the rest of it, including the economic provisions, in effect under a new title, the Puerto Rican Federal Relations Act. The second action occurred on June 4, 1951, when 77 percent of the Puerto Ricans voting in a referendum accepted the terms of Public Law 600. The third was their drafting and adopting a constitution during 1951 and 1952, and the fourth was the ratification of that document by Congress on July 3, 1952.

When the constitution took effect on July 25, 1952, the new Commonwealth of Puerto Rico came into existence. It also marked the attainment of internal self-government in the sense that the basic features of the system estabished by the new constitution were indistinguishable from those set forth in the U.S. state constitutions. They included a comprehensive bill of rights and a separation of powers into the familiar three branches, along with the customary provisions for their balancing and interaction.

In the meantime Muñoz began asserting that the significance of these events was that U.S.–Puerto Rican relations had undergone a profound change. His argument relied heavily on the first section of Public Law 600, which stated that "fully recognizing the principle of government by consent," Congress adopted the act "*in the nature of a compact* so that the people of Puerto Rico might organize a government pursuant to a constitution of its own adoption" (emphasis added). Reduced to its essentials, his "commonwealth" doctrine held that by virtue of the compact and the reciprocal process by which it was approved and implemented, Puerto Rico was no longer a colony of the United States. Instead, it had become an *estado libre asociado* (associated free state), or commonwealth, which remained linked to the United States by its own consent. The doctrine also maintained that changes in Puerto Rico's relationship with the United States could not thereafter be imposed unilaterally by Congress but could be accomplished only through procedures requiring the consent of both parties.

Advocates of independence and of statehood rejected the commonwealth doctrine out of hand. Supported by incontrovertible evidence, they argued that in enacting Public Law 600 and in ratifying the new

constitution Congress neither intended nor implied the revisions in U.S.–
Puerto Rican relations that Muñoz ascribed to their actions. Even members
of his own party found it difficult to accept his contention that the new
commonwealth arrangements had removed the last vestiges of colonialism
from Puerto Rico's relationship with the United States. One of their
objections to the "compact" was that it had not changed the Organic
Act provision giving federal legislation (except tax laws) the same force
and effect in Puerto Rico as in the United States. Since Puerto Ricans
still lacked voting representation, they pointed out, Congress would
continue unilaterally to enact laws on shipping, tariffs, environmental
protection, immigration, and hundreds of other matters that vitally
affected them. And since they still could not vote in presidential elections,
they argued, Puerto Ricans had little or no chance to influence the
president's decisions on foreign policy, defense, the federal budget, and
other things germane to their interests. More extreme autonomists
criticized the compact for neither recognizing Puerto Rican sovereignty
nor allowing the commonwealth to enter into commercial or other
relations with neighboring countries.

Muñoz acknowledged that these and other defects in the compact
needed to be corrected, and in 1959 he tried unsuccessfully to obtain
from Congress a modest amendment of the Federal Relations Act. In
1963 Congress again declined to revise the act, mainly because conflicting
testimony from procommonwealth, prostatehood, and proindependence
witnesses left congressional committees perplexed as to what the Puerto
Ricans themselves really wanted. In 1964, therefore, Congress established
a United States–Puerto Rican Commission to examine the three status
alternatives and submit a report. After two years of study the commission
recommended that Puerto Rico hold a plebiscite on the three options
and that "ad hoc advisory groups" be established after the plebiscite
to propose ways of implementing the option preferred by a majority—
"transition measures" if the choice was statehood or independence,
measures for its "further growth" if the choice was commonwealth. The
plebiscite was held on July 23, 1967. The results showed that 60.4
percent of those voting favored the commonwealth alternative, 39 percent
preferred statehood, and only .6 percent supported independence.

POLITICAL GROUPS: CHANGING PATTERNS
OF PARTY COMPETITION

Increasing prosperity in the private sector, expanding public services,
the novelty of commonwealth status, and the extraordinary personal
magnetism of Luis Muñoz Marín all contributed to the popularity of
the Popular Democratic party. It won at least 58 percent of the votes
cast and every office it contested in every election from 1944 through
1964. Its high-water mark was the 1952 election, held shortly after the
inauguration of the commonwealth, when Muñoz received 65 percent

of the gubernatorial vote. His margin of victory declined slightly in 1956 and 1960, but in the latter election he still won more than 58 percent of the vote. In the 1964 election his hand-picked successor, Roberto Sánchez Vilella, received 59 percent.

During the 1950s and 1960s the electoral fortunes of the statehood movement steadily improved, whereas those of the independence movement rapidly declined. The Republican Statehood party (PER) reached its lowest point in the 1952 election, when its gubernatorial nominee received only 13 percent of the vote. In each of the next three elections it improved its position, rising from 25 percent in 1956 to 35 percent in 1964. The head of the PER ticket in all three campaigns was Luis A. Ferré, a prominent industrialist whose prostatehood views attracted support from members of the rapidly expanding middle class. Having broken with the PER in 1967, he founded the New Progressive party in 1968 and won the governorship that year on the new PNP ticket. He accomplished that feat with only 43.6 percent of the vote, mainly because of factionalism within the Popular Democratic party: Repudiated by the old-guard PPD leadership, Governor Sánchez Vilella split the normal Popular Democratic vote by running for reelection as the candidate of his new People's party.

The Independence party reached its peak in the 1952 election when its candidate for governor received 19 percent of the vote, by far the most support ever received by a proindependence candidate. The party seems to have been the beneficiary of protest votes cast by resentful supporters of the old Liberal and Socialist parties that had been swept aside by the Popular Democratic juggernaut and by militant Catholics upset by the PPD government's birth-control clinics. In 1956 the PIP vote fell to 12.5 percent of the total, and in 1960 it plummeted to 3.1 percent—presumably because of losing many of its Catholic supporters to the short-lived Christian Action party, which contested the 1960 election and won 6.6 percent of the votes. Support for the PIP candidate deteriorated still further to 2.7 percent in the 1964 election, but recovered to 3.5 percent in 1968.

POLITICAL AND ECONOMIC CHANGES
AFTER 1968: THE POLICY RESPONSE

The inauguration of Luis Ferré as governor on January 2, 1969, was the beginning of a new era in Puerto Rican politics. It marked the end of Popular Democratic dominance, which had lasted twenty-eight years, and the beginning of a period in which the two major parties, roughly equal in strength, alternated in power every four years. The 1972 election restored control of the government to the Popular Democrats under the leadership of Rafael Hernández Colón, who replaced Ferré as governor. In 1976 the pendulum swung back: The New Progressive party won a majority of the seats in both legislative chambers and elected Carlos Romero Barceló to the governorship.

In 1980, however, the election results departed a bit from the pattern of party alternation, inasmuch as Governor Romero's reelection extended the New Progressive's control over the executive branch for another four years. But his margin of victory was only 3,500 votes, or .2 percent of the 1.6 million ballots cast, and the popular Democrats regained control of the legislature. In 1983 the PNP was further weakened by the defection of its popular mayor of San Juan, Hernán Padilla, who withdrew in order to form the Puerto Rican Renewal party (PRP) and to run as it gubernatorial candidate in the election of November 6, 1984. This development, so reminiscent of Governor Sánchez Vilella's ill-fated defection from the PPD in 1968, made it almost inevitable that the Popular Democrats would increase their majorities in the legislative chambers and elect Hernández Colón once again to the governorship in the 1984 contest.

The transfer of power from one party to the other made it difficult for the leadership of either party to accomplish much during its tenure of office in the period 1969–1981. Each new team of policymakers tended to modify or reverse the programs initiated by the team it supplanted and had all too little time to put alternative programs into effect. Governor Romero's second term, 1981–1985, so far has not remedied matters, for the Popular Democrat's control of the legislature produced stalemate on many issues. As will be seen in the following discussion, Governors Ferré, Hernández Colón, and Romero Barceló all made some attempt to promote their respective status objectives while in office, but they had little to show for their efforts when their terms expired. In any case, changed circumstances required all three governors to devote most of their time and attention to the island's economic difficulties.

The year 1969 marked the end of two decades of economic expansion in Puerto Rico. The U.S. recession of 1969–1970 badly damaged Puerto Rico's tourist business, private housing construction, and labor-intensive manufacturing, especially the apparel, leather goods, and textile industries. They had hardly begun to recover when the economy suffered the trip-hammer blows of the petroleum crisis of 1973–1974: the shortages, the quadrupling of crude oil prices, and the ensuing inflation and recession that afflicted the economies of even the most developed nations for the rest of the decade.

External recessions were not the only cause of Puerto Rico's economic troubles during the 1970s. More fundamental was the change of emphasis in Puerto Rican industry from labor-intensive to capital-intensive enterprises. Although labor-intensive industries had been the main engine of growth during the 1950s and 1960s and in 1970 were still accounting for 63 percent of total manufacturing output, by 1980 they were contributing only 31 percent. Capital-intensive industries' contribution, on the other hand, rose from 35 percent to 67 percent over the same period.

A basic factor in this reversal was the gradual rise in Puerto Rican wage levels, which by 1970 had nearly reached that of the U.S. minimum wage. Many U.S. entrepreneurs closed their labor-intensive plants in Puerto Rico and reestablished them in such places as Hong Kong, Singapore, South Korea, and the next-door Dominican Republic, where wages were less than half, sometimes only one-tenth, as high as in Puerto Rico. The corporate owners of Puerto Rico's capital-intensive industries, by contrast, had from the beginning paid wages far above the U.S. minimum but employed few workers.

One consequence of this change in the industrial pattern was to intensify the chronic problem of unemployment. In fiscal 1969 Puerto Rico's rate of unemployment had fallen to 10.3 percent of the labor force, an all-time low, but it started rising again in 1970. It reached 15.4 percent in 1975 and 20 percent in 1977. Thanks to a mild upturn in economic activity during 1977–1979, the rate fell to 17 percent by 1980; but the severe depression that began the following year caused the unemployment rate to reach a record 22.7 percent in 1982.

Widespread suffereing on the part of the unemployed and others disadvantaged by the hard times of the 1970s was to a considerable degree prevented by a dramatic expansion in federal-aid programs. Federal grants to the commonwealth and municipal governments in support of Medicaid, school lunches, aid to the unemployed, and many other programs, including highway construction and other public works, increased from $257 million in 1970 to $651 million in 1975 and $1,348 million in 1980. A far greater increase occurred in the amount of federal transfer payments made directly to individuals under such programs as old age and survivors' insurance, veterans' pensions, Medicare, and, beginning in July 1974, food stamps. Federal outlays in Puerto Rico for these programs rose from $303 million in 1970 to $1,167 million in 1975 and $2,360 million in 1980. Food stamp payments, which more than half of Puerto Rican families were receiving by 1980, accounted for $812 million of that year's total transfer payments.

In addition to the total of $3,708 million received in 1980 from federal grants and transfer payments, Puerto Rico received $543 million that year from other federal sources (customs duties, federal excise taxes on island rum sold in the states, and disbursements of federal departments and agencies to cover their operating expenses in Puerto Rico), for a grand total of $4,251 million. When reduced by $835 million in payments to the federal government, the net amount of federal funds received in Puerto Rico in 1980 came to $3,416 million, or 38.5 percent of the island's gross national product for that year.[3]

The Reagan administration began reducing federal outlays in Puerto Rico soon after taking office in January 1981. Its fiscal 1982 budget, which took effect in October 1981, cut about $650 million from the $4 billion (net) previously scheduled to be spent in Puerto Rico in FY1982. The largest single reduction was the excision of $300 million from funds totaling about $1.2 billion that had originally been proposed for food and nutritional assistance, including food stamps. Under the Reagan budget, the remaining $900 million was allocated to the Puerto Rican government in the form of a block grant to be distributed as it saw fit. Since July 1, 1982, the Romero Barceló administration has been mailing checks to eligible recipients instead of issuing food stamps, a simplification intended to save $15 million a year in administrative costs. Other Reagan budget cuts made substantial reductions in employment and job-training programs (eliminating about twenty-five thousand Comprehensive Employment and Training Act—CETA—jobs from commonwealth and municipal payrolls), education grants (eliminating such things as scholarships previously received by 95 percent of the students at some private colleges and universities), and public-works grants (eliminating such projects as water-supply and sewer-system improvements).[4]

Having become dependent on food stamps and other forms of direct aid, many beneficiaries of federal largess were ill prepared to deal with the cutbacks and began to suffer unaccustomed hardships. The reductions in federal outlays also intensified the severity of the 1981–1983 recession in Puerto Rico by reducing purchasing power and thereby contributing to a decline in economic activity, an increase in business closures and bankruptcies, and, as already noted, substantially increased unemployment.

THE STATUS ISSUE: PROSPECTS FOR CHANGE

In one sense, the perennial status debate still goes on in Puerto Rico, repeating old arguments for and against each of the three basic status alternatives, without seeming to get anywhere. Even less does a consensus in favor of any particular status outcome seem to be emerging. And yet, in another sense, the debate has entered a new stage—one in which a consensus on diagnosis, priorities, and even procedures may already have come into existence among leading proponents of each status option. Before examining that new development, however, let me briefly review some abortive actions that recent governors have taken with respect to the status issue.

Governors Ferré and Hernández Colón each tried unsuccessfully during his term of office to use the Ad Hoc Advisory Group as a device for directly or indirectly promoting greater popular support for his own status preference. Shrewdly exploiting the deep rift within the Popular Democratic party between those leaders who favored close association with the United States and those who preferred greater political autonomy for Puerto Rico, Governor Ferré appointed proassociation *populares* as the Puerto Rican members of the first Ad Hoc Advisory Group, established in 1970 to consider the "further growth" of commonwealth status. Its tacitly assimilationist recommendation that the right to vote in presidential elections be extended to Puerto Rico aroused widespread popular interest, but autonomist Popular Democrats in control of the Senate prevented the holding of a referendum on the issue.

A majority of the Puerto Rican members whom Governor Hernández appointed to the second advisory group in 1973 were autonomists. Under the chairmanship of Don Luis Muñoz Marín, they prepared a new Compact of Permanent Union Between Puerto Rico and the United States to replace the Federal Relations Act. Concurred in by the U.S. members with some reservations, the new compact proposed greatly increased autonomy for the commonwealth, including authority to control the admittance of aliens into the island, but nothing came of it. President Ford, to whom it was submitted in 1975, neither endorsed it nor forwarded it to Congress. Bills based on the document were nevertheless introduced in both houses, but they died in subcommittees. The Popular Democrats were powerless to revive the issue after their defeat at the polls in November 1976.

Governor Romero Barceló's frustrations in promoting statehood for Puerto Rico were of a different order. The main theme of his 1976 and 1980 campaigns was that "statehood is for the poor," but he received no commendation medals from the White House for using that argument. His thesis was the following: Under statehood most Puerto Ricans would not have to pay any federal income tax, for their incomes are too low to be taxable; but they would be certain to benefit greatly if Puerto Rico were to become a state, for in that case Congress could no longer discriminate against Puerto Rico by excluding its people from major welfare programs that the eligible citizens of every state in the union are entitled to benefit from. He would cite as examples the Supplemental Security Income program for the low-income blind, disabled, and aged; the minimum-income program for aged citizens ineligible for Social Security; revenue sharing; and several welfare programs in which allocations to Puerto Rico were "capped," that is, could not rise above a fixed amount. Although officials of the Reagan administration had said that its policy was "to treat Puerto Rico as if it were a state" in welfare matters,[5] its budget cuts gave a different impression.

In the 1960s the leading strategists of each major party began to think in terms of four successive favorable outcomes: (1) winning the next general election by a big enough majority to justify holding another plebiscite on the status alternatives; (2) winning impressive majority support for their party's status alternative in the plebiscite itself; (3) going to Congress with an irrefutable mandate from the Puerto Rican people for the enactment of legislation to implement the change they had endorsed; and, finally, (4) obtaining from Congress the requested legislation. The assumptions underlying this approach were that Congress would not act until a substantial proportion of the Puerto Rican people had rallied behind one of the status alternatives and that Congress would act in accordance with the majority preference once the plebiscite had identified it beyond any doubt.

These assumptions underlay the status strategies of the PPD and the PNP in every election campaign from that of 1968 through that of 1980. In the 1980 campaign, for example, one of Governor Romero's pledges to the electorate was to hold a plebiscite before 1985 if the New Progressives won the 1980 election by a handsome margin. In the event, his narrow plurality victory over Hernández Colón precluded recourse to a plebiscite during the ensuing four years. In the meantime, however, the leaders of the two major parties had hit upon a new strategy that has since changed the character of the status debate.

This process of basic reorientation began early in 1977 when pros-tatehood Puerto Ricans who had been Carter activitists among Hispanic voters during the 1976 campaign notified the new president and his staff that they intended to attack commonwealth status in the forthcoming hearings before the Decolonization Committee of the United Nations. In April 1977 Governor Romero announced that he would not defend commonwealth status before that committee, as his PDP predecessors had done from time to time at the behest of the U.S. State Department, because in his view it was flawed by "vestiges of colonialism."

These developments led the State Department to decide that the time had come to abandon its long-standing support for the commonwealth option and to adopt instead a policy of "self-determination and alternative futures"—that is, of leaving the status issue to the Puerto Rican people to decide for themselves and of supporting whichever alternative they preferred. At the hearings before the Decolonization Committee in 1978, representatives of all four Puerto Rican parties—including Governor Romero for the PNP and former Governor Hernández for the PPD—denounced the existing form of commonwealth for still containing colonialist features that had made it incompatible with full self-government ever since its adoption in 1952.

By 1978, in other words, the Puerto Rican party leaders had reached a consensus on the proposition that Puerto Rico's relations with the United States were fundamentally colonial in nature. Having agreed on a diagnosis of the problem, they proceeded to consider what should be done about it. The additional consensus that seems to be emerging is that the passive role for the United States implicit in its adherence to the "self-determination and alternative futures" policy is no longer acceptable. The current view is that as a colonial power the United States is the offending party and therefore has a positive obligation to take the lead in remedying what is in these times an unconscionable relationship. U.S. insistence on self-determination is seen as an evasion of responsibility: The issue, rather, "has become *decolonization*, a process that, by definition, requires an active involvement of the colonial power."[6]

Before Puerto Ricans can be expected to choose intelligently among status alternatives in a plebiscite, the argument runs, they must know as specifically as possible what Congress is or is not prepared to authorize in the case of each alternative. According to one exponent of this latest consensus, "Congress should establish a specialized body to deal with Puerto Rico's future. This body would formally explore the issues and provide a much-needed focus for debate. It could also spell out the conditions for each option in pragmatic, equitable ways, and formulate proposals that Congress could accept in advance and that Puerto Ricans could then decide on. . . . Washington must first tell Puerto Rico what the options are if it wishes Puerto Ricans to choose among them."[7]

It remains to be seen whether Congress can be prevailed upon to accept that responsibility and, if it does, what alternative a majority of the so-informed Puerto Rican electorate would adopt.

NOTES

1. The quotations are translated phrases from the second of a two-part article published by Muñoz Marín in *El Mundo* (San Juan, P.R.) on June 28 and 29, 1946, under the title "El Status Político: Nuevos caminos hacia viejos objetivos"; reprinted in Antonio Fernós Isern, *Puerto Rico Libre y Federado* (Biblioteca de Autores Puertorriqueños, San Juan, 1951), pp. 21–40, 36–37.

2. *New York Times,* August 3, 1967, p. 43; Puerto Rican Planning Board, *Informe Económico al Gobernador, 1970* (San Juan, 1971), table 17, p. A-22, percentages calculated from table 2, p. A-4, corrected to exclude net income from home needlework.

3. Unemployment data taken from Puerto Rican Planning Board, *Informe Económico al Gobernador, 1975* (San Juan, 1976), and *Informe Económico al Gobernador, 1982* (San Juan, 1983); and *Latin America Regional Reports: Caribbean* (London), July 16, 1982, p. 4. Data on federal grants, transfer payments, and disbursements taken from Puerto Rican Planning Board, *1982,* p. 410.

4. Ronald Walker, "Economic Storm Rips Puerto Rico," *San Francisco Chronicle,* November 10, 1982, p. A1.

5. Ibid.

6. Jorge Heine and Juan M. García-Passalacqua, *The Puerto Rican Question,* Headline Series, no. 266, Foreign Policy Association, New York, November/December 1983, p. 60. The Puerto Rican Independence party has long recognized that its best strategy is to convince opinion leaders in the United States, and especially in Congress and the executive branch, that it is in the interest of U.S. taxpayers and of the United States generally to grant independence to Puerto Rico. See Rubén Berríos Martínez, "Independence for Puerto Rico: The Only Solution,"*Foreign Affairs* 55 (April 1977):561–583.

7. Jeffrey M. Puryear, "Puerto Rico's Waiting," *New York Times,* April 14, 1981, p. A23.

SUGGESTIONS FOR FURTHER READING

Anderson, Robert W. *Party Politics in Puerto Rico.* Stanford University Press, Stanford, Calif., 1965.

Farr, Kenneth R. *Personalism and Party Politics: Institutionalization of the Popular Democratic Party of Puerto Rico.* Inter-American University Press, Hato Rey, P.R., 1973.

García-Passalacqua, Juan M. *La alternativa liberal*. Editorial Univeristaria, Universidad de Puerto Rico, Río Piedras, P.R., 1974.

Heine, Jorge, ed. *Time for Decision: The United States and Puerto Rico*. North-South Press, Lanham, Md., 1983.

Heine, Jorge, and Juan M. García-Passalacqua. *The Puerto Rican Question*. Headline Series, no. 266. Foreign Policy Association, New York, November/December 1983.

Johnson, Roberta Ann. *Puerto Rico: Commonwealth or Colony?* Praeger, New York, 1980.

Lewis, Gordon. *Puerto Rico: Freedom and Power in the Caribbean*. Monthly Review Press, New York, 1963.

Maldonado Denis, Manuel. *Puerto Rico: A Socio-Historic Interpretation*. Random House, New York, 1972.

————. *Puerto Rico y Estados Unidos: Emigración y colonialismo*. Siglo Veintiuno Editores, Mexico City, 1976.

Morales Carrión, Arturo. *Puerto Rico: A Political and Cultural History*. W.W. Norton, New York, 1983.

Nieves Falcón, Luis. *La opinión pública y las aspiraciones de los puertorriqueños*. Centro de Investigaciones Sociales, Universidad de Puerto Rico, Río Piedras, P.R., 1970.

Tumin, Melvin M., with Arnold Feldman. *Social Class and Social Change in Puerto Rico*. Princeton Unviersity Press, Princeton, N.J., 1961.

Wagenheim, Kal. *Puerto Rico: A Profile*. 2d ed. Praeger, New York, 1975.

Wells, Henry. *The Modernization of Puerto Rico*. Harvard University Press, Cambridge, 1969.

Part 4

Conclusion: Latin America and its alternative futures

HOWARD J. WIARDA
HARVEY F. KLINE

A LIVING LABORATORY

Latin America is one of the world's most exciting living laboratories of social and political change. Capitalist, socialist, feudal, and mercantilist economies exist in a variety of forms, along with numerous hybrids of these major types. The political structures vary from repressive authoritarian regimes that ignore democratic processes and ride roughshod over human rights to liberal and democratic polities whose citizens are as free as any in the world. In between are a variety of halfway houses, with combined civilian and military features, transitional regimes of various kinds, some tending toward democracy, others going back toward authoritarianism. The social systems also range from feudal and two class, to multiclass pluralistic, to socialist, again with many combinations from nation to nation and within single nations. The most primitive and backward conditions prevail in some areas, the most sophisticated and modern in others.

What helps make Latin America such a fascinating laboratory for comparative sociological and political science study is not only these differences, but the common background of the countries that make up the area. Few parts of the world offer such fruitful conditions for research on the processes of comparative change and modernization. Iberian institutions were set down in an unknown and almost virgin New World territory. Of course for a full understanding of the area, one must take account of the different patterns of the Spanish and Portuguese settlements—the distinct conditions encountered, the differing geographic and climatic conditions, the varying numbers and levels of native Indian civilizations, the distinct socioeconomic patterns that evolved, and the differential importance the colonizing countries assigned the far-flung territories—but still the point holds. Here was a new and largely unsettled territory that suddenly and dramatically experienced the indelible imprint of Iberian-style Westernization. The Spanish and the Portuguese gave the region a common language, religion, and legal system, common forms of social organization, common methods of economic enterprise, a common intellectual and educational tradition, a common structure of political authority, a common political culture, and a common way of behaving and mode of understanding. In Latin America, such shared conditions enable one to hold some factors constant, almost as though it were a scientific laboratory, in an examination of both the parallels and the divergences of national developmental experiences.

Although Latin America's common colonial and historical background should be emphasized with certain parallels in the developmental patterns, the diversity of the area is equally striking. Comparative analysis, after all, requires that both similar and differential aspects be studied. This book has sought to stress both aspects: the general and continental

633

patterns described in Part 1 and the diverse national experiences stressed in the chapters on specific countries.

Although both shared a Spanish colonial background, Argentina and Paraguay are quite different; though Peru, Bolivia, Ecuador, Mexico, and Guatemala all had large pre-Columbian Indian civilizations, their patterns of development have been far from identical. The developmental experiences of the plantation systems of the Caribbean nations and Brazil have similarly been distinctive; comparative Central American development, the comparative developmental experiences of the Andean nations, or those of the Southern Cone (Argentina, Chile, Uruguay) provide fascinating areas for study. Some countries, such as Mexico and Peru, were closely structured on the Spanish colonial system while other areas were characterized by colonial neglect. Those areas receiving the strongest Spanish influence were those with the greatest quantities of gold and silver and with large-scale Indian civilizations providing an abundance of cheap labor. These differing patterns of conquest and colonization in turn shaped the distinct developmental patterns—authoritarian or democratic—of the future Latin American nations.

The chapters on specific countries in this book point up the immense richness and diversity of the Latin American nations. Only with extreme care is it possible to generalize about all the nations of the area or to fashion a "Latin America policy" that applies to the region as a whole. The book has described traditional, liberal, socialist, and corporatist polities and influences as well as various combinations of them. It has examined civilian governments and military regimes and other situations where the distinction between civilian and military is blurred. Within the military category, there exist rightist and repressive regimes and leftist and nationalistic ones. There are countries that fit the general pattern of Latin American development as outlined in Part 1, other countries that fit the general pattern only partially, and still others that fit hardly at all. Hence, it is important to stress both the common currents in Latin America and the differences from country to country, both the main themes and the variations. The Latin American nations are incredibly complex and exceedingly diverse (and becoming more so), although the cultural and sociopolitical tradition in which they exist and behave politically is often a common one. In the book's discussion and study it is both the common patterns and the nuances that command attention, both the main roots and trunk *and* the several branches, both the constants and the variables in this intriguing living laboratory.

CONTINUITY AND CHANGE

Although the main structures of Latin American society and polity remained quite stable for a long period of time extending from the colonial period into the nineteenth century, in recent decades the change process has been greatly accelerated. The book identifies six major areas of change: political culture and values, the economic structure, social and class structure, political groups and organizations, the range of public policy, and the international environment.

The country chapters have made clear the degree to which Latin American political culture is undergoing transformation. New values and ideologies—socialism, corporatism, populism, Marxism, liberalism—have challenged the old belief systems. New communications and transportation grids are increasingly breaking down traditional isolation. Although there is enormous variation from country to country, it is plain that the older Catholic, authoritarian, and hierarchical assumptions are everywhere being questioned, the older bases of legitimacy are being challenged, and a great variety of new ideologies are competing for people's minds.

The economic system has also altered dramatically. Although one may still find a few countries that conform to the stereotype, these are no longer just sleepy rural, agricultural entities. Argentina, Brazil, Mexico, and Venezuela (and to a lesser degree Chile, Colombia, and Peru) have taken their place among the more industrialized nations of the world. In these and other countries, subsistence agriculture coexists with the most modern industries and agribusinesses. Manufacturing, mining, and services in many countries generate as much GNP as agriculture. The older feudalistic concepts and structures have given way to modern capitalist or socialist ones, and Latin America has become much more integrated than in the past with the international economic order.

These changes have served to accelerate social change. A new labor class has risen up. In many countries, a strong middle sector has also evolved, wresting power from the old elites but often so internally divided as to offer few possibilities for stable rule. The elite groups themselves are now increasingly differentiated between old landed wealth and new industrial, banking, commercial, and manufacturing elements. The social composition of the Church and the military officer corps has changed from upper to middle class. An urban subproletariat has emerged in all the countries of Latin America, and in the countryside the lethargic and tradition-bound peasant of the past has become restless and, in some cases, organized and mobilized.

The political system has changed concomitantly. New political parties have been formed, often replacing elite factions; they are organized around new ideological principles and often are mass based. Large-scale organizations of workers, peasants, university students, and professionals have emerged. These are no longer nations where a handful of oligarchs, clerics, and military officers dominate national life; increasingly competitive and pluralistic societies have evolved, with a great variety of competing interests. The United States, we have seen, is also a major actor within the Latin American political systems, bringing both benefits and a situation of dependency.

Not only have the major actors and the group structure changed, but the extent of governmental policy has greatly expanded. In addition to agrarian reform, economic development, urban policy, and family planning, major issue areas now encompass housing, water supplies, education, health care, electric power, literacy programs, irrigation, highways, and reforestation. New norms of honesty and efficiency exist, and governments are increasingly judged on the basis of their ability to deliver the services and programs the people have come to expect. Human rights have recently become a major issue.

The international environment in which the Latin American countries operate has also changed. The traditional isolation is breaking down at a rapid rate. Latin America no longer produces chiefly for itself but for the international market. At the same time, it is increasingly dependent on that market for goods it does not have or produce, such as oil (with some notable exceptions like Venezuela) and heavy machinery. The breakdown of the traditional isolation covers not just the economic marketplace but the marketplace of ideas as well. Latin America is caught up in all the social, cultural, and political transformations shaking the rest of the world. "Civilization" no longer stops at the Rio Grande; Latin America is as much a part of modern civilization as the United States is, and in some areas—international law and diplomacy, music, sociology and political science, the social and political experiments its regimes are undertaking, to say nothing of soccer—it may well be leading the way.

And yet, with all these changes, one should not lose sight of the continuities. Elitist and authoritarian structures persist. The pervasiveness of family structure, kinship, and patron-client relations is apparent. Corporatist and personalist politics usually predominate. The older belief systems and ways of behaving are powerful. Modern organizations and associational groups are often weak or nonexistent. Revolutionary breakthroughs have occurred in some countries, but in others the pace of change has been more gradual and evolutionary. Nor should one underestimate the ability of the traditional elites and ruling groups to accommodate and co-opt the new social forces as they have others in the past. In this way, although some limited change goes forward, the basic structure of power and society may be perpetuated. Indeed, it is largely the clash and conflict between these rival conceptions, the change-oriented forces on the one hand and the defenders of the status quo (albeit modified) on the other, that lie at the heart of contemporary Latin American politics. The struggle is certain to continue, as are the varied efforts of individual countries to reach some kind of compromise and reconciliation between them.

SOME NEW COMMON CURRENTS

Although Latin America is exceedingly diverse and the weight of the past hangs heavily over the area, there are some new common currents, highlighted in the country chapters, that command serious attention.

These changes have taken place relatively recently—over the last two decades—and they imply some profound present and future transformations for Latin American political society. Although the reader is encouraged to look for other commonalities and nuances derived from a systematic comparison of the country chapters, let us here offer, in the form of a set of hypotheses for further study, what to us as editors seem to be the most important nuances and departures stemming from these varied treatments.

1. *Accelerated change and the supplanting of the traditional order.* Since 1930 (a bit earlier in the cases of Mexico, Argentina, and Chile), the feudal, two-class, oligarchic, and elite-dominated systems have been set aside and in some cases eclipsed; now these changes are proceeding more rapidly and reaching deeper down into society. The Latin American countries are no longer a group of simple, traditional banana republics; they have become increasingly complex, mobilized, dynamic, multifaceted, even revolutionary nations.

2. *A growing differentiation among social and political groups.* Throughout the area, competitive labor and peasant movements, populist and middle-sector groups, political parties and other newer power contenders have challenged the wealth and position of the older elites. There is a growing pluralism in society and polity marked by increased competitiveness, challenge, division, and societal fragmentation.

3. *The emergence of a conflict society.* Although the older order is declining and a new one emerging, neither seems sufficiently well established or legitimate enough in most countries to rule effectively by itself or in coalition. The result in Latin America has been not a peaceful transition to bourgeois, moderate, middle-of-the-road, and democratic politics but a situation of conflict and discord.

4. *The radicalization of an entire younger generation.* We have been impressed by the degree to which the younger generation of opinion leaders in Latin America has been radicalized. Since roughly the mid-1960s, this new element (in many countries the majority of the population) has largely abandoned its older allegiance to liberalism and republicanism in favor of socialism. In some countries, the politically aware and involved younger generation is almost totally socialist and Marxist. Throughout Latin America, socialism is coming to represent the midpoint of the political spectrum, not the fringe. The question is no longer whether or not socialism is coming to Latin America, but when and in what form.

5. *The decline of U.S. influence.* Along with radicalization has come a downward slide in the position of the United States. Although many Latin American nations remain dependent on the United States, they have begun to take an increasingly independent stance. The U.S. model, culture, and society are no longer so widely admired; Latin America is expanding its trade and contacts with other parts of the world, including

the socialist one; U.S. foreign-assistance programs have largely failed; Cuba has definitively broken out of the U.S. sphere of influence; business people from other countries (Japan, Germany, Italy, France) are beating out U.S. competitors for the major contracts. The era of U.S. dominance and hegemony is ending as Latin America takes charge of its own future. Some attribute the trend to the declining international status of the United States; some believe that the United States has already lost the cold war in developing countries like Latin America. Whatever one decides on these questions—too complex to be resolved here—it seems that, along with the deterioration of the traditional order and the new thrust toward socialism on the part of the younger generation, the role and influence of the United States throughout the area have significantly diminished.

The strong U.S. presence in Central America probably represents a blip on this downward curve and not a reversal of it. Overall, what impresses is the pragmatism, despite the frequent rhetorical flourishes to the contrary, on the part of both parties: a growing sense of limits in the United States about what it can and cannot do in Latin America, and a corresponding realism on the part of the Latin American nations in dealing with the United States. For even with the decline of United States influence throughout the area, the United States remains a major presence and power with which the Latin Americans must deal pragmatically, and most Latin American leaders recognize that. At the same time, they have also, prudently, begun to diversify their international relations.

6. *The decline of Latin America's historic developmentalist model.* With the ebbing of U.S. influence in Latin America has come that of the classic Latin American developmentalist formula. That formula, as outlined in Chapter 7, involved the gradual accommodation and co-optation of the new and rising power contenders into the political system without the interests of the traditional elites being discarded in the process. That model is now not only being challenged by other, more radical alternatives, but it is collapsing from within. Rather than a peaceful and accommodative process of change, Latin American political society is now characterized by deep fragmentation of social and political groups, escalating conflict, increasing violence and class strife, and periodic long-term breakdowns. The consensual society of the past is being replaced by a society of discord and irreconcilable divisions. The old norms and institutions are deteriorating, and there are no adequate new ones to serve as replacements. A political and institutional vacuum is developing in which strife and violence are everyday occurrences, political disputes have polarized, and the middle way seems no longer to offer promise.

7. *Economic crisis.* One key cause of the current decline and malaise is economic crisis. Most of the Latin American nations are in desperate financial trouble. Relative to the industrialized countries of the north, they have been in a steadily worsening terms-of-trade situation ever

since the 1920s. Expenses and outflow far exceed income, inflation is rampant, expectations have outstripped production, growth has slowed and barely keeps pace with population. For many people, standards of living are falling. Spiraling oil prices have wreaked general disaster. Foreign debts have piled up, and some nations may be forced to default on their loans. The economic pie has stopped expanding in some countries and in some others may even be contracting. First, such a shrinking economic pie means some groups and individuals receive less and thus have increasing grounds for discontent. Second, it threatens the entire historical model of accommodative, co-optive politics since it means there are no new pieces to hand out to an increasingly impatient population.

8. *Military authoritarianism.* The immediate response to these series of crises was a rash of military coups and the coming to power of a host of generally right-wing authoritarian regimes. At the end of 1977, thirteen of the nineteen (excluding Puerto Rico) Latin American countries here analyzed were under military rule. The causes of this resurgence of military rule relate to the factors noted earlier: economic crisis, the failure of civilian politics and politicians and of the historic Latin American co-optive model, the challenge of rising revolutionary movements, and the like. The military regimes have frequently suspended or curbed human rights, sought to snuff out potential leftist challenges, and ruled brutally and oppressively. But military rule was a response to an existing vacuum and to the effort to stem chaos and disintegration. Along with a new web of political controls, the military initiated forms of state capitalist development, centralizing both public and private power in its own hands and desperately seeking to hold the nation together while it tried to fashion a new developmental formula.

But in the early 1980s the pendulum began to swing back the other way. Several military regimes had been thoroughly discredited by their mismanagement of their nation's economic accounts and their indiscriminate use of repression. A number of new democratically elected governments were inaugurated. But the military remain in the wings, and as the economic and political crisis intensifies it seems in several countries to be prepared to return to center stage.

9. *State socialism.* It is only a short step from state capitalism to state socialism, and given the socialist ideology of the Latin American younger generation—sometimes both civilian and military—that prospect has become a major alternative for the future. In countries where so large a share of the national product is already in state hands, all that is required for that transition to occur is a shift in the political leadership. That happened under General Velasco in Peru and partially under General Torrijos in Panama. Socialism may thus come to Latin America not through mass revolution from below but through decree-law from above. Venezuela and Costa Rica have opted for a gradual and parliamentary route to social democracy, but in other countries it could—and has—come quite abruptly.

The implications and corollaries of this transition are many and profound. One of importance has to do with Cuba and the internal settling down and bureaucratization of the Cuban Revolution, hence the increased willingness of the Latin American nations to accept the Cuban Revolution as a fact that may or may not have relevance for them. Our prognosis is that although the Cuban Revolution is unlikely to be repeated in very many other countries in Latin America in its Cuban forms (the Nicaraguan Revolution may be one of the exceptions), other socialist formulas may be tried. These would likely be eclectic and nationalistic efforts, however, growing from local needs and circumstances rather than as copies of what is a unique and in many ways distinctly Cuban experience.

Another fascinating area of study is provided by the varied left and nationalist military, or civil-military, regimes that do exist. In some countries, the struggles among left-wing factions within the military and their right and center counterparts, each intertwined with corresponding, similarly competitive civilian groups, provide the major focus of political conflict. Still another involves the longer-term transition from right to left regimes, from state capitalist systems to state socialist or syndicalist ones, or the increased blurring of the differences between them. Throughout Latin America, a search for new formulas to replace or supplement the older one is being conducted. Although we do not wish to make the process seem inevitable or entirely deterministic, our conclusion from the analyses presented in the country chapters is that the formulas arrived at are likely to involve increasing accommodation with socialist, syndicalist, and state socialist forms. These changes imply wrenching transformations in the Latin American social and political structures, but they open up new and exciting possibilities for innovation, development, and social justice.

THE FUTURE

Although it is probable that many of the Latin American countries will evolve toward left, statist, and socialist or syndicalist societies, the range of options will no doubt remain wide. We would anticipate that there will be civilian social democratic governments as in Costa Rica and Venezuela; left military regimes such as Peru, Panama, and to some degree Bolivia, Honduras, El Salvador, and Ecuador once had; and a variety of mixed civil-military regimes in other nations. There is a good chance that the appeal of a single-party integrating mechanism like Mexico's will continue. And the pressures from the left for a more thoroughgoing and radical restructuring as in Cuba or Nicaragua will also remain strong.

Nor should one underestimate the capacity of the authoritarian military regimes in Chile and elsewhere to hang on to power, although these regimes will probably evolve in new directions. One should not be surprised to see state capitalist systems become state socialist systems almost overnight in some cases.

One should not be surprised either at the adaptability of traditional elitist elements. Latin American elites tend to be very practical and flexible, and although it may sound ideologically inconsistent, they are capable of leading their nations in new directions. The elites, after all, frequently hold strong anti-American sentiments and are often strongly nationalist in their way. We would not be surprised if even those countries dominated by elites begin a pragmatic move toward the nationalization of major U.S. holdings, if the elites, who can be infinitely accommodative and flexible, decide that their best interests lie in leading the revolution rather than being overcome by it.

All this lends a dynamic flexibility and fascination to Latin American politics that we find exciting. It is healthy and exhilarating that there are not one or two routes to modernization but many and varied ones. We think it would be boring, as well as historically and factually inaccurate, to say that there is only one road for all nations to follow. That is too easy and too simple. It is far more interesting and invigorating, we find, to wrestle with the reality that Latin America has several alternative futures. Development may take a plurality of forms and need not correspond to any preconceived notions.

Whatever direction development takes in Latin America, one should bear in mind the following caveats.

1. Development is a long, difficult, arduous, wrenching process. It will not come through the use of antiseptic phrases and slogans. For some countries poor in resources, it may not come at all.

2. The capacity of the United States to influence future outcomes is likely to be limited. Latin America is highly nationalistic and has recently begun to expand its trade and relations outside the North American orbit. Latin America neither wishes to, nor by history and tradition can, follow the developmental model of the United States. Hence, there are likely to be increasing problems and tensions in North-South, U.S.–Latin American relations centering on major political and economic issues.

3. Latin American development will be carried out largely by the Latin American nations themselves and on their own terms. They will learn to devise developmental strategies and formulas attuned to their own desires and traditions rather than to imitate the already developed nations. Further, such development is likely to be in accord with the special nature of Latin American society and its institutions (as outlined in Part 1) and may not be in conformity with historical U.S. and West European experiences.

4. It is thus our obligation to seek to understand Latin America and its distinctive development processes on Latin America's own terms, through its perspectives, and not by means of our own rose-colored

lenses. We should keep our eyes and minds open to the distinct characteristics of another culture area, rather than seek to interpret it from a North American viewpoint. Only then can we begin to understand what Latin America is all about, develop an empathy for and comprehension of a foreign area whose assumptions and operating procedures are often different from our own, and appreciate Latin America's developmental aspirations not from some haughty or "superior" U.S. perspective but through the givens and dynamics of Latin American political society itself.

About the Editors
and Contributors

CONTRIBUTING EDITORS

Howard J. Wiarda is Professor of Political Science at the University of Massachusetts, Amherst, and a Resident Scholar and Director of the Center for Hemispheric Studies at the American Enterprise Institute for Public Policy Research in Washington, D.C. His publications include *Dictatorship and Development; The Dominican Republic: Nation in Transition; Dictatorship, Development, and Disintegration: Politics and Social Change in the Dominican Republic; The Brazilian Catholic Labor Movement; Politics and Social Change in Latin America; Corporatism and Development: The Portuguese Experience; Rift and Revolution: The Central American Imbroglio; In Search of Policy: The United States and Latin America; The Continuing Struggle for Democracy in Latin America* (Westview 1980); *Corporatism and National Development in Latin America* (Westview, 1981); and *The Dominican Republic: A Caribbean Crucible* (with Michael J. Kryzanek; Westview, 1981).

Harvey F. Kline is Professor of Political Science, University of Massachusetts, Amherst. His publications include *Legislative Behavior in Colombia* (coauthor); *Colombia: Portrait of Unity and Diversity* (Westview, 1983); *Energy Policy and the Colombian Elite: A Synthesis and Interpretation; Exxon and Colombian Coal: An Analysis of the North Cerrejon Debates;* and "Fidel Castro and the Cuban Revolution," in *Governments and Leaders,* edited by Edward Feit; as well as various articles about Colombian and Cuban politics. He is currently completing a book on Colombian coal policy.

CONTRIBUTORS

Charles F. Denton is Director of the Institute for Social and Population Studies, National University of Costa Rica, Heredia. He is the author of *Patterns of Costa Rican Politics* and (with Preston Lee Lawrence) *Latin American Politics: A Functional Approach.*

Kenneth Paul Erickson is Professor of Political Science at Hunter College, City University of New York. The author of *The Brazilian Corporate State and Working-Class Politics* and numerous scholarly articles, he has spent nearly three years researching in Brazil.

Ronald H. McDonald is Professor of Political Science at the Maxwell School, Syracuse University, and former Chairman of the department. He is the author of *Party Systems and Elections in Latin America* and numerous articles on Latin American politics.

James M. Malloy is Professor of Political Science and Chairman of the Department of Political Science at the University of Pittsburgh. He is the author of *Bolivia: The Uncompleted Revolution* and *The Politics of Social Security in Brazil* and editor of *Authoritarianism and Corporatism in Latin America.*

John D. Martz is Head of the Department of Political Science, the Pennsylvania State University. He is the coeditor of *The Colossus Challenged* (with E. Michael Erisman; Westview, 1982), and *Latin America, the United States, and The Inter-American System* (with Lars Schoultz; Westview, 1980). He is currently completing a book on the politics of petroleum in Ecuador.

Amparo Menéndez-Carrión is a doctoral candidate at the Johns Hopkins School of Advanced International Studies, where she is completing a dissertation, "Electoral Behavior Among the Urban Poor in Ecuador." Her book on electoral politics in Ecuador will appear in Spanish in 1985. She is the coauthor, with Riordan Roett, of a chapter on organized labor in Paraguay, to appear in *Latin American Labor Organizations,* edited by G. M. Greenfield and S. L. Maram (forthcoming).

James A. Morris has studied and traveled in Argentina, Uruguay, the Dominican Republic, Colombia, and Central America and been a consultant to the Department of State. He has written articles on Honduran political development for journals and periodicals. He is the author of *Honduras: Caudillo Politics and Military Rulers* (Westview, 1984) and coeditor of *Central America: Crisis and Adaptation* (with Steve C. Ropp).

David Scott Palmer is Chairman of Latin American and Caribbean Studies at the Foreign Service Institute and Professorial Lecturer at the School of Advanced International Studies, The Johns Hopkins University. He is the author of *Peru: The Authoritarian Tradition* (1980), also published in Spanish in 1984, as well as various monographs and articles. Current research interests include political participation, authoritarianism, development, and U.S. foreign policy.

Riordan Roett is Professor and Director of the Latin American Studies Program and Director of the Center of Brazilian Studies at the Johns Hopkins School of Advanced International Studies in Washington, D.C. He served as president of the Latin American Studies Association in 1978 and is a member of the Council on Foreign Relations. His books include *The Politics of Foreign Aid in the Brazilian Northeast, Brazil in the Sixties* (coeditor and coauthor), *Brazil in the Seventies* (editor), *Brazil: Politics in a Patrimonial Society,* and *Latin America, Western Europe, and the United States: A New Atlantic Triangle* (coeditor and author). He is the author of various journal articles and book reviews and testifies frequently before committees of the U.S. Congress.

Steve C. Ropp currently holds the position of Milward Simpson Distinguished Professor of Political Science at the University of Wyoming. He is the author of *Panamanian Politics: From Guarded Nation to National Guard* and coeditor with James A. Morris of *Central America: Crisis and Adaptation.*

Peter G. Snow, Professor, Department of Political Science at the University of Iowa, is the author of *Argentine Radicalism* and *Political Forces in Argentina* and many articles on Argentine politics published in Argentine, Mexican, Spanish, British, German, and U.S. scholarly journals.

Evelyn P. Stevens is a Research Associate at the Center for Latin American Studies at the University of California in Berkeley and a visiting lecturer in the Department of Political Science at that university. Dr. Stevens has lived and worked for more than twenty years in the Caribbean, Central America, and Mexico and has written numerous books and articles about those regions.

Philip B. Taylor, Jr., was a specialist on Latin American politics for nearly thirty years, retiring from the University of Houston in December 1984. He published materials on Uruguay, Mexico, Colombia, and Venezuela, including *Government and Politics of Uruguay* and a number of journal articles on that country. After 1977 he worked principally on Catalunya, publishing *Public Power in Catalunya: Incomplete Power Under Ambiguous Constraints* in 1983.

Arturo Valenzuela is Professor of Political Science and Director of the Council on Latin American Studies at Duke University. He is the author of *Political Brokers in Chile: Local Politics in a Centralized Polity* and *The Breakdown of Democratic Regimes: Chile.* With J. Samuel Valenzuela he is the coauthor of *The Origins of Democracy: Theoretical Reflections on* *the Chilean Case* and coeditor and coauthor of *Chile: Politics and Society* and *Military Rule in Chile: Dictatorship and Oppositions.* He has been a visiting fellow at the University of Sussex and the Woodrow Wilson International Center for Scholars.

J. Samuel Valenzuela is Assistant Professor of Sociology at Harvard University and 1984–1985 President of the New England Council of Latin American Studies. He is the author of *Democratización vía Reforma: La Expansión del Sufragio en Chile* and coeditor and author of *Chile: Politics and Society* and *Military Rule in Chile: Dictatorship and Oppositions.* His articles on labor movements, social change, political development, and the Chilean authoritarian regime have appeared in English, Spanish, and Italian publications.

Thomas W. Walker, Associate Professor of Political Science at Ohio University, is the author of *The Christian Democratic Movement in Nicaragua* and *Nicaragua: The Land of Sandino* (Westview, 1981 and 1985) and the editor/coauthor of *Nicaragua in Revolution, Nicaragua: The First Five Years,* and *Understanding Central America* (with John A. Booth; Westview, forthcoming). In 1982, he served on the National Task Force on Central America of the United Presbyterian Church. The following year he was named cochair of the Latin American Studies Association's Task Force on Scholarly Relations with Nicaragua.

Jerry L. Weaver was Director of the public administration program at UCLA. He has published two books on U.S. national health policy as well as numerous articles on various aspects of Latin American, particularly Guatemalan, affairs. He worked as a social science analyst with AID's Office of Rural Development and is presently Refugee Affairs Coordinator in the U.S. Embassy, Khartoum, Sudan.

Henry Wells, Professor of Political Science, University of Pennsylvania, is the author of *The Modernization of Puerto Rico* and articles and monographs on politics in Puerto Rico, the Dominican Republic, and Costa Rica.

Iêda Siqueira Wiarda is Adjunct Professor, Department of Political Science, University of Massachusetts, Amherst. She has been course chairperson, Foreign Service Institute, Department of State, and works as a consultant to various governmental and private agencies, especially on population and public policy issues in Latin America. She is the author of *Family Planning Activities in a Democratic Context: The Case of Venezuela; Women, Population and International Development in Latin America;* and several articles, chapters, and reviews.

About the Book

Latin American Politics and Development
SECOND EDITION, FULLY REVISED AND UPDATED
edited by Howard J. Wiarda and Harvey F. Kline

Six years have elapsed since this highly regarded text first appeared in print—years of change and upheaval in Latin America, a greatly increased U.S. presence throughout Central America and the Caribbean, and financial and economic instability throughout the hemisphere. In this second, fully revised and updated edition, the authors and editors rethink some of the general ideas and intellectual concepts about Latin America, emphasizing political economy, public policy, and the relations of dependency on a country-by-country basis. The book's contributors are among the leading scholars in the field of Latin American studies; all are experts on the countries about which they have written. The editors have sought not to impose any single conceptual framework or set of rigid orthodoxies on the contributors, but instead have cast the book in comparative terms within a broad framework of general development themes—economic, social, and political.

This provocative text is sufficiently flexible and the treatment of individual countries sufficiently independent from one another that the teacher or reader may use the text in several ways. In a one-semester course, the chapters in Part 1 can serve as a convenient introduction to Latin American politics, which may then be followed by a treatment of the countries the instructor feels are particularly important. In a two-semester sequence, the first semester might begin with the introductory chapters and conclude with a comparative analysis of Latin American revolutions; in the second semester, after a brief repetition of the introductory material for the benefit of new students, less politically incendiary countries could be covered. Other methods of organization might, of course, be devised. This widely adopted text has been specifically designed to accommodate a wide range of pedagogical approaches.

Other Titles of Interest
from Westview Press

†*Latin America, Its Problems and Its Promise: A Multidisciplinary Introduction,* edited by Jan Knippers Black

†*Politics and Public Policy in Latin America,* Steven W. Hughes and Kenneth J. Mijeski

†*The Dynamics of Latin American Foreign Policies: Challenges for the 1980s,* edited by Jennie K. Lincoln and Elizabeth G. Ferris

†*Latin American Nations in World Politics,* edited by Heraldo Muñoz and Joseph S. Tulchin

†*FOREIGN POLICY on Latin America, 1970–1980,* edited by the staff of *Foreign Policy*

†*Latin America and the U.S. National Interest: A Basis for U.S. Foreign Policy,* Margaret Daly Hayes

Controlling Latin American Conflicts: Ten Approaches, edited by Michael A. Morris and Victor Millán

†*The Caribbean Challenge: U.S. Policy in a Volatile Region,* edited by H. Michael Erisman

Political Change in Central America: Internal and External Dimensions, Wolf Grabendorff, Heinrich-W. Krumwiede, and Jörg Todt

†*The New Cuban Presence in the Caribbean,* edited by Barry B. Levine

†*Revolution in Central America,* edited by Stanford Central America Action Network

†*Revolution and Counterrevolution in Central America and the Caribbean,* edited by Donald E. Schulz and Douglas H. Graham

PROFILES OF CONTEMPORARY LATIN AMERICA:

†*Mexico: Paradoxes of Stability and Change,* Daniel Levy and Gabriel Székely

†*Nicaragua: The Land of Sandino,* Revised Edition, Thomas W. Walker

†*The Dominican Republic: A Caribbean Crucible,* Howard J. Wiarda and Michael J. Kryzanek

Colombia: Portrait of Unity and Diversity, Harvey F. Kline

Honduras: Caudillo Politics and Military Rulers, James A. Morris

†*Cuba: Dilemmas of a Revolution,* Juan M. del Aguila

Guatemala: A Nation in Turmoil, Peter Calvert

†Available in hardcover and paperback.

Index